Lecture Notes in Computer Science   11427

Commenced Publication in 1973
Founding and Former Series Editors:
Gerhard Goos, Juris Hartmanis, and Jan van Leeuwen

Advanced Research in Computing and Software Science
Subline of Lecture Notes in Computer Science

More information about this series at http://www.springer.com/series/7407

Tomáš Vojnar · Lijun Zhang (Eds.)

Tools and Algorithms for the Construction and Analysis of Systems

25th International Conference, TACAS 2019
Held as Part of the European Joint Conferences
on Theory and Practice of Software, ETAPS 2019
Prague, Czech Republic, April 6–11, 2019
Proceedings, Part I

Editors
Tomáš Vojnar
Brno University of Technology
Brno, Czech Republic

Lijun Zhang
Chinese Academy of Sciences
Beijing, China

ISSN 0302-9743   ISSN 1611-3349   (electronic)
Lecture Notes in Computer Science
ISBN 978-3-030-17461-3   ISBN 978-3-030-17462-0   (eBook)
https://doi.org/10.1007/978-3-030-17462-0

LNCS Sublibrary: SL1 – Theoretical Computer Science and General Issues

This Springer imprint is published by the registered company Springer Nature Switzerland AG
The registered company address is: Gewerbestrasse 11, 6330 Cham, Switzerland

ETAPS Foreword

Welcome to the 22nd ETAPS! This is the first time that ETAPS took place in the Czech Republic in its beautiful capital Prague.

ETAPS 2019 was the 22nd instance of the European Joint Conferences on Theory and Practice of Software. ETAPS is an annual federated conference established in 1998, and consists of five conferences: ESOP, FASE, FoSSaCS, TACAS, and POST. Each conference has its own Program Committee (PC) and its own Steering Committee (SC). The conferences cover various aspects of software systems, ranging from theoretical computer science to foundations to programming language developments, analysis tools, formal approaches to software engineering, and security.

Organizing these conferences in a coherent, highly synchronized conference program enables participation in an exciting event, offering the possibility to meet many researchers working in different directions in the field and to easily attend talks of different conferences. ETAPS 2019 featured a new program item: the Mentoring Workshop. This workshop is intended to help students early in the program with advice on research, career, and life in the fields of computing that are covered by the ETAPS conference. On the weekend before the main conference, numerous satellite workshops took place and attracted many researchers from all over the globe.

ETAPS 2019 received 436 submissions in total, 137 of which were accepted, yielding an overall acceptance rate of 31.4%. I thank all the authors for their interest in ETAPS, all the reviewers for their reviewing efforts, the PC members for their contributions, and in particular the PC (co-)chairs for their hard work in running this entire intensive process. Last but not least, my congratulations to all authors of the accepted papers!

ETAPS 2019 featured the unifying invited speakers Marsha Chechik (University of Toronto) and Kathleen Fisher (Tufts University) and the conference-specific invited speakers (FoSSaCS) Thomas Colcombet (IRIF, France) and (TACAS) Cormac Flanagan (University of California at Santa Cruz). Invited tutorials were provided by Dirk Beyer (Ludwig Maximilian University) on software verification and Cesare Tinelli (University of Iowa) on SMT and its applications. On behalf of the ETAPS 2019 attendants, I thank all the speakers for their inspiring and interesting talks!

ETAPS 2019 took place in Prague, Czech Republic, and was organized by Charles University. Charles University was founded in 1348 and was the first university in Central Europe. It currently hosts more than 50,000 students. ETAPS 2019 was further supported by the following associations and societies: ETAPS e.V., EATCS (European Association for Theoretical Computer Science), EAPLS (European Association for Programming Languages and Systems), and EASST (European Association of Software Science and Technology). The local organization team consisted of Jan Vitek and Jan Kofron (general chairs), Barbora Buhnova, Milan Ceska, Ryan Culpepper, Vojtech Horky, Paley Li, Petr Maj, Artem Pelenitsyn, and David Safranek.

The ETAPS SC consists of an Executive Board, and representatives of the individual ETAPS conferences, as well as representatives of EATCS, EAPLS, and EASST. The Executive Board consists of Gilles Barthe (Madrid), Holger Hermanns (Saarbrücken), Joost-Pieter Katoen (chair, Aachen and Twente), Gerald Lüttgen (Bamberg), Vladimiro Sassone (Southampton), Tarmo Uustalu (Reykjavik and Tallinn), and Lenore Zuck (Chicago). Other members of the SC are: Wil van der Aalst (Aachen), Dirk Beyer (Munich), Mikolaj Bojanczyk (Warsaw), Armin Biere (Linz), Luis Caires (Lisbon), Jordi Cabot (Barcelona), Jean Goubault-Larrecq (Cachan), Jurriaan Hage (Utrecht), Rainer Hähnle (Darmstadt), Reiko Heckel (Leicester), Panagiotis Katsaros (Thessaloniki), Barbara König (Duisburg), Kim G. Larsen (Aalborg), Matteo Maffei (Vienna), Tiziana Margaria (Limerick), Peter Müller (Zurich), Flemming Nielson (Copenhagen), Catuscia Palamidessi (Palaiseau), Dave Parker (Birmingham), Andrew M. Pitts (Cambridge), Dave Sands (Gothenburg), Don Sannella (Edinburgh), Alex Simpson (Ljubljana), Gabriele Taentzer (Marburg), Peter Thiemann (Freiburg), Jan Vitek (Prague), Tomas Vojnar (Brno), Heike Wehrheim (Paderborn), Anton Wijs (Eindhoven), and Lijun Zhang (Beijing).

I would like to take this opportunity to thank all speakers, attendants, organizers of the satellite workshops, and Springer for their support. I hope you all enjoy the proceedings of ETAPS 2019. Finally, a big thanks to Jan and Jan and their local organization team for all their enormous efforts enabling a fantastic ETAPS in Prague!

February 2019   Joost-Pieter Katoen
                                                       ETAPS SC Chair
                                                    ETAPS e.V. President

Preface

TACAS 2019 was the 25th edition of the International Conference on Tools and Algorithms for the Construction and Analysis of Systems conference series. TACAS 2019 was part of the 22nd European Joint Conferences on Theory and Practice of Software (ETAPS 2019). The conference was held at the Orea Hotel Pyramida in Prague, Czech Republic, during April 8–11, 2019.

Conference Description. TACAS is a forum for researchers, developers, and users interested in rigorously based tools and algorithms for the construction and analysis of systems. The conference aims to bridge the gaps between different communities with this common interest and to support them in their quest to improve the utility, reliability, flexibility, and efficiency of tools and algorithms for building systems. TACAS 2019 solicited four types of submissions:

– *Research papers*, identifying and justifying a principled advance to the theoretical foundations for the construction and analysis of systems, where applicable supported by experimental validation.
– *Case-study papers*, reporting on case studies and providing information about the system being studied, the goals of the study, the challenges the system poses to automated analysis, research methodologies and approaches used, the degree to which goals were attained, and how the results can be generalized to other problems and domains.
– *Regular tool papers*, presenting a new tool, a new tool component, or novel extensions to an existing tool, with an emphasis on design and implementation concerns, including software architecture and core data structures, practical applicability, and experimental evaluations.
– *Tool-demonstration papers* (short), focusing on the usage aspects of tools.

Paper Selection. This year, 164 papers were submitted to TACAS, among which 119 were research papers, 10 case-study papers, 24 regular tool papers, and 11 were tool-demonstration papers. After a rigorous review process, with each paper reviewed by at least three Program Committee members, followed by an online discussion, the Program Committee accepted 29 research papers, 2 case-study papers, 11 regular tool papers, and 8 tool-demonstration papers (50 papers in total).

Artifact-Evaluation Process. The main novelty of TACAS 2019 was that, for the first time, artifact evaluation was compulsory for all regular tool papers and tool demonstration papers. For research papers and case-study papers, artifact evaluation was optional. The artifact evaluation process was organized as follows:

– *Regular tool papers and tool demonstration papers.* The authors of the 35 submitted papers of these categories of papers were required to submit an artifact alongside their paper submission. Each artifact was evaluated independently by three reviewers. Out of the 35 artifact submissions, 28 were successfully evaluated, which corresponds to an acceptance rate of 80%. The AEC used a two-phase reviewing process: Reviewers first performed an initial check to see whether the artifact was technically usable and whether the accompanying instructions were consistent, followed by a full evaluation of the artifact. The main criterion for artifact acceptance was consistency with the paper, with completeness and documentation being handled in a more lenient manner as long as the artifact was useful overall. The reviewers were instructed to check whether results are consistent with what is described in the paper. Inconsistencies were to be clearly pointed out and explained by the authors. In addition to the textual reviews, reviewers also proposed a numeric value about (potentially weak) acceptance/rejection of the artifact. After the evaluation process, the results of the artifact evaluation were summarized and forwarded to the discussion of the papers, so as to enable the reviewers of the papers to take the evaluation into account. In all but three cases, tool papers whose artifacts did not pass the evaluation were rejected.

- *Research papers and case-study papers.* For this category of papers, artifact evaluation was voluntary. The authors of each of the 25 accepted papers were invited to submit an artifact immediately after the acceptance notification. Owing to the short time available for the process and acceptance of the artifact not being critical for paper acceptance, there was only one round of evaluation for this category, and every artifact was assigned to two reviewers. The artifacts were evaluated using the same criteria as for tool papers. Out of the 18 submitted artifacts of this phase, 15 were successfully evaluated (83% acceptance rate) and were awarded the TACAS 2019 AEC badge, which is added to the title page of the respective paper if desired by the authors.

TOOLympics. TOOLympics 2019 was part of the celebration of the 25th anniversary of the TACAS conference. The goal of TOOLympics is to acknowledge the achievements of the various competitions in the field of formal methods, and to understand their commonalities and differences. A total of 2^4 competitions joined TOOLympics and were presented at the event. An overview and competition reports of 11 competitions are included in the third volume of the TACAS 2019 proceedings, which are dedicated to the 25th anniversary of TACAS. The extra volume contains a review of the history of TACAS, the TOOLympics papers, and the papers of the annual Competition on Software Verification.

Competition on Software Verification. TACAS 2019 also hosted the 8th International Competition on Software Verification (SV-COMP), chaired and organized by Dirk Beyer. The competition again had high participation: 31 verification systems with developers from 14 countries were submitted for the systematic comparative evaluation, including three submissions from industry. The TACAS proceedings includes the competition report and short papers describing 11 of the participating verification systems. These papers were reviewed by a separate program committee (PC); each of the papers was assessed by four reviewers. Two sessions in the TACAS program (this year as part of the TOOLympics event) were reserved for the presentation of the results: the summary by the SV-COMP chair and the participating tools by the developer teams in the first session, and the open jury meeting in the second session.

Acknowledgments. We would like to thank everyone who helped to make TACAS 2019 successful. In particular, we would like to thank the authors for submitting their papers to TACAS 2019. We would also like to thank all PC members, additional reviewers, as well as all members of the artifact evaluation committee (AEC) for their detailed and informed reviews and, in the case of the PC and AEC members, also for their discussions during the virtual PC and AEC meetings. We also thank the Steering Committee for their advice. Special thanks go to the Organizing Committee of ETAPS 2019 and its general chairs, Jan Kofroň and Jan Vitek, to the chair of the ETAPS 2019 executive board, Joost-Pieter Katoen, and to the publication team at Springer.

March 2019

Tomáš Vojnar (PC Chair)
Lijun Zhang (PC Chair)
Marius Mikucionis (Tools Chair)
Radu Grosu (Use-Case Chair)
Dirk Beyer (SV-COMP Chair)
Ondřej Lengál (AEC Chair)
Ernst Moritz Hahn (AEC Chair)

Organization

Program Committee

Parosh Aziz Abdulla	Uppsala University, Sweden
Dirk Beyer	LMU Munich, Germany
Armin Biere	Johannes Kepler University Linz, Austria
Ahmed Bouajjani	IRIF, Paris Diderot University, France
Patricia Bouyer	LSV, CNRS/ENS Cachan, Université Paris Saclay, France
Yu-Fang Chen	Academia Sinica, Taiwan
Maria Christakis	MPI-SWS, Germany
Alessandro Cimatti	Fondazione Bruno Kessler, Italy
Rance Cleaveland	University of Maryland, USA
Leonardo de Moura	Microsoft Research, USA
Parasara Sridhar Duggirala	University of North Carolina at Chapel Hill, USA
Pierre Ganty	IMDEA Software Institute, Spain
Radu Grosu	Vienna University of Technology, Austria
Orna Grumberg	Technion – Israel Institute of Technology, Israel
Klaus Havelund	NASA/Caltech Jet Propulsion Laboratory, USA
Holger Hermanns	Saarland University, Germany
Falk Howar	TU Dortmund, Germany
Marieke Huisman	University of Twente, The Netherlands
Radu Iosif	Verimag, CNRS/University of Grenoble Alpes, France
Joxan Jaffar	National University of Singapore, Singapore
Stefan Kiefer	University of Oxford, UK
Jan Kretinsky	Technical University of Munich, Germany
Salvatore La Torre	Università degli studi di Salerno, Italy
Kim Guldstrand Larsen	Aalborg University, Denmark
Anabelle McIver	Macquarie University, Australia
Roland Meyer	TU Braunschweig, Germany
Marius Mikučionis	Aalborg University, Denmark
Sebastian A. Mödersheim	Technical University of Denmark, Denmark
David Parker	University of Birmingham, UK
Corina Pasareanu	CMU/NASA Ames Research Center, USA
Sanjit Seshia	University of California, Berkeley, USA
Bernhard Steffen	TU Dortmund, Germany
Jan Strejcek	Masaryk University, Czech Republic
Zhendong Su	ETH Zurich, Switzerland
Meng Sun	Peking University, China

Michael Tautschnig	Queen Mary University of London/Amazon Web Services, UK
Tomáš Vojnar (Co-chair)	Brno University of Technology, Czech Republic
Thomas Wies	New York University, USA
Lijun Zhang (Co-chair)	Institute of Software, Chinese Academy of Sciences, China
Florian Zuleger	Vienna University of Technology, Austria

Program Committee and Jury—SV-COMP

Dirk Beyer (Chair)	LMU Munich, Germany
Peter Schrammel (Representing 2LS)	University of Sussex, UK
Jera Hensel (Representing AProVE)	RWTH Aachen, Germany
Michael Tautschnig (Representing CBMC)	Amazon Web Services, UK
Kareem Khazem (Representing CBMC-Path)	University College London, UK
Vadim Mutilin (Representing CPA-BAM-BnB)	ISP RAS, Russia
Pavel Andrianov (Representing CPA-Lockator)	ISP RAS, Russia
Marie-Christine Jakobs (Representing CPA-Seq)	LMU Munich, Germany
Omar Alhawi (Representing DepthK)	University of Manchester, UK
Vladimír Štill (Representing DIVINE-Explicit)	Masaryk University, Czechia
Henrich Lauko (Representing DIVINE-SMT)	Masaryk University, Czechia
Mikhail R. Gadelha (Representing ESBMC-Kind)	University of Southampton, UK
Philipp Ruemmer (Representing JayHorn)	Uppsala University, Sweden
Lucas Cordeiro (Representing JBMC)	University of Manchester, UK
Cyrille Artho (Representing JPF)	KTH, Denmark
Omar Inverso (Representing Lazy-CSeq)	Gran Sasso Science Inst., Italy
Herbert Rocha (Representing Map2Check)	Federal University of Roraima, Brazil
Cedric Richter (Representing PeSCo)	University of Paderborn, Germany

Eti Chaudhary (Representing Pinaka)	IIT Hyderabad, India
Veronika Šoková (Representing PredatorHP)	BUT, Brno, Czechia
Franck Cassez (Representing Skink)	Macquarie University, Australia
Zvonimir Rakamaric (Representing SMACK)	University of Utah, USA
Willem Visser (Representing SPF)	Stellenbosch University, South Africa
Marek Chalupa (Representing Symbiotic)	Masaryk University, Czechia
Matthias Heizmann (Representing UAutomizer)	University of Freiburg, Germany
Alexander Nutz (Representing UKojak)	University of Freiburg, Germany
Daniel Dietsch (Representing UTaipan)	University of Freiburg, Germany
Priyanka Darke (Representing VeriAbs)	Tata Consultancy Services, India
R. K. Medicherla (Representing VeriFuzz)	Tata Consultancy Services, India
Pritom Rajkhowa (Representing VIAP)	Hong Kong UST, China
Liangze Yin (Representing Yogar-CBMC)	NUDT, China
Haining Feng (Representing Yogar-CBMC-Par.)	National University of Defense Technology, China

Artifact Evaluation Committee (AEC)

Pranav Ashok	TU Munich, Germany
Marek Chalupa	Masaryk University, Czech Republic
Gabriele Costa	IMT Lucca, Italy
Maryam Dabaghchian	University of Utah, USA
Bui Phi Diep	Uppsala, Sweden
Daniel Dietsch	University of Freiburg, Germany
Tom van Dijk	Johannes Kepler University, Austria
Tomáš Fiedor	Brno University of Technology, Czech Republic
Daniel Fremont	UC Berkeley, USA
Ondřej Lengál (Co-chair)	Brno University of Technology, Czech Republic
Ernst Moritz Hahn (Co-chair)	Queen's University Belfast, UK
Sam Huang	University of Maryland, USA
Martin Jonáš	Masaryk University, Czech Republic
Sean Kauffman	University of Waterloo, Canada
Yong Li	Chinese Academy of Sciences, China

Le Quang Loc   Teesside University, UK
Rasool Maghareh   National University of Singapore, Singapore
Tobias Meggendorfer   TU Munich, Germany
Malte Mues   TU Dortmund, Germany
Tuan Phong Ngo   Uppsala, Sweden
Chris Novakovic   University of Birmingham, UK
Thai M. Trinh   Advanced Digital Sciences Center, Illinois
                                  at Singapore, Singapore
Wytse Oortwijn   University of Twente, The Netherlands
Aleš Smrčka   Brno University of Technology, Czech Republic
Daniel Stan   Saarland University, Germany
Ilina Stoilkovska   TU Wien, Austria
Ming-Hsien Tsai   Academia Sinica, Taiwan
Jan Tušil   Masaryk University, Czech Republic
Pedro Valero   IMDEA, Spain
Maximilian Weininger   TU Munich, Germany

Additional Reviewers

Aiswarya, C.
Albarghouthi, Aws
Aminof, Benjamin
Américo, Arthur
Ashok, Pranav
Atig, Mohamed Faouzi
Bacci, Giovanni
Bainczyk, Alexander
Barringer, Howard
Basset, Nicolas
Bensalem, Saddek
Berard, Beatrice
Besson, Frédéric
Biewer, Sebastian
Bogomolov, Sergiy
Bollig, Benedikt
Bozga, Marius
Bozzano, Marco
Brazdil, Tomas
Caulfield, Benjamin
Chaudhuri, Swarat
Cheang, Kevin
Chechik, Marsha
Chen, Yu-Fang
Chin, Wei-Ngan
Chini, Peter

Ciardo, Gianfranco
Cohen, Liron
Cordeiro, Lucas
Cyranka, Jacek
Čadek, Pavel
Darulova, Eva
Degorre, Aldric
Delbianco, Germán Andrés
Delzanno, Giorgio
Devir, Nurit
Dierl, Simon
Dragoi, Cezara
Dreossi, Tommaso
Dutra, Rafael
Eilers, Marco
El-Hokayem, Antoine
Faella, Marco
Fahrenberg, Uli
Falcone, Ylies
Fox, Gereon
Freiberger, Felix
Fremont, Daniel
Frenkel, Hadar
Friedberger, Karlheinz
Frohme, Markus
Fu, Hongfei

Furbach, Florian
Garavel, Hubert
Ghosh, Bineet
Ghosh, Shromona
Gondron, Sebastien
Gopinath, Divya
Gossen, Frederik
Goyal, Manish
Graf-Brill, Alexander
Griggio, Alberto
Gu, Tianxiao
Guatto, Adrien
Gutiérrez, Elena
Hahn, Ernst Moritz
Hansen, Mikkel
Hartmanns, Arnd
Hasani, Ramin
Havlena, Vojtěch
He, Kangli
He, Pinjia
Hess, Andreas Viktor
Heule, Marijn
Ho, Mark
Ho, Nhut Minh
Holik, Lukas
Hsu, Hung-Wei
Inverso, Omar
Irfan, Ahmed
Islam, Md. Ariful
Itzhaky, Shachar
Jakobs, Marie-Christine
Jaksic, Stefan
Jasper, Marc
Jensen, Peter Gjøl
Jonas, Martin
Kaminski, Benjamin Lucien
Karimi, Abel
Katelaan, Jens
Kauffman, Sean
Kaufmann, Isabella
Khoo, Siau-Cheng
Kiesl, Benjamin
Kim, Eric
Klauck, Michaela
Kong, Hui
Kong, Zhaodan

Kopetzki, Dawid
Krishna, Siddharth
Krämer, Julia
Kukovec, Jure
Kumar, Rahul
Köpf, Boris
Lange, Martin
Le Coent, Adrien
Lemberger, Thomas
Lengal, Ondrej
Li, Yi
Lin, Hsin-Hung
Lluch Lafuente, Alberto
Lorber, Florian
Lu, Jianchao
Lukina, Anna
Lång, Magnus
Maghareh, Rasool
Mahyar, Hamidreza
Markey, Nicolas
Mathieson, Luke
Mauritz, Malte
Mayr, Richard
Mechtaev, Sergey
Meggendorfer, Tobias
Micheli, Andrea
Michelmore, Rhiannon
Monteiro, Pedro T.
Mover, Sergio
Mu, Chunyan
Mues, Malte
Muniz, Marco
Murano, Aniello
Murtovi, Alnis
Muskalla, Sebastian
Mutluergil, Suha Orhun
Neumann, Elisabeth
Ngo, Tuan Phong
Nickovic, Dejan
Nies, Gilles
Noller, Yannic
Norman, Gethin
Nowack, Martin
Olmedo, Federico
Pani, Thomas
Petri, Gustavo

Piazza, Carla
Poli, Federico
Poulsen, Danny Bøgsted
Prabhakar, Pavithra
Quang Trung, Ta
Ranzato, Francesco
Rasmussen, Cameron
Ratasich, Denise
Ravanbakhsh, Hadi
Ray, Rajarshi
Reger, Giles
Reynolds, Andrew
Rigger, Manuel
Rodriguez, Cesar
Rothenberg, Bat-Chen
Roveri, Marco
Rydhof Hansen, René
Rüthing, Oliver
Sadeh, Gal
Saivasan, Prakash
Sanchez, Cesar
Sangnier, Arnaud
Schlichtkrull, Anders
Schwoon, Stefan
Seidl, Martina
Shi, Xiaomu
Shirmohammadi, Mahsa
Shoukry, Yasser
Sighireanu, Mihaela
Soudjani, Sadegh
Spießl, Martin
Srba, Jiri

Srivas, Mandayam
Stan, Daniel
Stoilkovska, Ilina
Stojic, Ivan
Su, Ting
Summers, Alexander J.
Tabuada, Paulo
Tacchella, Armando
Tang, Enyi
Tian, Chun
Tonetta, Stefano
Trinh, Minh-Thai
Trtík, Marek
Tsai, Ming-Hsien
Valero, Pedro
van der Berg, Freark
Vandin, Andrea
Vazquez-Chanlatte, Marcell
Viganò, Luca
Villadsen, Jørgen
Wang, Shuai
Wang, Shuling
Weininger, Maximilian
Wendler, Philipp
Wolff, Sebastian
Wüstholz, Valentin
Xu, Xiao
Zeljić, Aleksandar
Zhang, Fuyuan
Zhang, Qirun
Zhang, Xiyue

Contents – Part I

Machine Learning

Contents – Part II

SAT and SMT I

Decomposing Farkas Interpolants

Martin Blicha[1,2(✉)] [ID], Antti E. J. Hyvärinen[1] [ID], Jan Kofroň[2] [ID],
and Natasha Sharygina[1] [ID]

[1] Università della Svizzera italiana (USI), Lugano, Switzerland
{martin.blicha,antti.hyvaerinen,natasha.sharygina}@usi.ch
[2] Faculty of Mathematics and Physics, Charles University, Prague, Czech Republic
{martin.blicha,jan.kofron}@d3s.mff.cuni.cz

Abstract. Modern verification commonly models software with
Boolean logic and a system of linear inequalities over reals and over-
approximates the reachable states of the model with Craig interpolation
to obtain, for example, candidates for inductive invariants. Interpolants
for the linear system can be efficiently constructed from a Simplex refu-
tation by applying the Farkas' lemma. However, Farkas interpolants do
not always suit the verification task and in the worst case they may
even be the cause of divergence of the verification algorithm. This work
introduces the decomposed interpolants, a fundamental extension of the
Farkas interpolants obtained by identifying and separating independent
components from the interpolant structure using methods from linear
algebra. We integrate our approach to the model checker Sally and show
experimentally that a portfolio of decomposed interpolants results in
immediate convergence on instances where state-of-the-art approaches
diverge. Being based on the efficient Simplex method, the approach is
very competitive also outside these diverging cases.

Keywords: Model checking · Satisfiability modulo theory ·
Linear arithmetic · Craig interpolation

1 Introduction

A central task in model checking systems with respect to safety properties [27]
consists of proving facts and attempting to generalize the obtained proofs. The
generalizations serve as a basis for inductive invariants needed for guiding the
search for a correctness proof in approaches such as IC3 [8] and k-induction [39],
both known to scale to the verification of highly complex systems.

Finding good proofs and generalizing them is hard. A widely used approach,
Satisfiability Modulo Theories (SMT) [7,13], models a system with propositional
logic and a range of first-order logics. Solvers for SMT combine a resolution-based
variant of the DPLL-algorithm [11,12,40] for propositional logic with decision
procedures for first-order logics. A vast range of first-order logics is maintained as
part of the SMT-LIB Initiative [6]. What is common to these logics is that their
solving requires typically only a handful of algorithms. Arguably, the two most

© The Author(s) 2019
T. Vojnar and L. Zhang (Eds.): TACAS 2019, Part I, LNCS 11427, pp. 3–20, 2019.
https://doi.org/10.1007/978-3-030-17462-0_1

important algorithms are a congruence closure algorithm for deciding quantifier-free equality logic with uninterpreted functions [31], and a Simplex-based procedure for linear arithmetic over real or rational numbers [16].

Generalizing proofs to inductive invariants is commonly done by Craig interpolation [10]. Here, the model is split into two parts, say, A and B, resulting in an *interpolation problem* (A, B). The proof of unsatisfiability for $A \wedge B$ is used to extract an *interpolant* I, a formula that is defined over the common symbols of A and B, is implied by A, and is unsatisfiable with B. Several interpolants can be computed for a given interpolation problem, and not all of them are useful for proving safety. Typically, this is a phenomenon used to construct a *portfolio* [20] of interpolation algorithms that is then applied in the hopes of aiding to find the safety proof.

The approaches to interpolation based on Farkas' lemma construct an LRA interpolant by summing all inequalities appearing in A into a single inequality. We call the resulting interpolant the *Farkas interpolant*. While a single inequality is desirable in some cases, it prevents IC3-style algorithms from converging in other ones [36]. We present how methods from linear algebra can be applied on a Farkas interpolant to obtain *decomposed interpolants* that do not consist of a single inequality and guarantee the convergence of the model-checking algorithm for some of the cases where Farkas interpolants do not converge. A major advantage of decomposed interpolants is that they can be computed using Simplex-based decision procedures as a black box, allowing us to make use of the highly tuned implementations present in many state-of-the-art SMT solvers.

Intuitively, while computing the decomposed interpolants we do not directly sum the inequalities in A, but, instead, we split the sum into sub-sums. The result is an interpolant that is a conjunction of often more than one component of the Farkas interpolant. This allows us not only to solve the convergence problem observed in model checking examples, but also to gain more control over the strength of LRA interpolants. In summary, the main contributions of this paper are

1. a new Farkas-lemma-based interpolation algorithm for LRA that is able to deal with convergence problems in model-checking benchmarks while still relying on a highly efficient Simplex-based decision procedure,
2. establishing properties regarding logical strength of interpolants produced by our interpolation algorithm with respect to the original Farkas interpolants,
3. implementation of our new interpolation algorithm in OPENSMT, our SMT solver, and integration of our approach with the model checker SALLY
4. experiments showing that the new approach is efficient in model checking, in particular in showing systems unsafe.

While the underlying intuition is simple, we quote here Jean D'Alembert (1717–1783) in saying that *Algebra is generous; she often gives more than is asked of her*: Our detailed analysis in Sects. 4 and 5 shows that the structure of the problem is surprisingly rich. Our experiments in Sect. 6 verify that the phenomena are practically relevant. Overall a portfolio constructed from our interpolation algorithm is significantly better than a portfolio based purely on Farkas interpolants. We furthermore show for individual instances that the effect is consistent instead of arising from random effects.

Related Work. The work on interpolation in LRA dates back to [32]. A compact set of rules for deriving LRA interpolants from the proof of unsatisfiability in an inference system was presented in [29]. The interpolants in these works were the Farkas interpolants. Current methods usually compute Farkas interpolants from explanations of unsatisfiability extracted directly from the Simplex-based decision procedure inside the SMT solver [16]. Recently in [3], we presented a way of computing an infinite family of interpolants between a primal and a dual interpolant with variable strength. However, those interpolants are still restricted to single inequalities.

The work most closely related to ours is [36] where the authors independently recognized the weakness of interpolation based on Farkas coefficients. They introduce a new interpolation procedure that gives guarantees of convergence of a special sequence of interpolation problems often occurring in model checking problems. However, this interpolation algorithm is based on a different decision procedure, called conflict resolution [26], which, based on the results reported in [36], is not as efficient as the Simplex-based decision procedure. In contrast, we show how the original approach based on the Simplex-based decision procedure and Farkas coefficients can be modified to produce interpolants not restricted to the single-inequality form, while additionally obtaining strength guarantees with respect to the original Farkas interpolants.

Other work on LRA interpolants include e.g. [1,35,37]. Both [1] and [37] focus on producing simple overall interpolants by attempting to reuse (partial) interpolants from pure LRA conflicts. Our focus is not on the overall interpolant, but on a single LRA conflict. However, in the context of interpolants from proofs produced by SMT solvers, our approach also has a potential for re-using components of interpolants for LRA conflicts across the whole proof. Beside algorithms for interpolants for LRA conflicts, there exist a large body of work on propositional interpolation [2,14,19,23].

The structure of the paper is as follows. In Sect. 2 we provide a concrete example model-checking problem where our approach guarantees immediate convergence but Farkas interpolation diverges. In Sect. 3 we define the notation used in the paper, and in Sects. 4 and 5 detail our main theoretical contribution. We provide experimental results in Sect. 6, and finally conclude in Sect. 7.

2 Motivation

Consider the transition system $S = (I, T, Err)$, where I and Err are, respectively, predicates that capture the initial and error states, and T is the transition function. The symbols x, y are real variables, and x', y' are their next-state versions.[1]

$$S = \begin{cases} I \equiv (x = 0) \wedge (y = 0), \\ T \equiv (x' = x + y) \wedge (y' = y + 1), \\ Err \equiv (x < 0) \end{cases} \tag{1}$$

---

[1] This example was first brought to our attention by Prof. Arie Gurfinkel. A similar example appears in [36].

The system is one variant from a family of similar transition systems that are known to not converge in straightforward implementations of IC3-based algorithms using LRA interpolation. For example, both SPACER [25] (using interpolation algorithm of Z3 [30]) and SALLY [24] (using interpolation algorithm of MATHSAT [9]) fail to compute a safe inductive invariant for this transition system. However, SALLY with our interpolation algorithm succeeds in computing the safe inductive invariant.[2] Closer examination of SALLY and SPACER reveals that the tools in their default configurations produce a divergent series of candidate invariants of the form $0 \leq kx + y$ for $k = 1, 2, 3, \ldots$. The reason for producing such a series is that both tools rely on Farkas interpolants that always consist of a single inequality. Instead of generalizing the Farkas interpolants, an approach advocated in this work, interpolation based on a different decision procedure was proposed for SALLY in [36], whereas SEAHORN [18] with SPACER as its underlying reasoning engine solves this issue with abstract interpretation.

In this work we show how to modify the interpolation algorithm to produce in the general case a *conjunction* of multiple inequalities, leading, in this case, to the discovery of an inductive safe invariant $x \geq 0 \wedge y \geq 0$. To avoid here a lengthy discussion on internals of IC3 but nevertheless provide a concrete example of the power of decomposed interpolants, we apply decomposed interpolants in a simple, interpolation-based procedure for computing inductive invariants for transition systems. This approach is a simplified version of k-induction (see, e.g., [28]). When applied to the system in Eq. (1), we show that computing the Farkas interpolant fails and decomposed interpolant succeeds in producing a safe inductive invariant. A safe, inductive invariant for (I, T, Err) is a predicate R that satisfies (1) $I(X) \rightarrow R(X)$, (2) $R(X) \wedge T(X, X') \rightarrow R(X)$, and (3) $R(X) \wedge Err(X) \rightarrow \bot$. We may opportunistically try to synthesise R by interpolating over the interpolation problem $(I(X), T(X, X') \wedge Err(X'))$. Using the system S of Eq. (1), we obtain $(x \geq 0 \wedge y \geq 0, x' = x + y \wedge y' = y + 1 \wedge x' < 0)$. A Farkas interpolant, the sum of the components from the A-part, is $x + y \geq 0$, which is neither safe nor inductive for S. However, the *decomposed interpolant* $x \geq 0 \wedge y \geq 0$ is an inductive invariant.

3 Preliminaries

We work in the domain of *Satisfiability Modulo Theories* (SMT) [7,13], where satisfiability of formulas is determined with respect to some background theory. In particular, we are concerned with the *lazy* approach to SMT, that combines SAT solver dealing with the propositional structure of a formula and *theory* solver for checking consistency of a conjunction of theory literals. The proof of unsatisfiability in this approach is basically a propositional proof that incorporates *theory lemmas* learnt by the theory solver and propagated to the SAT solver.

---

[2] Current implementation of SPACER does not support conjunctions of inequalities as interpolants, and therefore we are at the moment unable to try our approach on SPACER.

The proof-based interpolation algorithm then combines any propositional-proof-based interpolation algorithm with *theory interpolator*. Theory interpolator provides an interpolant for each theory conflict—an unsatisfiable conjunction of theory literals.

Linear Arithmetic and Linear Algebra. We use the letters x, y, z to denote variables and c, k to denote constants. Vector of n variables is denoted by $\mathbf{x} = (x_1, \ldots, x_n)^\mathsf{T}$ where n is usually known from context. $\mathbf{x}[i]$ denotes the element of $\mathbf{x}$ at position i, i.e. $\mathbf{x}[i] = x_i$. The vector of all zeroes is denoted as $\mathbf{0}$ and $\mathbf{e_i}$ denotes the unit vector with $\mathbf{e_i}[i] = 1$ and $\mathbf{e_i}[j] = 0$ for $j \neq i$. For two vectors $\mathbf{x} = (x_1, \ldots, x_n)^\mathsf{T}$ and $\mathbf{y} = (y_1, \ldots, y_n)^\mathsf{T}$ we say that $\mathbf{x} \leq \mathbf{y}$ iff $x_i \leq y_i$ for each $i \in \{1, \ldots, n\}$. $\mathbb{Q}$ denotes the set of rational numbers, $\mathbb{Q}^n$ the n-dimensional vector space of rational numbers and $\mathbb{Q}^{m \times n}$ the set of rational matrices with m rows and n columns. A transpose of matrix M is denoted as M^T. A kernel (also nullspace) of a matrix M is the vector space $ker(M) = \{\mathbf{x} \mid M\mathbf{x} = \mathbf{0}\}$.

We adopt the notation of matrix product for linear arithmetic. For a linear term $l = c_1 x_1 + \cdots + c_n x_n$, we write $\mathbf{c}^\mathsf{T} \mathbf{x}$ to denote l. Without loss of generality we assume that all linear inequalities are of the form $\mathbf{c}^\mathsf{T} \mathbf{x} \bowtie c$ with $\bowtie \in \{\leq, <\}$. By linear system over variables $\mathbf{x}$ we mean a finite set of linear inequalities $S = \{C_i \mid i = 1, \ldots, m\}$, where each C_i is a linear inequality over $\mathbf{x}$. Note that from the logical perspective, each C_i is an atom in the language of the theory of linear arithmetic, thus system S can be expressed as a formula $\bigwedge_{i=1}^{m} C_i$ and we use these representations interchangeably. A linear system is satisfiable if there exists an evaluation of variables that satisfies all inequalities; otherwise, it is unsatisfiable. This is the same as the (un)satisfiability of the formula representing the system.

We extend the matrix notation also to the whole linear system. For the sake of simplicity we use $\leq$ instead of $\bowtie$, even if the system contains a mix of strict and non-strict inequalities. The only important difference is that a (weighted) sum of a linear system (as defined below) results in a strict inequality, instead of a non-strict one, when at least one strict inequality is present in the sum with a non-zero coefficient. The theory, proofs and algorithm remain valid also in the presence of strict inequalities. We write $C\mathbf{x} \leq \mathbf{c}$ to denote the linear system S where C denotes the matrix of all coefficients of the system, $\mathbf{x}$ are the variables and $\mathbf{c}$ is the vector of the right sides of the inequalities. With the matrix notation, we can easily express the sum of (multiples) of inequalities. Given a system of inequalities $C\mathbf{x} \leq \mathbf{c}$ and a vector of "weights" (multiples) of the inequalities $\mathbf{k} \geq \mathbf{0}$, the inequality that is the (weighted) sum of the system can be expressed as $\mathbf{k}^\mathsf{T} C \mathbf{x} \leq \mathbf{k}^\mathsf{T} \mathbf{c}$.

Craig Interpolation. Given two formulas $A(\mathbf{x}, \mathbf{y})$ and $B(\mathbf{y}, \mathbf{z})$ such that $A \wedge B$ is unsatisfiable, a *Craig interpolant* [10] is a formula $I(\mathbf{y})$ such that $A \implies I$ and $I \implies \neg B$.

The pair of formulas (A, B) is also referred to as an *interpolation problem*. In linear arithmetic, the interpolation problem is a linear system S partitioned into two parts: A and B.

One way to compute a solution to an interpolation problem in linear arithmetic, used in many modern SMT solvers, is based on Farkas' lemma [17,38]. Farkas' lemma states that for an unsatisfiable system of linear inequalities $S \equiv C\mathbf{x} \leq \mathbf{c}$ there exist *Farkas* coefficients $\mathbf{k} \geq \mathbf{0}$ such that $\mathbf{k}^\mathsf{T} C\mathbf{x} \leq \mathbf{k}^\mathsf{T}\mathbf{c} \equiv 0 \leq -1$. In other words, the weighted sum of the system given by the Farkas coefficients is a contradictory inequality. If a strict inequality is part of the sum, the result might also be $0 < 0$.

The idea behind the interpolation algorithm based on Farkas coefficients is simple. Intuitively, given the partition of the linear system into A and B, we compute only the weighted sum of A. It is not hard to see that this sum is an interpolant. It follows from A because a weighted sum of a linear system with non-negative weights is always implied by the system. It is inconsistent with B because its sum with the weighted sum of B (using Farkas coefficients) is a contradictory inequality by Farkas lemma. Finally, it cannot contain any A-local variables, because in the weighted sum of the whole system all variables are eliminated, A-local variables are not present in B, so they must be eliminated already in the weighted sum of A.

More formally, for an unsatisfiable linear system $S \equiv C\mathbf{x} \leq \mathbf{c}$ over n variables, where $C \in \mathbb{Q}^{m \times n}, \mathbf{c} \in \mathbb{Q}^m$, and its partition to $A \equiv C_A\mathbf{x} \leq \mathbf{c_A}$ and $B \equiv C_B\mathbf{x} \leq \mathbf{c_B}$, where $C_A \in \mathbb{Q}^{k \times n}$, $C_B \in \mathbb{Q}^{l \times n}$, $\mathbf{c_A} \in \mathbb{Q}^k$, $\mathbf{c_B} \in \mathbb{Q}^l$ and $k + l = m$, there exist Farkas coefficients $\mathbf{k}^\mathsf{T} = (\mathbf{k_A^\mathsf{T}}\ \mathbf{k_B^\mathsf{T}})$ such that

$$(\mathbf{k_A^\mathsf{T}}\ \mathbf{k_B^\mathsf{T}}) \begin{pmatrix} C_A \\ C_B \end{pmatrix} = 0, (\mathbf{k_A^\mathsf{T}}\ \mathbf{k_B^\mathsf{T}}) \begin{pmatrix} \mathbf{c_A} \\ \mathbf{c_B} \end{pmatrix} = -1,$$

and the *Farkas interpolant* for (A, B) is the inequality

$$I^f \equiv \mathbf{k_A^\mathsf{T}} C_A \mathbf{x} \leq \mathbf{k_A^\mathsf{T}} \mathbf{c_A} \tag{2}$$

4 Decomposed Interpolants

In this section, we present our new approach to computing interpolants in linear arithmetic based on Farkas coefficients. The definition of Farkas interpolant of Eq. (2) corresponds to the weighted sum of A-part of the unsatisfiable linear system. This sum can be decomposed into j sums by decomposing the vector $\mathbf{k_A}$ into j vectors

$$\mathbf{k_A} = \sum_{i=1}^{j} \mathbf{k_{A,i}} \tag{3}$$

such that $\mathbf{0} \leq \mathbf{k_{A,i}} \leq \mathbf{k_A}$ for all i, thus obtaining j inequalities

$$I_i \equiv \mathbf{k_{A,i}^\mathsf{T}} C_A \mathbf{x} \leq \mathbf{k_{A,i}^\mathsf{T}} \mathbf{c_A} \tag{4}$$

If $\mathbf{k_{A,i}}$ are such that the left-hand side of the inequalities I_i contains only shared variables, the decomposition has an interesting application in interpolation, as illustrated below.

Definition 1 (decomposed interpolants). *Given an interpolation instance* (A, B), *if there exists a sum of the form Eq. (3) such that the left side of Eq. (4) contains only shared variables for all* $1 \leq i \leq j$, *then the set of inequalities* $S = \{I_1, \ldots, I_j\}$ *is a* decomposition. *In that case the formula* $\bigwedge_{i=1}^{j} I_i$ *is a decomposed interpolant (DI) of size* j *for* (A, B).

The decomposed interpolants are proper interpolants, as stated in the following theorem.

Theorem 1. *Let* (A, B) *be an interpolation problem in linear arithmetic. If* $S = \{I_1, \ldots, I_k\}$ *is a decomposition, then* $I^{DI} = I_1 \wedge \ldots \wedge I_k$ *is an interpolant for* (A, B).

Proof. Let $I^{DI} = I_1 \wedge \ldots \wedge I_k$. First, $A \implies I^{DI}$ holds since for all I_i, $A \implies I_i$. This is immediate from the fact that A is a system of linear inequalities $C_A \mathbf{x} \leq \mathbf{c_A}$, $I_i \equiv \mathbf{k_{A,i}^\top} C_A \mathbf{x} \leq \mathbf{k_{A,i}^\top} \mathbf{c_A}$ and $\mathbf{0} \leq \mathbf{k_{A,i}}$. Second, $I^{DI} \wedge B \implies \bot$ since I^{DI} implies Farkas interpolant I^f. This holds because $\mathbf{k_A} = \sum_i \mathbf{k_{A,i}}$ and $\mathbf{0} \leq \mathbf{k_{A,i}}$. Third, I^{DI} contains only shared variables by the definition of decomposition (Definition 1). Therefore, I^{DI} is an interpolant. □

Each interpolation instance has a *DI* of size one, a *trivial* decomposition, corresponding to the Farkas interpolant of Eq. (2). However, interpolation problems in general can admit bigger decompositions. In the following we give a concrete example of an instance with decomposition of size two.

Example 1. Let (A, B) be an interpolation problem in linear arithmetic with $A = (x_1 + x_2 \leq 0) \wedge (x_1 + x_3 \leq 0) \wedge (-x_1 \leq 0)$ and $B = (-x_2 - x_3 \leq -1)$. The linear systems corresponding to A and B are

$$C_A = \begin{pmatrix} 1 & 1 & 0 \\ 1 & 0 & 1 \\ -1 & 0 & 0 \end{pmatrix}, \quad \mathbf{c_A} = \begin{pmatrix} 0 \\ 0 \\ 0 \end{pmatrix}, \quad \text{and} \quad C_B = \begin{pmatrix} 0 & -1 & -1 \end{pmatrix}, \quad \mathbf{c_B} = \begin{pmatrix} -1 \end{pmatrix}.$$

Farkas coefficients are

$$\mathbf{k_A^\top} = \begin{pmatrix} 1 & 1 & 2 \end{pmatrix} \text{ and } \mathbf{k_B^\top} = \begin{pmatrix} 1 \end{pmatrix},$$

while Farkas interpolant for (A, B) is the inequality $I^f \equiv x_2 + x_3 \leq 0$. However, if we decompose $\mathbf{k_A}$ into

$$\mathbf{k_{A,1}^\top} = \begin{pmatrix} 1 & 0 & 1 \end{pmatrix} \text{ and } \mathbf{k_{A,2}^\top} = \begin{pmatrix} 0 & 1 & 1 \end{pmatrix},$$

we obtain the decomposition $\{x_2 \leq 0, x_3 \leq 0\}$ corresponding to the decomposed interpolant $I^{DI} \equiv x_2 \leq 0 \wedge x_3 \leq 0$ of size two.

4.1   Strength-Based Ordering of Decompositions

Decomposition of Farkas coefficients for a single interpolation problem is in general not unique. However, we can provide some structure to the space of possible interpolants by ordering interpolants with respect to their logical strength. To achieve this, we define the *coarseness* of a decomposition based on its ability to partition the terms of the interpolant into finer sums, and then prove that coarseness provides us with a way of measuring the interpolant strength.

Definition 2. *Let D_1, D_2 denote two decompositions of the same interpolation problem of size m, n, respectively, where $n < m$. Let $(\mathbf{q_1}, \ldots, \mathbf{q_m})$ denote the decomposition of Farkas coefficients corresponding to D_1 and let $(\mathbf{r_1}, \ldots, \mathbf{r_n})$ denote the decomposition of Farkas coefficients corresponding to D_2. We say that decomposition D_1 is finer than D_2 (or equivalently D_2 is coarser than D_1) and denote this as $D_1 \prec D_2$ when there exists a partition $P = \{p_1, \ldots, p_n\}$ of the set $\{\mathbf{q_1}, \ldots, \mathbf{q_m}\}$ such that for each i with $1 \le i \le n$, $\mathbf{r_i} = \sum_{\mathbf{q} \in p_i} \mathbf{q}$.*

Interpolants of decompositions ordered by their coarseness can be ordered by logical strength, as stated by the following lemma:

Lemma 1. *Assume D_1, D_2 are two decompositions of the same interpolation problem such that $D_1 \prec D_2$. Let I^{D_1}, I^{D_2} be the decomposed interpolants corresponding to D_1, D_2. Then I^{D_1} implies I^{D_2}.*

Proof. Informally, the implication follows from the fact that each linear inequality of I^{D_2} is a sum of some inequalities in I^{D_1}.

Formally, let I_i denote the i-th inequality in I^{D_2}. Then $I_i \equiv \mathbf{r_i}^\mathsf{T} C_A \mathbf{x} \le \mathbf{r_i}^\mathsf{T} \mathbf{c_A}$. Since $D_1 \prec D_2$, there is a set $\{I_{i_1}, \ldots, I_{i_j}\} \subseteq D_1$ such that for each k with $1 \le k \le j$, $I_{i_k} \equiv \mathbf{q_{i_k}}^\mathsf{T} C_A \mathbf{x} \le \mathbf{q_{i_k}}^\mathsf{T} \mathbf{c_A}$ and $\mathbf{r_i} = \sum_{k=1}^{j} \mathbf{q_{i_k}}$.

Since $\mathbf{q_{i_k}} \ge \mathbf{0}$, it holds that $I_{i_1} \wedge \cdots \wedge I_{i_j} \implies I_i$. This means that I^{D_1} implies every conjunct of I^{D_2}. $\square$

Note that the trivial, single-element decomposition corresponding to Farkas interpolant is the greatest element of this decomposition ordering. Also, for any decomposition of size more than one, replacing any number of elements by their sum yields a coarser decomposition. A possible reason to use a coarser decomposition may be that summing up some of the elements of a decomposition may result in eliminating a shared variable from the decomposition.

4.2   Strength of the Dual Interpolants

Let *Itp* denote an interpolation procedure and let *Itp*(A, B) stand for the interpolant computed by *Itp* for an interpolation problem (A, B). Then by *Itp*$'$ we denote the *dual* interpolation procedure, which works as follows: *Itp*$'(A, B) = \neg Itp(B, A)$. The duality theorem for interpolation states that *Itp*$'$ is correct interpolation procedure. This can be shown by verifying that the three interpolation conditions hold for *Itp*$'(A, B)$, given they hold for *Itp*(B, A).

Let us denote the interpolation procedure based on Farkas' lemma as Itp_F and the interpolation procedure computing decomposed interpolants as Itp_{DI}. The relation between Itp_F and its dual Itp'_F has been established in [3], namely that $Itp_F(A, B) \implies Itp'_F(A, B)$. We have shown in Lemma 1 that decomposed interpolant always implies Farkas interpolant computed from the same Farkas coefficients. This means that $Itp_{DI}(A, B) \implies Itp_F(A, B)$.

We can use this result to establish similar result for the dual interpolation procedures. Since $Itp_{DI}(B, A) \implies Itp_F(B, A)$, it follows that $\neg Itp_F(B, A) \implies \neg Itp_{DI}(B, A)$ and consequently $Itp'_F(A, B) \implies Itp'_{DI}(A, B)$.

Putting all the results on logical strength together, we obtain

$$Itp_{DI}(A, B) \implies Itp_F(A, B) \implies Itp'_F(A, B) \implies Itp'_{DI}(A, B).$$

Note that while both Itp_F and Itp'_F produce interpolants which are a single inequality and interpolants produced by Itp_{DI} are *conjunctions* of inequalities, interpolants produced by Itp'_{DI} are *disjunctions* of inequalities.

In the following section, we describe the details of the Itp_{DI} interpolation procedure.

5   Finding Decompositions

In this section we present our approach for finding decompositions for linear arithmetic interpolation problems given their Farkas coefficients.

We focus on the task of finding decomposition of $\mathbf{k_A^\mathsf{T}} C_A \mathbf{x}$. Recall that $C_A \in \mathbb{Q}^{l \times n}$ and $\mathbf{x}$ is a vector of variables of length n. Without loss of generality assume that there are no B-local variables since columns of C_A corresponding to B-local variables would contain all zeroes by definition in any case.

Furthermore, without loss of generality, assume the variables in the inequalities of A are ordered such that all A-local variables are before the shared ones. Then let us write

$$C_A = (L\ S), \quad \mathbf{x}^\mathsf{T} = \begin{pmatrix} \mathbf{x}_L{}^\mathsf{T} & \mathbf{x}_S{}^\mathsf{T} \end{pmatrix} \tag{5}$$

with $\mathbf{x}_L$ the vector of A-local variables of size p, $\mathbf{x}_S$ the vector of shared variables of size q, $n = p + q$, $L \in \mathbb{Q}^{l \times p}$ and $S \in \mathbb{Q}^{l \times q}$. We know that $\mathbf{k_A^\mathsf{T}} L = \mathbf{0}$ and the goal is to find $\mathbf{k_{A,i}}$ such that $\sum_i \mathbf{k_{A,i}} = \mathbf{k_A}$ and for each i $\mathbf{0} \le \mathbf{k_{A,i}} \le \mathbf{k_A}$ and $\mathbf{k_{A,i}^\mathsf{T}} L = \mathbf{0}$.

In the following we will consider two cases for computing the decompositions. We first study a common special case where the system A contains rows with no local variables, and give a linear-time algorithm for computing the decompositions. We then move to the general case where the rows of A contain local variables, and provide a decomposition algorithm based on computing a vector basis for a null space of a matrix obtained from A.

5.1   Trivial Elements

First, consider a situation where there is a linear inequality with no local variables. This means there is a row j in C_A (denoted as C_{Aj}) such that all entries in columns corresponding to local variables are 0, i.e., $L_j = \mathbf{0}^\mathsf{T}$. Then $\{I_1, I_2\}$ for $\mathbf{k}_{\mathbf{A},1} = \mathbf{k}_\mathbf{A}[j] \times \mathbf{e}_j$ and $\mathbf{k}_{\mathbf{A},2} = \mathbf{k}_\mathbf{A} - \mathbf{k}_{\mathbf{A},1}$ is a decomposition. Intuitively, any linear inequality that contains only shared variables can form a stand-alone element of a decomposition. When looking for finest decomposition, we do this iteratively for all inequalities with no local variables. In the next part we show how to look for a non-trivial decomposition when dealing with local variables.

5.2   Decomposing in the Presence of Local Variables

For this section, assume that L has no zero rows (we have shown above how to deal with such rows). We are going to search for a non-trivial decomposition starting with the following observation:

Observation. $\mathbf{k}_\mathbf{A}^\mathsf{T} L = 0$. Equivalently, there are no A-local variables in the Farkas interpolant. It follows that $L^\mathsf{T}\mathbf{k}_\mathbf{A} = 0$ and $\mathbf{k}_\mathbf{A}$ is in the *kernel* of L^T.

Let us denote by $\mathbb{K} = ker(L^\mathsf{T})$ the kernel of L^T.

Theorem 2. *Let* $\mathbf{v}_1, \ldots, \mathbf{v_n}$ *be* n *vectors from* $\mathbb{K}$ *such that* $\exists \alpha_1, \ldots, \alpha_n$ *with* $\alpha_i \mathbf{v}_i \geq \mathbf{0}$ *for all* i *and* $\mathbf{k}_\mathbf{A} = \sum_{i=1}^n \alpha_i \mathbf{v}_i$. *Then* $\{\mathbf{w}_1, \ldots, \mathbf{w_n}\}$ *for* $\mathbf{w_i} = \alpha_i \mathbf{v}_i$ *is a decomposition of* $\mathbf{k}_\mathbf{A}$ *and* $\{I_1, \ldots, I_n\}$ *for* $I_i \equiv \mathbf{w_i} C_A \mathbf{x} \leq \mathbf{c_A}$ *is a decomposition.*

Proof. The theorem follows from the definition of decomposition (Definition 1). From the assumptions of the theorem we immediately obtain $\mathbf{k}_\mathbf{A} = \sum_{i=1}^n \mathbf{w_i}$ and $\mathbf{w_i} \geq \mathbf{0}$. Moreover, $\mathbf{w_i} \in \mathbb{K}$, since $\mathbf{v_i} \in \mathbb{K}$ and $\mathbf{w_i} = \alpha_i \mathbf{v_i}$. As a consequence, $L^\mathsf{T}\mathbf{w_i} = 0$ and it follows that there are no A-local variables in $\mathbf{w_i}^\mathsf{T} C_A \mathbf{x}$.   □

Note that if the vectors are not linearly independent then the decomposition contains redundant elements. For example, if $w_3 = w_1 + w_2$ then $I_1 \wedge I_2 \implies I_3$ and I_3 is a redundant conjunct in the corresponding decomposed interpolant.

Good candidates that satisfy most of the assumptions of Theorem 2 (and avoid redundancies) are bases of the vector space $\mathbb{K}$. If $B = \{\mathbf{b}_1, \ldots, \mathbf{b_n}\}$ is a basis of $\mathbb{K}$ such that $\mathbf{k}_\mathbf{A} = \sum_{i=1}^n \alpha_i \mathbf{b_i}$ with $\alpha_i \mathbf{b_i} \geq \mathbf{0}$ for all i, then $\{\alpha_1 \mathbf{b}_1, \ldots, \alpha_n \mathbf{b_n}\}$ is a decomposition. Moreover, the decomposition generated by a basis cannot be refined (in the sense of the decomposition order $\prec$) without introducing redundancies. This follows from the fact that replacing one generator in a basis by more that one vector necessarily introduces linear dependency between the generators of the vector space. Thus, the decomposed interpolant from a basis has *maximal* logical strength. The search for a decomposition of Farkas coefficients $\mathbf{k}_\mathbf{A}$ by computing a basis of the kernel of the matrix of A-local variables L is described in Algorithm 1.

Function `Nullity` returns the dimension of the kernel. This can be efficiently computed for example using *Rank-Nullity Theorem* by computing Row Echelon Form of M by Gaussian elimination. Only if nullity is at least 2, we can hope to find any non-trivial decomposition. Function `KernelBasis` returns a basis of the kernel of a given matrix while function `Coordinates` returns the coordinates of the given vector with respect to the given basis. An algorithm to compute a basis of the kernel of a matrix can be found in any good introductory book on Linear

```
input  : matrix M, vector v such that v ∈ ker(M) and v > 0
output: (w₁, ..., wₘ), a decomposition of v, such that wᵢ ∈ ker(M), wᵢ ≥ 0
         and ∑ wᵢ = v
1 n ← Nullity(M)
2 if n ≤ 1 then return (v)
3 (b₁, ..., bₙ) ← KernelBasis(M)
4 (α₁, ..., αₙ) ← Coordinates(v, (b₁, ..., bₙ))
5 (w₁, ..., wₙ) ← (α₁b₁, ..., αₙbₙ)
6 if wᵢ ≥ 0 for each i then return (w₁, ..., wₙ)
7 else return (v)
```

Algorithm 1. Algorithm for decomposition of Farkas coefficients

Algebra, see e.g. [5]. If any component of the linear combination is negative, the combination cannot be used and we fall back to the trivial decomposition leading to the original Farkas interpolant. As a basis of a vector space is not unique, the implementation of KernelBasis may return an unsuitable basis even if a suitable one exists. This happened even in simple cases, so we implemented a strategy to replace unsuitable elements by a suitable sum of elements, if possible. Our preliminary results using this strategy are promising.

6   Experiments

We have implemented our algorithm in our SMT solver OPENSMT [21], which had already provided a variety of interpolation algorithms for propositional logic [22,33], theory of uninterpreted functions [4] and theory of linear real arithmetic [3]. We implemented both primal and dual versions of decomposed interpolation algorithm, which return the finest decomposition they can find.

We evaluated the effect of decomposed interpolants in a model-checking scenario using the model checker SALLY relying on OPENSMT for interpolation.[3] The PDKIND engine of SALLY was used, relying on YICES [15] for satisfiability queries and OPENSMT for interpolation queries. We experimented with four LRA interpolation algorithms: the original interpolation algorithms based on Farkas' lemma, Itp_F and Itp'_F, and the interpolation algorithm computing decomposed interpolants, Itp_{DI} and Itp'_{DI}. In each case, we used McMillan's interpolation rules [28] for the Boolean part. For comparison, we ran also a version of SALLY using MATHSAT in its default settings as an interpolation engine instead of OPENSMT. Since OPENSMT does not support the combination of incrementality and interpolation, MATHSAT was also used in non-incremental mode in this setting. The results are summarised in Figs. 1 and 2, and Table 1. The result of a portfolio is the virtual best of the results of individual algorithms

---

[3] Detailed description of the set-up and specifications of the experiments, together with all the results, can be found at http://verify.inf.usi.ch/content/decomposed-interpolants.

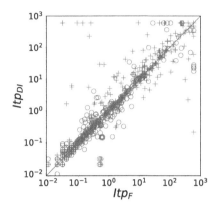
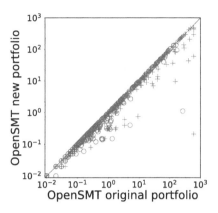

Fig. 1. Evaluation of the decomposed interpolants in model checking scenario. On the left, comparison of performance of SALLY using OPENSMT with different interpolation procedures, Itp_F and Itp_{DI}. On the right, the benefit of adding Itp_{DI} and Itp'_{DI} to the portfolio of interpolation procedures.

in the portfolio. The original portfolio of OPENSMT consists of Itp_F and Itp'_F, while in the new portfolio Itp_{DI} and Itp'_{DI} are added.

We used the same benchmarks as in [36]. They consist of several problem sets related to fault-tolerant algorithms (**om, ttesynchro, ttastartup, unifapprox, azadmanesh, approxagree, hacms, misc**), benchmarks from software model checking (**cav12, ctigar**), benchmark suite of KIND model checker (**lustre**), simple concurrent programs (**conc**), and problems modeling a lock-free hash table (**lfht**). Each benchmark is a transition system with formulas characterizing initial states, a transition relation and a property that should hold. SALLY can finish with two possible answers (or run out of resources without an answer): *valid* means the property holds and an invariant implying the property has been found; *invalid* means the property does not hold and a counterexample leading to a state where the property does not hold has been found. In the plots, we denote the answers as $+$ and $\circ$, respectively. The benchmarks were run on Linux machines with Intel E5-2650 v3 processor (2.3 GHz) with 64 GB of memory. Each benchmark was restricted to 600 s of running time and to 4 GB of memory.

Figure 1 illustrates the benefit of adding Itp_{DI} and Itp'_{DI} to the portfolio of OPENSMT interpolation algorithms. The direct comparison of Itp_F and Itp_{DI} clearly shows that in many cases the use of decomposed interpolants outperforms the original procedure, sometimes by an order of magnitude. The comparison of the old and the new portfolio shows that the importance of decomposition is still significant even after taking the capabilities of dual versions into account.

Figure 2 shows the benefit of the new portfolio by comparing the model checker performance to one using a different SMT solver. As far as we know, MATHSAT also computes interpolants from the proof of unsatisfiability and uses interpolation algorithm based on Farkas' lemma for LRA conflicts. Comparing to OPENSMT's Itp_F, we see that the version of SALLY using MATHSAT is superior, most probably

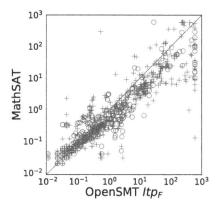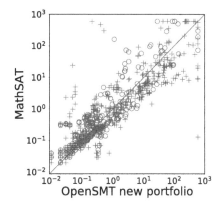

Fig. 2. Comparison of performance for the use of the interpolation procedure of MATH-SAT and OPENSMT—original Itp_F and the whole portfolio, respectively.

due to the differences in the implementation of the SMT solver. However, using the portfolio of interpolation procedures available in OPENSMT bridges the gap and allows SALLY to solve more benchmarks as can be seen in Table 1. This also shows a potential improvement for MATHSAT if it would offer the same portfolio of interpolation procedures as OPENSMT does.

Table 1 demonstrates the gain in the performance of the model checker from adding Itp_{DI} and Itp'_{DI} to the interpolation portfolio. The results are summarised *by category* with the name of the category and its number of benchmarks in the first column. The two columns per interpolation engine show the number of benchmarks successfully solved (validated/invalidated) within the limits and the total running time for *solved* benchmarks. Not only does the model checker with the extended portfolio solve *more* instances, but it also does so in *less* time.

Table 2 answers the question how often the new interpolation procedure manages to decompose Farkas coefficients, thus returning a different interpolant than the original procedure would. The statistics differ for Itp_{DI} and Itp'_{DI} due to the special nature of the interpolation problems in this model checking algorithm, as B-part *always* contains *only* shared symbols. Theoretically, this means Itp'_{DI} cannot discover any non-trivial elements of decomposition as there are no B-local variables. On the other hand, the decomposition to trivial elements is always possible, as all B-inequalities contain only shared variables. In our implementation, however, we consider the locality of a variable not from the global point of the whole interpolation problem, but from the local point of the current theory conflict. Consequently, even if a variable is shared in the whole problem, it can be local for the current theory conflict and the interpolant is not decomposed even if, from a global point, it could have been.

For Itp_{DI}, the first column reports the number of benchmarks with at least a *single* decomposition (any; with at least one trivial element; with at least one non-trivial element). The second column ("#non-triv. LRA itps") reports the total number of interpolation problems for theory conflict, not counting those without

Table 1. Performance of SALLY with old and new OPENSMT interpolation capabilities. Comparison with MATHSAT with its default interpolation included.

	OPENSMT portfolio Itp_F, Itp'_F		OPENSMT portfolio Itp_F, Itp'_F, Itp_{DI}, Itp'_{DI}		MATHSAT	
Problem set	solved (V/I)	Σ time(s)	solved (V/I)	Σ time(s)	solved (V/I)	Σ time(s)
approxagree (9)	9 (8/1)	101	9 (8/1)	72	9 (8/1)	173
azadmanesh (20)	16 (13/3)	74	16 (13/3)	69	19 (16/3)	102
cav12 (99)	63 (46/17)	3,427	63 (46/17)	2,960	64 (47/17)	796
conc (6)	3 (3/0)	48	4 (4/0)	347	3 (3/0)	38
ctigar (110)	70 (51/19)	1,812	72 (53/19)	1,493	75 (55/20)	1,803
hacms (5)	1 (1/0)	147	1 (1/0)	84	1 (1/0)	55
lfht (27)	17 (17/0)	502	17 (17/0)	502	16 (16/0)	518
lustre (790)	757 (423/334)	5,122	759 (425/334)	4,903	752 (420/332)	5,610
misc (10)	7 (6/1)	80	7 (6/1)	80	7 (6/1)	36
om (9)	9 (7/2)	7	9 (7/2)	7	9 (7/2)	6
ttastartup (3)	1 (1/0)	2	1 (1/0)	2	1 (1/0)	13
ttesynchro (6)	6 (3/3)	11	6 (3/3)	10	6 (3/3)	6
unifapprox (11)	10 (7/3)	21	10 (7/3)	20	11 (8/3)	125
	969 (586/383)	11,354	974 (591/383)	10,549	973 (591/382)	9,281

even theoretical possibility for decomposition. These include the problems where all inequalities were from one part of the problem (resulting in trivial interpolants, either ⊤ or ⊥) and the problems with a single inequality in the A-part (trivially yielding an interpolant equal to that inequality). The last column reports the number of successfully decomposed interpolants (with at least one trivial element; with at least one non-trivial element). Note that it can happen that a successful decomposition contains both trivial and non-trivial elements. For Itp'_{DI}, statistics regarding decompositions with non-trivial elements are left out as these decompositions were extremely rare. We see that at least one decomposition was possible in only roughly half of all the benchmarks. This explains why there are many points on the diagonal in Fig. 1. On the other hand, it shows that the test for the *possibility* of decomposition is very cheap and does not present a significant overhead. Another conclusion we can draw is that when the structure of the benchmark allows decomposition, the decomposition can often be discovered in many theory conflicts that appear during the solving.

During the evaluation we noticed that a small change in the solver sometimes had a huge effect on the performance of the model checker for a particular benchmark. It made previously unsolved instance easily solvable (or the other way around). To confirm that on some benchmarks Itp_{DI} is really better than Itp_F, we ran the model checker 100 times on chosen benchmarks, each time with a different random seed for the interpolating solver. For the benchmark **dillig03.c.mcmt** from category **ctigar** the model checker using Itp_F did *not* converge (in all runs) while Itp_{DI} ensured convergence in 0.2 s (in all runs). Itp_F also did not solve **fib_bench_safe_v1.mcmt** from category **conc**

Table 2. Interpolation statistics – pwd stands for "Number of problems with at least one decomposition". The numbers in parentheses denote "Decompositions with trivial and with non-trivial elements" (trivial/non-trivial).

Problem set	pwd	Itp_{DI} #non-triv. LRA itps	#decomp. itps	pwd	Itp'_{DI} #non-triv. LRA itps	#decomp. itps
approxagree (9)	1 (1/0)	7	7 (7/0)	1	18	18
azadmanesh (20)	4 (0/4)	4,831	266 (0/266)	4	4,353	4,353
cav12 (99)	31 (25/15)	1,368,187	7,399 (1,690/5,738)	45	204,036	57,127
conc (6)	3 (3/3)	424,145	215,376 (1,256/214,120)	3	13	13
ctigar (110)	73 (56/70)	2,982,559	826,621 (29,378/797,871)	77	152,613	152,612
hacms (5)	5 (5/5)	363,265	15,282 (532/14,750)	5	58,416	58,416
lfht (27)	13 (12/13)	838,094	12,785 (169/12,616)	14	111,060	111,060
lustre (790)	356 (356/192)	2,571,091	1,851,213 (855,958/1,054,516)	500	1,833,310	1,833,310
misc (10)	5 (4/5)	195,819	62,865 (8,700/55,042)	6	35,131	35,108
om (9)	4 (4/3)	1,150	236 (206/30)	3	168	168
ttastartup (3)	2 (2/2)	69,699	924 (16/908)	3	11,528	11,528
ttesynchro (6)	4 (4/0)	64	38 (38/0)	5	310	310
unifapprox (11)	0 (0/0)	0	0 (0/0)	2	25	25

and **large_const_c.mcmt** from category **ctigar**, while Itp_{DI} solved them in 42 runs on average in 377 s, and in 80 runs on average in 97 s, respectively. Finally, the benchmark **DRAGON_13.mcmt** from **lustre** was solved by Itp_F in 5 runs on average in 539 s, while it was solved by Itp_{DI} in 23 runs on average in 441 s.

7   Conclusion

In this paper, we have presented a new interpolation algorithm for linear real arithmetic that generalizes the interpolation algorithm based on Farkas' lemma used in modern SMT solvers. We showed that the algorithm is able to compute interpolants in the form of a *conjunction* of inequalities that are logically stronger than the single inequality returned by the original approach. This is useful in the IC3-style model-checking algorithms where Farkas interpolants have been shown to be a source of incompleteness. In our experiments, we have demonstrated that the opportunity to decompose Farkas interpolants occurs frequently in practice and that the decomposition often leads to (i) shortening of solving time and, in some cases, to (ii) solving a problem not solvable by the previous approach.

As the next steps, we plan to investigate how to automatically determine what kind of interpolant would be more useful for the current interpolation query in IC3-style model-checking algorithms. We also plan to investigate other uses of interpolation in model checking where stronger (or weaker) interpolants are desirable [34].

Acknowledgements. We would like to thank Dejan Jovanović for providing the benchmarks and for the help with integrating OPENSMT into SALLY. This work was supported by the Czech Science Foundation project 17-12465S and by the Swiss National Science Foundation (SNSF) grant 200020_166288.

References

1. Albarghouthi, A., McMillan, K.L.: Beautiful Interpolants. In: Sharygina, N., Veith, H. (eds.) CAV 2013. LNCS, vol. 8044, pp. 313–329. Springer, Heidelberg (2013). https://doi.org/10.1007/978-3-642-39799-8_22

2. Alt, L., Fedyukovich, G., Hyvärinen, A.E.J., Sharygina, N.: A proof-sensitive approach for small propositional interpolants. In: Gurfinkel, A., Seshia, S.A. (eds.) VSTTE 2015. LNCS, vol. 9593, pp. 1–18. Springer, Cham (2016). https://doi.org/10.1007/978-3-319-29613-5_1

3. Alt, L., Hyvärinen, A.E.J., Sharygina, N.: LRA interpolants from no man's land. In: Strichman, O., Tzoref-Brill, R. (eds.) HVC 2017. LNCS, vol. 10629, pp. 195–210. Springer, Cham (2017). https://doi.org/10.1007/978-3-319-70389-3_13

4. Alt, L., Hyvärinen, A.E.J., Asadi, S., Sharygina, N.: Duality-based interpolation for quantifier-free equalities and uninterpreted functions. In: Stewart, D., Weissenbacher, G. (eds.) FMCAD 2017, pp. 39–46. IEEE (2017)

5. Andrilli, S., Hecker, D.: Elementary Linear Algebra, 5th edn. Academic Press, Cambridge (2016). https://doi.org/10.1016/C2013-0-19116-7

6. Barrett, C., de Moura, L., Ranise, S., Stump, A., Tinelli, C.: The SMT-LIB initiative and the rise of SMT. In: Barner, S., Harris, I., Kroening, D., Raz, O. (eds.) HVC 2010. LNCS, vol. 6504, p. 3. Springer, Heidelberg (2011). https://doi.org/10.1007/978-3-642-19583-9_2

7. Barrett, C., Sebastiani, R., Seshia, S., Tinelli, C.: Satisfiability modulo theories. Frontiers in Artificial Intelligence and Applications, 1 edn., vol. 185, pp. 825–885 (2009)

8. Bradley, A.R.: SAT-based model checking without unrolling. In: Jhala, R., Schmidt, D. (eds.) VMCAI 2011. LNCS, vol. 6538, pp. 70–87. Springer, Heidelberg (2011). https://doi.org/10.1007/978-3-642-18275-4_7

9. Cimatti, A., Griggio, A., Schaafsma, B.J., Sebastiani, R.: The MathSAT5 SMT solver. In: Piterman, N., Smolka, S.A. (eds.) TACAS 2013. LNCS, vol. 7795, pp. 93–107. Springer, Heidelberg (2013). https://doi.org/10.1007/978-3-642-36742-7_7

10. Craig, W.: Three uses of the Herbrand-Gentzen theorem in relating model theory and proof theory. J. Symbolic Logic **22**(3), 269–285 (1957)

11. Davis, M., Logemann, G., Loveland, D.W.: A machine program for theorem-proving. Commun. ACM **5**(7), 394–397 (1962)

12. Davis, M., Putnam, H.: A computing procedure for quantification theory. J. ACM **7**(3), 201–215 (1960)

13. Detlefs, D., Nelson, G., Saxe, J.B.: Simplify: a theorem prover for program checking. J. ACM **52**(3), 365–473 (2005)

14. D'Silva, V., Kroening, D., Purandare, M., Weissenbacher, G.: Interpolant strength. In: Barthe, G., Hermenegildo, M. (eds.) VMCAI 2010. LNCS, vol. 5944, pp. 129–145. Springer, Heidelberg (2010). https://doi.org/10.1007/978-3-642-11319-2_12

15. Dutertre, B.: Yices 2.2. In: Biere, A., Bloem, R. (eds.) CAV 2014. LNCS, vol. 8559, pp. 737–744. Springer, Cham (2014). https://doi.org/10.1007/978-3-319-08867-9_49

16. Dutertre, B., de Moura, L.: A fast linear-arithmetic solver for DPLL(T). In: Ball, T., Jones, R.B. (eds.) CAV 2006. LNCS, vol. 4144, pp. 81–94. Springer, Heidelberg (2006). https://doi.org/10.1007/11817963_11

17. Farkas, G.: A Fourier-féle mechanikai elv alkalmazásai (Hungarian) (On the applications of the mechanical principle of Fourier) (1894)

18. Gurfinkel, A., Kahsai, T., Komuravelli, A., Navas, J.A.: The SeaHorn verification framework. In: Kroening, D., Păsăreanu, C.S. (eds.) CAV 2015. LNCS, vol. 9206, pp. 343–361. Springer, Cham (2015). https://doi.org/10.1007/978-3-319-21690-4_20

19. Gurfinkel, A., Rollini, S.F., Sharygina, N.: Interpolation properties and SAT-based model checking. In: Van Hung, D., Ogawa, M. (eds.) ATVA 2013. LNCS, vol. 8172, pp. 255–271. Springer, Cham (2013). https://doi.org/10.1007/978-3-319-02444-8_19

20. Huberman, B.A., Lukose, R.M., Hogg, T.: An economics approach to hard computational problems. Science **275**(5296), 51–54 (1997)

21. Hyvärinen, A.E.J., Marescotti, M., Alt, L., Sharygina, N.: OpenSMT2: An SMT solver for multi-core and cloud computing. In: Creignou, N., Le Berre, D. (eds.) SAT 2016. LNCS, vol. 9710, pp. 547–553. Springer, Cham (2016). https://doi.org/10.1007/978-3-319-40970-2_35

22. Jančík, P., Alt, L., Fedyukovich, G., Hyvärinen, A.E.J., Kofroň, J., Sharygina, N.: PVAIR: Partial Variable Assignment InterpolatoR. In: Stevens, P., Wąsowski, A. (eds.) FASE 2016. LNCS, vol. 9633, pp. 419–434. Springer, Heidelberg (2016). https://doi.org/10.1007/978-3-662-49665-7_25

23. Jančík, P., Kofroň, J., Rollini, S.F., Sharygina, N.: On interpolants and variable assignments. In: FMCAD 2014, pp. 123–130. IEEE (2014)

24. Jovanović, D., Dutertre, B.: Property-directed k-induction. In: FMCAD 2016, pp. 85–92. IEEE (2016)

25. Komuravelli, A., Gurfinkel, A., Chaki, S.: SMT-based model checking for recursive programs. In: Biere, A., Bloem, R. (eds.) CAV 2014. LNCS, vol. 8559, pp. 17–34. Springer, Cham (2014). https://doi.org/10.1007/978-3-319-08867-9_2

26. Korovin, K., Tsiskaridze, N., Voronkov, A.: Conflict resolution. In: Gent, I.P. (ed.) CP 2009. LNCS, vol. 5732, pp. 509–523. Springer, Heidelberg (2009). https://doi.org/10.1007/978-3-642-04244-7_41

27. Manna, Z., Pnueli, A.: Temporal Verification of Reactive Systems: Safety. Springer, Heidelberg (1995). https://doi.org/10.1007/978-1-4612-4222-2

28. McMillan, K.L.: Interpolation and SAT-based model checking. In: Hunt, W.A., Somenzi, F. (eds.) CAV 2003. LNCS, vol. 2725, pp. 1–13. Springer, Heidelberg (2003). https://doi.org/10.1007/978-3-540-45069-6_1

29. McMillan, K.L.: An interpolating theorem prover. Theoret. Comput. Sci. **345**(1), 101–121 (2005)

30. de Moura, L., Bjørner, N.: Z3: An efficient SMT solver. In: Ramakrishnan, C.R., Rehof, J. (eds.) TACAS 2008. LNCS, vol. 4963, pp. 337–340. Springer, Heidelberg (2008). https://doi.org/10.1007/978-3-540-78800-3_24

31. Nieuwenhuis, R., Oliveras, A.: Proof-producing congruence closure. In: Giesl, J. (ed.) RTA 2005. LNCS, vol. 3467, pp. 453–468. Springer, Heidelberg (2005). https://doi.org/10.1007/978-3-540-32033-3_33

32. Pudlák, P.: Lower bounds for resolution and cutting plane proofs and monotone computations. J. Symbolic Logic **62**(3), 981–998 (1997)

33. Rollini, S.F., Alt, L., Fedyukovich, G., Hyvärinen, A.E.J., Sharygina, N.: PeRIPLO: a framework for producing effective interpolants in SAT-based software verification. In: McMillan, K., Middeldorp, A., Voronkov, A. (eds.) LPAR 2013. LNCS, vol. 8312, pp. 683–693. Springer, Heidelberg (2013). https://doi.org/10.1007/978-3-642-45221-5_45

34. Rollini, S.F., Sery, O., Sharygina, N.: Leveraging interpolant strength in model checking. In: Madhusudan, P., Seshia, S.A. (eds.) CAV 2012. LNCS, vol. 7358, pp. 193–209. Springer, Heidelberg (2012). https://doi.org/10.1007/978-3-642-31424-7_18

35. Rybalchenko, A., Sofronie-Stokkermans, V.: Constraint solving for interpolation. In: Cook, B., Podelski, A. (eds.) VMCAI 2007. LNCS, vol. 4349, pp. 346–362. Springer, Heidelberg (2007). https://doi.org/10.1007/978-3-540-69738-1_25

36. Schindler, T., Jovanović, D.: Selfless interpolation for infinite-state model checking. In: Dillig, I., Palsberg, J. (eds.) VMCAI 2018. LNCS, vol. 10747, pp. 495–515. Springer, Cham (2018). https://doi.org/10.1007/978-3-319-73721-8_23

37. Scholl, C., Pigorsch, F., Disch, S., Althaus, E.: Simple interpolants for linear arithmetic. In: DATE 2014, pp. 1–6. IEEE (2014)

38. Schrijver, A.: Theory of Linear and Integer Programming. Wiley, New York (1998)

39. Sheeran, M., Singh, S., Stålmarck, G.: Checking safety properties using induction and a SAT-solver. In: Hunt, W.A., Johnson, S.D. (eds.) FMCAD 2000. LNCS, vol. 1954, pp. 127–144. Springer, Heidelberg (2000). https://doi.org/10.1007/3-540-40922-X_8

40. Silva, J.P.M., Sakallah, K.A.: GRASP: A search algorithm for propositional satisfiability. IEEE Trans. Comput. **48**(5), 506–521 (1999)

Parallel SAT Simplification
on GPU Architectures

Muhammad Osama(⊠)(iD) and Anton Wijs(⊠)(iD)

Eindhoven University of Technology, 5600 MB Eindhoven, The Netherlands
{o.m.m.muhammad,a.j.wijs}@tue.nl

Abstract. The growing scale of applications encoded to Boolean Satisfiability (SAT) problems imposes the need for accelerating SAT simplifications or preprocessing. Parallel SAT preprocessing has been an open
challenge for many years. Therefore, we propose novel parallel algorithms
for variable and subsumption elimination targeting Graphics Processing
Units (GPUs). Benchmarks show that the algorithms achieve an acceleration of 66× over a state-of-the-art SAT simplifier (SatELite). Regarding
SAT solving, we have conducted a thorough evaluation, combining both
our GPU algorithms and SatELite with MiniSat to solve the simplified
problems. In addition, we have studied the impact of the algorithms on
the solvability of problems with Lingeling. We conclude that our algorithms have a considerable impact on the solvability of SAT problems.

Keywords: Satisfiability · Variable elimination ·
Subsumption elimination · Parallel SAT preprocessing · GPU

1 Introduction

Algorithms to solve propositional Boolean Satisfiability (SAT) problems are
being used extensively for various applications, such as artificial intelligence, circuit design, automatic test pattern generation, automatic theorem proving, and
bounded model checking. Of course, SAT being NP-complete, scalability of these
algorithms is an issue. Simplifying SAT problems prior to solving them has proven
its effectiveness in modern conflict-driven clause learning (CDCL) SAT solvers [6,
9], particularly when applied on real-world applications relevant to software and
hardware verification [8,12,17,19]. It tends to produce reasonable reductions in
acceptable processing time. Many techniques based on, e.g., variable elimination,
clause elimination, and equivalence reasoning are being used to simplify SAT problems, whether prior to the solving phase (preprocessing) [8,10,12,15,16,24] or
during the search (inprocessing) [3,18]. However, applying variable and clause

M. Osama—This work is part of the GEARS project with project number TOP2.16.044,
which is (partly) financed by the Netherlands Organisation for Scientific Research
(NWO).
A. Wijs—We gratefully acknowledge the support of NVIDIA Corporation with the dona-
tion of the GeForce Titan Xp's used for this research.

T. Vojnar and L. Zhang (Eds.): TACAS 2019, Part I, LNCS 11427, pp. 21–40, 2019.
https://doi.org/10.1007/978-3-030-17462-0_2

elimination iteratively to large problems (in terms of the number of literals) can be a performance bottleneck in the whole SAT solving procedure, or even increase the number of literals, negatively impacting the solving time.

Recently, the authors of [2,11] discussed the current main challenges in parallel SAT solving. One of these challenges concerns the parallelisation of SAT simplification in modern SAT solvers. Massively parallel computing systems such as Graphics Processing Units (GPUs) offer great potential to speed up computations, but to achieve this, it is crucial to engineer new parallel algorithms and data structures from scratch to make optimal use of those architectures. GPU platforms have become attractive for general-purpose computing with the availability of the Compute Unified Device Architecture (CUDA) programming model [20]. CUDA is widely used to accelerate applications that are computationally intensive w.r.t. data processing and memory access. In recent years, for instance, we have applied GPUs to accelerate explicit-state model checking [26,27,30], state space decomposition [28,29] and minimisation [25], metaheuristic SAT solving [31], and SAT-based test generation [22].

In this paper, we introduce the first parallel algorithms for various techniques widely used in SAT simplification and discuss the various performance aspects of the proposed implementations and data structures. Also, we discuss the main challenges in CPU-GPU memory management and how to address them. In a nutshell, we aim to effectively simplify SAT formulas, even if they are extremely large, in only a few seconds using the massive computing capabilities of GPUs.

Contributions. We propose novel parallel algorithms to simplify SAT formulas using GPUs, and experimentally evaluate them, i.e., we measure both their runtime efficiency and their effect on the overall solving time, for a large benchmark set of SAT instances encoding real-world problems. We show how multiple variables can be eliminated simultaneously on a GPU while preserving the original satisfiability of a given formula. We call this technique Bounded Variable-Independent Parallel Elimination (BVIPE). The eliminated variables are elected first based on some criteria using the proposed algorithm Least-Constrained Variable Elections (LCVE). The variable elimination procedure includes both the so-called *resolution rule* and *gate equivalence reasoning*. Furthermore, we propose an algorithm for *parallel subsumption elimination* (PSE), covering both *subsumption elimination* and *self-subsuming resolution*.

The paper is organised as follows: Sect. 2 introduces the preliminaries. The main GPU challenges for SAT simplification are discussed in Sect. 3, and the proposed algorithms are explained in Sect. 4. Section 5 presents our experimental evaluation. Section 6 discusses related work, and Sect. 7 provides a conclusion and suggests future work.

2   Preliminaries

All SAT formulas in this paper are in conjunctive normal form (CNF). A CNF formula is a conjunction of clauses $\bigwedge_{i=1}^{m} C_i$ where each clause C_i is a disjunction of literals $\bigvee_{j=1}^{k} \ell_j$ and a literal is a Boolean variable x or its complement $\neg x$, which we refer to as $\bar{x}$. We represent clauses by sets of literals $C = \{\ell_1, \ldots, \ell_k\}$, i.e., $\{\ell_1, \ldots, \ell_k\}$ represents the formula $\ell_1 \vee \ldots \vee \ell_k$, and a SAT formula by a set of clauses $\{C_1, \ldots, C_m\}$, i.e., $\{C_1, \ldots, C_m\}$ represents the formula $C_1 \wedge \ldots \wedge C_m$.

Variable Elimination. Variables can be removed from clauses by either applying the *resolution rule* or *gate-equivalence reasoning*. Concerning the former, we represent application of the resolution rule w.r.t. some variable x using a *resolving operator* $\otimes_x$ on C_1 and C_2. The result of applying the rule is called the *resolvent* [24]. It is defined as $C_1 \otimes_x C_2 = C_1 \cup C_2 \setminus \{x, \bar{x}\}$, and can be applied iff $x \in C_1$, $\bar{x} \in C_2$. The $\otimes_x$ operator can be extended to resolve sets of clauses w.r.t. variable x. For a formula S, let $S_x \subseteq S$, $S_{\bar{x}} \subseteq S$ be the set of all clauses in S containing x and $\bar{x}$, respectively. The new resolvents are defined as $R_x(S) = \{C_1 \otimes_x C_2 \mid C_1 \in S_x \wedge C_2 \in S_{\bar{x}} \wedge \neg \exists y.\{y, \bar{y}\} \subseteq C_1 \otimes_x C_2\}$. The last condition addresses that a resolvent should not be a *tautology*, i.e. a self-satisfied clause in which a variable and its negation exist. The set of non-tautology resolvents can replace S, producing an equivalent SAT formula.

Gate-Equivalence Reasoning. This technique substitutes eliminated variables with deduced logical equivalent expressions. In this work, we focus on the reasoning of AND-OR gates since they are common in SAT-encoded problems and OR gates are likely to be found if AND-equivalence reasoning fails. In general, gate-equivalence reasoning can also be applied using other logical gates. A logical AND gate with k inputs $\ell_1, \ldots, \ell_k$ and output x can be captured by the two implications $x \implies \ell_1 \wedge \ldots \wedge \ell_k$ and $\ell_1 \wedge \ldots \wedge \ell_k \implies x$. In turn, these two implications can be encoded in SAT clauses $\{\{\bar{x}, \ell_1\}, \ldots, \{\bar{x}, \ell_k\}\}$ and $\{\{x, \bar{\ell}_1, \ldots, \bar{\ell}_k\}\}$, respectively. Similarly, the implications of an OR gate $x \implies \ell_1 \vee \ldots \vee \ell_k$ and $\ell_1 \vee \ldots \vee \ell_k \implies x$ are expressed by the SAT clauses $\{\{x, \bar{\ell}_1\}, \ldots, \{x, \bar{\ell}_k\}\}$ and $\{\{\bar{x}, \ell_1, \ldots, \ell_k\}\}$, respectively.

For instance, consider the following formula:

$$S = \{\{x, \bar{a}, \bar{b}\}, \{\bar{x}, a\}, \{\bar{x}, b\}, \{x, c\}, \{\bar{x}, \bar{b}\}, \{y, f\}, \{\bar{y}, d, e\}, \{y, \bar{d}\}, \{y, \bar{e}\}\}$$

The first three clauses in S capture the AND gate (x, a, b) and the last three clauses capture the OR gate (y, d, e). By substituting $a \wedge b$ for x and $d \vee e$ for y in the fourth, fifth, and sixth clauses, a new formula $\{\{a, c\}, \{b, c\}, \{\bar{a}, \bar{b}\}, \{d, e, f\}\}$ can be constructed. Combining AND/OR-gate equivalence reasoning with the resolution rule tends to result in smaller formulas compared to only applying the resolution rule [8,23].

Subsumption Elimination. A clause C_2 is said to *subsume* clause C_1 iff $C_2 \subseteq C_1$. The subsumed clause C_1 is redundant and can be deleted from the original SAT equation. A special form of subsumption is called *self-subsuming resolution*. It is applicable for two clauses C_1, C_2 iff for some variable x, we have $C_1 = C_1' \cup \{x\}$, $C_2 = C_2' \cup \{\bar{x}\}$, and $C_2' \subseteq C_1'$. Consider the clauses: $C_1 = \{x, a, b\}$ and $C_2 = \{\bar{x}, b\}$; C_2 self-subsumes C_1 since $x \in C_1$, $\bar{x} \in C_2$ and $\{b\} \subseteq \{a, b\}$. The self-subsuming literal x can be discarded, producing clause $C_1 = \{a, b\}$. In other words, we say that C_1 is *strengthened* by C_2.

3   GPU Challenges: Memory and Data

GPU Architecture. CUDA is a programming model developed by NVIDIA [20] to provide a general-purpose programming paradigm and allow using the massive capabilities of GPU resources to accelerate applications. Regarding the processing hardware, a GPU consists of multiple streaming multiprocessors (SMs) and each SM resembles an array of streaming processors (SPs) where every SP can execute multiple threads grouped together in 32-thread scheduling units called *warps*. On the programming level, a program can launch a *kernel* (GPU global function) to be executed by thousands of threads packed in thread *blocks* of up to 1,024 threads or 32 warps. All threads together form a *grid*. The GPU manages the execution of a launched kernel by evenly distributing the launched blocks to the available SMs through a hardware warp scheduler.

Concerning the memory hierarchy, a GPU has multiple types of memory:

- *Global memory* is accessible by all threads with high bandwidth but also high latency. The CPU (host) can access it as an interface to the GPU.
- *Shared memory* is on-chip memory shared by the threads in a block; it is smaller in size and has lower latency than global memory. It can be used to efficiently communicate data between threads in a block.
- *Registers* provide thread-local storage and provide the fastest memory.

To make optimal use of global memory bandwidth and hide its latency, using *coalesced accesses* is one of the best practices in global memory optimisation. When the threads in a warp try to access a consecutive block of 32-bit words, their accesses are combined into a single (coalesced) memory access. Uncoalesced memory accesses can for instance be caused by data sparsity or misalignment.

Regarding atomicity, a GPU is capable of executing *atomic* operations on both global and shared memory. A GPU *atomic* function typically performs a *read-modify-write* memory operation on one 32-bit or 64-bit word.

Memory Management. When small data packets need to be accessed frequently, both on the host (CPU) and device (GPU) side (which is the case in the current work), *unified memory* can play a crucial role in boosting the transfer rates by avoiding excessive memory copies. Unified memory creates a pool of managed memory that is shared between the CPU and GPU. This pool is accessible to both sides using a single pointer. Another advantage of unified memory is that it allows the CPU to allocate multidimensional pointers referencing global memory locations or nested structures. However, if a memory pool is required to be reallocated (resized), one must maintain memory coherency between the CPU-side and GPU-side memories. A reallocation procedure is necessary for our variable elimination algorithm, to make memory available when producing resolvents and reduce the memory use when removing clauses.

To better explain the coherency problem in reallocation, suppose there is an array A allocated and loaded with some data X, then X is visible from both the CPU and GPU memories. When A is reallocated from the host side, the memory is not physically allocated until it is first accessed, particularly when using an NVIDIA GPU with the Pascal architecture [20]. Once new data Y is written to A from the device side, both sides will observe a combination of X and Y, leading to memory corruptions and page faults. To avoid this problem, A must be reset on the host side directly after memory reallocation to assert the physical allocation. After that, each kernel may store its own data safely in the global memory. In the proposed algorithms, we introduce two types of optimisations addressing memory space and latency.

Regarding memory space optimisation, allocating memory dynamically each time a clause is added is not practical on a GPU while variables are eliminated in parallel. To resolve this, we initially launch a GPU kernel to calculate an upper bound for the number of resolvents to be added before the elimination procedure starts (Sect. 4.1). After this, reallocation is applied to store the new resolvents. Furthermore, a global counter is implemented inside our CNF data structure to keep track of new clauses. This counter is incremented atomically by each thread when adding a clause.

Concerning memory latency optimisation, when thread blocks produce resolvents, these can initially be stored in shared memory. Checking for tautologies can then be done by accessing shared memory, and non-tautologies can be written back to the global memory in a new CNF formula. Also, the definitions of AND-OR gates can be stored in shared memory, to be used later when applying clause substitution (see Sect. 4.1). This has the advantage of reducing the number of global memory accesses. Nevertheless, the size of shared memory in a GPU is very limited (48 KB in most architectures). If the potential size of a resolvent is larger than the amount pre-allocated for a single clause, our BVIPE algorithm automatically switches to the global memory and the resolvent is directly added to the new CNF formula. This mechanism reduces the global memory latency when applicable and deals with the shared memory size limitation dynamically.

Data Structures. The efficiency of state-of-the-art sequential SAT solving and preprocessing is to a large extent due to the meticulously coded data structures. When considering SAT simplification on GPUs, new data structures have to be tailored from scratch. In this work, we need two of them, one for the SAT formula in CNF form (which we refer to as *CNF*) and another for the literal *occurrence table* (*occurTAB*), via which one can efficiently iterate over all clauses containing a particular literal. In CPU implementations, typically, they are created using *heaps* and *auto-resizable vectors*, respectively. However, heaps and vectors are not suitable for GPU parallelisation, since data is inserted, reallocated and sorted dynamically. The best GPU alternative is to create a nested data structure with arrays using unified memory (see Fig. 1). The *CNF* contains a raw pointer (linear array) to store CNF literals and a child structure *Clause* to store clause info. Each clause has a *head pointer* referring to its first literal. The *occurTAB* structure has a raw pointer to store the clause occurrences (array pointers) for each literal in the formula and a child structure *occurList*. The creation of an *occurList* instance is done in parallel per literal using atomic operations. For each clause C, a thread is launched to insert the occurrences of C's literals in the associated *occurLists*. One important remark is that two threads storing the occurrences of different literals do not have to wait for each other. For instance, *occurTAB* in Fig. 1 shows two different atomic insertions executed at the same time for literals 2 and –1 (if an integer i represents a literal x, then $-i$ represents $\bar{x}$). This minimises the performance penalty of using atomics.

The advantages of the proposed data structures are: as mentioned above, *occurTAB* instances can be constructed in parallel. Furthermore, coalesced access is guaranteed since pointers are stored consecutively (the gray arrows in Fig. 1), and no explicit memory copying is done (host and device pointers are identical) making it easier to integrate the data structures with any sequential or parallel code.

4   Algorithm Design and Implementation

4.1   Parallel Variable Elimination

In order to eliminate Boolean variables simultaneously in SAT formulas without altering the original satisfiability, a set of variables should be selected for elimination checking that contains only variables that are *independent* of each other. The LCVE algorithm we propose is responsible for electing such a subset from a set of authorised candidates. The remaining variables relying on the elected ones are frozen.

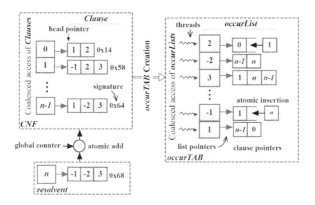

Fig. 1. An example of *CNF* and *occurTAB* data structures.

Algorithm 1: Constructing $\mathcal{A}$ - *GPU*

Input : __global__ $S[\,]$, n, μ
Output: __global__ $\mathcal{A}[\,]$

1 $h \leftarrow$ histogram(S, n);
2 $\mathcal{A} \leftarrow [\,]$; *scores* $\leftarrow [\,]$;
3 $\mathcal{A}$, *scores* $\leftarrow$ assignScores($h, \mathcal{A}, scores$);
4 $\mathcal{A} \leftarrow$ prune(sort($\mathcal{A}, scores$), h, μ);

Definition 1 (Authorised candidates). *Given a CNF formula S, we call $\mathcal{A}$ the set of* authorised candidates: $\mathcal{A} = \{x \mid 1 \leq h[x] \leq \mu \vee 1 \leq h[\bar{x}] \leq \mu\}$, *where*

- h is a histogram array ($h[x]$ is the number of occurrences of x in S)
- μ denotes a given maximum number of occurrences allowed for both x and its complement, representing the cut-off point for the LCVE algorithm

Definition 2 (Candidate Dependency Relation). *We call a relation* $\mathcal{D}$: $\mathcal{A} \times \mathcal{A}$ *a candidate dependency relation iff* $\forall x, y \in \mathcal{A}$, $x \mathcal{D} y$ *implies that* $\exists C \in S.(x \in C \vee \bar{x} \in C) \wedge (y \in C \vee \bar{y} \in C)$

Definition 3 (Elected candidates). *Given a set of authorised candidates* $\mathcal{A}$, *we call a set* $\varphi \subseteq \mathcal{A}$ *a set of* elected candidates *iff* $\forall x, y \in \varphi. \neg(x \mathcal{D} y)$

Definition 4 (Frozen candidates). *Given the sets* $\mathcal{A}$ *and* φ, *the set of* frozen candidates $\mathcal{F} \subseteq \mathcal{A}$ *is defined as* $\mathcal{F} = \{x \mid x \in \mathcal{A} \wedge \exists y \in \varphi. x \mathcal{D} y\}$

Before LCVE is executed, a sorted list of the variables in the CNF formula needs to be created, ordered by the number of occurrences in the formula, in ascending order (following the same rule as in [8]). From this list, the authorised candidates $\mathcal{A}$ can be straightforwardly derived, using μ as a cut-off point. Construction of this list can be done efficiently on a GPU using Algorithms 1 and 2. Algorithm 1 is labelled *GPU*, indicating that each individual step can be launched as a GPU computation. In contrast, algorithms providing kernel code, i.e., that describe the steps each individual GPU thread should perform as part of a GPU computation, such as Algorithm 2, are labelled *GPU kernel*.

Algorithm 2: Assign Scores to SAT formula variables - *GPU kernel*

Input   : __global__ $h[]$, $\mathcal{A}[]$, *scores*[]
Output: __global__ $\mathcal{A}[]$, *scores*[]

1 $tid \leftarrow xThread + blockDim \times xBlock$; $stride \leftarrow gridDim \times blockDim$;
2 **while** $tid < n$ **do**
3       $x \leftarrow tid + 1$;
4       $\mathcal{A}[tid] \leftarrow x$;
5   **if** $h[x] = 0 \vee h[\bar{x}] = 0$ **then**
6          $scores[x] \leftarrow \max(h[x], h[\bar{x}])$
7   **else**
8          $scores[x] \leftarrow h[x] \times h[\bar{x}]$
9       $tid \leftarrow tid + stride$

As input, Algorithm 1 requires a SAT formula S as an instance of *CNF*. Furthermore, it requires the number of variables n occurring in S and a cut-off point μ. At line 1, a histogram array h, providing for each literal the number of occurrences in S, is constructed. This histogram can be constructed on the GPU using the histogram method offered by the *Thrust* library [4,5]. At line 2, memory is allocated for the arrays $\mathcal{A}$ and *scores*. With h, these are input for the kernel *assignScores*. Once the kernel execution has terminated, at line 4, the candidates in $\mathcal{A}$ are sorted on the GPU based on their scores in *scores* and μ is used on the GPU to prune candidates with too many occurrences. We used the radix-sort algorithm as provided in the Thrust library [5].

In the kernel of Algorithm 2, at line 1, the *tid* variable refers to the thread identifier in the launched grid where *xThread* is the thread index inside a block of size *blockDim* and *xBlock* is the block index inside the entire grid of size *gridDim*.

The *stride* variable is used to determine the distance between variables that have to be processed by the same thread. In the subsequent **while** loop (lines 2–9), the thread index is used as a variable index (variable indices start at 1), jumping ahead *stride* variables at the end of each iteration. At lines 5–8, a score is computed for the currently considered variable x. This score should be indicative of the number of resolvents produced when eliminating x, which depends on the number of occurrences of both x and $\bar{x}$, and can be approximated by the formula $h[x] \times h[\bar{x}]$. To avoid score zero in case exactly one of the two literals does not occur in S, we consider that case separately. On average, Algorithm 1 outperforms the sequential counterpart 52×, when considering our benchmark set of problems [21].

LCVE Algorithm. Next, Algorithm 3 is executed on the host, given S, $\mathcal{A}$, h and an instance of *occurTAB* named OT. This algorithm accesses $2 \cdot |\mathcal{A}|$ number of *occurList* instances and parts of S. The use of unified memory significantly improves the rates of the resulting transfers and avoids explicitly copying entire data structures to the host side. The output is φ, implemented as a list. Function **abs** is defined as follows: $\mathbf{abs}(x) = x$ and $\mathbf{abs}(\bar{x}) = x$. The algorithm considers all variables x in $\mathcal{A}$ (line 2). If x has not yet been frozen (line 3), it adds x to φ (line 4). Next, the algorithm needs to identify all variables that depend on x. For this, the algorithm iterates over all clauses containing either x or $\bar{x}$ (line 5), and each literal ℓ in those clauses is compared to x (lines 6–8). If ℓ refers to a different variable v, and v is an authorised candidate, then v must be frozen (line 9).

Algorithm 3: The LCVE algorithm - *CPU*

Input : $S[], \mathcal{A}[], h[], OT[]$
Output: φ

1   $\mathcal{F} \leftarrow []$;
2   **foreach** $x \in \mathcal{A}$ **do**
3   **if** $\neg\mathcal{F}[x]$ **then**
4         $\varphi \leftarrow \varphi \mathbin{+\!\!+} x$;
5   **foreach** $C \in S[OT[x]] \cup S[OT[\bar{x}]]$ **do**
6   **foreach** $\ell \in C$ **do**
7               $v \leftarrow \mathbf{abs}(\ell)$;
8   **if** $v \neq x \wedge v \in \mathcal{A}$ **then**
9                  $\mathcal{F}[v] \leftarrow$ **true**;

BVIPE GPU Algorithm. After φ has been constructed, a kernel is launched to compute an upper bound for the number of resolvents (excluding tautologies) that may be produced by eliminating variables in φ. This kernel accumulates the number of resolvents of each variable using parallel reduction in shared memory within thread blocks. The resulting values (resident in shared memory) of all blocks are added up by atomic operations, resulting in the final output, stored in global memory (denoted by $|\tilde{S}|$). Afterwards, the *CNF* is reallocated according to the extra memory needed. The parallel variable elimination kernel (Algorithm 4) is now ready to be performed on the GPU, considering both the *resolution rule* and *gate-equivalence reasoning* (Sect. 2).

In Algorithm 4, first, each thread selects a variable in φ, based on tid (line 4). The *eliminated* array marks the variables that have been eliminated. It is used to distinguish eliminated and non-eliminated variabels when executing Algorithm 6.

Each thread checks the control condition at line 5 to determine whether the number of resolvents $(h[x] \times h[\bar{x}])$ of x will be less than the number of deleted clauses $(h[x]+h[\bar{x}])$. If the condition evaluates to **true**, a list *resolvents* is created in shared memory, which is then added to the simplified formula $\tilde{S}$ in global memory after discarding tautologies (line 8). The *markDeleted* routine marks resolved clauses as deleted. They are actually deleted on the host side, once the algorithm has terminated.

At line 10, definitions of AND and OR gates are deduced by the *gateReasoning* routine, and stored in shared memory in the lists α and β, respectively. If at least one gate definition is found, the *clauseSubstitution* routine substitutes the involved variable with the underlying definition (line 11), creating the resolvents.

In some situations, even if $h[x]$ or $h[\bar{x}]$ is greater than 1, the number of resolvents can be smaller than the deleted clauses, due to the fact that some resolvents may be tautologies that are subsequently discarded. For this reason, we provide a third alternative to lookahead for tautologies in order to conclusively decide whether to resolve a variable if the conditions at lines 5 and 10 both evaluate to **false**. This third option (line 15) has lower priority than gate equivalence reasoning (line 10), since the latter in practice tends to perform more reduction than the former.

Algorithm 4: The BVIPE algorithm - *GPU kernel*

> **Input** : __global__ $S, \varphi[\,], h, OT[\,], eliminated[\,]$
> **Input** : __shared__ $resolvents[\,], \alpha[\,], \beta[\,]$
> **Output:** __global__ $\tilde{S}$

1 $tid \leftarrow xThread + blockDim \times xBlock;$
2 $stride \leftarrow gridDim \times blockDim;$
3 **while** $tid < |\varphi|$ **do**
4      $x \leftarrow \varphi[tid], eliminated[x] \leftarrow$ **false**, $numTautologies \leftarrow 0;$
5   **if** $h[x] = 1 \vee h[\bar{x}] = 1$ **then**
6          $resolvents \leftarrow \text{resolve}(x, S, OT[x], OT[\bar{x}]);$ /* computes $R_x(S)$ */
7          $\text{markDeleted}(S, OT[x], OT[\bar{x}]);$
8          $\tilde{S} \leftarrow S \cup resolvents;$
9          $eliminated[x] \leftarrow$ **true**;
10   **else if** $(\alpha, \beta) \leftarrow \text{gateReasoning}(x, S, OT[x], OT[\bar{x}]) \neq (\emptyset, \emptyset)$ **then**
11         $resolvents \leftarrow \text{clauseSubstitution}(x, S, OT[x], OT[\bar{x}], \alpha, \beta);$
12         $\text{markDeleted}(S, OT[x], OT[\bar{x}]);$
13         $\tilde{S} \leftarrow S \cup resolvents;$
14         $eliminated[x] \leftarrow$ **true**;
15   **else**
16         $numTautologies \leftarrow \text{tautologyLookahead}(x, S, OT[x], OT[\bar{x}]);$
17         $numResolvents \leftarrow h[x] \times h[\bar{x}], numDeleted \leftarrow h[x] + h[\bar{x}];$
18   **if** $(numResolvents - numTautologies) < numDeleted$ **then**
19             $resolvents \leftarrow \text{resolve}(x, S, OT[x], OT[\bar{x}]);$
20             $\text{markDeleted}(S, OT[x], OT[\bar{x}]);$
21             $\tilde{S} \leftarrow S \cup resolvents;$
22             $eliminated[x] \leftarrow$ **true**;
23     $tid \leftarrow tid + stride;$

The sequential running time of Algorithm 4 is $\mathcal{O}(k \cdot |\varphi|)$, where k is the maximum length of a resolved clause in S. In practice, k often ranges between 2 and 10. Therefore, the worst case is linear w.r.t. $|\varphi|$. Consequently, the parallel complexity is $\mathcal{O}(|\varphi|/p)$, where p is the number of threads. Since a GPU is capable of launching thousands of threads, that is, $p \approx |\varphi|$, the parallel complexity is an amortised constant $\mathcal{O}(1)$. Our empirical results show an average speedup of $32\times$ compared to the sequential alternative [21].

4.2   Parallel Subsumption Elimination

Algorithm 5 presents our PSE algorithm. Notice that the subsumption check (lines 6–7) has a higher priority than self-subsumption (lines 8–12) because the former often results in deleting more clauses. We apply PSE on the *most constrained variables*, that is, the variables that occur most frequently in S, to maximise parallelism on the GPU. For each literal ℓ, the PSE algorithm is launched on a *two-dimensional* GPU grid, in which threads and blocks have two identifiers. Each thread compares the two clauses in $OT[\ell]$ that are associated with the thread coordinates in the grid. At line 4, those two clauses are obtained. At line 5, it is checked whether subsumption or self-subsumption may be applicable. For this to be the case, the length of one clause needs to be larger than the other. The *sig* routine compares the identifiers of two clauses. The identifier of a clause is computed by hashing its literals to a 64-bit value [8]. It has the property of refuting many non-subsuming clauses, but not all of them since hashing collisions may occur. At line 6, the *isSubset* routine runs a set intersection algorithm in linear time $\mathcal{O}(k)$ assuming that both clauses are sorted. If one clause is indeed a subset of the other, the latter clause is marked for deletion later (line 7).

Algorithm 5: The PSE algorithm - *GPU kernel*

Input: __global__ $S, \ell, OT[\,]$

1 $tx \leftarrow xThread + blockDim \times xBlock,\ ty \leftarrow yThread + blockDim \times yBlock$;
2 $stride \leftarrow gridDim \times blockDim$;
3 **while** $ty < |OT[\ell]| \land tx < |OT[\ell]|$ **do**
4      $C \leftarrow S[OT[\ell][ty]];\ \acute{C} \leftarrow S[OT[\ell][tx]]$;
5   **if** $|\acute{C}| < |C| \land sig(\acute{C}, C) \neq 0$ **then**
6   **if** $isSubset(\acute{C}, C)$ **then**
7   markDeleted(C);
8   **else if** $|C| > 1$ **then**
9              $litPos \leftarrow isSelfSub(\acute{C}, C)$;
10   **if** $litPos > -1$ **then**
11   atomicStrengthen($C, litPos$);
12   markSelfSub(C);
13     $ty \leftarrow ty + stride,\ tx \leftarrow tx + stride$;

As an alternative, the applicability of self-subsumption is checked at line 8. If C is not a unit clause, i.e., $|C| > 1$, then self-subsumption can be considered. We exclude unit clauses, because they cannot be reduced in size; instead, they should be propagated over the entire formula before being removed (doing so is planned for future work). If applicable, the routine *isSelfSub* returns the position in C of the literal to be removed, otherwise -1 is returned. This literal is marked for removal in C, using an atomic operation, to avoid race conditions on writing and reading the literal. Finally, the clause is marked as being altered by self-subsumption (line 12), as after execution of the algorithm, the marked literals need to be removed, and the clause resized accordingly.

Finally, following the concept of thread reuse, each thread jumps ahead *stride* variables in both dimensions at the end of each **while** loop iteration (line 13). Sequential subsumption elimination has time complexity $\mathcal{O}(k \cdot |OT[\ell]|^2)$. By launching enough threads in both dimensions (i.e., $|OT[\ell]|^2 \approx p$), the parallel complexity becomes $\mathcal{O}(k)$. In practice, the average speedup of PSE compared to sequential SE is $9\times$ [21].

Correctly Strenghtening Clauses in PSE. Strengthening self-subsumed clauses cannot be done directly at line 9 of Algorithm 5. Instead, clauses need to be altered in-place. Consider the case that a clause C can be self-subsumed by two different clauses C_1, C_2 on two different self-subsuming literals, and that this is detected by two different threads at the exact same time. We call this phenomenon the parallel-effect of self-subsumption. Notice that the same result can be obtained by applying self-subsumption sequentially in two successive rounds. In the first round, C is checked against C_1, while in the second round, what is left of C is checked against C_2. If C would be removed by t_1 and replaced by a new, strengthened clause, then t_2 may suddenly be accessing unallocated memory. Instead, C is atomically strengthened in-place at line 11; t marks the self-subsumed literal using an atomic Compare-And-Swap operation. At the end, all clauses marked as self-subsumed have to be shrunk in size, in essence, overwriting reset positions. This is performed in a separate kernel call.

Algorithm 6: The PHSE algorithm - *GPU kernel*

Input: ___global___ S, $\varphi[\,]$, *eliminated*$[\,]$, $OT[\,]$
Input: ___shared___ $sh\_C[\,]$

1 *tid* $\leftarrow$ *xThread* $+$ *blockDim* $\times$ *xBlock*, *stride* $\leftarrow$ *gridDim* $\times$ *blockDim*;
2 **while** *tid* $< |\varphi|$ **do**
3       $x \leftarrow \varphi[tid]$;
4   **if** $\neg eliminated[x]$ **then**
5   **foreach** $C \in S[OT[x]]$ **do**
6               $sh\_C \leftarrow C$;
7   **foreach** $C' \in S[OT[\bar{x}]]$ **do**
8   **if** $|C'| < |C| \wedge sig(C', C) \neq 0 \wedge isSelfSub(C', sh\_C)$ **then**
9   strengthenWT(C, sh_C, x);
10   **else if** $|C'| = |C| \wedge sig(C', C) \neq 0 \wedge isSelfSub(C', sh\_C)$ **then**
11   strengthenWT(C, sh_C, x);
12   markDeleted(C');
13   **foreach** $C'' \in S[OT[x]]$ **do**
14   **if** $|C''| < |C| \wedge sig(C'', C) \neq 0 \wedge isSubset(C'', sh\_C)$ **then**
15   markDeleted(C);

16   *tid* $\leftarrow$ *tid* $+$ *stride*;

Parallel Hybrid Subsumption Elimination (PHSE). PHSE is executed on elected variables that could not be eliminated earlier by variable elimination.

(Self)-subsumption elimination tends to reduce the number of occurrences of these non-eliminated variables as they usually eliminate many literals. After performing PHSE (Algorithm 6), the BVIPE algorithm can be executed again, after which PHSE can be executed, and so on, until no more literals can be removed.

Unlike PSE, the parallelism in the PHSE kernel is achieved on the variable level. In other words, each thread is assigned to a variable when executing PHSE. At line 4, previously eliminated variables are skipped. At line 6, a new clause is loaded, referenced by $OT[x]$, into shared memory (we call it the *shared clause*, sh_C).

The shared clause is then compared in the loop at lines 7–12 to all clauses referenced by $OT[\bar{x}]$ to check whether x is a self-subsuming literal. If so, both the original clause C, which resides in the global memory, and sh_C must be strengthened (via the *strengthenWT* function). Subsequently, the strengthened sh_C is used for subsumption checking in the loop at lines 13–15.

Regarding the complexity of Algorithm 6, the worst-case is that a variable x occurs in all clauses of S. However, in practice, the number of occurrences of x is bounded by the threshold value μ (see Definition 1). The same applies for its complement. Therefore, worst case, a variable and its complement both occur μ times. As PHSE considers all variables in φ and worst case has to traverse each loop μ times, its sequential worst-case complexity is $\mathcal{O}(|\varphi| \cdot \mu^2)$ and its parallel worst-case complexity is $\mathcal{O}(\mu^2)$.

5   Benchmarks

We implemented the proposed algorithms in CUDA C++ using CUDA toolkit v9.2. We conducted experiments using an NVIDIA Titan Xp GPU which has 30 SMs (128 cores each), 12 GB global memory and 48 KB shared memory. The machine equipped with the GPU was running Linux Mint v18. All GPU SAT simplifications were executed in four phases iteratively. Every two phases, the resulting CNF was reallocated to discard removed clauses. In general, the number of iterations can be configured, and the reallocation frequency can be also set to a desired value.

We selected 214 SAT problems from the industrial track of the 2013, 2016 and 2017 SAT competitions [13]. This set consists of almost all problems from those tracks that are more than 1 MB in file size. The largest size of problems occurring in this set is 1.2 GB. These problems have been encoded from 31 different real-world applications that have a whole range of dissimilar logical properties. Before applying any simplifications using the experimental tools, any occurring unit clauses were propagated. The presence of unit clauses immediately leads to simplification of the formula. By only considering formulas without unit clauses, the benchmark results directly indicate the true impact of our preprocessing algorithms.

In the benchmark experiments, besides the implementations of our new GPU algorithms, we involved the SatELite preprocessor [8], and the MiniSat and Lingeling [6] SAT solvers for the solving of problems, and executed these on the compute nodes of the DAS-5 cluster [1]. Each problem was analysed in isolation

on a separate computing node. Each computing node had an Intel Xeon E5-2630
CPU running at a core clock speed of 2.4 GHz with 128 GB of system memory,
and runs on the CentOS 7.4 operating system. We performed the equivalent of 6
months and 22 days of uninterrupted processing on a single node to measure how
GPU SAT simplification impacts SAT solving in comparison to using sequential
simplification or no simplification. The time out for solving experiments and
simplification experiments was set to 24 h and 5,000 s, respectively. Time outs
are marked 'T' in the tables in this section. Out-of-memory cases are marked
'M' in the tables.

The presented data shows that GPU+L solved many instances faster than
Table 1 gives the MiniSat solving performance summed over the CNF families
for both the original and simplified problems produced by GPU SAT simplification and SatELite. The $ve+$ and ve modes in GPU simplification represent variable elimination with and without PHSE, respectively. The all mode involves
both $ve+$ and PSE. The numbers between brackets of columns 2 to 7 denote
the number of solved instances at each family. Bold results in column 6 indicate
that the combination of GPU SAT simplification and MiniSat reduced the net
solution times (preprocessing + solving), or allowed more problems to be solved
compared to the ve column of SatElite + MiniSat (column 3). Likewise, the
all column for our results (column 7) is compared to column 4. The final four
columns summarise the number of instances solved faster by MiniSat when using
GPU SAT simplification (GPU+M) compared to not using GPU SAT simplification, and compared to using SatElite for simplification (SatElite+M). Numbers
in bold indicate that 50% or more of the CNF formulas were solved faster.

The final row accumulates all problems solved faster. The percentage expresses
the induced improvement by GPU SAT simplification over MiniSat and SatElite.
Similarly, Table 2 gives the performance of solving the problems with Lingeling and
GPU SAT simplification+Lingeling (GPU+L). Since SatELite is the groundwork
of preprocessing in Lingeling, there is no reason to apply it again.[1]

The presented data shows that GPU+L solved many instances faster than
SatElite with Lingeling, especially for the $ak128$, $blockpuzzle$, and $sokoban$ problems. In addition, GPU SAT simplification allowed Lingeling to solve more
instances of the $hwmcc$, $velev$, and $sncf$ models. This effect did not occur for
MiniSat.

Table 3 provides an evaluation of the achieved simplifications with GPU SAT
simplification and SatELite, where V, C, L are the number of variables, clauses,
and literals (in thousands), respectively, and $t(s)$ is the runtime in seconds. In
case of GPU SAT simplification, t includes the transfer time between host and
device. Bold results indicate significant improvements in reductions on literals
for more than 50% of the instances.

On average, SatElite managed to eliminate more variables and clauses at
the expense of literals explosion. Regarding scalability, GPU SAT simplification is able to preprocess extremely large problems (e.g., the $esawn$ problem,
$sokoban\text{-}p20.sas.ex.23$, and the high-depth $sncf$ model) in only a few seconds
while SatElite failed. For our benchmark set of SAT problems, GPU SAT

---

[1] The full tables with all obtained results are available at [21].

Table 1. MiniSat solving of original and simplified formulas (time in seconds).

Family (#CNF)	Minisat	SatElite + Minisat		GPU + Minisat			GPU+M vs MiniSat		GPU+M vs SatElite+M	
		ve	all	ve	ve+	all	ve+	all	ve+	all
dspam(8)	726(8)	143(8)	86(8)	194(8)	**127(8)**	**51(8)**	6	3	6	7
ACG(4)	10146(4)	5376(4)	2813(4)	9597(4)	4139(4)	3558(4)	4	4	3	1
ak128(30)	17353(11)	19604(11)	52185(11)	54302(11)	**34001(12)**	**5045(12)**	12	7	12	12
hwmcc(27)	291885(10)	294646(12)	408184(14)	205099(12)	145182(11)	262539(12)	11	11	8	7
UCG(3)	3048(3)	1467(3)	1022(3)	2186(3)	1831(3)	**725(3)**	2	3	1	3
UR(3)	12648(3)	12233(3)	4221(3)	27547(3)	**6431(3)**	20240(3)	3	1	2	0
UTI(1)	4594(1)	916(1)	1908(1)	2350(1)	4192(1)	1244(1)	1	1	0	1
itox(6)	7(6)	78(6)	151(6)	4.2(6)	**5.7(6)**	12(6)	3	0	6	6
manol-pipe(10)	1978(10)	3909(10)	3106(10)	1432(10)	1239(10)	1213(10)	7	7	5	5
blockpuzzle(14)	43584(13)	177545(13)	99569(10)	36698(14)	**55250(14)**	55317(14)	7	5	12	13
26-stack-cas(1)	0.9(1)	110(1)	110(1)	0.67(1)	**0.8(1)**	2.81(1)	1	0	1	1
9dlx-vliw(10)	14093(3)	141993(5)	133859(5)	76716(4)	**4553(1)**	112862(5)	1	4	0	4
dated(1)	3711(1)	4699(1)	3711(1)	3894(1)	4553(1)	3833(1)	0	0	1	0
podwr001(1)	14.5(1)	22(1)	53(1)	15.7(1)	**18(1)**	23(1)	0	0	1	1
transport(3)	2935(3)	1967(3)	2804(3)	5109(3)	2366(3)	7649(3)	1	1	0	1
valves(1)	3120(1)	770(1)	702(1)	1202(1)	1237(1)	873(1)	1	1	0	0
mizh-md5(6)	7492(6)	3272(6)	5091(6)	7519(6)	4457(6)	5805(6)	4	5	2	3
synthesis-aes(6)	15868(5)	10443(6)	54348(6)	7271(6)	**7645(6)**	8797(6)	5	5	3	5
test-c1-s(6)	32277(5)	86955(6)	23596(5)	23044(5)	28716(5)	81727(5)	4	5	1	2
cube-11-h13(1)	625(1)	324(1)	1173(1)	319(1)	**318(1)**	122(1)	1	1	1	1
esawn-uw3(1)	224(1)	M	M	426(1)	**563(1)**	610(1)	0	0	1	1
ibm-2002(1)	385(1)	66(1)	169(1)	61(1)	195(1)	**73(1)**	1	1	1	1
sin2(2)	38542(2)	44691(2)	39246(2)	45981(2)	54442(2)	**38016(2)**	1	1	1	2
traffic(1)	134(1)	133(1)	206(1)	133(1)	**41(1)**	282(1)	1	0	1	0
partial(8)	1696(1)	348(1)	605(1)	7062(2)	735(1)	T	1	0	0	0
newton(4)	24926(4)	6152(4)	5464(4)	15477(4)	19645(4)	13783(4)	4	4	2	2
safe(4)	5.5(4)	27(4)	102(4)	4.5(4)	**4.2(4)**	20(4)	2	0	4	4
arcfour(8)	1531(3)	831(3)	2196	1010(3)	1046(3)	**1051(3)**	3	3	0	1
sokoban(33)	127523(15)	116562(19)	91555(11)	119958(16)	101166(17)	**147564(18)**	11	11	8	13
#CNF solved faster (Percentage %)							98/135(73)	84/139(61)	82/140(59)	97/142(68)

Table 2. Lingeling solving of original and simplified formulas (time in seconds).

Family (#CNF)	Lingeling	GPU + Lingeling			GPU+L vs Lingeling	
		ve	ve+	all	ve+	all
dspam(8)	35(8)	52(8)	79(8)	65(8)	1	0
ACG(4)	1426(4)	1685(4)	1457(4)	**1392(4)**	3	3
ak128(30)	35692(16)	2602(16)	**41275(17)**	**2649(16)**	15	8
hwmcc15(27)	115970(27)	95530(27)	**96329(27)**	**109925(27)**	18	16
UCG(3)	605(3)	679(3)	762(3)	691(3)	0	1
UR(3)	2029(3)	1199(3)	2709(3)	**1739(3)**	1	2
UTI(1)	469(1)	412(1)	**402(1)**	362(1)	1	1
itox(6)	195(6)	153(6)	**92(6)**	**106(6)**	3	3
manol-pipe(10)	631(10)	662(10)	713(10)	659(10)	1	2
blockpuzzle(14)	30391(14)	57559(14)	57895(14)	**15328(14)**	7	7
26-stack-cas(1)	7(1)	1(1)	**1(1)**	3(1)	1	1
9dlx-vliw(10)	4287(10)	4713(10)	4579(10)	5121(10)	3	4
dated(1)	800(1)	704(1)	**751(1)**	**657(1)**	1	1
podwr001(1)	111(1)	108(1)	171(1)	**93(1)**	0	1
transport(3)	2526(3)	2246(3)	**1012(3)**	**2025(3)**	2	1
valves(1)	1536(1)	1501(1)	**1288(1)**	**1455(1)**	1	1
velev(2)	11717(2)	10645(2)	**10695(2)**	9381(2)	2	2
mizh-md5(6)	34104(6)	33327(6)	**32589(6)**	**23096(6)**	3	5
synthesis-aes(6)	49679(6)	16494(6)	**31927(6)**	16151(6)	3	6
test-c1-s(6)	84807(6)	55512(6)	17284(5)	4450(4)	3	2
cube-11-h13(1)	1495(1)	2022(1)	**1217(1)**	**813(1)**	1	1
esawn-uw3(1)	107(1)	271(1)	239(1)	463(1)	0	0
ibm-2002(1)	150(1)	191(1)	**129(1)**	194(1)	1	0
sin2(2)	4(1)	7(1)	4.2(1)	20(1)	0	0
traffic(1)	355(1)	694(1)	505(1)	869(1)	0	0
partial(8)	4691(2)	16026(2)	**1276(2)**	6735(2)	2	1
newton(4)	825(4)	913(4)	908(4)	861(4)	2	2
safe(4)	49(4)	57(4)	51(4)	63(4)	1	0
sncf-model(8)	73690(4)	135683(5)	T	**131301(5)**	0	4
arcfour(8)	1293(3)	1338(3)	1319(3)	1451(3)	0	1
sokoban(33)	339236(26)	139509(23)	248439(24)	166542(24)	14	17
#CNF solved faster (Percentage %)					90/179(50)	93/179(52)

simplification methods *ve+* and *all* achieve on average a speedup of 66× and 12× compared to SatElite *ve* and *all*, respectively [21].

Our appendix [21] presents larger tables, providing all our results related to Tables 1, 2 and 3. In addition, it presents a comparison between our GPU simplification algorithms and directly ported to the CPU versions of the algorithms, to provide more insight into the contribution of the GPU parallelisation. On average, subsumption elimination is performed 9× faster on the GPU, hybrid

Table 3. Comprehensive evaluation of simplification impact on original CNF size

Name	CNF (Original) V	C	L	SatElite ve V	C	L	t(s)	SatElite all V	C	L	t(s)	GPU ve+ V	C	L	t(s)	GPU all V	C	L	t(s)
dspam_dump_vc1103	275	920	2464	161	722	2190	12.9	155	695	2092	15.53	164	729	2182	0.69	164	729	2178	3.52
ACG-20-10p1	325	1316	3140	272	1293	3544	10.4	250	1194	3154	20.95	287	1243	3135	0.32	287	1242	3134	5.94
ak128astepbg2asisc	260	844	2144	130	681	2176	4.95	98	552	1853	11.32	162	617	1722	0.32	162	617	1722	1.12
hwmcc15deep-intel032	426	882	2051	69	334	1235	88.1	45	226	856	114.8	104	391	1171	0.47	104	390	1164	1.51
UCG-15-10p1	151	757	1845	119	739	2132	5.78	102	666	1849	13.51	122	700	1838	0.23	122	700	1837	3.50
UR-20-5p1	178	938	2320	140	918	2661	6.83	121	833	2332	15.97	145	874	2317	0.32	145	874	2317	9.37
UTI-20-10p1	203	1075	2656	160	1051	3042	7.74	138	954	2666	18.17	166	1001	2651	0.29	166	1001	2650	11.8
itox-vc1033	111	339	898	35	176	639	12.2	28	132	434	19.92	42	195	629	0.56	42	194	620	1.42
manol-pipe-f10ni	368	1100	2567	56	458	1855	15.2	56	456	1844	17.94	102	508	1590	0.75	102	508	1589	5.69
blockpuzzle_8x8_s1_f4	3	311	625	3	305	987	0.91	3	303	794	3.42	3	311	632	0.08	3	311	632	6.83
blockpuzzle_9x9_s1_f7	5	692	1389	5	681	2179	1.84	5	678	1764	8.53	5	691	1414	0.13	5	691	1414	6.18
26_stack_cas_longest	1505	3799	11287	1	11	44	110	1	10	39	110.4	3	14	43	0.84	3	14	41	2.80
9dlx_vliw_at_b_iq8	371	7170	20872	303	7042	22708	136	303	6994	21690	607.8	335	7098	21071	5.80	333	7069	20408	48.8
dated-10-17-u	177	813	1914	134	740	2074	8.49	67	425	1112	15.96	127	678	1764	0.43	127	678	1764	4.22
valves-gates-1-k617	970	3062	7842	302	1777	6027	30.9	249	1368	4454	52.40	371	1680	4970	1.21	366	1655	4856	18.5
velev-pipe-oun-1.1-05	236	7676	22782	143	7491	23933	45.0	143	7488	23914	84.85	178	7561	22683	11.5	178	7557	22530	109
velev-vliw-uns-2.0-uq5	151	2465	7141	120	2407	7653	41.2	120	2391	7388	99.17	131	2424	7181	1.55	130	2411	6963	20.3
esawn_uw3.debugged	12200	48049	133127	n/a	n/a	n/a	M	n/a	n/a	n/a	M	7361	36184	108331	16.0	7385	36189	108187	333
mizh-md5-12	69	226	585	28	171	576	1.53	28	163	552	2.17	37	163	482	0.07	37	163	482	0.32
mizh-md5-48-5	61	238	689	34	193	641	1.36	26	157	533	2.31	26	167	563	0.12	26	167	563	2.05
slp-synthesis-aes-top30	97	304	745	37	211	1110	41.9	37	191	1043	90.04	42	215	658	0.07	42	196	599	1.71
ibm-2002-23r-k90	209	864	2176	80	601	2179	9.93	72	523	1796	17.74	107	652	1899	0.38	107	645	1834	5.26
newton.2.3.i.smt2-cvc4	302	1309	3625	193	1116	3669	19.5	183	1025	3320	29.79	215	1079	3193	0.77	215	1074	3160	7.12
partial-10-19-s	269	1282	3033	207	1175	3293	13.0	168	995	2750	25.59	198	1089	2845	0.56	198	1089	2845	7.64
safe029	62	305	1048	41	261	1204	7.92	40	251	1095	23.66	56	291	1025	0.27	56	290	932	3.01
sin2.c.20.smt2-cvc4	1962	7954	21638	1063	6684	22579	136	867	5647	19591	306	1196	6072	18167	3.24	1196	6056	18057	35.2
sncf_model_depth_07	814	2641	6565	n/a	n/a	n/a	T	n/a	n/a	n/a	T	423	1778	5089	1.97	424	1778	5084	7.82
test_s18160	411	1831	5104	266	1595	5170	23.0	266	1595	5102	30.2	306	1607	4770	0.75	306	1599	4731	10.6
traffic_3_uc_sat	142	1312	4558	141	1311	4556	3.15	141	1311	4556	3.22	141	1311	4557	1.06	141	1310	4554	28.5
arcfour_6.14	105	404	1172	60	316	1365	4.99	60	316	1364	6.13	72	341	1114	0.09	72	341	1114	1.21
sokoban-p17.sas.ex.11	606	876	2312	6	151	1023	49.1	6	134	718	179	34	283	1180	0.53	34	282	1026	2.44
sokoban-p20.sas.ex.23	3632	7258	48119	111	2929	40787	11.0	n/a	n/a	n/a	n/a	276	3716	41536	0.34	276	3714	38205	5.96

subsumption elimination is performed 15× faster on the GPU, and BVE is conducted 32× faster on the GPU.

6   Related Work

Subbarayan and Pradhan [24] provided the first Bounded Variable Elimination (BVE) technique, called NiVER, based on the resolution rule of Davis-Putnam-Logemann-Loveland (DPLL) [7]. Eén and Biere [8] extended NiVER with subsumption elimination and clause substitution. However, the subsumption check is only performed on the clauses resulting from variable elimination, hence no reductions are obtained if there are no variables to resolve.

Heule *et al.* [14,16] introduced several approaches for clause elimination that can be effective in SAT simplifications, such as Blocked Clause Elimination. Bao *et al.* [3], on the other hand, have presented an efficient implementation of Common Sub-clause Elimination (CSE) performed periodically during SAT solving. CSE trims the search space, thereby decreasing the solving time, and is stable, i.e., the outcome of CSE does not depend on the chosen clause ordering. Gebhardt and Manthey [10] presented the first attempt to parallelise SAT preprocessing on a multi-core CPU using a locking scheme to prevent threads corrupting the SAT formula. However, they reported only a very limited speedup of on average 1.88× when running on eight cores.

All the above methods apply sound simplifications, but none are tailored for GPU parallelisation. They may consume considerable time when processing large problems.

Finally, it should be noted that BVE, as introduced in [8,10,16,24], is not confluent, as noted by the authors of [16]. Due to dependency between variables, altering the elimination order of these variables may result in different simplified formulas. This drawback is circumvented by our LCVE algorithm, which makes it possible to perform parallel variable elimination while achieving the confluence property.

7   Conclusion

We have shown that SAT simplifications can be performed efficiently on many-core systems, producing impactful reductions in a fraction of a second, even for larger problems consisting of millions of variables and tens of millions of clauses. The proposed BVIPE algorithm provides the first methodology to eliminate multiple variables in parallel while preserving satisfiability. Finally, PSE and PHSE have proven their effectiveness in removing many clauses and literals in a reasonable amount of time.

Concerning future work, the results of this work motivate us to take the capabilities of GPU SAT simplification further by supporting more simplification techniques or balancing the workload on multiple GPUs.

References

1. Bal, H., et al.: A medium-scale distributed system for computer science research: infrastructure for the long term. IEEE Comput. **49**(5), 54–63 (2016)
2. Balyo, T., Sinz, C.: Parallel satisfiability. In: Hamadi, Y., Sais, L. (eds.) Handbook of Parallel Constraint Reasoning, pp. 3–29. Springer, Cham (2018). https://doi.org/10.1007/978-3-319-63516-3_1
3. Bao, F.S., Gutierrez, C., Charles-Blount, J.J., Yan, Y., Zhang, Y.: Accelerating boolean satisfiability (SAT) solving by common subclause elimination. Artif. Intell. Rev. **49**(3), 439–453 (2018)
4. Bell, N., Hoberock, J.: Thrust: a productivity-oriented library for CUDA. In: GPU computing gems Jade edition, pp. 359–371. Elsevier, Atlanta (2012)
5. Bell, N., Hoberock, J.: A parallel algorithms library. Thrust Github (2018). https://thrust.github.io/
6. Biere, A.: Lingeling, plingeling and treengeling entering the SAT competition 2013. In: Proceedings of SAT Competition, pp. 51–52 (2013)
7. Davis, M., Logemann, G., Loveland, D.: A machine program for theorem-proving. Commun. ACM **5**(7), 394–397 (1962)
8. Eén, N., Biere, A.: Effective preprocessing in SAT through variable and clause elimination. In: Bacchus, F., Walsh, T. (eds.) SAT 2005. LNCS, vol. 3569, pp. 61–75. Springer, Heidelberg (2005). https://doi.org/10.1007/11499107_5
9. Eén, N., Sörensson, N.: An extensible SAT-solver. In: Giunchiglia, E., Tacchella, A. (eds.) SAT 2003. LNCS, vol. 2919, pp. 502–518. Springer, Heidelberg (2004). https://doi.org/10.1007/978-3-540-24605-3_37
10. Gebhardt, K., Manthey, N.: Parallel variable elimination on CNF formulas. In: Timm, I.J., Thimm, M. (eds.) KI 2013. LNCS (LNAI), vol. 8077, pp. 61–73. Springer, Heidelberg (2013). https://doi.org/10.1007/978-3-642-40942-4_6
11. Hamadi, Y., Wintersteiger, C.: Seven challenges in parallel SAT solving. AI Mag. **34**(2), 99 (2013)
12. Han, H., Somenzi, F.: Alembic: an efficient algorithm for CNF preprocessing. In: Proceedings of 44th ACM/IEEE Design Automation Conference, pp. 582–587. IEEE (2007)
13. Heule, M., Järvisalo, M., Balyo, T., Balint, A., Belov, A.: SAT Competition, vol. 13, pp. 16–17 (2018). https://satcompetition.org/
14. Heule, M., Järvisalo, M., Biere, A.: Clause elimination procedures for CNF formulas. In: Fermüller, C.G., Voronkov, A. (eds.) LPAR 2010. LNCS, vol. 6397, pp. 357–371. Springer, Heidelberg (2010). https://doi.org/10.1007/978-3-642-16242-8_26
15. Heule, M., Järvisalo, M., Lonsing, F., Seidl, M., Biere, A.: Clause elimination for SAT and QSAT. J. Artif. Intell. Res. **53**, 127–168 (2015)
16. Järvisalo, M., Biere, A., Heule, M.: Blocked clause elimination. In: Esparza, J., Majumdar, R. (eds.) TACAS 2010. LNCS, vol. 6015, pp. 129–144. Springer, Heidelberg (2010). https://doi.org/10.1007/978-3-642-12002-2_10
17. Järvisalo, M., Biere, A., Heule, M.J.: Simulating circuit-level simplifications on CNF. J. Autom. Reasoning **49**(4), 583–619 (2012)
18. Järvisalo, M., Heule, M.J.H., Biere, A.: Inprocessing rules. In: Gramlich, B., Miller, D., Sattler, U. (eds.) IJCAR 2012. LNCS (LNAI), vol. 7364, pp. 355–370. Springer, Heidelberg (2012). https://doi.org/10.1007/978-3-642-31365-3_28
19. Jin, H., Somenzi, F.: An incremental algorithm to check satisfiability for bounded model checking. ENTCS **119**(2), 51–65 (2005)

20. NVIDIA: CUDA C Programming Guide (2018). https://docs.nvidia.com/cuda/cuda-c-programming-guide/index.html
21. Osama, M., Wijs, A.: Parallel SAT Simplification on GPU Architectures -Appendix (2019). http://www.win.tue.nl/~awijs/suppls/pss-app.pdf
22. Osama, M., Gaber, L., Hussein, A.I., Mahmoud, H.: An efficient SAT-based test generation algorithm with GPU accelerator. J. Electron. Test. **34**(5), 511–527 (2018)
23. Ostrowski, R., Grégoire, É., Mazure, B., Saïs, L.: Recovering and exploiting structural knowledge from CNF formulas. In: Van Hentenryck, P. (ed.) CP 2002. LNCS, vol. 2470, pp. 185–199. Springer, Heidelberg (2002). https://doi.org/10.1007/3-540-46135-3_13
24. Subbarayan, S., Pradhan, D.K.: NiVER: non-increasing variable elimination resolution for preprocessing SAT instances. In: Hoos, H.H., Mitchell, D.G. (eds.) SAT 2004. LNCS, vol. 3542, pp. 276–291. Springer, Heidelberg (2005). https://doi.org/10.1007/11527695_22
25. Wijs, A.: GPU accelerated strong and branching bisimilarity checking. In: Baier, C., Tinelli, C. (eds.) TACAS 2015. LNCS, vol. 9035, pp. 368–383. Springer, Heidelberg (2015). https://doi.org/10.1007/978-3-662-46681-0_29
26. Wijs, A.: BFS-based model checking of linear-time properties with an application on GPUs. In: Chaudhuri, S., Farzan, A. (eds.) CAV 2016. LNCS, vol. 9780, pp. 472–493. Springer, Cham (2016). https://doi.org/10.1007/978-3-319-41540-6_26
27. Wijs, A., Bošnački, D.: Many-core on-the-fly model checking of safety properties using GPUs. Int. J. Softw. Tools Technol. Transfer **18**(2), 169–185 (2016)
28. Wijs, A., Katoen, J.-P., Bošnački, D.: GPU-based graph decomposition into strongly connected and maximal end components. In: Biere, A., Bloem, R. (eds.) CAV 2014. LNCS, vol. 8559, pp. 310–326. Springer, Cham (2014). https://doi.org/10.1007/978-3-319-08867-9_20
29. Wijs, A., Katoen, J.P., Bošnački, D.: Efficient GPU algorithms for parallel decomposition of graphs into strongly connected and maximal end components. Formal Methods Syst. Des. **48**(3), 274–300 (2016)
30. Wijs, A., Neele, T., Bošnački, D.: GPUexplore 2.0: unleashing GPU explicit-state model checking. In: Fitzgerald, J., Heitmeyer, C., Gnesi, S., Philippou, A. (eds.) FM 2016. LNCS, vol. 9995, pp. 694–701. Springer, Cham (2016). https://doi.org/10.1007/978-3-319-48989-6_42
31. Youness, H., Ibraheim, A., Moness, M., Osama, M.: An efficient implementation of ant colony optimization on GPU for the satisfiability problem. In: 2015 23rd Euromicro International Conference on Parallel, Distributed, and Network-Based Processing, pp. 230–235, March 2015

Encoding Redundancy
for Satisfaction-Driven Clause Learning

Marijn J. H. Heule[1], Benjamin Kiesl[2,3], and Armin Biere[4(✉)]

[1] Department of Computer Science, The University of Texas, Austin, USA
[2] Institute of Logic and Computation, TU Wien, Vienna, Austria
[3] CISPA Helmholtz Center for Information Security, Saarbrücken, Germany
[4] Institute for Formal Models and Verification,
Johannes Kepler University, Linz, Austria
`armin.biere@jku.at`

Abstract. Satisfaction-Driven Clause Learning (SDCL) is a recent SAT solving paradigm that aggressively trims the search space of possible truth assignments. To determine if the SAT solver is currently exploring a dispensable part of the search space, SDCL uses the so-called positive reduct of a formula: The positive reduct is an easily solvable propositional formula that is satisfiable if the current assignment of the solver can be safely pruned from the search space. In this paper, we present two novel variants of the positive reduct that allow for even more aggressive pruning. Using one of these variants allows SDCL to solve harder problems, in particular the well-known Tseitin formulas and mutilated chessboard problems. For the first time, we are able to generate and automatically check clausal proofs for large instances of these problems.

1 Introduction

Conflict-driven clause learning (CDCL) [26, 28] is the most successful paradigm for solving satisfiability (SAT) problems and therefore CDCL solvers are pervasively used as reasoning engines to construct and verify systems. However, CDCL solvers still struggle to handle some important applications within reasonable time. These applications include the verification of arithmetic circuits, challenges from cryptanalysis, and hard combinatorial problems. There appears to be a theoretical barrier to dealing with some of these applications efficiently.

At its core, CDCL is based on the resolution proof system, which means that the same limitations that apply to resolution also apply to CDCL. Most importantly, there exist only exponentially large resolution proofs for several seemingly easy problems [15, 33], implying that CDCL solvers require exponential time to solve them. A recent approach to breaking this exponential barrier is

Supported by NSF under grant CCF-1813993, by AFRL Award FA8750-15-2-0096, and by the Austrian Science Fund (FWF) under projects W1255-N23 and S11409-N23 (RiSE).

T. Vojnar and L. Zhang (Eds.): TACAS 2019, Part I, LNCS 11427, pp. 41–58, 2019.
https://doi.org/10.1007/978-3-030-17462-0_3

the *satisfaction-driven clause learning* (SDCL) paradigm [20], which can automatically find short proofs of pigeon-hole formulas in the PR proof system [19].

SDCL extends CDCL by pruning the search space of truth assignments more aggressively. While a pure CDCL solver learns only clauses that can be efficiently derived via resolution, an SDCL solver also learns stronger clauses. The initial approach to learning these clauses is based on the so-called *positive reduct*: Given a formula and a partial truth assignment, the positive reduct is a simple propositional formula encoding the question of whether the assignment can be pruned safely from the search space. In cases where the positive reduct is satisfiable, the solver performs the pruning by learning a clause that blocks the assignment.

Although the original SDCL paradigm can solve the hard pigeon-hole formulas, we observe that it is not sophisticated enough to deal with other hard formulas that require exponential-size resolution proofs, such as Tseitin formulas over expander graphs [32,33] or mutilated chessboard problems [1,13,27]. In this paper, we deal with this issue and present techniques that improve the SDCL paradigm. In particular, we introduce new variants of the above-mentioned positive reduct that allow SDCL to prune the search space even more aggressively.

In a first step, we explicitly formalize the notion of a *pruning predicate*: For a formula F and a (partial) assignment α, a pruning predicate is a propositional formula that is satisfiable if α can be pruned in a satisfiability-preserving way. Ideally, a pruning predicate is easily solvable while still pruning the search space as much as possible. We then present two novel pruning predicates of which one, the *filtered positive reduct*, is easier to solve and arguably more useful in practice while the other, the PR *reduct*, allows for stronger pruning.

In many applications, it is not enough that a solver just provides a simple yes/no answer. Especially when dealing with mathematical problems or safety-critical systems, solvers are required to provide automatically checkable proofs that certify the correctness of their answers. The current state of the art in proof generation and proof checking is to focus on *clausal proofs*, which are specific sequences of clause additions and clause removals. Besides the requirement that SAT solvers in the main track of the SAT competition must produce such clausal proofs, there also exist corresponding proof checkers whose correctness has been verified by theorem provers, as first proposed in a seminal TACAS'17 paper [12].

We implemented a new SDCL solver, called SADICAL, that can solve the pigeon-hole formulas, the Tseitin formulas, and the mutilated chessboard problems due to using the filtered positive reduct. Our solver also produces PR proofs [19]. We certify their correctness by translating them via DRAT proofs [17] to LRAT proofs, which are then validated by a formally verified proof checker [18].

Existing approaches to solving the Tseitin formulas are based on symmetry breaking [14] or algebraic reasoning, in particular Gaussian elimination [3,9,21,31]. However, the respective tools do not output machine-checkable proofs. Moreover, approaches based on symmetry breaking and Gaussian elimination depend strongly on the syntactic structure of formulas to identify symmetries and cardinality constraints, respectively. They are therefore vulnerable to syntactic changes that do not affect the semantics of a formula. In contrast, SDCL reasons on the semantic level, making it less prone to syntactic changes.

The main contributions of this paper are as follows: (1) We explicitly formulate the notion of a pruning predicate, which was used only implicitly in the original formulation of SDCL. (2) We present two novel pruning predicates that generalize the positive reduct. (3) We implemented a new SDCL solver, called SADICAL, that uses one of our new pruning predicates. (4) We show by an experimental evaluation that this new pruning predicate enables SADICAL to produce short proofs (without new variables) of Tseitin formulas and of mutilated chessboard problems.

2   Preliminaries

Propositional logic. We consider propositional formulas in *conjunctive normal form* (CNF), which are defined as follows. A *literal* is defined to be either a variable x (a *positive literal*) or the negation $\overline{x}$ of a variable x (a *negative literal*). The *complement* $\overline{l}$ of a literal l is defined as $\overline{l} = \overline{x}$ if $l = x$ and $\overline{l} = x$ if $l = \overline{x}$. Accordingly, for a set L of literals, we define $\overline{L} = \{\overline{l} \mid l \in L\}$. A *clause* is a disjunction of literals. A *formula* is a conjunction of clauses. We view clauses as sets of literals and formulas as sets of clauses. For a set L of literals and a formula F, we define $F_L = \{C \in F \mid C \cap L \neq \emptyset\}$. By $var(F)$ we denote the variables of a literal, clause, or formula F. For convenience, we treat $var(F)$ as a variable if F is a literal, and as a set of variables otherwise.

Satisfiability. An *assignment* is a function from a set of variables to the truth values 1 (*true*) and 0 (*false*). An assignment is *total* w.r.t. a formula F if it assigns a truth value to all variables $var(F)$ occurring in F; otherwise it is *partial*. A literal l is *satisfied* by an assignment α if l is positive and $\alpha(var(l)) = 1$ or if it is negative and $\alpha(var(l)) = 0$. A literal is *falsified* by an assignment α if its complement is satisfied by α. A clause is satisfied by an assignment α if it contains a literal that is satisfied by α. Finally, a formula is satisfied by an assignment α if all its clauses are satisfied by α. A formula is *satisfiable* if there exists an assignment that satisfies it. We often denote assignments by sequences of the literals they satisfy. For instance, $x\,\overline{y}$ denotes the assignment that assigns 1 to x and 0 to y. For an assignment α, $var(\alpha)$ denotes the variables assigned by α. For a set L of non-contradictory literals, we denote by α_L the assignment obtained from α by making all literals in L true and assigning the same value as α to other variables not in $var(L)$.

Formula simplification. We refer to the empty clause by $\bot$. Given an assignment α and a clause C, we define $C\lceil\alpha = \top$ if α satisfies C; otherwise, $C\lceil\alpha$ denotes the result of removing from C all the literals falsified by α. For a formula F, we define $F\lceil\alpha = \{C\lceil\alpha \mid C \in F \text{ and } C\lceil\alpha \neq \top\}$. We say that an assignment α *touches* a clause C if $var(\alpha) \cap var(C) \neq \emptyset$. A *unit clause* is a clause with only one literal. The result of applying the *unit clause rule* to a formula F is the formula

$F \upharpoonright l$ where (l) is a unit clause in F. The iterated application of the unit clause rule to a formula F, until no unit clauses are left, is called *unit propagation*. If unit propagation yields the empty clause $\bot$, we say that unit propagation applied to F derived a *conflict*.

```
      SDCL ( formula F )
 1  α := ∅
 2  forever do
 3      α := UnitPropagate (F, α)
 4      if α falsifies a clause in F then
 5          C := AnalyzeConflict()
 6          F := F ∧ C
 7          if C is the empty clause ⊥ then return UNSAT
 8          α := BackJump(C, α)
 9      else if the pruning predicate Pα(F) is satisfiable then
10          C := AnalyzeWitness()
11          F := F ∧ C
12          α := BackJump(C, α)
13      else
14          if all variables are assigned then return SAT
15          l := Decide()
16          α := α ∪ {l}
```

Fig. 1. SDCL algorithm [20]. The lines 9 to 12 extend CDCL [26].

Formula relations. Two formulas are *logically equivalent* if they are satisfied by the same total assignments. Two formulas are *equisatisfiable* if they are either both satisfiable or both unsatisfiable. Furthermore, by $F \vdash_1 G$ we denote that for every clause $(l_1 \vee \cdots \vee l_n) \in G$, unit propagation applied to $F \wedge (\bar{l}_1) \wedge \cdots \wedge (\bar{l}_n)$ derives a conflict. If $F \vdash_1 G$, we say that F implies G via unit propagation. For example, $(\bar{a} \vee c) \wedge (\bar{b} \vee \bar{c})$ implies $(\bar{a} \vee \bar{b})$ via unit propagation since unit propagation derives a conflict on $(\bar{a} \vee c) \wedge (\bar{b} \vee \bar{c}) \wedge (a) \wedge (b)$.

Conflict-Driven Clause Learning (CDCL). To determine whether a formula is satisfiable a CDCL solver iteratively performs the following operations (obtained from the pseudo code in Fig. 1 by removing the lines 9 to 12): First, the solver performs unit propagation until either it derives a conflict or the formula contains no more unit clauses. If it derives a conflict, it analyzes the conflict to learn a clause that prevents it from repeating similar (bad) decisions in the future ("clause learning"). If this learned clause is the (unsatisfiable) empty clause $\bot$, the solver can conclude that the formula is unsatisfiable. In case it is not the empty clause, the solver revokes some of its variable assignments ("backjumping") and then repeats the whole procedure again by performing unit propagation. If, however, the solver does not derive a conflict, there are two options: Either all variables are assigned, in which case the solver can conclude that the formula is satisfiable, or there are still unassigned variables, in which case the solver first assigns a truth value to an unassigned variable (the actual variable and the truth value are chosen based on a so-called *decision heuristic*) and then continues by again performing unit propagation. For more details see the chapter on CDCL [25] in the Handbook of Satisfiability [7].

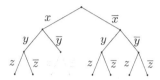

Fig. 2. By learning the clause $\overline{x} \vee y$, a solver prunes all branches where x is true and y is false from the search space. SDCL can prune satisfying branches too (unlike CDCL).

Satisfaction-Driven Clause Learning (SDCL). The SDCL algorithm [20], shown in Fig. 1, is a generalization of CDCL that is obtained by adding lines 9 to 12 to the CDCL algorithm. In CDCL, if unit propagation does not derive a conflict, the solver picks a variable and assigns a truth value to it. In contrast, an SDCL solver does not necessarily assign a new variable in this situation. Instead, it first checks if the current assignment can be pruned from the search space without affecting satisfiability. If so, the solver prunes the assignment by learning a new clause (Fig. 2 illustrates how clause learning can prune the search space). This clause is returned by the AnalyzeWitness() function and usually consists of the decision literals of the current assignment (although other ways of computing the clause are possible, c.f. [20]). If the assignment cannot be pruned, the solver proceeds by assigning a new variable—just as in CDCL. To check if the current assignment can be pruned, the solver produces a propositional formula that should be easier to solve than the original formula and that can only be satisfiable if the assignment can be pruned. Thus, an SDCL solver solves several easier formulas in order to solve a hard formula. In this paper, we call these easier formulas *pruning predicates*. We first formalize the pruning predicate used in the original SDCL paper before we introduce more powerful pruning predicates.

3 Pruning Predicates and Redundant Clauses

As already explained informally, a pruning predicate is a propositional formula whose satisfiability guarantees that an assignment can be pruned from the search space. The actual pruning is then performed by adding the clause that *blocks* the assignment (or a subclause of this clause, as explained in detail later):

Definition 1. *Given an assignment* $\alpha = a_1 \ldots a_k$, *the clause* $(\overline{a}_1 \vee \cdots \vee \overline{a}_k)$ *is the clause that* blocks α.

The clause that blocks α is thus the unique maximal clause falsified by α. Based on this notion, we define pruning predicates as follows:

Definition 2. *Let F be a formula and C the clause that blocks a given (partial) assignment α. A* pruning predicate *for F and α is a formula $P_\alpha(F)$ such that the following holds: if $P_\alpha(F)$ is satisfiable, then F and $F \wedge C$ are equisatisfiable.*

Thus, if a pruning predicate for a formula F and an assignment α is satisfiable, we can add the clause that blocks α to F without affecting satisfiability. We thus say that this clause is *redundant* with respect to F. In the paper that introduces SDCL [20], the so-called *positive reduct* (see Definition 3 below) is used as a pruning predicate. The positive reduct is obtained from satisfied clauses of the original formula by removing unassigned literals.

In the following, given a clause C and an assignment α, we write $\mathsf{touched}_\alpha(C)$ to denote the subclause of C that contains exactly the literals assigned by α. Analogously, we denote by $\mathsf{untouched}_\alpha(C)$ the subclause of C that contains the literals *not* assigned by α [20].

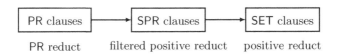

Fig. 3. Relationship between types of redundant clauses and the corresponding pruning predicates. An arrow from X to Y means that X is a superset of Y.

Definition 3. *Let F be a formula and α an assignment. Then, the* positive reduct $\mathsf{p}_\alpha(F)$ *of F and α is the formula $G \wedge C$ where C is the clause that blocks α and $G = \{\mathsf{touched}_\alpha(D) \mid D \in F \text{ and } D\!\restriction_\alpha = \top\}$.*

Example 1. Let $F = (x \vee \overline{y} \vee z) \wedge (w \vee \overline{y}) \wedge (\overline{w} \vee \overline{z})$ and $\alpha = x\,y\,\overline{z}$. Then, the positive reduct $\mathsf{p}_\alpha(F)$ of F w.r.t. α is the formula $(x \vee \overline{y} \vee z) \wedge (\overline{z}) \wedge (\overline{x} \vee \overline{y} \vee z)$.

The positive reduct is satisfiable if and only if the clause blocked by α is a *set-blocked clause* [23], short SET clause, with respect to F. Since the addition of set-blocked clauses to a formula preserves satisfiability, it follows that the positive reduct is a pruning predicate. Moreover, since the problem of deciding whether a given clause is a set-blocked clause is NP-complete, it is natural to use a SAT solver for finding set-blocked clauses.

Although set-blocked clauses can be found efficiently with the positive reduct, there are more general kinds of clauses whose addition can prune the search space more aggressively, namely *propagation-redundant clauses* (PR clauses) and their subclass of *set-propagation-redundant clauses* (SPR clauses) [19].

In the following, we thus introduce two different kinds of pruning predicates. Given a formula F and an assignment α, the first pruning predicate, called the *filtered positive reduct*, is satisfiable if and only if the clause that blocks α is an

SPR clause in F. The second pruning predicate, called PR *reduct*, is satisfiable if and only if the clause that blocks α is a PR clause; it allows us to prune more assignments than the filtered positive reduct but it is also harder to solve. The relationship between the redundant clause types and pruning predicates is shown in Fig. 3. According to [19], the definition of PR clauses is as follows:

Definition 4. *Let F be a formula, C a clause, and α the assignment blocked by C. Then, C is* propagation redundant (PR) *with respect to F if there exists an assignment ω such that $F{\upharpoonright}\alpha \vdash_1 F{\upharpoonright}\omega$ and ω satisfies C.*

The clause C can be seen as a constraint that prunes all assignments that extend α from the search space. Since $F{\upharpoonright}\alpha$ implies $F{\upharpoonright}\omega$ via unit propagation, every assignment that satisfies $F{\upharpoonright}\alpha$ also satisfies $F{\upharpoonright}\omega$, and so we say that F is *at least as satisfiable* under ω as it is under α. Moreover, since ω satisfies C, it must disagree with α. Consider the following example [19]:

Example 2. Let $F = (x \vee y) \wedge (\overline{x} \vee y) \wedge (\overline{x} \vee z)$ be a formula, $C = (x)$ a clause, and $\omega = x\,z$ an assignment. Then, $\alpha = \overline{x}$ is the assignment blocked by C. Now, consider $F{\upharpoonright}\alpha = (y)$ and $F{\upharpoonright}\omega = (y)$. Since unit propagation clearly derives a conflict on $F{\upharpoonright}\alpha \wedge (\overline{y}) = (y) \wedge (\overline{y})$, we have $F{\upharpoonright}\alpha \vdash_1 F{\upharpoonright}\omega$ and thus C is propagation redundant with respect to F.

The key property of propagation-redundant clauses is that their addition to a formula preserves satisfiability [19]. A strict subclass of propagation-redundant clauses are set-propagation-redundant clauses, which have the additional requirement that ω must assign the same variables as α. For the following definition, recall (from the preliminaries) that α_L denotes the assignment obtained from α by assigning 1 to the literals in L [19]:

Definition 5. *Let F be a formula, C a clause, and α the assignment blocked by C. Then, C is* set-propagation redundant (SPR) *with respect to F if it contains a non-empty set L of literals such that $F{\upharpoonright}\alpha \vdash_1 F{\upharpoonright}\alpha_L$.*

If $F{\upharpoonright}\alpha \vdash_1 F{\upharpoonright}\alpha_L$, we say C is SPR *by L with respect to F.*

Example 3. Let $F = (x \vee y) \wedge (x \vee \overline{y} \vee z) \wedge (\overline{x} \vee z) \wedge (\overline{x} \vee u) \wedge (\overline{u} \vee x)$, $C = x \vee u$, and $L = \{x, u\}$. Then, $\alpha = \overline{x}\,\overline{u}$ is the assignment blocked by C, and $\alpha_L = x\,u$. Now, consider $F{\upharpoonright}\alpha = (y) \wedge (\overline{y} \vee z)$ and $F{\upharpoonright}\alpha_L = (z)$. Clearly, $F{\upharpoonright}\alpha \vdash_1 F{\upharpoonright}\alpha_L$ and so C is set-propagation redundant by L with respect to F.

Most known types of redundant clauses are SPR clauses [19]. This includes *blocked clauses* [24], *set-blocked clauses* [23], *resolution asymmetric tautologies* (RATs) [22], and many more. By introducing pruning predicates that allow us to add SPR clauses and even PR clauses to a formula, we thus allow for more effective pruning than with the positive reduct originally used in SDCL. We start by presenting our new *filtered* positive reduct.

4   The Filtered Positive Reduct

The original positive reduct of a formula F and an assignment α is obtained by first taking all clauses of F that are satisfied by α and then removing from these clauses the literals that are not touched (assigned) by α. The resulting clauses are then conjoined with the clause C that blocks α. We obtain the *filtered* positive reduct by not taking *all* satisfied clauses of F but only those for which the untouched part is not implied by $F\!\restriction\!\alpha$ via unit propagation:

Definition 6. *Let F be a formula and α an assignment. Then, the* filtered *positive reduct* $f_\alpha(F)$ *of F and α is the formula $G \wedge C$ where C is the clause that blocks α and $G = \{\mathsf{touched}_\alpha(D) \mid D \in F \text{ and } F\!\restriction\!\alpha \not\vdash_1 \mathsf{untouched}_\alpha(D)\}$.*

Clearly the filtered positive reduct is a subset of the positive reduct because $F\!\restriction\!\alpha \not\vdash_1 \mathsf{untouched}_\alpha(D)$ implies $D\!\restriction\!\alpha = \top$. To see this, suppose $D\!\restriction\!\alpha \neq \top$. Then, $D\!\restriction\!\alpha$ is contained in $F\!\restriction\!\alpha$ and since $\mathsf{untouched}_\alpha(D) = D\!\restriction\!\alpha$, it follows that $F\!\restriction\!\alpha \vdash_1 \mathsf{untouched}_\alpha(D)$. Therefore, the filtered positive reduct is obtained from the positive reduct by removing ("filtering") every clause $D' = \mathsf{touched}_\alpha(D)$ such that $F\!\restriction\!\alpha \vdash_1 \mathsf{untouched}_\alpha(D)$.

The following example illustrates how the filtered positive reduct allows us to prune assignments that cannot be pruned when using only the positive reduct:

Example 4. Let $F = (x \vee y) \wedge (\overline{x} \vee y)$ and consider the assignment $\alpha = x$. The positive reduct $p_\alpha(F) = (x) \wedge (\overline{x})$ is unsatisfiable and so it does not allow us to prune α. In contrast, the filtered positive reduct $f_\alpha(F) = (\overline{x})$, obtained by filtering out the clause (x), is satisfied by the assignment $\overline{x}$. The clause (x) is not contained in the filtered reduct because $\mathsf{untouched}_\alpha(x \vee y) = (y)$ and $F\!\restriction\!\alpha = (y)$, which implies $F\!\restriction\!\alpha \vdash_1 \mathsf{untouched}_\alpha(x \vee y)$. Note that the clause $(\overline{x})$ is contained both in the positive reduct and in the filtered positive reduct since it blocks α.

The filtered positive reduct has a useful property: If a non-empty assignment α falsifies a formula F, then the filtered positive reduct $f_\alpha(F)$ is satisfiable. To see this, observe that $\bot \in F\!\restriction\!\alpha$ and so $F\!\restriction\!\alpha \vdash_1 \mathsf{untouched}_\alpha(D)$ for every clause $D \in F$ because unit propagation derives a conflict on $F\!\restriction\!\alpha$ alone (note that this also holds if $\mathsf{untouched}_\alpha(D)$ is the empty clause $\bot$). Therefore, $f_\alpha(F)$ contains only the clause that blocks α, which is clearly satisfiable. The ordinary positive reduct does not have this property.

Note that the filtered positive reduct contains only variables of $var(\alpha)$. Since it also contains the clause that blocks α, any satisfying assignment of the filtered positive reduct must disagree with α on at least one literal. Hence, every satisfying assignment of the filtered positive reduct is of the form α_L where L is a set of literals that are contained in the clause that blocks α. With the filtered positive reduct, we can identify exactly the clauses that are set-propagation redundant with respect to a formula:

Theorem 1. *Let F be a formula, α an assignment, and C the clause that blocks α. Then, C is SPR by an $L \subseteq C$ with respect to F if and only if the assignment α_L satisfies the filtered positive reduct $f_\alpha(F)$.*

Proof. For the "only if" direction, suppose C is SPR by an $L \subseteq C$ in F, meaning that $F\lceil\alpha \vdash_1 F\lceil\alpha_L$. We show that α_L satisfies all clauses of $f_\alpha(F)$. Let therefore $D' \in f_\alpha(F)$. By definition, D' is either the clause that blocks α or it is of the form $\mathsf{touched}_\alpha(D)$ for some clause $D \in F$ such that $F\lceil\alpha \nvdash_1 \mathsf{untouched}_\alpha(D)$. In the former case, D' is clearly satisfied by α_L since α_L must disagree with α. In the latter case, since $F\lceil\alpha \vdash_1 F\lceil\alpha_L$, it follows that either $F\lceil\alpha \vdash_1 D\lceil\alpha_L$ or α_L satisfies D. Now, if $D\lceil\alpha_L \neq \top$, it cannot be the case that $F\lceil\alpha \vdash_1 D\lceil\alpha_L$ since $var(\alpha_L) = var(\alpha)$ and thus $D\lceil\alpha_L = \mathsf{untouched}_\alpha(D)$, which would imply $F\lceil\alpha \vdash_1 \mathsf{untouched}_\alpha(D)$. Therefore, α_L must satisfy D. But then α_L must satisfy $D' = \mathsf{touched}_\alpha(D)$, again since $var(\alpha_L) = var(\alpha)$.

For the "if" direction, assume that α_L satisfies the filtered positive reduct $f_\alpha(F)$. We show that $F\lceil\alpha \vdash_1 F\lceil\alpha_L$. Let $D\lceil\alpha_L \in F\lceil\alpha_L$. Since $D\lceil\alpha_L$ is contained in $F\lceil\alpha_L$, we know that α_L does not satisfy D and so it does not satisfy $\mathsf{touched}_\alpha(D)$. Hence, $\mathsf{touched}_\alpha(D)$ cannot be contained in $f_\alpha(F)$, implying that $F\lceil\alpha \vdash_1 \mathsf{untouched}_\alpha(D)$. But, $D\lceil\alpha_L = \mathsf{untouched}_\alpha(D)$ since $var(\alpha_L) = var(\alpha)$ and thus it follows that $F\lceil\alpha \vdash_1 D\lceil\alpha_L$. □

When the (ordinary) positive reduct is used for SDCL solving, the following property holds [20]: Assume the solver has a current assignment $\alpha = \alpha_d \cup \alpha_u$ where α_d consists of all the assignments that were made by the decision heuristic and α_u consists of all assignments that were derived via unit propagation. If the solver then finds that the positive reduct of its formula and the assignment α is satisfiable, it can learn the clause that blocks α_d instead of the longer clause that blocks α, thus pruning the search space more effectively. This is allowed because the clause that blocks α_d is guaranteed to be propagation redundant.

The same holds for the filtered positive reduct and the argument is analogous to the earlier one [20]: Assume the filtered positive reduct of F and $\alpha = \alpha_d \cup \alpha_u$ is satisfiable. Then, the clause that blocks α is set-propagation redundant with respect to F and thus there exists an assignment α_L such that $F\lceil\alpha \vdash_1 F\lceil\alpha_L$. But then, since unit propagation derives all the assignments of α_u from $F\lceil\alpha_d$, it must also hold that $F\lceil\alpha_d \vdash_1 F\lceil\alpha_L$, and so the clause that blocks α_d is propagation redundant with respect to F and (witness) assignment $\omega = \alpha_L$.

Finally, observe that the filtered positive reducts $f_{\alpha_d}(F)$ and $f_\alpha(F)$ are not always equisatisfiable. To see this, consider the formula $F = (\overline{x} \vee y) \wedge (x \vee \overline{y})$ and the assignments $\alpha = x\,y$ and $\alpha_d = x$. Clearly, the unit clause y is derived from $F\lceil\alpha_d$. Now, observe that $f_\alpha(F)$ is satisfiable while $f_{\alpha_d}(F)$ is unsatisfiable. It thus makes sense to first compute the filtered positive reduct with respect to α and then—in case it is satisfiable—remove the propagated literals to obtain a shorter clause.

5   The PR Reduct

We showed in the previous section that the filtered positive reduct characterizes precisely the set-propagation-redundant clauses. Since set-propagation-redundant clauses are a subset of propagation-redundant clauses [19], it is natural to search for an encoding that characterizes the propagation-redundant clauses, which could possibly lead to an even more aggressive pruning of the search space. As we will see in the following, such an encoding must necessarily be large because it has to reason over all possible clauses of a formula. We thus believe that it is hardly useful for practical SDCL solving.

The positive reduct and the filtered positive reduct yield small formulas that can be easily solved in practice. The downside, however, is that nothing can be learned from their unsatisfiability. This is different for a pruning predicate that encodes propagation redundancy:

Theorem 2. *If a clause $l_1 \vee \cdots \vee l_k$ is not propagation redundant with respect to a formula F, then F implies $\bar{l}_1 \wedge \cdots \wedge \bar{l}_k$.*

Proof. Assume $l_1 \vee \cdots \vee l_k$ is not propagation redundant with respect to F, or equivalently that all assignments ω with $F\lceil_{\bar{l}_1 \ldots \bar{l}_k} \vdash F\lceil_\omega$ agree with $\bar{l}_1 \ldots \bar{l}_k$. Then, no assignment that disagrees with $\bar{l}_1 \ldots \bar{l}_k$ can satisfy F. As a consequence, F implies $\bar{l}_1 \wedge \cdots \wedge \bar{l}_k$. □

By solving a pruning predicate for propagation-redundant clauses, we thus not only detect if the current assignment can be pruned (in case the predicate is satisfiable), but also if the formula can only possibly be satisfied by extensions of the current assignment (in case the predicate is unsatisfiable). This is in contrast to the positive reduct and the filtered positive reduct, which often only need to consider a small subpart of the original formula. We thus believe that such an encoding is not useful in practice. In the following, we present a possible encoding which—due to the above reasons—we did not evaluate in practice. Nevertheless, performing such an evaluation is still part of our future work.

In the definition of propagation-redundant clauses, the assignment ω does not necessarily assign the same variables as α. To deal with this, we use the idea of the so-called *dual-rail encoding* [8,10,30]. In the dual-rail encoding, a given variable x is replaced by two new variables x^p and x^n. The intuitive idea is that x^p is true whenever the original variable x is supposed to be true and x^n is true whenever x is supposed to be false. If both x^p and x^n are false, then x is supposed to be unassigned. Finally, x^p and x^n cannot be true at the same time. Thus, the *dual-rail encodings* of a clause are defined as follows: Let $C = P \vee N$ be a clause with $P = x_1 \vee \cdots \vee x_k$ containing only positive literals and $N = \overline{x}_{k+1} \vee \cdots \vee \overline{x}_m$ containing only negative literals. Further, let $x_1^p, x_1^n, \ldots, x_m^p, x_m^n$ be new variables. Then, the *positive dual-rail encoding* C^p of C is the clause

$$x_1^p \vee \cdots \vee x_k^p \vee x_{k+1}^n \vee \cdots \vee x_m^n,$$

and the *negative dual-rail encoding* C^n of C is the clause

$$x_1^n \vee \cdots \vee x_k^n \vee x_{k+1}^p \vee \cdots \vee x_m^p.$$

We can now define the PR reduct as follows:

Definition 7. *Let F be a formula and α an assignment. Then, the PR reduct $\mathrm{pr}_\alpha(F)$ of F and α is the formula $G \wedge C$ where C is the clause that blocks α and G is the union of the following sets of clauses where all the s_i are new variables:*

$$\{\overline{x^p} \vee \overline{x^n} \mid x \in var(F) \setminus var(\alpha)\},$$

$$\{\overline{s}_i \vee \mathsf{touched}_\alpha(D_i) \vee \mathsf{untouched}_\alpha(D_i)^p \mid D_i \in F\},$$

$$\{\overline{L^n} \vee s_i \mid D_i \in F \ \text{and} \ L \subseteq \mathsf{untouched}_\alpha(D_i)$$
$$\text{such that } F{\restriction}\alpha \not\vDash \mathsf{untouched}_\alpha(D_i) \setminus L\}.$$

In the last set, if L is empty, we obtain a unit clause with the literal s_i.

We thus keep all the variables assigned by α but introduce the dual-rail variants for variables of F not assigned by α. The clauses of the form $\overline{x^p} \vee \overline{x^n}$ ensure that for a variable x, the two variables x^p and x^n cannot be true at the same time.

The main idea is that satisfying assignments of the PR reduct correspond to assignments of the formula F: from a satisfying assignment τ of the PR reduct we obtain an assignment ω over the variables of the original formula F as follows:

$$\omega(x) = \begin{cases} \tau(x) & \text{if } x \in var(\tau) \cap var(F), \\ 1 & \text{if } \tau(x^p) = 1, \\ 0 & \text{if } \tau(x^n) = 1. \end{cases}$$

Analogously, we obtain from ω a satisfying assignment τ of the filtered positive reduct $\mathrm{pr}_\alpha(F)$ as follows:

$$\tau(x) = \begin{cases} \omega(x) & \text{if } x \in var(\alpha); \\ 1 & \text{if } x = x^p \text{ and } \omega(x) = 1, \text{ or} \\ & \text{if } x = x^n \text{ and } \omega(x) = 0, \text{ or} \\ & \text{if } x = s_i \text{ and } \omega \text{ satisfies } D_i; \\ 0 & \text{otherwise.} \end{cases}$$

To prove that the clause that blocks an assignment α is propagation redundant w.r.t. a formula F if the PR reduct of F and α is satisfiable, we use the following:

Lemma 1. *Let F be a formula and let α and ω be two assignments such that $F{\restriction}\alpha \vdash F{\restriction}\omega$. Then, $F{\restriction}\alpha \vdash F{\restriction}\omega x$ for every literal x such that $var(x) \in var(\alpha)$.*

Proof. Let $D{\restriction}\omega x \in F{\restriction}\omega x$. We show that $F{\restriction}\alpha \vdash D{\restriction}\omega x$. Clearly, $x \notin D$ for otherwise $D{\restriction}\omega x = \top$, which would imply $D{\restriction}\omega x \notin F{\restriction}\omega x$. Therefore, the only possible difference between $D{\restriction}\omega$ and $D{\restriction}\omega x$ is that $\overline{x}$ is contained in $D{\restriction}\omega$ but not in $D{\restriction}\omega x$. Now, since $var(x) \in var(\alpha)$, we know that $var(x) \notin F{\restriction}\alpha$. But then, $F{\restriction}\alpha \vdash D{\restriction}\omega x$ if and only if $F{\restriction}\alpha \vdash D{\restriction}\omega$ and thus $F{\restriction}\alpha \vdash F{\restriction}\omega x$. $\qquad\square$

We can now show that the PR reduct precisely characterizes the propagation-redundant clauses:

Theorem 3. *Let F be a formula, α an assignment, and C the clause that blocks α. Then, C is propagation redundant with respect to F if and only if the PR reduct $\mathrm{pr}_\alpha(F)$ of F and α is satisfiable.*

Proof. For the "only if" direction, assume that C is propagation redundant with respect to F, meaning that there exists an assignment ω such that ω satisfies C and $F\lceil\alpha \vdash_1 F\lceil\omega$. By Lemma 1, we can without loss of generality assume that $var(\alpha) \subseteq var(\omega)$. Now consider the assignment τ that corresponds to ω as explained before Lemma 1. We show that τ satisfies $\mathrm{pr}_\alpha(F)$. Since the clause C that blocks α is in $\mathrm{pr}_\alpha(F)$, it must be satisfied by ω. Since ω satisfies C, τ satisfies C. Also, by construction, τ never satisfies both x^p and x^n for a variable x and so it satisfies the clauses $\overline{x^p} \vee \overline{x^n}$. If, for a clause $\overline{s}_i \vee \mathsf{touched}_\alpha(D_i) \vee \mathsf{untouched}_\alpha(D_i)^p$, τ satisfies s_i, then we know that ω satisfies D_i and thus τ must satisfy $\mathsf{touched}_\alpha(D_i) \vee \mathsf{untouched}_\alpha(D_i)^p$.

It remains to show that τ satisfies the clause $\overline{L^n} \vee s_i$ for every $D_i \in F$ and every set $L \subseteq \mathsf{untouched}_\alpha(D_i)$ such that $F\lceil\alpha \nvdash_1 \mathsf{untouched}_\alpha(D_i) \setminus L$. Assume to the contrary that, for such a clause, $\tau(s_i) = 0$ and τ falsifies all literals in $\overline{L^n}$. Then, ω does not satisfy D_i and it falsifies all literals in L. But, from $var(\alpha) \subseteq var(\omega)$ we know that $D_i\lceil\omega \subseteq \mathsf{untouched}_\alpha(D_i)$ and thus it follows that $D_i\lceil\omega \subseteq \mathsf{untouched}_\alpha(D_i) \setminus L$. Hence, since $F\lceil\alpha \nvdash_1 \mathsf{untouched}_\alpha(D_i) \setminus L$, we conclude that $F\lceil\alpha \nvdash_1 D_i\lceil\omega$, a contradiction.

For the "if" direction, assume that there exists a satisfying assignment τ of $\mathrm{pr}_\alpha(F)$ and consider the assignment ω that corresponds to τ as explained before Lemma 1. Since $C \in \mathrm{pr}_\alpha(F)$, ω must satisfy C. It remains to show that $F\lceil\alpha \vdash_1 F\lceil\omega$. Let $D_i\lceil\omega \in F\lceil\omega$. Then, ω does not satisfy D_i and so $\mathsf{touched}_\alpha(D_i) \vee \mathsf{untouched}_\alpha(D_i)^p$ is falsified by τ, implying that τ must falsify s_i. As $var(\alpha) \subseteq var(\omega)$, we know that $D_i\lceil\omega \subseteq \mathsf{untouched}_\alpha(D_i)$, meaning that $D_i\lceil\omega$ is of the form $\mathsf{untouched}_\alpha(D_i) \setminus L$ for some set $L \subseteq \mathsf{untouched}_\alpha(D_i)$ such that ω falsifies L. But then the clause $\overline{L^n} \vee s_i$ cannot be contained in $\mathrm{pr}_\alpha(F)$ since it would be falsified by τ. We thus conclude that $F\lceil\alpha \vdash_1 \mathsf{untouched}_\alpha(D_i) \setminus L$ and so $F\lceil\omega \vdash_1 D_i\lceil\omega$. $\square$

Note that the last set of clauses of the PR reduct, in principle has exponentially many clauses w.r.t. the length of the largest original clause. We leave it to future work to answer the question whether non-exponential encodings exist. But even if a polynomial encoding can be found, we doubt its usefulness in practice.

6   Implementation

We implemented a clean-slate SDCL solver, called SADICAL, that can learn PR clauses using either the positive reduct or the filtered positive reduct. It consists of around 3K lines of C and is based on an efficient CDCL engine using state-of-the-art algorithms, data structures, and heuristics, including a variable-move-to-front decision heuristic [4], a sophisticated restart policy [5], and aggressive clause-data-based reduction [2]. Our implementation provides a simple but efficient framework to evaluate new SDCL-inspired ideas and heuristics.

The implementation closely follows the pseudo-code shown in Fig. 1 and computes the pruning predicate before every decision. This is costly in general, but allows the solver to detect PR clauses as early as possible. Our goal is to determine whether short PR proofs can be found automatically. The solver produces PR proofs and we verified all the presented results using proof checkers. The source code of SADiCAL is available at http://fmv.jku.at/sadical.

Two aspects of SDCL are crucial: the pruning predicate and the decision heuristics. For the pruning predicate we ran experiments with both the positive reduct and the filtered positive reduct. The initially proposed decision heuristics for SDCL [20] are as follows: Pick the variable that occurs most frequently in short clauses. Also, apart from the root-node branch, assign only literals that occur in clauses that are touched but not satisfied by the current assignment.

We added another restriction: whenever a (filtered) positive reduct is satisfiable, make all literals in the witness (i.e., the satisfying assignment of the pruning predicate) that disagree with the current assignment more important than any other literal in the formula. This restriction is removed when the solver backtracks to the root node (i.e., when a unit clause is learned) and added again when a new PR clause is found. The motivation of this restriction is as follows: we observed that literals in the witness that disagree with the current assignment typically occur in short PR clauses; making them more important than other literals increases the likelihood of learning short PR clauses.

7   Evaluation

In the following, we demonstrate that the filtered positive reduct allows our SDCL solver to prove unsatisfiability of formulas well-known for having only exponential-size resolution proofs. We start with Tseitin formulas [11,32]. In short, a Tseitin formula represents the following graph problem: Given a graph with 0/1-labels for each vertex such that an odd number of vertices has label 1, does there exist a subset of the edges such that (after removing edges not in the subset) every vertex with label 0 has an even degree and every vertex with label 1 has an odd degree? The answer is *no* as the sum of all degrees is always even. The formula is therefore unsatisfiable by construction. Tseitin formulas defined over expander graphs require resolution proofs of exponential size [33] and also appear hard for SDCL when using the ordinary positive reduct as pruning predicate. We compare three settings, all with proof logging:

    (1) plain CDCL,
    (2) SDCL with the positive reduct $p_\alpha(F)$, and
    (3) SDCL with the filtered positive reduct $f_\alpha(F)$.

Additionally, we include the winner of the 2018 SAT Competition: the CDCL-based solver MapleLCMDistChronoBT (short MLBT) [29]. The results are shown in Table 1. The last column shows the proof-validation times by the formally verified checker in ACL2. To verify the proofs for all our experiments, we did the following: We started with the PR proofs produced by our SDCL solver using the filtered positive reduct. We then translated them into DRAT proofs using the pr2drat tool [17]. Finally, we used the drat-trim checker to optimize the proofs (i.e., to remove redundant proof parts) and to convert them into the LRAT format, which is the format supported by the formally verified proof checker.

Table 1 shows the performance on small (Urquhart-s3*), medium (Urquhart-s4*), and large (Urquhart-s5*) Tseitin formulas running on a Xeon E5-2690 CPU 2.6 GHz with 64 GB memory.[1] Only our solver with the filtered positive reduct is able to efficiently prove unsatisfiability of all these instances. Notice that with the ordinary positive reduct it is impossible to solve any of the formulas. There may actually be a theoretical barrier here. The LSDCL solver also uses the positive reduct, but only for assignments with at most two decision literals. As a consequence, the overhead of the positive reduct is small. In the future we plan to develop meaningful limits for SADICAL as well.

Table 1. Runtime Comparison (in Seconds) on the Tseitin Benchmarks [11,33].

formula	MLBT [29]	LSDCL [20]	plain	$p_\alpha(F)$	$f_\alpha(F)$	ACL2
Urquhart-s3-b1	2.95	5.86	16.31	> 3600	**0.02**	0.09
Urquhart-s3-b2	1.36	2.4	2.82	> 3600	**0.03**	0.13
Urquhart-s3-b3	2.28	19.94	2.08	> 3600	**0.03**	0.16
Urquhart-s3-b4	10.74	32.42	7.65	> 3600	**0.03**	0.17
Urquhart-s4-b1	86.11	583.96	> 3600	> 3600	**0.32**	2.37
Urquhart-s4-b2	154.35	1824.95	183.77	> 3600	**0.11**	0.78
Urquhart-s4-b3	258.46	> 3600	129.27	> 3600	**0.16**	1.12
Urquhart-s4-b4	> 3600	> 3600	> 3600	> 3600	**0.14**	1.17
Urquhart-s5-b1	> 3600	> 3600	> 3600	> 3600	**1.27**	9.86
Urquhart-s5-b2	> 3600	> 3600	> 3600	> 3600	**0.58**	4.38
Urquhart-s5-b3	> 3600	> 3600	> 3600	> 3600	**1.67**	17.99
Urquhart-s5-b4	> 3600	> 3600	> 3600	> 3600	**2.91**	24.24

Table 2. Runtime Comparison (in Seconds) on the Pigeon-Hole Formulas.

formula	MLBT [29]	LSDCL [20]	plain	$p_\alpha(F)$	$f_\alpha(F)$	ACL2
hole20	> 3600	1.13	> 3600	**0.22**	0.55	6.78
hole30	> 3600	8.81	> 3600	**1.71**	4.30	87.58
hole40	> 3600	43.10	> 3600	**7.94**	20.38	611.24
hole50	> 3600	149.67	> 3600	**25.60**	68.46	2792.39

We also ran experiments with the pigeon-hole formulas. Although these formulas are hard for resolution, they can be solved efficiently with SDCL using

---

[1] Log files, benchmarks and source code are available at http://fmv.jku.at/sadical.

the positive reduct [20]. Table 2 shows a runtime comparison, again including PR proof logging, for pigeon-hole formulas of various sizes. Notice that the computational costs of the solver with the filtered positive reduct are about 3 to 4 times as large compared to the solver with the positive reduct. This is caused by the overhead of computing the filtering. The sizes of the PR proofs produced by both versions are similar. Our solver with the positive reduct is about four times as fast compared to the SDCL version (only positive reduct) of LINGELING [20], in short LSDCL. As the heuristics and proof sizes of our solver and LSDCL are similar, the better performance is due to our dedicated SDCL implementation.

Finally, we performed experiments with the recently released 2018 SAT Competition benchmarks. We expected slow performance on most benchmarks due to the high overhead of solving pruning predicates before making decisions. However, our solver outperformed the participating solvers on mutilated chessboard problems [27] which were contributed by Alexey Porkhunov (see Table 3).

For example, our solver can prove unsatisfiability of the 18×18 mutilated chessboard in 43.88 seconds. The filtered positive reduct was crucial to obtain this result. The other solvers, apart from CADICAL solving it in 828 seconds, timed out after 5000 seconds during the competition (on competition hardware). Resolution proofs of mutilated chessboard problems are exponential in size [1], which explains the poor performance of CDCL solvers. On these problems, like on the Tseitin formulas, our solver performed much better with the filtered positive reduct than with the positive reduct. The results are robust with respect to partially and completely scrambling formulas as suggested by [6], with the exception of the pigeon hole formulas, which needs to be investigated.

Table 3. Runtime Comparison (in Seconds) on the Mutilated Chessboard Formulas.

formula	MLBT [29]	LSDCL [20]	plain	$p_\alpha(F)$	$f_\alpha(F)$	ACL2
mchess_15	51.53	1473.11	2480.67	> 3600	**13.14**	29.12
mchess_16	380.45	> 3600	2115.75	> 3600	**15.52**	36.86
mchess_17	2418.35	> 3600	> 3600	> 3600	**25.54**	57.83
mchess_18	> 3600	> 3600	> 3600	> 3600	**43.88**	100.71

8   Conclusion

We introduced two new SAT encodings for pruning the search space in satisfaction-driven clause learning (SDCL). The first encoding, called the filtered positive reduct, is easily solvable and prunes the search space more aggressively than the positive reduct (which was used when SDCL was initially introduced). The second encoding, called the PR reduct, might not be useful in practice though it precisely characterizes propagation redundancy.

Based on the filtered positive reduct, we implemented an SDCL solver and our experiments show that the solver can efficiently prove the unsatisfiability of the Tseitin formulas, the pigeon-hole formulas, and the mutilated chessboard problems. For all these formulas, CDCL solvers require exponential time due to theoretical restrictions. Moreover, to the best of our knowledge, our solver is the first to generate machine-checkable proofs of unsatisfiability of these formulas. We certified our results using a formally verified proof checker.

Although our SDCL solver can already produce proofs of formulas that are too hard for CDCL solvers, it is still outperformed by CDCL solvers on many simpler formulas. This seems to suggest that also in SAT solving, there is no free lunch. Nevertheless, we believe that the performance of SDCL on simple formulas can be improved by tuning the solver more carefully, e.g., by only learning propagation-redundant clauses when this is really beneficial, or by coming up with a dedicated decision heuristic. To deal with these problems, we are currently investigating an approach based on reinforcement learning.

Considering our results, we believe that SDCL is a promising SAT-solving paradigm for formulas that are too hard for ordinary CDCL solvers. Finally, proofs of challenging problems can be enormous in size, such as the 2 petabytes proof of Schur Number Five [16]; SDCL improvements have the potential to produce proofs that are substantially smaller and faster to verify.

References

1. Alekhnovich, M.: Mutilated chessboard problem is exponentially hard for resolution. Theoret. Comput. Sci. **310**(1–3), 513–525 (2004)
2. Audemard, G., Simon, L.: Predicting learnt clauses quality in modern SAT solvers. In: Proceedings of the 21st International Joint Conference on Artificial Intelligence (IJCAI 2019), pp. 399–404 (2009)
3. Biere, A.: Splatz, Lingeling, Plingeling, Treengeling, YalSAT entering the SAT competition 2016. In: Proceedings of SAT Competition 2016 - Solver and Benchmark Descriptions. Department of Computer Science Series of Publications B, vol. B-2016-1, pp. 44–45. University of Helsinki (2016)
4. Biere, A., Fröhlich, A.: Evaluating CDCL variable scoring schemes. In: Heule, M.J.H., Weaver, S. (eds.) SAT 2015. LNCS, vol. 9340, pp. 405–422. Springer, Cham (2015)
5. Biere, A., Fröhlich, A.: Evaluating CDCL restart schemes. In: Proceedings of the 6th Pragmatics of SAT Workshop (PoS 2015). EPiC Series in Computing, vol. 59, pp. 1–17 (2019)
6. Biere, A., Heule, M.J.H.: The effect of scrambling CNFs. In: Proceedings of the 9th Pragmatics of SAT Workshop (PoS 2018) (2018, to be published)
7. Biere, A., Heule, M.J.H., van Maaren, H., Walsh, T. (eds.): Handbook of Satisfiability. IOS Press, Amsterdam (2009)
8. Bonet, M.L., Buss, S., Ignatiev, A., Marques-Silva, J., Morgado, A.: MaxSAT resolution with the dual rail encoding. In: Proceedings of the 32nd AAAI Conference on Artificial Intelligence (AAAI 2018). AAAI Press (2018)
9. Brickenstein, M., Dreyer, A.: PolyBoRi: a framework for Gröbner-basis computations with boolean polynomials. J. Symbolic Comput. **44**(9), 1326–1345 (2009). Effective Methods in Algebraic Geometry

10. Bryant, R.E., Beatty, D., Brace, K., Cho, K., Sheffler, T.: COSMOS: a compiled simulator for MOS circuits. In: Proceedings of the 24th ACM/IEEE Design Automation Conference (DAC 87), pp. 9–16. ACM (1987)
11. Chatalic, P., Simon, L.: Multi-resolution on compressed sets of clauses. In: Proceedings of the 12th IEEE International Conference on Tools with Artificial Intelligence (ICTAI 2000), pp. 2–10 (2000)
12. Cruz-Filipe, L., Marques-Silva, J., Schneider-Kamp, P.: Efficient certified resolution proof checking. In: Legay, A., Margaria, T. (eds.) TACAS 2017. LNCS, vol. 10205, pp. 118–135. Springer, Heidelberg (2017)
13. Dantchev, S.S., Riis, S.: "Planar" tautologies hard for resolution. In: Proceedings of the 42nd Annual Symposium on Foundations of Computer Science (FOCS 2001), pp. 220–229. IEEE Computer Society (2001)
14. Devriendt, J., Bogaerts, B., Bruynooghe, M., Denecker, M.: Improved static symmetry breaking for SAT. In: Creignou, N., Le Berre, D. (eds.) SAT 2016. LNCS, vol. 9710, pp. 104–122. Springer, Cham (2016)
15. Haken, A.: The intractability of resolution. Theoret. Comput. Sci. **39**, 297–308 (1985)
16. Heule, M.J.H.: Schur number five. In: Proceedings of the 32nd AAAI Conference on Artificial Intelligence (AAAI 2018). AAAI Press (2018)
17. Heule, M.J.H., Biere, A.: What a difference a variable makes. In: Beyer, D., Huisman, M. (eds.) TACAS 2018. LNCS, vol. 10806, pp. 75–92. Springer, Cham (2018)
18. Heule, M.J.H., Hunt Jr., W.A., Kaufmann, M., Wetzler, N.: Efficient, verified checking of propositional proofs. In: Ayala-Rincón, M., Muñoz, C.A. (eds.) ITP 2017. LNCS, vol. 10499, pp. 269–284. Springer, Cham (2017)
19. Heule, M.J.H., Kiesl, B., Biere, A.: Short proofs without new variables. In: de Moura, L. (ed.) CADE 2017. LNCS (LNAI), vol. 10395, pp. 130–147. Springer, Cham (2017)
20. Heule, M.J.H., Kiesl, B., Seidl, M., Biere, A.: PRuning through satisfaction. In: Strichman, O., Tzoref-Brill, R. (eds.) HVC 2017. LNCS, vol. 10629, pp. 179–194. Springer, Cham (2017)
21. Heule, M.J.H., van Maaren, H.: Aligning CNF- and equivalence-reasoning. In: Hoos, H.H., Mitchell, D.G. (eds.) SAT 2004. LNCS, vol. 3542, pp. 145–156. Springer, Heidelberg (2005)
22. Järvisalo, M., Heule, M.J.H., Biere, A.: Inprocessing rules. In: Gramlich, B., Miller, D., Sattler, U. (eds.) IJCAR 2012. LNCS (LNAI), vol. 7364, pp. 355–370. Springer, Heidelberg (2012)
23. Kiesl, B., Seidl, M., Tompits, H., Biere, A.: Super-blocked clauses. In: Olivetti, N., Tiwari, A. (eds.) IJCAR 2016. LNCS (LNAI), vol. 9706, pp. 45–61. Springer, Cham (2016)
24. Kullmann, O.: On a generalization of extended resolution. Discrete Appl. Math. **96–97**, 149–176 (1999)
25. Marques-Silva, J., Lynce, I., Malik, S.: Conflict-driven clause learning SAT solvers. In: Biere, A., Heule, M.J.H., van Maaren, H., Walsh, T. (eds.) Handbook of Satisfiability, pp. 131–153. IOS Press, Amsterdam (2009)
26. Marques Silva, J.P., Sakallah, K.A.: GRASP: a search algorithm for propositional satisfiability. IEEE Trans. Comput. **48**(5), 506–521 (1999)
27. McCarthy, J.: A tough nut for proof procedures. Memo 16, Stanford Artificial Intelligence Project, July 1964
28. Moskewicz, M.W., Madigan, C.F., Zhao, Y., Zhang, L., Malik, S.: Chaff: engineering an efficient SAT solver. In: Proceedings of the 38th Design Automation Conference (DAC 2001), pp. 530–535. ACM (2001)

29. Nadel, A., Ryvchin, V.: Chronological backtracking. In: Beyersdorff, O., Winter-steiger, C.M. (eds.) SAT 2018. LNCS, vol. 10929, pp. 111–121. Springer, Cham (2018)
30. Palopoli, L., Pirri, F., Pizzuti, C.: Algorithms for selective enumeration of prime implicants. Artif. Intell. **111**(1), 41–72 (1999)
31. Soos, M., Nohl, K., Castelluccia, C.: Extending SAT solvers to cryptographic prob-lems. In: Kullmann, O. (ed.) SAT 2009. LNCS, vol. 5584, pp. 244–257. Springer, Heidelberg (2009)
32. Tseitin, G.S.: On the complexity of derivation in propositional calculus. In: Siek-mann, J.H., Wrightson, G. (eds.) Automation of Reasoning: 2: Classical Papers on Computational Logic 1967–1970, pp. 466–483. Springer, Heidelberg (1983)
33. Urquhart, A.: Hard examples for resolution. J. ACM **34**(1), 209–219 (1987)

WAPS: Weighted and Projected Sampling

Rahul Gupta[1(✉)], Shubham Sharma[1], Subhajit Roy[1], and Kuldeep S. Meel[2]

[1] Indian Institute of Technology Kanpur, Kanpur, India
{grahul,smsharma,subhajit}@iitk.ac.in
[2] National University of Singapore, Singapore, Singapore
meel@comp.nus.edu.sg

Abstract. Given a set of constraints F and a user-defined weight function W on the assignment space, the problem of constrained sampling is to sample satisfying assignments of F conditioned on W. Constrained sampling is a fundamental problem with applications in probabilistic reasoning, synthesis, software and hardware testing. Consequently, the problem of sampling has been subject to intense theoretical and practical investigations over the years. Despite such intense investigations, there still remains a gap between theory and practice. In particular, there has been significant progress in the development of sampling techniques when W is a uniform distribution, but such techniques fail to handle general weight functions W. Furthermore, we are, often, interested in Σ_1^1 formulas, i.e., $G(X) := \exists Y F(X, Y)$ for some F; typically the set of variables Y are introduced as auxiliary variables during encoding of constraints to F. In this context, one wonders *whether it is possible to design sampling techniques whose runtime performance is agnostic to the underlying weight distribution and can handle Σ_1^1 formulas?*

The primary contribution of this work is a novel technique, called WAPS, for sampling over Σ_1^1 whose runtime is agnostic to W. WAPS is based on our recently discovered connection between knowledge compilation and uniform sampling. WAPS proceeds by compiling F into a well studied compiled form, d-DNNF, which allows sampling operations to be conducted in linear time in the size of the compiled form. We demonstrate that WAPS can significantly outperform existing state-of-the-art weighted and projected sampler WeightGen, by up to 3 orders of magnitude in runtime while achieving a geometric speedup of $296\times$ and solving 564 more instances out of 773. The distribution generated by WAPS is statistically indistinguishable from that generated by an ideal weighted and projected sampler. Furthermore, WAPS is almost oblivious to the number of samples requested.

The original version of this chapter was revised: The acknowledgement was modified. The correction to this chapter is available at https://doi.org/10.1007/978-3-030-17462-0_29

Appendix along with open source tool is available at https://github.com/meelgroup/waps.

This work was supported in part by NUS ODPRT Grant R-252-000-685-133 and National Research Foundation Singapore under its AI Singapore Programme [Award Number: AISG-RP-2018-005]. The computational work for this article was performed on resources of the National Supercomputing Centre, Singapore https://www.nscc.sg.

© The Author(s) 2019
T. Vojnar and L. Zhang (Eds.): TACAS 2019, Part I, LNCS 11427, pp. 59–76, 2019.
https://doi.org/10.1007/978-3-030-17462-0_4

1 Introduction

Boolean satisfiability (SAT) has gathered applications in bounded model checking of hardware and software systems [5,7,51], classical planning [35] and scheduling [27]. Despite the worst-case hardness of SAT, the past few decades have witnessed a significant improvement in the runtime performance of the state-of-the-art SAT solvers [41]. This improvement has led to the usage of SAT solvers as oracles to handle problems whose complexity lies beyond NP. Among these problems, *constrained sampling*, that concerns with sampling from the space of solutions of a set of constraints F, subject to a user-defined weight function W, has witnessed a surge of interest owing to the wide range of applications ranging from machine learning, probabilistic reasoning, software and hardware verification to statistical physics [3,32,39,45].

Not surprisingly, the problem of sampling is known to be computationally intractable. When the weight function W is fixed to a uniform distribution, the problem of constrained sampling is also known as uniform sampling. Uniform sampling has witnessed a long-standing interest from theoreticians and practitioners alike [4,33,38,45]. The past few years, however, have witnessed a significant improvement in the runtime performance of the sampling tools when the weight function W is fixed to a uniform distribution owing to the rise of hashing-based paradigm [2,11,13,22]. While the significant progress for uniform sampling has paved the way for its usage in constrained random simulation [45], the restriction of uniform distribution is limiting, and several applications of constrained sampling require the underlying techniques to be able to handle a wide variety of distributions and related problem formulations as listed below:

Literal-Weighted Sampling. In case of literal-weighted sampling, we consider the weight function over assignments defined as the product of the weight of literals, which is specified using a weight function $W(\cdot)$ that assigns a non-negative weight to each literal l in a boolean formula F. As argued in [12], literal-weighted weight function suffices for most of the practical applications ranging from constrained random simulation, probabilistic reasoning, and reliability of power-grids [10,14,21,45].

Projected Sampling. Typically, users define constraints in high-level modeling languages such as Verilog [1], Bayesian networks [14] and configuration of grids [21] and then CNF encodings are employed to convert them into a CNF [6]. Commonly used schemes like *Tseitin encoding* [50] introduce auxiliary variables during encoding; though the encoded formulas are equisatisfiable, they typically do not preserve the number of satisfying assignments. In particular, given an initial set of constraints G expressed over a set of variables X, we obtain another formula F such that $G(X) = \exists Y F(X, Y)$. Therefore, we are concerned with sampling over solutions of F *projected over a subset of variables* (such as X in this case). In other words, we are concerned with sampling over Σ_1^1 formulas.

Conditioned Sampling. Given a boolean formula Φ and a partial assignment σ, conditioned sampling refers to sampling from the models of Φ *that satisfy σ*. Conditioning has interesting applications in testing where one is interested in fuzzing the system with inputs that satisfy certain patterns (preconditions). Conditioning has been applied in the past for fault diagnosis [23], conformant planning [46] and databases [15].

Typically, practical applications require sampling techniques that can handle all the above formulations. While techniques based on interval propagation, binary decision diagrams and random perturbation of solution space [22,25,44] cannot handle projection, conditioned, and weighted sampling efficiently, the hashing-based techniques have significantly improved the scalability of sampling techniques and are capable of handling projection and literal-weighted scheme [11,42]. However, the performance of hashing-based techniques is extremely limited in their ability to handle literal-weighted sampling, and one observes a drastic drop in their performance as the weight distribution shifts away from uniform. In this context, one wonders: *whether it is possible to design techniques which can handle projection, conditioned, and literal-weighted sampling without degradation in their performance?*

In this work, we answer the above question in affirmative: we extend our previously proposed knowledge compilation framework in the context of uniform sampling to handle all the three variants. We have implemented a prototype of our framework, named WAPS, and demonstrate that within a time limit of 1800 s, WAPS performs better than the current state-of-the-art weighted and projected sampler WeightGen [10], by up to 3 orders of magnitude in terms of runtime while achieving a geometric speedup of 296×. Out of the 773 benchmarks available, WAPS was able to sample from 588 benchmarks while WeightGen was able to sample from only 24 benchmarks. Furthermore, WAPS is almost oblivious to the number of samples requested.

A significant advantage of our framework is its simplicity: we show that our previously proposed framework in the context of uniform sampling, KUS [49], can be lifted to handle literal-weighted, projection and conditioned sampling. We demonstrate that unlike hashing-based techniques, the runtime performance of WAPS is not dependent on the underlying weight distribution. We want to assert that the simplicity of our framework, combined with its runtime performance and its ability to be agnostic to the underlying distribution is a significant novel contribution to the area of constrained sampling. Besides, an important contribution of our work is the theoretical analysis of sampling techniques that employ knowledge compilation.

The rest of the paper is organized as follows. We first discuss the related work in Sect. 2. We then introduce notations and preliminaries in Sect. 3. In Sect. 4 we present WAPS and do theoretical analysis of WAPS in Sect. 5. We then describe the experimental methodology and discuss results in Sect. 6. Finally, we conclude in Sect. 7.

2   Related Work

Weighted sampling is extensively studied in the literature with the objective of providing scalability while ensuring strong theoretical guarantees. Markov Chain Monte Carlo (MCMC) sampling [32,40] is the most popular technique for weighted sampling; several algorithms like Metropolis-Hastings and simulated annealing have been extensively studied in the literature [36,40]. While MCMC based sampling is guaranteed to converge to a target distribution under mild requirements, convergence is often impractically slow [31]. The practical adaptations for MCMC-based sampling in the context of constrained-random verification has been proposed in [37]. Unfortunately, practical MCMC based sampling tools use heuristics that destroy the theoretical guarantees. Interval-propagation and belief networks have also been employed for sampling [20,26,29], but, though these techniques are scalable, the generated distributions can deviate significantly from the uniform distribution, as shown in [38].

To bridge the wide gap between scalable algorithms and those that give strong guarantees of uniformity several hashing-based techniques have been proposed [10,11,24,28] for weighted sampling. The key idea behind hashing-based techniques is to employ random parity constraints as pairwise independent hash functions to partition the set of satisfying assignments of CNF formula into cells. The hashing-based techniques have achieved significant runtime performance improvement in case of uniform sampling but their scalability suffers for weight distribution and depends strongly on parameters such as *tilt*, which are unlikely to be small for most practical distributions [42].

In recent past, a significant amount of work has been done to compile propositional theory, often represented as a propositional formula in CNF into tractable knowledge representations. One of the prominent and earliest representations is Ordered Binary Decision Diagrams (OBDDs), which have been effectively used for circuit analysis and synthesis [9]. Another family of representations known as Deterministic Decomposable Negation Normal Form (d-DNNF) [19] have proved to be influential in many probabilistic reasoning applications [14,17,18]. Recently, another representation called as Sentential Decision Diagram (SDD) [16] was proposed which maintains canonicity and polytime support for boolean combinations and bridged the gap of succinctness between OBDDs and d-DNNFs. In our recent work [49], we were able to tackle the problem of uniform sampling by exploiting the properties of d-DNNF. Specifically, we were able to take advantage of recent advancements made in the field of knowledge compilation and use the compiled structure to generate uniform samples while competing with the state-of-the-art tools for uniform sampling.

3   Notations and Preliminaries

A literal is a boolean variable or its negation. A clause is a disjunction of a set of literals. A propositional formula F in conjunctive normal form (CNF) is a conjunction of clauses. Let $Vars(F)$ be the set of variables appearing in F. The set $Vars(F)$

is called *support* of F. A *satisfying assignment* or *witness* of F, denoted by σ, is an assignment of truth values to variables in its support such that F evaluates to true. We denote the set of all witnesses of F as R_F. Let $var(l)$ denote the variable of literal l, i.e., $var(l) = var(\neg l)$ and $F_{|l}$ denotes the formula obtained when literal l is set to true in F. Given an assignment σ over $Vars(F)$ and a set of variables $P \subseteq Vars(F)$, define $\sigma_P = \{l \mid l \in \sigma, var(l) \in P\}$ and $R_{F\downarrow P}$ to be the projection of R_F onto P, i.e., $R_{F\downarrow P} = \{\sigma_P \mid \sigma \in R_F\}$.

Given a propositional formula F and a weight function $W(\cdot)$ that assigns a non-negative weight to every literal, the weight of assignment σ denoted as $W(\sigma)$ is the product of weights of all the literals appearing in σ, i.e., $W(\sigma) = \prod_{l \in \sigma} W(l)$. The weight of a set of assignments Y is given by $W(Y) = \sum_{\sigma \in Y} W(\sigma)$. Note that, we have overloaded the definition of weight function $W(\cdot)$ to support different arguments – a literal, an assignment and a set of assignments. We want to highlight that the assumption about weight distribution being generated solely by a literal-weighted function stands well, as many real-world applications like probabilistic inference can be efficiently reduced to literal-weighted sampling [14]. Also, for notational convenience, whenever the formula F, weight function W and sampling set P is clear from the context, we omit mentioning it.

3.1 Weighted and Projected Generators

A *weighted and projected probabilistic generator* is a probabilistic algorithm that generates a witness from $R_{F\downarrow P}$ with respect to weight distribution generated by weight function W. A *weighted and projected generator* $\mathcal{G}^{wp}(\cdot, \cdot, \cdot)$ is a probabilistic generator that guarantees

$$\forall y \in R_{F\downarrow P}, \Pr\left[\mathcal{G}^{wp}(F, P, W) = y\right] = \frac{W(y)}{W(R_{F\downarrow P})},$$

An *almost weighted and projected generator* $\mathcal{G}^{awp}(\cdot, \cdot, \cdot)$ relaxes this requirement, ensuring that: given a tolerance $\varepsilon > 0$, $\forall y \in R_{F\downarrow P}$ we have

$$\frac{W(y)}{(1+\varepsilon)W(R_{F\downarrow P})} \leq \Pr\left[\mathcal{G}^{awp}(F, P, W) = y\right] \leq \frac{(1+\varepsilon)W(y)}{W(R_{F\downarrow P})},$$

Probabilistic generators are allowed to occasionally "fail" in the sense that no witness may be returned even if $R_{F\downarrow P}$ is non-empty. The failure probability for such generators must be bounded by a constant strictly less than 1.

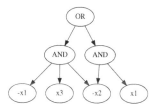

Fig. 1. Example of d-DNNF

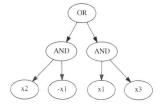

Fig. 2. The projected d-DNNF of Example 1

3.2   Deterministic Decomposable Negation Normal Form (d-DNNF)

To formally define d-DNNF, we first define the Negation Normal Form (NNF):

Definition 1 [19]. *Let X be the set of propositional variables. A sentence in NNF is a rooted, directed acyclic graph (DAG) where each leaf node i is labeled with true, false, x or $\neg x$, $x \in X$; and each internal node is labeled with $\vee$ or $\wedge$ and can have arbitrarily many children.*

d-DNNF further imposes that the representation is:

- **Deterministic:** An NNF is deterministic if the operands of $\vee$ in all well-formed boolean formula in the NNF are mutually inconsistent.
- **Decomposable:** An NNF is decomposable if the operands of $\wedge$ in all well-formed boolean formula in the NNF are expressed on a mutually disjoint set of variables.

The deterministic and decomposable properties are conveniently expressed by AND-OR graphs (DAGs) where a node is either an AND node, an OR node or a literal. The operands of AND/OR nodes appear as children of the node. Figure 1 shows an example of d-DNNF representation. For every node t, the subformula corresponding to t is the formula corresponding to d-DNNF obtained by removing all the nodes u such that there does not exist a path from t to u. $T(t)$ represents the set of all partial satisfying assignments for the subformula corresponding to t. The siblings of a node t are the children of the parent of t excluding t itself and the set of such children is given by $Siblings(t)$.

Decision-DNNF is a subset of d-DNNF where the deterministic OR nodes are decision nodes [18]. The state-of-the-art d-DNNF construction tools like C2D [18], DSHARP [43] and D4 [30], construct the Decision-DNNF representation where each OR node has exactly two children while an AND node may have multiple children. Since our framework WAPS employs modern d-DNNF compilers, we assume that the OR node has exactly two children. This assumption is only for the simplicity of exposition as our algorithms can be trivially adopted to the general d-DNNF representations.

4   Algorithm

In this section, we discuss our primary technical contribution: WAPS, weighted and projected sampler that samples from $R_{F \downarrow P}$ with respect to weight function W by employing the knowledge compilation techniques.

WAPS takes a CNF formula F, a set of sampling variables P, a function assigning weights to literals W and required number of samples s as inputs and returns SampleList, a list of size s which contain samples such that each sample is independently drawn from the weighted distribution generated by W over $R_{F \downarrow P}$.

Similar to KUS, WAPS (Algorithm 1) mainly comprises of three phases: Compilation, Annotation and Sampling. For d-DNNF compilation, WAPS invokes a specialized compilation routine PCompile over the formula F and the sampling set P (line 1). This is followed by the normalization of weights such that for any literal l, $W'(l) + W'(\neg l) = 1$, where W' is the normalized weight returned in line 2. Then for annotation, WAnnotate is invoked in line 3 which uses the weight function W' to annotate weights to all the nodes of the d-DNNF tree. Finally, subroutine Sampler (line 4) is invoked which returns s independently drawn samples over P following the weighted distribution generated by W over $R_{F \downarrow P}$. We now describe these three phases in detail.

4.1   Compilation

The compilation phase is performed using the subroutine PCompile. PCompile is a modified procedure over the component caching and clause learning based algorithm of the d-DNNF compiler DSHARP [43,47]. It is presented in Algorithm 2. The changes from the existing algorithm are underlined. The rest of the procedure which is similar to DSHARP is mentioned here for completeness. The description of PCompile is as follows:

PCompile takes in a CNF formula F in the clausal form and a set of sampling variables P as input and returns a d-DNNF over P. If the formula does not contain any variable from P, PCompile invokes SAT (line 2) which returns a $True$ node if the formula is satisfiable, else it returns a $False$ node. Otherwise, DecideLiteral is invoked to choose a literal appearing in F such that $var(l) \in P$ (line 3). This decision is then recursively propagated by invoking CompileBranch to create t_1, the d-DNNF of $F_{|l}$ (line 4) and t_2, the d-DNNF of $F_{|\neg l}$ (line 5). Disjoin is invoked in line 6 which takes t_1 and t_2 as input and returns t_2 if t_1 is $False$ node, t_1 if t_2 is $False$ node otherwise a new tree composed by an OR node as the parent of t_1 and t_2. The result of Disjoin is then stored in the cache (line 7) and returned as an output of PCompile (line 8).

We now discuss the subroutine CompileBranch. It is presented in Algorithm 3. It takes in a CNF formula F, set of sampling variables P and literal l as input and returns a d-DNNF tree of $F_{|l}$ on P. It first invokes BCP (Binary Constraint Propagation), with F, l and P which performs unit-propagation to return a tuple of reduced formula F' and a set of implied literals $(term)$ projected over variables in P (line 1). Then CompileBranch checks if F' contains an empty clause and returns $False$ node to indicate that $F_{|l}$ is not satisfiable, else the formula is solved using component decomposition as described below.

At line 6 it breaks the formula F' into separate components formed by disjoint set of clauses such that no two components share any variables. Then each component is solved independently (lines 8–15). For each component, it first examines the cache to see if this component has been solved earlier and is present in the cache (line 9). If cache lookup fails, it solves the component with a recursive call to PCompile (line 11). If any component is found to be unsatisfiable, $False$ node is returned implying that the overall formula is unsatisfiable too, else CompileBranch simply conjoins the components' d-DNNFs together with the decided l and implied literals $(term)$ and returns this after storing it in the cache for the formula $F_{|l}$ (lines 16–18).

We illustrate PCompile procedure on the following example formula F:

Example 1. $F = \{\{x_1, x_2\}, \{\neg x_3, \neg x_5, x_6\}, \{\neg x_2, x_4, \neg x_1\}, \{x_3, \neg x_6, \neg x_1\}, \{x_6,$ $x_5, \neg x_1, x_3\}, \{x_3, x_6, \neg x_5, \neg x_1\}\}$

Figure 2 represents the d-DNNF of Example 1 on $P = \{x_1, x_2, x_3\}$. For detailed discussion about applying PCompile on F please refer to Appendix.

Algorithm 1. WAPS(F, P, W, s)

1: dag ← PCompile(F, P)
2: W' ← Normalize(W)
3: WAnnotate(dag.$root$, W')
4: SampleList ← Sampler(dag.$root$, s)
5: **return** SampleList

Algorithm 2. PCompile(F, P)

1: **if** $Vars(F) \cap P = \phi$ **then**
2:     **return** $\underline{SAT(F)}$
3: l ← DecideLiteral(F, P)
4: t_1 ← CompileBranch(F, P, l)
5: t_2 ← CompileBranch($F, P, \neg l$)
6: t ← Disjoin(t_1, t_2)
7: CacheStore(F, t)
8: **return** t

Algorithm 3. CompileBranch(F, P, l)

1: $(F', term)$ ← BCP(F, l, P)
2: **if** $\emptyset \in F'$ **then**
3:     CacheStore($F_{|l}, False$)
4:     **return** $False$ ▷ CDCL is done
5: **else**
6:     $Comps$ ← DisjointComponents(F')
7:     $dcomps$ ← {}
8:     **for** C ← $Comps$ **do**
9:         $ddnnf$ ← GetCache(C)
10:         **if** $ddnnf$ is not found **then**
11:             $ddnnf$ ← PCompile(C, P)
12:         $dcomps$.Add($ddnnf$)
13:         **if** $ddnnf = False$ **then**
14:             CacheStore($F_{|l}, False$)
15:             **return** $False$
16: $t = $ Conjoin($l, term, dcomps$)
17: CacheStore($F_{|l}, t$)
18: **return** t

4.2 Annotation

The subroutine WAnnotate is presented in Algorithm 4. WAnnotate takes in a d-DNNF dag and a weight function W as inputs and returns an annotated d-DNNF dag whose each node t is annotated with a weight, given by the sum of weights of all the partial assignments represented by subtree rooted at t. The weights subsequently annotated on children of an OR node indicate the probability with which it would be selected in the sampling phase.

WAnnotate performs a bottom up traversal on d-DNNF dag in a reverse topological order. For each node in the d-DNNF dag, WAnnotate maintains an attribute, weight, as per the label of the node given as follows:

Literal (lines 2–3): The weight of a literal node is taken as the weight of the literal given by the weight function W.

OR (lines 4–8): The weight of OR node is made equal to the sum of weights of both of its children.

AND (lines 9–13): The weight of AND node is made equal to the product of weights of all its children.

Algorithm 4. Bottom-Up Pass to annotate d-DNNF with weights on literals

---

1: **function** WAnnotate(t, W)
2:     **if** $label(t) = Literal$ **then**
3:         $t.weight \leftarrow W(t)$
4:     **else if** $label(t) = \text{OR}$ **then**
5:         $t.weight \leftarrow 0$
6:         **for** $c \in \{t.left, t.right\}$ **do**
7:             WAnnotate(c)
8:             $t.weight \leftarrow t.weight + c.weight$
9:     **else if** $label(t) = \text{AND}$ **then**
10:        $t.weight \leftarrow 1$
11:        **for** $c \in Childrens(t)$ **do**
12:            WAnnotate(c)
13:            $t.weight \leftarrow t.weight \times c.weight$

4.3 Sampling

Algorithm Sampler takes the annotated d-DNNF dag and the required number of samples s and returns SampleList, a list of s samples conforming to the distribution of their weights as governed by weight function W given to WAnnotate. The subroutine Sampler is very similar to the sampling procedure in our previous work [49] except that we take the annotated weight of the node instead of the annotated count in the previous work as the probability for Bernoulli trials. We refer the readers to Appendix for a detailed discussion.

4.4 Conditioned Sampling

The usage of samplers in testing environment necessitates sampling from F conditioned on fixing assignment to a subset of variables. The state of the art techniques, such as those based on universal hashing, treat every query as independent and are unable to reuse computation across different queries. In contrast, the compilation to d-DNNF allows WAPS to reuse the same d-DNNF. In particular, for a given conditioning expressed as conjunction of different literals, i.e., $\hat{C} = \bigwedge_i l_i$.

In particular, instead of modifying computationally expensive d-DNNF, we modify the weight function as follows:

$$\hat{W}(l) = \begin{cases} 0, & l \notin \hat{C} \\ W(l) & otherwise \end{cases}$$

5 Theoretical Analysis

We now present theoretical analysis of WAPS, which consists of two components: correctness of WAPS and analysis of behavior of Sampler on the underlying d-DNNF graph. First, we prove that WAPS is an exact weighted and projected sampler in Theorem 1. To this end, we prove the correctness of our projected d-DNNF dag compilation procedure PCompile in Lemma 1. In Lemma 2, we show that WAnnotate annotates each node of the d-DNNF with weights that represent the weight of assignments represented by subtree rooted at that node. This enables us to sample as per the weight distribution in the sampling phase which is proved in Theorem 1 using Lemmas 1 and 2. Secondly, further probing into the behavior of subroutine Sampler, we provide an analysis of the probability of visiting any node in the d-DNNF dag while sampling. For this, we first find a probability of visiting a node by following a particular path in Lemma 3 and then we use this result to prove an upper bound for the general case of visiting a node from all possible paths in Theorem 2. We believe that this analysis will motivate the researchers to find new ways to speed up or device new methods to find exact or approximate sampling techniques over a given compiled representation.

The proofs of Theorem 1 and Lemmas 1, 2 and 3 can be found in Appendix.

Lemma 1. *Given a formula F and set of sampling variables P, the tree returned by PCompile(F, P) is a d-DNNF dag which represents the set of satisfying assignments of the formula F projected over the set of sampling variables P.*

Lemma 2. *Every node t in the d-DNNF dag returned by WAnnotate is annotated by $W(T(t))$, where $T(t)$ is the set of all the partial assignments corresponding to the subtree rooted at t.*

Theorem 1. *For a given F, P and s, SampleList is the list of samples generated by WAPS. Let SampleList$[i]$ indicate the sample at the ith index of the list. Then for each $y \in R_{F \downarrow P}$, $\forall i \in [s]$, we have $\Pr[y = \text{SampleList}[i]] = \frac{W(y)}{W(R_{F \downarrow P})}$.*

Lemma 3. *For a given F and P, let fol(ρ) be the event of following a path ρ, which start at root and ends at node t, then $\Pr[\text{fol}(\rho)] = \frac{W(T(t)) \times c_\rho}{W(R_{F \downarrow P})}$ where c_ρ is the product of weight of all the OR nodes' siblings encountered in the path ρ from root to t and $T(t)$ is the set of all the partial satisfying assignments represented by subtree rooted at t.*

Theorem 2. *For a given F and P, let visit(t) be the event of visiting a node t to fetch one sample as per subroutine Sampler, then $\Pr[\text{visit}(t)] \leq \frac{W(\Gamma(t))}{W(R_{F \downarrow P})}$ where $\Gamma(t) = \{\sigma \mid \sigma \in R_{F \downarrow P}, \sigma_{\downarrow Vars(t)} \in T(t)\}$ and $T(t)$ is a set of all the partial satisfying assignments represented by subtree rooted at t.*

Proof. In Lemma 3 we have calculated the probability of visiting a node t by taking a particular path from root to node t. So the probability of visiting a node t will be the sum of probability of visiting t by all possible paths. Let $\mathcal{P} = \{\rho_1, \rho_2, \cdots, \rho_m\}$ be the set of all paths from root to node t and visit(t) be the event of visiting a node t in subroutine Sampler then,

$$\Pr[\text{visit}(t)] = \sum_{\rho \in \mathcal{P}} \Pr[\text{visit}(t) \mid \text{fol}(\rho)] \times \Pr[\text{fol}(\rho)] = \sum_{\rho \in \mathcal{P}} 1 \times \Pr[\text{fol}(\rho)]$$

From Lemma 3, $\Pr[\text{visit}(t)] = \sum_{\rho \in \mathcal{P}} \frac{W(T(t)) \times c_\rho}{W(R_{F \downarrow P})}$ where c_ρ is the product of the weight of all the OR nodes' siblings encountered in a path ρ from root to t. For any such path, we call $\{t_\rho^1, t_\rho^2, \cdots, t_\rho^n\}$ as the set of all the OR node siblings encountered on the path ρ. Now, let σ_ρ^{ext} be the set of assignments over P represented by path ρ. Therefore,

$$\sigma_\rho^{ext} = T(t_\rho^1) \times T(t_\rho^2) \cdots \times T(t_\rho^n) \times T(t)$$

where, $T(\cdot)$ are set of assignments and $\times$ is a cross product. Now, any tuple from σ_ρ^{ext} represents a satisfying assignment in the d-DNNF. Therefore, $\sigma_\rho^{ext} \subseteq R_{F \downarrow P}$. Note that, from Lemma 2, it follows that weight annotated by WAnnotate at t is equal to $W(T(t))$. Therefore,

$$c_\rho = W(T(t_\rho^1)) \times W(T(t_\rho^2)) \cdots \times W(T(t_\rho^n))$$

And, $W(\sigma_\rho^{ext}) = W(T(t)) \times c_\rho$. Notice that, $\sigma_\rho^{ext} \subseteq \Gamma(t)$ as σ_ρ^{ext} represents satisfying extensions of partial assignments contained in $T(t)$ itself. This is true $\forall \rho \in \mathcal{P}$. Therefore as $W(.)$ is an increasing function,

$$\bigcup_{\rho \in \mathcal{P}} \sigma_\rho^{ext} \quad \subseteq \quad \Gamma(t) \quad \Longrightarrow \quad \sum_{\rho \in \mathcal{P}} W(T(t)) \times c_\rho \quad \leq \quad W(\Gamma(t))$$

Note that, the inequality indeed holds as the intersection of sets of partial assignments represented by t and any other node not lying on the path from root to t may not be ϕ (empty). Therefore,

$$\sum_{\rho \in \mathcal{P}} \frac{W(T(t)) \times c_\rho}{W(R_{F \downarrow P})} \quad \leq \quad \frac{W(\Gamma(t))}{W(R_{F \downarrow P})} \quad \Longrightarrow \quad \Pr[\text{visit}(t)] \quad \leq \quad \frac{W(\Gamma(t))}{W(R_{F \downarrow P})}$$

6   Evaluation

In order to evaluate the runtime performance and analyze the quality of samples generated by WAPS, we implemented a prototype in Python. For d-DNNF compilation, our prototype makes use of DSHARP [43] when sampling set is available else we use D4 [30]. We would have preferred to use state-of-the-art d-DNNF compiler D4 but owing to its closed source implementation, we could not modify it as per our customized compilation procedure PCompile. Therefore, for projected compilation, we have modified DSHARP which has an open-source implementation. We have conducted our experiments on a wide range of publicly available benchmarks. In all, our benchmark suite consisted of 773 benchmarks arising from a wide range of real-world applications. Specifically, we used constraints arising from DQMR networks, bit-blasted versions of SMT-LIB (SMT) benchmarks, and ISCAS89 circuits [8] with parity conditions on randomly chosen subsets of outputs and nextstate variables [34,48]. We assigned random weights to literals wherever weights were not already available in our benchmarks. All our experiments were conducted on a high performance compute cluster whose each node consists of E5-2690 v3 CPU with 24 cores and 96 GB of RAM. We utilized single core per instance of benchmark with a timeout of 1800 s.

Table 1. Run time (in seconds) for 1000 samples

Benchmark	Vars	Clauses	$|P|$	WeightGen	WAPS			Speedup
					Compile	A+S	Total	on WeightGen
s526a_3_2	366	944	24	490.34	15.37	1.96	17.33	28.29
LoginService	11511	41411	36	1203.93	15.02	0.75	15.77	76.34
blockmap_05_02	1738	3452	1738	1140.87	0.04	5.30	5.34	213.65
s526_3_2	365	943	24	417.24	0.06	0.67	0.73	571.56
or-100-5-4-UC-60	200	500	200	1795.52	0.01	0.74	0.74	2426.38
or-50-5-10-UC-40	100	250	100	1292.67	0.01	0.36	0.36	3590.75
blasted_case35	400	1414	46	TO	0.57	1.46	2.03	-
or-100-20-4-UC-50	200	500	200	TO	0.19	2.48	2.67	-

The objective of our evaluation was to answer the following questions:

1. How does WAPS perform in terms of runtime in comparison to WeightGen, the current state-of-the-art weighted and projected sampler?
2. How does WAPS perform for *incremental sampling* and scales when asked for different number of samples?
3. How does the distribution of samples generated by WAPS compare with the distribution generated by an ideal weighted and projected sampler?
4. How does WAPS perform for conditioning on arbitrary variables?
5. How does our knowledge compilation based sampling techniques perform in comparison to hashing based sampling techniques for the task of generalizing to arbitrary weight distributions?

Our experiment demonstrated that within a time limit of 1800 s, WAPS is able to significantly outperform existing state-of-the-art weighted and projected sampler WeightGen, by up to 3 orders of magnitude in terms of runtime while achieving a geometric speedup of 296×. Out of the 773 benchmarks available WAPS was able to sample from 588 benchmarks while WeightGen was able to sample from only 24 benchmarks. For *incremental sampling*, WAPS achieves a geometric speedup of 3.69. Also, WAPS is almost oblivious to the number of samples requested. Empirically, the distribution generated by WAPS is statistically indistinguishable from that generated by an ideal weighted and projected sampler. Also, while performing conditioned sampling in WAPS, we incur no extra cost in terms of runtime in most of the cases. Moreover, the performance of our knowledge compilation based sampling technique is found to be oblivious to weight distribution. We present results for only a subset of representative benchmarks here. Detailed data along with the expanded versions of all the tables presented here is available at https://github.com/meelgroup/waps.

Number of Instances Solved. We compared the runtime performance of WAPS with WeightGen [10] (state-of-the-art weighted and projected sampler) by generating 1000 samples from each tool with a timeout of 1800 s. Figure 3 shows the cactus plot for WeightGen and WAPS. We present the number of benchmarks on the

x−axis and the time taken on y−axis. A point (x, y) implies that x benchmarks took less than or equal to y seconds to sample. All our runtime statistics for WAPS include the time for the knowledge compilation phase (via D4 or DSHARP). From all the 773 available benchmarks WeightGen was able to sample from only 24 benchmarks while WAPS was able to sample from 588 benchmarks. Table 1 shows the runtimes of some of the benchmarks on the two tools. The columns in the table give the benchmark name, number of variables, number of clauses, size of sampling set, time taken in seconds by WeightGen and WAPS divided into time taken by Compilation and A+S: Annotation and Sampling followed by speedup of WAPS with respect to WeightGen. Table 1 clearly shows that WAPS outperforms WeightGen by upto 3 orders of magnitude. For all the 24 benchmarks that WeightGen was able to solve WAPS outperformed WeightGen with a geometric speedup of 296×.

Incremental Sampling. Incremental sampling involves fetching multiple, relatively small-sized samples until the objective (such as desired coverage or violation of property) is achieved. We benefit from pre-compiled knowledge representations in this scenario, as they allow us to perform repeated sampling as per varied distributions. If weights are changed, we simply Annotate the tree again followed by sampling, else, we directly move to the sampling phase, thus saving a significant amount of time by bypassing the compilation phase.

In our experiments, we have evaluated the time taken by WAPS for 1000 samples in 10 successive calls with same weights. The results are presented in Table 2 for a subset of benchmarks. The first column mentions the benchmark name with the number of variables, clauses and size of sampling set in subsequent columns. The time taken by WAPS for first run to fetch 1000 samples is given in the fifth column while the overall time taken for first run together with the subsequent 9 incremental runs is presented in sixth column. The final column shows the average gain in terms of speedup calculated by taking the ratio of time taken by WAPS for first run with the average time taken by WAPS for subsequent 9 incremental runs thus resulting in a total of 10000 samples. Overall, WAPS achieves a geometric speedup of 3.69× on our set of benchmarks.

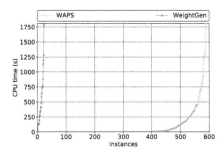

Fig. 3. Cactus Plot comparing WeightGen and WAPS.

Benchmark	Vars	Clauses	$|P|$	WAPS 1000	WAPS 10,000	Speedup
case110	287	1263	287	1.14	9.28	1.26
or-70-10-10-UC-20	140	350	140	2.75	9.02	6.56
s526_7_4	383	1019	24	60.38	143.16	13.20
or-60-5-2-UC-10	120	300	120	12.10	20.35	16.50
s35932_15_7	17918	44709	1763	69.01	106.65	20.73
case121	291	975	48	35.85	51.41	20.73
s641_15_7	576	1399	54	729.38	916.83	35.01
squaring7	1628	5837	72	321.95	365.13	67.10
LoginService	11511	41411	36	15.89	18.12	64.13
ProjectService	3175	11019	55	184.51	195.25	154.61

Table 2. Runtimes (in sec.) of WAPS for incremental sampling

Table 3. Runtime (in sec.) of WAPS to generate different size samples

Benchmark	Vars	Clauses	$|P|$	Sampling Size				
				1000	2000	4000	8000	10000
s1488_7_4	872	2499	14	0.5	0.75	1.29	2.2	2.9
s444_15_7	377	1072	24	0.74	1.29	1.91	3.46	4.12
s526_3_2	365	943	24	0.84	1.03	1.86	3.71	4.22
s820a_3_2	598	1627	23	0.63	1.03	2.04	3.92	4.81
case35	400	1414	46	2.38	3.22	5.31	9.38	11.41
LoginService	11511	41411	36	15.8	16.12	16.68	18.3	18.36
ProjectService	3175	11019	55	184.22	184.99	188.33	191.16	193.92
or-60-20-6-UC-10	120	300	120	1465.34	1458.23	1494.46	1499.67	1488.23

Effect of Number of Samples. To check how WAPS scales with different number of samples, we invoked WAPS for fetching different number of samples: 1000, 2000, 4000, 8000, 10000 with a timeout of 1800 s. Table 3 presents the runtime of WAPS for different samples on some benchmarks. The first column represents the benchmark name. Second, third and fourth columns represent the number of variables, clauses and size of sampling set. The next five columns represent the time taken by WAPS for 1000, 2000, 4000, 8000 and 10000 samples. Table 3 clearly demonstrates that WAPS is almost oblivious to the number of samples requested.

Uniform Sampling Generalized for Weighted Sampling. To explore the trend in performance between uniform and weighted sampling on the dimension of hashing based techniques pitched against our newly proposed sampling techniques based on knowledge compilation, we compared WAPS to KUS in a parallel comparison between WeightGen and UniGen2. Specifically, we ran WAPS for weighted sampling and KUS for uniform sampling without utilizing the sampling set as KUS does not support the sampling set. On the other hand, for hashing based sampling techniques, we compared WeightGen to UniGen2 while using the sampling set. Figure 4 shows the cactus plot for WeightGen and UniGen2 and Fig. 5 shows a cactus plot for WAPS and KUS. From all the 773 benchmarks, WeightGen was able to sample from only 24 benchmarks while UniGen2 was able to sample from 208 benchmarks. In comparison, WAPS was able to sample from 606 benchmarks while KUS was able to sample from 602 benchmarks. Our experiments demonstrated that the performance of hashing-based techniques is extremely limited in their ability to handle literal-weighted sampling and there is a drastic drop in their performance as the weight distribution shifts away from uniform. While for our knowledge compilation based sampling techniques we observe that their performance is oblivious to the weight distribution.

Distribution Comparison. We measure the distribution of WAPS vis-a-vis an *ideal weighted and projected sampler* (IS) and observed that WAPS is statistically indistinguishable from IS. Please refer to Appendix for more detailed discussion.

Effect of Conditioning on Variables. We evaluated the performance of WAPS in the context of conditioned sampling. We observed a slight improvement in average runtime as more and more variables get constrained. For detailed results, please refer to Appendix.

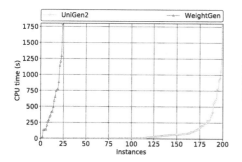
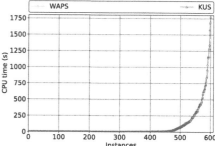

Fig. 4. Cactus Plot comparing WeightGen and UniGen2.

Fig. 5. Cactus Plot comparing WAPS and KUS.

7 Conclusion

In this paper, we designed a knowledge compilation-based framework, called WAPS, for literal-weighted, projected and conditional sampling. WAPS provides strong theoretical guarantees and its runtime performance upon the existing state-of-the-art weighted and projected sampler WeightGen, by up to 3 orders of magnitude in terms of runtime. Out of the 773 benchmarks available, WAPS is able to sample from 588 benchmarks while WeightGen is only able to sample from 24 benchmarks. WAPS achieves a geometric speedup of 3.69 for *incremental sampling*. It is worth noting that WeightGen has weaker guarantees than WAPS. Furthermore, WAPS is almost oblivious to the number of samples requested.

References

1. System Verilog (2015). http://www.systemverilog.org
2. Achlioptas, D., Hammoudeh, Z.S., Theodoropoulos, P.: Fast sampling of perfectly uniform satisfying assignments. In: Beyersdorff, O., Wintersteiger, C.M. (eds.) SAT 2018. LNCS, vol. 10929, pp. 135–147. Springer, Cham (2018). https://doi.org/10.1007/978-3-319-94144-8_9
3. Bacchus, F., Dalmao, S., Pitassi, T.: Algorithms and complexity results for #SAT and Bayesian inference. In: Proceedings of FOCS, pp. 340–351 (2003)

4. Bellare, M., Goldreich, O., Petrank, E.: Uniform generation of NP-witnesses using an NP-oracle. Inf. Comput. **163**(2), 510–526 (2000)
5. Biere, A., Cimatti, A., Clarke, E., Fujita, M., Zhu, Y.: Symbolic model checking using SAT procedures instead of BDDs. In: Proceedings of DAC, pp. 317–320 (1999)
6. Biere, A., Heule, M., van Maaren, H., Walsh, T.: Handbook of Satisfiability. IOS Press, Amsterdam (2009)
7. Bjesse, P., Leonard, T., Mokkedem, A.: Finding bugs in an Alpha microprocessor using satisfiability solvers. In: Berry, G., Comon, H., Finkel, A. (eds.) CAV 2001. LNCS, vol. 2102, pp. 454–464. Springer, Heidelberg (2001). https://doi.org/10.1007/3-540-44585-4_44
8. Brglez, F., Bryan, D., Kozminski, K.: Combinational profiles of sequential benchmark circuits. In: Proceedings of ISCAS, pp. 1929–1934 (1989)
9. Bryant, R.E.: Symbolic Boolean manipulation with ordered binary-decision diagrams. ACM Comput. Surv. (CSUR) **24**(3), 293–318 (1992)
10. Chakraborty, S., Fremont, D.J., Meel, K.S., Seshia, S.A., Vardi, M.Y.: Distribution-aware sampling and weighted model counting for SAT. In: Proceedings of AAAI, pp. 1722–1730 (2014)
11. Chakraborty, S., Fremont, D.J., Meel, K.S., Seshia, S.A., Vardi, M.Y.: On parallel scalable uniform SAT witness generation. In: Baier, C., Tinelli, C. (eds.) TACAS 2015. LNCS, vol. 9035, pp. 304–319. Springer, Heidelberg (2015). https://doi.org/10.1007/978-3-662-46681-0_25
12. Chakraborty, S., Fried, D., Meel, K.S., Vardi, M.Y.: From weighted to unweighted model counting. In: Proceedings of IJCAI, pp. 689–695 (2015)
13. Chakraborty, S., Meel, K.S., Vardi, M.Y.: A scalable and nearly uniform generator of SAT witnesses. In: Sharygina, N., Veith, H. (eds.) CAV 2013. LNCS, vol. 8044, pp. 608–623. Springer, Heidelberg (2013). https://doi.org/10.1007/978-3-642-39799-8_40
14. Chavira, M., Darwiche, A.: On probabilistic inference by weighted model counting. Artif. Intell. **172**(6), 772–799 (2008)
15. Dalvi, N.N., Schnaitter, K., Suciu, D.: Computing query probability with incidence algebras. In: Proceedings of PODS, pp. 203–214 (2010)
16. Darwiche, A.: SDD: a new canonical representation of propositional knowledge bases. In: Proceedings of 22nd International Joint Conference on Artificial Intelligence, pp. 819–826 (2011)
17. Darwiche, A.: On the tractable counting of theory models and its application to belief revision and truth maintenance. CoRR (2000)
18. Darwiche, A.: New advances in compiling CNF to decomposable negation normal form. In: Proceedings of ECAI, pp. 318–322 (2004)
19. Darwiche, A., Marquis, P.: A knowledge compilation map. J. Artif. Intell. Res. **17**, 229–264 (2002)
20. Dechter, R., Kask, K., Bin, E., Emek, R.: Generating random solutions for constraint satisfaction problems. In: Proceedings of AAAI, pp. 15–21 (2002)
21. Duenas-Osorio, L., Meel, K.S., Paredes, R., Vardi, M.Y.: Counting-based reliability estimation for power-transmission grids. In: Proceedings of AAAI (2017)
22. Dutra, R., Laeufer, K., Bachrach, J., Sen, K.: Efficient sampling of SAT solutions for testing. In: Proceedings of ICSE, pp. 549–559 (2018)
23. Elliott, P., Williams, B.: DNNF-based belief state estimation. In: Proceedings of AAAI, pp. 36–41 (2006)
24. Ermon, S., Gomes, C.P., Sabharwal, A., Selman, B.: Embed and project: discrete sampling with universal hashing. In: Proceedings of NIPS, pp. 2085–2093 (2013)

25. Ermon, S., Gomes, C.P., Selman, B.: Uniform solution sampling using a constraint solver as an Oracle. In: Proceedings of UAI, pp. 255–264 (2012)
26. Gogate, V., Dechter, R.: A new algorithm for sampling CSP solutions uniformly at random. In: Benhamou, F. (ed.) CP 2006. LNCS, vol. 4204, pp. 711–715. Springer, Heidelberg (2006). https://doi.org/10.1007/11889205_56
27. Gomes, C.P., Selman, B., McAloon, K., Tretkoff, C.: Randomization in backtrack search: exploiting heavy-tailed profiles for solving hard scheduling problems. In: Proceedings of AIPS (1998)
28. Ivrii, A., Malik, S., Meel, K.S., Vardi, M.Y.: On computing minimal independent support and its applications to sampling and counting. Constraints **21**, 1–18 (2015). https://doi.org/10.1007/s10601-015-9204-z
29. Iyer, M.A.: RACE: a word-level ATPG-based constraints solver system for smart random simulation. In: Proceedings of ITC, pp. 299–308 (2003)
30. Lagniez, J.-M ., Marquis, P.: An improved decision-DNNF compiler. In: Proceedings of IJCAI, pp. 667–673 (2017)
31. Jerrum, M.R., Sinclair, A.: Approximating the permanent. SIAM J. Comput. **18**(6), 1149–1178 (1989)
32. Jerrum, M.R., Sinclair, A.: The Markov Chain Monte Carlo method: an approach to approximate counting and integration. In: Hochbaum, D.S. (ed.) Approximation Algorithms for NP-Hard Problems, pp. 482–520. ACM, New York (1996)
33. Jerrum, M.R., Valiant, L.G., Vazirani, V.V.: Random generation of combinatorial structures from a uniform distribution. Theoret. Comput. Sci. **43**(2–3), 169–188 (1986)
34. John, A.K., Chakraborty, S.: A quantifier elimination algorithm for linear modular equations and disequations. In: Gopalakrishnan, G., Qadeer, S. (eds.) CAV 2011. LNCS, vol. 6806, pp. 486–503. Springer, Heidelberg (2011). https://doi.org/10.1007/978-3-642-22110-1_39
35. Kautz, H., Selman, B.: Pushing the envelope: planning, propositional logic, and stochastic search. In: Proceedings of AAAI (1996)
36. Kirkpatrick, S., Gelatt, C.D., Vecchi, M.P.: Optimization by simulated annealing. Science **220**(4598), 671–680 (1983)
37. Kitchen, N.: Markov Chain Monte Carlo stimulus generation for constrained random simulation. Ph.D. thesis, University of California, Berkeley (2010)
38. Kitchen, N., Kuehlmann, A.: Stimulus generation for constrained random simulation. In: Proceedings of ICCAD, pp. 258–265 (2007)
39. Madras, N., Piccioni, M.: Importance sampling for families of distributions. Ann. Appl. Probab. **9**, 1202–1225 (1999)
40. Madras, N.: Lectures on Monte Carlo Methods, Fields Institute Monographs, vol. 16. American Mathematical Society, Providence (2002)
41. Malik, S., Zhang, L.: Boolean satisfiability from theoretical hardness topractical success. Commun. ACM **52**(8), 76–82 (2009)
42. Meel, K.S.: Constrained counting and sampling: bridging the gap between theory and practice. Ph.D. thesis, Rice University (2017)
43. Muise, C., McIlraith, S.A., Beck, J.C., Hsu, E.I.: DSHARP: fast d-DNNF compilation with sharpSAT. In: Proceedings of AAAI, pp. 356–361 (2016)
44. Naveh, R., Metodi, A.: Beyond feasibility: CP usage in constrained-random functional hardware verification. In: Schulte, C. (ed.) CP 2013. LNCS, vol. 8124, pp. 823–831. Springer, Heidelberg (2013). https://doi.org/10.1007/978-3-642-40627-0_60
45. Naveh, Y., et al.: Constraint-based random stimuli generation for hardware verification. In: Proceedings of IAAI, pp. 1720–1727 (2006)

46. Palacios, H., Bonet, B., Darwiche, A., Geffner, H.: Pruning conformant plans by counting models on compiled d-DNNF representations. In: Proceedings of ICAPS, pp. 141–150 (2005)
47. Sang, T., Bacchus, F., Beame, P., Kautz, H.A., Pitassi, T.: Combining component caching and clause learning for effective model counting. In: Proceedings of SAT (2004)
48. Sang, T., Beame, P., Kautz, H.: Performing Bayesian inference by weighted model counting. In: Proceedings of AAAI, pp. 475–481 (2005)
49. Sharma, S., Gupta, R., Roy, S., Meel, K.S.: Knowledge compilation meets uniform sampling. In: Proceedings of LPAR-22, pp. 620–636 (2018)
50. Tseitin, G.S.: On the complexity of derivation in propositional calculus. In: Siekmann, J.H., Wrightson, G. (eds.) Automation of Reasoning. Symbolic Computation (Artificial Intelligence). Springer, Berlin, Heidelberg (1983). https://doi.org/10.1007/978-3-642-81955-1_28
51. Velev, M.N., Bryant, R.E.: Effective use of Boolean satisfiability procedures in the formal verification of superscalar and VLIW microprocessors. J. Symb. Comput. **2**, 73–106 (2003)

SAT and SMT II

Building Better Bit-Blasting
for Floating-Point Problems

Martin Brain[1]([⊠]), Florian Schanda[2]([⊠]), and Youcheng Sun[1]

[1] Oxford University, Oxford, UK
{martin.brain,youcheng.sun}@cs.ox.ac.uk
[2] Zenuity GmbH, Unterschleißheim, Germany
florian.schanda@zenuity.com

Abstract. An effective approach to handling the theory of floating-point is to reduce it to the theory of bit-vectors. Implementing the required encodings is complex, error prone and requires a deep understanding of floating-point hardware. This paper presents SymFPU, a library of encodings that can be included in solvers. It also includes a verification argument for its correctness, and experimental results showing that its use in CVC4 out-performs all previous tools. As well as a significantly improved performance and correctness, it is hoped this will give a simple route to add support for the theory of floating-point.

Keywords: IEEE-754 · Floating-point ·
Satisfiability modulo theories · SMT

1 Introduction

From the embedded controllers of cars, aircraft and other "cyber-physical" systems, via JavaScript to the latest graphics, computer vision and machine learning accelerator hardware, floating-point computation is everywhere in modern computing. To reason about contemporary software, we must be able to efficiently reason about floating-point. To derive proofs, counter-examples, test cases or attack vectors we need bit-accurate results.

The vast majority of systems use IEEE-754 [1] floating-point implementations, or slight restrictions or relaxations. This makes unexpected behaviour rare; floating-point numbers behave enough like real numbers that programmers largely do not (need to) think about the difference. This gives a challenge for software verification: finding the rarely considered edge-cases that may result in incorrect, unsafe or insecure behaviour.

All of the authors would like to thank ATI project 113099, SECT-AIR; additionally Martin Brain would like to thank DSTL CDE Project 30713 and BTC-ES AG; Florian Schanda was employed at Altran UK when most of the work was done, this paper is not a result of Florian's work at Zenuity GmbH. Florian would like to thank Elisa Barboni for dealing with a last-minute issue in benchmarking.

T. Vojnar and L. Zhang (Eds.): TACAS 2019, Part I, LNCS 11427, pp. 79–98, 2019.
https://doi.org/10.1007/978-3-030-17462-0_5

Of the many verification tools that can address these challenges, almost all use SMT solvers to find solutions to sets of constraints, or show they are infeasible. So there is a pressing need for SMT solvers to be able to reason about floating-point variables. An extension to the ubiquitous SMT-LIB standard to support floating-point [13] gives a common interface, reducing the wider problem to a question of efficient implementation within SMT solvers.

Most solvers designed for verification support the theory of bit-vectors. As floating-point operations can be implemented with circuits, the "bit-blasting" approach of reducing the floating-point theory to bit-vectors is popular. This method is conceptually simple, makes use of advances in bit-vector theory solvers and allows mixed floating-point/bit-vector problems to be solved efficiently.

Implementing the theory of floating-point should be as simple as adding the relevant circuit designs to the bit-blaster. However, encodings of floating-point operations in terms of bit-vectors, similarly to implementation of floating-point units in hardware, are notoriously complex and detailed. Getting a high degree of assurance in their correctness requires a solid understanding of floating-point operations and significant development effort.

Then there are questions of performance. Floating-point units designed for hardware are generally optimised for low latency, high throughput or low power consumption. Likewise software implementations of floating-point operations tend to focus on latency and features such as arbitrary precision. However, there is nothing to suggest that a design that produces a 'good' circuit will also produce a 'good' encoding or vice-versa.

To address these challenges this paper presents the following contributions:

- A comprehensive overview of the literature on automated reasoning for floating-point operations (Section 2).
- An exploration of the design space for floating-point to bit-vector encodings (Section 3) and the choices made when developing the SymFPU; a library of encodings that can be integrated into SMT solvers that support the theory of bit-vectors (Section 4).
- A verification case for the correctness of the SymFPU encodings and various other SMT solvers (Section 5).
- An experimental evaluation five times larger than previous works gives a comprehensive evaluation of existing tools and shows that the SymFPU encodings, even used in a naïve way significantly out-perform all other approaches (Section 6). These experiments subsume the evaluations performed in many previous works, giving a robust replication of their results.

2   The Challenges of Floating-Point Reasoning

Floating-point number systems are based on computing with a fixed number of *significant digits*. Only the significant digits are stored (the *significand*), along with their distance from the decimal point (the *exponent*) as the power of a fixed base. The following are examples of decimals numbers with three significant digits and their floating-point representations.

Arithmetic is performed as normal, but the result may have more than the specified number of digits and need to be rounded to a representable value. This gives the first major challenge for reasoning about floating-point numbers: rounding after each operation means that addition and multiplication are no longer associative, nor are they distributive.

Existence of identities, additive inverses[1] and symmetry are preserved except for special cases (see below) and in some cases addition even gains an absorptive property ($a+b = a$ for some non-zero b). However, the resulting structure is not a well studied algebra and does not support many symbolic reasoning algorithms.

Rounding ensures the significand fits in a fixed number of bits, but it does not deal with exponent overflow or underflow. Detecting, and graceful and efficient handling of these edge-cases was a significant challenge for older floating-point systems. To address these challenges, IEEE-754 defines floating-point numbers representing $\pm\infty$ and ± 0[2] and a class of fixed-point numbers known as *denormal* or *subnormal* numbers.

To avoid intrusive branching and testing code in computational hot-spots, all operations have to be defined for these values. This gives troubling questions such as "What is $\infty + -\infty$?" or "Is 0/0 equal to 1/0, $-1/0$, or neither?". The standard resolves these with a fifth class of number, not-a-number (NaN).

The proliferation of classes of number is the second source of challenges for automated reasoning. An operation as simple as an addition can result in a 125-way case split if each class of input number and rounding mode is considered individually. Automated reasoning systems for floating-point numbers need an efficient way of controlling the number of side conditions and edge cases.

As well as the two major challenges intrinsic to IEEE-754 floating-point, there are also challenges in how programmers use floating-point numbers. In many systems, floating-point values are used to represent some "real world" quantity – light or volume levels, velocity, distance, etc. Only a small fraction of the range of floating-point numbers are then meaningful. For example, a 64-bit floating-point number can represent the range $[1 * 10^{-324}, 1 * 10^{308}]$ which dwarfs the range of likely speeds (in m/s) of any vehicle[3] $[1 * 10^{-15}, 3 * 10^8]$. Apart from languages like Ada [35] or SPARK [3] that have per-type ranges, the required information on what are meaningful ranges is rarely present in – or can be inferred from – the program alone. This makes it hard to create "reasonable" preconditions or avoid returning laughably infeasible verification failures.

Despite the challenges, there are many use-cases for floating-point reasoning: testing the feasibility of execution paths, preventing the generation of ∞ and NaN, locating absorptive additions and catastrophic cancellation, finding language-level undefined behaviour (such as the much-cited Ariane 5 Flight 501 incident), showing run-time exception freedom, checking hardware and FPGA

---

[1] But not multiplicative ones for subtle reasons.

[2] Two distinct zeros are supported so that underflow from above and below can be distinguished, helping handle some branch cuts such as tan.

[3] Based on the optimistic use of the classical electron radius and the speed of light.

designs (such as the equally well cited Intel FDIV bug) and proving functional correctness against both float-valued and real-valued specifications.

2.1   Techniques

Current fully automatic[4] floating-point reasoning tools can be roughly grouped into four categories: bit-blasting, interval techniques, black-box optimisation approaches and axiomatic schemes.

Bit-Blasting. CBMC [17] was one of the first tools to convert from bit-vector formulae to Boolean SAT problems (so called "bit-blasting"). It benefited from the contemporaneous rapid improvement in SAT solver technology and lead to the DPLL(T) [29] style of SMT solver. Later versions of CBMC also converted floating-point constraints directly into Boolean problems [15]. These conversions were based on the circuits given in [44] and served as inspiration for a similar approach in MathSAT [16] and independent development of similar techniques in Z3 [24] and SONOLAR [39]. SoftFloat [34] has been used to simulate floating-point support for integer only tools [48] but is far from a satisfactory approach as the algorithms used for efficient software implementation of floating-point are significantly different from those used for hardware [45] and efficient encodings.

The principle disadvantage of bit-blasting is that the bit-vector formulae generated can be very large and complex. To mitigate this problem, there have been several approaches [15,56,57] to approximating the bit-vector formulae. This remains an under-explored and promising area.

Interval Techniques. One of the relational properties preserved by IEEE-754 is a weak form of monotonicity, e.g.: $0 < s \wedge a < b \Rightarrow a + s \leqslant b + s$. These properties allow efficient and tight interval bounds to be computed for common operations. This is used by the numerical methods communities and forms the basis for three independent lineages of automated reasoning tools.

Based on the formal framework of abstract interpretation, a number of techniques that partition abstract domains to compute an exact result[5] have been proposed. These include the ACDL framework [26] that generalises the CDCL algorithm used in current SAT solvers. Although this is applicable to a variety of domains, the use of intervals is widespread as an efficient and "precise enough" foundation. CDFPL [27] applied these techniques to programs and [11] implemented them within MathSAT. Absolute [47] uses a different partitioning scheme without learning, but again uses intervals.

---

[4] Machine assisted proof, such as interactive theorem provers are outside the scope of the current discussion. There has been substantial work in Isabelle, HOL, HOL Light, ACL2, PVS, Coq and Meta-Tarski on floating-point.

[5] This approach is operationally much closer to automated reasoning than classical abstract interpreters such as Fluctuat [31], Astrée [8], Polyspace [54], and CodePeer [2], as well as more modern tools such as Rosa [22] and Daisy [36] which compute over-approximate bounds or verification results.

From the automated reasoning community similar approaches have been developed. Originally implemented in the nlsat tool [37], mcSAT [25] can be seen as an instantiation of the ACDL framework using a constant abstraction and tying the generalisation step to a particular approach to variable elimination. Application of this technique to floating-point would likely either use intervals or a conversion to bit-vectors [58]. iSAT3 [51] implements an interval partitioning and learning system, which could be seen as another instance of ACDL. Independently, dReal [30] and raSAT [55] have both developed interval partitioning techniques which would be directly applicable to floating-point systems.

A third strand of convergent evolution in the development of interval based techniques comes from the constraint programming community. FPCS [43] uses intervals with sophisticated back-propagation rules [4] and smart partitioning heuristics [59]. Colibri [42] takes a slightly different approach, using a more expressive constraint representation of difference bounded matrices[6]. This favours more powerful inference over a faster search.

These approaches all have compact representations of spaces of possibilities and fast propagation which allow them to efficiently tackle "large but easy" problems. However they tend to struggle as the relations between expressions become more complex, requiring some kind or relational reasoning such as the learning in MathSAT, or the relational abstractions of Colibri. As these advantages and disadvantages fit well with those of bit-blasting, hybrid systems are not uncommon. Both MathSAT and Z3 perform simple interval reasoning during pre-processing and iSAT3 has experimented with using CBMC and SMT solvers for problems that seem to be UNSAT [46,52].

Optimisation Approaches. It is possible to evaluate many formulae quickly in hardware, particularly those derived from software verification tasks. Combined with a finite search space for floating-point variables, this makes local-search and other "black-box" techniques an attractive proposition. XSat [28] was the first tool to directly make use of this approach (although Ariadne [5] could be seen as a partial precursor), making use of an external optimisation solver. goSAT [38] improved on this by compiling the formulae to an executable form. A similar approach using an external fuzz-testing tool is taken by JFS [40].

These approaches have considerable promise, particularly for SAT problems with relatively dense solution spaces. The obvious limitation is that these techniques are often unable to identify UNSAT problems.

Axiomatic. Although rounding destroys many of the obvious properties, the algebra of floating-point is not without non-trivial results. Gappa [23] was originally created as a support tool for interactive theorem provers, but can be seen a solver in its own right. It instantiates a series of theorems about floating-point numbers until a sufficient error bound is determined. Although its saturation process is naïve, it is fast and effective, especially when directed by a more conventional SMT solver [20]. Why3 [9] uses an axiomatisation of floating-point

---

[6] In the abstract interpretation view this could be seen as a relational abstraction.

numbers based on reals when producing verification conditions for provers that only support real arithmetic. Combining these approaches Alt-Ergo [19] ties the instantiation of relevant theorems to its quantifier and non-linear real theory solvers. Finally, KLEE-FP [18] can be seen as a solver in the axiomatic tradition but using rewriting rather than theorem instantiation.

3   Floating-Point Circuits

Floating-point circuits have been the traditional choice for bit-blasting encoding. The 'classical' design[7] for floating-point units is a four stage pipeline [45]: unpacking, operation, rounding, and packing.

Unpacking. IEEE-754 gives an encoding for all five kinds of number. To separate the encoding logic from the operation logic, it is common to *unpack*; converting arguments from the IEEE-754 format to a larger, redundant format used within the floating-point unit (FPU). The unpacking units and intermediate format are normally the same for all operations within an FPU. A universal feature is splitting the number into three smaller bit-vectors: the sign, exponent and significand. Internal formats may also include some of the following features:

– Flags to record if the number is an infinity, NaN, zero or subnormal.
– The leading 1 for normal numbers (the so-called *hidden-bit*) may be added. Thus the significand may be regarded as a fix-point number in the range $[0, 1)$ or $[1, 2)$. Some designs go further allowing the significand range to be larger, allowing lazy normalisation.
– The exponent may be biased or unbiased[8].
– Subnormal numbers may be normalised (requiring an extended exponent), flagged, transferred to a different unit or even trapped to software.

Operate. Operations, such as addition or multiplication are performed on unpacked numbers, significantly simplifying the logic required. The result will be another unpacked number, often with an extended significand (two or three extra bits for addition, up to twice the number of bits for multiplication) and extended exponent (typically another one or two bits). For example, using this approach multiplication is relatively straight forward:

1. Multiply the two significands, giving a fixed-point number with twice the precision, in the range $[1, 4)$.

---

[7] Modern high-performance processors often only implement a fused mulitply-add (FMA) unit that computes $round(x * y + z)$ and then use a mix of table look-ups and Newton-Raphson style iteration to implement divide, square-root, etc.
[8] Although the exponent is interpreted as a signed number, it is encoded, in IEEE-754 format using a biased representation, so that the $000 \ldots 00$ bit-vector represents the smallest negative number rather than 0 and $111 \ldots 11$ represents the largest positive rather than the -1 in 2's complement encodings. This makes the ordering of bit-vectors and IEEE-754 floating-point numbers compatible.

2. Add the exponents ($2^{e_1} * 2^{e_2} = 2^{e_1 + e_2}$) and subtract the bias if they are stored in a biased form.
3. Potentially renormalise the exponent into the range $[1, 2)$ (right shift the significand one place and increment the exponent).
4. Use the classification flags to handle special cases (∞, NaN, etc.).

Addition is more involved as the two significands must be aligned before they can be added or subtracted. In most cases, the location of the leading 1 in the resulting significand is roughly known, meaning that the renormalisation is simple (for example $s_1 \in [1, 2), s_2 \in [1, 2) \Rightarrow s_1 + s_2 \in [2, 4)$). However in the case of catastrophic cancellation the location of the leading 1 is non-obvious. Although this case is rare, it has a disproportionate effect on the design of floating-point adders: it is necessary to locate the leading 1 to see how many bits have been cancelled to determine what changes are needed for the exponent.

Round. Given the exact result in extended precision, the next step is to round to the nearest representable number in the target output format. Traditionally, the rounder would have been a common component of the FPU, shared between the functional units and would be independent of the operations. The operation of the rounder is relatively simple but the order of operations is very significant:

1. Split the significand into the representable bits, the first bit after (the *guard bit*) and the OR of the remaining bits (the *sticky bit*).
2. The guard bit and sticky bit determine whether the number is less than half way to the previous representable number, exact half way, or over half way. Depending on the rounding mode the significand may be incremented (i.e. rounded up).
3. The exponent is checked to see if it is too large (*overflow*) or too small (*underflow*) for the target format, and the output is set to infinity/the largest float or 0/the smallest float depending on the rounding mode.

To work out which bits to convert to the guard and sticky bits, *it is critical to know the position of the leading 1*, and if the number is subnormal or not.

Pack. The final step is to convert the result back into the packed IEEE-754 format. This is the converse of the unpacking stage, with flags for the type of number being used to set special values. Note that this can result in the carefully calculated and rounded result being ignored in favour of outputting the fixed bit-pattern for ∞ or NaN.

4 SymFPU

SymFPU is a C++ library of bit-vector encodings of floating-point operations. It is available at https://github.com/martin-cs/symfpu. The types used to represent signed and unsigned bit-vectors, Booleans, rounding-modes and floating-point formats are templated so that multiple "back-ends" can be implemented. This allows SymFPU to be used as an executable multi-precision library and to generate symbolic encodings of the operations. As well as the default executable back-end, integrations into CVC4 [6] and CBMC [17] have been developed. These typically require 300–500 effective lines of code, the majority of which is routine interfacing.

Packing Removal. By choosing an unpacked format that is bijective with the packed format, the following property holds: $pack \circ unpack = id = unpack \circ pack$. The encodings in CBMC do not have this property as the packing phase is used to mask out the significand and exponent when special values are generated. The property allows a key optimisation: the final unpack stage of an operation and the pack of the next can be eliminated. Hence values can be kept in unpacked form and whole chains of operations can be performed without packing. Although this is not necessarily a large saving on its own, it allows the use of unpacked formats which would be too expensive if every operation was packed.

Unpacked Format. Key to SymFPU's performance is the unpacked format. Flags are used for ∞, NaN and zero. This means that special cases can be handled at the end of the operation, bypassing the need to reason about the actual computation if one of the flags is set. Special cases share the same 'default' significand and exponent, so assignment to the flags will propagate values through the rest of the circuit.

The exponent is a signed bit-vector without bias, moving a subtract from the multiplier into the packing and unpacking (avoided as described above) and allowing decision procedures for signed bit-vectors to be used [32].

The significand is represented with the leading one and subnormal numbers are normalised. This adds considerable cost to the packing and unpacking but means that the leading one can be tracked at design time, avoiding the expensive normalisation phase before rounding that CBMC's encodings have. A normalisation phase is needed in the adder for catastrophic cancellation and the subnormal case of rounding is more expensive but critically both of these cases are rare (see below). Z3's encodings use a more complex system of lazy normalisation. This works well when operations include packing but is harder to use once packing has been removed. Integrating this approach is a challenge for future work.

Additional Bit-Vector Operations. SymFPU uses a number of non-standard bit-vector operations including add-with-carry (for including the renormalisation bit into exponents during multiply), conditional increment, decrement and left-shift (used for normalisation), max and min, count leading zeros, order encode (output has input number of bits), right sticky shift, and normalise. Work on creating optimal encodings [12] of these operations is on-going.

Invariants. As the significand in the unpacked format always has a leading one, it is possible to give strong invariants on the location of leading ones during the algorithms. Other invariants are general properties of IEEE-754 floating-point, for example the exponent of an effective addition is always $max(e_a, e_b)$ or $max(e_a, e_b) + 1$ regardless of rounding. Where possible, bit-vectors operations are used so that no overflows or underflows occur – a frustrating source of bugs in the CBMC encodings. Invariants in SymFPU can be checked with executable back-ends and used as auxiliary constraints in symbolic ones.

Probability Annotations. There are many sub-cases within operations which are unlikely or rare, for example rounding the subnormal result of a multiplication, catastrophic cancellation, or late detection of significand overflow during rounding. These are often more expensive to handle than the common cases. SymFPU contains probability annotations that mark likely and unlikely cases so that these can be handled separately.

5   Correctness

Developing a floating-point implementation, literal and symbolic, is a notoriously detailed and error prone task. For SymFPU we developed a substantial verification process which is summarised in Figure 1. Our verification case is based on system-level testing of SymFPU in CVC4, and double/triple diversity of checks, developers, references and implementations:

1. We use five test suites, four developed specifically for this project. These were developed independently by three different developers using different methodologies and different "ground truth" references. Where hardware was a reference, several different chips from different vendors were used.
2. The results of three different solvers (CVC4 with SymFPU, MathSAT, and Z3) are compared and each test is only regarded as passed when any discrepancy, between solvers or with the reference results, has been resolved. Each solver has its own, independently developed encodings and there is diversity in the algorithms used.

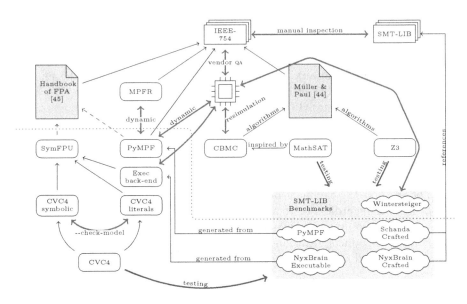

Fig. 1. The verification case for SymFPU. The contributions of this paper are below the dotted line. Thicker arrows are verification activities, and black arrows the usage of various documents and libraries.

As described above, SymFPU contains a significant number of dynamically-checked invariants. CVC4 also checks the models generated for satisfiable formulae, checking the symbolic back-end against the literal one. The experiments described in Section 6 also acted as system-level tests. This approach uncovered numerous bugs in the SymFPU encodings, the solvers and even our reference libraries. However, as it is a testing based verification argument, it cannot be considered to be complete. [41] used a similar technique successfully in a more limited setting without the emphasis on ground truth.

5.1 PyMPF

Testing-based verification is at best as good as the reference results for the tests – a high-quality test oracle is vital. Various solvers have their own multi-precision libraries, using these would not achieve the required diversity. MPFR [33] was considered but it does not support all of the operations in SMT-LIB, and has an awkward approach to subnormals.

To act as an oracle, we developed PyMPF [49], a Python multi-precision library focused on correctness through simplicity rather than performance. Unlike other multi-precision floating-point libraries it represents numbers as rationals rather than significand and exponent, and explicitly rounds to the nearest representable rational after each operation using a simple binary search. Where possible, all calculations are dynamically checked against a compiled C version of the operation and MPFR, giving triple diversity.

Using PyMPF as an oracle, a test suite was generated covering all combination of classes: ± 0, subnormal (smallest, random, largest), normal (smallest, random, largest, 1, $\frac{1}{2}$), $\pm\infty$, and NaN along with all combination of five rounding modes. The majority of these require only forwards reasoning, but some require backwards reasoning. Benchmarks are generated for both SAT and UNSAT problems; in addition some benchmarks correctly exploit the unspecified behaviour in the standard. This suite proved particularly effective, finding multiple soundness bugs in all implementations we were able to test.

6   Experimental Results

We had two experimental objectives: (a) compare SymFPU with the state of the art, (b) reproduce, validate, or update results from previous papers.

6.1   Experimental Setup

All benchmarks are available online [50], along with the scripts to run them. Experiments were conducted in the TACAS artefact evaluation virtual machine, hosted on an Intel i7-7820HQ laptop with 32 GiB RAM running Debian Stretch. All experiments were conducted with a one minute timeout[9] and 2500 MiB memory limit, set with a custom tool (rather than ulimit) that allowed us to reliably distinguish between tool crashes, timeouts, or memory use limits.

Solver responses were split into six classes: solved ("sat" or "unsat" response), unknown ("unknown" response), timeout, oom (out-of-memory), unsound ("sat" or "unsat" response contradicting the :status annotation), and error (anything else, including "unsupported" messages, parse errors or other tool output).

Although one minute is a relatively short limit, it best matches the typical industrial use-cases with SPARK; and trial runs with larger time-outs suggest that the additional time does not substantially change the qualitative nature of the results.

6.2   Benchmarks

We have tried to avoid arbitrary choices in benchmark selection as we want to demonstrate that SymFPU's encodings are a good general-purpose solution. As such we compare with some solvers in their specialised domain. Benchmarks are in logics QF_FP or QF_FPBV except for: Heizmann benchmarks include quantifiers and arrays; SPARK benchmarks (including Industrial_1) include arrays, datatypes, quantifiers, uninterpreted functions, integer and reals, and bitvectors. SAT, UNSAT or unknown here refers to the :status annotations in the benchmarks, not to our results.

---

[9] Except for the Wintersteiger suite where we used a 1 s timeout to deal with Alt-Ergo's behaviour.

Schanda 200 problems (34.0% SAT, 63.0% UNSAT, 3.0% unknown). Hand-written benchmarks accumulated over the years working on SPARK, user-supplied axioms, industrial code and problems, and reviewing papers and the SMT-LIB theory [13,14].

PyMPF 72,925 problems (52.3% SAT, 47.7% UNSAT). A snapshot of benchmarks generated using PyMPF [49] as described above.

NyxBrain 52,500 problems (99.5% SAT, 0.5% UNSAT). Hand-written edge-cases, and generated problems based on bugs in existing implementations.

Wintersteiger 39,994 problems (50.0% SAT, 50.0% UNSAT). Randomly generated benchmarks that cover many aspects of the floating-point theory.

Griggio 214 problems (all unknown). Benchmark set deliberately designed to highlight the limitations of bit-blasting and the advantages of interval techniques. They were the most useful in reproducing other paper's results.

Heizmann 207 problems (1.0% SAT, 99.0% unknown). Taken from the Ultimate Automizer model checker.

Industrial_1 388 problems (all UNSAT). Extracted from a large industrial Ada 2005 code base. We used the SPARK 2014 tools to produce (identifier obfuscated) verification conditions.

Industrial_1 QF 388 problems (all unknown). As above, but with quantifiers and data-types removed.

SPARK FP 2950 problems (5.3% UNSAT, 94.7% unknown). The floating-point subset of the verification conditions from the SPARK test suite[10], generated using a patched[11] SPARK tool to map the square root function of the Ada Standard library to `fp.sqrt`.

SPARK FP QF 2950 problems (all unknown). As above, but with all quantifiers and data-types removed.

CBMC 54 problems (7.4% UNSAT, 92.6% unknown). Non-trivial benchmarks from SV-COMP's floating-point collection [7], fp-bench [21] benchmarks that contained checkable post-conditions, the benchmarks used by [5], and the sample programs from [59]. The benchmarks are provided in SMT-LIB and the original C program for comparing to CBMC's floating-point solver.

Not all SMT solvers support all features of SMT-LIB, hence we provide alternative encodings in some cases. In particular Alt-Ergo does not parse moden SMT-LIB at all; so Griggio and Wintersteiger have been translated with the `fp-smt2-to-why3`[12] tool from [19] and the SPARK FP benchmarks have been generated by SPARK directly for Alt-Ergo, where possible (since Alt-Ergo does not support the `ite` contruct, there is a translation step inside Why3 that attempts to remove it, but it sometimes runs out of memory).

---

[10] Github: AdaCore/spark2014, directory testsuite/gnatprove/tests.

[11] Github: florianschanda/spark_2014 and florianschanda/why3.

[12] https://gitlab.com/OCamlPro-Iguernlala/Three-Tier-FPA-Benchs/tree/master/translators/fp-smt2-to-why3.

6.3   Solvers

We have benchmarked the following solvers in the following configurations on the benchmarks described above: CVC4 [6] (with SymFPU)[13], Z3 (4.8.1) [24], Z3 Smallfloats (3a3abf82) [57], MathSAT (5.5.2) [16], MathSAT (5.5.2) using ACDCL [11], SONOLAR (2014-12-04) [39], Colibri (r1981) [42], Alt-Ergo (2.2.0) [19], and goSAT (4e475233) [38].

We have also attempted to benchmark XSat [28], but we were unable to reliably use the tools as distributed at the required scale (≈ 200k benchmarks). However, we understand that goSAT is an evolution of the ideas implemented in XSat, and its results should be representative.

We would have liked to benchmark iSAT3 [51], Coral [53] and Gappa [23], but they do not provide SMT-LIB front-ends and there are no automatic translators we are aware of to their native input language. Binaries for FPCS [43] and Alt-Ergo/Gappa [20] were not available.

6.4   Results

Overall. Table 1 shows the overall summary of how many benchmarks any given solver was able to solve (correct SAT or UNSAT answer). CVC4 using the SymFPU encodings solves the most problems in all but two categories. In the case of the "Griggio" suite this is not surprising, given it's purpose. A detailed breakdown of that benchmark suite can be found in Table 2.

Griggio Suite. Table 2 shows the detailed results for the Griggio suite. Since the benchmark suite was designed to be difficult for bit-blasting solvers, it is not surprising that MathSAT (ACDCL) and Colibri do very well here, as they are not bit-blasting solvers. Though it is claimed in [19] that "Bit-blasting based techniques perform better on Griggio benchmarks", this is evidently not the case.

Heizmann Suite. Table 3 shows the detailed results for the benchmarks from the Ultimate Automizer project. These benchmarks were particularly useful to include as they are industrial in nature and are generated independent of all solver developers and the authors of this paper. The errors mainly relate to quantifiers (MathSAT, Colibri, SONOLAR), conversions (MathSAT-ACDCL), sorts (Colibri), and arrays (SONOLAR).

CBMC Suite. Table 4 shows a comparison between CBMC and SMT Solvers when attempting to solve the same problem. The original benchmark in C is given to CBMC, and SMT Solvers attempt to either solve a hand-encoding of the same problem or the encoding of the problem generated by CBMC.

---

[13] https://github.com/martin-cs/cvc4/tree/floating-point-symfpu.

Table 1. Percentage of solved benchmarks. Solver names abbreviated: AE (Alt-Ergo), Col (Colibri), MS (MathSAT), MS-A (MathSAT ACDCL), SON (SONOLAR), Z3-SF (Z3 SmallFloats), VBS (Virtual Best Solver). A ✓ indicates that all problems are solved, a blank entry indicates that the solver did not solve any problem for the given benchmark suite. In this table and all subsequent tables a * indicates that at least one benchmark was expressed in a solver-specific dialect, and the best result for each benchmark is typeset in bold.

Benchmark	AE	Col	CVC4	goSAT	MS	MS-A	SON	Z3	Z3-SF	VBS
CBMC		**66.7**	55.6	9.3	50.0	**66.7**	38.9	42.6	46.3	83.3*
Schanda		82.5	**85.5**	1.0	68.0*	28.0*		84.0	82.0	96.0*
Griggio	0.9*	61.7	61.2	41.1	59.3	**69.2**	67.8	33.2	46.3	89.3
Heizmann		14.0	**74.9**		58.5	27.5	2.9	51.7	42.0	91.8
Industrial 1		**91.2**						65.2	62.9	91.8
Industrial 1 (QF)		93.0	**98.2**		97.2	88.1		85.8	83.2	99.7
NyxBrain		99.8	**99.9**	34.2	95.4	95.0	99.2	99.9	99.9	>99.9
PyMPF		92.2	**99.7**	0.3	39.4	35.9		99.3	98.4	99.8
SPARK FP	68.6*		**85.6**					82.0	73.6	90.2*
SPARK FP (QF)		94.0	**95.8**		83.3	78.9		90.3	90.3	99.7
Wintersteiger	49.9*	✓	✓	13.9	85.8	85.8		✓	✓	✓*

Table 2. Results for benchmark 'Griggio' 214 problems (all unknown), ordered by % solved. Total time includes timeouts. A ✓ in "Unsound" indicates 0 unsound results.

Solver	Solved	Unknown	Timeout	Oom	Error	Unsound	Total time (m:s)
MathSAT (ACDCL)	**69.2%**	0	66	**0**	✓	✓	1:11:03
SONOLAR	67.8%	0	59	10	✓	✓	1:19:35
Colibri	61.7%	0	73	2	7	✓	1:22:13
CVC4	61.2%	0	77	6	✓	✓	1:40:47
MathSAT	59.3%	0	85	2	✓	✓	1:53:26
Z3 (SmallFloat)	46.3%	0	99	16	✓	✓	2:13:28
goSAT	41.1%	120	**6**	**0**	✓	✓	**8:28**
Z3	33.2%	0	124	19	✓	✓	2:34:16
Alt-Ergo FPA	0.9%*	2	210	**0**	✓	✓	3:32:40
Virtual best	89.3%	17	6	0	✓	✓	12:53

6.5   Replication

As part of our evaluation we have attempted to reproduce, validate or update results from previous papers. We have encountered issues with unclear solver configurations and versions and arbitrary benchmark selections.

The Z3 approximation paper [57] uses the Griggio test suite with a 20 minute timeout. It reported that there is little difference between Z3 and Z3-SmallFloats, and MathSAT outperformed both. Our results in Table 2 confirm this.

The MathSAT ACDCL [11] paper also looks at the Griggio test suite with a 20 minute timeout, our results in Table 2 are roughly ordered as theirs and can be considered to confirm these results.

Although the total number of SAT/UNSAT varied based on algorithm selection (i.e. the tool was clearly unsound) in [38], goSAT has been fixed and the results are broadly reproducible. We discovered some platform dependent behaviour (different SAT/UNSAT answers) between AMD and Intel processors. This can likely be fixed with appropriate compilation flags.

Table 3. Results for benchmark 'Heizmann' 207 problems (1.0% SAT, 99.0% unknown), ordered by % solved. Total time includes timeouts.

Solver	Solved	Unknown	Timeout	Oom	Error	Unsound	Total time (m:s)
CVC4	**74.9%**	48	0	0	4	✓	0:39.20
MathSAT	58.5%	0	0	0	86	✓	0:35.48
Z3	51.7%	0	91	9	✓	✓	2:03:36
Z3 (SmallFloat)	42.0%	0	111	9	✓	✓	2:13:13
MathSAT (ACDCL)	27.5%	0	0	0	150	✓	0:25.33
Colibri	14.0%	0	0	0	178	✓	0:30.34
SONOLAR	2.9%	0	0	0	201	✓	**0:7.92**
Virtual best	91.8%	17	0	0	✓	✓	5:36

Table 4. Results for benchmark 'CBMC' 54 problems (7.4% UNSAT, 92.6% unknown), ordered by number of unsound answers and then by % solved. Total time includes timeouts.

Solver	Solved	Unknown	Timeout	Oom	Error	Unsound	Total time (m:s)
Colibri	**66.7%**	0	14	0	4	✓	16:04
CBMC	61.1%*	0	17	4	✓	✓	19:25
CBMC –refine	61.1%*	0	21	0	✓	✓	23:30
CVC4	55.6%	0	17	7	✓	✓	23:41
MathSAT	50.0%	0	22	5	✓	✓	26:34
Z3 (SmallFloat)	46.3%	0	22	7	✓	✓	27:32
Z3	42.6%	0	22	9	✓	✓	29:29
SONOLAR	38.9%	0	0	0	33	✓	0:19.20
goSAT	9.3%	0	0	0	49	✓	**0:0.55**
MathSAT (ACDCL)	**66.7%**	0	9	0	7	2	9:51
Virtual best	83.3%*	0	9	0	✓	✓	9:55

We were unable to reproduce the results of the XSat [28] paper, as we could not get the tools to work reliably. In particular the docker instance cannot be used in our testing infrastructure as the constant-time overhead of running docker ruins performance, and eventually the docker daemon crashes.

We were only able to reproduce small parts from the Alt-Ergo FPA [19] paper. The biggest problem is benchmark selection and generation, which was not repeatable from scratch. Two particular measurements are worth commenting on: while they have roughly equal solved rate for SPARK VCs for Alt-Ergo and Z3 (40% and 36% respectively), as can be seen in Table 1 we get (68% and 86%) - although as noted we could not fully replicate their benchmark selection. However even more surprising are their results for the Griggio suite where they report a mere 4% for MathSAT-ACDCL which does not match our results of 69% as seen in Table 2.

7   Conclusion

By careful consideration of the challenges of floating-point reasoning (Section 2) and the fundamentals of circuit design (Section 3) we have designed a library of encodings that reduce the cost of developing a correct and efficient floating-point solver to a few hundred lines of interface code (Section 4). Integration into CVC4 gives a solver that substantially out-performs all previous systems (Section 6) despite using the most direct and naïve approach[14]. The verification process used to develop SymFPU ensures a high-level of quality, as well as locating tens of thousands of incorrect answers from hundreds of bugs across all existing solvers.

At a deeper level our experimental work raises some troubling questions about how developments in solver technology are practically evaluated. It shows that the quality of implementation (even between mature systems) can make a larger difference to performance than the difference between techniques [10]. Likewise the difficulty we had in replicating the trends seen in previous experimental work underscores the need for diverse and substantial benchmark sets.

References

1. IEEE standard for floating-point arithmetic. IEEE Std 754-2008, pp. 1–70, August 2008. https://doi.org/10.1109/IEEESTD.2008.4610935
2. AdaCore: CodePeer. https://www.adacore.com/codepeer
3. Altran, AdaCore: SPARK 2014. https://adacore.com/sparkpro
4. Bagnara, R., Carlier, M., Gori, R., Gotlieb, A.: Filtering floating-point constraints by maximum ULP (2013). https://arxiv.org/abs/1308.3847v1
5. Barr, E.T., Vo, T., Le, V., Su, Z.: Automatic detection of floating-point exceptions. In: Proceedings of the 40th Annual ACM SIGPLAN-SIGACT Symposium on Principles of Programming Languages, POPL 2013, pp. 549–560. ACM, New York (2013). https://doi.org/10.1145/2429069.2429133

---

[14] SymFPU (as it is used in CVC4) is an eager bit-blasting approach. These were first published in 2006, predating all approaches except some interval techniques.

6. Barrett, C., et al.: CVC4. In: Gopalakrishnan, G., Qadeer, S. (eds.) CAV 2011. LNCS, vol. 6806, pp. 171–177. Springer, Heidelberg (2011). https://doi.org/10.1007/978-3-642-22110-1_14
7. Beyer, D.: SV-COMP. https://github.com/sosy-lab/sv-benchmarks
8. Blanchet, B., et al.: A static analyzer for large safety-critical software. In: Proceedings of the ACM SIGPLAN 2003 Conference on Programming Language Design and Implementation, PLDI 2003, pp. 196–207. ACM, New York (2003). https://doi.org/10.1145/781131.781153
9. Bobot, F., Filliâtre, J.C., Marché, C., Paskevich, A.: Why3: shepherd your herd of provers. In: Boogie 2011: First International Workshop on Intermediate Verification Languages, pp. 53–64. Wroclaw, Poland (2011). https://hal.inria.fr/hal-00790310
10. Brain, M., De Vos, M.: The significance of memory costs in answer set solver implementation. J. Logic Comput. **19**(4), 615–641 (2008). https://doi.org/10.1093/logcom/exn038
11. Brain, M., D'Silva, V., Griggio, A., Haller, L., Kroening, D.: Deciding floating-point logic with abstract conflict driven clause learning. Formal Methods Syst. Des. **45**(2), 213–245 (2014). https://doi.org/10.1007/s10703-013-0203-7
12. Brain, M., Hadarean, L., Kroening, D., Martins, R.: Automatic generation of propagation complete SAT encodings. In: Jobstmann, B., Leino, K.R.M. (eds.) VMCAI 2016. LNCS, vol. 9583, pp. 536–556. Springer, Heidelberg (2016). https://doi.org/10.1007/978-3-662-49122-5_26
13. Brain, M., Tinelli, C.: SMT-LIB floating-point theory, April 2015. http://smtlib.cs.uiowa.edu/theories-FloatingPoint.shtml
14. Brain, M., Tinelli, C., Rümmer, P., Wahl, T.: An automatable formal semantics for IEEE-754, June 2015. http://smtlib.cs.uiowa.edu/papers/BTRW15.pdf
15. Brillout, A., Kroening, D., Wahl, T.: Mixed abstractions for floating-point arithmetic. In: FMCAD, pp. 69–76. IEEE (2009). https://doi.org/10.1109/FMCAD.2009.5351141
16. Cimatti, A., Griggio, A., Schaafsma, B.J., Sebastiani, R.: The MathSAT5 SMT solver. In: Piterman, N., Smolka, S.A. (eds.) TACAS 2013. LNCS, vol. 7795, pp. 93–107. Springer, Heidelberg (2013). https://doi.org/10.1007/978-3-642-36742-7_7
17. Clarke, E., Kroening, D., Lerda, F.: A tool for checking ANSI-C programs. In: Jensen, K., Podelski, A. (eds.) TACAS 2004. LNCS, vol. 2988, pp. 168–176. Springer, Heidelberg (2004). https://doi.org/10.1007/978-3-540-24730-2_15
18. Collingbourne, P., Cadar, C., Kelly, P.H.: Symbolic crosschecking of floating-point and SIMD code. In: Proceedings of the Sixth Conference on Computer Systems, EuroSys 2011, pp. 315–328. ACM, New York (2011). https://doi.org/10.1145/1966445.1966475
19. Conchon, S., Iguernlala, M., Ji, K., Melquiond, G., Fumex, C.: A three-tier strategy for reasoning about floating-point numbers in SMT. In: Majumdar, R., Kunčak, V. (eds.) CAV 2017. LNCS, vol. 10427, pp. 419–435. Springer, Cham (2017). https://doi.org/10.1007/978-3-319-63390-9_22
20. Conchon, S., Melquiond, G., Roux, C., Iguernelala, M.: Built-in treatment of an axiomatic floating-point theory for SMT solvers. In: Fontaine, P., Goel, A. (eds.) 10th International Workshop on Satisfiability Modulo Theories, pp. 12–21. Manchester, United Kingdom, June 2012. https://hal.inria.fr/hal-01785166
21. Damouche, N., Martel, M., Panchekha, P., Qiu, C., Sanchez-Stern, A., Tatlock, Z.: Toward a standard benchmark format and suite for floating-point analysis. In: Bogomolov, S., Martel, M., Prabhakar, P. (eds.) NSV 2016. LNCS, vol. 10152, pp. 63–77. Springer, Cham (2017). https://doi.org/10.1007/978-3-319-54292-8_6

22. Darulova, E., Kuncak, V.: Sound compilation of reals. In: Proceedings of the 41st ACM SIGPLAN-SIGACT Symposium on Principles of Programming Languages, POPL 2014, pp. 235–248. ACM, New York (2014). https://doi.org/10.1145/2535838.2535874

23. Daumas, M., Melquiond, G.: Certification of bounds on expressions involving rounded operators. ACM Trans. Math. Softw. **37**(1), 2:1–2:20 (2010). https://doi.org/10.1145/1644001.1644003

24. de Moura, L., Bjørner, N.: Z3: an efficient SMT solver. In: Ramakrishnan, C.R., Rehof, J. (eds.) TACAS 2008. LNCS, vol. 4963, pp. 337–340. Springer, Heidelberg (2008). https://doi.org/10.1007/978-3-540-78800-3_24

25. de Moura, L., Jovanović, D.: A model-constructing satisfiability calculus. In: Giacobazzi, R., Berdine, J., Mastroeni, I. (eds.) VMCAI 2013. LNCS, vol. 7737, pp. 1–12. Springer, Heidelberg (2013). https://doi.org/10.1007/978-3-642-35873-9_1

26. D'Silva, V., Haller, L., Kroening, D.: Abstract conflict driven learning. In: Proceedings of the 40th Annual ACM SIGPLAN-SIGACT Symposium on Principles of Programming Languages, POPL 2013, pp. 143–154. ACM, New York (2013). https://doi.org/10.1145/2429069.2429087

27. D'Silva, V., Haller, L., Kroening, D., Tautschnig, M.: Numeric bounds analysis with conflict-driven learning. In: Flanagan, C., König, B. (eds.) TACAS 2012. LNCS, vol. 7214, pp. 48–63. Springer, Heidelberg (2012). https://doi.org/10.1007/978-3-642-28756-5_5

28. Fu, Z., Su, Z.: XSat: a fast floating-point satisfiability solver. In: Chaudhuri, S., Farzan, A. (eds.) CAV 2016. LNCS, vol. 9780, pp. 187–209. Springer, Cham (2016). https://doi.org/10.1007/978-3-319-41540-6_11

29. Ganzinger, H., Hagen, G., Nieuwenhuis, R., Oliveras, A., Tinelli, C.: DPLL(T): fast decision procedures. In: Alur, R., Peled, D.A. (eds.) CAV 2004. LNCS, vol. 3114, pp. 175–188. Springer, Heidelberg (2004). https://doi.org/10.1007/978-3-540-27813-9_14

30. Gao, S., Kong, S., Clarke, E.M.: dReal: an SMT solver for nonlinear theories over the reals. In: Bonacina, M.P. (ed.) CADE 2013. LNCS (LNAI), vol. 7898, pp. 208–214. Springer, Heidelberg (2013). https://doi.org/10.1007/978-3-642-38574-2_14

31. Goubault, E., Putot, S.: Static analysis of numerical algorithms. In: Yi, K. (ed.) SAS 2006. LNCS, vol. 4134, pp. 18–34. Springer, Heidelberg (2006). https://doi.org/10.1007/11823230_3

32. Hadarean, L., Bansal, K., Jovanović, D., Barrett, C., Tinelli, C.: A tale of two solvers: eager and lazy approaches to bit-vectors. In: Biere, A., Bloem, R. (eds.) CAV 2014. LNCS, vol. 8559, pp. 680–695. Springer, Cham (2014). https://doi.org/10.1007/978-3-319-08867-9_45

33. Hanrot, G., Zimmermann, P., Lefèvre, V., Pèlissier, P., Thèveny, P., et al.: The GNU MPFR Library. http://www.mpfr.org

34. Hauser, J.R.: SoftFloat. http://www.jhauser.us/arithmetic/SoftFloat.html

35. ISO/IEC JTC 1/SC 22/WG 9 Ada Rapporteur Group: Ada reference manual. ISO/IEC 8652:2012/Cor.1:2016 (2016). http://www.ada-auth.org/standards/rm12_w_tc1/html/RM-TOC.html

36. Izycheva, A., Darulova, E.: On sound relative error bounds for floating-point arithmetic. In: Proceedings of the 17th Conference on Formal Methods in Computer-Aided Design, FMCAD 2017, pp. 15–22. FMCAD Inc, Austin, TX (2017). http://dl.acm.org/citation.cfm?id=3168451.3168462

37. Jovanović, D., de Moura, L.: Solving non-linear arithmetic. In: Gramlich, B., Miller, D., Sattler, U. (eds.) IJCAR 2012. LNCS (LNAI), vol. 7364, pp. 339–354. Springer, Heidelberg (2012). https://doi.org/10.1007/978-3-642-31365-3_27

38. Khadra, M.A.B., Stoffel, D., Kunz, W.: goSAT: floating-point satisfiability as global optimization. In: Formal Methods in Computer Aided Design, FMCAD 2017, pp. 11–14. IEEE (2017). https://doi.org/10.23919/FMCAD.2017.8102235
39. Lapschies, F.: SONOLAR the solver for non-linear arithmetic (2014). http://www.informatik.uni-bremen.de/agbs/florian/sonolar
40. Liew, D.: JFS: JIT fuzzing solver. https://github.com/delcypher/jfs
41. Liew, D., Schemmel, D., Cadar, C., Donaldson, A.F., Zähl, R., Wehrle, K.: Floating-point symbolic execution: a case study in n-version programming, pp. 601–612. IEEE, October 2017. https://doi.org/10.1109/ASE.2017.8115670
42. Marre, B., Bobot, F., Chihani, Z.: Real behavior of floating point numbers. In: SMT Workshop (2017). http://smt-workshop.cs.uiowa.edu/2017/papers/SMT2017_paper_21.pdf
43. Michel, C., Rueher, M., Lebbah, Y.: Solving constraints over floating-point numbers. In: Walsh, T. (ed.) CP 2001. LNCS, vol. 2239, pp. 524–538. Springer, Heidelberg (2001). https://doi.org/10.1007/3-540-45578-7_36
44. Mueller, S.M., Paul, W.J.: Computer Architecture: Complexity and Correctness. Springer, Heidelberg (2000). https://doi.org/10.1007/978-3-662-04267-0
45. Muller, J.M., et al.: Handbook of Floating-Point Arithmetic. Birkhäuser (2009). https://doi.org/10.1007/978-0-8176-4705-6
46. Neubauer, F., et al.: Accurate dead code detection in embedded C code by arithmetic constraint solving. In: Ábrahám, E., Davenport, J.H., Fontaine, P. (eds.) Proceedings of the 1st Workshop on Satisfiability Checking and Symbolic Computation. CEUR, vol. 1804, pp. 32–38, September 2016. http://ceur-ws.org/Vol-1804/paper-07.pdf
47. Pelleau, M., Miné, A., Truchet, C., Benhamou, F.: A constraint solver based on abstract domains. In: Giacobazzi, R., Berdine, J., Mastroeni, I. (eds.) VMCAI 2013. LNCS, vol. 7737, pp. 434–454. Springer, Heidelberg (2013). https://doi.org/10.1007/978-3-642-35873-9_26
48. Romano, A.: Practical floating-point tests with integer code. In: McMillan, K.L., Rival, X. (eds.) VMCAI 2014. LNCS, vol. 8318, pp. 337–356. Springer, Heidelberg (2014). https://doi.org/10.1007/978-3-642-54013-4_19
49. Schanda, F.: Python arbitrary-precision floating-point library (2017). https://www.github.com/florianschanda/pympf
50. Schanda, F., Brain, M., Wintersteiger, C., Griggio, A., et al.: SMT-LIB floating-point benchmarks, June 2017. https://github.com/florianschanda/smtlib_schanda
51. Scheibler, K., Kupferschmid, S., Becker, B.: Recent improvements in the SMT solver iSAT. In: Haubelt, C., Timmermann, D. (eds.) Methoden und Beschreibungssprachen zur Modellierung und Verifikation von Schaltungen und Systemen (MBMV), Warnemünde, Germany, pp. 231–241, 12–14 March 2013. Institut für Angewandte Mikroelektronik und Datentechnik, Fakultät für Informatik und Elektrotechnik, Universität Rostock (2013), http://www.avacs.org/fileadmin/Publikationen/Open/scheibler.mbmv2013.pdf
52. Scheibler, K., et al.: Accurate ICP-based floating-point reasoning. In: Proceedings of the 16th Conference on Formal Methods in Computer-Aided Design FMCAD 2016, pp. 177–184. FMCAD Inc, Austin, TX (2016). http://dl.acm.org/citation.cfm?id=3077629.3077660
53. Souza, M., Borges, M., d'Amorim, M., Păsăreanu, C.S.: CORAL: solving complex constraints for symbolic PathFinder. In: Bobaru, M., Havelund, K., Holzmann, G.J., Joshi, R. (eds.) NFM 2011. LNCS, vol. 6617, pp. 359–374. Springer, Heidelberg (2011). https://doi.org/10.1007/978-3-642-20398-5_26

54. The MathWorks Inc: Polyspace. https://www.mathworks.com/polyspace
55. Tung, V.X., Van Khanh, T., Ogawa, M.: raSAT: an SMT solver for polynomial constraints. Formal Methods Syst. Des. **51**(3), 462–499 (2017). https://doi.org/10.1007/s10703-017-0284-9
56. Zeljic, A., Backeman, P., Wintersteiger, C.M., Rümmer, P.: Exploring approximations for floating-point arithmetic using UppSAT. In: Automated Reasoning - 9th International Joint Conference, IJCAR 2018, Held as Part of the Federated Logic Conference, FloC 2018, Oxford, UK, 14–17 July 2018, Proceedings, pp. 246–262 (2018). https://doi.org/10.1007/978-3-319-94205-6_17
57. Zeljić, A., Wintersteiger, C.M., Rümmer, P.: Approximations for model construction. In: Demri, S., Kapur, D., Weidenbach, C. (eds.) IJCAR 2014. LNCS (LNAI), vol. 8562, pp. 344–359. Springer, Cham (2014). https://doi.org/10.1007/978-3-319-08587-6_26
58. Zeljić, A., Wintersteiger, C.M., Rümmer, P.: Deciding bit-vector formulas with mcSAT. In: Creignou, N., Le Berre, D. (eds.) SAT 2016. LNCS, vol. 9710, pp. 249–266. Springer, Cham (2016). https://doi.org/10.1007/978-3-319-40970-2_16
59. Zitoun, H., Michel, C., Rueher, M., Michel, L.: Search strategies for floating point constraint systems. In: Beck, J.C. (ed.) CP 2017. LNCS, vol. 10416, pp. 707–722. Springer, Cham (2017). https://doi.org/10.1007/978-3-319-66158-2_45

The Axiom Profiler: Understanding and Debugging SMT Quantifier Instantiations

Nils Becker, Peter Müller, and Alexander J. Summers[(⊠)]

Department of Computer Science, ETH Zurich, Zurich, Switzerland
nbecker@student.ethz.ch, {peter.mueller,alexander.summers}@inf.ethz.ch

Abstract. SMT solvers typically reason about universal quantifiers via E-matching: syntactic matching patterns for each quantifier prescribe shapes of ground terms whose presence in the SMT run will trigger quantifier instantiations. The effectiveness and performance of the SMT solver depend crucially on well-chosen patterns. Overly restrictive patterns cause relevant quantifier instantiations to be missed, while overly permissive patterns can cause performance degradation including non-termination if the solver gets stuck in a matching loop. Understanding and debugging such instantiation problems is an overwhelming task, due to the typically large number of quantifier instantiations and their non-trivial interactions with each other and other solver aspects. In this paper, we present the Axiom Profiler, a tool that enables users to analyse instantiation problems effectively, by filtering and visualising rich logging information from SMT runs. Our tool implements novel techniques for automatically detecting matching loops and explaining why they repeat indefinitely. We evaluated the tool on the full test suites of five existing program verifiers, where it discovered and explained multiple previously-unknown matching loops.

1 Introduction

SMT solvers are in prevalent use for a wide variety of applications, including constraint solving, program synthesis, software model checking, test generation and program verification. They combine highly-efficient propositional reasoning with natively supported theories and first-order quantifiers. Quantifiers are used frequently, for instance, to model additional mathematical theories and other domain-specific aspects of an encoded problem. In a program verification setting, for example, one might model a factorial function using an uninterpreted function `fact` from integers to integers and (partially) defining its meaning by means of quantified formulas such as $\forall i\!:\!\texttt{Int} :: \texttt{i > 1} \Rightarrow \texttt{fact(i) = i * fact(i-1)}$.

The support for quantifiers in SMT is not without a price; satisfiability of SMT assertions with quantifiers is undecidable in general. SMT solvers employ a range of heuristics for quantifier instantiation, the most widely-used (and the one focused on in this paper) being *E-matching* [7]. The E-matching approach

© The Author(s) 2019
T. Vojnar and L. Zhang (Eds.): TACAS 2019, Part I, LNCS 11427, pp. 99–116, 2019.
https://doi.org/10.1007/978-3-030-17462-0_6

attaches syntactic *patterns* to each universal quantifier, prescribing shapes of ground terms which, when encountered during the SMT solver's run, will trigger[1] a quantifier instantiation. For example, the pattern {fact(i)} on the quantifier above would indicate that a quantifier instantiation should be made whenever a function application fact(t) (for some term t) is encountered; the term t then prescribes the corresponding instantiation for the quantified variable.

The success of E-matching as a quantifier instantiation strategy depends crucially on well-chosen patterns: poorly chosen patterns can result in *too few* quantifier instantiations and failure to prove unsatisfiability of a formula, or *too many* quantifier instantiations, leading to poor and unpredictable performance, and even non-termination. For the factorial example above, a ground term fact(n) will match the pattern {fact(i)}, yielding an instantiation of the quantifier body, which includes the ground term fact(n-1); this term again matches the pattern, and, if it is never *provable* that n - x > 1 is definitely false, this process continues generating terms and quantifier instantiations indefinitely, in a *matching loop*.

Choosing suitable matching patterns is one of the main difficulties in using E-matching effectively [14,16]. It is extremely difficult to analyse *how* and *why* quantifier instantiations misbehave, especially for SMT problems with a large number of quantifiers[2]. Some solvers report high-level statistics (e.g. total number of quantifier instantiations); these are insufficient to determine whether quantifiers were instantiated as intended, and what the root causes of unintended instantiations are. SMT problems with poor performance are typically highly *brittle* with respect to changes in the input (due to internal pseudo-random heuristics), making performance problems difficult to reproduce or minimise; altering the example often unpredictably changes its behaviour. Conversely, problems with poor quantifier instantiation behaviour are not *always* slow; slowdowns typically manifest only when sufficiently many *interactions* with other aspects of the solver (e.g. theory reasoning) arise: extending problematic examples can cause sudden performance degradation, while the underlying cause existed in the original problem. There is therefore a clear need for tool support for uncovering, understanding and debugging quantifier instantiations made during SMT queries.

In this paper, we present the *Axiom Profiler*, a tool that addresses these challenges, providing comprehensive support for the manual and automated analysis of the quantifier instantiations performed by an SMT solver run, enabling a user to uncover and explain the underlying causes for quantifier-related problems. Our tool takes a log file generated by an SMT solver (in our case, Z3 [6]), interprets it, and provides a wide array of features and algorithms for displaying, navigating and analysing the data. Specifically, we present the following key contributions:

---

[1] In some tools, patterns are themselves alternatively called *triggers*.

[2] Such problems are common in e.g. program verification: for example, queries generated from Dafny's [13] test suite include an average of 2,500 quantifiers; it is not uncommon for hundreds to be instantiated hundreds of times for a single query: *cf.* Sect. 7.

1. We propose a *debugging recipe*, identifying the essential information needed and typical steps performed to analyse quantifier-related problems (Sect. 3).
2. We devise and present detailed *justifications* for each quantifier instantiation, including equality reasoning steps that enable the pattern match (Sect. 4).
3. We define an *instantiation graph* which reflects the causal relationships between quantifier instantiations, that is, which instantiations generate terms or equalities used to trigger which other instantiations (Sect. 5).
4. We present a novel automatic analysis over the causal graph which detects matching loops and explains why they occur (Sect. 6).
5. We provide an implementation. Our evaluation on test suites from five existing program verifiers reveals and explains (confirmed) previously-unknown matching loops (Sect. 7).

Our implementation extends the *VCC Axiom Profiler* [16], developed during the VCC [3] project at Microsoft Research. While this older tool (as well as the prior logging mechanism implemented for Z3) has been invaluable as a basis for our implementation, the features and contributions presented in this paper did not exist in the prior tool (aside from a basic explanation of single instantiations, omitting, e.g., equality reasoning steps used to justify a match). Our tool is open source and is available at https://bitbucket.org/viperproject/axiom-profiler/.

2   Background and Running Example

SMT Solving. SMT solvers handle input problems expressed as first-order logic assertions, including both *uninterpreted* function symbols and combinations of natively-supported *interpreted theories* (e.g., integers or reals). SMT problems can contain free uninterpreted symbols (e.g., unknown constants); the problem of SMT solving is to decide whether some interpretation for these symbols results in a model of the assertion (the assertion is *satisfiable*), or not (it is *unsatisfiable*).

The core of an SMT solver is a boolean SAT solving engine, which searches for a model by case-splitting on boolean literals, building up a *candidate model*. This core engine natively represents only quantifier-free propositional logic (including uninterpreted function symbols and equality). Transitive reasoning about equalities, as well as congruence closure properties (i.e., $a = b \Rightarrow f(a) = f(b)$ for functions f), is handled using an *E-graph* data structure [7], which efficiently represents the equivalence classes induced by currently-assumed equality facts (and represents disequality facts) over terms in the candidate model.

Running Example. Figure 1 shows our running example, an SMT query including a simplified modelling of program heaps and arrays, along with assertions (facts) encoding several properties: injectivity of the `slot` mapping (from integers to array locations), meaning of a `next` function (C-style pointer increment), and sortedness of an array `a`. The last two assertions represent an index `i` being somewhere early in array `a`, and an attempt to *prove* that the next array entry cannot be smaller than that at `i`; this proof goal is negated: any model found by the SMT solver is a counterexample to the proof goal. The `check-sat` command tells the solver to try to find a model for the conjunction of the assertions.

```
 1   ; ... uninterpreted sorts: Heap, Loc, Arr
 2   (declare-fun slot (Arr Int) Loc)           ; heap location for array slot
 3   (declare-fun lookup (Heap Loc) Int)        ; dereference on the heap
 4   (declare-fun next (Loc) Loc)               ; next slot: pointer increment
 5   (assert ∀ar:Arr, i: Int, k:Int :: {slot(ar,i),slot(ar,k)}
 6    i = k ∨ slot(ar,i) != slot(ar,k))         ; injectivity of slot (Q_inj)
 7   (assert ∀ar:Arr, i: Int :: {slot(ar,i)}
 8    next(slot(ar,i)) = slot(ar,i+1))          ; definition of next (Q_nxt)
 9   ; ... declare uninterpreted constants h : Heap, a : Arr, len,j : Int
10   (assert ∀i: Int. {lookup(h, slot(a,i))}  ; sortedness property (Q_srt)
11    i < 0 ∨ i >= len ∨ lookup(h, slot(a,i)) >= lookup(h, next(slot(a,i))))
12   (assert 0 <= j ∧ j+100 < len)  ; avoids trivial models (e.g., len = 0)
13   (assert (not (lookup(h, slot(a,j)) > (lookup(h, next(slot(a,j)))))))
14   (check-sat)
```

Fig. 1. Running example: a simple SMT encoding of a problem with heaps and arrays. We use pseudocode roughly based on the smtlib format, with presentational liberties.

Quantifier Instantiation via E-matching. The most commonly-employed method for supporting first-order quantifiers in an SMT solver is *E-matching* [7]. Each $\forall$-quantified subformula (after conversion to negation normal form) must be equipped with at least one *pattern*: a set of terms to pattern-match against in order to trigger a quantifier instantiation. We write patterns in braces preceding a quantifier body, such as {slot(ar,i)} in line 7 of Fig. 1. This pattern prescribes instantiating the quantifier when a ground term of the form slot(ar',i') is present (for some terms ar', i') in the E-graph. In this instantiation, ar is bound to (replaced by) ar' and i to i'. Patterns may contain multiple terms (e.g. {slot(ar,i),slot(ar,k)} in line 5), meaning that the quantifier is instantiated only if the E-graph contains a matching term for *each* of these pattern terms. It is also possible to specify multiple (alternative) patterns for the same quantifier.

The choice of patterns is critical to the behaviour of the SMT solver. Since quantifier instantiations will *only* be considered when matching terms are encountered, overly restrictive patterns cause relevant quantifier instantiations to be missed (in the extreme case, if *no* ground term matching the pattern is encountered, the solver will behave as if the quantified formula were not present). But overly *permissive* patterns can cause too many quantifier instantiations, resulting in bad performance and even non-termination. The example in Fig. 1 performs around 5000 quantifier instantiations before *unknown* is reported, indicating that the solver can neither deduce unsatisfiability, nor confirm that its candidate model is correct (the solver cannot be certain whether the candidate model could be ruled out by extra quantifier instantiations not allowed by the patterns).

Why are so many quantifier instantiations made, for such a simple problem? One issue is the quantifier labelled Q_{nxt}, with a matching term slot(ar',i'). The resulting instantiation yields the assertion next(slot(ar',i')) = slot(ar',i'+1), in which the (new) ground term slot(ar',i'+1) occurs; when added to the E-graph, this will trigger a new match, in a sequence which can continue indefinitely (the solver terminates only because we bound the depth to 100). Such a repeating instantiation pattern is called a *matching loop*, and is a key cause of poorly performing solver runs. We will show in the next sections how we can systematically discover this matching loop and other quantifier-related problems in our example.

As illustrated by the quantifier Q_{srt}, terms in patterns may include nested function applications. Matching of ground terms against such patterns is not purely syntactic, but is performed modulo the *equalities* in the candidate model. For example, adding `x = slot(a,3)` $\wedge$ `lookup(h, x) = 42` to the example will trigger a match against the pattern `{lookup(h, slot(a,j))}`. The application of `lookup` can be rewritten via the assumed equality to `lookup(h, slot(a,3))`, which matches the pattern. Thus, understanding an instantiation requires knowledge not only of the available terms, but also of the equalities derived by the solver.

3   A Debugging Recipe for SMT Quantifiers

Even with input problems as simple as that of Fig. 1, undesirable quantifier instantiations easily occur; realistic problems generated by, for instance, program verification tools typically include many hundreds of quantifiers, thousands of terms, and a complex mixture of propositional and theory-specific constraints. Diagnosing and understanding performance problems is further complicated by the fact that the observed slow-downs may not be due to the quantifier instantiations alone; quantifier instantiations may generate many additional theory-specific terms which slow theory reasoning in the SMT solver, and disjunctive formulas which slow the case-splitting boolean search.

In order to systematically understand a quantifier-related SMT problem, we identify (based on our experience) the following sequence of debugging questions:

1. *Are there suspicious numbers of quantifier instantiations?* If not, poor performance is due to other causes, such as non-linear arithmetic reasoning.
2. *Which quantifiers exist in the given SMT problem, and what are their patterns?* The answer to this question is crucial for the subsequent steps and is by no means trivial: in many SMT applications, some quantifiers may be generated by client tools, the SMT solver itself may preprocess input formulas heavily (and heuristically select missing patterns), and nested quantifiers may be added only when outer quantifiers are instantiated.
3. *Which quantifiers are instantiated many times?* Our experience shows that most quantifier instantiation problems are caused by relatively few quantifiers. The quantifiers identified here will be further examined in the next steps.
4. To identify problematic quantifiers, it is often useful to explore the interactions between several quantifiers by asking:
   (a) *Does the causal relationship between quantifier instantiations exhibit high branching: that is, a single quantifier instantiation leads directly to many subsequent instantiations?* A typical example is when an instantiation produces new terms that lead to a combinatorial explosion of matches for another quantifier. Once we have identified such a situation, we analyse the involved quantifiers according to step 5.

(b) *Are there long sequences of instantiations causing one another?* Long sequences often indicate matching loops. To determine whether that's the case, we ask: *Is there a repeating sequence which indicates a matching loop?* If so, we analyse the involved quantifiers (as described in step 5) to determine whether and how this sequence can repeat indefinitely.

5. Once we have identified potentially problematic quantifiers, we analyse their individual instantiations by asking:

   (a) *Which pattern of the instantiated quantifier is matched, and to which terms?* The answer is needed to understand the cause of the instantiation, and particularly for identifying overly-permissive matching patterns.

   (b) *What do these terms mean with respect to the input problem?* SMT terms can often get very large and, thus, difficult to understand; tracing them back to the original problems facilitates the analysis.

   (c) *Is the match triggered via equality reasoning? Where do the necessary terms and equalities originate from?* Such matches are difficult to detect by manually inspecting the input problem because the patterns and the matching terms look syntactically different; instantiation problems that involve equality reasoning are especially difficult to debug by hand.

Except for the very first step in this recipe, efficiently answering these questions is impractical without tool support; our Axiom Profiler now provides this support.

4   Visualising Quantifier Instantiations

The Axiom Profiler takes as input a log file produced by Z3 and provides a wide range of features for analysing the performed quantifier instantiations. In this section, we show the key features for visualising and navigating the data from the log file. In the subsequent sections, we demonstrate how to analyse quantifier instantiation problems, both manually and automatically.

Figure 2 shows a screenshot for the example from Fig. 1. The tool shows in the middle panel raw data on quantifier instantiations from the log file plus some summary statistics, in the right-hand panel an instantiation graph with causal relationships between instantiations, and in the left-hand panel details of selected instantiations. We describe the three panels in the following.

Raw Data. The middle panel displays the raw data on quantifier instantiations, organised per quantifier as an (XML-like) hierarchy of fields; we inherited this view from the VCC Axiom Profiler [16]. The top-level statistics are useful as an overview for steps 1–3 of our debugging recipe (Sect. 3). Each line corresponds to an individual quantifier and shows its total number of instantiations ("`#instances`"). Manually navigating the underlying raw data is possible, but typically impractical.

In our example 11 quantifiers are listed: the first 3 are from our input problem; the remaining 8 are generated internally by Z3 (they are never instantiated, and we ignore them for our discussion). We can see there are more than 5000 quantifier instantiations in total; all three quantifiers are instantiated many times.

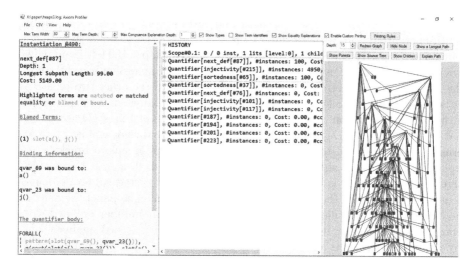

Fig. 2. A visualisation of the quantifier instantiations for the example in Fig. 1. (Colour figure online)

Instantiation Graph. The right-hand panel is one of the most important features of our tool. The *instantiation graph* visualises *causal relationships* between quantifier instantiations, which allows us to identify the high-branching and long-sequence scenarios described in step 4 of our debugging recipe. The nodes in the graph represent quantifier instantiations; a (directed) edge indicates that the source node provides either a term which was matched in order to trigger the successor node, or an equality used to trigger the match. Information about equalities is important for step 5c of our recipe, as we will discuss in Sect. 5.

Graph nodes are coloured, where each colour indicates a different quantifier; all instantiations of the same quantifier are coloured identically. The colours make it easy to spot prevalent quantifiers, and to visually identify patterns such as repeating sequences down a long path, which often indicate a matching loop.

Since instantiation graphs can get very large, we provide various filters, for instance, to control the maximum depth to which the graph is displayed, or to expand and collapse the children of a node. It is also possible to display the nodes with the highest number of children (to detect high branching, see step 4a) or the nodes starting the longest paths, as well as longest path starting from a node, which are features especially useful for detecting matching loops.

Our running example contains several instantiation problems. For instance, the instantiation graph in Fig. 2 shows a very large number of purple nodes (the quantifier labelled Q_{inj} in Fig. 1) and two sequences of yellow (the Q_{nxt} quantifier) and green (Q_{srt}) nodes, which indicate potential matching loops. Whereas the *number* of instantiations is also visible from the raw data, identifying such groupings and patterns is made possible by the instantiation graph.

Instantiation Details. The raw data and instantiation graph allow one to identify potentially-problematic quantifiers according to the first four steps of our debugging recipe. To support the analysis described in step 5, the left-hand panel provides details of all relevant information about specific quantifier instantiations. The instantiation of interest can be selected in either of the other two panels.

Selecting the top node in the graph from our example yields an explanation of the first instantiation of the (Q_{nxt}) quantifier. The panel lists *blamed terms*: that is, terms in the E-graph whose subterms were matched against the patterns; here, the blamed term is `slot(a,j)` (the numbers in square brackets are explained below). The subterm of a blamed term matched against the pattern (here, the whole term) is highlighted in gold, while the nested subterms bound to quantified variables (here, `a` and `j`) are shown in blue. The panel then shows the bindings per quantified variable (named by a unique number prefixed with "`qvar_`"), the quantifier itself (highlighting the pattern matched against), and any new resulting terms added to the E-graph. In particular, the bound terms and pattern matched against provide the information needed for step 5a of the debugging recipe.

In realistic examples, presenting the relevant terms readably can be a challenge, for which we provide a variety of features. Since the E-graph often contains only partial information about interpreted literals, it can be useful to annotate function applications and constants with a numeric *term identifier* (shown in square brackets); these identifiers are generated by Z3. For example, all integer-typed terms are simply represented by `Int()` here; the term identifiers allow us to identify identical terms, even though their precise meanings are unknown. Since identifiers can also make large terms harder to read, enabling them is optional.

For some problems, the relevant terms can get extremely large. To present terms in a meaningful form (see step 5b of our recipe), our tool provides facilities for defining custom printing rules. Typical use cases include simplifying names, and rendering those representing operators (such as a list append function) with infix syntax. In addition, our tool allows one to choose the depth to which terms are printed; we use ... to replace subterms below this depth.

5   Manual Analysis of Instantiation Problems

In this section, we demonstrate on the example from Fig. 1 how to use the features of the Axiom Profiler to manually analyse and debug quantifier instantiation problems. The *automatic* analyses provided by our tool will be discussed in Sect. 6.

Simple Matching Loops. Since all three quantifiers in our example lead to many instantiations, we start narrowing down the problem by looking for matching loops (step 4b in the recipe). Filtering for nodes starting the longest paths displays the sub-graph on the left of Fig. 3. One can see two parallel sequences of instantiations; an initial one of yellow (Q_{nxt}) instantiations, and a second of green (Q_{srt}) instantiations. Since the (Q_{nxt}) sequence is self-contained (there are

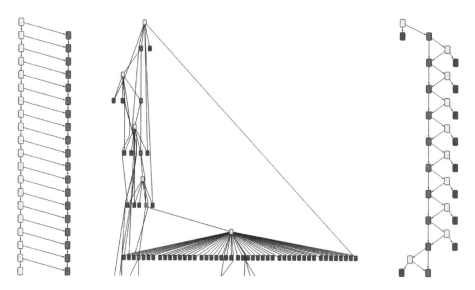

Fig. 3. Sub-graphs of the instantiation graph for the example in Fig. 1 showing the simple matching loop, high branching, and the matching loop with equality reasoning. Instantiations of Q_{nxt} are yellow, Q_{srt} is green, and Q_{inj} is purple. (Colour figure online)

no incoming edges from outside of these nodes), we investigate this one first. By selecting and inspecting the details of these instantiations (in the left-hand panel) in turn, we see that all after the first look very similar: each blames a term of the shape `slot(a, Int() + j)` (`Int()` abstracts all constants from the integer theory) and produces (among others) a new term of this same shape. The term identifiers show that the new term from each instantiation is the one blamed by the next, indicating a matching loop. In Sect. 6, we will show how the Axiom Profiler can perform this entire analysis automatically.

The detected matching loop for Q_{nxt} is the one we discussed in Sect. 2. It can be fixed by selecting a more restrictive pattern for the Q_{nxt} quantifier, namely `{next(slot(a,i))}`, only allowing instantiations when the `next` function is applied to an array slot. In particular, instantiating the quantifier does not produce a new term of this shape, which breaks the matching loop. Re-running Z3 on the fixed example reduces the number of quantifier instantiations to around 1400.

High Branching. Besides long paths, high branching may point to potentially problematic quantifiers (see step 4a of our debugging recipe). Once we have fixed the matching loop described above, we use the "Most Children" filter (available from "Redraw Graph") to identify the nodes with highest branching factor; subsequently using "Show Children" on one of these nodes results in the sub-graph in the middle of Fig. 3. This node has 42 child nodes, of which 41 are instantiations of the injectivity property (Q_{inj}). The pattern for this quantifier is `{slot(a,i),slot(a,k)}`, so each instantiation requires two applications of the `slot` function. Examining the instantiation details reveals that the 41 instantiations all share one of the two `slot` terms, while the other varies. The common term is produced by the parent node, and then combined with many previously-existing terms to trigger the instantiation 41 times.

The underlying problem is that the pattern yields a number of instantiations that is quadratic in the number of `slot` terms. This is a known "anti-pattern" for expressing injectivity properties; an alternative is to add an inverse function and axioms expressing this fact [5], which can then match linearly in the number of `slot` terms. For simple injectivity axioms such as that from our example, Z3 will even perform this rewriting for us; we disabled this option for the sake of illustration. Enabling this reduces the number of quantifier instantiations to 152.

Equality Explanations. The remaining instantiations in our example form a long path, which may indicate another matching loop. As shown on the right of Fig. 3, the path alternates the quantifiers Q_{nxt} and Q_{srt}. Unlike for the simple matching loop we uncovered earlier in this section, neither of the two quantifiers now produces a term that *directly* matches the pattern for Q_{srt}. Instead, subsequent instantiations are triggered by rewriting terms via equalities.

The Axiom Profiler explains the required rewriting steps to support step 5c of the recipe. In particular, the instantiation details shown include, besides the blamed terms, the equalities used and how they can yield a term that matches the necessary pattern. In our example, the very first instantiation blames a term `lookup(h, next(slot(a, j)))` and shows the following relevant equality:

```
(2)  next(slot(a, j))
       = (next_def[#56])
     slot(a, +(Int(), j))
```

where (2) is a number for this equality, and the (`next_def[#56]`) annotation after the equality symbol is the *justification* for the equality; in this case, it names a quantifier (the Q_{nxt} quantifier in Fig. 1). In general, equality justifications can be more complex; we contributed code for Z3 to log relevant information, letting us reconstruct transitive equality steps, theory-generated equalities, and congruence closure steps (for which a recursive equality explanation can also be generated).

By inspecting each node's blamed terms and relevant equality information, it is possible to indeed uncover a matching loop still present in this version of our example. In brief: instantiating the Q_{srt} quantifier produces a term that triggers an instantiation of the Q_{nxt} quantifier, which produces equality (2). This equality is then used to rewrite the same term, resulting in another match for the Q_{srt} quantifier, and so on. Matching up all relevant terms and assembling the details of this explanation manually remains somewhat laborious; in the next section, we show a more detailed explanation which our tool produces *automatically*.

6   Automated Explanation of Matching Loops

The previous section illustrated how the Axiom Profiler supports the manual analysis of quantifier instantiation problems. For the common and severe problem of matching loops, our tool is also able to produce such explanations *automatically*, reducing the necessary debugging effort significantly.

Consider the example from Fig. 1, after fixing the first of the two matching loops as explained in the previous section. Recall that our *manual analysis* revealed that the second matching loop consists of repeated instantiations of quantifier Q_{srt}, which are sustained via equalities obtained from the quantifier Q_{nxt}. Applying our *automated analysis* produces the following explanation: (1) It identifies a potential matching loop involving the quantifiers Q_{nxt} and Q_{srt}. (2) It synthesises a template term `lookup(h, next(slot(a,`T_1`))` whose presence, for any term T_1, sets off the matching loop. (3) It explains step by step: (a) how such a term triggers the quantifier Q_{nxt} (recall that we fixed the pattern to `{next(slot(ar,i))}`) to produce the equality `next(slot(a,`T_1`))=slot(a,`T_1`+Int())`, (b) how this equality is used to rewrite the template term to `lookup(h, slot(a,`T_1`+Int())`, (c) that the resulting term causes an instantiation of quantifier Q_{srt} to produce the term `lookup(h, next(slot(a,`T_1`+Int()))`, and (d) how this term sets off the next iteration by using T_1`+Int()` for T_1. Our algorithm to produce such explanations consists of four main steps, which we explain in the remainder of this section.

Step 1: Selecting Paths. Our algorithm starts by selecting a path through the instantiation graph that represents a likely matching loop. The user can influence this choice by selecting a node that must be on the path and by selecting a sub-graph that must contain the path. The algorithm then chooses a path heuristically, favouring long paths and paths with many instantiations per quantifier (more precisely, per matched pattern). Since it is common that paths contain several instantiations before actually entering a matching loop, our algorithm prunes path prefixes if their quantifiers do not occur frequently in the rest of the path.

Step 2: Identifying Repeating Sequences. Matching loops cause repeated sequences of quantifier instantiations. We abstract the instantiations on a path to a *string* (instantiations of the same quantifier and pattern get the same character), and efficiently find the substring (subsequence of instantiations) repeating *most often* using suffix trees [23]; in our example, this subsequence is Q_{nxt}, Q_{srt}.

Step 3: Generalising Repetitions. Each repetition of the subsequence identified in the previous step potentially represents an iteration of a matching loop. To produce a generalised explanation for the entire loop, we first produce explanations of each individual repetition and then generalise those explanations.

The automatic explanation of the individual repetitions works as summarised in steps 5a and 5c of our debugging recipe, and uses the same functionality that we used for the manual analysis in the previous section. In our example, the analysis reveals that the first repetition of the sequence is triggered by the term lookup(h,slot(a,i)), which comes from the assertion in line 13. This term triggers an instantiation of the quantifier Q_{srt}, which in turn triggers the quantifier Q_{nxt} to produce the equality next(slot(a,i))=next(slot(a,i+1)). Rewriting the term lookup(h,next(slot(a,i))) from the quantifier Q_{srt} with this equality produces lookup(h,slot(a,i+1)). Performing this analysis on the second repetition shows that it is triggered by exactly this term and, after the analogous sequence of steps, produces lookup(h,slot(a,i+2)), and so on.

The explanations for the individual repetitions of the sequence will differ in the exact terms they blame and equalities they use. However, since each repetition triggers the same patterns of the same quantifiers, these terms and equalities have term structure in common. We extract this common structure by performing anti-unification [19], that is, by replacing each position in which subterms *disagree* with fresh symbolic variables. In our example, anti-unification of the blamed terms for the first instantiation of each repetition produces lookup(h,slot(a,T_1)), that is, the disagreeing terms i, i+1, etc. have been replaced by the fresh symbolic variable T_1. Similarly, the used equalities are anti-unified to next(slot(a,T_2))=next(slot(a,T_3+Int())).

Introducing a fresh symbolic variable in *each* such position loses information for terms originally occurring multiple times. For instance, in our example, anti-unifying the blamed terms and the used equalities introduces three symbolic variables T_1, T_2, T_3 even though the disagreeing terms are equal in each repetition of the sequence. This equality is vital for the explanation of the matching loop.

In simple examples such as this one, we need only keep the first introduced symbolic variable T; in general there may be different choices which can mutually express each other via function applications (e.g. $T = f(T')$ and $T' = g(T)$, for which *either* symbolic variable would be sufficient). We handle the general problem of selecting which symbolic variables to keep by building a directed graph to represent this expressibility relation between symbolic variables. We have developed an algorithm to efficiently select *some* subset of the symbolic variables with no redundant elements based on this graph; we then rewrite all generalised terms and equalities using only these variables. In our example, the graph reflects $T_1 \rightleftarrows T_2 \rightleftarrows T_3$ and, thus, we are able to rewrite the generalised equality to use only T_1 resulting in next(slot(a,T_1))=next(slot(a,T_1+Int())).

Step 4: Characterising Matching Loops. Once we have generalised templates of the blamed terms and equalities, we use these to express the terms used to begin the *next* iteration of the repeating pattern; if this is a term with *additional* structure, we classify the overall path explained as a matching loop. In our example, we see that where T_1 was used, T_1+Int() is used in the next iteration, from which we conclude that this is indeed a matching loop. We add the information about these terms used to start the *next* iteration of the loop to our finalised explanations (*cf.* (d) in the explanation starting this section).

7   Implementation and Evaluation

Our work is implemented as a stand-alone application. We also submitted (accepted) patches to Z3 to obtain the full logging information that our tool requires; we now record equalities used for matching patterns, and justifications for *how* these equalities were derived from the solver's E-graph. These logging mechanisms are enabled via the additional `trace=true proof=true` logging options. Other SMT solvers could produce the same information (information on terms, equalities and matches), and reuse our work.

Example	Tool	#quants	#instantiations	#loops	longest	= used
compiler	Why3	1,473	195,961	1	12	
kmp	Why3	35	1,376	1	18	
blocking_semantics5	Why3	86	210,291	2	10	
fibonacci	Why3	234	32,647	2	19	
induction	Why3	2	197	1	20	
sf	Why3	5	2,020	2	16	
sumrange	Why3	10	1,837	2	19	
vstte10_queens	Why3	16	194	1	18	
unionfind	Viper	98	285,311	1	100	✓
linked_list_qp_append	Viper	196	17,470	1	96	
testHistoryLemmasPVL	Viper	4	271	2	100	✓
testHistoryThreadsLemmasPVL	Viper	4	270	2	100	✓
tree_delete_min	Viper	19	6,709	1	96	✓
list_insert	Viper	24	287,559	1	94	✓
list_insert_heuristics	Viper	23	181,392	1	94	✓
tree_delete_min_heuristics	Viper	19	29,747	1	96	✓
tree_delete_min_no_assert	Viper	19	120,776	1	98	✓
ComputationsLoop	Dafny	16	518	1	33	
ComputationsLoop2	Dafny	20	519	1	33	
NoTypeArgs	Dafny	59	40,110	1	98	✓
Lucas-down	Dafny	86	3,412	1	99	
Lucas-up	Dafny	129	46,877	1	91	

Fig. 4. An overview of the matching loops found in examples flagged by the automated analysis. "#quants" indicated the no. of quantifiers present (we only count those instantiated at least once). "longest" indicates the length of the longest path; "= used" indicates whether equality explanations occur in the generalised path explanation for this matching loop. Examples exhibiting similar matching loops are grouped together.

In order to demonstrate that the Axiom Profiler can be used to identify and help explain matching loops in real world problems, we ran experiments on a total of 34,159 SMT files, corresponding to the full test suites of a selection of verification tools which use Z3 as a backend: F* [22] (6,281 files), Why3 [10] (26,258 files), Viper (887 files) [18], Nagini [9] (266 files) and Dafny [13] (467 files)). Using a command-line interface for our tool, we analysed each of these files in an attempt to find matching loops. We note that since these are expert-written, polished (and, presumably performant) test suite examples, one might expect most, if not all such issues to have been eliminated.

For each file, the tool analysed the 40 longest paths in the instantiation graph, searching for matching loops using the analysis of Sect. 6. In order to eliminate most false positives (since paths were found with no user introspection, and repeating patterns do not always indicate matching loops), we searched for paths with at least *10* repetitions of some quantifier instantiation sequence. We found 51 such files, and inspected each by hand for matching loops, using the techniques of Sects. 4 and 6 to identify whether matching loops are present (false positives also occurred: for example, in tools which model lookups in program heaps using axioms, there are often long chains of instantiations of the same axiom but for different versions of the heap). For all investigated examples, our tool analyses these paths in a second or two: this manual classification is very efficient.

Figure 4 summarises the matching loops we discovered. We found 28 previously-unknown matching loops: 13 from Why3, 10 from Viper and 5 from Dafny; we didn't find any matching loops in the F* or Nagini suites (which could be due to highly-tuned or restrictive triggers). The matching loops we detected were of many varieties. In Why3, 10 stemmed from modelling recursively-defined concepts (e.g. $\forall$x: Int even(x). even(x) $\implies$ even(x + 2)). We also found more complex matching loops in Why3's axiomatization of lists and arrays. For example, an array axiom $\forall$x, y. {mk_ref(x,y)}. sort(ref(x),mk_ref(x,y)) yields a term matching a second axiom, yielding contents(ref(T_1), mk_ref(ref(T_1), mk_ref(T_1, T_2))). The outer mk_ref term is new; we can instantiate the first axiom again. Why3 leaves the selection of most patterns to the SMT-solver, and uses a timeout (along with alternative solvers); this explains the potential for matching loops.

Viper provides two verifiers; we extracted and ran SMT queries for both. We found 4 causes of matching loops; some manifested in multiple files. These include direct matching loops and more complex cases: e.g. in the testHistoryLemmasPVL example, an associativity axiom allows repeatedly generating new term structure, which feeds a parallel matching loop concerning a recursive function definition.

For Dafny, we also found some simple and some complex cases. One axiom $\forall$a, b, c {app(a, app(b, c))}. app(a, app(b, c)) = app(app(a, b), c) expressing associativity of a concatenation operator[3], in combination with a case-split assumption made by Z3 that one term a' instantiated for a is equal to Nil, and the known property Nil=app(Nil,Nil), allows rewriting the right-hand-side term learned from each instantiation with a new app application on which the same axiom can be matched. A similar problem is described by Moskal [16].

In all cases (including those which, when inspected manually turned out to be false positives), following our debugging recipe and applying the Axiom Profiler's features allowed us to quickly isolate and explain the matching loops present. We have communicated our findings to the respective tool authors, who all confirmed that these matching loops were previously-unknown and that they plan to investigate them further (potentially using the Axiom Profiler itself).

---

[3] The actual function name is concat; we abbreviate for readability.

8   Related Work

Since its origin in the Simplify prover [7], E-matching has been adapted and improved in implementations for a variety of SMT solvers [1, 2, 4, 11, 17]. Since E-matching-based instantiation gives weak guarantees for *satisfiable* problems (typically returning *unknown* as an outcome), for problem domains where satisfiability (and a corresponding model) is the desired outcome, alternative instantiation techniques have been proposed [12, 20, 21]. For specific domains, these are often preferable, but for problems in which many external concepts need to be modelled with quantifiers, such as deductive program verification, E-matching remains the only general solution. While our work focuses on E-matching support, it would be interesting future work to investigate to what extent we could also provide useful information about other quantifier instantiation strategies.

As discussed in the Introduction, we build upon the *VCC Axiom Profiler* [16] tool, which defined first versions of the logging in Z3 (without equality information), the raw data display (retained in our middle panel) and a basic display of information per quantifier, without explanations of equalities used to justify matches. The contributions of this paper make it practical to quickly navigate and understand even complicated SMT runs, in ways impossible with the previous tool. Nonetheless, this prior tool was a very helpful basis for our implementation.

The serious challenges of pattern selection have warranted papers both on expert strategies [14, 16], and for formalising the logical meaning of quantifiers equipped with patterns [8]. Various SMT solvers select patterns for quantifiers automatically (if omitted by the user). To reduce the uncertainty introduced in this way, many program verification tools select their own patterns when encoding to SMT (e.g., VCC [3], Viper [18], Dafny [13]). Leino and Pit-Claudel [15] present a technique for selecting patterns in Dafny while avoiding direct matching loops; the matching loops we found in Dafny tests arose in spite of this functionality.

9   Conclusions

In this paper, we presented a comprehensive solution for the analysis of quantifier instantiations in SMT solvers. Our newly-developed Axiom Profiler enables a user to effectively explore and understand the quantifier instantiations performed by an SMT run, their connections and potentially-problematic patterns which arise (e.g. due to matching loops). Our instantiation graph, customisable visualisation of information and automatic explanations for matching loops make investigating even complex SMT queries practical in reasonable time. Furthermore, we were able to script these analyses to uncover matching loops in a variety of test suites for existing tools; it would be interesting to analyse further tools in this way.

As future work, we plan to investigate tighter integration with tools that build on SMT solvers, e.g. to represent terms at a higher level of abstraction. We also plan to investigate whether theory-reasoning steps in the SMT solver can be made less opaque to our tool, especially with respect to justifying equalities. Automating explanations for matching loops with repeating structures more complex than single paths would be a challenging extension of our techniques.

Acknowledgements. We thank Frederik Rothenberger for his substantial work on visualisation features. We are grateful to Marco Eilers, Jean-Christophe Filliâtre, Rustan Leino, Nikhil Swamy for providing their test suites and advice on their verification tools. We thank Nikolaj Bjørner for his assistance with Z3, and Michał Moskal for generous advice and feedback on earlier versions of the tool. Finally, we are very grateful to Marco Eilers, Malte Schwerhoff and Arshavir Ter-Gabrielyan, for providing extensive feedback on our tool and paper drafts.

References

1. Bansal, K., Reynolds, A., King, T., Barrett, C., Wies, T.: Deciding local theory extensions via E-matching. In: Kroening, D., Păsăreanu, C.S. (eds.) CAV 2015, Part II. LNCS, vol. 9207, pp. 87–105. Springer, Cham (2015). https://doi.org/10.1007/978-3-319-21668-3_6

2. Barrett, C., et al.: CVC4. In: Gopalakrishnan, G., Qadeer, S. (eds.) CAV 2011. LNCS, vol. 6806, pp. 171–177. Springer, Heidelberg (2011). https://doi.org/10.1007/978-3-642-22110-1_14

3. Cohen, E., et al.: VCC: a practical system for verifying concurrent C. In: Berghofer, S., Nipkow, T., Urban, C., Wenzel, M. (eds.) TPHOLs 2009. LNCS, vol. 5674, pp. 23–42. Springer, Heidelberg (2009). https://doi.org/10.1007/978-3-642-03359-9_2

4. de Moura, L., Bjørner, N.: Efficient E-matching for SMT solvers. In: Pfenning, F. (ed.) CADE 2007. LNCS (LNAI), vol. 4603, pp. 183–198. Springer, Heidelberg (2007). https://doi.org/10.1007/978-3-540-73595-3_13

5. de Moura, L., Bjørner, N.: Z3 - a tutorial. Technical report, Microsoft Research (2010)

6. de Moura, L., Bjørner, N.: Z3: an efficient SMT solver. In: Ramakrishnan, C.R., Rehof, J. (eds.) TACAS 2008. LNCS, vol. 4963, pp. 337–340. Springer, Heidelberg (2008). https://doi.org/10.1007/978-3-540-78800-3_24

7. Detlefs, D., Nelson, G., Saxe, J.B.: Simplify: a theorem prover for program checking. J. ACM **52**(3), 365–473 (2005)

8. Dross, C., Conchon, S., Kanig, J., Paskevich, A.: Reasoning with triggers. In: Fontaine, P., Goel, A. (eds.) Satisfiability Modulo Theories (SMT). EPiC Series in Computing, vol. 20, pp. 22–31. EasyChair (2012)

9. Eilers, M., Müller, P.: Nagini: a static verifier for Python. In: Chockler, H., Weissenbacher, G. (eds.) CAV 2018. LNCS, vol. 10981, pp. 596–603. Springer, Cham (2018). https://doi.org/10.1007/978-3-319-96145-3_33

10. Filliâtre, J.-C., Paskevich, A.: Why3 — where programs meet provers. In: Felleisen, M., Gardner, P. (eds.) ESOP 2013. LNCS, vol. 7792, pp. 125–128. Springer, Heidelberg (2013). https://doi.org/10.1007/978-3-642-37036-6_8

11. Ge, Y., Barrett, C., Tinelli, C.: Solving quantified verification conditions using satisfiability modulo theories. In: Pfenning, F. (ed.) CADE 2007. LNCS (LNAI), vol. 4603, pp. 167–182. Springer, Heidelberg (2007). https://doi.org/10.1007/978-3-540-73595-3_12

12. Ge, Y., de Moura, L.: Complete instantiation for quantified formulas in satisfiabiliby modulo theories. In: Bouajjani, A., Maler, O. (eds.) CAV 2009. LNCS, vol. 5643, pp. 306–320. Springer, Heidelberg (2009). https://doi.org/10.1007/978-3-642-02658-4_25

13. Leino, K.R.M.: Dafny: an automatic program verifier for functional correctness. In: Clarke, E.M., Voronkov, A. (eds.) LPAR 2010. LNCS (LNAI), vol. 6355, pp. 348–370. Springer, Heidelberg (2010). https://doi.org/10.1007/978-3-642-17511-4_20

14. Leino, K.R.M., Monahan, R.: Reasoning about comprehensions with first-order SMT solvers. In: Proceedings of the 2009 ACM Symposium on Applied Computing, SAC 2009, pp. 615–622. ACM, New York (2009)

15. Leino, K.R.M., Pit-Claudel, C.: Trigger selection strategies to stabilize program verifiers. In: Chaudhuri, S., Farzan, A. (eds.) CAV 2016, Part I. LNCS, vol. 9779, pp. 361–381. Springer, Cham (2016). https://doi.org/10.1007/978-3-319-41528-4_20

16. Moskal, M.: Programming with triggers. In: SMT. ACM International Conference Proceeding Series, vol. 375, pp. 20–29. ACM (2009)

17. Moskal, M., Lopuszański, J., Kiniry, J.R.: E-matching for fun and profit. Electron. Notes Theor. Comput. Sci. **198**(2), 19–35 (2008)

18. Müller, P., Schwerhoff, M., Summers, A.J.: Viper: a verification infrastructure for permission-based reasoning. In: Jobstmann, B., Leino, K.R.M. (eds.) VMCAI 2016. LNCS, vol. 9583, pp. 41–62. Springer, Heidelberg (2016). https://doi.org/10.1007/978-3-662-49122-5_2

19. Plotkin, G.D.: A note on inductive generalization. In: Meltzer, B., Michie, D. (eds.) Machine Intelligence, pp. 153–163. Edinburgh University Press, Edinburgh (1970)

20. Reynolds, A., Tinelli, C., de Moura, L.: Finding conflicting instances of quantified formulas in SMT. In: Proceedings of the 14th Conference on Formal Methods in Computer-Aided Design, FMCAD 2014, pp. 31:195–31:202. FMCAD Inc., Austin (2014)

21. Reynolds, A., Tinelli, C., Goel, A., Krstić, S., Deters, M., Barrett, C.: Quantifier instantiation techniques for finite model finding in SMT. In: Bonacina, M.P. (ed.) CADE 2013. LNCS (LNAI), vol. 7898, pp. 377–391. Springer, Heidelberg (2013). https://doi.org/10.1007/978-3-642-38574-2_26

22. Swamy, N., Chen, J., Fournet, C., Strub, P.-Y., Bhargavan, K., Yang, J.: Secure distributed programming with value-dependent types. In: Proceedings of the 16th ACM SIGPLAN International Conference on Functional Programming, ICFP 2011, pp. 266–278. ACM, New York (2011)

23. Weiner, P.: Linear pattern matching algorithms. In: Switching and Automata Theory (SWAT), pp. 1–11. IEEE (1973)

On the Empirical Time Complexity of Scale-Free 3-SAT at the Phase Transition

Thomas Bläsius[1]([⊠]), Tobias Friedrich[1], and Andrew M. Sutton[2]

[1] Hasso Plattner Institute, Potsdam, Germany
thomas.blaesius@hpi.de
[2] University of Minnesota Duluth, Duluth, MN, USA

Abstract. The hardness of formulas at the solubility phase transition of random propositional satisfiability (SAT) has been intensely studied for decades both empirically and theoretically. Solvers based on stochastic local search (SLS) appear to scale very well at the critical threshold, while complete backtracking solvers exhibit exponential scaling. On industrial SAT instances, this phenomenon is inverted: backtracking solvers can tackle large industrial problems, where SLS-based solvers appear to stall. Industrial instances exhibit sharply different structure than uniform random instances. Among many other properties, they are often *heterogeneous* in the sense that some variables appear in many while others appear in only few clauses.

We conjecture that the *heterogeneity* of SAT formulas alone already contributes to the trade-off in performance between SLS solvers and complete backtracking solvers. We empirically determine how the run time of SLS vs. backtracking solvers depends on the heterogeneity of the input, which is controlled by drawing variables according to a scale-free distribution. Our experiments reveal that the efficiency of complete solvers at the phase transition is strongly related to the heterogeneity of the degree distribution. We report results that suggest the depth of satisfying assignments in complete search trees is influenced by the level of heterogeneity as measured by a power-law exponent. We also find that incomplete SLS solvers, which scale well on uniform instances, are not affected by heterogeneity. The main contribution of this paper utilizes the scale-free random 3-SAT model to isolate heterogeneity as an important factor in the scaling discrepancy between complete and SLS solvers at the uniform phase transition found in previous works.

1 Introduction

The worst-case time complexity of propositional satisfiability (SAT) entails that no known algorithm can solve it in polynomial time [12]. Nevertheless, many large industrial SAT instances can be solved efficiently in practice by modern solvers. So far, this discrepancy is not well-understood.

Studying random SAT instances provides a way to explain this discrepancy between theory and practice as it replaces the worst case with the average case.

T. Vojnar and L. Zhang (Eds.): TACAS 2019, Part I, LNCS 11427, pp. 117–134, 2019.
https://doi.org/10.1007/978-3-030-17462-0_7

A large amount of both theoretical and experimental research effort focuses almost exclusively on the *uniform random* distribution. Uniform random SAT instances are generated by choosing, for each clause, the variables included in this clause uniformly at random among all variables. Uniform random formulas are easy to construct, and are comparatively more accessible to probabilistic analysis due to their uniformity and the stochastic independence of choices. The analysis of this model can provide valuable insights into the SAT problem in general and has led to the development of tools that are useful also in other areas. However, considering the average-case complexity of solving uniform random formulas cannot explain why SAT solvers work well in practice: in the interesting case that the clause-variable ratio is close to the satisfiability threshold (i.e., the formulas are not trivially satisfiable or trivially unsatisfiable), SAT solvers that perform well on industrial instances struggle to solve the randomly generated formulas fast and algorithms tuned for random formulas perform poorly on industrial instances [14,27,33].

The comparative efficiency of existing solvers on real-world SAT instances is somewhat surprising given not only worst-case complexity theoretic results, but also the apparent hardness of uniform random formulas sampled from the critically-constrained regime [8,31]. Katsirelos and Simon [26] comment that even though the ingredients for building a good SAT solver are mostly known, we still currently cannot explain their strong performance on real-world problems.

This picture is further complicated by the fact that solvers based on stochastic local search (SLS) appear to scale *polynomially* in the critically constrained region of uniform random SAT, whereas complete backtracking solvers scale *exponentially* on these formulas [32]. We are interested in identifying structural aspects of formulas that do not occur in uniform random instances, but can somehow be exploited by solvers.

Industrial SAT instances are complex, and possess many structural characteristics. Among these are *modularity* [4], *heterogeneity* [2], *self-similarity* [1], and *locality* [22]. Modularity measures how well the formula (when modeled as a graph representing the inclusion relation between variables and clauses) can be separated into communities with many internal and few external connections. It is generally assumed that the high modularity of industrial instances is one of the main reasons for the good performance of SAT solvers. Though it is possible to develop models that generate formulas with high modularity [21,35], there is, however, no established model with this property. Enforcing high modularity can lead to complicated stochastic dependencies, making analysis difficult.

Heterogeneity measures the imbalance in distribution of variables over the clauses of the formula. A highly heterogeneous formula contains only few variables that appear in many clauses and many variables appearing in few clauses. Many industrial instances, particularly from formal verification, exhibit a high heterogeneity. Ansótegui, Bonet, and Levy [3] proposed a number of non-uniform models that produce heterogeneous instances. One such model they introduced was the *scale-free* model. Often, the degree distribution (the *degree* of a variable is the number of clauses containing it as a literal) roughly follows a *power-law* [2], i.e., the number of variables of degree d is proportional to $d^{-\beta}$.

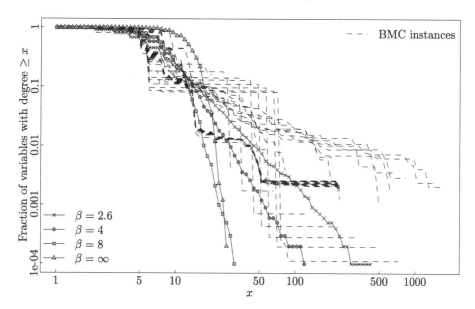

Fig. 1. Empirical cumulative degree distributions on power-law formulas for different β, $n = 10000$, and hardware model checking instances from SAT 2017 competition. Power-law distributions appear as a line on a log-log plot with slope determined by β. As β increases, we observe the power-law distributions converging to uniform ($\beta = \infty$).

Here β is the *power-law exponent*. Figure 1 illustrates a number of empirical cumulative degree distributions for both industrial and synthetic power-law formulas. The industrial formulas come from the SAT-encoded deep bound hardware model checking instance benchmarks submitted to the 2017 SAT competition [7] that had measured empirical power law exponents below 5.

A degree distribution that follows a power law is only a sufficient condition for heterogeneity. Nevertheless, we argue that the scale-free model allows for fine-tuned parametric control over the extent of heterogeneity in the form of the power-law exponent β (see Proposition 1).

No single one of the above properties (e.g., heterogeneity, modularity, locality, etc.) can completely characterize the time scaling effects observed on industrial instances vs. uniform random instances. However, a first step toward explaining the performance of SAT solvers in different environments is to isolate these features and determine what kinds of structural properties do influence the run time of different solvers. Our goal in this paper is to empirically determine the impact of heterogeneity (as produced by a scale-free degree distribution) on the run time of SLS-based vs. complete backtracking solvers.[1]

Though it seems natural that a more realistic model is better suited to explain the run times observed in practice, it is unclear whether the heterogeneity is

---

[1] A solver is *complete* if it always finds a solution or a proof that no solution exists. In contrast, SLS-based solvers only terminate if they find a solution.

actually even a relevant factor. It might as well be that other mentioned properties, such as modularity, or self-similarity lead to good run times independent of
the degree distribution. The experiments Ansótegui et al. [3] performed on their
different models indicate that the heterogeneity in fact helps solvers that also
perform well on industrial instances. However, these experiments did not address
the phenomenon observed by Mu and Hoos [32] where SLS solvers outperform
complete solvers. Our goal is to demonstrate that heterogeneity of the degree
distribution has a strong positive impact on the scaling of complete solvers, but
not on SLS-based solvers.

To study this impact, we perform large-scale experiments on scale-free random 3-SAT instances with varying power-law exponents β. We note that small
power-law exponents lead to heterogeneous degree distributions while increasing β makes the instances more and more homogeneous; see Fig. 1. In fact, for
$\beta \to \infty$, scale-free random 3-SAT converges to the uniform random 3-SAT model.
Thus, it can be seen as a generalization of the uniform model with a parameter
β that directly adjusts the heterogeneity.

Our experiments clearly show a distinct crossover in performance with respect
to a set of complete backtracking (CDCL- and DPLL-based) SAT solvers and
a set of SLS-based solvers as we interpolate between highly heterogeneous
instances and uniform random instances. Moreover, the performance of SLS-
based solvers remain relatively unaffected by the degree distribution. These
results might partially explain the effect observed on uniform random instances
by Mu and Hoos [32]. In this case, complete backtracking solvers scale poorly
on random instances with a homogeneous degree distribution, while SLS-based
solvers perform best.

2   Scale-Free Formulas and Heterogeneity

A random 3-SAT formula Φ on n Boolean variables $x_1, \ldots, x_n$ and m clauses is a
conjunction of m clauses $\Phi := C_1 \wedge C_2 \wedge \cdots \wedge \cdots \wedge C_m$ where $C_i := (\ell_{i,1} \vee \ell_{i,2} \vee \ell_{i,3})$
is a disjunction of exactly three literals. A literal is a possibly negated variable. A
formula Φ is satisfiable if there is exists variable assignment for which Φ evaluates
to true.

The canonical distribution for random 3-SAT formulas is the *uniform distribution*, which is the uniform measure taken over all formulas with n variables
and m clauses. The uniform 3-SAT distribution is sampled by selecting uniformly
m 3-sets of variables and negating each variable with probability $1/2$ to form
the clauses of the formula. The *scale-free* random 3-SAT distribution is similar,
except the degree distribution of the variables is not homogeneous.

In the scale-free model introduced by Ansótegui, Bonet and Levy [3], a formula is constructed by sampling each clause independently at random. In contrast to the classical uniform random model, however, the variable probabilities
$p_i := \Pr(X = x_i)$ to choose a variable x_i are non-uniform. In particular, a
scale-free formula is generated by using a *power-law* distribution for the variable
distribution. To this end, we assign each variable x_i a *weight* w_i and sample it
with probability $p_i := \Pr(X = x_i) = \frac{w_i}{\sum_j w_j}$. To achieve a power-law distribution,

we use the following concrete sequence of weights.

$$w_i := \frac{\beta - 2}{\beta - 1} \left(\frac{n}{i}\right)^{\frac{1}{\beta - 1}} \tag{1}$$

for $i = 1, 2 \ldots, n$, which is a canonical choice for power-law weights, cf. [9]. This sequence guarantees $\sum_j w_j \to n$ for $n \to \infty$ and therefore

$$p_i \to \frac{1}{n} \frac{\beta - 2}{\beta - 1} \left(\frac{n}{i}\right)^{\frac{1}{\beta - 1}}. \tag{2}$$

To draw Φ, we generate each clause C_i as follows. (1) Sample three variables independently at random according to the distribution p_i. Repeat until no variables coincide. (2) Negate each of the three variables independently at random with probability $1/2$.

Note that Ansótegui et al. [3] use α instead of β as the power-law exponent and define $\beta := 1/(\alpha - 1)$. We instead follow the notational convention of Chung and Lu, cf. [9].

As already noted in the introduction, the power-law exponent β can be seen as a measure of how heterogeneous the resulting formulas are. This can be formalized as follows.

Proposition 1. *For a fixed number of variables, scale-free random 3-SAT converges to uniform random 3-SAT as $\beta \to \infty$.*

Proof. First observe that, for any fixed n and $\beta \to \infty$, the weights w_i as defined in Eq. (1) converge to 1. When generating a scale-free random 3-SAT instance, variables are chosen to be included in a clause with probability proportional to w_i. Thus, for $\beta \to \infty$, each variable is chosen with the same probability $1/n$ as it is the case for uniform random 3-SAT. □

We note that the model converges rather quickly: The difference between the weights is maximized for w_1 and w_n (with w_1 being the largest and w_n being the smallest). By choosing $\beta = c \log n$, the maximum weight difference $w_1 - w_n$ converges to the small constant $e^{1/c} - 1$ for growing n. Thus, when choosing $\beta \in \omega(\log n)$ (i.e., β grows asymptotically faster than $\log n$), this difference actually goes to 0 for $n \to \infty$, leading to the uniform model. This quick convergence can also be observed in Fig. 1 where the difference between $\beta = 8$ and the uniform case ($\beta = \infty$) is rather small.

2.1 The Solubility Phase Transition

The *constraint density* of a distribution of formulas on n variables and m clauses is measured as the ratio of clauses to variables m/n. A *phase transition* in a random satisfiability model is the phenomenon of a sharp transition as a function of constraint density between formulas that are almost surely satisfiable and formulas that are almost surely not satisfiable. The location of such a transition is called the *critical density* or *threshold*.

Threshold phenomena in the uniform random model have been studied for decades. The *satisfiability threshold conjecture* maintains that if Φ is a formula drawn uniformly at random from the set of all k-CNF formulas with n variables and m clauses, there exists a real number r_k such that

$$\lim_{n \to \infty} \Pr\{\Phi \text{ is satisfiable}\} = \begin{cases} 1 & m/n < r_k; \\ 0 & m/n > r_k. \end{cases}$$

This transition is sharp [18] in the sense that the probability of satisfiability as a function of constraint density m/n approaches a unit step function as $n \to \infty$. For $k = 2$, the location of the transition is known exactly to be $r_2 = 1$ [10]. For $k \geq 3$, bounds asymptotic in k [11] and exact results for large constant k [16] are now known.

The phenomenon of a sharp solubility transition is also interesting from the perspective of computational complexity and algorithm engineering, since it appears to coincide with a regime of formulas that are particularly difficult to solve by complete SAT solvers [31].

In the scale-free model, the location of the critical threshold $r_k(\beta)$ is a function of power-law exponent β. In the case of $k = 2$, it was proved that the critical density is bounded as $r_2(\beta) \leq \frac{(\beta-1)(\beta-3)}{(\beta-2)^2}$ [19]. Recently, Levy [28] proved this bound for $k = 2$ is tight. Similar to the uniform model, the critical density $r_k(\beta)$ for $k > 2$ seems to be more elusive.

2.2 Characterizing the Scale-Free Phase Transition

Ansótegui et al. [3] empirically located the phase transition of the scale-free 3-SAT model and noted that the critical density for very low β was small, and the threshold approaches the critical point of the uniform model at ≈ 4.26 as $\beta \to \infty$.[2] They report the critical threshold values as a function of β by testing 200 formulas at each value of β in the set $\{2, 7/3, 3, 5, \infty\}$.

Nevertheless, a number of details about the nature of the scale-free phase transition is still lacking from this picture. First, the sharpness of the phase transition as β evolves is not immediately clear. Furthermore, even though most previous work assumes the hardest instances are located at the phase transition region [3, Section 4], it is not obvious what the shape and extent of an easy-hard-easy transition (if it even exists) would be for scale-free formulas, nor is it known how the effect is influenced by β. Finally, previous works have so far not addressed the curious phenomenon of SLS solvers and complete solvers that seem to scale so differently on uniform random and industrial problems. We tackle this issue in the next section.

To better characterize the phase transition in the scale-free model, we generated formulas as follows. For any particular n and β, taking a sequence of 300 equidistant values $\alpha_i \in [2, 5]$ for $i \in \{1, \ldots, 300\}$, we sample 100 formulas from

---

[2] We are translating the term they refer to as β to the term we refer to as β, as mentioned above.

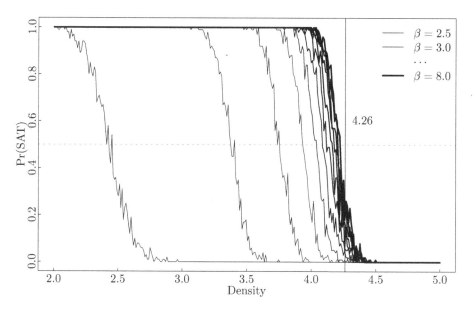

Fig. 2. Proportion of satisfiable formulas ($n = 500$) as a function of constraint density m/n for various power-law exponents β. Threshold approaches the critical density of the uniform random 3-SAT model: $r_3 \approx 4.26$.

the scale-free distribution with n variables, power-law exponent β, and density α_i (i.e., $m = \alpha_i n$). In other words, each value of n and β corresponds to 30000 formulas at various densities.

To estimate the location of the critical threshold, we decide the satisfiability of each formula with the DPLL-based solver march_hi [25]. We then find the density α_i yielding half the formulas satisfiable. This is the approach for locating the threshold in the uniform model [13]. However, in the case of the random scale-free model, the threshold depends on β.

Using this approach, we generated sets of formulas at the phase transition varying both n and β. For each $n \in \{500, 600, 700\}$, we generated formulas with $\beta \in \{2.5, 2.6, \ldots, 5.0\}$. We find the run times of the complete solvers exhibit a strong positive correlation with β. This is consistent with complete solvers performing poorly on uniform random ($\beta = \infty$) problems of even modest sizes, but it unfortunately restricts us to more modest formula sizes. To determine the effect of very large power-law exponents, we also generated formulas for $n = 500$, $\beta \in \{5, 6, 7, 8\}$.

The sharpness of the transition appears to evolve with β. Figure 2 reports the proportion of satisfiable formulas as a function of constraint density with $n = 500$. As $\beta \to \infty$, the solubility transition shifts toward the supposed critical density of the uniform random 3-SAT model, i.e., $r_3 \approx 4.26$. This is consistent with previous work on this model, but we also can see from this that the transition becomes steeper with increasing β, despite the fact that n is held constant.

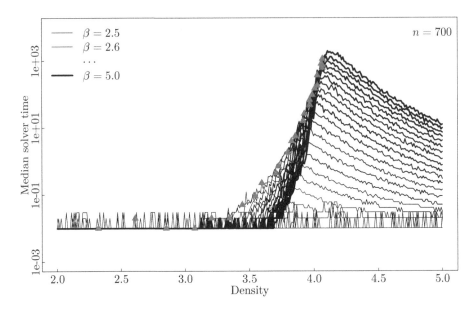

Fig. 3. Median solver times for march_hi on formulas of size $n = 700$ as β evolves toward the uniform distribution. Red triangles (▲) mark the exact density at which empirical threshold was determined. (Color figure online)

On the uniform random model, the hardest formulas for complete backtracking solvers lie at the solubility phase transition because they produce deeper search trees [31]. We also observe this so-called easy-hard-easy pattern for the scale free model in the trends for median time for march_hi to solve formulas of size $n = 700$ in Fig. 3. Moreover, the power-law exponent β is strongly correlated with the height of the hardness peak and we conjecture that the complexity of the resulting search tree is strongly coupled to the heterogeneity of the degree distribution. The empirically determined critical point, indicated in the figure with a red triangle (▲) tightly corresponds with the hardness peaks.

3   Scaling Across Solver Types

Our main goal is to understand the influence of the heterogeneity of the degree distribution at the phase transition on SLS-based solvers and complete backtracking solvers. The original paper by Mu and Hoos [32] investigated three DPLL-based SAT solvers: kcnfs [15], march_hi [25], and march_br [24]; and three SLS-based solvers: WalkSAT/SKC [34], BalancedZ [29], and ProbSAT [5]. They found the three DPLL-based solvers scaled exponentially at the uniform critical threshold and the SLS-based solvers did not. To investigate the role of heterogeneity in this context, we used the same solvers as the original Mu and Hoos paper.

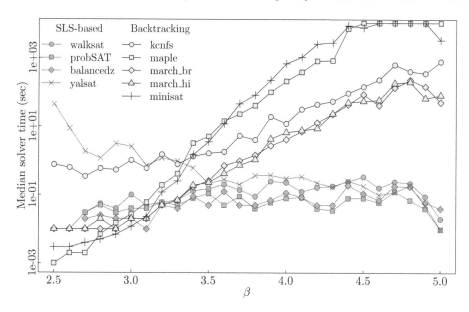

Fig. 4. Median solver time at the phase transition for all solvers on formulas with $n = 700$. Top of plot corresponds to one hour cutoff.

In addition to the DPLL solvers, we tested MiniSAT [17], and the MiniSAT-based CDCL solver MapleCOMSPS [30]. These choices are motivated by a number of reasons. First, MiniSAT has performed well in industrial categories in previous SAT competitions, as has MapleCOMSPS on the Applications Benchmark at the SAT 2016 competition and the Main Track and No Limit Track at the SAT 2017 competition. Second, we want to know if architectural decisions such as branching heuristic, look-ahead, backtracking strategy, or clause learning has any effect. We also supplemented the SLS-based solvers with YalSAT [6], which won first place in the Random Track of the SAT 2017 competition.

SLS-based solvers are *incomplete* in the sense that they can only decide satisfiability. Studies that involve such solvers need to be constrained to satisfiable formulas [20,32,36]. We use the standard rejection sampling approach to filtering for satisfiable formulas. For each n and β value, we filtered out the unsatisfiable formulas at the phase transition located as described above. For each of these formulas, we ran each of the above SLS-based and complete solvers to compare the required CPU time until a solution was determined. We imposed a solver cutoff time of one hour. In Fig. 4, we chart the median solution time on formulas of size $n = 700$ at the phase transition as a function of power law exponent β. For low β (highly heterogeneous) formulas, the complete solvers outpace the SLS-based solvers (though solution time for both is fast). We observe a crossover point around $\beta = 3.5$ where the required time for complete solvers begins to dominate the median time for the SLS techniques.

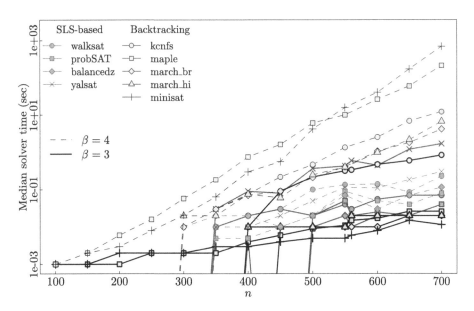

Fig. 5. Median solver time at the phase transition for all solvers on formulas with $\beta = 3$ (——) and $\beta = 4$ (- -).

Figure 4 reveals that the CDCL-based solvers MiniSAT and MapleCOM-SPS had worse performance degradation with decreasing heterogeneity than the DPLL-based solvers. Moreover, YalSAT seems to perform worse on highly heterogeneous formulas. This is interesting behavior, as YalSAT implements variants of ProbSAT with a Luby restart strategy and is conjectured to be identical to ProbSAT on uniform random instances [6]. Our results confirm that YalSAT and ProbSAT are indistinguishable as β increases, but we have evidence that the restart schedule might somehow affect performance on heterogeneous formulas.

To better quantify the influence of scaling with n, we consider the median solver time as a function of n for two representative values of β (3 and 4) in Fig. 5. To obtain a clearer picture, we repeated the formula generation process for smaller formulas ($n = 100, 200, \ldots$). The exponential scaling in complete solvers with large β (dashed lines) is easy to observe in this plot. On smaller β (solid lines), the complete solvers scale more efficiently.

To take variance into account, we compare solver performance in Fig. 6.[3] Here we have removed the CDCL-based solvers and YalSAT for clarity. This is therefore the solver set originally investigated by Mu and Hoos [32]. We again can identify a distinct crossover point at $\beta = 3.5$. Figure 7 repeats the results for $n = 500$. For this size of formula, the small β regime is extremely easy, and the results are somewhat obscured. However, these formulas are small enough that

---

[3] In all box blots, the boxes show the interquartile range, the bold line is the median, and the whiskers extend to $3/2 \cdot$ IQR below (respectively, above) the 25th (respectively, the 75th) percentile. All points beyond this are outliers.

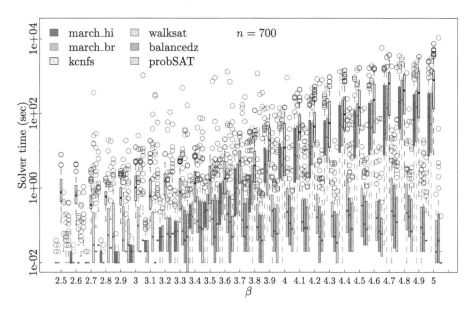

Fig. 6. CPU time to solve formulas at the scale-free phase transition with $n = 700$.

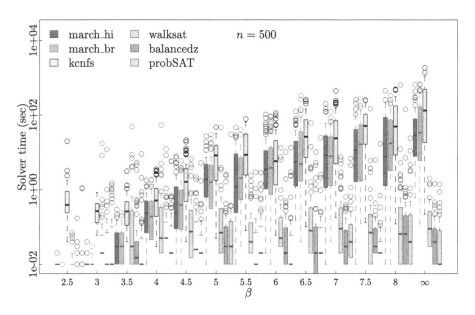

Fig. 7. CPU time to solve formulas at the scale-free phase transition with $n = 500$. Rightmost group ($\beta = \infty$) denotes satisfiable uniform random formulas with $n = 500$ and $m = 2131$.

we are able to consistently solve high β formulas, and we report the results up to $\beta = 8$. The rightmost group of the figure represents filtered uniform random formulas with $n = 500$ and $m = 2131$. To estimate the correct critical density for the uniform formulas, we used the parametric model from [32, Eq. (3)].

4 Effect of Heterogeneity on Search Trees

The discrepancy in solver efficiency across different levels of heterogeneity observed in the preceding section suggests that the degree distribution strongly affects the decisions of a wide range of solvers in a systematic way. We hypothesize that, for fixed n and m, heterogeneous 3-SAT formulas have more satisfying assignments on average, and these assignments tend to be more quickly reachable, because partial assignments tend to produce more implied literals.

Even for small formulas, it is infeasible to enumerate all satisfying assignments. Propositional model counting offers a technique in the form of an exhaustive extension to DPLL in which the branchpoint after a satisfying assignment is followed [23]. When a branch corresponding to a partial assignment of t fixed variables is marked as satisfiable at depth d, it is already possible to conclude that there are 2^{n-t} solutions at depth at least d. Using this technique, we can count the satisfying assignments to formulas generated by the scale-free model to measure the influence of heterogeneity on the solution count. The left panel of Fig. 8 reports the number of satisfying assignments found in satisfiable scale-free formulas generated at each β value.

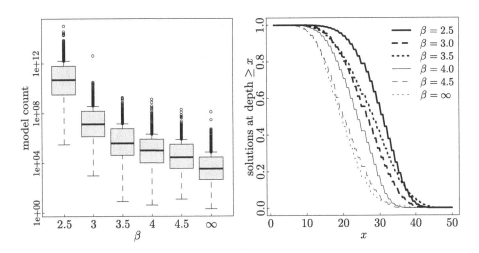

Fig. 8. Left: count of satisfying assignments on satisfiable scale-free formulas at each power-law exponent at the phase transition. For each $\beta \in \{2.5, 3.0, \ldots, 4.5, \infty\}$, we filter from 1000 generated random formulas at the phase transition with $n = 100$. Right: empirical degree distributions reporting the proportion of solutions at depth equal or greater than x aggregated over all formulas at each β value.

To obtain a more detailed picture, we plot the empirical cumulative distribution functions of solution depth on the right panel of Fig. 8. The curves represent the proportion $P(x)$ of solutions at a depth equal or greater than x.

As mentioned above, shallower solutions arise from the abundance of implied literals. We find that highly heterogeneous formulas tend to have many more constraint propagations leading to either satisfying assignments or contradictions. We recorded this data and display it in Fig. 9.

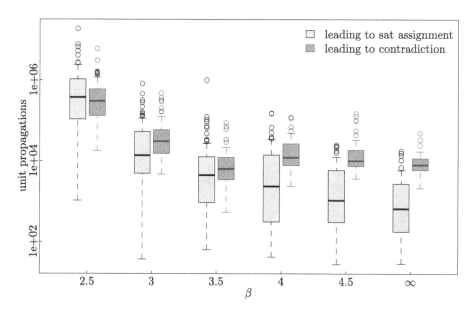

Fig. 9. Number of constraint propagations leading to a satisfying assignment or contradiction as a function of β.

4.1   Relaxed Bounded Model Checking Instances

Our aim has been to isolate heterogeneity as an impacting factor in the relative performance discrepancy between SLS solvers and complete solvers. Nevertheless, we also conjecture that the behavior of complete solvers on synthetic scale-free formulas is comparable to their behavior on certain industrial instances with power-law degree distributions. To investigate this, we compare the complexity of the remaining formula after selecting a branching literal during runs of march_hi, which was the highest performing backtracking solver for our data. Each solid line in Fig. 10 displays the average remaining formula complexity measured as clauses not yet satisfied as a percentage of original formula size. These run averages are taken over all satisfiable powerlaw formulas of $n = 500$ for different values of β. Note that some early averages exceed 100%, which likely occurs because march_hi also adds binary resolvents during the solving process. Moreover, the complexity may increase during the run, as complete solvers utilize backtracking.

We compare this with the well-known BMC DIMACS benchmark set from CMU[4]. Our motivation for this choice was to utilize a widely available set of bounded model checking formulas of reasonable size. To provide a fair comparison to the filtered scale-free formulas, we "relaxed" each BMC formula by iteratively removing a single clause at random until the first time it was satisfiable. This preserves the statistical characteristics of the degree distribution while producing a satisfiable formula.

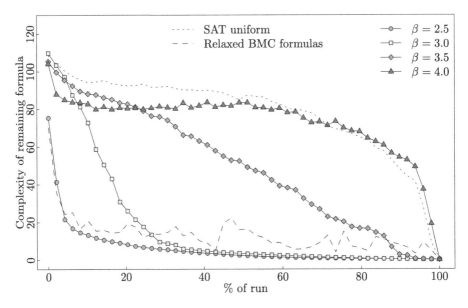

Fig. 10. Average complexity of the remaining formula depending on the percentage of already made branching decisions in a run. Reported are runs of march_hi on scale-free formulas of varying β, and satisfiable real-world model checking formulas: uniform $(\cdots)$, industrial $(--)$, and synthetic $(—)$.

The profile of the industrial bounded model checking formulas closely matches the solver behavior on the heterogeneous scale-free formulas, whereas the solver behavior on the uniform suite corresponds to the behavior on more homogeneous formulas. We conjecture that the power-law degree distribution in the bounded model checking formulas (cf. Fig. 1) affect the search tree in similar ways.

5   Conclusions

We have investigated a parameterized distribution over propositional formulas that allows us to carefully control the heterogeneity (via the power-law exponent) to interpolate smoothly between highly heterogeneous random formulas

---

[4] http://fmv.jku.at/bmc/.

and nearly-uniform random formulas. This allows us to observe the exact influence of this kind of heterogeneity on hardness for two different solver classes. Our empirical analysis uncovers an interesting crossover effect in the performance of SLS-based vs. complete backtracking solvers, depending on the heterogeneity.

We summarize our main findings as follows. (1) Complete solvers tuned for industrial instances perform significantly better on heterogeneous formulas than uniform formulas. This is likely due to the fact that the search space of highly heterogeneous formulas have more solutions, and solutions tend to be shallower in the decision tree. (2) Incomplete SLS-based solvers, which are typically recognized for their performance on uniform random k-SAT, do not benefit much (if at all) from heterogeneity. (3) Random instances (even heterogeneous ones) close to the satisfiability threshold are harder to solve than many industrial instances.

The first two insights are a step towards understanding the disaccording runtime behaviors of different solvers on industrial and random instances. Moreover, these findings suggest that the behavior of SLS-based solvers are relatively heterogeneity-invariant, whereas complete solvers are far more sensitive to the homogeneous degree distributions of uniform random formulas. This may explain, at least in part, the exponential scaling of complete solvers at the uniform phase transition observed by Mu and Hoos [32].

On the other hand, the third insight shows that heterogeneity alone cannot explain why industrial instances can be solved so fast in practice. On the upside, this means that random scale-free formulas chosen close to the satisfiability threshold can serve as hard benchmark instances. It would be interesting to see whether incomplete solvers can be tuned to catch up to (or even outperform) complete solvers on heterogeneous instances. Due to the similarities between heterogeneous random formulas and industrial instances with respect to runtime behavior, we believe that tuning solvers for heterogeneous random formulas can actually lead to techniques that also help solving industrial instances faster.

The behavior of solvers on uniform random formulas is well-studied. However, there is no obvious reason to believe that solver performance near the scale-free phase transition is identical to performance near the uniform phase transition. Our work suggests that there is some kind of structure in formulas with heavy-tailed degree distributions that is being exploited by complete solvers. It is important to stress that a scale-free degree distribution alone is not enough to characterize the complex structure of real problems. Our results provide context by isolating heterogeneity (as realized by the power-law exponent) as an important feature impacting the performance of state-of-the-art CDCL- and DPLL-based SAT solvers. Other non-uniform models exist, and a future avenue of work is to investigate such models, especially the Popularity-Similarity model recently introduced by Giráldez-Cru and Levy [22], which can generate formulas with both a scale-free degree distribution and high modularity.

References

1. Ansótegui, C., Bonet, M.L., Giráldez-Cru, J., Levy, J.: The fractal dimension of SAT formulas. In: Demri, S., Kapur, D., Weidenbach, C. (eds.) IJCAR 2014. LNCS (LNAI), vol. 8562, pp. 107–121. Springer, Cham (2014). https://doi.org/10.1007/978-3-319-08587-6_8

2. Ansótegui, C., Bonet, M.L., Levy, J.: On the structure of industrial SAT instances. In: Gent, I.P. (ed.) CP 2009. LNCS, vol. 5732, pp. 127–141. Springer, Heidelberg (2009). https://doi.org/10.1007/978-3-642-04244-7_13

3. Ansótegui, C., Bonet, M.L., Levy, J.: Towards industrial-like random SAT instances. In: Proceedings of the Twenty-First International Joint Conference on Artificial Intelligence (IJCAI), pp. 387–392 (2009)

4. Ansótegui, C., Giráldez-Cru, J., Levy, J.: The community structure of SAT formulas. In: Cimatti, A., Sebastiani, R. (eds.) SAT 2012. LNCS, vol. 7317, pp. 410–423. Springer, Heidelberg (2012). https://doi.org/10.1007/978-3-642-31612-8_31

5. Balint, A., Schöning, U.: probSAT and pprobSAT. In: Proceedings of the 2014 SAT Competition, p. 63 (2014)

6. Biere, A.: CaDiCaL, Lingeling, Plingeling, Treengeling and YalSAT. In: Proceedings of SAT Competition 2017, pp. 14–15 (2017)

7. Biere, A.: Deep bound hardware model checking instances, quadratic propagations benchmarks and reencoded factorization problems submitted to the SAT competition 2017. In: Proceedings of SAT Competition 2017, pp. 40–41 (2017)

8. Cheeseman, P., Kanefsky, B., Taylor, W.M.: Where the really hard problems are. In: Proceedings of the Twelfth International Joint Conference on Artificial Intelligence (IJCAI), pp. 331–340 (1991)

9. Chung, F., Lu, L.: The average distances in random graphs with given expected degrees. PNAS **99**(25), 15879–15882 (2002)

10. Chvátal, V., Reed, B.: Mick gets some (the odds are on his side). In: Proceedings of the Thirty-Third IEEE Annual Symposium on Foundations of Computer Science (FOCS), pp. 620–627, October 1992

11. Coja-Oghlan, A.: The asymptotic k-SAT threshold. In: Proceedings of the Forty-Sixth Annual Symposium on Theory of Computing (STOC), pp. 804–813 (2014)

12. Cook, S.A.: The complexity of theorem-proving procedures. In: Proceedings of the Third Annual Symposium on Theory of Computing (STOC), pp. 151–158 (1971)

13. Crawford, J.M., Auton, L.D.: Experimental results on the crossover point in random 3-SAT. Artif. Intell. **81**(1–2), 31–57 (1996)

14. Crawford, J.M., Baker, A.B.: Experimental results on the application of satisfiability algorithms to scheduling problems. In: Proceedings of the Tweltfh AAAI Conference on Artificial Intelligence, pp. 1092–1097 (1994)

15. Dequen, G., Dubois, O.: *kcnfs*: an efficient solver for random k-SAT formulae. In: Giunchiglia, E., Tacchella, A. (eds.) SAT 2003. LNCS, vol. 2919, pp. 486–501. Springer, Heidelberg (2004). https://doi.org/10.1007/978-3-540-24605-3_36

16. Ding, J., Sly, A., Sun, N.: Proof of the satisfiability conjecture for large k. In: Proceedings of the Forty-Seventh Annual Symposium on Theory of Computing (STOC), pp. 59–68 (2015)

17. Eén, N., Sörensson, N.: An extensible SAT-solver. In: Giunchiglia, E., Tacchella, A. (eds.) SAT 2003. LNCS, vol. 2919, pp. 502–518. Springer, Heidelberg (2004). https://doi.org/10.1007/978-3-540-24605-3_37

18. Friedgut, E.: Sharp thresholds of graph properties, and the k-SAT problem. J. Am. Math. Soc. **12**(4), 1017–1054 (1999)

19. Friedrich, T., Krohmer, A., Rothenberger, R., Sutton, A.M.: Phase transitions for scale-free SAT formulas. In: Proceedings of the Twenty-First AAAI Conference on Artificial Intelligence, pp. 3893–3899 (2017)
20. Gent, I.P., Walsh, T.: Towards an understanding of hill-climbing procedures for SAT. In: Proceedings of the Eleventh AAAI Conference on Artificial Intelligence, pp. 28–33 (1993)
21. Giráldez-Cru, J., Levy, J.: A modularity-based random SAT instances generator. In: Proceedings of the Twenty-Fourth International Joint Conference on Artificial Intelligence (IJCAI), pp. 1952–1958 (2015)
22. Giráldez-Cru, J., Levy, J.: Locality in random SAT instances. In: Proceedings of the Twenty-Sixth International Joint Conference on Artificial Intelligence (IJCAI), pp. 638–644 (2017)
23. Gomes, C.P., Sabharwal, A., Selman, B.: Model counting. In: Biere, A., Heule, M., van Maaren, H., Walsh, T. (eds.) Handbook of Satisfiability. Frontiers in Artificial Intelligence and Applications, vol. 185, pp. 633–654. IOS Press, Amsterdam (2009)
24. Heule, M.J.H.: march_br. In: Proceedings of SAT Competition 2013 (2013)
25. Heule, M., van Maaren, H.: march_hi. In: Proceedings of the 2009 SAT Competition, pp. 27–28 (2009)
26. Katsirelos, G., Simon, L.: Eigenvector centrality in industrial SAT instances. In: Milano, M. (ed.) CP 2012. LNCS, pp. 348–356. Springer, Heidelberg (2012). https://doi.org/10.1007/978-3-642-33558-7_27
27. Konolige, K.: Easy to be hard: difficult problems for greedy algorithms. In: Proceedings of the Fourth International Conference on Principles of Knowledge Representation and Reasoning (KR), pp. 374–378 (1994)
28. Levy, J.: Percolation and phase transition in SAT. ArXiv e-prints, July 2017. arXiv:1708.06805
29. Li, C., Huang, C., Xu, R.: Balance between intensification and diversification: a unity of opposites. In: Proceedings of SAT Competition 2014, pp. 10–11 (2014)
30. Liang, J.H., Oh, C., Ganesh, V., Czarnecki, K., Poupar, P.: MapleCOMSPS, MapleCOMSPS_lrb, MapleCOMSPS_CHB. In: Proceedings of the 2016 SAT Competition, pp. 52–53 (2016)
31. Mitchell, D.G., Selman, B., Levesque, H.J.: Hard and easy distributions of SAT problems. In: Proceedings of the Tenth AAAI Conference on Artificial Intelligence, pp. 459–465 (1992)
32. Mu, Z., Hoos, H.H.: On the empirical time complexity of random 3-SAT at the phase transition. In: Proceedings of the Twenty-Fourth International Joint Conference on Artificial Intelligence (IJCAI), pp. 367–373 (2015)
33. Rish, I., Dechter, R.: Resolution versus search: two strategies for SAT. J. Autom. Reasoning **24**(1–2), 225–275 (2000)
34. Selman, B., Kautz, H.A., Cohen, B.: Noise strategies for improving local search. In: Proceedings of the Twelfth AAAI Conference on Artificial Intelligence, pp. 337–343 (1994)
35. Slater, A.: Modelling more realistic SAT problems. In: McKay, B., Slaney, J. (eds.) AI 2002. LNCS (LNAI), vol. 2557, pp. 591–602. Springer, Heidelberg (2002). https://doi.org/10.1007/3-540-36187-1_52
36. Yokoo, M.: Why adding more constraints makes a problem easier for hill-climbing algorithms: analyzing landscapes of CSPs. In: Smolka, G. (ed.) CP 1997. LNCS, vol. 1330, pp. 356–370. Springer, Heidelberg (1997). https://doi.org/10.1007/BFb0017451

Modular and Efficient
Divide-and-Conquer SAT Solver on Top
of the Painless Framework

Ludovic Le Frioux[1,2(✉)], Souheib Baarir[2,3], Julien Sopena[2,4],
and Fabrice Kordon[2]

[1] LRDE, EPITA, 94270 Le Kremlin-Bicêtre, France
ludovic@lrde.epita.fr
[2] Sorbonne Université, CNRS, LIP6, UMR 7606, 75005 Paris, France
{ludovic.le-frioux,souheib.baarir,julien.sopena,fabrice.kordon}@lip6.fr
[3] Université Paris Nanterre, 92000 Nanterre, France
[4] Inria, DELYS Team, 75005 Paris, France

Abstract. Over the last decade, parallel SATisfiability solving has been
widely studied from both theoretical and practical aspects. There are
two main approaches. First, divide-and-conquer (D&C) splits the search
space, each solver being in charge of a particular subspace. The second
one, portfolio launches multiple solvers in parallel, and the first to find a
solution ends the computation. However although D&C based approaches
seem to be the natural way to work in parallel, portfolio ones experimentally provide better performances.

An explanation resides on the difficulties to use the native formulation of the SAT problem (*i.e.,* the CNF form) to compute an *a priori*
good search space partitioning (*i.e.,* all parallel solvers process their subspaces in comparable computational time). To avoid this, dynamic load
balancing of the search subspaces is implemented. Unfortunately, this is
difficult to compare load balancing strategies since state-of-the-art SAT
solvers appropriately dealing with these aspects are hardly adaptable to
various strategies than the ones they have been designed for.

This paper aims at providing a way to overcome this problem by
proposing an implementation and evaluation of different types of divide-
and-conquer inspired from the literature. These are relying on the
Painless framework, which provides concurrent facilities to elaborate
such parallel SAT solvers. Comparison of the various strategies are then
discussed.

Keywords: Divide-and-conquer · Parallel satisfiability · SAT solver ·
Tool

1 Introduction

Modern SAT solvers are now able to handle complex problems involving millions of variables and billions of clauses. These tools have been used successfully

T. Vojnar and L. Zhang (Eds.): TACAS 2019, Part I, LNCS 11427, pp. 135–151, 2019.
https://doi.org/10.1007/978-3-030-17462-0_8

to solve constraints' systems issued from many contexts, such as planning decision [16], hardware and software verification [7], cryptology [23], and computational biology [20], etc.

State-of-the-art complete SAT solvers are based on the well-known Conflict-
Driven Clause Learning (CDCL) algorithm [21,28,30]. With the emergence of
many-core machines, multiple parallelisation strategies have been conducted on
these solvers. Mainly, two classes of parallelisation techniques have been studied:
divide-and-conquer (D&C) and portfolio. Divide-and-conquer approaches, often
based on the guiding path method, decompose recursively and dynamically,
the original search space in subspaces that are solved separately by sequential
solvers [1,2,12,14,26,29]. In the portfolio setting, many sequential SAT solvers
compete for the solving of the whole problem [4,5,11]. The first to find a solution, or proving the problem to be unsatisfiable ends the computation. Although
divide-and-conquer approaches seem to be the natural way to parallelise SAT
solving, the outcomes of the parallel track in the annual SAT Competition show
that the best state-of-the-art parallel SAT solvers are portfolio ones.

The main problem of divide-and-conquer based approaches is the search space
division so that load is balanced over solvers, which is a theoretical hard problem.
Since no optimal heuristics has been found, solvers compensate non optimal
space division by enabling dynamic load balancing. However, state-of-the-art
SAT solvers appropriately dealing with these aspects are hardly adaptable to
various strategies than the ones they have been designed for [1,2,6]. Hence, it
turns out to be very difficult to make fair comparisons between techniques (*i.e.,*
using the same basic implementation). Thus, we believe it is difficult to conclude
on the (non-) effectiveness of a technique with respect to another one and this
may lead to premature abortion of potential good ideas.

This paper tries to solve these problems by proposing a simple, generic, and
efficient divide-and-conquer component on top of the `Painless` [18] framework.
This component eases the implementation and evaluation of various strategies,
without any compromise on efficiency. Main contributions of this paper are the
followings:

- an overview of state-of-the-art divide-and-conquer methods;
- a complete divide-and-conquer component that has been integrated to the
  `Painless` framework;
- a fair experimental evaluation of different types of divide-and-conquer
  inspired from the literature, and implemented using this component.

These implementations have often similar and sometimes better performances
compared with state-of-the-art divide-and-conquer SAT solvers.

Let us outline several results of this work. First, our `Painless` framework
is able to support implementation of multiple D&C strategies in parallel solvers.
Moreover, we have identified "axes" for customization and adaptation of heuristics. Thus, we foresee it will be much easier to explore next D&C strategies.
Second, our best implementation at this stage is comparable in terms of performance, with the best state-of-the-art D&C solvers, which shows our framework's
efficiency.

This paper is organized as follows: Sect. 2 introduces useful background to deal with the SAT problem. Section 3 is dedicated to divide-and-conquer based parallel SAT solving. Section 4 explains the mechanism of divide-and-conquer we have implemented in `Painless`. Section 5 analyses the results of our experiments, and Sect. 6 concludes and gives some perspectives.

2 Background

A *propositional variable* can have two possible values $\top$ (True), or $\bot$ (False). A *literal l* is a propositional variable (x) or its negation ($\neg x$). A *clause* ω is a finite disjunction of literals (noted $\omega = \bigvee_{i=1}^{k} \ell_i$). A clause with a single literal is called *unit clause*. A *conjunctive normal form (CNF) formula* φ is a finite conjunction of clauses (noted $\varphi = \bigwedge_{i=1}^{k} \omega_i$). For a given formula φ, the set of its variables is noted: V_φ. An *assignment* $\mathcal{A}$ of variables of φ, is a function $\mathcal{A} : V_\varphi \to \{\top, \bot\}$. $\mathcal{A}$ is total (complete) when all elements of V_φ have an image by $\mathcal{A}$, otherwise it is partial. For a given formula φ, and an assignment $\mathcal{A}$, a clause of φ is satisfied when it contains at least one literal evaluating to true, regarding $\mathcal{A}$. The formula φ is satisfied by $\mathcal{A}$ iff $\forall \omega \in \varphi, \omega$ is satisfied. φ is said to be SAT if there is at least one assignment that makes it satisfiable. It is defined as UNSAT otherwise.

Algorithm 1. CDCL algorithm

```
1  function CDCL()
2      dl ← 0                                    // Current decision level
3      while not all variables are assigned do
4          conflict ← unitPropagation()
5          if conflict then
6              if dl = 0 then
7                  return ⊥                        // φ is UNSAT
8              end
9              ω ← conflictAnalysis()
10             addLearntClause(ω)
11             dl ← backjump(ω)
12         end
13         else
14             assignDecisionLiteral()
15             dl ← dl + 1
16         end
17     end
18     return ⊤                                   // φ is SAT
```

Conflict Driven Clause Leaning. The majority of the complete state-of-the-art sequential SAT solvers are based on the Conflict Driven Clause Learning (CDCL) algorithm [21,28,30], that is an enhancement of the DPLL algorithm [9, 10]. The main components of a CDCL are presented in Algorithm 1.

At each step of the main loop, `unitPropagation`[1] (line 4) is applied on the formula. In case of conflict (line 5), two situations can be observed: the conflict is detected at decision level 0 ($dl == 0$), thus the formula is declared UNSAT (lines 6–7); otherwise, a new asserting clause is derived by the conflict analysis and the algorithm backjumps to the assertion level [21] (lines 8–10). If there is no conflict (lines 11–13), a new decision literal is chosen (heuristically) and the algorithm continues its progression (adding a new decision level: $dl \leftarrow dl + 1$). When all variables are assigned (line 3), the formula is said to be SAT.

The Learning Mechanism. The effectiveness of the CDCL lies in the *learning mechanism* (line 10). Each time a conflict is encountered, it is analyzed (`conflictAnalysis` function in Algorithm 1) in order to compute its reasons and derive a *learnt clause*. While present in the system, this clause will avoid the same mistake to be made another time, and therefore allows faster deductions (conflicts/unit propagations).

Since the number of conflicts is very huge (in avg. 5000/s [3]), controlling the size of the database storing learnt clauses is a challenge. It can dramatically affect performance of the `unitPropagation` function. Many strategies and heuristics have been proposed to manage the cleaning of the stored clauses (*e.g.*, the Literal Block Distance (LBD) [3] measure).

3   Divide-and-Conquer Based Parallel SAT Solvers

The divide-and-conquer strategy in parallel SAT solving is based on splitting the search space into subspaces that are submitted to different workers. If a subspace is proven SAT then the initial formula is SAT. The formula is UNSAT if all the subspaces are UNSAT. The challenging points of the divide-and-conquer mechanism are: *dividing the search space*, *balancing jobs between workers*, and *exchanging learnt clauses*.

3.1   Dividing the Search Space

This section describes how to create multiple search subspaces for the studied problem, and the heuristics to balance their estimated computational costs.

Techniques to Divide the Search Space. To divide the search space, the most often used technique is the *guiding path* [29]. It is a conjunction of literals (called cube) that are assumed by the invoked solver (worker). Let φ be a formula, and $x \in \mathcal{V}_\varphi$ a variable. Thanks to Shannon decomposition, we can rewrite φ as $\varphi = (\varphi \wedge x) \vee (\varphi \wedge \neg x)$. The two guiding paths here are reduced to a single literal: (x) and $(\neg x)$. This principle can be applied recursively on each subspaces to create multiple guiding paths.

---

[1] The `unitPropagation` function implements the Boolean Constraint Propagation (BCP) procedure that forces (in cascade) the values of the variables in unit clauses [9].

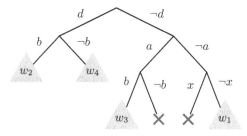

Fig. 1. Using guiding path to divide the search space

Figure 1 illustrates such an approach where six subspaces have been created from the original formula. They are issued from the following guiding paths: $(d \wedge b)$, $(d \wedge \neg b)$, $(\neg d \wedge a \wedge b)$, $(\neg d \wedge a \wedge \neg b)$, $(\neg d \wedge \neg a \wedge x)$, $(\neg d \wedge \neg a \wedge \neg x)$. The subspaces that have been proven UNSAT, are highlighted with red crosses. The rest of the subspaces are submitted to workers (noted w_i).

It is worth noting that other partitioning techniques exist that were initially developed for distributed systems rather than many-cores machines. We can cite the *scattering* [13], and the *xor partitioning* [27] approaches.

Choosing Division Variables. Choosing the best *division variable* is a hard problem, requiring the use of heuristics. A good division heuristic should decrease the overall total solving time[2]. Besides, it should create balanced subspaces w.r.t. their solving time: if some subspaces are too easy to solve this will lead to repeatedly asking for new jobs and redividing the search space (phenomenon known as *ping pong effect* [15]).

Division heuristics can be classified in two categories: *look ahead* and *look back*. Look ahead heuristics rely on the possible future behaviour of the solver. Contrariwise, look back heuristics rely on statistics gathered during the past behaviour of the solver. Let us present the most important ones.

Look Ahead. In stochastic SAT solving (chapters 5 and 6 in [8]), look ahead heuristics are used to choose the variable implying the biggest number of unit propagations as a decision variable. When using this heuristic for the division, one tries to create the smallest possible subspaces (*i.e.,* with the least unassigned variables). The main difficulty of this technique is the generated cost of applying the unit propagation for the different variables. The so-called "cube-and-conquer" solver presented in [12] relies on such an heuristic.

Look Back. Since sequential solvers are based on heuristics to select their decision variables, these can naturally be used to operate the search space division. The idea is to use the variables' VSIDS-based [25] order[3] to decompose the search

---

[2] Compared to the solving time using a sequential solver.
[3] The number of their implications in propagation conflicts.

in subspaces. Actually, when a variable is highly ranked w.r.t. to this order, then it is commonly admitted that it is a good starting point for a separate exploration [2,13,22].

Another explored track is the number of *flips* of the variables [1]. A flip is when a variable is propagated to the reverse of its last propagated value. Hence, ranking the variables according to the number of their flips, and choosing the highest one as a division point helps to generate search subspaces with comparable computational time. This can be used to limit the number of variables on which the look ahead propagation is applied by preselecting a predefined percentage of variables with the highest number of flips.

Another look back approach, called propagation rate (PR), tends to produce the same effect as the look ahead heuristics [26]. The PR of a variable v is the ratio between the numbers of propagations due to the branching of v divided by the number of time v has been chosen as a decision. The variable with the highest PR is chosen as division point.

3.2 Load Balancing

Despite all the effort to produce balanced subspaces, it is practically impossible to ensure the same difficulty for each of them. Hence, some workers often become quickly idle, thus requiring a dynamic load balancing mechanism.

A first solution to achieve dynamic load balancing is to rely on *work stealing*: each time a solver proves its subspace to be UNSAT[4], it asks for a new job. A target worker is chosen to divide its search space (*e.g.,* extends its guiding path). Hence, the target is assigned to one of the new generated subspaces, while the idle solver works on the other. The most common architecture to implement this strategy is based on a master/slave organization, where slaves are solvers.

When a new division is needed, choosing the best target is a challenging problem. For example, the Dolius solver [1] uses a FIFO order to select targets: the next one is the worker that is working for the longest time on its search space. This strategy guarantees fairness between workers. Moreover the target has a better knowledge of its search space, resulting in a better division when using a look back heuristic.

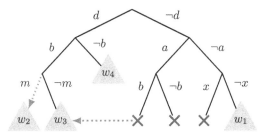

Fig. 2. Load balancing through work stealing

---

[4] If the result is SAT the global resolution ends.

Let us suppose in the example of Fig. 1 that worker w_3 proves its subspace to be UNSAT, and asks for a new one. Worker w_2 is chosen to divide and share its subspace. In Fig. 2, m is chosen as division variable and two new guiding paths are created, one for w_2 and one for w_3. Worker w_3 now works on a new subspace and its new guiding path is $(d \wedge b \wedge \neg m)$, while the guiding path of w_2 is $(d \wedge b \wedge m)$.

Another solution to perform dynamic load balancing is to create more search subspaces (jobs) than available parallel workers (cube-and-conquer [12]). These jobs are then managed via a work queue where workers pick new jobs. To increase the number of available jobs at runtime, a target job is selected to be divided. The strategy implemented in `Treengeling` [6] is to choose the job with the smallest number of variables; this favours SAT instances.

3.3 Exchanging Learnt Clauses

Dividing the search space can be subsumed to the definition of constraints on the values of some variables. Technically, there exist two manners to implement such constraints: (i) constrain the original formula; (ii) constrain the decision process initialisation of the used solver.

When the search space division is performed using (i), some learnt clauses cannot be shared between workers. This is typically the case of learnt clauses deduced from at least one clause added for space division, otherwise, correctness is not preserved. The simplest solution to preserve correctness is then to disable clause sharing [6]. Another (more complex) approach is to mark the clauses that must not be shared [17]. Clauses added for the division are initially marked. Then, the tag is propagated to each learnt clause that is deduced from at least one already marked clause.

When the search space division is performed using (ii), some decisions are forced. With this technique there is no sharing restrictions for any learnt clauses. This solution is often implemented using the assumption mechanisms [1,2].

4 Implementation of a Divide-and-Conquer

This section presents the divide-and-conquer component we have built on top of the `Painless` framework. First, we recall the general architecture and operations of `Painless`. Then we describe the generic divide-and-conquer component's mechanisms. Finally we detail the different heuristics we have instantiated using this component.

4.1 About the Painless Framework

`Painless` [18] is a framework that aims at simplifying the implementation and evaluation of parallel SAT solvers for many-core environments. Thanks to its genericity and modularity, the components of `Painless` can be instantiated independently to produce new complete solvers.

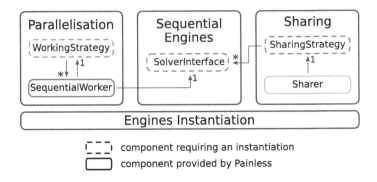

Fig. 3. Architecture of `Painless`

The main idea of the framework is to separate the technical components (*e.g.*, those dedicated to the management of concurrent programming aspects) from those implementing heuristics and optimizations embedded in a parallel SAT solver. Hence, the developer of a (new) parallel solver concentrates his efforts on the functional aspects, namely parallelisation and sharing strategies, thus delegating implementation issues (*e.g.*, data concurrent access protection mechanisms) to the framework.

Three main components arise when treating parallel SAT solvers: *sequential engines*, *parallelisation*, and *sharing*. These form the global architecture of `Painless` depicted in Fig. 3.

Sequential Engines. The core element considered in the framework is a sequential SAT solver. This can be any CDCL state-of-the art solver. Technically, these engines are operated through a generic interface providing basics of sequential solvers: *solve, interrupt, add clauses*, etc.

Thus, to instantiate `Painless` with a particular solver, one needs to implement the interface according to this engine.

Parallelisation. To build a parallel solver using the aforementioned engines, one needs to define and implement a parallelisation strategy. Portfolio and divide-and-conquer are the basic known ones. Also, they can be arbitrarily composed to form new strategies.

In `Painless`, a strategy is represented by a tree-structure of arbitrarily depth. The internal nodes of the tree represent parallelisation strategies, and leaves are core engines. Technically, the internal nodes are implemented using `WorkingStrategy` component and the leaves are instances of `SequentialWorker` component.

Hence, to develop its own parallelisation strategy, the user should create one or more strategies, and build the required tree-structure.

Sharing. In parallel SAT solving, the exchange of learnt clauses warrants a particular focus. Indeed, besides the theoretical aspects, a bad implementation of a good sharing strategy may dramatically impact the solver's efficiency.

In `Painless`, solvers can export (import) clauses to (from) the others during the resolution process. Technically, this is done by using lockfree queues [24]. The sharing of these learnt clauses is dedicated to particular components called `Sharers`. Each `Sharer` in charge of sets of producers and consumers and its behaviour reduces to a loop of sleeping and exchange phases.

Hence, the only part requiring a particular implementation is the exchange phase, that is user defined.

4.2   The Divide-and-Conquer Component in Painless

To implement divide-and-conquer solvers with `Painless`, we define a new component. It is based on a master/slaves architecture.

Figure 4 shows the architecture of our tool. It contains several entities. The *master* is a thread executing the only D&C instance of the `WorkingStrategy` class. The *workers* are slave threads executing instances of the `SequentialWorker` class. An instance of the `Sharing` class allows workers to share clauses.

The master and the workers interact asynchronously by means of events. In the initialisation phase, the master may send asynchronous events to himself too.

Master. The master (1) initialises the D&C component; (2) selects targets to divide their search spaces; (3) and operates the division along with the relaunch of the associated solvers. These actions are triggered by the events INIT, NEED_JOB, and READY_TO_DIV, respectively. In the remainder of this section we consider a configuration with N workers.

The master can be in two states: either it is sleeping, or it is currently processing an incoming event. Initially the master starts a first solver on the whole formula by sending it the SOLVE event. It then generates $N - 1$ NEED_JOB events to himself. This will provoke the division of the search space in N subspaces according the to implemented policy. At the end of this initialisation phase, it returns to its sleeping state. At this point, all workers are processing their subspaces.

Each time a worker needs a job, it notifies the master with a NEED_JOB event.

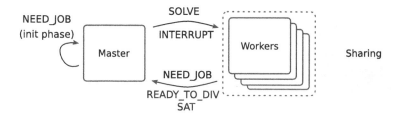

Fig. 4. Architecture of the divide-and-conquer SAT solver

All over its execution, the master reacts to the NEED_JOB event as follows:

1. it selects a target using the current policy[5], and requests this target to interrupt by sending an INTERRUPT event. Since this is an asynchronous communication, the master may process other events until it receives a READY_TO_DIV event;
2. once it receives a READY_TO_DIV event, the master proceeds to the effective division of the subspace of the worker which emitted the event. Both the worker which emitted the event and the one which requested a job are then invited to solve their new subspaces through the send of a SOLVE event.

The master may receive a SAT event from its workers. It means a solution has been computed and the whole execution must end. When a worker ends in an UNSAT situation, it makes a request for a new job (NEED_JOB event). When the master has no more division of the search space to perform, it states the SAT problem is UNSAT.

Slaves. A slave may be in three different states: *idle*, *work*, and *work_interrupt_requested*. Initially, it is *idle* until it receives a SOLVE request from the master. Then, it moves to the *work* state and starts to process its assigned subspace. It may:

- find a solution, then emit a SAT event to the master, and move back to *idle*;
- end processing of the subspace, with an UNSAT result, then it emits a NEED_JOB event to the master, and move back to *idle*;
- receive an INTERRUPT event from the master, then, it moves to the *work_interrupt_requested* state and continues its processing until it reaches a stable state[6] according to the underlying sequential engine implementation. Then, it sends a READY_TO_DIV event to the master prior to move back to *idle*.

4.3   Implemented Heuristics

The divide-and-conquer component presented in the previous section should be generic enough to allow the implementation of any of the state-of-the-art strategies presented in Sect. 3. We selected some strategies to be implemented, keeping in mind that at least one of each family should be retained:

1. Techniques to Divide the Search Space (Sect. 3.1):
   we have implemented the guiding path method based on the use of assumptions. Since we want to be as generic as possible, we have not considered techniques adding constraints to the formula (because they require tagging mechanisms complex to implement to enable clause sharing).

---

[5] This policy may change dynamically over the execution of the solver.
[6] For example, in Minisat-based solvers, a stable state could correspond to the configuration of the solver after a restart.

2. Choosing Division Variables (Sect. 3.1):
   the different division heuristics we have implemented in the `MapleCOMSPS` solver[7], are: VSIDS, number of flips, and propagation rate.
3. Load Balancing (Sect. 3.2):
   a work-stealing mechanism was implemented to operate dynamic load balancing. The master selects targets using a FIFO policy (as in `Dolius`) moderated by a minimum computation time (2 s) for the workers in order to let these acquire a sufficient knowledge of the subspace.

The exchange of learnt clauses (Sect. 3.3) on any of the strategies we implemented is not restricted. This allows to reuse any of the already off-the-shelf strategies provided by the `Painless` framework.

Another important issue deals with the way new subspaces are allocated to workers. We provide two strategies:

- **Reuse:** the worker reuses the same object-solver all over its execution and the master feeds it with guiding paths;
- **Clone:** each time a new subspace is assigned to a worker, the master clones the object-solver from the target and provides the copy to the idle worker. Thus, the idle worker will benefit form the knowledge (VSIDS, locally learned clauses, etc.) of the target worker.

Hence, our `Painless`-based `D&C` component can thus be instantiated to produces solvers over six orthogonal axes: (1) technique to divide the search space; (2) technique to choose the division variables; (3) load balancing strategy; (4) the sharing strategy; (5) the subspace allocation technique; (6) and the used underlying sequential solver.

By lack of time for experimentations, we select for this paper 6 solvers: all based on `MapleCOMSPS`, and sharing all learnt clauses which LBD ≤ 4 (this value has been experimentally deduced). Table 1 summarizes the implemented `D&C` solvers we have used for our experiments in the next section.

Table 1. The `D&C` solvers we use for experiments in this paper

	VSIDS	Number of flips	Propagation Rate
Reuse	`P-REUSE-VSIDS`	`P-REUSE-FLIPS`	`P-REUSE-PR`
Clone	`P-CLONE-VSIDS`	`P-CLONE-FLIPS`	`P-CLONE-PR`

5 Evaluation

This section presents the results of experiments done with the six `D&C` solvers we presented in Sect. 4.3. We also did comparative experiments with state-of-art `D&C` solvers (`Treengeling` [6] and `MapleAmpharos` [26]).

---

[7] We used the version that won the main track of the SAT Competition in 2016 [19].

Treengeling is a cube-and-conquer solver based on the Lingeling sequential solver. MapleAmpharos is an adaptive divide-and-conquer based on the solver Ampharos [2], and using MapleCOMSPS as sequential solver. Comparing our new solvers with state-of-the-art ones (*e.g.,* not implemented on Painless) is a way to assess if our solution is competitive despite the genericity introduced by Painless and ad-hoc optimizations implemented in other solvers.

All experiments were executed on a multi-core machine with 12 physical cores (2 x Intel Xeon E5645 @ 2.40 GHz), and 64 GB of memory. Hyper-threading has been activated porting the number of logical cores to 24. We used the 400 instances of the parallel track of the SAT Competition 2018[8]. All experiments have been conducted using the following settings:

- each solver has been run once on each instance with a time-out of 5000 s (as in the SAT Competition);
- the number of used cores is limited to 23 (the remaining core is booked to the operating system);
- instances that were trivially solved by a solver (at the preprocessing phase) were removed, indeed in this case the D&C component of solvers is not enabled, these instances are then irrelevant for our case study.

Results of these experiences are summarized in Table 2. The different columns represent respectively: the total number of solved instances, the number of UNSAT solved instances, the number of SAT solved instances, and the PAR-2 score[9].

Table 2. Results of the different solvers

Solver	ALL (360)	UNSAT	SAT	PAR-2
P-CLONE-FLIPS	198	87	111	1732696.65
P-CLONE-PR	183	73	110	1871614.48
P-CLONE-VSIDS	183	77	106	1880281.54
P-REUSE-FLIPS	190	83	107	1796426.72
P-REUSE-PR	180	72	108	1938621.48
P-REUSE-VSIDS	184	75	109	1868619.43
MapleAmpharos	153	29	124	2190680.55
Treengeling	200	84	116	1810471.56

5.1   Comparing the Implemented Divide-and-Conquer Solvers

Figure 5 presents the cactus plot of the performances of the different D&C solvers. These differ in two orthogonal axes: the used subspace allocation technique, and the used division heuristic. We analyse here each axe separately.

---

[8] http://sat2018.forsyte.tuwien.ac.at/benchmarks/Main.zip.
[9] The used measure in the annual SAT Competition.

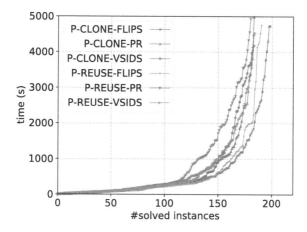

Fig. 5. Cactus plot of the different divide-and-conquer based solvers

When considering the allocation technique (clone *vs.* reuse), we can observe that the cloning based strategy is globally more efficient, even if it has a supplementary cost (due to the cloning phase). The scatter plots of Fig. 6 confirm this observation (most plots are below the diagonal, showing evidence of a better average performance). We believe this is due to the local knowledge that is implicitly shared between the (cloned) workers.

When considering the division heuristics (VSIDS, number of flips, and propagation rate), we observe that number of flips based approach is better than the two others. Both, by the number of solved instances and the PAR-2 measure. This is particularly true when considering the cloning based strategy. VSIDS and propagation rate based solvers are almost identical.

5.2   Comparison with State-of-the-Art Divide-and-Conquer

Figure 7 shows a cactus plot comparing our best divide-and-conquer (*i.e.*, P-CLO-NE-FLIPS) against `Treengeling` and `MapleAmpharos`.

The `MapleAmpharos` solver seems to be less efficient than our tool, and solves less instances. When considering only the 123 instances that both solvers were able to solve, we can calculate the cumulative execution time of this intersection (CTI) for `MapleAmpharos` and P-CLONE-FLIPS: it is, respectively, 24h33min and 14h34min.

Although our tool solves 2 less instances as `Treengeling`, it has better PAR-2 measure. The CTI calculated on the 169 instances solved by both solvers, is 49h14min and 22h23min, respectively for `Treengeling` and P-CLONE-FLIPS. We can say that even if both solve almost the same number of instances, our D&C solver is faster. We clearly observe this phenomenon in Fig. 7.

Thus, in addition to highlight the performance of our instantiation, this shows the effectiveness of the flip-based approach with respect to the well-proven cube-and-conquer strategies.

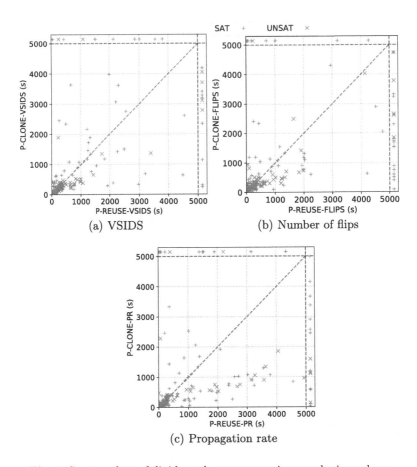

(a) VSIDS

(b) Number of flips

(c) Propagation rate

Fig. 6. Scatter plots of divide-and-conquer reusing *vs.* cloning solvers

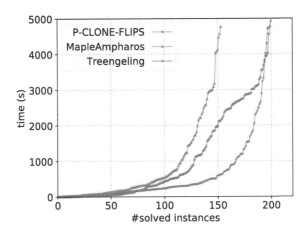

Fig. 7. Cactus plot of the best instantiated divide-and-conquer and state-of-the-art solvers

6   Conclusion

This paper proposed an optimal implementation of several parallel SAT solvers using the divide-and-conquer (D&C) strategy that handle parallelisms by performing successive divisions of the search space.

Such an implementation was performed on top of the `Painless` framework that allows to easily deal with variants of strategies. Our `Painless`-based implementation can be customized and adapted over six orthogonal axes: (1) technique to divide the search space; (2) technique to choose the division variables; (3) load balancing strategy; (4) the sharing strategy; (5) the subspace allocation technique; (6) and the used underlying sequential solver.

This work shows that we have now a modular and efficient framework to explore new D&C strategies along these six axes. We were then able to make a fair comparison between numerous strategies.

Among the numerous solvers we have available, we selected six of them for performance evaluation. Charts are provided to show how they competed, but also how they cope face to natively implemented D&C state-of-the-art solvers.

This study shows that the flip-based approach in association with the clone policy outperforms the other strategies whatever the used standard metrics is. Moreover, when compared with the state-of-the-art D&C-based solvers, our best solver shows to be very efficient and allows us to conclude the effectiveness of our modular platform based approach with respect to the well-competitive D&C solvers.

In the near future, we want to conduct more massive experiments to measure the impact of clauses sharing strategies in the D&C context, and evaluate the scalability of the various D&C approaches.

References

1. Audemard, G., Hoessen, B., Jabbour, S., Piette, C.: Dolius: a distributed parallel SAT solving framework. In: Pragmatics of SAT International Workshop (POS) at SAT, pp. 1–11. Citeseer (2014)
2. Audemard, G., Lagniez, J.-M., Szczepanski, N., Tabary, S.: An adaptive parallel SAT solver. In: Rueher, M. (ed.) CP 2016. LNCS, vol. 9892, pp. 30–48. Springer, Cham (2016). https://doi.org/10.1007/978-3-319-44953-1_3
3. Audemard, G., Simon, L.: Predicting learnt clauses quality in modern SAT solvers. In: Proceedings of the 21st International Joint Conferences on Artifical Intelligence (IJCAI), pp. 399–404. AAAI Press (2009)
4. Audemard, G., Simon, L.: Lazy clause exchange policy for parallel SAT solvers. In: Sinz, C., Egly, U. (eds.) SAT 2014. LNCS, vol. 8561, pp. 197–205. Springer, Cham (2014). https://doi.org/10.1007/978-3-319-09284-3_15
5. Balyo, T., Sanders, P., Sinz, C.: HordeSat: a massively parallel portfolio SAT solver. In: Heule, M., Weaver, S. (eds.) SAT 2015. LNCS, vol. 9340, pp. 156–172. Springer, Cham (2015). https://doi.org/10.1007/978-3-319-24318-4_12
6. Biere, A.: CaDiCaL, Lingeling, Plingeling, Treengeling and YalSAT entering the SAT competition 2018. In: Proceedings of SAT Competition 2018: Solver and Benchmark Descriptions, pp. 13–14. Department of Computer Science, University of Helsinki, Finland (2018)

7. Biere, A., Cimatti, A., Clarke, E., Zhu, Y.: Symbolic model checking without BDDs. In: Cleaveland, W.R. (ed.) TACAS 1999. LNCS, vol. 1579, pp. 193–207. Springer, Heidelberg (1999). https://doi.org/10.1007/3-540-49059-0_14

8. Biere, A., Heule, M., van Maaren, H.: Handbook of Satisfiability, vol. 185. IOS Press, Amsterdam (2009)

9. Davis, M., Logemann, G., Loveland, D.: A machine program for theorem-proving. Commun. ACM **5**(7), 394–397 (1962)

10. Davis, M., Putnam, H.: A computing procedure for quantification theory. J. ACM **7**(3), 201–215 (1960)

11. Hamadi, Y., Jabbour, S., Sais, L.: ManySAT: a parallel SAT solver. J. Satisfiability Boolean Model. Comput. **6**(4), 245–262 (2009)

12. Heule, M.J.H., Kullmann, O., Wieringa, S., Biere, A.: Cube and conquer: guiding CDCL SAT solvers by lookaheads. In: Eder, K., Lourenço, J., Shehory, O. (eds.) HVC 2011. LNCS, vol. 7261, pp. 50–65. Springer, Heidelberg (2012). https://doi.org/10.1007/978-3-642-34188-5_8

13. Hyvärinen, A.E.J., Junttila, T., Niemelä, I.: A distribution method for solving SAT in grids. In: Biere, A., Gomes, C.P. (eds.) SAT 2006. LNCS, vol. 4121, pp. 430–435. Springer, Heidelberg (2006). https://doi.org/10.1007/11814948_39

14. Hyvärinen, A.E.J., Manthey, N.: Designing scalable parallel SAT solvers. In: Cimatti, A., Sebastiani, R. (eds.) SAT 2012. LNCS, vol. 7317, pp. 214–227. Springer, Heidelberg (2012). https://doi.org/10.1007/978-3-642-31612-8_17

15. Jurkowiak, B., Li, C.M., Utard, G.: Parallelizing satz using dynamic workload balancing. Electron. Notes Discrete Math. **9**, 174–189 (2001)

16. Kautz, H.A., Selman, B., et al.: Planning as satisfiability. In: Proceedings of the 10th European Conference on Artificial Intelligence (ECAI), vol. 92, pp. 359–363 (1992)

17. Lanti, D., Manthey, N.: Sharing information in parallel search with search space partitioning. In: Nicosia, G., Pardalos, P. (eds.) LION 2013. LNCS, vol. 7997, pp. 52–58. Springer, Heidelberg (2013). https://doi.org/10.1007/978-3-642-44973-4_6

18. Le Frioux, L., Baarir, S., Sopena, J., Kordon, F.: PaInleSS: a framework for parallel SAT solving. In: Gaspers, S., Walsh, T. (eds.) SAT 2017. LNCS, vol. 10491, pp. 233–250. Springer, Cham (2017). https://doi.org/10.1007/978-3-319-66263-3_15

19. Liang, J.H., Oh, C., Ganesh, V., Czarnecki, K., Poupart, P.: MapleCOMSPS, mapleCOMSPS LRB, mapleCOMSPS CHB. In: Proceedings of SAT Competition 2016: Solver and Benchmark Descriptions, p. 52. Department of Computer Science, University of Helsinki, Finland (2016)

20. Lynce, I., Marques-Silva, J.: SAT in bioinformatics: making the case with haplotype inference. In: Biere, A., Gomes, C.P. (eds.) SAT 2006. LNCS, vol. 4121, pp. 136–141. Springer, Heidelberg (2006). https://doi.org/10.1007/11814948_16

21. Marques-Silva, J.P., Sakallah, K.: GRASP: a search algorithm for propositional satisfiability. IEEE Trans. Comput. **48**(5), 506–521 (1999)

22. Martins, R., Manquinho, V., Lynce, I.: Improving search space splitting for parallel SAT solving. In: Proceedings of the 22nd IEEE International Conference on Tools with Artificial Intelligence (ICTAI), vol. 1, pp. 336–343. IEEE (2010)

23. Massacci, F., Marraro, L.: Logical cryptanalysis as a SAT problem. J. Autom. Reasoning **24**(1), 165–203 (2000)

24. Michael, M.M., Scott, M.L.: Simple, fast, and practical non-blocking and blocking concurrent queue algorithms. In: Proceedings of the 15th ACM Symposium on Principles of Distributed Computing (PODC), pp. 267–275. ACM (1996)

25. Moskewicz, M.W., Madigan, C.F., Zhao, Y., Zhang, L., Malik, S.: Chaff: engineering an efficient SAT solver. In: Proceedings of the 38th Design Automation Conference (DAC), pp. 530–535. ACM (2001)
26. Nejati, S., et al.: A propagation rate based splitting heuristic for divide-and-conquer solvers. In: Gaspers, S., Walsh, T. (eds.) SAT 2017. LNCS, vol. 10491, pp. 251–260. Springer, Cham (2017). https://doi.org/10.1007/978-3-319-66263-3_16
27. Plaza, S., Markov, I., Bertacco, V.: Low-latency SAT solving on multicore processors with priority scheduling and XOR partitioning. In: the 17th International Workshop on Logic and Synthesis (IWLS) at DAC (2008)
28. Silva, J.P.M., Sakallah, K.A.: GRASP–a new search algorithm for satisfiability. In: Proceedings of the 16th IEEE/ACM International Conference on Computer-Aided Design (ICCAD), pp. 220–227. IEEE (1997)
29. Zhang, H., Bonacina, M.P., Hsiang, J.: PSATO: a distributed propositional prover and its application to quasigroup problems. J. Symb. Comput. **21**(4), 543–560 (1996)
30. Zhang, L., Madigan, C.F., Moskewicz, M.H., Malik, S.: Efficient conflict driven learning in a boolean satisfiability solver. In: Proceedings of the 20th IEEE/ACM International Conference on Computer-Aided Design (ICCAD), pp. 279–285. IEEE (2001)

SAT Solving and Theorem Proving

Quantitative Verification of Masked Arithmetic Programs Against Side-Channel Attacks

Pengfei Gao[1], Hongyi Xie[1], Jun Zhang[1], Fu Song[1(✉)], and Taolue Chen[2]

[1] School of Information Science and Technology,
ShanghaiTech University, Shanghai, China
`songfu@shanghaitech.edu.cn`
[2] Department of Computer Science and Information Systems,
Birkbeck, University of London, London, UK

Abstract. Power side-channel attacks, which can deduce secret data via statistical analysis, have become a serious threat. Masking is an effective countermeasure for reducing the statistical dependence between secret data and side-channel information. However, designing masking algorithms is an error-prone process. In this paper, we propose a hybrid approach combing type inference and model-counting to verify masked arithmetic programs against side-channel attacks. The type inference allows an efficient, lightweight procedure to determine most observable variables whereas model-counting accounts for completeness. In case that the program is not perfectly masked, we also provide a method to quantify the security level of the program. We implement our methods in a tool QMVERIF and evaluate it on cryptographic benchmarks. The experiment results show the effectiveness and efficiency of our approach.

1 Introduction

Side-channel attacks aim to infer secret data (e.g. cryptographic keys) by exploiting statistical dependence between secret data and non-functional observations such as execution time [33], power consumption [34], and electromagnetic radiation [46]. They have become a serious threat in application domains such as cyber-physical systems. As a typical example, the power consumption of a device executing the instruction $c = p \oplus k$ usually depends on the secret k, and this can be exploited via *differential power analysis* (DPA) [37] to deduce k.

Masking is one of the most widely-used and effective countermeasure to thwart side-channel attacks. Masking is essentially a randomization technique for reducing the statistical dependence between secret data and side-channel information (e.g. power consumption). For example, using Boolean masking scheme, one can mask the secret data k by applying the exclusive-or ($\oplus$) operation with a random variable r, yielding a masked secret data $k \oplus r$. It can be readily verified that the distribution of $k \oplus r$ is independent of the value of k when r is

This work is supported by NSFC (61532019, 61761136011), EPSRC (EP/P00430X/1), and ARC (DP160101652, DP180100691).

T. Vojnar and L. Zhang (Eds.): TACAS 2019, Part I, LNCS 11427, pp. 155–173, 2019.
https://doi.org/10.1007/978-3-030-17462-0_9

uniformly distributed. Besides Boolean masking scheme, there are other masking schemes such as additive masking schemes (e.g. $(k + r) \bmod n$) and multiplicative masking schemes (e.g. $(k \times r) \bmod n$). A variety of masking implementations such as AES and its non-linear components (S-boxes) have been published over the years. However, designing effective and efficient masking schemes is still a notoriously difficult task, especially for non-linear functions. This has motivated a large amount of work on verifying whether masked implementations, as either (hardware) circuits or (software) programs, are statistically independent of secret inputs. Typically, masked hardware implementations are modeled as (probabilistic) Boolean programs where all variables range over the Boolean domain (i.e. $\mathbb{GF}(2)$), while masked software implementations, featuring a richer set of operations, require to be modeled as (probabilistic) arithmetic programs.

Verification techniques for masking schemes can be roughly classified into type system based approaches [3–5,14,16,19,38] and model-counting based approaches [24,25,50]. The basic idea of type system based approaches is to infer a *distribution type* for observable variables in the program that are potentially exposed to attackers. From the type information one may be able to show that the program is secure. This class of approaches is generally very efficient mainly because of their static analysis nature. However, they may give inconclusive answers as most existing type systems do not provide completeness guarantees.

Model-counting based approaches, unsurprisingly, encode the verification problem as a series of model-counting problems, and typically leverage SAT/SMT solvers. The main advantage of this approach is its completeness guarantees. However, the size of the model-counting constraint is usually exponential in the number of (bits of) random variables used in masking, hence the approach poses great challenges to its scalability. We mention that, within this category, some work further exploits Fourier analysis [11,15], which considers the Fourier expansion of the Boolean functions. The verification problem can then be reduced to checking whether certain coefficients of the Fourier expansion are zero or not. Although there is no hurdle in principle, to our best knowledge currently model-counting based approaches are limited to Boolean programs only.

While verification of masking for Boolean programs is well-studied [24,50], generalizing them to arithmetic programs brings additional challenges. First of all, arithmetic programs admit more operations which are absent from Boolean programs. A typical example is field multiplication. In the Boolean domain, it is nothing more than $\oplus$ which is a bit operation. However for $\mathbb{GF}(2^n)$ (typically $n = 8$ in cryptographic algorithm implementations), the operation is nontrivial which prohibits many optimization which would otherwise be useful for Boolean domains. Second, verification of arithmetic programs often suffers from serious scalability issues, especially when the model-counting based approaches are applied. We note that transforming arithmetic programs into equivalent Boolean versions is theoretically possible, but suffer from several deficiencies: (1) one has to encode complicated arithmetic operations (e.g. finite field multiplication) as bitwise operations; (2) the resulting Boolean program needs to be checked against higher-order attacks which are supposed to observe multiple observations simultaneously. This is a far more difficult problem. Because of this, we believe such as approach is practically, if not infeasible, unfavourable.

Perfect masking is ideal but not necessarily holds when there are flaws or only a limited number of random variables are allowed for efficiency consideration. In case that the program is not perfectly masked (i.e., a potential side channel does exist), naturally one wants to tell how severe it is. For instance, one possible measure is the resource the attacker needs to invest in order to infer the secret from the side channel. For this purpose, we adapt the notion of *Quantitative Masking Strength*, with which a correlation of the number of power traces to successfully infer secret has been established empirically [26,27].

Main Contributions. We mainly focus on the verification of masked *arithmetic* programs. We advocate a hybrid verification method combining type system based and model-counting based approaches, and provide additional quantitative analysis. We summarize the main contributions as follows.

- We provide a hybrid approach which integrates type system based and model-counting based approaches into a framework, and support a sound and complete reasoning of masked arithmetic programs.
- We provide quantitative analysis in case when the masking is not effective, to calculate a quantitative measure of the information leakage.
- We provide various heuristics and optimized algorithms to significantly improve the scalability of previous approaches.
- We implement our approaches in a software tool and provide thorough evaluations. Our experiments show orders of magnitude of improvement with respect to previous verification methods on common benchmarks.

We find, perhaps surprisingly, that for model-counting, the widely adopted approaches based on SMT solvers (e.g. [24,25,50]) may not be the best approach, as our experiments suggest that an alternative brute-force approach is comparable for Boolean programs, and significantly outperforms for arithmetic programs.

Related Work. The d-threshold probing model is the de facto standard leakage model for order-d power side-channel attacks [32]. This paper focuses on the case that $d = 1$. Other models like noise leakage model [17,45], bounded moment model [6], and threshold probing model with transitions/glitch [15,20] could be reduced to the threshold probing model, at the cost of introducing higher orders [3]. Other work on side channels such as execution-time, faults, and cache do exist ([1,2,7,8,12,28,31,33] to cite a few), but is orthogonal to our work.

Type systems have been widely used in the verification of side channel attacks with early work [9,38], where masking compilers are provided which can transform an input program into a functionally equivalent program that is resistant to first-order DPA. However, these systems either are limited to certain operations (i.e., $\oplus$ and table look-up), or suffer from unsoundness and incompleteness under the threshold probing model. To support verification of higher-order masking, Barthe et al. introduced the notion of noninterference (NI, [3]), and strong t-noninterference (SNI, [4]), which were extended to give a unified framework for both software and hardware implementations in `maskVerif` [5]. Further work along this line includes improvements for efficiency [14,19], generalization for assembly-level code [15], and extensions with glitches for hardware programs [29]. As mentioned earlier, these approaches are incomplete, i.e., secure programs may fail to pass their verification.

[24,25] proposed a model-counting based approach for Boolean programs by leveraging SMT solvers, which is complete but limited in scalability. To improve efficiency, a hybrid approach integrating type-based and model-counting based approaches [24,25] was proposed in [50], which is similar to the current work in spirit. However, it is limited to Boolean programs and qualitative analysis only. [26,27] extended the approach of [24,25] for quantitative analysis, but is limited to Boolean programs. The current work not only extends the applicability but also achieves significant improvement in efficiency even for Boolean programs (cf. Sect. 5). We also find that solving model-counting via SMT solvers [24,50] may not be the best approach, in particular for arithmetic programs.

Our work is related to quantitative information flow (QIF) [13,35,43,44,49] which leverages notions from information theory (typically Shannon entropy and mutual information) to measure the flow of information in programs. The QIF framework has also been specialized to side-channel analysis [36,41,42]. The main differences are, first of all, QIF targets fully-fledged programs (including branching and loops) so program analysis techniques (e.g. symbolic execution) are needed, while we deal with more specialized (transformed) masked programs in straight-line forms; second, to measure the information leakage quantitatively, our measure is based on the notion QMS which is correlated with the number of power traces needed to successfully infer the secret, while QIF is based on a more general sense of information theory; third, for calculating such a measure, both works rely on model-counting. In QIF, the constraints over the input are usually linear, but the constraints in our setting involve arithmetic operations in rings and fields. Randomized approximate schemes can be exploited in QIF [13] which is not suitable in our setting. Moreover, we mention that in QIF, input variables should in principle be partitioned into public and private variables, and the former of which needs to be existentially quantified. This was briefly mentioned in, e.g., [36], but without implementation.

2   Preliminaries

Let us fix a bounded integer domain $\mathbb{D} = \{0, \cdots, 2^n - 1\}$, where n is a fixed positive integer. Bit-wise operations are defined over $\mathbb{D}$, but we shall also consider arithmetic operations over $\mathbb{D}$ which include $+, -, \times$ modulo 2^n for which $\mathbb{D}$ is consider to be a ring and the Galois field multiplication $\odot$ where $\mathbb{D}$ is isomorphic to $\mathbb{GF}(2)[x]/(p(x))$ (or simply $\mathbb{GF}(2^n)$) for some irreducible polynomial p. For instance, in AES one normally uses $\mathbb{GF}(2^8)$ and $p(x) = x^8 + x^4 + x^3 + x^2 + 1$.

2.1   Cryptographic Programs

We focus on programs written in C-like code that implement cryptographic algorithms such as AES, as opposed to arbitrary software programs. To analyze such programs, it is common to assume that they are given in straight-line forms (i.e., branching-free) over $\mathbb{D}$ [3,24]. The syntax of the program under consideration is given as follows, where $c \in \mathbb{D}$.

Operation: $\mathcal{O} \ni \circ ::= \oplus \mid \wedge \mid \vee \mid \odot \mid + \mid - \mid \times$
Expression: $e ::= c \mid x \mid e \circ e \mid \neg e \mid e \ll c \mid e \gg c$
Statememt: $\mathtt{stmt} ::= x \leftarrow e \mid \mathtt{stmt}; \mathtt{stmt}$
Program: $P(X_p, X_k, X_r) ::= \mathtt{stmt}; \mathtt{return}\ x_1, ..., x_m$

A program P consists of a sequence of assignments followed by a return statement. An assignment $x \leftarrow e$ assigns the value of the expression e to the variable x, where e is built up from a set of variables and constants using (1) bit-wise operations *negation* ($\neg$), *and* ($\wedge$), *or* ($\vee$), *exclusive-or* ($\oplus$), *left shift* $\ll$ and *right shift* $\gg$; (2) modulo 2^n arithmetic operations: *addition* ($+$), *subtraction* ($-$), *multiplication* ($\times$); and (3) finite-field *multiplication* ($\odot$) (over $\mathbb{GF}(2^n)$)[1]. We denote by $\mathcal{O}^*$ the extended set $\mathcal{O} \cup \{\ll, \gg\}$ of operations.

Given a program P, let $X = X_p \uplus X_k \uplus X_i \uplus X_r$ denote the set of variables used in P, where X_p, X_k and X_i respectively denote the set of public input, private input and internal variables, and X_r denotes the set of (uniformly distributed) random variables for *masking* private variables. We assume that the program is given in the *single static assignment* (SSA) form (i.e., each variable is defined exactly once) and each expression uses at most one operator. (One can easily transform an arbitrary straight-line program into an equivalent one satisfying these conditions.) For each assignment $x \leftarrow e$ in P, **the computation $\mathcal{E}(x)$ of** x is an expression obtained from e by iteratively replacing all the occurrences of the internal variables in e by their defining expressions in P. SSA form guarantees that $\mathcal{E}(x)$ is well-defined.

Semantics. A *valuation* is a function $\sigma : X_p \cup X_k \to \mathbb{D}$ assigning to each variable $x \in X_p \cup X_k$ a value $c \in \mathbb{D}$. Let Θ denote the set of all valuations. Two valuations $\sigma_1, \sigma_2 \in \Theta$ are *Y-equivalent*, denoted by $\sigma_1 \approx_Y \sigma_2$, if $\sigma_1(x) = \sigma_2(x)$ for all $x \in Y$.

Given an expression e in terms of $X_p \cup X_k \cup X_r$ and a valuation $\sigma \in \Theta$, we denote by $e(\sigma)$ the expression obtained from e by replacing all the occurrences of variables $x \in X_p \cup X_k$ by their values $\sigma(x)$, and denote by $\llbracket e \rrbracket_\sigma$ the distribution of e (with respect to the uniform distribution of random variables $e(\sigma)$ may contain). Concretely, $\llbracket e \rrbracket_\sigma(v)$ is the probability of the expression $e(\sigma)$ being evaluated to v for each $v \in \mathbb{D}$. For each variable $x \in X$ and valuation $\sigma \in \Theta$, we denote by $\llbracket x \rrbracket_\sigma$ the distribution $\llbracket \mathcal{E}(x) \rrbracket_\sigma$. The semantics of the program P is defined as a (partial) function $\llbracket P \rrbracket$ which takes a valuation $\sigma \in \Theta$ and an internal variable $x \in X_i$ as inputs, returns the distribution $\llbracket x \rrbracket_\sigma$ of x.

Threat Models and Security Notions. We assume that the adversary has access to public input X_p, but not to private input X_k or random variables X_r, of a program P. However, the adversary may have access to an internal variable $x \in X_i$ via side-channels. Under these assumptions, the goal of the adversary is to deduce the information of X_k.

---

[1] Note that addition/subtraction over Galois fields is essentially bit-wise exclusive-or.

```
1 Cube(k, r₀, r₁){        6    x₃ = x₁ ⊙ x ;         11    x₈ = x₁ ⊙ r₀ ;
2    x = k ⊕ r₀ ;         7    x₄ = r₁ ⊕ x₂ ;        12    x₉ = x₈ ⊕ x₅ ;
3    x₀ = x ⊙ x ;         8    x₅ = x₄ ⊕ x₃ ;        13    return (x₇, x₉) ;
4    x₁ = r₀ ⊙ r₀ ;       9    x₆ = x₀ ⊙ x ;         14 }
5    x₂ = x₀ ⊙ r₀ ;      10    x₇ = x₆ ⊕ r₁ ;
```

Fig. 1. A buggy version of Cube from [47]

Definition 1. *Let P be a program. For every internal variable $x \in X_i$,*

- *x is* uniform *in P, denoted by x-**UF**, if $[\![P]\!](\sigma)(x)$ is uniform for all $\sigma \in \Theta$.*
- *x is* statistically independent *in P, denoted by x-**SI**, if $[\![P]\!](\sigma_1)(x) = [\![P]\!](\sigma_2)(x)$ for all $(\sigma_1, \sigma_2) \in \Theta^2_{X_p}$, where $\Theta^2_{X_p} := \{(\sigma_1, \sigma_2) \in \Theta \times \Theta \mid \sigma_1 \approx_{X_p} \sigma_2\}$.*

Proposition 1. *If the program P is x-**UF**, then P is x-**SI**.*

Definition 2. *For a program P, a variable x is* perfectly masked *(a.k.a. secure under 1-threshold probing model [32]) in P if it is x-**SI**, otherwise x is* leaky.
P is perfectly masked *if all internal variables in P are perfectly masked.*

2.2 Quantitative Masking Strength

When a program is not perfectly masked, it is important to quantify how secure it is. For this purpose, we adapt the notion of *Quantitative Masking Strength* (QMS) from [26,27] to quantify the strength of masking countermeasures.

Definition 3. *The* quantitative masking strength QMS_x *of a variable $x \in X$, is defined as:* $1 - \max_{(\sigma_1, \sigma_2) \in \Theta^2_{X_p}, c \in \mathbb{D}} \left([\![x]\!]_{\sigma_1}(c) - [\![x]\!]_{\sigma_2}(c) \right)$.
Accordingly, the quantitative masking strength of the program P is defined by $\mathsf{QMS}_P := \min_{x \in X_i} \mathsf{QMS}_x$.

The notion of QMS generalizes that of perfect masking, i.e., P is x-**SI** iff $\mathsf{QMS}_x = 1$. The importance of QMS has been highlighted in [26,27] where it is empirically shown that, for Boolean programs the number of power traces needed to determine the secret key is exponential in the QMS value. This study suggests that computing an *accurate* QMS value for leaky variables is highly desirable.

Example 1. Let us consider the program in Fig. 1, which implements a buggy Cube in $\mathrm{GF}(2^8)$ from [47]. Given a secret key k, to avoid first-order side-channel attacks, k is masked by a random variable r_0 leading to two shares $x = k \oplus r_0$ and r_0. Cube(k, r_0, r_1) returns two shares x_7 and x_9 such that $x_7 \oplus x_9 = k^3 := k \odot k \odot k$, where r_1 is another random variable.

Cube computes $k \odot k$ by $x_0 = x \odot x$ and $x_1 = r_0 \odot r_0$ (Lines 3–4), as $k \odot k = x_0 \oplus x_1$. Then, it computes k^3 by a secure multiplication of two pairs of shares (x_0, x_1) and (x, r_0) using the random variable r_1 (Lines 5–12). However, this program is vulnerable to first-order side-channel attacks, as it is neither x_2-**SI** nor x_3-**SI**. As shown in [47], we shall refresh (x_0, x_1) before computing $k^2 \odot k$ by inserting

$x_0 = x_0 \oplus r_2$ and $x_1 = x_1 \oplus r_2$ after Line 4, where r_2 is a random variable. We use this buggy version as a running example to illustrate our techniques.

As setup for further use, we have: $X_p = \emptyset$, $X_k = \{k\}$, $X_r = \{r_0, r_1\}$ and $X_i = \{x, x_0, \cdots, x_9\}$. The computations $\mathcal{E}(\cdot)$ of internal variables are:

$\mathcal{E}(x) = k \oplus r_0 \qquad \mathcal{E}(x_0) = (k \oplus r_0) \odot (k \oplus r_0) \qquad \mathcal{E}(x_1) = r_0 \odot r_0$

$\mathcal{E}(x_2) = ((k \oplus r_0) \odot (k \oplus r_0)) \odot r_0 \qquad\qquad \mathcal{E}(x_3) = (r_0 \odot r_0) \odot (k \oplus r_0)$

$\mathcal{E}(x_4) = r_1 \oplus (((k \oplus r_0) \odot (k \oplus r_0)) \odot r_0) \qquad \mathcal{E}(x_6) = ((k \oplus r_0) \odot (k \oplus r_0)) \odot (k \oplus r_0)$

$\mathcal{E}(x_5) = (r_1 \oplus ((k \oplus r_0) \odot (k \oplus r_0)) \odot r_0) \oplus ((r_0 \odot r_0) \odot (k \oplus r_0))$

$\mathcal{E}(x_7) = (((k \oplus r_0) \odot (k \oplus r_0)) \odot (k \oplus r_0)) \oplus r_1 \quad \mathcal{E}(x_8) = (r_0 \odot r_0) \odot r_0$

$\mathcal{E}(x_9) = ((r_0 \odot r_0) \odot r_0) \oplus ((r_1 \oplus ((k \oplus r_0) \odot (k \oplus r_0) \odot r_0)) \oplus ((r_0 \odot r_0) \odot (k \oplus r_0)))$

3 Three Key Techniques

In this section, we introduce three key techniques: type system, model-counting based reasoning and reduction techniques, which will be used in our algorithm.

3.1 Type System

We present a type system for formally inferring *distribution types* of internal variables, inspired by prior work [3,14,40,50]. We start with some basic notations.

Definition 4 (Dominant variables). *Given an expression e, a random variable r is called a* dominant variable *of e if the following two conditions hold: (i) r occurs in e exactly once, and (ii) each operator on the path between the leaf r and the root in the abstract syntax tree of e is from either $\{\oplus, \neg, +, -\}$ or $\{\odot\}$ such that one of the children of the operator is a non-zero constant.*

Remark that in Definition 4, for efficiency consideration, we take a purely syntactic approach meaning that we do not simplify e when checking the condition (i) that r occurs once. For instance, x is *not* a dominant variable in $((x \oplus y) \oplus x) \oplus x$, although intuitively e is equivalent to $y \oplus x$.

Given an expression e, let $\mathsf{Var}(e)$ be the set of variables occurring in e, and $\mathsf{RVar}(e) := \mathsf{Var}(e) \cap X_r$. We denote by $\mathsf{Dom}(e) \subseteq \mathsf{RVar}(e)$ the set of all dominant random variables of e, which can be computed in linear time in the size of e.

Proposition 2. *Given a program P with $\mathcal{E}(x)$ defined for each variable x of P, if $\mathsf{Dom}(\mathcal{E}(x)) \neq \emptyset$, then P is x-$\mathbf{UF}$.*

Definition 5 (Distribution Types). *Let $\mathcal{T} = \{\mathsf{RUD}, \mathsf{SID}, \mathsf{SDD}, \mathsf{UKD}\}$ be the set of distribution types, where for each variable $x \in X$,*

- *$\mathcal{E}(x) : \mathsf{RUD}$ meaning that the program is x-$\mathbf{UF}$;*
- *$\mathcal{E}(x) : \mathsf{SID}$ meaning that the program is x-$\mathbf{SI}$;*
- *$\mathcal{E}(x) : \mathsf{SDD}$ meaning that the program is not x-$\mathbf{SI}$;*
- *$\mathcal{E}(x) : \mathsf{UKD}$ meaning that the distribution type of x is unknown.*

where RUD is a subtype of SID (cf. Proposition 1).

$$\frac{\mathsf{Dom}(e) \neq \emptyset}{\vdash e : \mathsf{RUD}} \ (\mathrm{Dom}) \qquad \frac{\vdash e_1 \star e_2 : \tau}{\vdash e_2 \star e_1 : \tau} \ (\mathrm{Com}) \qquad \frac{\vdash e : \tau}{\vdash \neg e : \tau} \ (\mathrm{IDE}_1)$$

$$\frac{\vdash e : \mathsf{SID}}{\vdash e \bullet e : \mathsf{SID}} \ (\mathrm{IDE}_2) \qquad \frac{}{\vdash e \diamond e : \mathsf{SID}} \ (\mathrm{IDE}_3) \qquad \frac{\vdash e : \mathsf{SDD}}{\vdash e \bowtie e : \mathsf{SDD}} \ (\mathrm{IDE}_4)$$

$$\frac{\mathsf{Var}(e) \cap X_k = \emptyset}{\vdash e : \mathsf{SID}} \ (\mathrm{NoKey}) \qquad \frac{x \in X_k}{\vdash x : \mathsf{SDD}} \ (\mathrm{Key}) \qquad \frac{\vdash e_1 : \mathsf{RUD} \ \vdash e_2 : \mathsf{RUD}}{\mathsf{Dom}(e_1) \setminus \mathsf{RVar}(e_2) \neq \emptyset}{\vdash e_1 \circ e_2 : \mathsf{SID}} \ (\mathrm{SID}_1)$$

$$\frac{\vdash e_1 : \mathsf{SID} \ \vdash e_2 : \mathsf{SID}}{\mathsf{RVar}(e_1) \cap \mathsf{RVar}(e_2) = \emptyset}{\vdash e_1 \bullet e_2 : \mathsf{SID}} \ (\mathrm{SID}_2) \qquad \frac{\vdash e_1 : \mathsf{SDD} \ \vdash e_2 : \mathsf{RUD}}{\mathsf{Dom}(e_2) \setminus \mathsf{RVar}(e_1) \neq \emptyset}{\vdash e_1 \circ e_2 : \mathsf{SDD}} \ (\mathrm{SDD}) \qquad \frac{\text{No rule is}}{\text{appliable to } e}{\vdash e : \mathsf{UKD}} \ (\mathrm{UKD})$$

Fig. 2. Type inference rules, where $\star \in \mathcal{O}$, $\circ \in \{\wedge, \vee, \odot, \times\}$, $\bullet \in \mathcal{O}^*$, $\bowtie \in \{\wedge, \vee\}$ and $\diamond \in \{\oplus, -\}$.

Type judgements, as usual, are defined in the form of $\vdash e : \tau$, where e is an expression in terms of $X_r \cup X_k \cup X_p$, and $\tau \in \mathcal{T}$ denotes the distribution type of e. A type judgement $\vdash e : \mathsf{RUD}$ (resp. $\vdash e : \mathsf{SID}$ and $\vdash e : \mathsf{SDD}$) is valid iff P is x-**UF** (resp. x-**SI** and not x-**SI**) for all variables x such that $\mathcal{E}(x) = e$. A sound proof system for deriving valid type judgements is given in Fig. 2.

Rule (Dom) states that e containing some dominant variable has type RUD (cf. Proposition 2). Rule (Com) captures the commutative law of operators $\star \in \mathcal{O}$. Rules (IDE$_i$) for $i = 1, 2, 3, 4$ are straightforward. Rule (NoKey) states that e has type SID if e does not use any private input. Rule (Key) states that each private input has type SDD. Rule (SID$_1$) states that $e_1 \circ e_2$ for $\circ \in \{\wedge, \vee, \odot, \times\}$ has type SID, if both e_1 and e_2 have type RUD, and e_1 has a dominant variable r which is not used by e_2. Indeed, $e_1 \circ e_2$ can be seen as $r \circ e_2$, then for each valuation $\eta \in \Theta$, the distributions of r and $e_2(\eta)$ are independent. Rule (SID$_2$) states that $e_1 \bullet e_2$ for $\bullet \in \mathcal{O}^*$ has type SID, if both e_1 and e_2 have type SID (as well as its subtype RUD), and the sets of random variables used by e_1 and e_2 are disjoint. Likewise, for each valuation $\eta \in \Theta$, the distributions on $e_1(\eta)$ and $e_2(\eta)$ are independent. Rule (SDD) states that $e_1 \circ e_2$ for $\circ \in \{\wedge, \vee, \odot, \times\}$ has type SDD, if e_1 has type SDD, e_2 has type RUD, and e_2 has a dominant variable r which is not used by e_1. Intuitively, $e_1 \circ e_2$ can be safely seen as $e_1 \circ r$.

Finally, if no rule is applicable to an expression e, then e has unknown distribution type. Such a type is needed because our type system is—by design—incomplete. However, we expect—and demonstrate empirically—that for cryptographic programs, most internal variables have a definitive type other than UKD. As we will show later, to resolve UKD-typed variables, one can resort to model-counting (cf. Sect. 3.2).

Theorem 1. If $\vdash \mathcal{E}(x) : \mathsf{RUD}$ (resp. $\vdash \mathcal{E}(x) : \mathsf{SID}$ and $\vdash \mathcal{E}(x) : \mathsf{SDD}$) is valid, then P is x-**UF** (resp. x-**SI** and not x-**SI**).

Example 2. Consider the program in Fig. 1, we have:

$$\vdash \mathcal{E}(x) : \mathsf{RUD}; \quad \vdash \mathcal{E}(x_0) : \mathsf{SID}; \quad \vdash \mathcal{E}(x_1) : \mathsf{SID}; \quad \vdash \mathcal{E}(x_2) : \mathsf{UKD};$$
$$\vdash \mathcal{E}(x_3) : \mathsf{UKD}; \quad \vdash \mathcal{E}(x_4) : \mathsf{RUD}; \quad \vdash \mathcal{E}(x_5) : \mathsf{RUD}; \quad \vdash \mathcal{E}(x_6) : \mathsf{UKD};$$
$$\vdash \mathcal{E}(x_7) : \mathsf{RUD}; \quad \vdash \mathcal{E}(x_8) : \mathsf{SID}; \quad \vdash \mathcal{E}(x_9) : \mathsf{RUD}.$$

3.2   Model-Counting Based Reasoning

Recall that for $x \in X_i$, $\text{QMS}_x := 1 - \max_{(\sigma_1,\sigma_2) \in \Theta^2_{X_p}, c \in \mathbb{D}}(\llbracket x \rrbracket_{\sigma_1}(c) - \llbracket x \rrbracket_{\sigma_2}(c))$.

To compute QMS_x, one naive approach is to use brute-force to enumerate all possible valuations σ and then to compute distributions $\llbracket x \rrbracket_\sigma$ again by enumerating the assignments of random variables. This approach is exponential in the number of (bits of) variables in $\mathcal{E}(x)$.

Another approach is to lift the SMT-based approach [26,27] from Boolean setting to the arithmetic one. We first consider a "decision" version of the problem, i.e., checking whether $\text{QMS}_x \geq q$ for a given rational number $q \in [0,1]$. It is not difficult to observe that this can be reduced to checking the satisfiability of the following logic formula:

$$\exists \sigma_1, \sigma_2 \in \Theta^2_{X_p}.\exists c \in \mathbb{D}.\big(\sharp(c = \llbracket x \rrbracket_{\sigma_1}) - \sharp(c = \llbracket x \rrbracket_{\sigma_2})\big) > \Delta^q_x, \qquad (1)$$

where $\sharp(c = \llbracket x \rrbracket_{\sigma_1})$ and $\sharp(c = \llbracket x \rrbracket_{\sigma_2})$ respectively denote the number of satisfying assignments of $c = \llbracket x \rrbracket_{\sigma_1}$ and $c = \llbracket x \rrbracket_{\sigma_2}$, $\Delta^q_x = (1-q) \times 2^m$, and m is the number of bits of random variables in $\mathcal{E}(x)$.

We further encode (1) as a (quantifier-free) first-order formula Ψ^q_x to be solved by an off-the-shelf SMT solver (e.g. Z3 [23]):

$$\Psi^q_x := \big(\bigwedge_{f:\text{RVar}(\mathcal{E}(x)) \to \mathbb{D}} (\Theta_f \wedge \Theta'_f)\big) \wedge \Theta_{\text{b2i}} \wedge \Theta'_{\text{b2i}} \wedge \Theta^q_{\text{diff}}$$

where

- **Program logic** (Θ_f and Θ'_f): for every $f : \text{RVar}(\mathcal{E}(x)) \to \mathbb{D}$, Θ_f encodes $c_f = \mathcal{E}(x)$ into a logical formula with each occurrence of a random variable $r \in \text{RVar}(\mathcal{E}(x))$ being replaced by its value $f(r)$, where c_f is a fresh variable. There are $|\mathbb{D}|^{|\text{RVar}(\mathcal{E}(x))|}$ distinct copies, but share the same X_p and X_k. Θ'_f is similar to Θ_f except that all variables $k \in X_k$ and c_f are replaced by fresh variables k' and c'_f respectively.
- **Boolean to integer** (Θ_{b2i} and Θ'_{b2i}): $\Theta_{\text{b2i}} := \bigwedge_{f:\text{RVar}(\mathcal{E}(x)) \to \mathbb{D}} I_f = (c = c_f)$? 1 : 0. It asserts that for each $f : \text{RVar}(\mathcal{E}(x)) \to \mathbb{D}$, a fresh integer variable I_f is 1 if $c = c_f$, otherwise 0. Θ'_{b2i} is similar to Θ_{b2i} except that I_f and c_f are replaced by I'_f and c'_f respectively.
- **Different sums** (Θ^q_{diff}): $\sum_{f:\text{RVar}(\mathcal{E}(x)) \to \mathbb{D}} I_f - \sum_{f:\text{RVar}(\mathcal{E}(x)) \to \mathbb{D}} I'_f > \Delta^q_x$.

Theorem 2. Ψ^q_x is unsatisfiable iff $\text{QMS}_x \geq q$, and the size of Ψ^q_x is polynomial in $|P|$ and exponential in $|\text{RVar}(\mathcal{E}(x))|$ and $|\mathbb{D}|$.

Based on Theorem 2, we present an algorithm for computing QMS_x in Sect. 4.2.

Note that the qualitative variant of Ψ^q_x (i.e. $q = 1$) can be used to decide whether x is statistically independent by checking whether $\text{QMS}_x = 1$ holds. This will be used in Algorithm 1.

Example 3. By applying the model-counting based reasoning to the program in Fig. 1, we can conclude that x_6 is perfectly masked, while x_2 and x_3 are leaky. This cannot be done by our type system or the ones in [3,4]. To give a sample encoding, consider the variable x_3 for $q = \frac{1}{2}$ and $\mathbb{D} = \{0,1,2,3\}$. We have that $\Psi^{\frac{1}{2}}_{x_3}$ is

$$\begin{pmatrix} c_0 = (0 \odot 0) \odot (k \oplus 0) & \wedge & c_0' = (0 \odot 0) \odot (k' \oplus 0) & \wedge \\ c_1 = (1 \odot 1) \odot (k \oplus 1) & \wedge & c_1' = (1 \odot 1) \odot (k' \oplus 1) & \wedge \\ c_2 = (2 \odot 2) \odot (k \oplus 2) & \wedge & c_2' = (2 \odot 2) \odot (k' \oplus 2) & \wedge \\ c_3 = (3 \odot 3) \odot (k \oplus 3) & \wedge & c_3' = (3 \odot 3) \odot (k' \oplus 3) & \wedge \end{pmatrix}$$

$$\begin{pmatrix} I_0 = (c = c_0) \ ? \ 1 : 0 & \wedge & I_1 = (c = c_1) \ ? \ 1 : 0 & \wedge \\ I_2 = (c = c_2) \ ? \ 1 : 0 & \wedge & I_3 = (c = c_3) \ ? \ 1 : 0 & \wedge \end{pmatrix}$$

$$\begin{pmatrix} I_0' = (c = c_0') \ ? \ 1 : 0 \ \wedge \ I_1' = (c = c_1') \ ? \ 1 : 0 \ \wedge \\ I_2' = (c = c_2') \ ? \ 1 : 0 \ \wedge \ I_3' = (c = c_3') \ ? \ 1 : 0 \ \wedge \end{pmatrix}$$

$$(I_0 + I_1 + I_2 + I_3) - (I_0' + I_1' + I_2' + I_3') > (1 - \tfrac{1}{2})^2$$

3.3   Reduction Heuristics

In this section, we provide various heuristics to reduce the size of formulae. These can be both applied to type inference and model-counting based reasoning.

Ineffective Variable Elimination. A variable x is *ineffective* in an expression e if for all functions $\sigma_1, \sigma_2 : \mathsf{Var}(e) \to \mathbb{D}$ that agree on their values on the variables $\mathsf{Var}(e) \setminus \{x\}$, e has same values under σ_1 and σ_2. Otherwise, we say x is *effective* in e. Clearly if x is ineffective in e, then e and $e[c/x]$ are equivalent for any $c \in \mathbb{D}$ while $e[c/x]$ contains less variables, where $e[c/x]$ is obtained from e by replacing all occurrences of x with c. Checking whether x is effective or not in e can be performed by a satisfiability checking of the logical formula: $e[c/x] \neq e[c'/x]$. Obviously, $e[c/x] \neq e[c'/x]$ is satisfiable iff x is effective in e.

Algebraic Laws. For every sub-expression e' of the form $e_1 \oplus e_1, e_2 - e_2, e \circ 0$ or $0 \circ e$ with $\circ \in \{\times, \odot, \wedge\}$ in the expression e, it is safe to replace e' by 0, namely, e and $e[0/e']$ are equivalent. Note that the constant 0 is usually introduced by instantiating ineffective variables by 0 when eliminating ineffective variables.

Dominated Subexpression Elimination. Given an expression e, if e' is a r-dominated sub-expression in e and r does not occur in e elsewhere, then it is safe to replace each occurrence of e' in e by the random variable r. Intuitively, e' as a whole can be seen as a random variable when evaluating e. Besides this elimination, we also allow to add mete-theorems specifying forms of sub-expressions e' that can be replaced by a fresh variable. For instance, $r \oplus ((2 \times r) \wedge e'')$ in e, when the random variable r does not appear elsewhere, can be replaced by the random variable r.

Let $\widehat{e}$ denote the expression obtained by applying the above heuristics on the expression e.

Transformation Oracle. We suppose there is an oracle Ω which, whenever possible, transforms an expression e into an equivalent expression $\Omega(e)$ such that the type inference can give a non-UKD type to $\Omega(e)$.

Lemma 1. $\mathcal{E}(x)(\sigma)$ *and* $\widehat{\mathcal{E}(x)}(\sigma)$ *have same distribution for any* $\sigma \in \Theta$.

Example 4. Consider the variable x_6 in the program in Fig. 1, $(k \oplus r_0)$ is r_0-dominated sub-expression in $\mathcal{E}(x_6) = ((k \oplus r_0) \odot (k \oplus r_0)) \odot (k \oplus r_0)$, then, we can simplify $\mathcal{E}(x_6)$ into $\widehat{\mathcal{E}(x_6)} = r_0 \odot r_0 \odot r_0$. Therefore, we can deduce that $\vdash \mathcal{E}(x_6) : \mathsf{SID}$ by applying the NoKey rule on $\widehat{\mathcal{E}(x_6)}$.

Algorithm 1. PMCHECKING(P, X_p, X_k, X_r, X_i)

---

1 **Function** PMCHECKING(P, X_p, X_k, X_r, X_i)
2   **foreach** $x \in X_i$ **do**
3   **if** $\vdash \mathcal{E}(x) : \mathsf{UKD}$ *is valid* **then**
4   **if** $\vdash \widehat{\mathcal{E}(x)} : \mathsf{UKD}$ *is valid* **then**
5   **if** $\Omega(\widehat{\mathcal{E}(x)})$ *exists* **then**
6   Let $\vdash \mathcal{E}(x) : \tau$ be valid for valid $\vdash \Omega(\widehat{\mathcal{E}(x)}) : \tau$;
7   **else if** $\mathsf{ModelCountingBasedSolver}(\widehat{\mathcal{E}(x)}) = \mathsf{SAT}$ **then**
8   Let $\vdash \mathcal{E}(x) : \mathsf{SDD}$ be valid;
9   **else** Let $\vdash \mathcal{E}(x) : \mathsf{SID}$ be valid;
10   **else** Let $\vdash \mathcal{E}(x) : \tau$ be valid for valid $\vdash \widehat{\mathcal{E}(x)} : \tau$;

---

4 Overall Algorithms

In this section, we present algorithms to check perfect masking and to compute the QMS values.

4.1 Perfect Masking Verification

Given a program P with the sets of public (X_p), secret (X_k), random (X_r) and internal (X_i) variables, PMCHECKING, given in Algorithm 1, checks whether P is perfectly masked or not. It iteratively traverses all the internal variables. For each variable $x \in X_i$, it first applies the type system to infer its distribution type. If $\vdash \mathcal{E}(x) : \tau$ for $\tau \neq \mathsf{UKD}$ is valid, then the result is conclusive. Otherwise, we will simplify the expression $\mathcal{E}(x)$ and apply the type inference to $\widehat{\mathcal{E}(x)}$.

If it fails to resolve the type of x and $\Omega(\widehat{\mathcal{E}(x)})$ does not exist, we apply the model-counting based (SMT-based or brute-force) approach outlined in Sect. 3.2, in particular, to check the expression $\widehat{\mathcal{E}(x)}$. There are two possible outcomes: either $\widehat{\mathcal{E}(x)}$ is SID or SDD. We enforce $\mathcal{E}(x)$ to have the same distributional type as $\widehat{\mathcal{E}(x)}$ which might facilitate the inference for other expressions.

Theorem 3. *P is perfectly masked iff $\vdash \mathcal{E}(x) : \mathsf{SDD}$ is not valid for any $x \in X_i$, when Algorithm 1 terminates.*

We remark that, if the model-counting is disabled in Algorithm 1 where UKD-typed variables are interpreted as potentially leaky, Algorithm 1 would degenerate to a type inference procedure that is fast and potentially more accurate than the one in [3], owing to the optimization introduced in Sect. 3.3.

4.2 QMS Computing

After applying Algorithm 1, each internal variable $x \in X_i$ is endowed by a distributional type of either SID (or RUD which implies SID) or SDD. In the former case, x is perfectly masked meaning observing x would gain nothing for

---

Algorithm 2. Procedure QMSCOMPUTING(P, X_p, X_k, X_r, X_i)

---

1 **Function** QMSCOMPUTING(P, X_p, X_k, X_r, X_i)
2   PMCHECKING(P, X_p, X_k, X_r, X_i);
3   **foreach** $x \in X_i$ **do**
4   **if** $\vdash \mathcal{E}(x) : \mathsf{SID}$ *is valid* **then** $\mathsf{QMS}_x := 1$;
5   **else**
6   **if** $\mathsf{RVar}(\widehat{\mathcal{E}(x)}) = \emptyset$ **then** $\mathsf{QMS}_x := 0$;
7   **else**
8                  $\mathtt{low} := 0; \mathtt{high} := 2^{n \times |\mathsf{RVar}(\widehat{\mathcal{E}(x)})|}$;
9   **while** $\mathtt{low} < \mathtt{high}$ **do**
10                     $\mathtt{mid} := \lceil \frac{\mathtt{low+high}}{2} \rceil; q := \frac{\mathtt{mid}}{2^{n \times |\mathsf{RVar}(\mathcal{E}(x))|}}$;
11   **if** SMTSolver$(\widehat{\Psi}_x^q) =$SAT **then** $\mathtt{high} := \mathtt{mid} - 1$;
12   **else** $\mathtt{low} := \mathtt{mid}$;
13                 $\mathsf{QMS}_x := \frac{\mathtt{low}}{2^{n \times |\mathsf{RVar}(\widehat{\mathcal{E}(x)})|}}$;

---

side-channel attackers. In the latter case, however, x becomes a side-channel and it is natural to ask how many power traces are required to infer secret from x of which we have provided a measure formalized via QMS.

QMSCOMPUTING, given in Algorithm 2, computes QMS_x for each $x \in X_i$. It first invokes the function PMCHECKING for perfect masking verification. For SID-typed variable $x \in X_i$, we can directly infer that QMS_x is 1. For each leaky variable $x \in X_i$, we first check whether $\widehat{\mathcal{E}(x)}$ uses any random variables or not. If it does not use random variables, we directly deduce that QMS_x is 0. Otherwise, we use either the brute-force enumeration or an SMT-based binary search to compute QMS_x. The former one is trivial, hence not presented in Algorithm 2. The latter one is based on the fact that $\mathsf{QMS}_x = \frac{i}{2^{n \cdot |\mathsf{RVar}(\widehat{\mathcal{E}(x)})|}}$ for some integer $0 \leq i \leq 2^{n \cdot |\mathsf{RVar}(\widehat{\mathcal{E}(x)})|}$. Hence the while-loop in Algorithm 2 executes at most $\mathsf{O}(n \cdot |\mathsf{RVar}(\widehat{\mathcal{E}(x)})|)$ times for each x.

Our SMT-based binary search for computing QMS values is different from the one proposed by Eldib et al. [26,27]. Their algorithm considers Boolean programs *only* and computes QMS values by directly binary searching the QMS value q between 0 to 1 with a pre-defined step size ϵ ($\epsilon = 0.01$ in [26,27]). Hence, it only *approximate* the actual QMS value and the binary search iterates $\mathsf{O}(\log(\frac{1}{\epsilon}))$ times for each internal variable. Our approach works for more general arithmetic programs and computes the accurate QMS value.

5   Practical Evaluation

We have implemented our methods in a tool named QMVERIF, which uses Z3 [23] as the underlying SMT solver (fixed size bit-vector theory). We conducted experiments perfect masking verification and QMS computing on both Boolean and arithmetic programs. Our experiments were conducted on a server with 64-bit Ubuntu 16.04.4 LTS, Intel Xeon CPU E5-2690 v4, and 256 GB RAM.

Table 1. Results on masked Boolean programs for perfect masking verification.

Name	$|X_i|$	♯SDD	♯Count	QMVERIF		SCINFER [50]
				SMT	B.F.	
P12	197k	0	0	2.9s	**2.7s**	3.8s
P13	197k	4.8k	4.8k	2m 8s	**2m 6s**	47m 8s
P14	197k	3.2k	3.2k	1m 58s	**1m 45s**	53m 40s
P15	198k	1.6k	3.2k	**2m 25s**	2m 43s	69m 6s
P16	197k	4.8k	4.8k	1m 50s	**1m 38s**	61m 15s
P17	205k	17.6k	12.8k	1m 24s	**1m 10s**	121m 28s

5.1 Experimental Results on Boolean Programs

We use the benchmarks from the publicly available cryptographic software implementations of [25], which consists of 17 Boolean programs (P1-P17). We conducted experiments on P12-P17, which are the regenerations of MAC-Keccak reference code submitted to the SHA-3 competition held by NIST. (We skipped tiny examples P1-P11 which can be verified in less than 1 second.) P12-P17 are transformed into programs in straight-line forms.

Perfect Masking Verification. Table 1 shows the results of perfect masking verification on P12-P17, where Columns 2–4 show basic statistics, in particular, they respectively give the number of internal variables, leaky internal variables, and internal variables which required model-counting based reasoning. Columns 5–6 respectively show the total time of our tool QMVERIF using SMT-based and brute-force methods. Column 7 shows the total time of the tool SCINFER [50].

We can observe that: (1) our reduction heuristics significantly improve performance compared with SCINFER [50] (generally 22–104 times faster for imperfect masked programs; note that SCINFER is based on SMT model-counting), and (2) the performance of the SMT-based and brute-force counting methods for verifying perfect masking of Boolean programs is largely comparable.

Computing QMS. For comparison purposes, we implemented the algorithm of [24,25] for computing QMS values of leaky internal variables. Table 2 shows the results of computing QMS values on P13-P17 (P12 is excluded because it does not contain any leaky internal variable), where Column 2 shows the number of leaky internal variables, Columns 3–7 show the total number of iterations in the binary search (cf. Sect. 4.2), time, the minimal, maximal and average of QMS values using the algorithm from [24,25]. Similarly, Columns 8–13 shows statistics of our tool QMVERIF, in particular, Column 9 (resp. Column 10) shows the time of using SMT-based (resp. brute-force) method. The time reported in Table 2 *excludes* the time used for perfect masking checking.

We can observe that (1) the brute-force method outperforms the SMT-based method for computing QMS values, and (2) our tool QMVERIF using SMT-based methods takes significant less iterations and time, as our binary search step

Table 2. Results of masked Boolean programs for computing QMS Values.

Name	♯SDD	SC Sniffer [26,27]					QMVᴇʀɪꜰ					
		♯Iter	Time	Min	Max	Avg.	♯Iter	SMT	B.F.	Min	Max	Avg.
P13	4.8k	480k	97m 23s	0.00	1.00	0.98	**0**	0	0	0.00	1.00	0.98
P14	3.2k	160k	40m 13s	0.51	1.00	0.99	9.6k	2m 56s	**39s**	0.50	1.00	0.99
P15	1.6k	80k	23m 26s	0.51	1.00	1.00	4.8k	1m 36s	**1m 32s**	0.50	1.00	1.00
P16	4.8k	320k	66m 27s	0.00	1.00	0.98	6.4k	1m 40s	**8s**	0.00	1.00	0.98
P17	17.6k	1440k	337m 46s	0.00	1.00	0.93	4.8k	51s	**1s**	0.00	1.00	0.94

Table 3. Results of masked arithmetic programs, where P.M.V. denotes perfect masking verification, B.F. denotes brute-force, 12 S.F. denotes that Z3 emits segmentation fault after verifying 12 internal variables.

Description	$|X_i|$	♯SDD	♯Count	P.M.V.		QMS		
				SMT	B.F.	SMT	B.F.	Value
SecMult [47]	11	0	0	≈0s	≈0s	-	-	1
Sbox (4) [22]	66	0	0	≈0s	≈0s	-	-	1
B2A [30]	8	**0**	1	17s	**2s**	-	-	1
A2B [30]	46	0	0	≈0s	≈0s	-	-	1
B2A [21]	82	0	0	≈0s	≈0s	-	-	1
A2B [21]	41	0	0	≈0s	≈0s	-	-	1
B2A [18]	11	**0**	1	**1m 35s**	10m 59s	-	-	1
B2A [10]	16	0	0	≈0s	≈0s	-	-	1
Sbox [47]	45	0	0	≈0s	≈0s	-	-	1
Sbox [48]	772	2	1	≈0s	≈0s	0.9s	≈0s	0
k^3	11	2	2	96m 59s	**0.2s**		32s	0.988
k^{12}	15	2	2	101m 34s	**0.3s**		27s	0.988
k^{15}	21	4	4	93m 27s (12 S.F.)	**28m 17s**		≈64h	0.988, 0.980
k^{240}	23	4	4	93m 27s (12 S.F.)	**30m 9s**		≈64h	0.988, 0.980
k^{252}	31	4	4	93m 27s (12 S.F.)	**32m 58s**		≈64h	0.988, 0.980
k^{254}	39	4	4	93m 27s (12 S.F.)	**30m 9s**		≈64h	0.988, 0.980

depends on the number of bits of random variables, but not a pre-defined value (e.g. 0.01) as used in [24,25]. In particular, the QMS values of leaky variables whose expressions contain no random variables, e.g., P13 and P17, do not need binary search.

5.2 Experimental Results on Arithmetic Programs

We collect arithmetic programs which represent non-linear functions of masked cryptographic software implementations from the literature. In Table 3, Column 1 lists the name of the functions under consideration, where $k^3, \ldots, k^{254}$ are buggy fragments of first-order secure exponentiation [47] without the first RefreshMask function; A2B and B2A are shorthand for ArithmeticToBoolean and BooleanToArithmetic, respectively. Columns 2–4 show basic statistics. For all the experiments, we set $\mathbb{D} = \{0, \cdots, 2^8 - 1\}$.

Perfect Masking Verification. Columns 5–6 in Table 3 show the results of perfect masking verification on these programs using SMT-based and brute-force methods respectively.

We observe that (1) some UKD-typed variables (e.g., in B2A [30], B2A [18] and Sbox [48], meaning that the type inference is inconclusive in these cases) are resolved (as SID-type) by model-counting, and (2) on the programs (except B2A [18]) where model-counting based reasoning is required (i.e., $\sharp$Count is non-zero), the brute-force method is significantly faster than the SMT-based method. In particular, for programs $k^{15}, \ldots, k^{254}$, Z3 crashed with segment fault after verifying 12 internal variables in 93 min, while the brute-force method comfortably returns the result. To further explain the performance of these two classes of methods, we manually examine these programs and find that the expressions of the UKD-typed variable (using type inference) in B2A [18] (where the SMT-based method is faster) only use exclusive-or ($\oplus$) operations and one subtraction ($-$) operation, while the expressions of the other UKD-typed variables (where the brute-force method is faster) involve the finite field multiplication ($\odot$).

We remark that the transformation oracle and meta-theorems (cf. Sect. 3.3) are only used for A2B [30] by manually utilizing the equations of Theorem 3 in [30]. We have verified the correctness of those equations by SMT solvers. In theory model-counting based reasoning could verify A2B [30]. However, in our experiments both SMT-based and brute-force methods failed to terminate in 3 days, though brute-force methods had verified more internal variables. For instance, on the expression $((2 \times r_1) \oplus (x - r) \oplus r_1) \wedge r$ where x is a private input and r, r_1 are random variables, Z3 cannot terminate in 2 days, while brute-force methods successfully verified in a few minutes. We also tested the SMT solver Boolector [39] (the winner of SMT-COMP 2018 on QF-BV, Main Track), which crashed with being out of memory. Undoubtedly more systematic experiments are required in the future, but our results suggest that, contrary to the common belief, currently SMT-based approaches are not promising, which calls for more scalable techniques.

Computing QMS. Columns 7–9 in Table 3 show the results of computing QMS values, where Column 7 (resp. Column 8) shows the time of the SMT-based (resp. brute-force) method for computing QMS values (*excluding* the time for perfect masking verification) and Column 9 shows QMS values of all leaky variables (note that duplicated values are omitted).

6   Conclusion

We have proposed a hybrid approach combing type inference and model-counting to verify masked arithmetic programs against first-order side-channel attacks. The type inference allows an efficient, lightweight procedure to determine most observable variables whereas model-counting accounts for completeness, bringing the best of two worlds. We also provided model-counting based methods to quantify the amount of information leakage via side channels. We have presented the tool support QMVERIF which has been evaluated on standard cryptographic benchmarks. The experimental results showed that our method significantly outperformed state-of-the-art techniques in terms of both accuracy and scalability.

Future work includes further improving SMT-based model counting techniques which currently provide no better, if not worse, performance than the naïve brutal-force approach. Furthermore, generalizing the work in the current paper to the verification of higher-order masking schemes remains to be a very challenging task.

References

1. Almeida, J.B., Barbosa, M., Barthe, G., Dupressoir, F., Emmi, M.: Verifying constant-time implementations. In: USENIX Security Symposium, pp. 53–70 (2016)
2. Antonopoulos, T., Gazzillo, P., Hicks, M., Koskinen, E., Terauchi, T., Wei, S.: Decomposition instead of self-composition for proving the absence of timing channels. In: ACM SIGPLAN Conference on Programming Language Design and Implementation, pp. 362–375 (2017)
3. Barthe, G., Belaïd, S., Dupressoir, F., Fouque, P.-A., Grégoire, B., Strub, P.-Y.: Verified proofs of higher-order masking. In: Oswald, E., Fischlin, M. (eds.) EUROCRYPT 2015. LNCS, Part I, vol. 9056, pp. 457–485. Springer, Heidelberg (2015). https://doi.org/10.1007/978-3-662-46800-5_18
4. Barthe, G., et al.: Strong non-interference and type-directed higher-order masking. In: ACM Conference on Computer and Communications Security, pp. 116–129 (2016)
5. Barthe, G., Belaïd, S., Fouque, P., Grégoire, B.: maskVerif: a formal tool for analyzing software and hardware masked implementations. IACR Cryptology ePrint Archive 2018:562 (2018)
6. Barthe, G., Dupressoir, F., Faust, S., Grégoire, B., Standaert, F.-X., Strub, P.-Y.: Parallel implementations of masking schemes and the bounded moment leakage model. In: Coron, J.-S., Nielsen, J.B. (eds.) EUROCRYPT 2017. LNCS, Part I, vol. 10210, pp. 535–566. Springer, Cham (2017). https://doi.org/10.1007/978-3-319-56620-7_19
7. Barthe, G., Dupressoir, F., Fouque, P., Grégoire, B., Zapalowicz, J.: Synthesis of fault attacks on cryptographic implementations. In: Proceedings of the ACM SIGSAC Conference on Computer and Communications Security, pp. 1016–1027 (2014)
8. Barthe, G., Köpf, B., Mauborgne, L., Ochoa, M.: Leakage resilience against concurrent cache attacks. In: Abadi, M., Kremer, S. (eds.) POST 2014. LNCS, vol. 8414, pp. 140–158. Springer, Heidelberg (2014). https://doi.org/10.1007/978-3-642-54792-8_8
9. Bayrak, A.G., Regazzoni, F., Novo, D., Ienne, P.: Sleuth: automated verification of software power analysis countermeasures. In: Bertoni, G., Coron, J.-S. (eds.) CHES 2013. LNCS, vol. 8086, pp. 293–310. Springer, Heidelberg (2013). https://doi.org/10.1007/978-3-642-40349-1_17
10. Bettale, L., Coron, J., Zeitoun, R.: Improved high-order conversion from boolean to arithmetic masking. IACR Trans. Cryptogr. Hardw. Embed. Syst. 2018(2), 22–45 (2018)

11. Bhasin, S., Carlet, C., Guilley, S.: Theory of masking with codewords in hardware: low-weight dth-order correlation-immune boolean functions. IACR Cryptology ePrint Archive 2013:303 (2013)
12. Biham, E., Shamir, A.: Differential fault analysis of secret key cryptosystems. In: Kaliski, B.S. (ed.) CRYPTO 1997. LNCS, vol. 1294, pp. 513–525. Springer, Heidelberg (1997). https://doi.org/10.1007/BFb0052259
13. Biondi, F., Enescu, M.A., Heuser, A., Legay, A., Meel, K.S., Quilbeuf, J.: Scalable approximation of quantitative information flow in programs. In: Dillig, I., Palsberg, J. (eds.) VMCAI 2018. LNCS, vol. 10747, pp. 71–93. Springer, Cham (2018). https://doi.org/10.1007/978-3-319-73721-8_4
14. Bisi, E., Melzani, F., Zaccaria, V.: Symbolic analysis of higher-order side channel countermeasures. IEEE Trans. Comput. **66**(6), 1099–1105 (2017)
15. Bloem, R., Gross, H., Iusupov, R., Könighofer, B., Mangard, S., Winter, J.: Formal verification of masked hardware implementations in the presence of glitches. In: Nielsen, J.B., Rijmen, V. (eds.) EUROCRYPT 2018. LNCS, Part II, vol. 10821, pp. 321–353. Springer, Cham (2018). https://doi.org/10.1007/978-3-319-78375-8_11
16. Breier, J., Hou, X., Liu, Y.: Fault attacks made easy: differential fault analysis automation on assembly code. Cryptology ePrint Archive, Report 2017/829 (2017). https://eprint.iacr.org/2017/829
17. Chari, S., Jutla, C.S., Rao, J.R., Rohatgi, P.: Towards sound approaches to counteract power-analysis attacks. In: Wiener, M. (ed.) CRYPTO 1999. LNCS, vol. 1666, pp. 398–412. Springer, Heidelberg (1999). https://doi.org/10.1007/3-540-48405-1_26
18. Coron, J.-S.: High-order conversion from boolean to arithmetic masking. In: Fischer, W., Homma, N. (eds.) CHES 2017. LNCS, vol. 10529, pp. 93–114. Springer, Cham (2017). https://doi.org/10.1007/978-3-319-66787-4_5
19. Coron, J.-S.: Formal verification of side-channel countermeasures via elementary circuit transformations. In: Preneel, B., Vercauteren, F. (eds.) ACNS 2018. LNCS, vol. 10892, pp. 65–82. Springer, Cham (2018). https://doi.org/10.1007/978-3-319-93387-0_4
20. Coron, J.-S., Giraud, C., Prouff, E., Renner, S., Rivain, M., Vadnala, P.K.: Conversion of security proofs from one leakage model to another: a new issue. In: Schindler, W., Huss, S.A. (eds.) COSADE 2012. LNCS, vol. 7275, pp. 69–81. Springer, Heidelberg (2012). https://doi.org/10.1007/978-3-642-29912-4_6
21. Coron, J.-S., Großschädl, J., Vadnala, P.K.: Secure conversion between boolean and arithmetic masking of any order. In: Batina, L., Robshaw, M. (eds.) CHES 2014. LNCS, vol. 8731, pp. 188–205. Springer, Heidelberg (2014). https://doi.org/10.1007/978-3-662-44709-3_11
22. Coron, J.-S., Prouff, E., Rivain, M., Roche, T.: Higher-order side channel security and mask refreshing. In: Moriai, S. (ed.) FSE 2013. LNCS, vol. 8424, pp. 410–424. Springer, Heidelberg (2014). https://doi.org/10.1007/978-3-662-43933-3_21
23. de Moura, L., Bjørner, N.: Z3: An efficient SMT solver. In: Ramakrishnan, C.R., Rehof, J. (eds.) TACAS 2008. LNCS, vol. 4963, pp. 337–340. Springer, Heidelberg (2008). https://doi.org/10.1007/978-3-540-78800-3_24
24. Eldib, H., Wang, C., Schaumont, P.: Formal verification of software countermeasures against side-channel attacks. ACM Trans. Softw. Eng. Methodol. **24**(2), 11 (2014)
25. Eldib, H., Wang, C., Schaumont, P.: SMT-based verification of software countermeasures against side-channel attacks. In: Ábrahám, E., Havelund, K. (eds.) TACAS 2014. LNCS, vol. 8413, pp. 62–77. Springer, Heidelberg (2014). https://doi.org/10.1007/978-3-642-54862-8_5

26. Eldib, H., Wang, C., Taha, M., Schaumont, P.: QMS: evaluating the side-channel resistance of masked software from source code. In: ACM/IEEE Design Automation Conference, vol. 209, pp. 1–6 (2014)

27. Eldib, H., Wang, C., Taha, M.M.I., Schaumont, P.: Quantitative masking strength: quantifying the power side-channel resistance of software code. IEEE Trans. CAD Integr. Circ. Syst. **34**(10), 1558–1568 (2015)

28. Eldib, H., Wu, M., Wang, C.: Synthesis of fault-attack countermeasures for cryptographic circuits. In: Chaudhuri, S., Farzan, A. (eds.) CAV 2016. LNCS, Part II, vol. 9780, pp. 343–363. Springer, Cham (2016). https://doi.org/10.1007/978-3-319-41540-6_19

29. Faust, S., Grosso, V., Pozo, S.M.D., Paglialonga, C., Standaert, F.: Composable masking schemes in the presence of physical defaults and the robust probing model. IACR Cryptology ePrint Archive 2017:711 (2017)

30. Goubin, L.: A sound method for switching between boolean and arithmetic masking. In: Koç, Ç.K., Naccache, D., Paar, C. (eds.) CHES 2001. LNCS, vol. 2162, pp. 3–15. Springer, Heidelberg (2001). https://doi.org/10.1007/3-540-44709-1_2

31. Guo, S., Wu, M., Wang, C.: Adversarial symbolic execution for detecting concurrency-related cache timing leaks. In: Proceedings of the ACM SIGSOFT Symposium on the Foundations of Software Engineering, pp. 377–388 (2018)

32. Ishai, Y., Sahai, A., Wagner, D.: Private circuits: securing hardware against probing attacks. In: Boneh, D. (ed.) CRYPTO 2003. LNCS, vol. 2729, pp. 463–481. Springer, Heidelberg (2003). https://doi.org/10.1007/978-3-540-45146-4_27

33. Kocher, P.C.: Timing attacks on implementations of Diffie-Hellman, RSA, DSS, and other systems. In: Koblitz, N. (ed.) CRYPTO 1996. LNCS, vol. 1109, pp. 104–113. Springer, Heidelberg (1996). https://doi.org/10.1007/3-540-68697-5_9

34. Kocher, P., Jaffe, J., Jun, B.: Differential power analysis. In: Wiener, M. (ed.) CRYPTO 1999. LNCS, vol. 1666, pp. 388–397. Springer, Heidelberg (1999). https://doi.org/10.1007/3-540-48405-1_25

35. Malacaria, P., Heusser, J.: Information theory and security: quantitative information flow. In: Aldini, A., Bernardo, M., Di Pierro, A., Wiklicky, H. (eds.) SFM 2010. LNCS, vol. 6154, pp. 87–134. Springer, Heidelberg (2010). https://doi.org/10.1007/978-3-642-13678-8_3

36. Malacaria, P., Khouzani, M.H.R., Pasareanu, C.S., Phan, Q., Luckow, K.S.: Symbolic side-channel analysis for probabilistic programs. In: Proceedings of the 31st IEEE Computer Security Foundations Symposium (CSF), pp. 313–327 (2018)

37. Moradi, A., Barenghi, A., Kasper, T., Paar, C.: On the vulnerability of FPGA bitstream encryption against power analysis attacks: extracting keys from xilinx virtex-ii fpgas. In: Proceedings of ACM Conference on Computer and Communications Security (CCS), pp. 111–124 (2011)

38. Moss, A., Oswald, E., Page, D., Tunstall, M.: Compiler assisted masking. In: Prouff, E., Schaumont, P. (eds.) CHES 2012. LNCS, vol. 7428, pp. 58–75. Springer, Heidelberg (2012). https://doi.org/10.1007/978-3-642-33027-8_4

39. Niemetz, A., Preiner, M., Biere, A.: Boolector 2.0 system description. J. Satisf. Boolean Model. Comput. **9**, 53–58 (2014). (published 2015)

40. Ouahma, I.B.E., Meunier, Q., Heydemann, K., Encrenaz, E.: Symbolic approach for side-channel resistance analysis of masked assembly codes. In: Security Proofs for Embedded Systems (2017)

41. Pasareanu, C.S., Phan, Q., Malacaria, P.: Multi-run side-channel analysis using symbolic execution and Max-SMT. In: Proceedings of the IEEE 29th Computer Security Foundations Symposium (CSF), pp. 387–400 (2016)

42. Phan, Q., Bang, L., Pasareanu, C.S., Malacaria, P., Bultan, T.: Synthesis of adaptive side-channel attacks. In: Proceedings of the 30th IEEE Computer Security Foundations Symposium (CSF), pp. 328–342 (2017)

43. Phan, Q., Malacaria, P.: Abstract model counting: a novel approach for quantification of information leaks. In: Proceedings of the 9th ACM Symposium on Information, Computer and Communications Security (ASIACCS), pp. 283–292 (2014)

44. Phan, Q., Malacaria, P., Pasareanu, C.S., d'Amorim, M.: Quantifying information leaks using reliability analysis. In: Proceedings of 2014 International Symposium on Model Checking of Software (SPIN), pp. 105–108 (2014)

45. Prouff, E., Rivain, M.: Masking against side-channel attacks: a formal security proof. In: Johansson, T., Nguyen, P.Q. (eds.) EUROCRYPT 2013. LNCS, vol. 7881, pp. 142–159. Springer, Heidelberg (2013). https://doi.org/10.1007/978-3-642-38348-9_9

46. Quisquater, J.-J., Samyde, D.: ElectroMagnetic Analysis (EMA): measures and counter-measures for smart cards. In: Attali, I., Jensen, T. (eds.) E-smart 2001. LNCS, vol. 2140, pp. 200–210. Springer, Heidelberg (2001). https://doi.org/10.1007/3-540-45418-7_17

47. Rivain, M., Prouff, E.: Provably secure higher-order masking of AES. In: Mangard, S., Standaert, F.-X. (eds.) CHES 2010. LNCS, vol. 6225, pp. 413–427. Springer, Heidelberg (2010). https://doi.org/10.1007/978-3-642-15031-9_28

48. Schramm, K., Paar, C.: Higher order masking of the AES. In: Pointcheval, D. (ed.) CT-RSA 2006. LNCS, vol. 3860, pp. 208–225. Springer, Heidelberg (2006). https://doi.org/10.1007/11605805_14

49. Val, C.G., Enescu, M.A., Bayless, S., Aiello, W., Hu, A.J.: Precisely measuring quantitative information flow: 10k lines of code and beyond. In: Proceedings of IEEE European Symposium on Security and Privacy (EuroS&P), pp. 31–46 (2016)

50. Zhang, J., Gao, P., Song, F., Wang, C.: SCInfer: refinement-based verification of software countermeasures against side-channel attacks. In: Chockler, H., Weissenbacher, G. (eds.) CAV 2018. LNCS, Part II, vol. 10982, pp. 157–177. Springer, Cham (2018). https://doi.org/10.1007/978-3-319-96142-2_12

Incremental Analysis of Evolving Alloy Models

Wenxi Wang[1]([envelope]), Kaiyuan Wang[2]([envelope]), Milos Gligoric[1]([envelope]),
and Sarfraz Khurshid[1]([envelope])

[1] The University of Texas at Austin, Austin, USA
{wenxiw,gligoric,khurshid}@utexas.edu
[2] Google Inc., Sunnyvale, USA
kaiyuanw@google.com

Abstract. Alloy is a well-known tool-set for building and analyzing software designs and models. Alloy's key strengths are its intuitive notation based on relational logic, and its powerful analysis engine backed by propositional satisfiability (SAT) solvers to help users find subtle design flaws. However, scaling the analysis to the designs of real-world systems remains an important technical challenge. This paper introduces a new approach, iAlloy, for more efficient analysis of Alloy models. Our key insight is that users often make small and frequent changes and repeatedly run the analyzer when developing Alloy models, and the development cost can be reduced with the incremental analysis over these changes. iAlloy is based on two techniques – a static technique based on a lightweight *impact* analysis and a dynamic technique based on solution *re-use* – which in many cases helps avoid potential costly SAT solving. Experimental results show that iAlloy significantly outperforms Alloy analyzer in the analysis of evolving Alloy models with more than 50% reduction in SAT solver calls on average, and up to 7x speedup.

1 Introduction

Building software models and analyzing them play an important role in the development of more reliable systems. However, as the complexity of the modeled systems increases, both the cost of creating the models and the complexity of analyzing these models become high [24].

Our focus in this paper is to reduce the cost of analyzing models written in Alloy [5] – a relational, first-order logic with transitive closure. The Alloy analyzer provides automatic analysis of Alloy models. To analyze the model, the user writes Alloy *paragraphs* (e.g., signatures, predicates, functions, facts and assertions), and the analyzer executes the *commands* that define constraint solving problems. The analyzer translates the commands and related Alloy paragraphs into propositional satisfiability (SAT) formulas and then solves them using off-the-shelf SAT solvers. We focus on successive runs of the analyzer as the model undergoes development and modifications. The key insight is that during model development and validation phases, the user typically makes many changes that

© The Author(s) 2019
T. Vojnar and L. Zhang (Eds.): TACAS 2019, Part I, LNCS 11427, pp. 174–191, 2019.
https://doi.org/10.1007/978-3-030-17462-0_10

are relatively small, which enables the incremental analysis to reduce the subsequent analysis cost [1].

We introduce a novel technique called iAlloy that incrementally computes the analysis results. iAlloy introduces a two-fold optimization for Alloy analyzer. Firstly, iAlloy comes with a *static* technique that computes the *impact* of a change on commands based on a lightweight dependency analysis, and *selects* for execution a subset of commands that may be impacted. We call this technique *regression command selection* (RCS), since it shares the spirit of regression test selection for imperative code [4] and adapts it to declarative models in Alloy. Secondly, iAlloy comes with a *dynamic* technique that uses memoization to enable *solution reuse* (SR) by efficiently checking if an existing solution already works for a command that must be executed. SR uses a partial-order based on sets of parameters in predicate paragraphs to enable effective re-use of solutions across different commands.

To evaluate iAlloy we conduct experiments using two sets of Alloy models that have multiple versions. One set, termed *mutant version set*, uses simulated evolving Alloy models where different versions are created using the MuAlloy [21,27] tool for generating *mutants* with small syntactic modifications of the given base Alloy models. This set includes 24 base Alloy models and 5 mutant versions for each base model. The other set, termed *real version set*, uses base Alloy models that had real faults and were repaired using the ARepair [25,26] tool for fixing faulty Alloy models. For each faulty base model, its evolution is the corresponding fixed model. This set includes 36 base Alloy models and 2 versions for each model.

The experimental results show that iAlloy is effective at reducing the overall analysis cost for both sets of subject models. Overall, iAlloy provides more than 50% command execution reduction on average, and up to 7x speed up. In addition, SR performs surprisingly well in the real version set with 58.3% reduction of the selected commands, which indicates that our approach is promising for incrementally analyzing real-world evolving Alloy models.

This paper makes the following contributions:

- **Approach.** We introduce a novel approach, iAlloy, based on static analysis (regression command selection) and dynamic analysis (solution re-use) for incrementally analyzing evolving Alloy models, and embody the approach as a prototype tool on top of the Alloy analyzer.
- **Evaluation.** We conduct an extensive experimental evaluation of our approach using two sets of subject Alloy models, one based on syntactic mutation changes and the other based on fault fixing changes. The results show that iAlloy performs well on both sets.
- **Dataset.** We publicly release our subject Alloy models and their versions at the following URL: https://github.com/wenxiwang/iAlloy-dataset. Given the lack of common availability of Alloy models with evolution history, we believe that our dataset will be particularly useful for other researchers who want to evaluate their incremental analysis techniques for Alloy.

While our focus in this paper is the Alloy modeling language and tool-set, we believe our technique can generalize to optimize analysis for models in other declarative languages, e.g., Z [17] and OCL [2].

2   Background

In this section, we first introduce Alloy [5] based on an example which we use through the paper. Then, we describe MuAlloy [21,27] – a mutation testing framework for Alloy, which we apply to create different versions of an Alloy model to simulate model evolutions. Finally, we briefly describe regression test selection (RTS) for imperative code. Although our regression command selection (RCS) applies to declarative code, the two methods share similar ideas.

2.1   Alloy

Alloy [5] is a declarative language for lightweight modeling and software analysis. The language is based on first-order logic with transitive closure. Alloy comes with an analyzer which is able to perform a bounded exhaustive analysis. The input of the Alloy analyzer is an Alloy model that describes the system properties. The analyzer translates the model into conjunctive normal form (CNF) and invokes an off-the-shelf SAT solver to search for solutions, i.e., boolean instances. The boolean instances are then mapped back to Alloy level instances and displayed to the end user.

Figure 1 shows the Dijkstra Alloy model which illustrates how mutexes are grabbed and released by processes, and how Dijkstra's mutex ordering constraint can prevent deadlocks. This model comes with the standard Alloy distribution (version 4.2). An Alloy model consists of a set of *relations* (e.g., signatures, fields and variables) and constraints (e.g., predicates, facts and assertions) which we call *paragraphs*. A signature (`sig`) defines a set of atoms, and is the main data type specified in Alloy. The running example defines 3 signatures (lines 3–6), namely `Process`, `Mutex` and `State`.

Facts (`fact`) are formulas that take no arguments and define constraints that must be satisfied by every instance that exists. The formulas can be further structured using predicates (`pred`) and functions (`fun`) which are parameterized formulas that can be invoked. Users can use Alloy's built-in `run` command to invoke a predicate and the Alloy analyzer either returns an instance if the predicate is satisfiable or reports that the predicate is unsatisfiable. The `IsStalled` predicate (lines 12–14) is invoked by the `GrabMutex` predicate (line 16) and the `run` command (line 53). The parameters of the `IsStalled` predicate are s and p with signature types `State` and `Process`, respectively. An assertion (`assert`) is also a boolean formula that can be invoked by the built-in `check` command to check if any counter example can refute the asserted formula. Assertions does not take any parameter. The `DijkstraPreventsDeadlocks` assertion (lines 45–47) is invoked by the `check` command (line 60) with a scope of up to 6 atoms for each signature.

2.2   MuAlloy

MuAlloy [21,27] automatically generates mutants and filters out mutants that are semantically equivalent to the original base model. Table 1 shows the mutation operators supported in MuAlloy. *MOR* mutates signature multiplicity,

```
1. open util/ordering [State] as so
2. open util/ordering [Mutex] as mo
3. sig Process {}
4. sig Mutex {}
5. sig State { holds, waits: Process -> Mutex }
6. pred Initial [s: State] {
7.   no (s.holds + s.waits)
8. }
9. pred IsFree [s: State, m: Mutex] {
10.   no m.~(s.holds) // no process holds this mutex
11. }
12. pred IsStalled [s: State, p: Process] {
13.   some p.(s.waits)
14. }
15. pred GrabMutex [s: State, p: Process, m: Mutex, s': State] {
16.   !s.IsStalled[p] // a process can only act if it is not waiting for a mutex
17.   m !in p.(s.holds) // can only grab a mutex that is not yet hold
18.   all m': p.(s.holds) | mo/lt[m',m] // mutexes must be grabbed in order
19.   s.IsFree[m] => {
20.     p.(s'.holds) = p.(s.holds) + m // if the mutex is free, the process now holds it
21.     no p.(s'.waits) // the process is not stalled any more
22.   } else {
23.     p.(s'.holds) = p.(s.holds) // if the mutex is not free, the process still hold the same mutexes.
24.     p.(s'.waits) = m // and wait on the new mutex.
25.   }
26.   all otherProc: Process - p | { // other processes maintain the same state
27.     otherProc.(s'.holds) = otherProc.(s.holds)
28.     otherProc.(s'.waits) = otherProc.(s.waits)
29.   }
30. }
31. pred ReleaseMutex [s: State, p: Process, m: Mutex, s': State] {
32.   !s.IsStalled[p]
33.   ...
34. }
35. pred GrabOrRelease {
36.   Initial[so/first] &&
37.   (all pre: State - so/last | let post = so/next[pre] | // for every pre and post state
38.   (post.holds = pre.holds && post.waits = pre.waits) || // either nothing happens
39.   (some p: Process, m: Mutex | pre.GrabMutex [p, m, post]) || // or a process grabs a mutex
40.   (some p: Process, m: Mutex | pre.ReleaseMutex [p, m, post])) // or releases a mutex
41. }
42. pred Deadlock {
43.   ...
44. }
45. assert DijkstraPreventsDeadlocks {
46.   GrabOrRelease => ! Deadlock
47. }
48. pred ShowDijkstra {
49.   GrabOrRelease && Deadlock
50.   some waits
51. }
52. run Initial for 10
53. run IsStalled for 10
54. run IsFree for 10
55. run GrabMutex for 30
56. run ReleaseMutex for 35
57. run GrabOrRelease for 16
58. run Deadlock for 50 expect 1
59. run ShowDijkstra for 5 expect 1
60. check DijkstraPreventsDeadlocks for 6 expect 0
```

Fig. 1. Dijkstra Alloy model from standard Alloy distribution (version 4.2); the line written in red was absent from the faulty version

e.g., `lone sig` to `one sig`. QOR mutates quantifiers, e.g., `all` to `some`. UOR, BOR and LOR define operator replacement for unary, binary and formula list operators, respectively. For example, UOR mutates `a.*b` to `a.^b`; BOR mutates `a=>b` to `a<=>b`; and LOR mutates `a&&b` to `a||b`. UOI inserts an unary operator before expressions, e.g., `a.b` to `a.~b`. UOD deletes an unary operator, e.g., `a.* ~b` to `a.*b`.

Table 1. Mutation Operators Supported in MuAlloy

Mutation Operator	Description
MOR	Multiplicity Operator Replacement
QOR	Quantifier Operator Replacement
UOR	Unary Operator Replacement
BOR	Binary Operator Replacement
LOR	Formula List Operator Replacement
UOI	Unary Operator Insertion
UOD	Unary Operator Deletion
LOD	Logical Operand Deletion
PBD	Paragraph Body Deletion
BOE	Binary Operand Exchange
IEOE	Imply-Else Operand Exchange

LOD deletes an operand of a logical operator, e.g., a||b to b. *PBD* deletes the body of an Alloy paragraph. *BOE* exchanges operands for a binary operator, e.g., a=>b to b=>a. *IEOE* exchanges the operands of imply-else operation, e.g., a => b else c to a => c else b.

2.3   Regression Test Selection for Imperative Code

Regression test selection (RTS) techniques select a subset of test cases from an initial test suite. The subset of tests checks if the affected sources of a project continue to work correctly. RTS is *safe* if it guarantees that the subset of selected tests includes all tests whose behavior may be affected by the changes [4, 32]. RTS is *precise* if tests that are not affected are also not selected. Typical RTS techniques has three phases: the *analysis phase* selects tests to run, the *execution phase* runs the selected tests, and the *collection phase* collects information from the current version for future analysis. RTS techniques can perform at different granularities. For example, FaultTracer [35] analyzes dependencies at the method level while Ekstazi [3] does it at the file level, and both tools target projects written in Java.

During the analysis phase, RTS tools commonly compute a checksum, i.e., a unique identifier, of each code entity (e.g., method or file) on which a test depends. If the checksum changes, we view its source code as changed, in which case the test is selected and executed; otherwise it is not selected. The execution phase is tightly integrated with the analysis phase and simply executes selected tests. During the collection phase, RTS either dynamically monitors the test execution [3] or statically analyzes the test [7] to collect accessed/used entities, which are saved for the analysis phase in the next run.

3   Motivating Example

This section describes how iAlloy works using two versions of the Dijkstra Alloy model. Line 18 (highlighted in red) in Fig. 1 was absent in a faulty version of the model which we denote as Version 1. The model in Fig. 1 is the correct version which we denote as Version 2.

First, we apply iAlloy to Version 1. iAlloy invokes commands `Initial` (line 52), `IsStalled` (line 53), `IsFree` (line 54) and `GrabMutex` (line 55) with the SAT solver. Before invoking command `ReleaseMutex` (line 56), iAlloy finds that the solution obtained from invoking `GrabMutex` can be reused as the solution of `ReleaseMutex`. Therefore, command `ReleaseMutex` is solved without invoking SAT. iAlloy continues to invoke the rest of the commands and finds that command `Deadlock` (line 58) can reuse the solution of `IsStalled`, and command `DijkstraPreventsDeadlocks` can reuse the solution of `ShowDijkstra`. Next, we apply iAlloy again to Version 2. iAlloy performs dependency analysis between Version 1 and Version 2, and only selects the commands that are affected by the change (Line 18 in Fig. 1), namely commands `GrabMutex`, `GrabOrRelease`, `ShowDijkstra` and `DijkstraPreventsDeadlocks`. iAlloy tries to reuse the solutions of previous runs when invoking the four selected commands and `GrabMutex` reuses the solution of command `GrabMutex` in Version 1.

Traditionally, Alloy analyzer needs to execute 18 commands with expensive SAT solving, which takes total of 103.01 seconds. In comparison, iAlloy only invokes 9 commands where 5 commands are saved by regression command selection and 4 commands are saved by solution reuse. In total, iAlloy takes 84.14 seconds. Overall, iAlloy achieves 1.22x speed-up with 18.87 seconds time saving. Section 5 evaluates more subjects and shows that iAlloy achieves 1.59x speed-up on average and reduces unnecessary command invocations by more than 50%.

4   Techniques

In an evolving Alloy model scenario, we propose a two-step incremental analysis to reduce the time overhead of command execution. The first step is regression command selection (RCS) based on static dependency analysis (Sect. 4.1). The second step is solution reuse (SR) using fast instance evaluation (Sect. 4.2). Note that RCS handles paragraph-level dependency analysis, while SR covers more sophisticated expression-level dependency analysis.

Algorithm 1 shows the general algorithm of our incremental analysis. For each version (m_v) in a sequence of model evolutions ($ModelVersionSeq$), iAlloy first applies RCS ($RCmdSelection$) to select the commands ($SelectCmdList$) that are affected since the last version. Then, for each command in $SelectCmdList$, iAlloy further checks whether the solutions of previous commands can be reused in the new commands ($CheckReuse$). Note that the solutions of commands in the same version can also be reused. However, if the signatures change in the current version, then SR is not applicable and all commands are executed. If none of the old solutions can be reused for the current command c, then iAlloy invokes the SAT solver ($Execute$) to find a new solution which may be used for the next run.

Algorithm 1. General Algorithm for Incremental Alloy Model Solving

Input: model version sequence $ModelVersionSeq$
Output: solution for each command

1: **for** $m_v \in ModelVersionSeq$ **do**
2:     $SelectCmdList = \text{RCmdSelection}(m_v)$;
3:     **for** $c \in SelectCmdList$ **do**
4:         **if** $\text{Changed}(c.Dependency.SigList)$ **then**
5:             $\text{Execute}(c, SolutionSet)$;
6:         **else if** $!\text{CheckReuse}(c, SolutionSet)$ **then**
7:             $\text{Execute}(c, SolutionSet)$;
8:         **end if**
9:     **end for**
10: **end for**

Algorithm 2. Algorithm for Regression Command Selection

Input: one model version m_v
Output: selected command list

1: **procedure** RCMDSELECTION(Model m_v)
2:     List<Cmd> $SelectCmdList$;
3:     Map<Cmd, Nodes> $Cmd2DpdParagraphs = \text{DpdAnalysis}(m_v.AllCmd)$;
4:     **for** $c \in m_v.AllCmd$ **do**
5:         $DpdParagraphs = Cmd2DpdParagraphs.\text{get}(c)$;
6:         **if** $\text{Exist}(c.Dependency)$ **then**   ▷ old dependency
7:             $newDependency = \text{CheckSum}(DpdParagraphs)$;
8:             **if** $\text{Changed}(c.Dependency, newDependency)$ **then**
9:                 $\text{Update}(c, newDependency)$;
10:                 $SelectCmdList.\text{add}(c)$; ▷ update dependency and select commands
11:             **end if**
12:         **else**
13:             $dependency = \text{CheckSum}(DpdParagraphs)$
14:             $\text{Update}(c, dependency)$;
15:             $SelectCmdList.\text{add}(c)$;   ▷ update dependency and select commands
16:         **end if**
17:     **end for**
18:     **return** $SelectCmdList$;
19: **end procedure**

4.1 Regression Command Selection (RCS)

Algorithm 2 presents the algorithm for RCS. iAlloy first gets the dependent paragraphs of each command ($Cmd2DpdParagraphs$) based on the dependency analysis ($DpdAnalysis$). For each command c in model version m_v, iAlloy generates a unique identifier, as described in Sect. 2.3, for each dependent paragraph ($CheckSum$). If the checksum of any dependent paragraph changes, iAlloy selects the corresponding command as the command execution candidate ($SelectCmdList$) and updates the dependency with new checksum.

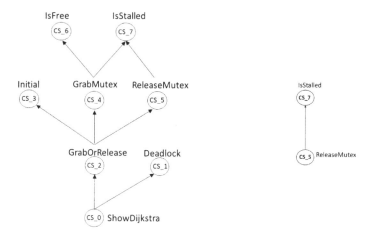

Fig. 2. Dependency graph for ShowDijkstra (left) and ReleaseMutex (right) command in the Dijkstra model

The dependency information of each command is the key for RCS. The dependency analysis for Alloy models can be either at the paragraph level or at the expression level. For safety reasons as we mentioned in Sect. 2.3, we do dependency analysis on the paragraph level in RCS. And we address further fine-grained expression level analysis in SR to achieve a better precision. To filter out the changes in comments and spaces, we traverse the AST of each paragraph and output the canonicalized string of the paragraph. The canonicalized string is hashed into a checksum which represents the unique version of the paragraph.

We take the Dijkstra Alloy model in Fig. 1 as an example. The dependency graph of command ShowDijkstra is shown in Fig. 2 (left), including transitively dependent Alloy paragraphs and their corresponding checksums CS_i. Since the checksum CS_4 of predicate GrabMutex is changed (line 18 in Fig. 1) and GrabMutex is in the dependency graph of command ShowDijkstra, command ShowDijkstra is selected. In comparison, the dependency graph of command ReleaseMutex is shown in Fig. 2 (right). Since the checksums of both IsStalled and ReleaseMutex do not change, command ReleaseMutex is not selected.

4.2 Solution Reuse (SR)

Algorithm 3 illustrates how iAlloy checks if a solution can be reused by the current command. The input to Algorithm 3 is each selected command (c) from RCS and a solution set containing all the previous solutions (*SolutionSet*). If the solution s from *SolutionSet* includes valuations of parameters of the Alloy paragraph (represented as *CheckList* which includes implicit Alloy facts) invoked by c (Sect. 4.2.1), and *CheckList* is satisfiable under s (Sect. 4.2.2), then s can be reused as the Alloy instance if c is invoked and c need not be invoked with expensive SAT solving (return true). Otherwise, SAT solving is involved to generate a

---

Algorithm 3. Algorithm for Solution Reuse Checking

Input: one command and the solution set
Output: if the command can reuse any solution in the solution set

1: **procedure** CHECKREUSE(Cmd c, Set<Solution> $SolutionSet$)
2:    List<Nodes> $CheckList$;
3:    $CheckList$.add($c.Dependency.FactList$);
4:    **if** CheckCmd(c) **then**   ▷ c is *check* command
5:        $CheckList$.add($c.Dependency.Assert$);
6:    **else**   ▷ c is *run* command
7:        $CheckList$.add($c.Dependency.Pred$);
8:    **end if**
9:    **for** $s \in SolutionSet$ **do**
10:        **if** $c.param \subseteq s.cmd.param$ && $s.sol$.evaluator($CheckList$) = true **then**
11:            **return** true;
12:        **end if**
13:    **end for**
14:    **return** false;
15: **end procedure**

---

new solution (if there is any) which is stored for subsequent runs (Algorithm 4, Sect. 4.2.3).

Note that SR not only filters out the semantically equivalent regression changes, but also covers the sophisticated expression-level dependency analysis. For example, suppose the only change in an Alloy model is a boolean expression changed from A to A || B where || stands for disjunction and B is another boolean expression, the old solution of the corresponding command is still valid and can be reused. Besides, SR allows solutions from other commands to be reused for the current command, which further reduces SAT solving overhead.

4.2.1   Solution Reuse Condition

As described in Sect. 2, each command invokes either a predicate or an assert. Each predicate has multiple parameter types which we denote as *parameter set* for simplicity in the rest of the paper. The parameter set of any assertion is an empty set ($\varnothing$). As shown in the following equation, we define the parameter set of a command c (c.param) as the parameter set of the directly invoked predicate (ParamSet(c.pred)) or assertion ($\varnothing$).

$$c.param = \begin{cases} ParamSet(c.pred), & c \text{ is run command} \\ \varnothing, & c \text{ is check command} \end{cases}$$

A command that invokes an Alloy paragraph with parameters implicitly checks if there exists a set of valuations of the corresponding parameters that satisfies the paragraph. We observe that command c_2 can reuse the solution s_1 obtained by invoking c_1 if the parameter set of c_2 is a subset of that of c_1, namely $c_2.param \subseteq c_1.param$. The solution reuse complies to a partial order based on

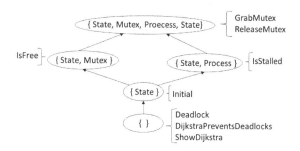

Fig. 3. Parameter relations of commands in the Dijkstra model

---

Algorithm 4. Algorithm for Command Execution

Input: one command and the solution set
Output: save the solution if it is SAT or print out UNSAT

```
 1: procedure CMDEXECUTE(Cmd c, Set<Solution> SolutionSet)
 2:     A4Solution sol = Alloy.solve(c);
 3:     if sol.IsSat() then                          ▷ if the solution is SAT;
 4:         Solution s;
 5:         s.sol = sol;               ▷ store the instance and corresponding command;
 6:         s.cmd = c;
 7:         SolutionSet.add(s);
 8:     else
 9:         print UNSAT
10:     end if
11: end procedure
```

---

the subset relation of command parameters. On the other hand, solution s_1 cannot be reused by c_2 if $c_2.param \subsetneq c_1.param$, in which case we do not know all the valuations of c_2's parameters.

Figure 3 shows how solution reuse is conducted based on the subset relations of command parameter set in the Dijkstra model. For instance, since the parameter set {} ($\varnothing$) is the subset of all parameter sets above it, the corresponding commands Deadlock, DijkstraPreventsDeadlocks and ShowDijkstra with parameter set {} can reuse all solutions of commands whose parameter sets are the super set of {}, namely Initial, IsFree, IsStalled, GrabMutex and ReleaseMutex. Since any parameter set is a subset of itself, a solution $s1$ of command c_1 can be reused by the command c_2 which has the same parameter set as c_1.

4.2.2 Solution Reuse Evaluation

Once a solution s can be reused for command c, we need to further check if s is actually the solution of c that satisfies the corresponding constraints. As described in Sect. 2, the constraints of a command come from all facts and the transitively invoked predicate/assertion. To reuse s in the old version, s must be

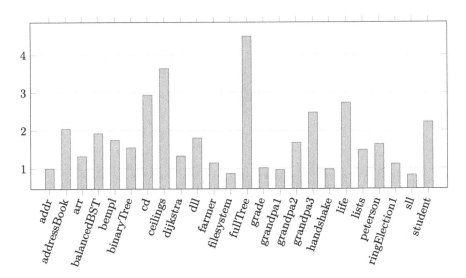

Fig. 4. Speedup results on Mutant Version Set

satisfiable for c in the new version. If c is unsatisfiable under the valuations of s, it does not imply that c is unsatisfiable in the solution space and thus c must be invoked with SAT solving. The satisfiability of command c is determined by the Alloy built-in evaluator under the valuation of s.

4.2.3 Command Execution

If none of the solutions can be reused by command c, iAlloy executes the command as described in Algorithm 4. If a solution *sol* is found (`Sol.IsSat()`), the solution *sol* together with the command c is saved for subsequent runs. To avoid saving too many solutions as the model evolves (which may slow down the SR and reduce the overall gain), we only keep the most recent solution for each command. In future work, we plan to evaluate how long a solution should be kept.

5   Experimental Evaluation

In this paper, we answer the following research questions to evaluate iAlloy:

- RQ1: How does iAlloy perform compared to traditional Alloy Analyzer (which we treat as the baseline)?
- RQ2: How much reduction of the commands executed does Regression Command Selection and Solution Reuse contribute in the two subject sets?
- RQ3: What is the time overhead of Regression Command Selection, Solution Reuse and command execution in iAlloy, respectively?

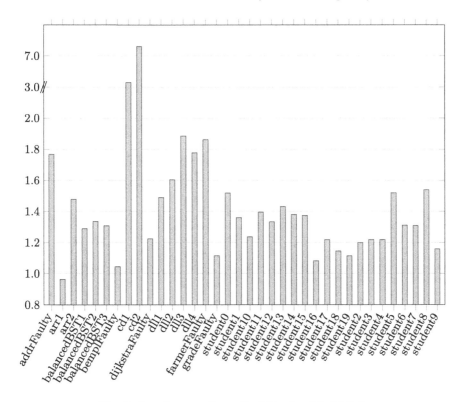

Fig. 5. Speedup results on Real Version Model Set

5.1   Experimental Setup

Subjects: There are two subject sets in the experiment. The first set of subjects is the simulated evolving Alloy model version sets, which we call Mutant Version Set. In this set, we take 24 Alloy models from the standard Alloy distribution (version 4.2) and use them as the first version. For each model in version 1, we use MuAlloy [27] to generate several mutants and randomly select one as version 2. This process continues until we get the fifth version. Thus, each subject in the Mutant Version Set includes five versions. The second subject set is called Real Version Set. Each subject in this set consists of two model versions: the real faulty model (version 1) from the ARepair [26] distribution and the correct model after the fix (version 2). There are 36 subjects in this set.

Baseline: The baseline in this experiment is the traditional Alloy Analyzer, which executes each command for each version.

Platform: We conduct all our experiments on Ubuntu Linux 16.04, an Intel Core-i7 6700 CPU (3.40 GHz) and 16 GB RAM. The version of Alloy we did experiments on is version 4.2.

Table 2. RCS, SR and Command Execution Results in Mutant Version Set

Model	cmd	select	reuse	execute	T_select (%)	T_reuse (%)	T_execute (%)
addr	5	5 (100%)	0 (0%)	5 (100%)	4.2	0.0	95.8
addressBook	10	9 (90%)	3 (33.3%)	6 (66.7%)	0.3	53.5	46.2
arr	5	5 (100%)	2 (40%)	3 (60%)	3.6	1.9	94.5
balancedBST	20	16 (80%)	13 (81.3%)	3 (18.7%)	12.3	23.7	64.0
bempl	10	10 (100%)	4 (40%)	6 (60%)	1.4	1.8	96.8
binaryTree	5	5 (100%)	3 (60%)	2 (40%)	1.7	0.9	97.4
cd	20	13 (65%)	9 (69.2%)	4 (30.8%)	0.7	0.8	98.5
ceilings	30	18 (60%)	13 (72.2%)	5 (27.8%)	2.9	5.3	91.7
dijkstra	30	23 (76.7%)	9 (39.1%)	14 (60.9%)	0.6	36.3	63.2
dll	20	14 (70%)	9 (64.3%)	5 (35.7%)	11.4	14.8	73.9
farmer	15	15 (100%)	3 (20%)	12 (80%)	0.3	1.6	98.1
filesystem	15	11 (73.3%)	3 (27.3%)	8 (72.7%)	27.9	17.4	54.7
fullTree	15	13 (86.7%)	11 (84.6%)	2 (15.4%)	1.6	2.3	96.1
grade	10	10 (100%)	0 (0%)	10 (100%)	1.2	0.9	97.9
grandpa1	15	15 (100%)	0 (0%)	15 (100%)	0.6	0.0	99.4
grandpa2	10	7 (70%)	3 (42.9%)	4 (57.1%)	1.2	1.0	97.8
grandpa3	25	16 (64%)	6 (37.5%)	10 (62.5%)	0.3	0.5	99.2
handshake	20	20 (100%)	0 (0%)	20 (100%)	0.5	0.0	99.5
life	15	7 (46.7%)	1 (14.3%)	6 (85.7%)	0.9	2.2	96.9
lists	20	20 (100%)	9 (45%)	11 (55%)	0.2	0.4	99.4
peterson	85	69 (81.2%)	41 (59.4%)	28 (40.6%)	0.8	7.8	91.5
ringElection1	30	30 (100%)	7 (23.3%)	23 (76.7%)	0.4	1.7	97.9
sll	5	5 (100%)	0 (0%)	5 (100%)	29.9	6.2	63.9
student	25	23 (92%)	20 (87.0%)	3 (13.0%)	9.2	21.5	69.3
Overall	460	379 (82.4%)	169 (44.6%)	210 (55.4%)	4.7	8.4	86.8

5.2   RQ1: Speed-up Effectiveness

Figures 4 and 5 show the speedup of iAlloy compared to the baseline on Mutant Version Set and Real Version Set, respectively. The x-axis denotes the subject names and the y-axis denotes the speed up. In Mutant Version Set, iAlloy achieves speed-up for 19 subjects (75% of the subject set), with up to 4.5x speed-up and 1.79x on average. The reason iAlloy did not speed up on the remaining 5 subjects is that either the change is in the signatures or many commands are unsatisfiable under the previous solutions, where the analysis time overhead in iAlloy (RCS and SR) is larger than the savings. In Real Version Set, we observe that iAlloy achieves a speedup of up to 7.66x and 1.59x on average over all subjects except one (97% of the subject set). iAlloy does not save any time on arr1 because there exists a single command in the subject and the command is unsatisfiable (in which case neither RCS nor SR can save any command executions).

5.3   RQ2: Command Selection and Solution Reuse Effectiveness

Columns 2–5 in Tables 2 and 3 show the total number of commands in each subject (cmd), the number of the selected commands and their percentage compared to the total number of commands (select), the number of solution reuse

Table 3. RCS, SR and Command Execution Results in Real Version Set

Model	cmd	select	reuse	execute	T_select (%)	T_reuse (%)	T_execute (%)
addr	2	2 (100%)	1 (50%)	1 (50%)	24.9	4.7	70.4
arr1	2	2 (100%)	0 (0%)	2 (100%)	7.4	0.0	92.6
arr2	2	2 (100%)	1 (50%)	1 (50%)	7.2	1.4	91.4
bBST1	8	8 (100%)	6 (75%)	2 (25%)	13.4	15.2	71.4
bBST2	8	8 (100%)	6 (75%)	2 (25%)	14.0	15.0	70.9
bBST3	8	8 (100%)	6 (75%)	2 (25%)	13.5	14.9	71.5
bempl	4	4 (100%)	0 (0%)	4 (100%)	1.8	0.4	97.8
cd1	8	7 (87.5%)	5 (71.4%)	2 (28.6%)	1.1	0.9	97.9
cd2	8	7 (87.5%)	6 (85.7%)	1 (14.3%)	3.5	3.0	93.5
dijk	12	10 (83.3%)	5 (50%)	5 (50%)	0.7	23.2	76.2
dll1	8	8 (100%)	6 (75%)	2 (25%)	13.2	16.0	70.8
dll2	8	8 (100%)	6 (75%)	2 (25%)	12.7	17.0	70.3
dll3	8	8 (100%)	7 (87.5%)	1 (12.5%)	16.3	22.3	61.3
dll4	8	8 (100%)	7 (87.5%)	1 (12.5%)	17.6	22.3	60.1
farmer	7	7 (100%)	2 (28.6%)	5 (71.4%)	0.7	2.5	96.8
grade	4	4 (100%)	1 (25%)	3 (75%)	3.6	1.7	94.8
stu0	10	10 (100%)	7 (70%)	3 (30%)	8.1	11.0	80.9
stu1	10	10 (100%)	6 (60%)	4 (40%)	5.8	8.3	85.9
stu10	10	10 (100%)	5 (50%)	5 (50%)	6.7	10.1	83.2
stu11	10	10 (100%)	7 (70%)	3 (30%)	7.6	10.4	81.9
stu12	10	10 (100%)	7 (70%)	3 (30%)	7.6	9.2	83.2
stu13	10	10 (100%)	7 (70%)	3 (30%)	6.4	9.5	84.1
stu14	10	10 (100%)	6 (60%)	4 (40%)	6.6	8.7	84.8
stu15	10	10 (100%)	6 (60%)	4 (40%)	6.9	6.7	86.4
stu16	10	10 (100%)	4 (40%)	6 (60%)	9.4	13.3	77.4
stu17	10	10 (100%)	5 (50%)	5 (50%)	6.7	8.0	85.3
stu18	10	10 (100%)	4 (40%)	6 (60%)	7.7	10.5	81.8
stu19	10	10 (100%)	4 (40%)	6 (60%)	6.1	9.8	84.1
stu2	10	10 (100%)	4 (40%)	6 (60%)	6.2	8.6	85.2
stu3	11	11 (100%)	5 (45.5%)	6 (54.5%)	5.3	8.9	85.8
stu4	10	10 (100%)	4 (40%)	6 (60%)	7.1	9.6	83.3
stu5	10	10 (100%)	7 (70%)	3 (30%)	8.1	8.2	83.7
stu6	10	10 (100%)	6 (60%)	4 (40%)	7.0	9.1	84.0
stu7	10	10 (100%)	6 (60%)	4 (40%)	6.6	8.9	84.5
stu8	10	10 (100%)	7 (70%)	3 (30%)	6.7	7.4	85.9
stu9	10	10 (100%)	4 (40%)	6 (60%)	7.1	11.0	81.9
Overall	306	302 (98.7%)	176 (58.3%)	126 (41.7%)	8.1	9.7	82.2

and their percentage in selected commands (reuse), and the number of actually executed commands and their percentage in selected commands (execute), for the Mutant and Real Version Set respectively. We can see that, both RCS and SR help reduce command execution in both subject sets, but to different extent. A smaller portion of commands are selected in Mutant Set (82.4%) than in Real Set (98.7%). This is due to the fact that there are more changes between versions in Real Set than in Mutant Set. However, smaller portion (41.7% vs. 55.4%) of the selected commands are executed and a larger portion (58.3% vs. 44.6%) of selected commands successfully reuse solutions in Real Set, comparing with Mutant Set. Besides, there are 54.3% command execution reduction ($\frac{cmd - execute}{cmd}$) in Mutant Set and 58.8% in Real Set. The result shows that iAlloy is promising in reducing the command executions in analyzing real world Alloy models as they evolve.

5.4 RQ3: Time Consumption

Columns 6–8 in Tables 2 and 3 present the percentage of time consumption in RCS (T_select), SR (T_reuse), and command execution (T_execute) in the Mutant Version Set and Real Version Set, respectively. We can see that in both subject sets, execution takes most of the time while RCS and SR are lightweight.

6   Related Work

A lot of work has been done to improve [20,22,24] and extend [10–13,16,19,25, 28–31,33] Alloy. We discuss work that is closely related to iAlloy.

Incremental Analysis for Alloy. Li et al. [9] first proposed the incremental analysis idea for their so-called consecutive Alloy models which are similar to the evolving models. They exploit incremental SAT solving to solve only the *delta* which is the set of boolean formulas describing the changed part between two model versions. Solving only the delta would result in a much improved SAT solving time than solving the new model version from scratch. Titanium [1] is an incremental analysis tool for evolving Alloy models. It uses all the solutions of the previous model version to potentially calculate tighter bounds for certain relational variables in the new model version. By tightening the bounds, Titanium reduces the search space, enabling SAT solver to find the new solutions at a fraction of the original solving time. These two approaches are the most relevant to our work that both focus on improving solving efficiency in the translated formulas. Whereas our incremental approach is to avoid the SAT solving phase completely, which is fundamentally different from existing approaches. In addition, Titanium has to find all the solutions in order to tighten the bounds, which would be inefficient when only certain number of solutions are needed.

Regression Symbolic Execution. Similar to the SAT solving applications such as Alloy analyzer, symbolic execution tools also face the scalability problems, in which case a lot of work has been done to improve the performance [6,14,23,34]. The most closely related to our work is regression symbolic execution [14,15,34]. Similar to our RCS, symbolic execution on the new version is guided through the changed part with the previous versions. In addition, there is also work on verification techniques that reuses or caches the results [8,18].

7 Conclusion and Future Work

In this paper, we proposed a novel incremental analysis technique with regression command selection and solution reuse. We implemented our technique in a tool called iAlloy. The experimental results show that iAlloy can speed up 90% of our subjects. Furthermore, it performs surprisingly well in models of the real faulty versions with up to 7.66 times speed up and above 50% command execution reduction. This indicates that iAlloy is promising in reducing time overhead of analyzing real-world Alloy models. In the future, we plan to extend iAlloy to support changes that involve Alloy signatures and perform a more fine-grained analysis to improve command selection.

Acknowledgments. We thank the anonymous reviewers for their valuable comments. This research was partially supported by the US National Science Foundation under Grants Nos. CCF-1566363, CCF-1652517, CCF-1704790 and CCF-1718903.

References

1. Bagheri, H., Malek, S.: Titanium: efficient analysis of evolving alloy specifications. In: International Symposium on Foundations of Software Engineering, pp. 27–38 (2016)
2. Rational Software Corporation: Object constraint language specification. Version 1.1 (1997)
3. Gligoric, M., Eloussi, L., Marinov, D.: Practical regression test selection with dynamic file dependencies. In: International Symposium on Software Testing and Analysis, pp. 211–222 (2015)
4. Graves, T.L., Harrold, M.J., Kim, J.-M., Porter, A., Rothermel, G.: An empirical study of regression test selection techniques. Trans. Softw. Eng. Methodol. **10**(2), 184–208 (2001)
5. Jackson, D.: Alloy: a lightweight object modelling notation. Trans. Softw. Eng. Methodol. **11**(2), 256–290 (2002)
6. Jia, X., Ghezzi, C., Ying, S.: Enhancing reuse of constraint solutions to improve symbolic execution. In: International Symposium on Software Testing and Analysis, pp. 177–187 (2015)
7. Legunsen, O., Shi, A., Marinov, D.: STARTS: STAtic regression test selection. In: Automated Software Engineering, pp. 949–954 (2017)
8. Leino, K.R.M., Wüstholz, V.: Fine-grained caching of verification results. In: Kroening, D., Păsăreanu, C.S. (eds.) CAV 2015. LNCS, Part I, vol. 9206, pp. 380–397. Springer, Cham (2015). https://doi.org/10.1007/978-3-319-21690-4_22
9. Li, X., Shannon, D., Walker, J., Khurshid, S., Marinov, D.: Analyzing the uses of a software modeling tool. Electron. Notes Theoret. Comput. Sci. **164**(2), 3–18 (2006)
10. Montaghami, V., Rayside, D.: Extending alloy with partial instances. In: Derrick, J., et al. (eds.) ABZ 2012. LNCS, vol. 7316, pp. 122–135. Springer, Heidelberg (2012). https://doi.org/10.1007/978-3-642-30885-7_9
11. Montaghami V., Rayside D.: Staged evaluation of partial instances in a relational model finder. In: Ait Ameur Y., Schewe KD. (eds) Abstract State Machines, Alloy, B, TLA, VDM, and Z. ABZ 2014. LNCS, vol. 8477, pp. 318–323. Springer, Heidelberg (2014). https://doi.org/10.1007/978-3-662-43652-3_32

12. Nelson, T., Saghafi, S., Dougherty, D.J., Fisler, K., Krishnamurthi, S.: Aluminum: principled scenario exploration through minimality. In: International Conference on Software Engineering, pp. 232–241 (2013)
13. Nijjar, J., Bultan, T.: Bounded verification of ruby on rails data models. In: International Symposium on Software Testing and Analysis, pp. 67–77 (2011)
14. Person, S., Yang, G., Rungta, N., Khurshid, S.: Directed incremental symbolic execution. SIGPLAN Not. 46(6), 504–515 (2011)
15. Ramos, D.A., Engler, D.R.: Practical, low-effort equivalence verification of real code. In: Gopalakrishnan, G., Qadeer, S. (eds.) CAV 2011. LNCS, vol. 6806, pp. 669–685. Springer, Heidelberg (2011). https://doi.org/10.1007/978-3-642-22110-1_55
16. Regis, G., et al.: DynAlloy analyzer: a tool for the specification and analysis of alloy models with dynamic behaviour. In: Foundations of Software Engineering, pp. 969–973 (2017)
17. Spivey, J.M.: The Z Notation: A Reference Manual. Prentice-Hall Inc., Upper Saddle River (1989)
18. Strichman, O., Godlin, B.: Regression verification - a practical way to verify programs. In: Meyer, B., Woodcock, J. (eds.) VSTTE 2005. LNCS, vol. 4171, pp. 496–501. Springer, Heidelberg (2008). https://doi.org/10.1007/978-3-540-69149-5_54
19. Sullivan, A., Wang, K., Khurshid, S.: AUnit: a test automation tool for alloy. In: International Conference on Software Testing, Verification, and Validation, pp. 398–403 (2018)
20. Sullivan, A., Wang, K., Khurshid, S., Marinov, D.: Evaluating state modeling techniques in alloy. In: Software Quality Analysis, Monitoring, Improvement, and Applications (2017)
21. Sullivan, A., Wang, K., Zaeem, R.N., Khurshid, S.: Automated test generation and mutation testing for alloy. In: International Conference on Software Testing, Verification, and Validation, pp. 264–275 (2017)
22. Torlak, E., Jackson, D.: Kodkod: a relational model finder. In: Grumberg, O., Huth, M. (eds.) TACAS 2007. LNCS, vol. 4424, pp. 632–647. Springer, Heidelberg (2007). https://doi.org/10.1007/978-3-540-71209-1_49
23. Visser, W., Geldenhuys, J., Dwyer, M.B.: Green: reducing, reusing and recycling constraints in program analysis. In: International Symposium on the Foundations of Software Engineering, pp. 58:1–58:11 (2012)
24. Wang, J., Bagheri, H., Cohen, M.B.: An evolutionary approach for analyzing Alloy specifications. In: International Conference on Automated Software Engineering, pp. 820–825 (2018)
25. Wang, K., Sullivan, A., Khurshid, S.: ARepair: a repair framework for alloy. In: International Conference on Software Engineering, pp. 577–588 (2018)
26. Wang, K., Sullivan, A., Khurshid, S.: Automated model repair for alloy. In: Automated Software Engineering, pp. 577–588 (2018)
27. Wang, K, Sullivan, A., Khurshid, S.: MuAlloy: a mutation testing framework for alloy. In: International Conference on Software Engineering, pp. 29–32 (2018)
28. Wang, K., Sullivan, A., Koukoutos, M., Marinov, D., Khurshid, S.: Systematic generation of non-equivalent expressions for relational algebra. In: Butler, M., Raschke, A., Hoang, T.S., Reichl, K. (eds.) ABZ 2018. LNCS, vol. 10817, pp. 105–120. Springer, Cham (2018). https://doi.org/10.1007/978-3-319-91271-4_8
29. Wang, K., Sullivan, A., Marinov, D., Khurshid, S.: ASketch: a sketching framework for alloy. In: Symposium on the Foundations of Software Engineering, pp. 916–919 (2018)

30. Wang, K., Sullivan, A., Marinov, D., Khurshid, S.: Fault localization for declarative models in alloy. eprint arXiv:1807.08707 (2018)
31. Wang, K., Sullivan, A., Marinov, D., Khurshid, S.: Solver-based sketching of alloy models using test valuations. In: Butler, M., Raschke, A., Hoang, T.S., Reichl, K. (eds.) ABZ 2018. LNCS, vol. 10817, pp. 121–136. Springer, Cham (2018). https://doi.org/10.1007/978-3-319-91271-4_9
32. Wang, K., Zhu, C., Celik, A., Kim, J., Batory, D., Gligoric, M.: Towards refactoring-aware regression test selection. In: IEEE/ACM 40th International Conference on Software Engineering (ICSE), pp. 233–244 (2018)
33. Wang, W., Wang, K., Zhang, M., Khurshid, S.: Learning to optimize the alloy analyzer. In: International Conference on Software Testing, Verification and Validation (2019, to appear)
34. Yang, G., Păsăreanu, C.S., Khurshid, S.: Memoized symbolic execution. In: International Symposium on Software Testing and Analysis, pp. 144–154 (2012)
35. Zhang, L., Kim, M., Khurshid, S.: Localizing failure-inducing program edits based on spectrum information. In: International Conference on Software Maintenance and Evolution, pp. 23–32 (2011)

Extending a Brainiac Prover
to Lambda-Free Higher-Order Logic

Petar Vukmirović[1]([✉]), Jasmin Christian Blanchette[1,2], Simon Cruanes[3],
and Stephan Schulz[4]

[1] Vrije Universiteit Amsterdam, Amsterdam, The Netherlands
p.vukmirovic@vu.nl
[2] Max-Planck-Institut für Informatik, Saarland Informatics Campus,
Saarbrücken, Germany
[3] Aesthetic Integration, Austin, TX, USA
[4] DHBW Stuttgart, Stuttgart, Germany

Abstract. Decades of work have gone into developing efficient proof
calculi, data structures, algorithms, and heuristics for first-order automatic theorem proving. Higher-order provers lag behind in terms of efficiency. Instead of developing a new higher-order prover from the ground
up, we propose to start with the state-of-the-art superposition-based
prover E and gradually enrich it with higher-order features. We explain
how to extend the prover's data structures, algorithms, and heuristics to
λ-free higher-order logic, a formalism that supports partial application
and applied variables. Our extension outperforms the traditional encoding and appears promising as a stepping stone towards full higher-order
logic.

1 Introduction

Superposition-based provers, such as E [26], SPASS [33], and Vampire [18], are
among the most successful first-order reasoning systems. They serve as back-
ends in various frameworks, including software verifiers (Why3 [15]), automatic
higher-order theorem provers (Leo-III [27], Satallax [12]), and "hammers" in
proof assistants (HOLyHammer for HOL Light [17], Sledgehammer for Isabelle
[21]). Decades of research have gone into refining calculi, devising efficient data
structures and algorithms, and developing heuristics to guide proof search. This
work has mostly focused on first-order logic with equality, with or without arithmetic.

Research on higher-order automatic provers has resulted in systems such as
LEO [8], Leo-II [9], and Leo-III [27], based on resolution and paramodulation,
and Satallax [12], based on tableaux. These provers feature a "cooperative"
architecture, pioneered by LEO: They are full-fledged higher-order provers that
regularly invoke an external first-order prover in an attempt to finish the proof
quickly using only first-order reasoning. However, the first-order backend will
succeed only if all the necessary higher-order reasoning has been performed,

© The Author(s) 2019
T. Vojnar and L. Zhang (Eds.): TACAS 2019, Part I, LNCS 11427, pp. 192–210, 2019.
https://doi.org/10.1007/978-3-030-17462-0_11

meaning that much of the first-order reasoning is carried out by the slower higher-order prover. As a result, this architecture leads to suboptimal performance on first-order problems and on problems with a large first-order component. For example, at the 2017 installment of the CADE ATP System Competition (CASC) [30], Leo-III, using E as one of its backends, proved 652 out of 2000 first-order problems in the Sledgehammer division, compared with 1185 for E on its own and 1433 for Vampire.

To obtain better performance, we propose to start with a competitive first-order prover and extend it to full higher-order logic one feature at a time. Our goal is a *graceful* extension, so that the system behaves as before on first-order problems, performs mostly like a first-order prover on typical, mildly higher-order problems, and scales up to arbitrary higher-order problems, in keeping with the zero-overhead principle: *What you don't use, you don't pay for.*

As a stepping stone towards full higher-order logic, we initially restrict our focus to a higher-order logic without λ-expressions (Sect. 2). Compared with first-order logic, its distinguishing features are partial application and applied variables. This formalism is rich enough to express the recursive equations of higher-order combinators, such as the map operation on finite lists:

$$\text{map } f \text{ nil} \approx \text{nil} \qquad \text{map } f \text{ (cons } x \text{ } xs) \approx \text{cons } (f \text{ } x) \text{ (map } f \text{ } xs)$$

Our vehicle is E, a prover developed primarily by Schulz. It is written in C and offers good performance, with the emphasis on "brainiac" heuristics rather than raw speed. E regularly scores among the top systems at CASC, and usually is the strongest open source[1] prover in the relevant divisions. It also serves as a backend for competitive higher-order provers. We refer to our extended version of E as Ehoh. It corresponds to E version 2.3 configured with `-enable-ho`. A prototype of Ehoh is described in Vukmirović's MSc thesis [31].

The three main challenges are generalizing the term representation (Sect. 3), the unification algorithm (Sect. 4), and the indexing data structures (Sect. 5). We also adapted the inference rules (Sect. 6) and the heuristics (Sect. 7). This paper explains the key ideas. Details, including correctness proofs, are given in a separate technical report [32].

A novel aspect of our work is *prefix optimization*. Higher-order terms contain twice as many proper subterms as first-order terms; for example, the term f (g a) b contains not only the argument subterms g a, a, b but also the "prefix" subterms f, f (g a), g. Using prefix optimization, the prover traverses subterms recursively in a first-order fashion, considering all the prefixes of the current subterm together, at no significant additional cost. Our experiments (Sect. 8) show that Ehoh is effectively as fast as E on first-order problems and can also prove higher-order problems that do not require synthesizing λ-terms. As a next step, we plan to add support for λ-terms and higher-order unification.

---

[1] http://wwwlehre.dhbw-stuttgart.de/~sschulz/WORK/E_DOWNLOAD/V_2.3/.

2   Logic

Our logic corresponds to the intensional λ-free higher-order logic (λfHOL) described by Bentkamp, Blanchette, Cruanes, and Waldmann [7, Sect. 2]. Another possible name for this logic would be "applicative first-order logic." Extensionality can be obtained by adding suitable axioms [7, Sect. 3.1].

A type is either an atomic type ι or a function type $\tau \to \upsilon$, where τ and υ are themselves types. Terms, ranged over by s, t, u, v, are either *variables* $x, y, z, \ldots$, (*function*) *symbols* a, b, c, d, f, g, ... (often called "constants" in the higher-order literature), or binary applications $s\,t$. Application associates to the left, whereas $\to$ associates to the right. The typing rules are as for the simply typed λ-calculus. A term's *arity* is the number of extra arguments it can take; thus, if f has type $\iota \to \iota \to \iota$ and a has type ι, then f is binary, f a is unary, and f a a is nullary. Terms have a unique "flattened" decomposition of the form $\zeta\, s_1 \ldots s_m$, where ζ, the *head*, is a variable x or symbol f. We abbreviate tuples $(a_1, \ldots, a_m)$ to $\overline{a_m}$ or $\overline{a}$; abusing notation, we write $\zeta\, \overline{s_m}$ for the curried application $\zeta\, s_1 \ldots s_m$.

An equation $s \approx t$ corresponds to an unordered pair of terms. A literal L is an equation or its negation. Clauses C, D are finite multisets of literals, written $L_1 \vee \cdots \vee L_n$. E and Ehoh clausify the input as a preprocessing step.

A well-known technique to support λfHOL using first-order reasoning systems is to employ the *applicative encoding*. Following this scheme, every n-ary symbol is converted to a nullary symbol, and application is represented by a distinguished binary symbol @. For example, the λfHOL term f $(x\, a)$ b is encoded as the first-order term @(@(f, @(x, a)), b). However, this representation is not graceful; it clutters data structures and impacts proof search in subtle ways, leading to poorer performance, especially on large benchmarks. In our empirical evaluation, we find that for some prover modes, the applicative encoding incurs a 15% decrease in success rate (Sect. 8). For these and further reasons (Sect. 9), it is not an ideal basis for higher-order reasoning.

3   Types and Terms

The term representation is a fundamental question when building a theorem prover. Delicate changes to E's term representation were needed to support partial application and especially applied variables. In contrast, the introduction of a higher-order type system had a less dramatic impact on the prover's code.

Types. For most of its history, E supported only untyped first-order logic. Cruanes implemented support for atomic types for E 2.0 [13, p. 117]. Symbols f are declared with a type signature: $f : \tau_1 \times \cdots \times \tau_m \to \tau$. Atomic types are represented by integers in memory, leading to efficient type comparisons.

In λfHOL, a type signature consists of types τ, in which the function type constructor $\to$ can be nested—e.g., $(\iota \to \iota) \to \iota \to \iota$. A natural way to represent such types is to mimic their recursive structures using tagged unions. However, this leads to memory fragmentation, and a simple operation such as querying the type of a function's ith argument would require dereferencing i pointers.

We prefer a flattened representation, in which a type $\tau_1 \to \cdots \to \tau_n \to \iota$ is represented by a single node labeled with $\to$ and pointing to the array $(\tau_1, \ldots, \tau_n, \iota)$. Applying $k \leq n$ arguments to a function of the above type yields a term of type $\tau_{k+1} \to \cdots \to \tau_n \to \iota$. In memory, this corresponds to skipping the first k array elements.

To speed up type comparisons, Ehoh stores all types in a shared bank and implements perfect sharing, ensuring that types that are structurally the same are represented by the same object in memory. Type equality can then be implemented as a pointer comparison.

Terms. In E, terms are represented as perfectly shared directed acyclic graphs. Each node, or *cell*, contains 11 fields, including `f_code`, an integer that identifies the term's head symbol (if ≥ 0) or variable (if < 0); `arity`, an integer corresponding to the number of arguments passed to the head symbol; `args`, an array of size `arity` consisting of pointers to argument terms; and `binding`, which possibly stores a substitution for a variable used for unification and matching.

In higher-order logic, variables may have function type and be applied, and symbols can be applied to fewer arguments than specified by their type signatures. A natural representation of λfHOL terms as tagged unions would distinguish between variables x, symbols f, and binary applications $s\,t$. However, this scheme suffers from memory fragmentation and linear-time access, as with the representation of types, affecting performance on purely or mostly first-order problems. Instead, we propose a flattened representation, as a generalization of E's existing data structures: Allow arguments to variables, and for symbols let `arity` be the number of *actual* arguments.

A side effect of the flattened representation is that prefix subterms are not shared. For example, the terms f a and f a b correspond to the flattened cells f(a) and f(a, b). The argument subterm a is shared, but not the prefix f a. Similarly, x and x b are represented by two distinct cells, $x()$ and $x(b)$, and there is no connection between the two occurrences of x. In particular, despite perfect sharing, their `binding` fields are unconnected, leading to inconsistencies.

A potential solution would be to systematically traverse a clause and set the `binding` fields of all cells of the form $x(\bar{s})$ whenever a variable x is bound, but this would be inefficient and inelegant. Instead, we implemented a hybrid approach: Variables are applied by an explicit application operator @, to ensure that they are always perfectly shared. Thus, x b c is represented by the cell @(x, b, c), where x is a shared subcell. This is graceful, since variables never occur applied in first-order terms. The main drawback of this technique is that some normalization is necessary after substitution: Whenever a variable is instantiated by a term with a symbol head, the @ symbol must be eliminated. Applying the substitution $\{x \mapsto f\,a\}$ to the cell @(x, b, c) must produce the cell f(a, b, c) and not @(f(a), b, c), for consistency with other occurrences of f a b c.

There is one more complication related to the `binding` field. In E, it is easy and useful to traverse a term as if a substitution has been applied, by following all set `binding` fields. In Ehoh, this is not enough, because cells must also be normalized. To avoid repeatedly creating the same normalized cells, we introduced a `binding_cache` field that connects a $@(x, \overline{s})$ cell with its substitution. However, this cache can easily become stale when the `binding` pointer is updated. To detect this situation, we store x's `binding` value in the $@(x, \overline{s})$ cell's `binding` field (which is otherwise unused). To find out whether the cache is valid, it suffices to check that the `binding` fields of x and $@(x, \overline{s})$ are equal.

Term Orders. Superposition provers rely on term orders to prune the search space. To ensure completeness, the order must be a simplification order that can be extended to a simplification order that is total on variable-free terms. The Knuth–Bendix order (KBO) and the lexicographic path order (LPO) meet this criterion. KBO is generally regarded as the more robust and efficient option for superposition. E implements both. In earlier work, Blanchette and colleagues have shown that only KBO can be generalized gracefully while preserving all the necessary properties for superposition [5]. For this reason, we focus on KBO.

E implements the linear-time algorithm for KBO described by Löchner [19], which relies on the tupling method to store intermediate results, avoiding repeated computations. It is straightforward to generalize the algorithm to compute the graceful λfHOL version of KBO [5]. The main difference is that when comparing two terms f $\overline{s_m}$ and f $\overline{t_n}$, because of partial application we may now have $m \neq n$; this required changing the implementation to perform a length-lexicographic comparison of the tuples $\overline{s_m}$ and $\overline{t_n}$.

4   Unification and Matching

Syntactic unification of λfHOL terms has a definite first-order flavor. It is decidable, and most general unifiers (MGUs) are unique up to variable renaming. For example, the unification constraint f $(y \ a) \stackrel{?}{=} y$ (f a) has the MGU $\{y \mapsto f\}$, whereas in full higher-order logic it would admit infinitely many independent solutions of the form $\{y \mapsto \lambda x. \ f \ (f \ (\cdots (f \ x) \cdots))\}$. Matching is a special case of unification where only the variables on the left-hand side can be instantiated.

An easy but inefficient way to implement unification and matching for λfHOL is to apply the applicative encoding (Sect. 1), perform first-order unification or matching, and decode the result. Instead, we propose to generalize the first-order unification and matching procedures to operate directly on λfHOL terms.

We present our unification procedure as a transition system, generalizing Baader and Nipkow [3]. A unification problem consists of a finite set S of unification constraints $s_i \stackrel{?}{=} t_i$, where s_i and t_i are of the same type. A problem is in *solved form* if it has the form $\{x_1 \stackrel{?}{=} t_1, \ldots, x_n \stackrel{?}{=} t_n\}$, where the x_i's are distinct and do not occur in the t_j's. The corresponding unifier is $\{x_1 \mapsto t_1, \ldots, x_n \mapsto t_n\}$. The transition rules attempt to bring the input constraints into solved form.

The first group of rules consists of operations that focus on a single constraint and replace it with a new (possibly empty) set of constraints:

Delete $\{t \stackrel{?}{=} t\} \uplus S \Longrightarrow S$

Decompose $\{f \ \overline{s_m} \stackrel{?}{=} f \ \overline{t_m}\} \uplus S \Longrightarrow S \cup \{s_1 \stackrel{?}{=} t_1, \ldots, s_m \stackrel{?}{=} t_m\}$

DecomposeX $\{x\ \overline{s_m} \overset{?}{=} u\ \overline{t_m}\} \uplus S \Longrightarrow S \cup \{x \overset{?}{=} u,\ s_1 \overset{?}{=} t_1,\ldots,s_m \overset{?}{=} t_m\}$
            if x and u have the same type and $m > 0$

Orient $\{f\ \overline{s} \overset{?}{=} x\ \overline{t}\} \uplus S \Longrightarrow S \cup \{x\ \overline{t} \overset{?}{=} f\ \overline{s}\}$

OrientXY $\{x\ \overline{s_m} \overset{?}{=} y\ \overline{t_n}\} \uplus S \Longrightarrow S \cup \{y\ \overline{t_n} \overset{?}{=} x\ \overline{s_m}\}$ if $m > n$

Eliminate $\{x \overset{?}{=} t\} \uplus S \Longrightarrow \{x \overset{?}{=} t\} \cup \{x \mapsto t\}(S)$ if $x \in \mathit{Var}(S) \setminus \mathit{Var}(t)$

The Delete, Decompose, and Eliminate rules are essentially as for first-order terms. The Orient rule is generalized to allow applied variables and complemented by a new OrientXY rule. DecomposeX, also a new rule, can be seen as a variant of Decompose that analyzes applied variables; the term u may be an application.

The rules belonging to the second group detect unsolvable constraints:

Clash $\{f\ \overline{s} \overset{?}{=} g\ \overline{t}\} \uplus S \Longrightarrow \bot$ if $f \neq g$

ClashTypeX $\{x\ \overline{s_m} \overset{?}{=} u\ \overline{t_m}\} \uplus S \Longrightarrow \bot$ if x and u have different types

ClashLenXF $\{x\ \overline{s_m} \overset{?}{=} f\ \overline{t_n}\} \uplus S \Longrightarrow \bot$ if $m > n$

OccursCheck $\{x \overset{?}{=} t\} \uplus S \Longrightarrow \bot$ if $x \in \mathit{Var}(t)$ and $x \neq t$

The derivations below demonstrate the computation of MGUs for the unification problems $\{f\ (y\ a) \overset{?}{=} y\ (f\ a)\}$ and $\{x\ (z\ b\ c) \overset{?}{=} g\ a\ (y\ c)\}$:

$$
\begin{array}{ll}
& \{f\ (y\ a) \overset{?}{=} y\ (f\ a)\} \\
\Longrightarrow_{\text{Orient}} & \{y\ (f\ a) \overset{?}{=} f\ (y\ a)\} \\
\Longrightarrow_{\text{DecomposeX}} & \{y \overset{?}{=} f,\ f\ a \overset{?}{=} y\ a\} \\
\Longrightarrow_{\text{Eliminate}} & \{y \overset{?}{=} f,\ f\ a \overset{?}{=} f\ a\} \\
\Longrightarrow_{\text{Delete}} & \{y \overset{?}{=} f\}
\end{array}
\qquad
\begin{array}{ll}
& \{x\ (z\ b\ c) \overset{?}{=} g\ a\ (y\ c)\} \\
\Longrightarrow_{\text{DecomposeX}} & \{x \overset{?}{=} g\ a,\ z\ b\ c \overset{?}{=} y\ c\} \\
\Longrightarrow_{\text{OrientXY}} & \{x \overset{?}{=} g\ a,\ y\ c \overset{?}{=} z\ b\ c\} \\
\Longrightarrow_{\text{DecomposeX}} & \{x \overset{?}{=} g\ a,\ y \overset{?}{=} z\ b,\ c \overset{?}{=} c\} \\
\Longrightarrow_{\text{Delete}} & \{x \overset{?}{=} g\ a,\ y \overset{?}{=} z\ b\}
\end{array}
$$

E stores open constraints in a double-ended queue. Constraints are processed from the front. New constraints are added at the front if they involve complex terms that can be dealt with swiftly by Decompose or Clash, or to the back if one side is a variable. Soundness and completeness proofs as well as the pseudocode for unification and matching algorithms are included in our report [32].

During proof search, E repeatedly needs to test a term s for unifiability not only with some other term t but also with t's subterms. Prefix optimization speeds up this test: The subterms of t are traversed in a first-order fashion; for each such subterm $\zeta\ \overline{t_n}$, at most one prefix $\zeta\ \overline{t_k}$, with $k \leq n$, is possibly unifiable with s, by virtue of their having the same arity. Using this technique, Ehoh is virtually as efficient as E on first-order terms.

5   Indexing Data Structures

Superposition provers like E work by saturation. Their main loop heuristically selects a clause and searches for potential inference partners among a possibly large set of other clauses. Mechanisms such as simplification and subsumption also require locating terms in a large clause set. For example, when E derives a new equation $s \approx t$, if s is larger than t according to the term order, it will rewrite all instances $\sigma(s)$ of s to $\sigma(t)$ in existing clauses.

To avoid iterating over all terms (including subterms) in large clause sets, superposition provers store the potential inference partners in indexing data structures. A term index stores a set of terms S. Given a *query term* t, a query returns all terms $s \in S$ that satisfy a given *retrieval condition*: $\sigma(s) = \sigma(t)$ (s and t are unifiable), $\sigma(s) = t$ (s generalizes t), or $s = \sigma(t)$ (s is an instance of t), for some substitution σ. *Perfect* indices return exactly the subset of terms satisfying the retrieval condition. In contrast, *imperfect* indices return a superset of eligible terms, and the retrieval condition needs to be checked for each candidate.

E relies on two term indexing data structures, perfect discrimination trees [20] and fingerprint indices [24], that needed to be generalized to λfHOL. It also uses feature vector indices [25] to speed up clause subsumption and related techniques, but these require no changes to work with λfHOL clauses.

Perfect Discrimination Trees. Discrimination trees [20] are tries in which every node is labeled with a symbol or a variable. A path from the root to a leaf node corresponds to a "serialized term"—a term expressed without parentheses and commas. Consider the following discrimination trees:

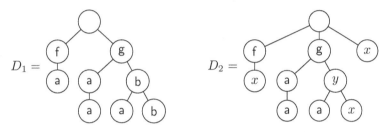

Assuming $a, b, x, y : \iota$, $f : \iota \to \iota$, and $g : \iota^2 \to \iota$, the trees D_1 and D_2 represent the term sets $\{f(a), g(a, a), g(b, a), g(b, b)\}$ and $\{f(x), g(a, a), g(y, a), g(y, x), x\}$.

E uses perfect discrimination trees for finding generalizations of query terms. For example, if the query term is $g(a, a)$, it would follow the path g.a.a in the tree D_1 and return $\{g(a, a)\}$. For D_2, it would also explore paths labeled with variables, binding them as it proceeds, and return $\{g(a, a), g(y, a), g(y, x), x\}$.

The data structure relies on the observation that serializing is unambiguous. Conveniently, this property also holds for λfHOL terms. Assume that two distinct λfHOL terms yield the same serialization. Clearly, they must disagree on parentheses; one will have the subterm $s\ t\ u$ where the other has $s\ (t\ u)$. However, these two subterms cannot both be well typed.

When generalizing the data structure to λfHOL, we face a slight complication due to partial application. First-order terms can only be stored in leaf nodes, but in Ehoh we must also be able to represent partially applied terms, such as f, g, or g a (assuming, as above, that f is unary and g is binary). Conceptually, this can be solved by storing a Boolean on each node indicating whether it is an accepting state. In the implementation, the change is more subtle, because several parts of E's code implicitly assume that only leaf nodes are accepting.

The main difficulty specific to λfHOL concerns applied variables. To enumerate all generalizing terms, E needs to backtrack from child to parent nodes. To achieve this, it relies on two stacks that store subterms of the query term: term_stack stores the terms that must be matched in turn against the current subtree, and term_proc stores, for each node from the root to the current subtree, the corresponding processed term, including any arguments yet to be matched.

The matching procedure starts at the root with an empty substitution σ. Initially, term_stack contains the query term, and term_proc is empty. The procedure advances by moving to a suitable child node:

A. If the node is labeled with a symbol f and the top item t of term_stack is $f(\overline{t_n})$, replace t by n new items $t_1, \ldots, t_n$, and push t onto term_proc.
B. If the node is labeled with a variable x, there are two subcases. If x is already bound, check that $\sigma(x) = t$; otherwise, extend σ so that $\sigma(x) = t$. Next, pop a term t from term_stack and push it onto term_proc.

The goal is to reach an accepting node. If the query term and all the terms stored in the tree are first-order, term_stack will then be empty, and the entire query term will have been matched.

Backtracking works in reverse: Pop a term t from term_proc; if the current node is labeled with an n-ary symbol, discard term_stack's topmost n items; finally, push t onto term_stack. Variable bindings must also be undone.

As an example, looking up $g(b, a)$ in the tree D_1 would result in the following succession of stack states, starting from the root ϵ along the path g.b.a:

	ϵ	g	g.b	g.b.a
term_stack:	$[g(b, a)]$	$[b, a]$	$[a]$	$[]$
term_proc:	$[]$	$[g(b, a)]$	$[b, g(b, a)]$	$[a, b, g(b, a)]$

(The notation $[a_1, \ldots, a_n]$ represents the n-item stack with a_1 on top.) Backtracking amounts to moving leftwards: When backtracking from the node g to the root, we pop $g(b, a)$ from term_proc, we discard two items from term_stack, and we push $g(b, a)$ onto term_stack.

To adapt the procedure to λfHOL, the key idea is that an applied variable is not very different from an applied symbol. A node labeled with an n-ary symbol or variable ζ matches a prefix t' of the k-ary term t popped from term_stack and leaves $n - k$ arguments $\overline{u}$ to be pushed back, with $t = t' \, \overline{u}$. If ζ is a variable, it must be bound to the prefix t'. Backtracking works analogously: Given the arity n of the node label ζ and the arity k of the term t popped from term_proc, we discard the topmost $n - k$ items $\overline{u}$ from term_proc.

To illustrate the procedure, we consider the tree D_2 but change y's type to $\iota \to \iota$. This tree represents the set $\{f \, x, \, g \, a \, a, \, g \, (y \, a), \, g \, (y \, x), \, x\}$. Let $g \, (g \, a \, b)$ be the query term. We have the following sequence of substitutions and stacks:

	ϵ	g	$g.y$	$g.y.x$
σ:	$\emptyset$	$\emptyset$	$\{y \mapsto g\,a\}$	$\{y \mapsto g\,a,\, x \mapsto b\}$
term_stack:	$[g\,(g\,a\,b)]$	$[g\,a\,b]$	$[b]$	$[]$
term_proc:	$[]$	$[g\,(g\,a\,b)]$	$[g\,a\,b,\, g\,(g\,a\,b)]$	$[b,\, g\,a\,b,\, g\,(g\,a\,b)]$

Finally, to avoid traversing twice as many subterms as in the first-order case, we can optimize prefixes: Given a query term $\zeta\,\overline{t_n}$, we can also match prefixes $\zeta\,\overline{t_k}$, where $k < n$, by allowing term_stack to be nonempty at the end.

Fingerprint Indices. Fingerprint indices [24] trade perfect indexing for a compact memory representation and more flexible retrieval conditions. The basic idea is to compare terms by looking only at a few predefined sample positions. If we know that term s has symbol f at the head of the subterm at 2.1 and term t has g at the same position, we can immediately conclude that s and t are not unifiable.

Let A ("at a variable"), B ("below a variable"), and N ("nonexistent") be distinguished symbols. Given a term t and a position p, the *fingerprint function* $\mathcal{G\!fpf}$ is defined as

$$\mathcal{G\!fpf}(t,p) = \begin{cases} f & \text{if } t|_p \text{ has a symbol head f} \\ A & \text{if } t|_p \text{ is a variable} \\ B & \text{if } t|_q \text{ is a variable for some proper prefix } q \text{ of } p \\ N & \text{otherwise} \end{cases}$$

Based on a fixed tuple of sample positions $\overline{p_n}$, the *fingerprint* of a term t is defined as $\mathcal{F}p(t) = \big(\mathcal{G\!fpf}(t,p_1), \ldots, \mathcal{G\!fpf}(t,p_n)\big)$. To compare two terms s and t, it suffices to check that their fingerprints are componentwise compatible using the following unification and matching matrices:

	f_1	f_2	A	B	N
f_1		✗			✗
A					✗
B					
N	✗	✗		✗	

	f_1	f_2	A	B	N
f_1		✗	✗	✗	✗
A				✗	✗
B					
N	✗	✗	✗	✗	

The rows and columns correspond to s and t, respectively. The metavariables f_1 and f_2 represent arbitrary distinct symbols. Incompatibility is indicated by ✗.

As an example, let $(\epsilon, 1, 2, 1.1, 1.2, 2.1, 2.2)$ be the sample positions, and let $s = f(a, x)$ and $t = f(g(x), g(a))$ be the terms to unify. Their fingerprints are

$$\mathcal{F}p(s) = (f, a, A, N, N, B, B) \qquad \mathcal{F}p(t) = (f, g, g, A, N, a, N)$$

Using the left matrix, we compute the compatibility vector $(-, ✗, -, ✗, -, -, -)$. The mismatches at positions 1 and 1.1 indicate that s and t are not unifiable.

A fingerprint index is a trie that stores a term set T keyed by fingerprint. The term $f(g(x), g(a))$ above would be stored in the node addressed by $f.g.g.A.N.a.N$, possibly together with other terms that share the same fingerprint. This organization makes it possible to unify or match a query term s against all the terms T in one traversal. Once a node storing the terms $U \subseteq T$ has been reached, due to overapproximation we must apply unification or matching on s and each $u \in U$.

When adapting this data structure to λfHOL, we must first choose a suitable notion of position in a term. Conventionally, higher-order positions are strings over $\{1, 2\}$ indicating, for each binary application $t_1 \, t_2$, which term t_i to follow. Given that this is not graceful, it seems preferable to generalize the first-order notion to flattened λfHOL terms—e.g., $x \, \mathsf{a} \, \mathsf{b} \,|_1 = \mathsf{a}$ and $x \, \mathsf{a} \, \mathsf{b} \,|_2 = \mathsf{b}$. However, this approach fails on applied variables. For example, although $x \, \mathsf{b}$ and $\mathsf{f} \, \mathsf{a} \, \mathsf{b}$ are unifiable (using $\{x \mapsto \mathsf{f} \, \mathsf{a}\}$), sampling position 1 would yield a clash between b and a. To ensure that positions remain stable under substitution, we propose to number arguments in reverse: $t|^\epsilon = t$ and $\zeta \, t_n \, \ldots \, t_1 |^{i.p} = t_i |^p$ if $1 \leq i \leq n$.

Let $t \langle^p$ denote the subterm $t|^q$ such that q is the longest prefix of p for which $t|^q$ is defined. The λfHOL version of the fingerprint function is defined as follows:

$$\mathcal{G}\!fpf'(t, p) = \begin{cases} \mathsf{f} & \text{if } t|^p \text{ has a symbol head } \mathsf{f} \\ \mathsf{A} & \text{if } t|^p \text{ has a variable head} \\ \mathsf{B} & \text{if } t|^p \text{ is undefined but } t\langle^p \text{ has a variable head} \\ \mathsf{N} & \text{otherwise} \end{cases}$$

Except for the reversed numbering scheme, $\mathcal{G}\!fpf'$ coincides with $\mathcal{G}\!fpf$ on first-order terms. The fingerprint $\mathcal{F}p'(t)$ of a term t is defined analogously as before, and the same compatibility matrices can be used.

The most interesting new case is that of an applied variable. Given the sample positions $(\epsilon, 2, 1)$, the fingerprint of x is $(\mathsf{A}, \mathsf{B}, \mathsf{B})$ as before, whereas the fingerprint of $x \, \mathsf{c}$ is $(\mathsf{A}, \mathsf{B}, \mathsf{c})$. As another example, let $(\epsilon, 2, 1, 2.2, 2.1, 1.2, 1.1)$ be the sample positions, and let $s = x \, (\mathsf{f} \, \mathsf{b} \, \mathsf{c})$ and $t = \mathsf{g} \, \mathsf{a} \, (y \, \mathsf{d})$. Their fingerprints are

$$\mathcal{F}p(s) = (\mathsf{A}, \mathsf{B}, \mathsf{f}, \mathsf{B}, \mathsf{B}, \mathsf{b}, \mathsf{c}) \qquad\qquad \mathcal{F}p(t) = (\mathsf{g}, \mathsf{a}, \mathsf{A}, \mathsf{N}, \mathsf{N}, \mathsf{B}, \mathsf{d})$$

The terms are not unifiable due to the incompatibility at position 1.1 (c versus d).

We can easily support prefix optimization for both terms s and t being compared: We ensure that s and t are fully applied, by adding enough fresh variables as arguments, before computing their fingerprints.

6   Inference Rules

Saturating provers try to show the unsatisfiability of a set of clauses by systematically adding logical consequences (up to simplification and redundancy), eventually deriving the empty clause as an explicit witness of unsatisfiability. They employ two kinds of inference rules: *generating rules* produce new clauses and are necessary for completeness, whereas *simplification rules* delete existing clauses or replace them by simpler clauses. This simplification is crucial for success, and most modern provers spend a large part of their time on simplification.

Ehoh implements essentially the same logical calculus as E, except that it is generalized to λfHOL terms. The standard inference rules and completeness proof of superposition can be reused verbatim; the only changes concern the basic definitions of terms and substitutions [7, Sect. 1].

The Generating Rules. The superposition calculus consists of the following four core generating rules, whose conclusions are added to the proof state:

$$\frac{s \not\approx s' \vee C}{\sigma(C)}\ \text{ER} \qquad\qquad \frac{s \approx t \vee s' \approx u \vee C}{\sigma(t \not\approx u \vee s \approx u \vee C)}\ \text{EF}$$

$$\frac{s \approx t \vee C \qquad u[s'] \not\approx v \vee D}{\sigma(u[t] \not\approx v \vee C \vee D)}\ \text{SN} \qquad \frac{s \approx t \vee C \qquad u[s'] \approx v \vee D}{\sigma(u[t] \approx v \vee C \vee D)}\ \text{SP}$$

In each rule, σ denotes the MGU of s and s'. Not shown are order- and selection-based side conditions that restrict the rules' applicability.

Equality resolution and factoring (ER and EF) work on entire terms that occur on either side of a literal occurring in the given clause. To generalize them, it suffices to disable prefix optimization for our unification algorithm. By contrast, the rules for superposition into negative and positive literals (SN and SP) are more complex. As two-premise rules, they require the prover to find a partner for the given clause. There are two cases to consider.

To cover the case where the given clause acts as the left premise, the prover relies on a fingerprint index to compute a set of clauses containing terms possibly unifiable with a side s of a positive literal of the given clause. Thanks to our generalization of fingerprints, in Ehoh this candidate set is guaranteed to overapproximate the set of all possible inference partners. The unification algorithm is then applied to filter out unsuitable candidates. Thanks to prefix optimization, we can avoid gracelessly polluting the index with all prefix subterms.

For the case where the given clause is the right premise, the prover traverses its subterms s' looking for inference partners in another fingerprint index, which contains only entire left- and right-hand sides of equalities. Like E, Ehoh traverses subterms in a first-order fashion. If prefix unification succeeds, Ehoh determines the unified prefix and applies the appropriate inference instance.

The Simplifying Rules. Unlike generating rules, simplifying rules do not necessarily add conclusions to the proof state—they can also remove premises. E implements over a dozen simplifying rules, with unconditional rewriting and clause subsumption as the most significant examples. Here, we restrict our attention to a single rule, which best illustrates the challenges of supporting λfHOL:

$$\frac{s \approx t \qquad u[\sigma(s)] \approx u[\sigma(t)] \vee C}{s \approx t}\ \text{ES}$$

Given an equation $s \approx t$, equality subsumption (ES) removes a clause containing a literal whose two sides are equal except that an instance of s appears on one side where the corresponding instance of t appears on the other side.

E maintains a perfect discrimination tree that stores clauses of the form $s \approx t$ indexed by s and t. When applying the ES rule, E considers each literal $u \approx v$ of the given clause in turn. It starts by taking the left-hand side u as a query term. If an equation $s \approx t$ (or $t \approx s$) is found in the tree, with $\sigma(s) = u$, the prover checks whether $\sigma'(t) = v$ for some extension σ' of σ. If so, ES is applicable. To consider nonempty contexts, the prover traverses the subterms u' and v' of u and v in lockstep, as long as they appear under identical contexts. Thanks to prefix optimization, when Ehoh is given a subterm u', it can find an equation $s \approx t$ in the tree such that $\sigma(s)$ is equal to some prefix of u', with n arguments $\overline{u_n}$ remaining as unmatched. Checking for equality subsumption then amounts to checking that $v' = \sigma'(t)\, \overline{u_n}$, for some extension σ' of σ.

For example, let $\mathsf{f}\,(\mathsf{g}\,\mathsf{a}\,\mathsf{b}) \approx \mathsf{f}\,(\mathsf{h}\,\mathsf{g}\,\mathsf{b})$ be the given clause, and suppose that $x\,\mathsf{a} \approx \mathsf{h}\,x$ is indexed. Under context $\mathsf{f}\,[\;]$, Ehoh considers the subterms $\mathsf{g}\,\mathsf{a}\,\mathsf{b}$ and $\mathsf{h}\,x\,\mathsf{b}$. It finds the prefix $\mathsf{g}\,\mathsf{a}$ of $\mathsf{g}\,\mathsf{a}\,\mathsf{b}$ in the tree, with $\sigma = \{x \mapsto \mathsf{g}\}$. The prefix $\mathsf{h}\,\mathsf{g}$ of $\mathsf{h}\,\mathsf{g}\,\mathsf{b}$ matches the indexed equation's right-hand side $\mathsf{h}\,x$ using the same substitution, and the remaining argument in both subterms, b, is identical.

7   Heuristics

E's heuristics are largely independent of the prover's logic and work unchanged for Ehoh. On first-order problems, Ehoh's behavior is virtually the same as E's. Yet, in preliminary experiments, we observed that some λfHOL benchmarks were proved quickly by E in conjunction with the applicative encoding (Sect. 1) but timed out with Ehoh. Based on these observations, we extended the heuristics.

Term Order Generation. The inference rules and the redundancy criterion are parameterized by a term order (Sect. 3). E can generate a *symbol weight* function (for KBO) and a *symbol precedence* (for KBO and LPO) based on criteria such as the symbols' frequencies and whether they appear in the conjecture.

In preliminary experiments, we discovered that the presence of an explicit application operator @ can be beneficial for some problems. With the applicative encoding, generation schemes can take the symbols $@_{\tau,\upsilon}$ into account, effectively exploiting the type information carried by such symbols. To simulate this behavior, we introduced four generation schemes that extend E's existing symbol-frequency-based schemes by partitioning the symbols by type. To each symbol, the new schemes assign a frequency corresponding to the sum of all symbol frequencies for its class. In addition, we designed four schemes that combine E's type-agnostic and Ehoh's type-aware approaches.

To generate symbol precedences, E can sort symbols by weight and use the symbol's position in the sorted array as the basis for precedence. To account for the type information introduced by the applicative encoding, we implemented four type-aware precedence generation schemes.

Literal Selection. The side conditions of the superposition rules (SN and SP, Sect. 6) allow the use of a literal selection function to restrict the set of *inference literals*, thereby pruning the search space. Given a clause, a literal selection function returns a (possibly empty) subset of its literals. For completeness, any nonempty subset selected must contain at least one negative literal. If no literal is selected, all *maximal* literals become inference literals. The most widely used function in E is probably `SelectMaxLComplexAvoidPosPred`, which we abbreviate to `SelectMLCAPP`. It selects at most one negative literal, based on size, groundness, and maximality of the literal in the clause. It also avoids negative literals that share a predicate symbol with a positive literal in the same clause.

Clause Selection. Selection of the given clause is a critical choice point. E heuristically assigns *clause priorities* and *clause weights* to the candidates. E's main loop visits, in round-robin fashion, a set of priority queues. From each queue, it selects a number of clauses with the highest priorities, breaking ties by preferring smaller weights.

E provides template weight functions that allow users to fine-tune parameters such as weights assigned to variables or function symbols. The most widely used template is `ConjectureRelativeSymbolWeight`. It computes term and clause weights according to eight parameters, notably *conj_mul*, a multiplier applied to the weight of conjecture symbols. We implemented a new type-aware template function, called `ConjectureRelativeSymbolTypeWeight`, that applies the *conj_mul* multiplier to all symbols whose type occurs in the conjecture.

Configurations and Modes. A combination of parameters—including term order, literal selection, and clause selection—is called a *configuration*. For years, E has provided an *auto* mode, which analyzes the input problem and chooses a configuration known to perform well on similar problems. More recently, E has been extended with an *autoschedule* mode, which applies a portfolio of configurations in sequence on the given problem. Configurations that perform well on a wide range of problems have emerged over time. One of them is the configuration that is most often chosen by E's *auto* mode. We call it *boa* ("best of *auto*").

8   Evaluation

In this section, we consider the following questions: How useful are Ehoh's new heuristics? And how does Ehoh perform compared with the previous version of E, 2.2, used directly or in conjunction with the applicative encoding, and compared with other provers? To answer the first question, we evaluated each new parameter independently. From the empirical results, we derived a new configuration optimized for λfHOL problems. To answer the second question, we compared Ehoh's success rate on λfHOL problems with native higher-order provers and with E's on their applicatively encoded counterparts. We also included first-order benchmarks to measure Ehoh's overhead with respect to E.

We set a CPU time limit of 60 s per problem. The experiments were performed on StarExec [28] nodes equipped with Intel Xeon E5-2609 0 CPUs clocked at 2.40 GHz and with 8192 MB of memory. Our raw data are publicly available.[2]

We used the *boa* configuration as the basis to evaluate the new heuristic schemes. For each heuristic parameter we tuned, we changed only its value while keeping the other parameters the same as for *boa*. All heuristic parameters were tested on a 5012 problem suite generated using Sledgehammer, consisting of four versions of the Judgment Day [11] suite. Our main findings are as follows:

- The combination of the weight generation scheme `invtypefreqrank` and the precedence generation scheme `invtypefreq` performs best.
- The literal selection heuristics `SelectMLCAPP`, `SelectMLCAPPPreferAppVar`, and `SelectMLCAPPAvoidAppVar` give virtually the same results.
- The clause selection function `ConjectureRelativeSymbolTypeWeight` with `ConstPrio` priority and an *appv_mul* factor of 1.41 performs best.

We derived a new configuration from *boa*, called *hoboa*, by enabling the features identified in the first and third points. Below, we present a more detailed evaluation of *hoboa*, along with other configurations, on a larger benchmark suite. The benchmarks are partitioned as follows: (1) 1147 first-order TPTP [29] problems belonging to the FOF (untyped) and TF0 (monomorphic) categories, excluding arithmetic; (2) 5012 Sledgehammer-generated problems from the Judgment Day [11] suite, targeting the monomorphic first-order logic embodied by TPTP TF0; (3) all 530 monomorphic higher-order problems from the TH0 category of the TPTP library belonging to the λfHOL fragment; (4) 5012 Judgment Day problems targeting the λfHOL fragment of TPTP TH0.

For the first group of benchmarks, we randomly chose 1000 FOF problems (out of 8172) and all monomorphic TFF problems that are parsable by E. Both groups of Sledgehammer problems include two subgroups of 2506 problems, generated to include 32 or 512 Isabelle lemmas (SH32 and SH512), to represent both smaller and larger problems arising in interactive verification. Each subgroup itself consists of two sub-subgroups of 1253 problems, generated by using either λ-lifting or SK-style combinators to encode λ-expressions.

We evaluated Ehoh against Leo-III and Satallax and a version of E, called @+E, that first performs the applicative encoding. Leo-III and Satallax have the advantage that they can instantiate higher-order variables by λ-terms. Thus, some formulas that are provable by these two systems may be nontheorems for @+E and Ehoh. A simple example is the conjecture $\exists f.\ \forall x\ y.\ f\ x\ y \approx g\ y\ x$, whose proof requires taking $\lambda x\ y.\ g\ y\ x$ as the witness for f.

We also evaluated E, @+E, Ehoh, and Leo-III on first-order benchmarks. The number of problems each system proved is given in Fig. 1. We considered the E modes *auto* (a) and *autoschedule* (as) and the configurations *boa* (b) and *hoboa* (hb).

---

[2] http://matryoshka.gforge.inria.fr/pubs/ehoh_results.tar.gz.

	First-order			Higher-order		
	TPTP	SH32	SH512	TPTP	SH32	SH512
E a	598	939	1234			
E as	**645**	950	**1311**			
E b	546	944	1243			
@+E a	526	943	1114	395	962	1119
@+E as	567	950	1151	397	965	1155
@+E b	538	942	1228	397	960	1272
Ehoh a	599	938	1233	396	962	1240
Ehoh as	644	949	1310	395	**973**	**1325**
Ehoh b	547	944	1243	396	966	1244
Ehoh hb	502	944	1231	393	968	1262
Leo-III	542	**951**	1126	**421**	963	1145
Satallax				406	768	790

Fig. 1. Number of proved problems

We observe the following:

- Comparing the Ehoh rows with the corresponding E rows, we see that Ehoh's overhead is barely noticeable—the difference is at most one problem. The raw evaluation data reveal that Ehoh's time overhead is about 3.7%.
- Ehoh generally outperforms the applicative encoding, on both first-order and higher-order problems. On Sledgehammer benchmarks, the best Ehoh mode (*autoschedule*) clearly outperforms all @+E modes and configurations. Despite this, there are problems that @+E proves faster than Ehoh.
- Especially on large benchmarks, the E variants are substantially more successful than Leo-III and Satallax. On the other hand, Leo-III emerges as the winner on the first-order SH32 benchmark set, presumably thanks to the combination of first-order backends (CVC4, E, and iProver) it depends on.
- The new *hoboa* configuration outperforms *boa* on higher-order problems, suggesting that it could be worthwhile to re-train *auto* and *autoschedule* based on λfHOL benchmarks and to design further heuristics.

9   Discussion and Related Work

Most higher-order provers were developed from the ground up. Two exceptions are Otter-λ by Beeson [6] and Zipperposition by Cruanes [14]. Otter-λ adds λ-terms and second-order unification to the superposition-based Otter. The approach is pragmatic, with little emphasis on completeness. Zipperposition is a superposition-based prover written in OCaml. It was initially designed for first-order logic but subsequently extended to higher-order logic. Its performance is a far cry from E's, but it is easier to modify. It is used by Bentkamp et al. [7] for experimenting with higher-order features. Finally, there is noteworthy preliminary work by the developers of Vampire [10] and of CVC4 and veriT [4].

Native higher-order reasoning was pioneered by Robinson [22], Andrews [1], and Huet [16]. TPS, by Andrews et al. [2], was based on expansion proofs and let users specify proof outlines. The Leo systems, developed by Benzmüller and his colleagues, are based on resolution and paramodulation. LEO [8] introduced the cooperative paradigm to integrate first-order provers. Leo-III [27] expands the cooperation with SMT (satisfiability modulo theories) solvers and introduces term orders. Brown's Satallax [12] is based on a higher-order tableau calculus, guided by a SAT solver; recent versions also cooperate with first-order provers.

An alternative to all of the above is to reduce higher-order logic to first-order logic by means of a translation. Robinson [23] outlined this approach decades before tools such as Sledgehammer [21] and HOLyHammer [17] popularized it in proof assistants. In addition to performing an applicative encoding, such translations must eliminate the λ-expressions and encode the type information.

By removing the need for the applicative encoding, our work reduces the translation gap. The encoding buries the λfHOL terms' heads under layers of @ symbols. Terms double in size, cluttering the data structures, and twice as many subterm positions must be considered for inferences. Moreover, encoding is incompatible with interpreted operators, notably for arithmetic. A further complication is that in a monomorphic logic, @ is not a single symbol but a type-indexed family of symbols $@_{\tau,\upsilon}$, which must be correctly introduced and recognized. Finally, the encoding must be undone in the generated proofs. While it should be possible to base a higher-order prover on such an encoding, the prospect is aesthetically and technically unappealing, and performance would likely suffer.

10   Conclusion

Despite considerable progress since the 1970s, higher-order automated reasoning has not yet assimilated some of the most successful methods for first-order logic with equality, such as superposition. We presented a graceful extension of a state-of-the-art first-order theorem prover to a fragment of higher-order logic devoid of λ-terms. Our work covers both theoretical and practical aspects. Experiments show promising results on λ-free higher-order problems and very little overhead for first-order problems, as we would expect from a graceful generalization.

The resulting Ehoh prover will form the basis of our work towards strong higher-order automation. Our aim is to turn it into a prover that excels on proof obligations emerging from interactive verification; in our experience, these tend to be large but only mildly higher-order. Our next steps will be to extend E's term data structure with λ-expressions and investigate techniques for computing higher-order unifiers efficiently.

Acknowledgment. We are grateful to the maintainers of StarExec for letting us use their service. We thank Ahmed Bhayat, Alexander Bentkamp, Daniel El Ouraoui, Michael Färber, Pascal Fontaine, Predrag Janičić, Robert Lewis, Tomer Libal, Giles Reger, Hans-Jörg Schurr, Alexander Steen, Mark Summerfield, Dmitriy Traytel, and the anonymous reviewers for suggesting many improvements to this text. We also want to thank the other members of the Matryoshka team, including Sophie Tourret and Uwe Waldmann, as well as Christoph Benzmüller, Andrei Voronkov, Daniel Wand, and Christoph Weidenbach, for many stimulating discussions.

Vukmirović and Blanchette's research has received funding from the European Research Council (ERC) under the European Union's Horizon 2020 research and innovation program (grant agreement No. 713999, Matryoshka). Blanchette has received funding from the Netherlands Organization for Scientific Research (NWO) under the Vidi program (project No. 016.Vidi.189.037, Lean Forward). He also benefited from the NWO Incidental Financial Support scheme.

References

1. Andrews, P.B.: Resolution in type theory. J. Symb. Log. **36**(3), 414–432 (1971)
2. Andrews, P.B., Bishop, M., Issar, S., Nesmith, D., Pfenning, F., Xi, H.: TPS: a theorem-proving system for classical type theory. J. Autom. Reason. **16**(3), 321–353 (1996)
3. Baader, F., Nipkow, T.: Term Rewriting and All That. Cambridge University Press, Cambridge (1998)
4. Barbosa, H., Reynolds, A., Fontaine, P., Ouraoui, D.E., Tinelli, C.: Higher-order SMT solving (work in progress). In: Dimitrova, R., D'Silva, V. (eds.) SMT 2018 (2018)
5. Becker, H., Blanchette, J.C., Waldmann, U., Wand, D.: A transfinite Knuth–Bendix order for lambda-free higher-order terms. In: de Moura, L. (ed.) CADE 2017. LNCS (LNAI), vol. 10395, pp. 432–453. Springer, Cham (2017). https://doi.org/10.1007/978-3-319-63046-5_27
6. Beeson, M.: Lambda logic. In: Basin, D., Rusinowitch, M. (eds.) IJCAR 2004. LNCS (LNAI), vol. 3097, pp. 460–474. Springer, Heidelberg (2004). https://doi.org/10.1007/978-3-540-25984-8_34
7. Bentkamp, A., Blanchette, J.C., Cruanes, S., Waldmann, U.: Superposition for lambda-free higher-order logic. In: Galmiche, D., Schulz, S., Sebastiani, R. (eds.) IJCAR 2018. LNCS (LNAI), vol. 10900, pp. 28–46. Springer, Cham (2018). https://doi.org/10.1007/978-3-319-94205-6_3
8. Benzmüller, C., Kohlhase, M.: System description: Leo—a higher-order theorem prover. In: Kirchner, C., Kirchner, H. (eds.) CADE 1998. LNCS (LNAI), vol. 1421, pp. 139–143. Springer, Heidelberg (1998). https://doi.org/10.1007/BFb0054256
9. Benzmüller, C., Sultana, N., Paulson, L.C., Theiss, F.: The higher-order prover LEO-II. J. Autom. Reason. **55**(4), 389–404 (2015)
10. Bhayat, A., Reger, G.: Set of support for higher-order reasoning. In: Konev, B., Urban, J., Rümmer, P. (eds.) PAAR-2018, CEUR Workshop Proceedings, vol. 2162, pp. 2–16. CEUR-WS.org (2018)
11. Böhme, S., Nipkow, T.: Sledgehammer: Judgement Day. In: Giesl, J., Hähnle, R. (eds.) IJCAR 2010. LNCS (LNAI), vol. 6173, pp. 107–121. Springer, Heidelberg (2010). https://doi.org/10.1007/978-3-642-14203-1_9
12. Brown, C.E.: Satallax: an automatic higher-order prover. In: Gramlich, B., Miller, D., Sattler, U. (eds.) IJCAR 2012. LNCS (LNAI), vol. 7364, pp. 111–117. Springer, Heidelberg (2012). https://doi.org/10.1007/978-3-642-31365-3_11
13. Cruanes, S.: Extending Superposition with Integer Arithmetic, Structural Induction, and Beyond. PhD thesis, École polytechnique (2015). https://who.rocq.inria.fr/Simon.Cruanes/files/thesis.pdf

14. Cruanes, S.: Superposition with structural induction. In: Dixon, C., Finger, M. (eds.) FroCoS 2017. LNCS (LNAI), vol. 10483, pp. 172–188. Springer, Cham (2017). https://doi.org/10.1007/978-3-319-66167-4_10

15. Filliâtre, J.-C., Paskevich, A.: Why3—where programs meet provers. In: Felleisen, M., Gardner, P. (eds.) ESOP 2013. LNCS, vol. 7792, pp. 125–128. Springer, Heidelberg (2013). https://doi.org/10.1007/978-3-642-37036-6_8

16. Huet, G.P.: A mechanization of type theory. In: Nilsson, N.J. (ed.) IJCAI-73, pp. 139–146. Morgan Kaufmann Publishers Inc., Burlington (1973)

17. Kaliszyk, C., Urban, J.: HOL(y)Hammer: online ATP service for HOL light. Math. Comput. Sci. **9**(1), 5–22 (2015)

18. Kovács, L., Voronkov, A.: First-order theorem proving and VAMPIRE. In: Sharygina, N., Veith, H. (eds.) CAV 2013. LNCS, vol. 8044, pp. 1–35. Springer, Heidelberg (2013). https://doi.org/10.1007/978-3-642-39799-8_1

19. Löchner, B.: Things to know when implementing KBO. J. Autom. Reason. **36**(4), 289–310 (2006)

20. McCune, W.: Experiments with discrimination-tree indexing and path indexing for term retrieval. J. Autom. Reason. **9**(2), 147–167 (1992)

21. Paulson, L.C., Blanchette, J.C.: Three years of experience with Sledgehammer, a practical link between automatic and interactive theorem provers. In: Sutcliffe, G., Schulz, S., Ternovska, E. (eds.) IWIL-2010. EPiC, vol. 2, pp. 1–11. EasyChair (2012)

22. Robinson, J.: Mechanizing higher order logic. In: Meltzer, B., Michie, D. (eds.) Machine Intelligence, vol. 4, pp. 151–170. Edinburgh University Press, Edinburgh (1969)

23. Robinson, J.: A note on mechanizing higher order logic. In: Meltzer, B., Michie, D. (eds.) Machine Intelligence, vol. 5, pp. 121–135. Edinburgh University Press, Edinburgh (1970)

24. Schulz, S.: Fingerprint indexing for paramodulation and rewriting. In: Gramlich, B., Miller, D., Sattler, U. (eds.) IJCAR 2012. LNCS (LNAI), vol. 7364, pp. 477–483. Springer, Heidelberg (2012). https://doi.org/10.1007/978-3-642-31365-3_37

25. Schulz, S.: Simple and efficient clause subsumption with feature vector indexing. In: Bonacina, M.P., Stickel, M.E. (eds.) Automated Reasoning and Mathematics. LNCS (LNAI), vol. 7788, pp. 45–67. Springer, Heidelberg (2013). https://doi.org/10.1007/978-3-642-36675-8_3

26. Schulz, S.: System description: E 1.8. In: McMillan, K., Middeldorp, A., Voronkov, A. (eds.) LPAR 2013. LNCS, vol. 8312, pp. 735–743. Springer, Heidelberg (2013). https://doi.org/10.1007/978-3-642-45221-5_49

27. Steen, A., Benzmüller, C.: The higher-order prover Leo-III. In: Galmiche, D., Schulz, S., Sebastiani, R. (eds.) IJCAR 2018. LNCS (LNAI), vol. 10900, pp. 108–116. Springer, Cham (2018). https://doi.org/10.1007/978-3-319-94205-6_8

28. Stump, A., Sutcliffe, G., Tinelli, C.: StarExec: a cross-community infrastructure for logic solving. In: Demri, S., Kapur, D., Weidenbach, C. (eds.) IJCAR 2014. LNCS (LNAI), vol. 8562, pp. 367–373. Springer, Cham (2014). https://doi.org/10.1007/978-3-319-08587-6_28

29. Sutcliffe, G.: The TPTP problem library and associated infrastructure. From CNF to TH0, TPTP v6.4.0. J. Autom. Reason. **59**(4), 483–502 (2017)

30. Sutcliffe, G.: The CADE-26 automated theorem proving system competition–CASC-26. AI Commun. **30**(6), 419–432 (2017)

31. Vukmirović, P.: Implementation of Lambda-Free Higher-Order Superposition. MSc thesis, Vrije Universiteit Amsterdam (2018). http://matryoshka.gforge.inria.fr/pubs/vukmirovic_msc_thesis.pdf

32. Vukmirović, P., Blanchette, J.C., Cruanes, S., Schulz, S.: Extending a brainiac prover to lambda-free higher-order logic (technical report). Technical report (2019). http://matryoshka.gforge.inria.fr/pubs/ehoh_report.pdf
33. Weidenbach, C., Dimova, D., Fietzke, A., Kumar, R., Suda, M., Wischnewski, P.: SPASS version 3.5. In: Schmidt, R.A. (ed.) CADE 2009. LNCS (LNAI), vol. 5663, pp. 140–145. Springer, Heidelberg (2009). https://doi.org/10.1007/978-3-642-02959-2_10

Verification and Analysis

LCV: A Verification Tool for Linear Controller Software

Junkil Park[1(✉)], Miroslav Pajic[2],
Oleg Sokolsky[1], and Insup Lee[1]

[1] Department of Computer and Information Science,
University of Pennsylvania, Philadelphia, PA, USA
{park11,sokolsky,lee}@cis.upenn.edu
[2] Department of Electrical and Computer Engineering,
Duke University, Durham, NC, USA
miroslav.pajic@duke.edu

Abstract. In the model-based development of controller software, the use of an unverified code generator/transformer may result in introducing unintended bugs in the controller implementation. To assure the correctness of the controller software in the absence of verified code generator/transformer, we develop Linear Controller Verifier (LCV), a tool to verify a linear controller implementation against its original linear controller model. LCV takes as input a Simulink block diagram model and a C code implementation, represents them as linear time-invariant system models respectively, and verifies an input-output equivalence between them. We demonstrate that LCV successfully detects a known bug of a widely used code generator and an unknown bug of a code transformer. We also demonstrate the scalability of LCV and a real-world case study with the controller of a quadrotor system.

1 Introduction

Most safety-critical embedded and cyber-physical systems have a software-based controller at their core. The safety of these systems rely on the correct operation of the controller. Thus, in order to have a high assurance for such systems, it is imperative to ensure that controller software is correctly implemented.

Nowadays, controller software is developed in a model-based fashion, using industry-standard tools such as Simulink [31] and Stateflow [36]. In this development process, first of all, the controller model is designed and analyzed. Controller design is performed using a mathematical model of the control system that captures both the dynamics of the "plant", the entity to be controlled, and the controller itself. With this model, analysis is performed to conclude whether the plant model adequately describes the system to be controlled, and whether the controller achieves the desired goals of the control system. Once the control engineer is satisfied with the design, a software implementation is automatically produced by code generation from the mathematical model of the controller. Code generation tools such as Embedded Coder [30] and Simulink Coder [32]

© The Author(s) 2019
T. Vojnar and L. Zhang (Eds.): TACAS 2019, Part I, LNCS 11427, pp. 213–225, 2019.
https://doi.org/10.1007/978-3-030-17462-0_12

are widely used. The generated controller implementation is either used as it is in the control system, or sometimes transformed into another code before used for various reasons such as numerical accuracy improvement [8,9] and code protection [2,4,5]. For simplicity's sake herein, we will call code generation even when code generation is potentially followed by code transformation.

To assure the correctness of the controller implementation, it is necessary to check that code generation is done correctly. Ideally, we would like to have verified tools for code generation. In this case, no verification of the controller implementation would be needed because the tools would guarantee that any produced controller correctly implements its model. In practice, however, commercial code generators are complex black-box software that are generally not amenable to formal verification. Subtle bugs have been found in commercially available code generators that consequently generate incorrect code [29]. Unverified code transformers may introduce unintended bugs in the output code.

In the absence of verified code generators, it is desirable to verify instances of implementations against their original models. Therefore, this work considers the problem of such instance verification for a given controller model and software implementation. To properly address this verification problem, the following challenges should be considered: First of all, such verification should be performed from the input-output perspective (i.e., input-output conformance). Correct implementations may have different state representations to each other for several possible reasons (e.g., code generator's choice of state representation, optimization used in the code generation process). In other words, the original controller model and a correct implementation of the model may be different from each other in state representation, while being functionally equivalent from the input-output perspective. Thus, it is necessary to develop the verification technique that is not sensitive to the state representation of the controller. Moreover, there is an inherent discrepancy between controller models and their implementations. The controller software for embedded systems uses a finite precision arithmetic (e.g., floating-point arithmetic) which introduces rounding errors in the computation. In addition to these rounding errors, the implementations may be inexact in the numeric representation of controller parameters due to the potential rounding errors in the code generation/optimization process. Thus, it is reasonable to allow a tolerance in the conformance verification as long as the implementation has the same desired property to the model's. Finally, such verification is desired to be automatic and scalable because verification needs to be followed by each instance of code generation.

We, therefore, present LCV (shown in Fig. 1), a tool that automatically verifies controller implementations against their models from the input-output perspective with given tolerance thresholds.[1] The verification technique behind this tool is based on the work of [24]. LCV uses the state-space representation form of the linear time-invariant (LTI) system to represent both the Simulink block

---

[1] We assume that a threshold value ϵ is given by a control engineer as a result of the robustness analysis that guarantees the desired properties of the control system in the presence of uncertain disturbances.

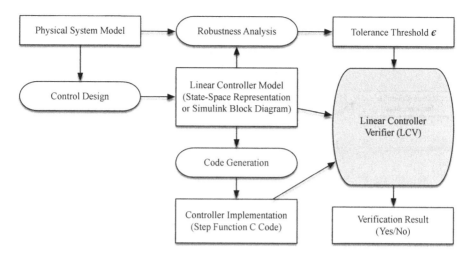

Fig. 1. LCV in the model-based development process.

diagram (i.e., controller model) and the C code (i.e., controller implementation). LCV checks the input-output equivalence relation between the two LTI models by similarity checking. The contribution of this work compared to the previous work [24] is as follows: As controller specifications are often given in the form of block diagrams, LCV extends the preliminary prototype [24] to take not only the state-space representation of an LTI system but also the Simulink block diagram as an input specification model. As a result, a real-world case study, where the controller specification of a quadrotor called Erle-Copter [11] is given as a Simulink block diagram, was conducted using LCV and demonstrated in this paper. In the case study with a proportional-integral-derivative (PID) controller, we demonstrate that LCV successfully detects a known (reproduced) bug of Embedded Coder as well as an unknown bug of Salsa [8], a code transformation method/tool for numerical accuracy.[2] Moreover, LCV has been enhanced in many ways such as improving in scalability, supporting fully automatic verification procedures, providing informative output messages and handling customized user inputs.

2   Related Work

To ensure the correctness of the controller implementation against the controller model, a typically used method in practice is equivalence testing (or back-to-back testing) [6,7,28] which compares the outputs of the executable model and code for the common input sequence. The limitation of this testing-based method is that it does not provide a thorough verification. Static analysis-based approaches [3,12,14] have been used to analyze the controller code,

---

[2] This bug has been confirmed by the author of the tool.

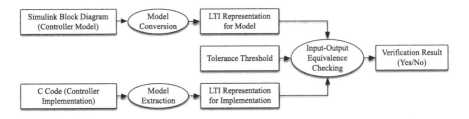

Fig. 2. The verification flow of LCV.

but focuses on checking common properties such as numerical stability, the absence of buffer overflow or arithmetic exceptions rather than verifying the code against the model. The work of [17,27] proposes translation validation techniques for Simulink diagrams and the generated codes. The verification relies on the structure of the block diagram and the code, thus being sensitive to the controller state while our method verifies code against the model from the input-output perspective, not being sensitive to the controller state. Due to optimization and transformation during a code generation process, a generated code which is correct, may have a different state representation than the model's. In this case, our method can verify that the code is correct w.r.t. the model, but the state-sensitive methods [17,27] cannot. [13,16,37,38] present a control software verification approach based on the concept of proof-carrying code. In their approach, the code annotation based on the Lyapunov function and its proof are produced at the time of code generation. The annotation asserts control theory related properties such as stability and convergence, but not equivalence between the controller specifications and the implementations. In addition, their approach requires the internal knowledge and control of the code generator to use, and may not be applicable to the off-the-shelf black-box code generators. The work of [19,24,25] presents methods to verify controller implementations against LTI models, but does not relate the block diagram models with the implementation code.

3   Verification Flow of Linear Controller Verifier

The goal of LCV is to verify linear controller software. Controllers are generally specified as a function that, given the current state of the controller and a set of input sensor values, computes control output that is sent to the system actuators and the new state of the controller. In this work, we focus on linear-time invariant (LTI) controllers [26], since these are the most commonly used controllers in control systems. In software, controllers are implemented as a subroutine (or a function in the C language). This function is known as the *step function* (see [23] for an example). The step function is invoked by the control system periodically, or upon arrival of new sensor data (i.e., measurements).

This section describes the verification flow (shown in Fig. 2) and the implementation details of LCV. LCV takes as input a Simulink block diagram (i.e., controller model), a C code (i.e., controller implementation) and a tolerance threshold as a real number. In addition, LCV requires the following information to be given as input: the name of the step function and the interface of the step function. LCV assumes that the step function interfaces through the given input and output global variables. In other words, the input and output variables are declared in the global scope, and the input variables are written (or set) before the execution (or entrance) of the step function. Likewise, the output variables are read (or used) after the execution (or exit) of the step function.[3] Thus, the step function interface comprises the list of input (and output) variables of the step function in the same order of the corresponding input (and output) ports of the block diagram model. Since LCV verifies controllers from the input-output perspective, LCV does not require any state related information (i.e., the dimension of the controller state, or the list of state variables of the step function). Instead, LCV automatically obtains such information about the controller state from the analysis of the input C code and the input Simulink block diagram.

A restriction on this work is that LCV only focuses on verifying linear controller software. Thus, the scope of inputs of LCV is limited as follows: the input C program is limited to be a step function that only has a deterministic and finite execution path for a symbolic input, which is often found to be true for many embedded linear controllers. Moreover, the input Simulink block diagram is limited to be essentially an LTI system model (i.e., satisfying the superposition property). The block diagram that LCV can handle may include basic blocks (e.g., constant block, gain block, sum block), subsystem blocks (i.e., hierarchy) and series/parallel/feedback connections of those blocks. Extending LCV to verify a broader class of controllers is an avenue for future work.

The key idea in the verification flow (shown in Fig. 2) is that LCV represents both the Simulink block diagram and the C code in the same form of mathematical representation (i.e., the state space representation of an LTI system), and compares the two LTI models from the input-output perspective. Thus, the first step of the verification is to transform the Simulink block diagram into a state space representation of an LTI system, which is defined as follows:

$$\mathbf{z}_{k+1} = \mathbf{A}\mathbf{z}_k + \mathbf{B}\mathbf{u}_k$$
$$\mathbf{y}_k = \mathbf{C}\mathbf{z}_k + \mathbf{D}\mathbf{u}_k. \tag{1}$$

where $\mathbf{u}_k$, $\mathbf{y}_k$ and $\mathbf{z}_k$ are the input vector, the output vector and the state vector at time k respectively. The matrices $\mathbf{A}$, $\mathbf{B}$, $\mathbf{C}$ and $\mathbf{D}$ are controller parameters. We convert the Simulink block diagram into the LTI model employing the 'exact linearization' (or block-by-block linearization) feature of Simulink Control Design [33] which is implemented in the built-in Matlab function `linearize`. In this step, each individual block is linearized first and then combined together with others to produce the overall block diagram's LTI model.

---

[3] This convention is used by Embedded Coder, a code generation toolbox for Matlab/Simulink.

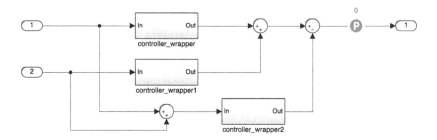

Fig. 3. The simulink block diagram for checking the additivity of the controller

This step assumes that the block diagram represents a linear controller model. A systematic procedure[4] can remove this assumption: one can check whether a given Simulink block diagram is linear (i.e., both additive and homogeneous) using Simulink Design Verifier [34], a model checker for Simulink. For example, to check if a controller block in Simulink is additive or not, as shown in Fig. 3, one can create two additional duplicates of the controller block, generate two different input sequences, and exhaustively check if the output of the controller in response to the sum of two inputs is equal to the sum of two outputs of the controllers in response the two inputs respectively. In Fig. 3, `controller_wrapper` wraps the actual controller under test, and internally performs multiplexing and demultiplexing to handle the multiple inputs and outputs of the controller. Simulink Design Verifier serves checking if this holds for all possible input sequences. However, a limitation of the current version of Simulink Design Verifier is that it does not support all Simulink blocks and does not properly handle non-linear cases. In these cases, alternatively, one can validate the linearity of controllers using simulation-based testing instead of model checking, which can be systematically done by Simulink Test [35]. This method is not limited by any types of Simulink blocks, and can effectively disprove the linearity of controllers for non-linear cases. However, this alternative method using Simulink Test may not be as rigorous as the model-checking based method using Simulink Design Verifier because not all possible input cases are considered.

The next step in the LCV's verification flow is to extract the LTI model from the controller implementation C code. The idea behind this step is to exploit the fact that linear controller codes (i.e., step function) used for embedded systems generally have simple control flows for the sake of deterministic real-time behaviors (e.g., fixed upper bound of loops). Thus, the semantics of such linear controller codes can be represented as a set of mathematical functions that are loop-free, which can be further transformed into the form of an LTI model. To do this specifically, LCV uses the symbolic execution technique which is capable of

---

[4] This procedure is currently not implemented in LCV because the required tools such as Simulink Design Verifier and Simulink Test mostly provide their features through GUIs rather than APIs. Thus, this procedure will be implemented in the future work once such APIs are available. Until then, this procedure can be performed manually.

identifying the computation of the step function (i.e., C function which implements the controller). By the computation, we mean the big-step transition relation on global states between before and after the execution of the step function. The big-step transition relation is represented as symbolic formulas that describe how the global variables change as the effect of the step function execution. The symbolic formulas associate each global variable representing the controller's state and output with the symbolic expression to be newly assigned to the global variable, where the symbolic expression consists of the old values of the global variables representing the controller's state and input. Then, LCV transforms the set of equations (i.e., symbolic formulas) that represent the transition relation into a form of matrix equation, from which an LTI model for the controller implementation is extracted [24]. LCV employs the off-the-shelf symbolic execution tool PathCrawler [39], which outputs the symbolic execution paths and the path conditions of a given C program in an extensible markup language (XML) file format.

Finally, LCV performs the input-output equivalence checking between the LTI model obtained from the block diagram and the LTI model extracted from the C code implementation. To do this, we employ the notion of similarity transformation [26], which implies that two minimal LTI models $\Sigma(\mathbf{A}, \mathbf{B}, \mathbf{C}, \mathbf{D})$ and $\hat{\Sigma}(\hat{\mathbf{A}}, \hat{\mathbf{B}}, \hat{\mathbf{C}}, \hat{\mathbf{D}})$ are input-output equivalent if and only if they are *similar* to each other, meaning that there exists a non-singular matrix $\mathbf{T}$ such that

$$\hat{\mathbf{A}} = \mathbf{TAT}^{-1}, \qquad \hat{\mathbf{B}} = \mathbf{TB}, \qquad \hat{\mathbf{C}} = \mathbf{CT}^{-1}, \qquad \text{and} \qquad \hat{\mathbf{D}} = \mathbf{D} \qquad (2)$$

where $\mathbf{T}$ is referred to as the *similarity transformation matrix* [26].

Given the extracted LTI model (from the C Code) and the original LTI model (obtained from the Simulink block diagram), we first minimize both LTI models via Kalman Decomposition [26] (Matlab function `minreal`). Then, the input-output equivalence checking problem is reduced to the problem of finding the existence of $\mathbf{T}$ (i.e., similarity checking problem). LCV formulates the similarity checking problem as a convex optimization problem[5], and employs CVX [15], a convex optimization solver to find $\mathbf{T}$. In the formulation, the equality relation is relaxed up to a given tolerance threshold ϵ in order to tolerate the numerical errors that come from multiple sources (e.g., the controller parameters, the computation of the implementation, the verification process). We assume that the tolerance threshold ϵ is given by a control engineer as the result of robustness analysis so that the verified controller implementation preserves the certain desired properties of the original controller model (e.g., stability). ϵ is chosen to be 10^{-5} for the case study that we performed in the next section.

The output of LCV is as follows: First of all, when LCV fails to extract an LTI model from code, it tells the reason (e.g., non-deterministic execution paths for a symbolic input due to branching over a symbolic expression condition, non-linear arithmetic computation due to the use of trigonometric functions). Moreover, for the case of non-equivalent model and code, LCV provides the LTI models obtained from the Simulink block diagram model and the C code respectively, so that the user can simulate both of the models and easily find

---

[5] Please refer [24] for the details of the formulation.

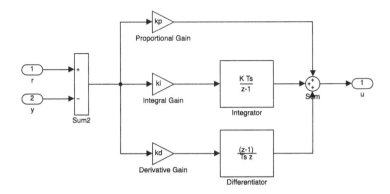

Fig. 4. The block diagram of the PID controller.

an input sequence that leads to a discrepancy between their output behaviors.[6] Finally, for the case of equivalent model and code, LCV additionally provides a similarity transformation matrix $\mathbf{T}$ between the two LTI models, which is the key evidence to prove the input-output equivalence between the model and code.

4   Evaluation

We evaluate LCV through conducting a case study using a standard PID controller and a controller used in a quadrotor. We also evaluate the scalability of LCV in the subsequent subsection.

4.1   Case Study

PID Controller. In our case study, we first consider a proportional-integral-derivative (PID) controller, which is a closed-loop feedback controller commonly used in various control systems (e.g., industrial control systems, robotics, automotive). A PID controller attempts to minimize the error value e_t over time which is defined as the difference between a reference point r_t (i.e., desired value) and a measurement value y_t (i.e., $e_t = r_t - y_t$). To do this, the PID controller adjusts a control input u_t computing the sum of the proportion term $k_p e_t$, integral term $k_i T \sum_{i=1}^{t} e_t$ and derivative term $k_d \frac{e_t - e_{t-1}}{T}$ so that

$$u_t = k_p e_t + k_i T \sum_{i=1}^{t} e_t + k_d \frac{e_t - e_{t-1}}{T}. \tag{3}$$

where k_p, k_i and k_d are gain constants for the corresponding term, and T is the sampling time. Figure 4 shows the Simulink block diagram for the PID controller, where the gain constants are defined as $k_p = 9.4514, k_i = 0.69006, k_d = 2.8454$, and the sampling period is 0.2 s.

---

[6] This feature to generate counterexamples will be implemented in a future version of LCV.

Table 1. Summary of the case study with the PID controller (Fig. 4) and its different versions of implementation

Impl.	Description	Buggy?	LCV output
PID1	Generated by Embedded Coder	No	Equivalent
PID2	Optimized from PID1 by Salsa (Level 1)	No	Equivalent
PID3	Optimized from PID1 by Salsa (Level 2)	Yes (due to a bug in Salsa)	Not equivalent
PID3'	Corrected from PID3 manually	No	Equivalent
PID4	Generated by Embedded Coder with a buggy option triggered	Yes (due to a bug in Embedded Coder)	Not equivalent

For the PID controller model, we check various different versions of implementations such as PID1, PID2, PID3, PID3' and PID4 (summarized in Table 1). PID1 is obtained by code generation from the model using Embedded Coder. PID2 is obtained from PID1 by the transformation (or optimization) of Salsa [8] to improve the numerical accuracy (using the first transformation technique (referred to as Level 1) presented in [8]). In a similar way, PID3 is obtained by the transformation from PID1 for an even better numerical accuracy (following the second transformation technique (referred to as Level 2) as Listing 3 in [8]). However, this transformation for PID3 contains an unintended bug by mistake that has been confirmed by the authors of the paper (i.e., variable s is not computed correctly, and the integral term is redundantly added to the output), which makes PID3 incorrect. PID3' is an implementation that manually corrects PID3. Using LCV, we can verify that PID1, PID2 and PID3' are correct implementations, but PID3 is not (see the verification result for PID3 [21]).

Moreover, PID4 is obtained by injecting a known bug of Embedded Coder into the implementation PID1. The bug with the ID 1658667 [29] that exists in the Embedded Coder version from 2015a through 2017b (7 consecutive versions) causes the generated code to have state variable declarations in a wrong scope. The state variables which are affected by the bug are mistakenly declared as local variables inside the step function instead of being declared as global variables. Thus, those state variables affected by the bug are unable to preserve their values throughout the consecutive step function executions. LCV can successfully detect the injected bug by identifying that the extracted model from the controller code does not match the original controller model (see the verification result for PID4 [22]).

Quadrotor Controller. The second and more complex application in our case study is a controller of the quadrotor called Erle-Copter. The quadrotor controller controls the quadrotor to be in certain desired angles in roll, yaw and pitch. The quadrotor uses the controller software from the open source project Ardupilot [1]. Inspired by the controller software, we obtained the Simulink block diagram shown in Fig. 5. In the names of the Inport blocks, the suffix _d indicates the desired angle, _d, the measured angle, and _rate_y, the angular speed. Each component of the coordinate of the quadrotor is separately controlled by its own

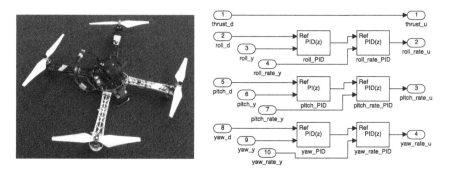

Fig. 5. Our quadrotor platform (Left). The quadrotor controller block diagram (Right).

cascade PID controller [18]. A cascade of PID controller is a sequential connection of two PID controllers such that one PID controller controls the reference point of another. In Fig. 5, there are three cascade controllers for the controls of roll, pitch and yaw. For example, for the roll control, `roll_pid` controls the angle of roll, while `roll_rate_PID` controls the rate of roll using the output of `roll_PID` as the reference point. The sampling time T of each PID controller is 2.5 ms. This model uses the built-in PID controller block of Simulink to enable the PID auto-tuning software in Matlab (i.e., `pidtune()`). The required physical quantities for controlling roll and pitch are identified by physical experiments [10]. We use Embedded Coder to generate the controller code for the model, and verify that the generated controller code correctly implements the controller model using LCV (see the verification result for the quadrotor controller [20]).

4.2 Scalability

To evaluate the scalability of LCV, we measure the running time of LCV verifying the controllers of different dimensions (i.e., the size of the LTI model). We randomly generate LTI controller models using Matlab function `drss` varying the controller dimension n from 2 to 50. The range of controller sizes was chosen based on our observation of controller systems in practice. We construct Simulink models with LTI system blocks that contain the generated LTI models, and use Embedded Coder to generate the implementations for the controllers. The running time of LCV for verifying the controllers with different dimensions is presented in Fig. 6, which shows that LCV is scalable for the realistic size of controller dimension. Compared to the previous version (or the preliminary prototype) of LCV [24], the new version of LCV has been much improved in scalability by tighter integration with the symbolic execution engine PathCrawler (i.e., in the model extraction phase, the invocation of constraint solver along with symbolic execution has been significantly reduced).

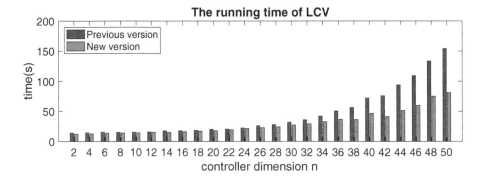

Fig. 6. The running time of LCV for verifying controllers with dimension n.

5 Conclusion

We have presented our tool LCV which verifies the equivalence between a given Simulink block diagram and a given C implementation from the input-output perspective. Through an evaluation, we have demonstrated that LCV is applicable to the verification of a real-world system's controller and scalable for the realistic controller size. Our current/future development work includes: relating the equivalence precision and the controller's performance, and handling nonlinear controllers.

Acknowledgments. This work is sponsored in part by the ONR under agreement N00014-17-1-2504, as well as the NSF CNS-1652544 grant. This research was supported in part by ONR N000141712012, Global Research Laboratory Program (2013K1A1A2A02078326) through NRF, and the DGIST Research and Development Program (CPS Global Center) funded by the Ministry of Science, ICT & Future Planning, and NSF CNS-1505799 and the Intel-NSF Partnership for Cyber-Physical Systems Security and Privacy.

References

1. Ardupilot Dev Team: Ardupilot, September 2018. http://ardupilot.org/
2. Behera, C.K., Bhaskari, D.L.: Different obfuscation techniques for code protection. Procedia Comput. Sci. **70**, 757–763 (2015)
3. Blanchet, B., et al.: A static analyzer for large safety-critical software. In: ACM SIGPLAN Notices, vol. 38, pp. 196–207. ACM (2003)
4. Cappaert, J.: Code obfuscation techniques for software protection, pp. 1–112. Katholieke Universiteit Leuven (2012)
5. Collberg, C., Thomborson, C., Low, D.: A taxonomy of obfuscating transformations. Technical report, Department of Computer Science, The University of Auckland, New Zealand (1997)
6. Conrad, M.: Testing-based translation validation of generated code in the context of IEC 61508. Form Methods Syst. Des. **35**(3), 389–401 (2009)

7. Conrad, M.: Verification and validation according to ISO 26262: a workflow to facilitate the development of high-integrity software. Embedded Real Time Software and Systems (ERTS2 2012) (2012)

8. Damouche, N., Martel, M., Chapoutot, A.: Transformation of a PID controller for numerical accuracy. Electron. Notes Theor. Comput. Sci. **317**, 47–54 (2015)

9. Damouche, N., Martel, M., Chapoutot, A.: Improving the numerical accuracy of programs by automatic transformation. Int. J. Softw. Tools Technol. Transfer **19**(4), 427–448 (2017). https://doi.org/10.1007/s10009-016-0435-0

10. Derafa, L., Madani, T., Benallegue, A.: Dynamic modelling and experimental identification of four rotors helicopter parameters. In: 2006 IEEE International Conference on Industrial Technology (2006)

11. Erle Robotics: Erle-copter, September 2018. http://erlerobotics.com/blog/erle-copter/

12. Feret, J.: Static analysis of digital filters. In: Schmidt, D. (ed.) ESOP 2004. LNCS, vol. 2986, pp. 33–48. Springer, Heidelberg (2004). https://doi.org/10.1007/978-3-540-24725-8_4

13. Feron, E.: From control systems to control software. IEEE Control Syst. **30**(6), 50–71 (2010)

14. Goubault, E., Putot, S.: Static analysis of finite precision computations. In: Jhala, R., Schmidt, D. (eds.) VMCAI 2011. LNCS, vol. 6538, pp. 232–247. Springer, Heidelberg (2011). https://doi.org/10.1007/978-3-642-18275-4_17

15. Grant, M., Boyd, S.: CVX: Matlab software for disciplined convex programming, version 2.1, March 2014. http://cvxr.com/cvx

16. Herencia-Zapana, H., et al.: PVS linear algebra libraries for verification of control software algorithms in C/ACSL. In: Goodloe, A.E., Person, S. (eds.) NFM 2012. LNCS, vol. 7226, pp. 147–161. Springer, Heidelberg (2012). https://doi.org/10.1007/978-3-642-28891-3_15

17. Majumdar, R., Saha, I., Ueda, K., Yazarel, H.: Compositional equivalence checking for models and code of control systems. In: 52nd Annual IEEE Conference on Decision and Control (CDC), pp. 1564–1571 (2013)

18. Michael, N., Mellinger, D., Lindsey, Q., Kumar, V.: The GRASP multiple micro-UAV test bed. IEEE Robot. Autom. Mag. **17**(3), 56–65 (2010)

19. Pajic, M., Park, J., Lee, I., Pappas, G.J., Sokolsky, O.: Automatic verification of linear controller software. In: 12th International Conference on Embedded Software (EMSOFT), pp. 217–226. IEEE Press (2015)

20. Park, J.: Erle-copter verification result. https://doi.org/10.5281/zenodo.2565035

21. Park, J.: Pid3 verification result. https://doi.org/10.5281/zenodo.2565023

22. Park, J.: Pid4 verification result. https://doi.org/10.5281/zenodo.2565030

23. Park, J.: Step function example. https://doi.org/10.5281/zenodo.44338

24. Park, J., Pajic, M., Lee, I., Sokolsky, O.: Scalable verification of linear controller software. In: Chechik, M., Raskin, J.-F. (eds.) TACAS 2016. LNCS, vol. 9636, pp. 662–679. Springer, Heidelberg (2016). https://doi.org/10.1007/978-3-662-49674-9_43

25. Park, J., Pajic, M., Sokolsky, O., Lee, I.: Automatic verification of finite precision implementations of linear controllers. In: Legay, A., Margaria, T. (eds.) TACAS 2017. LNCS, vol. 10205, pp. 153–169. Springer, Heidelberg (2017). https://doi.org/10.1007/978-3-662-54577-5_9

26. Rugh, W.J.: Linear System Theory. Prentice Hall, London (1996)

27. Ryabtsev, M., Strichman, O.: Translation validation: from simulink to C. In: Bouajjani, A., Maler, O. (eds.) CAV 2009. LNCS, vol. 5643, pp. 696–701. Springer, Heidelberg (2009). https://doi.org/10.1007/978-3-642-02658-4_57

28. Stuermer, I., Conrad, M., Doerr, H., Pepper, P.: Systematic testing of model-based code generators. IEEE Trans. Software Eng. **33**(9), 622–634 (2007)
29. The Mathworks, Inc.: Bug reports for incorrect code generation. http://www.mathworks.com/support/bugreports/?product=ALL&release=R2015b&keyword=Incorrect+Code+Generation
30. The Mathworks, Inc.: Embedded coder, September 2017. https://www.mathworks.com/products/embedded-coder.html
31. The Mathworks, Inc.: Simulink, September 2018. https://www.mathworks.com/products/simulink.html
32. The Mathworks, Inc.: Simulink coder, September 2018. https://www.mathworks.com/products/simulink-coder.html
33. The Mathworks, Inc.: Simulink control design, September 2018. https://www.mathworks.com/products/simcontrol.html
34. The Mathworks, Inc.: Simulink design verifier, September 2018. https://www.mathworks.com/products/sldesignverifier.html
35. The Mathworks, Inc.: Simulink test, September 2018. https://www.mathworks.com/products/simulink-test.html
36. The Mathworks, Inc.: Stateflow, September 2018. https://www.mathworks.com/products/stateflow.html
37. Wang, T., et al.: From design to implementation: an automated, credible autocoding chain for control systems. arXiv preprint arXiv:1307.2641 (2013)
38. Wang, T.E., Ashari, A.E., Jobredeaux, R.J., Feron, E.M.: Credible autocoding of fault detection observers. In: American Control Conference (ACC), pp. 672–677 (2014)
39. Williams, N., Marre, B., Mouy, P., Roger, M.: PathCrawler: automatic generation of path tests by combining static and dynamic analysis. In: Dal Cin, M., Kaâniche, M., Pataricza, A. (eds.) EDCC 2005. LNCS, vol. 3463, pp. 281–292. Springer, Heidelberg (2005). https://doi.org/10.1007/11408901_21

Semantic Fault Localization
and Suspiciousness Ranking

Maria Christakis[1](✉), Matthias Heizmann[2](✉), Muhammad Numair Mansur[1](✉), Christian Schilling[3](✉) (iD), and Valentin Wüstholz[4](✉)

[1] MPI-SWS, Kaiserslautern, Saarbrücken, Germany
{maria,numair}@mpi-sws.org
[2] University of Freiburg, Freiburg im Breisgau, Germany
heizmann@informatik.uni-freiburg.de
[3] IST Austria, Klosterneuburg, Austria
christian.schilling@ist.ac.at
[4] ConsenSys Diligence, Berlin, Germany
valentin.wustholz@consensys.net

Abstract. Static program analyzers are increasingly effective in checking correctness properties of programs and reporting any errors found, often in the form of error traces. However, developers still spend a significant amount of time on debugging. This involves processing long error traces in an effort to localize a bug to a relatively small part of the program and to identify its cause. In this paper, we present a technique for automated fault localization that, given a program and an error trace, efficiently narrows down the cause of the error to a few statements. These statements are then ranked in terms of their suspiciousness. Our technique relies only on the semantics of the given program and does not require any test cases or user guidance. In experiments on a set of C benchmarks, we show that our technique is effective in quickly isolating the cause of error while out-performing other state-of-the-art fault-localization techniques.

1 Introduction

In recent years, program analyzers are increasingly applied to detect errors in real-world software. When detecting an error, static (or dynamic) analyzers often present the user with an error trace (or a failing test case), which shows how an assertion can be violated. Specifically, an error trace refers to a sequence of statements through the program that leads to the error. The user then needs to process the error trace, which is often long for large programs, in order to localize the problem to a manageable number of statements and identify its actual cause. Therefore, despite the effectiveness of static program analyzers in detecting errors and generating error traces, users still spend a significant amount of time on debugging.

Our Approach. To alleviate this situation, we present a technique for automated fault localization, which significantly reduces the number of statements

© The Author(s) 2019
T. Vojnar and L. Zhang (Eds.): TACAS 2019, Part I, LNCS 11427, pp. 226–243, 2019.
https://doi.org/10.1007/978-3-030-17462-0_13

that might be responsible for a particular error. Our technique takes as input a program and an error trace, generated by a static analyzer, and determines which statements along the error trace are potential causes of the error. We identify the potential causes of an error by checking, for each statement along the error trace, whether there exists a local fix such that the trace verifies. We call this technique *semantic fault localization* because it exclusively relies on the semantics of the given program, without for instance requiring any test cases or guidance from the user.

Although there is existing work that also relies on program semantics for fault localization, our technique is the first to semantically rank the possible error causes in terms of suspiciousness. On a high level, we compute a *suspiciousness score* for a statement by taking into account how much code would become unreachable if we were to apply a local fix to the statement. Specifically, suspiciousness is inversely proportional to the amount of unreachable code. The key insight is that developers do not intend to write unreachable code, and thus the cause of the error is more likely to be a statement that, when fixed, renders fewer parts of the program unreachable.

Our experimental evaluation compares our technique to six fault-localization approaches from the literature on the widely-used TCAS benchmarks (of the Siemens test suite [19]). We show that in 30 out of 40 benchmarks, our technique narrows down the cause of the error more than any of the other approaches and is able to pin-point the faulty statement in 14 benchmarks. In addition, we evaluate our technique on several seeded bugs in SV-COMP benchmarks [5].

Contributions. We make the following contributions:

- We present an automated fault-localization technique that is able to quickly narrow down the error cause to a small number of suspicious statements.
- We describe an effective ranking mechanism for the suspicious statements.
- We implement this technique in a tool architecture for localizing and ranking suspicious statements along error traces reported by the Ultimate Automizer [16] software model checker.
- We evaluate the effectiveness of our technique on 51 benchmarks.

2 Guided Tour

This section uses a motivating example to give an overview of our technique for semantic fault localization and suspiciousness ranking.

Example. Let us consider the simple program on the left of Fig. 1. The statement on line 2 denotes that y is assigned a non-deterministic value, denoted by ⋆. The conditional on line 3 has a non-deterministic predicate, but in combination with the `assume` statements (lines 4 and 7), it is equivalent to a conditional of the following form:

```
if (y < 3) { x := 0; } else { x := 1; }
```

```
1 x := 2;
2 y := *;
3 if (*) {
4     assume y < 3;
5     x := 0;
6 } else {
7     assume 3 ≤ y;
8     x := 1;
9 }
10 assert 0 < x;
```

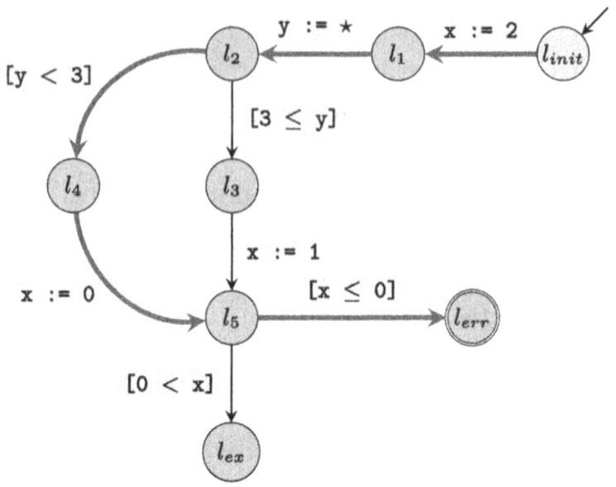

Fig. 1. The running example (left) and its control-flow graph (right).

The assertion on line 10 fails when program execution takes the **then** branch of the **if** statement, and thus, it cannot be verified by a (sound) static analyzer. The error trace that is generated by a static analyzer for this program is

$$x := 2;\ y := *;\ assume\ y < 3;\ x := 0;\ assume\ x \leq 0;\ assert\ false$$

and we mark it in bold on the control-flow graph of the program, which is shown on the right of Fig. 1. Statement assume $x \leq 0$ indicates that the error trace takes the failing branch of the assertion on line 10 of the program. The **assert false** statement denotes that this trace through the program results in an error.

Fault Localization. From such an error trace, our technique is able to determine a set of suspicious assignment statements, which we call *trace-aberrant statements*. Intuitively, these are statements along the error trace for which there exists a *local fix* that makes the trace verify. An assignment statement has a local fix if there exists an expression that may replace the right-hand side of the assignment such that the error becomes unreachable along this error trace. (In Sect. 5, we explain how our technique is able to identify other suspicious statements, apart from assignments.)

For example, statement x := 0 of the error trace is trace-aberrant because there exists a value that may be assigned to variable x such that the trace verifies. In particular, when x is assigned a positive value, assume $x \leq 0$ terminates execution before reaching the error. Statement y := * is trace-aberrant for similar reasons. These are all the trace-aberrant statements along this error trace. For instance, x := 2 is not trace-aberrant because the value of x is over-written by the second assignment to the variable, thus making the error reachable along this trace, regardless of the initial value of x.

Suspiciousness Ranking. So far, we have seen that, when given the above error trace and the program of Fig. 1, semantic fault localization detects two trace-aberrant statements, y := * and x := 0. Since for real programs there can be

many trace-aberrant statements, our technique computes a semantic suspiciousness score for each of them. Specifically, the computed score is inversely proportional to how much code would become unreachable if we applied a local fix to
the statement. This is because developers do not intentionally write unreachable
code. Therefore, when they make a mistake, they are more likely to fix a statement that renders fewer parts of the program unreachable relatively to other
suspicious statements.

For example, if we were to fix statement x := 0 as discussed above (that
is, by assigning a positive value to x), no code would become unreachable. As
a result, this statement is assigned the highest suspiciousness score. On the
other hand, if we were to fix statement y := $\star$ such that $3 \leq$ y holds and the
trace verifies, the **then** branch of the **if** statement would become unreachable.
Consequently, y := $\star$ is assigned a lower suspiciousness score than x := 0.

As we show in Sect. 6, this ranking mechanism is very effective at narrowing
down the cause of an error to only a few lines in the program.

Program $\mathcal{P} ::= s$

Statement $s ::= s_1; s_2 \mid v := \star \mid v := e \mid$ **assert** $p \mid$ **assume** $p \mid$ **if** ($\star$) $\{s_1\}$ **else** $\{s_2\}$
   $\mid$ **while** ($\star$) $\{s\}$

Expression $e ::= v \mid c \mid e_1 \oplus e_2 \quad (\oplus \in \{+, -, \times\})$

Predicate $p ::= e_1 \oslash e_2 \quad (\oslash \in \{<, >, \leq, \geq, =\})$

Fig. 2. A simple programming language.

3   Semantic Fault Localization

As mentioned in the previous section, our technique consists of two steps, where
we determine (trace-)aberrant statements in the first step and compute their
suspiciousness ranks in the next one.

3.1   Programming Language

To precisely describe our technique, we introduce a small programming language,
shown in Fig. 2. As shown in the figure, a program consists of a statement, and
statements include sequencing, assignments, assertions, assumptions, conditionals, and loops. Observe that conditionals and loops have non-deterministic predicates, but note that, in combination with assumptions, they can express any
conditional or loop with a predicate p. To simplify the discussion, we do not
introduce additional constructs for procedure definitions and calls.

We assume that program execution terminates as soon as an assertion or
assumption violation in encountered (that is, when the corresponding predicate
evaluates to false). For simplicity, we also assume that our technique is applied
to one failing assertion at a time.

3.2 Trace-Aberrant Statements

Recall from the previous section that trace-aberrant statements are assignments along the error trace for which there exists a local fix that makes the trace verify (that is, the error becomes unreachable along this trace):

Definition 1 (Trace aberrance). *Let τ be a feasible error trace and s an assignment statement of the form $v := \star$ or $v := e$ along τ. Statement s is* trace-aberrant *iff there exists an expression e' that may be assigned to variable v such that the trace verifies.*

To determine which assignments along an error trace are trace-aberrant, we first compute, in the post-state of each assignment, the weakest condition that ensures that the trace verifies. We, therefore, define a predicate transformer WP such that, if $WP(S, Q)$ holds in a state along the error trace, then the error is unreachable and Q holds after executing statement S. The definition of this weakest-precondition transformer is standard [9] for all statements that may appear in an error trace:

- $WP(s_1; s_2, Q) \equiv WP(s_1, WP(s_2, Q))$
- $WP(v := \star, Q) \equiv \forall v'.Q[v := v']$, where $v' \notin \mathit{freeVars}(Q)$
- $WP(v := e, Q) \equiv Q[v := e]$
- $WP(\texttt{assert false}, Q) \equiv \mathit{false}$
- $WP(\texttt{assume } p, Q) \equiv p \Rightarrow Q$

In the weakest precondition of the non-deterministic assignment, v' is fresh in Q and $Q[v := v']$ denotes the substitution of v by v' in Q.

To illustrate, we compute this condition in the post-state of each assignment along the error trace of Sect. 2. Weakest precondition

$$WP(\texttt{assume } \texttt{x} \leq \texttt{0}; \texttt{assert false}, \mathit{true}) \equiv 0 < \texttt{x}$$

should hold in the pre-state of statement $\texttt{assume } \texttt{x} \leq \texttt{0}$, and thus in the post-state of assignment $\texttt{x} := \texttt{0}$, for the trace to verify. Similarly, $3 \leq \texttt{y}$ and false should hold in the post-state of assignments $\texttt{y} = \star$ and $\texttt{x} := \texttt{2}$, respectively. Note that condition false indicates that the error is always reachable after assignment $\texttt{x} := \texttt{2}$.

Second, we compute, in the pre-state of each assignment along the error trace, the strongest condition that holds when executing the error trace until that state. We define a predicate transformer SP such that condition $SP(P, S)$ describes the post-state of statement S for an execution of S that starts from an initial state satisfying P. The definition of this strongest-postcondition transformer is also standard [10] for all statements that may appear in an error trace:

- $SP(P, s_1; s_2) \equiv SP(SP(P, s_1), s_2)$
- $SP(P, v := \star) \equiv \exists v'.P[v := v']$, where $v' \notin \mathit{freeVars}(P)$
- $SP(P, v := e) \equiv \exists v'.P[v := v'] \wedge v = e[v := v']$,
  where $v' \notin \mathit{freeVars}(P) \cup \mathit{freeVars}(e)$

- $SP(P, \texttt{assert false}) \equiv \mathit{false}$
- $SP(P, \texttt{assume } p) \equiv P \wedge p$

In the strongest postcondition of the assignment statements, v' represents the previous value of v.

For example, strongest postcondition

$$SP(\mathit{true}, \texttt{x := 2}) \equiv \texttt{x} = 2$$

holds in the post-state of assignment $\texttt{x := 2}$, and therefore in the pre-state of $\texttt{y := } \star$. Similarly, the strongest such conditions in the pre-state of assignments $\texttt{x := 2}$ and $\texttt{x := 0}$ along the error trace are true and $\texttt{x} = 2 \wedge \texttt{y} < 3$, respectively.

Third, our technique determines if an assignment a (of the form $v := \star$ or $v := e$) along the error trace is trace-aberrant by checking whether the Hoare triple [17] $\{\phi\}\ v := \star\ \{\psi\}$ is valid. Here, ϕ denotes the strongest postcondition in the pre-state of assignment a, v the left-hand side of a, and ψ the negation of the weakest precondition in the post-state of a. If this Hoare triple is *invalid*, then assignment statement a is trace-aberrant, otherwise it is not.

Intuitively, the validity of the Hoare triple implies that, when starting from the pre-state of a, the error is always reachable no matter which value is assigned to v. In other words, there is no local fix for statement a that would make the trace verify. Consequently, assignment a is not trace-aberrant since it cannot possibly be the cause of the error. As an example, consider statement $\texttt{x := 2}$. For this assignment, our technique checks the validity of the Hoare triple $\{\mathit{true}\}\ \texttt{x := } \star\ \{\mathit{true}\}$. Since any value for $\texttt{x}$ satisfies the true postcondition, assignment $\texttt{x := 2}$ is not trace-aberrant.

If, however, the Hoare triple is invalid, there exists a value for variable v such that the weakest precondition in the post-state of a holds. This means that there is a local fix for a that makes the error unreachable. As a result, statement a is found to be trace-aberrant. For instance, for statement $\texttt{x := 0}$, we construct the following Hoare triple: $\{\texttt{x} = 2 \wedge \texttt{y} < 3\}\ \texttt{x := } \star\ \{\texttt{x} \leq 0\}$. This Hoare triple is invalid because there are values that may be assigned to $\texttt{x}$ such that $\texttt{x} \leq 0$ does not hold in the post-state. Assignment $\texttt{x := 0}$ is, therefore, trace-aberrant. Similarly, for $\texttt{y := } \star$, the Hoare triple $\{\texttt{x} = 2\}\ \texttt{y := } \star\ \{\texttt{y} < 3\}$ is invalid.

3.3   Program-Aberrant Statements

We now define *program-aberrant statements*; these are assignments for which there exists a local fix that makes *every* trace through them verify:

Definition 2 (Program aberrance). *Let τ be a feasible error trace and s an assignment statement of the form $v := \star$ or $v := e$ along τ. Statement s is* program-aberrant *iff there exists an expression e' that may be assigned to variable v such that all traces through s verify.*

Based on the above definition, the trace-aberrant assignments in the program of Fig. 1 are also program-aberrant. This is because there is only one error trace through these statements.

As another example, let us replace the assignment on line 8 of the program by x := -1. In this modified program, the assertion on line 10 fails when program execution takes either branch of the if statement. Now, assume that a static analyzer, which clearly fails to verify the assertion, generates the same error trace that we described in Sect. 2 (for the then branch of the if statement). Like before, our technique determines that statements y := ⋆ and x := 0 along this error trace are trace-aberrant. However, although there is still a single error trace through statement x := 0, there are now two error traces through y := ⋆, one for each branch of the conditional. We, therefore, know that x := 0 is program-aberrant, but it is unclear whether assignment y := ⋆ is.

To determine which trace-aberrant assignments along an error trace are also program-aberrant, one would need to check if there exists a local fix for these statements such that all traces through them verify. Recall that there exists a fix for a trace-aberrant assignment if there exists a right-hand side that satisfies the weakest precondition in the post-state of the assignment *along the error trace*. Therefore, checking the existence of a local fix for a program-aberrant statement involves computing the weakest precondition in the post-state of the statement *in the program*, which amounts to program verification and is undecidable.

Identifying which trace-aberrant statements are also program-aberrant is desirable since these are precisely the statements that can be fixed for the program to verify. However, determining these statements is difficult for the reasons indicated above. Instead, our technique uses the previously-computed weakest preconditions to decide which trace-aberrant assignments *must* also be program-aberrant, in other words, it can under-approximate the set of program-aberrant statements. In our experiments, we find that many trace-aberrant statements are *must-program-aberrant*.

To compute the must-program-aberrant statements, our technique first identifies the trace-aberrant ones, for instance, y := ⋆ and x := 0 for the modified program. In the following, we refer to the corresponding error trace as ϵ.

As a second step, our technique checks whether all traces through the trace-aberrant assignments verify with the most permissive local fix that makes ϵ verify. To achieve this, we instrument the faulty program as follows. We replace a trace-aberrant statement a_i of the form $v := e$ by a non-deterministic assignment $v := \star$ with the same left-hand side v. Our technique then introduces an **assume** statement right after the non-deterministic assignment. The predicate of the assumption corresponds to the weakest precondition that is computed in the post-state of the assignment along error trace ϵ[1]. We apply this instrumentation separately for each trace-aberrant statement a_i, where $i = 0, \ldots, n$, and we refer to the instrumented program that corresponds to trace-aberrant statement a_i as P_{a_i}. (Note that our technique uses this instrumentation for ranking aberrant statements in terms of suspiciousness, as we explain in Sect. 4.) Once we obtain a program P_{a_i}, we instrument it further to add a flag that allows the error to

---

[1] Any universal quantifier appearing in the weakest precondition can be expressed within the language of Fig. 2 by using non-deterministic assignments.

manifest itself only for traces through statement a_i (as per Definition 2). We denote each of these programs by $P_{a_i}^\dagger$.

For example, the light gray boxes on the right show the instrumentation for checking whether statement x := 0 of the modified program is program-aberrant (the darker boxes should be ignored). Lines 8–9 constitute the instrumentation that generates program $P_{\text{x} := 0}$. As explained in Sect. 3.2, when the computed weakest precondition holds on line 9, it implies that trace ϵ verifies. Consequently, this instrumentation represents a hypothetical local fix for assignment x := 0. Lines 1, 10, and 15 block any program execution that does not go through statement x := 0. As a result, the assertion may fail only due to failing executions through this statement. Similarly, when considering the dark gray boxes in addition to lines 1 and 15 (and ignoring all other light boxes), we obtain $P_{\text{y} := \star}^\dagger$. Line 4 alone constitutes the instrumentation that generates program $P_{\text{y} := \star}$.

```
1  flag := 0;
2  x := 2;
3  y := *;
4  assume 3 ≤ y;
5  flag := 1;
6  if (*)
7      assume y < 3;
8      x := *;
9      assume 0 < x;
10     flag := 1;
11 } else {
12     assume 3 ≤ y;
13     x := -1;
14 }
15 assume flag = 1;
16 assert 0 < x;
```

Third, our technique runs the static analyzer on each of the n instrumented programs $P_{a_i}^\dagger$. If the analyzer does not generate a new error trace, then statement a_i must be program-aberrant, otherwise we do not know. For instance, when running the static analyzer on $P_{\text{x} := 0}^\dagger$ from above, no error is detected. Statement x := 0 is, therefore, program-aberrant. However, an error trace is reported for program $P_{\text{y} := \star}^\dagger$ (through the else branch of the conditional). As a result, our technique cannot determine whether y := $\star$ is program-aberrant. Notice, however, that this statement is, in fact, not program-aberrant because there is no fix that we can apply to it such that both traces verify.

3.4 k-Aberrance

So far, we have focused on (trace- or program-) aberrant statements that may be fixed to single-handedly make one or more error traces verify. The notion of aberrance, however, may be generalized to sets of statements that make the corresponding error traces verify only when fixed together:

Definition 3 (k-Trace aberrance). *Let τ be a feasible error trace and $\bar{s}$ a set of assignment statements of the form $v := \star$ or $v := e$ along τ. Statements $\bar{s}$ are $|\bar{s}|$-trace-aberrant, where $|\bar{s}|$ is the cardinality of $\bar{s}$, iff there exist local fixes for all statements in $\bar{s}$ such that trace τ verifies.*

Definition 4 (k-Program aberrance). *Let $\bar{\tau}$ be the set of all feasible error traces through any assignment statement s in a set $\bar{s}$. Each statement s is of the form $v := \star$ or $v := e$ along an error trace τ in $\bar{\tau}$. Statements $\bar{s}$ are $|\bar{s}|$-program-aberrant, where $|\bar{s}|$ is the cardinality of $\bar{s}$, iff there exist local fixes for all statements in $\bar{s}$ such that all traces $\bar{\tau}$ verify.*

For example, consider the modified version of the program in Fig. 1 that we discussed above. Assignments x := 0 and x := -1 are 2-program-aberrant because their right-hand side may be replaced by a positive value such that both traces through these statements verify.

Our technique may be adjusted to compute k-aberrant statements by exploring all combinations of k assignments along one or more error traces.

4   Semantic Suspiciousness Ranking

In this section, we present how aberrant statements are ranked in terms of their suspiciousness. As mentioned earlier, the suspiciousness score of an aberrant statement is inversely proportional to how much code would become unreachable if we applied a local fix to the statement.

First, for each aberrant statement a_i, where $i = 0, \ldots, n$, our technique generates the instrumented program P_{a_i} (see Sect. 3.3 for the details). Recall that the trace-aberrant statements for the program of Fig. 1 are y := * and x := 0.

Second, we check reachability of the code in each of these n instrumented programs P_{a_i}. Reachability may be simply checked by converting all existing assertions into assumptions and introducing an assert false at various locations in the program. An instrumentation for checking reachability in $P_{\text{x := 0}}$ is shown on the right; all changes are highlighted. In particular, we detect whether the injected assertion on line 7 is

```
1 x := 2;
2 y := *;
3 if (*)
4     assume y < 3;
5     x := *;
6     assume 0 < x;
7     assert false;
8 } else {
9     assume 3 ≤ y;
10    x := 1;
11    assert false;
12 }
13 assume 0 < x;
```

reachable by passing the above program (without the dark gray box) to an off-the-shelf analyzer. We can similarly check reachability of the other assertion. In the above program, both assertions are reachable, whereas in the corresponding program for assignment y := *, only one of them is. The number of reachable assertions in a program P_{a_i} constitutes the suspiciousness score of statement a_i.

As a final step, our technique ranks the aberrant statements in order of decreasing suspiciousness. Intuitively, this means that, by applying a local fix to the higher-ranked statements, less code would become unreachable in comparison to the statements that are ranked lower. Since developers do not typically intend to write unreachable code, the cause of the error in P is more likely to be a higher-ranked aberrant statement. For our running example, trace-aberrant statement x := 0 is ranked higher than y := *.

As previously discussed, when modifying the program of Fig. 1 to replace assignment x := 1 by x := -1, our technique determines that only x := 0 must be program-aberrant. For the error trace through the other branch of the conditional, we would similarly identify statement x := -1 as must-program-aberrant. Note that, for this example, must program aberrance does not miss any program-aberrant statements. In fact, in our experiments, must program aberrance does not miss any error causes, despite its under-approximation.

5   Implementation

We have implemented our technique in a toolchain for localizing and ranking suspicious statements in C programs. We used UAutomizer in the Ultimate analysis
framework to obtain error traces (version 0.1.23). UAutomizer is a software model
checker that translates C programs to Boogie [4] and then employs an automata-
based verification approach [16]. Our implementation extends UAutomizer to identify (trace- or program-) aberrant statements along the generated error traces, as
we describe in Sect. 3. Note that, due to abstraction (for instance, of library calls),
UAutomizer may generate spurious error traces. This is an orthogonal issue that
we do not address in this work.

To also identify aberrant expressions, for instance, predicates of conditionals
or call arguments, we pre-process the program by first assigning these expressions
to temporary variables, which are then used instead. This allows us to detect
error causes relating to statements other than assignments.

Once the aberrant statements have been determined, we instrument the
Boogie code to rank them (see Sect. 4). Specifically, our implementation inlines
procedures and injects an **assert false** statement at the end of each basic block
(one at a time). Instead of extending the existing support for "smoke checking"
in Boogie, we implemented our own reachability checker in order to have more
control over where the assertions are injected. While this might not be as efficient due to the larger number of Boogie queries (each including the time for parsing, pre-processing, and SMT solving), one could easily optimize or replace this
component.

6   Experimental Evaluation

We evaluate the effectiveness of our technique in localizing and ranking suspicious statements by applying our toolchain to several faulty C programs. In the
following, we introduce our set of benchmarks (Sect. 6.1), present the experimental setup (Sect. 6.2), and investigate four research questions (Sect. 6.3).

6.1   Benchmark Selection

For our evaluation, we used 51 faulty C programs from two independent sources.
On the one hand, we used the faulty versions of the TCAS task from the Siemens
test suite [19]. The authors of the test suite manually introduced faults in several
tasks while aiming to make these bugs as realistic as possible. In general, the
Siemens test suite is widely used in the literature (e.g., [14, 20, 22, 25–28]) for
evaluating and comparing fault-localization techniques.

The TCAS task implements an aircraft-collision avoidance system and consists of 173 lines of C code; there are no specifications. This task also comes with
1608 test cases, which we used to introduce assertions in the faulty program versions. In particular, in each faulty version, we specified the correct behavior as
this was observed by running the tests against the original, correct version of the

code. This methodology is commonly used in empirical studies with the Siemens test suite, and it was necessary for obtaining an error trace from UAutomizer.

On the other hand, we randomly selected 4 correct programs (with over 250 lines of code) from the SV-COMP software-verification competition [5], which includes standard benchmarks for evaluating program analyzers. We automatically injected faults in each of these programs by randomly mutating statements within the program. All SV-COMP benchmarks are already annotated with assertions, so faults manifest themselves by violating the existing assertions.

6.2   Experimental Setup

We ran all experiments on an Intel® Core i7 CPU @ 2.67 GHz machine with 16 GB of memory, running Linux. Per analyzed program, we imposed a timeout of 120 s and a memory limit of 6 GB to UAutomizer.

To inject faults in the SV-COMP benchmarks, we developed a mutator that randomly selects an assignment statement, mutates the right-hand side, and checks whether the assertion in the program is violated. If it is, the mutator emits a faulty program version. Otherwise, it generates up to two additional mutations for the same assignment before moving on to another.

6.3   Experimental Results

To evaluate our technique, we consider the following research questions:

- **RQ1:** How effective is our technique in narrowing down the cause of an error to a small number of suspicious statements?
- **RQ2:** How efficient is our technique?
- **RQ3:** How does under-approximating program-aberrant statements affect fault localization?
- **RQ4:** How does our technique compare against state-of-the-art approaches for fault localization in terms of effectiveness and efficiency?

RQ1 (Effectiveness). Tables 1 and 2 summarize our experimental results on the TCAS and SV-COMP benchmarks, respectively. The first column of Table 1 shows the faulty versions of the program, and the second column the number of trace-aberrant statements that were detected for every version. Similarly, in Table 2, the first column shows the program version[2], the second column the lines of source code in every version, and the third column the number of trace-aberrant statements. For all benchmarks, the actual cause of each error is always

---

[2] A version is denoted by $<correct\text{-}program\text{-}id>.<faulty\text{-}version\text{-}id>$. We mutate the following correct programs from SV-COMP: 1. `mem_slave_tlm.1_true-unreach-call_false-termination.cil.c` (4 faulty versions), 2. `kundu_true-unreach-call_false-termination.cil.c` (4 faulty versions), 3. `mem_slave_tlm.2_true-unreach-call_false-termination.cil.c` (2 faulty versions), and 4. `pc_sfifo_1_true-unreach-call_false-termination.cil.c` (1 faulty version). All versions are at: https://github.com/numairmansur/SemanticFaultLocalization_Benchmarks.

Table 1. Our experimental results for the TCAS benchmarks.

Prg	Abr stmts		Rank		Time (m:s)		Program reduction (%)							
ver	trc	prg	trc	prg	trc	prg	trc	prg	A	B	C	D	E	F
1	16	11	5	3	2:24	1:17	8.1	5.7	1.7	1.7	1.7	1.7	1.7	8.6
2	15	13	1	1	2:33	1:46	1.7	1.7	6.3	5.7	5.7	6.3	5.7	4.6
3	4	4	1	1	0:29	0:31	1.7	1.7	12.7	12.1	10.4	12.7	12.1	9.8
4	16	14	4	4	2:59	1:53	7.5	7.5	1.7	1.7	1.7	1.7	1.7	9.2
5	4	4	1	1	0:28	0:33	1.7	1.7	14.4	10.9	9.8	14.4	10.9	8.6
6	13	13	5	5	1:51	1:53	7.5	7.5	2.8	2.8	2.8	2.8	2.8	8.6
7	15	13	5	5	2:28	1:57	6.9	6.3	12.1	12.1	9.8	12.1	12.1	9.2
8	14	13	5	5	2:14	1:51	6.9	5.7	12.7	12.7	12.7	12.7	12.7	8.6
9	16	14	1	1	2:21	1:55	1.7	1.7	7.5	7.5	7.5	7.5	7.5	5.2
10	15	14	2	2	2:12	1:53	3.4	2.8	11.5	11.5	15.0	11.5	16.1	9.2
11	15	7	2	1	1:58	0:56	2.8	1.7	2.8	2.8	2.3	2.8	2.8	6.3
12	16	14	3	3	2:38	1:46	5.7	5.2	12.7	12.1	9.8	12.7	12.1	9.2
13	17	15	5	5	2:40	1:56	6.3	5.2	15.6	12.1	10.4	15.6	12.1	9.2
14	4	4	1	1	0:30	0:29	1.7	1.7	5.7	5.7	5.7	5.7	5.7	8.1
15	17	15	4	4	2:52	2:02	7.5	6.3	15.0	13.2	10.4	15.0	13.2	7.5
16	16	14	5	5	2:22	1:57	6.3	6.3	12.1	12.1	12.1	12.1	12.1	9.2
17	16	14	5	5	2:37	2:03	8.0	7.5	12.1	12.1	9.8	12.1	12.1	9.2
18	16	14	5	5	2:02	1:51	8.0	7.5	14.4	11.5	9.8	14.4	11.5	6.9
19	16	14	5	5	2:20	1:55	8.0	7.5	12.1	12.1	9.8	12.1	12.1	9.2
20	15	11	1	1	2:16	1:23	1.7	1.7	7.5	7.5	7.5	7.5	7.5	9.2
21	16	12	1	1	2:16	1:27	1.7	1.7	7.5	7.5	7.5	7.5	7.5	8.6
22	17	8	1	1	2:45	1:03	2.3	1.7	7.5	7.5	7.5	7.5	7.5	5.7
23	14	11	1	1	2:22	1:30	1.7	1.7	7.5	7.5	7.5	7.5	7.5	6.3
24	17	13	1	1	2:39	1:57	2.3	1.7	7.5	7.5	7.5	7.5	7.5	8.6
25	16	14	3	3	1:44	1:51	9.2	8.1	1.1	1.1	1.1	1.1	1.1	6.9
26	15	13	3	3	2:17	1:52	2.8	1.7	13.8	12.7	10.4	13.8	12.7	9.2
27	15	13	4	4	2:36	1:58	8.6	8.1	14.4	10.9	9.8	14.4	10.9	10.9
28	15	13	1	1	2:03	1:50	1.7	1.7	6.3	5.7	4.0	6.3	5.7	5.7
29	12	8	3	2	1:46	1:09	1.7	1.7	6.3	6.3	5.7	6.3	5.7	5.7
30	14	8	2	2	1:47	1:06	1.7	1.7	6.3	5.7	5.7	6.3	5.7	5.7
31	17	15	4	4	2:32	1:57	8.1	6.3	2.8	2.8	2.8	2.8	2.8	10.9
32	14	13	5	5	1:55	1:54	6.3	6.3	2.8	2.8	2.8	2.8	2.8	10.9
33	17	15	4	4	2:48	2:05	2.8	2.8	14.4	12.7	10.9	14.4	12.7	—
34	16	14	4	4	2:43	2:13	8.0	6.9	13.2	12.7	10.4	13.2	12.7	8.6
35	14	8	2	2	1:59	0:59	2.3	1.7	6.3	5.7	4.0	6.3	5.7	5.7
36	6	3	1	1	0:43	0:26	3.4	1.7	13.2	13.2	10.4	13.2	13.2	2.9
37	17	8	6	3	2:43	1:04	9.8	4.6	1.1	1.1	0.5	1.1	0.5	8.6
39	16	7	5	1	2:45	0:55	9.2	4.6	1.1	1.1	1.1	1.1	1.1	6.9
40	16	14	4	4	2:48	1:46	6.3	6.3	15.0	15.0	15.0	15.0	15.6	6.3
41	17	15	4	4	2:50	2:00	9.8	8.6	1.7	1.7	1.7	1.7	1.7	8.6
Avg	14.4	11.5	3.1	2.9	2:12	1:34	5.1	4.3	8.6	8.0	7.3	8.6	8.1	7.9

included in the statements that our technique identifies as trace-aberrant. This is to be expected since the weakest-precondition and strongest-postcondition transformers that we use for determining trace aberrance are known to be sound.

The fourth column of Table 1 and the fifth column of Table 2 show the suspiciousness rank that our technique assigns to the actual cause of each error. For both sets of benchmarks, the average rank of the faulty statement is 3, and all faulty statements are ranked in the top 6. A suspiciousness rank of 3 means that users need to examine *at least* three statements to identify the problem; they might have to consider more in case multiple statements have the same rank.

To provide a better indication of how much code users have to examine to identify the bug, the eighth column of Table 1 and the seventh column of Table 2 show the percentage reduction in the program size. On average, our technique reduces the code size down to 5% for TCAS and less than 1% for SV-COMP.

RQ2 (Efficiency). The sixth column of Table 1 shows the time that our technique requires for identifying the trace-aberrant statements in a given error trace as well as for ranking them in terms of suspiciousness. This time does not include the generation of the error trace by UAutomizer. As shown in the table, our technique takes only a little over 2 min on average to reduce a faulty program to about 5% of its original size.

Table 2. Our experimental results for the SV-COMP benchmarks.

Prg ver	LoSC	Abr stmts		Rank		Rdc (%)	
		trc	prg	trc	prg	trc	prg
1.1	1336	34	29	4	2	0.4	0.2
1.2	1336	34	28	4	2	0.4	0.2
1.3	1336	34	31	2	1	0.2	0.1
1.4	1336	34	30	3	1	0.4	0.1
2.1	630	23	10	3	2	1.3	0.3
2.2	630	16	8	1	1	0.3	0.3
2.3	630	22	9	3	2	1.3	0.3
2.4	630	27	25	4	3	1.2	1.1
3.1	1371	37	33	3	1	0.3	0.2
3.2	1371	37	32	3	1	0.3	0.1
4.1	360	18	8	4	2	3.3	0.8
Average		28.7	22.0	3.0	1.6	0.8	0.3

Note that most of this time (98.5% on average) is spent on the suspiciousness ranking. The average time for determining the trace-aberrant statements in an error trace is only 1.7 s. Recall from Sect. 5 that our reachability analysis, which is responsible for computing the suspiciousness score of each aberrant statement, is not implemented as efficiently as possible (see Sect. 5 for possible improvements).

RQ3 (Program aberrance). In Sect. 3.3, we discussed that our technique can under-approximate the set of program-aberrant statements along an error trace. The third, fifth, seventh, and ninth columns of Table 1 as well as the fourth, sixth, and eighth columns of Table 2 show the effect of this under-approximation.

There are several observations to be made here, especially in comparison to the experimental results for trace aberrance. First, there are fewer aberrant statements, which is to be expected since (must-)program-aberrant statements may only be a subset of trace-aberrant statements. Perhaps a bit surprisingly, the actual cause of each error is always included in the must-program-aberrant statements. In other words, the under-approximation of program-aberrant statements does not miss any error causes in our benchmarks. Second, the suspiciousness rank assigned to the actual cause of each error is slightly higher, and all faulty statements are ranked in the top 5. Third, our technique requires about 1.5 min for fault localization and ranking, which is faster due to the smaller number of aberrant statements. Fourth, the code is reduced even more, down to 4.3 for TCAS and 0.3% for SV-COMP.

RQ4 (Comparison). To compare our technique against state-of-the-art fault-localization approaches, we evaluated how five of the most popular [35] spectrum-based fault-localization (SBFL) techniques [20,24,34] perform on our benchmarks. In general, SBFL is the most well-studied and evaluated fault-localization technique in the literature [26]. SBFL techniques essentially compute suspiciousness scores based on statement-execution frequencies. Specifically, the more frequently a statement is executed by failing test cases and the less frequently it is executed by successful tests, the higher its suspiciousness score. We also compare against an approach that reduces fault localization to the maximal satisfiability problem (MAX-SAT) and performs similarly to SBFL.

The last eight columns of Table 1 show the comparison in code reduction across different fault-localization techniques. Columns A, B, C, D, and E refer to the SBFL techniques, and in particular, to Tarantula [20], Ochiai [2], Op2 [24], Barinel [1], and DStar [34], respectively. The last column (F) corresponds to BugAssist [21,22], which uses MAX-SAT. To obtain these results, we implemented all SBFL techniques and evaluated them on TCAS using the existing test suite. For BugAssist, we used the published percentages of code reduction for these benchmarks [22]. Note that we omit version 38 in Table 1 as is common in experiments with TCAS. The fault is in a non-executable statement (array declaration) and its frequency cannot be computed by SBFL.

The dark gray boxes in the table show which technique is most effective with respect to code reduction for each version. Our technique for must program aberrance is the most effective for 30 out of 40 versions. The light gray boxes in the trace-aberrance column denote when this technique is the most effective in comparison with columns A–F (that is, without considering program aberrance). As shown in the table, our technique for trace aberrance outperforms approaches A–F in 28 out of 40 versions. In terms of lines of code, users need to inspect 7–9 statements when using our technique, whereas they would need to look at 13–15 statements when using other approaches. This is a reduction of 4–8 statements, and every statement that users may safely ignore saves them valuable time.

Regarding efficiency, our technique is comparable to SBFL (A–E); we were not able to run BugAssist (F), but it should be very lightweight for TCAS. SBFL techniques need to run the test suite for every faulty program. For the TCAS tests, this takes 1 min 11 s on average on our machine. Parsing the statement-execution frequencies and computing the suspiciousness scores takes about 5 more seconds. Therefore, the average difference with our technique ranges from a few seconds (for program aberrance) to a little less than a minute (for trace aberrance). There is definitely room for improving the efficiency of our technique, but despite it being slightly slower than SBFL for these benchmarks, it saves the user the effort of inspecting non-suspicious statements. Moreover, note that the larger the test suite, the higher the effectiveness of SBFL, and the longer its running time. Thus, to be as effective as our technique, SBFL would require more test cases, and the test suite would take longer to run. We do not consider the time for test case generation just like we do not consider the running time of the static analysis that generates the error traces.

7 Related Work

Among the many fault-localization techniques [35], SBFL [20,24,34] is the most well-studied and evaluated. Mutation-based fault localization (MBFL) [23,25] is almost as effective as SBFL but significantly more inefficient [26]. In general, MBFL extends SBFL by considering, not only how frequently a statement is executed in tests, but also whether a mutation to the statement affects the test outcomes. So, MBFL generates many mutants per statement, which requires running the test suite per mutant, and not per faulty program as in SBFL. Our local fixes resemble mutations, but they are performed *symbolically* and can be seen as applying program-level abductive reasoning [6,11,12] or angelic verification [8] for fault localization.

The use of error invariants [7,13,18,29] is a closely-related fault-localization technique. Error invariants are computed from Craig interpolants along an error trace and capture which states will produce the error from that point on. They are used for slicing traces by only preserving statements whose error invariants before and after the statement differ. Similarly, Wang et al. [32] use a syntactic-level weakest-precondition computation for a given error trace to produce a minimal set of word-level predicates, which explain why the program fails. In contrast, we use the novel notion of trace aberrance for this purpose and compute a suspiciousness ranking to narrow down the error cause further.

Griesmayer et al. [14] use an error trace from a bounded model checker to instrument the program with "abnormal predicates". These predicates allow expressions in the program to take arbitrary values, similarly to how our technique replaces a statement $v := e$ by a non-deterministic one. Unlike our technique, their approach may generate a prohibitively large instrumentation, requires multiple calls to the model checker, and does not rank suspicious statements.

Several fault-localization algorithms leverage the differences between faulty and successful traces [3,15,27,36]. For instance, Ball et al. [3] make several calls to a model checker and compare any generated counterexamples with successful traces. In contrast, we do not require successful traces for comparisons.

Zeller [36] uses delta-debugging, which identifies suspicious parts of the input by running the program multiple times. Slicing [31,33] removes statements that are definitely not responsible for the error based on data and control dependencies. Shen et al. [30] use unsatisfiable cores for minimizing counterexamples. Our technique is generally orthogonal to these approaches, which could be run as a pre-processing step to reduce the search space.

8 Conclusion

We have presented a novel technique for fault localization and suspiciousness ranking of statements along an error trace. We demonstrated its effectiveness in narrowing down the error cause to a small fraction of the entire program.

As future work, we plan to evaluate the need for k-aberrance by analyzing software patches and to combine our technique with existing approaches for program repair to improve their effectiveness.

Acknowledgments. This work was supported by the German Research Foundation (DFG) as part of CRC 248 (https://www.perspicuous-computing.science), the Austrian Science Fund (FWF) under grants S11402-N23 (RiSE/SHiNE) and Z211-N23 (Wittgenstein Award), and the European Union's Horizon 2020 research and innovation programme under the Marie Skłodowska-Curie grant agreement No. 754411.

References

1. Abreu, R., Zoeteweij, P., van Gemund, A.J.C.: Spectrum-based multiple fault localization. In: ASE, pp. 88–99. IEEE Computer Society (2009)
2. Abreu, R., Zoeteweij, P., Golsteijn, R., van Gemund, A.J.C.: A practical evaluation of spectrum-based fault localization. JSS **82**, 1780–1792 (2009)
3. Ball, T., Naik, M., Rajamani, S.K.: From symptom to cause: localizing errors in counterexample traces. In: POPL, pp. 97–105. ACM (2003)
4. Barnett, M., Chang, B.-Y.E., DeLine, R., Jacobs, B., Leino, K.R.M.: Boogie: a modular reusable verifier for object-oriented programs. In: de Boer, F.S., Bonsangue, M.M., Graf, S., de Roever, W.-P. (eds.) FMCO 2005. LNCS, vol. 4111, pp. 364–387. Springer, Heidelberg (2006). https://doi.org/10.1007/11804192_17
5. Beyer, D.: Competition on software verification (SV-COMP) (2017). https://sv-comp.sosy-lab.org
6. Calcagno, C., Distefano, D., O'Hearn, P.W., Yang, H.: Compositional shape analysis by means of bi-abduction. In: POPL, pp. 289–300. ACM (2009)
7. Christ, J., Ermis, E., Schäf, M., Wies, T.: Flow-sensitive fault localization. In: Giacobazzi, R., Berdine, J., Mastroeni, I. (eds.) VMCAI 2013. LNCS, vol. 7737, pp. 189–208. Springer, Heidelberg (2013). https://doi.org/10.1007/978-3-642-35873-9_13
8. Das, A., Lahiri, S.K., Lal, A., Li, Y.: Angelic verification: precise verification modulo unknowns. In: Kroening, D., Păsăreanu, C.S. (eds.) CAV 2015. LNCS, vol. 9206, pp. 324–342. Springer, Cham (2015). https://doi.org/10.1007/978-3-319-21690-4_19
9. Dijkstra, E.W.: Guarded commands, nondeterminacy and formal derivation of programs. CACM **18**, 453–457 (1975)
10. Dijkstra, E.W., Scholten, C.S.: Predicate Calculus and Program Semantics. Springer, New York (1990). https://doi.org/10.1007/978-1-4612-3228-5
11. Dillig, I., Dillig, T.: EXPLAIN: a tool for performing abductive inference. In: Sharygina, N., Veith, H. (eds.) CAV 2013. LNCS, vol. 8044, pp. 684–689. Springer, Heidelberg (2013). https://doi.org/10.1007/978-3-642-39799-8_46
12. Dillig, I., Dillig, T., Aiken, A.: Automated error diagnosis using abductive inference. In: PLDI, pp. 181 192. ACM (2012)

13. Ermis, E., Schäf, M., Wies, T.: Error invariants. In: Giannakopoulou, D., Méry, D. (eds.) FM 2012. LNCS, vol. 7436, pp. 187–201. Springer, Heidelberg (2012). https://doi.org/10.1007/978-3-642-32759-9_17

14. Griesmayer, A., Staber, S., Bloem, R.: Automated fault localization for C programs. ENTCS **174**, 95–111 (2007)

15. Groce, A., Chaki, S., Kroening, D., Strichman, O.: Error explanation with distance metrics. STTT **8**, 229–247 (2006)

16. Heizmann, M., Hoenicke, J., Podelski, A.: Software model checking for people who love automata. In: Sharygina, N., Veith, H. (eds.) CAV 2013. LNCS, vol. 8044, pp. 36–52. Springer, Heidelberg (2013). https://doi.org/10.1007/978-3-642-39799-8_2

17. Hoare, C.A.R.: An axiomatic basis for computer programming. CACM **12**, 576–580 (1969)

18. Holzer, A., Schwartz-Narbonne, D., Tabaei Befrouei, M., Weissenbacher, G., Wies, T.: Error invariants for concurrent traces. In: Fitzgerald, J., Heitmeyer, C., Gnesi, S., Philippou, A. (eds.) FM 2016. LNCS, vol. 9995, pp. 370–387. Springer, Cham (2016). https://doi.org/10.1007/978-3-319-48989-6_23

19. Hutchins, M., Foster, H., Goradia, T., Ostrand, T.J.: Experiments of the effectiveness of dataflow- and controlflow-based test adequacy criteria. In: ICSE, pp. 191–200. IEEE Computer Society/ACM (1994)

20. Jones, J.A., Harrold, M.J.: Empirical evaluation of the Tarantula automatic fault-localization technique. In: ASE, pp. 273–282. ACM (2005)

21. Jose, M., Majumdar, R.: Bug-assist: assisting fault localization in ANSI-C programs. In: Gopalakrishnan, G., Qadeer, S. (eds.) CAV 2011. LNCS, vol. 6806, pp. 504–509. Springer, Heidelberg (2011). https://doi.org/10.1007/978-3-642-22110-1_40

22. Jose, M., Majumdar, R.: Cause clue clauses: error localization using maximum satisfiability. In: PLDI, pp. 437–446. ACM (2011)

23. Moon, S., Kim, Y., Kim, M., Yoo, S.: Ask the mutants: mutating faulty programs for fault localization. In: ICST, pp. 153–162. IEEE Computer Society (2014)

24. Naish, L., Lee, H.J., Ramamohanarao, K.: A model for spectra-based software diagnosis. TOSEM **20**, 11:1–11:32 (2011)

25. Papadakis, M., Le Traon, Y.: Metallaxis-FL: mutation-based fault localization. Softw. Test. Verif. Reliab. **25**, 605–628 (2015)

26. Pearson, S., et al.: Evaluating and improving fault localization. In: ICSE, pp. 609–620. IEEE Computer Society/ACM (2017)

27. Renieris, M., Reiss, S.P.: Fault localization with nearest neighbor queries. In: ASE, pp. 30–39. IEEE Computer Society (2003)

28. Santelices, R.A., Jones, J.A., Yu, Y., Harrold, M.J.: Lightweight fault-localization using multiple coverage types. In: ICSE, pp. 56–66. IEEE Computer Society (2009)

29. Schäf, M., Schwartz-Narbonne, D., Wies, T.: Explaining inconsistent code. In: ESEC/FSE, pp. 521–531. ACM (2013)

30. Shen, S.Y., Qin, Y., Li, S.K.: Minimizing counterexample with unit core extraction and incremental SAT. In: Cousot, R. (ed.) VMCAI 2005. LNCS, vol. 3385, pp. 298–312. Springer, Heidelberg (2005). https://doi.org/10.1007/978-3-540-30579-8_20

31. Tip, F.: A survey of program slicing techniques. J. Program. Lang. **3**, 121–189 (1995)

32. Wang, C., Yang, Z., Ivančić, F., Gupta, A.: Whodunit? Causal analysis for counterexamples. In: Graf, S., Zhang, W. (eds.) ATVA 2006. LNCS, vol. 4218, pp. 82–95. Springer, Heidelberg (2006). https://doi.org/10.1007/11901914_9

33. Weiser, M.: Program slicing. In: ICSE, pp. 439–449. IEEE Computer Society (1981)

34. Wong, W.E., Debroy, V., Gao, R., Li, Y.: The DStar method for effective software fault localization. Trans. Reliab. **63**, 290–308 (2014)
35. Wong, W.E., Gao, R., Li, Y., Abreu, R., Wotawa, F.: A survey on software fault localization. TSE **42**, 707–740 (2016)
36. Zeller, A.: Isolating cause-effect chains from computer programs. In: FSE, pp. 1–10. ACM (2002)

Computing Coupled Similarity

Benjamin Bisping[(✉)] [iD] and Uwe Nestmann [iD]

Technische Universität Berlin, Berlin, Germany
{benjamin.bisping,uwe.nestmann}@tu-berlin.de

Abstract. *Coupled similarity* is a notion of equivalence for systems with internal actions. It has outstanding applications in contexts where internal choices must transparently be distributed in time or space, for example, in process calculi encodings or in action refinements. No tractable algorithms for the computation of coupled similarity have been proposed up to now. Accordingly, there has not been any tool support.

We present a *game-theoretic algorithm to compute coupled similarity*, running in cubic time and space with respect to the number of states in the input transition system. We show that one cannot hope for much better because deciding the coupled simulation preorder is at least as hard as deciding the weak simulation preorder.

Our results are backed by an *Isabelle/HOL* formalization, as well as by a parallelized implementation using the *Apache Flink* framework. Data or code related to this paper is available at: [2].

1 Introduction

Coupled similarity hits a sweet spot within the *linear-time branching-time spectrum* [9]. At that spot, one can encode between brands of process calculi [14,22,25], name a branching-time semantics for Communicating Sequential Processes [10], distribute synchronizations [23], and refine atomic actions [5,28]. Weak bisimilarity is too strong for these applications due to the occurrence of situations with *partially commited states* like in the following example.

Example 1 (Gradually committing philosophers). Three philosophers A, B, and C want to eat pasta. To do so, they must first sit down on a bench s and grab a fork f. Unfortunately, only either A alone or the thinner B and C together can fit on the bench, and there is just one fork. From the outside, we are only interested in the fact which of them gets to eat. So we consider the whole bench-and-fork business internal to the system. The following CCS structure models the situation in the notation of [21]. The resources correspond to output actions (which can be consumed only once) and obtaining the resources corresponds to input actions.

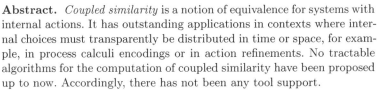

$$P_g \overset{\text{def}}{=} \left(\bar{s} \mid \bar{f} \mid s.f.A \mid s.(f.B \mid f.C) \right) \setminus \{s, f\}$$

$$A \overset{\text{def}}{=} aEats.A \qquad B \overset{\text{def}}{=} bEats.B$$

$$C \overset{\text{def}}{=} cEats.C$$

T. Vojnar and L. Zhang (Eds.): TACAS 2019, Part I, LNCS 11427, pp. 244–261, 2019.
https://doi.org/10.1007/978-3-030-17462-0_14

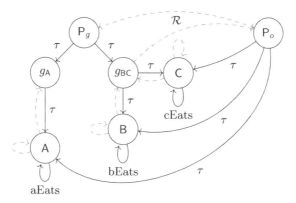

Fig. 1. A non-maximal weak/coupled simulation $\mathcal{R}$ on the philosopher system from Example 1. (Color figure online)

One might now be inclined to ponder that exactly one of the philosophers will get both resources and that we thus could merge s and f into a single resource sf:

$$P_o \stackrel{\text{def}}{=} \left(\overline{\text{sf}} \quad | \quad \text{sf.A} \mid \text{sf.B} \mid \text{sf.C}\right) \setminus \{\text{sf}\}$$

The structure of P_g and P_o has the transition system in Fig. 1 as its semantics. Notice that the internal communication concerning the resource allocation turns into internal τ-actions, which in P_g, g_A, and g_{BC} *gradually decide* who is going to eat the pasta, whereas P_o *decides in one step*.

P_g and P_o are mutually related by a weak simulation (blue dashed lines in Fig. 1) and hence *weakly similar*. However, there cannot be a *symmetric* weak simulation relating them because $P_g \xrightarrow{\tau} g_{BC}$ cannot be matched symmetrically by P_o as no other reachable state shares the weakly enabled actions of g_{BC}. Thus, they are *not weakly bisimilar*. This counters the intuition that weak bisimilarity ignores how much internal behavior happens between visible actions. There seems to be no good argument how an outside observer should notice the difference whether an internal choice is made in one or two steps.

So how to fix this overzealousness of weak bisimilarity? Falling back to weak similarity would be too coarse for many applications because it lacks the property of weak bisimilarity to coincide with strong bisimilarity on systems without internal behavior. This property, however, is present in notions that refine *contrasimilarity* [31]. There is an easy way to having the cake and eating it, here: *Coupled similarity* is precisely the intersection of contrasimilarity and weak similarity (Fig. 2). It can be defined by adding a weak form of symmetry (*coupling*) to weak simulation. The weak simulation in Fig. 1 fulfills coupling and thus is a coupled simulation. This shows that coupled similarity is coarse enough for situations with gradual commitments. At the same time, it is a close fit for weak bisimilarity, with which it coincides for many systems.

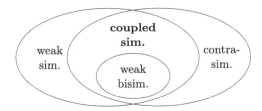

Fig. 2. Notions of equivalence for systems with internal actions.

Up to now, no algorithms and tools have been developed to enable a wider use of coupled similarity in automated verification settings. Parrow and Sjödin [24] have only hinted at an exponential-space algorithm and formulated as an open research question whether coupled similarity can be decided in **P**. For similarity and bisimilarity, polynomial algorithms exist. The best algorithms for weak bisimilarity [3,19,26] are slightly sub-cubic in time, $\mathcal{O}(|S|^2 \log |S|)$ for transition systems with $|S|$ states. The best algorithms for similarity [15,27], adapted for weak similarity, are cubic. Such a slope between similarity and bisimilarity is common [18]. As we show, coupled similarity inherits the higher complexity of weak similarity. Still, the closeness to weak bisimilarity can be exploited to speed up computations.

Contributions. This paper makes the following contributions.

- We prove that action-based single-relation *coupled similarity can be defined in terms of coupled delay simulation* (Subsect. 2.2).
- We *reduce weak similarity to coupled similarity*, thereby showing that deciding coupled similarity inherits the complexity of weak similarity (Subsect. 2.4).
- We present and verify a simple polynomial-time *coupled simulation fixed-point algorithm* (Sect. 3).
- We *characterize the coupled simulation preorder by a game and give an algorithm*, which runs in cubic time and can be nicely optimized (Sect. 4)
- We *implement the game algorithm for parallel computation using Apache Flink* and benchmark its performance (Sect. 5).

Technical details can be found in the first author's Master's thesis [1]. Isabelle/HOL [32] proofs are available from https://coupledsim.bbisping.de/isabelle/.

2   Coupled Similarity

This section characterizes the coupled simulation preorder for transition systems with silent steps in terms of coupled delay simulation. We prove properties that are key to the correctness of the following algorithms.

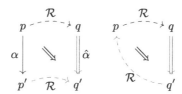

A: Weak simulation **B:** Coupling

Fig. 3. Illustration of weak simulation and coupling on transition systems (Definition 4, black part implies red part). (Color figure online)

2.1 Transition Systems with Silent Steps

Labeled transition systems capture a discrete world view, where there is a current state and a branching structure of possible state changes ("transitions") to future states.

Definition 1 (Labeled transition system). *A* labeled transition system *is a tuple $\mathcal{S} = (S, \Sigma_\tau, \rightarrow)$ where S is a set of* states, *Σ_τ is a set of* actions *containing a special* internal action *$\tau \in \Sigma_\tau$, and $\rightarrow \subseteq S \times \Sigma_\tau \times S$ is the* transition relation. *We call $\Sigma := \Sigma_\tau \setminus \{\tau\}$ the* visible actions.

The weak transition relation $\overset{\hat{\tau}}{\Rightarrow}$ *is defined as the reflexive transitive closure of internal steps $\overset{\hat{\tau}}{\Rightarrow} := \overset{\tau}{\rightarrow}^*$ combined with $\overset{\hat{a}}{\Rightarrow} := \overset{\hat{\tau}}{\Rightarrow}\overset{a}{\rightarrow}\overset{\hat{\tau}}{\Rightarrow}$ ($a \in \Sigma$).*

As a shorthand for $\overset{\hat{\tau}}{\Rightarrow}$, we also write just $\Rightarrow$. We call an $\overset{\hat{a}}{\Rightarrow}$-step "weak" whereas an $\overset{\alpha}{\rightarrow}$-step is referred to as "strong" ($\alpha \in \Sigma_\tau$). A visible action $a \in \Sigma$ is said to be *weakly enabled* in p iff there is some p' such that $p \overset{\hat{a}}{\Rightarrow} p'$.

Definition 2 (Stability and divergence). *A state p is called* stable *iff it has no τ-transitions, $p \overset{\tau}{\nrightarrow}$. A state p is called* divergent *iff it is possible to perform an infinite sequence of τ-transitions beginning in this state, $p \overset{\tau}{\rightarrow}^\omega$.*

2.2 Defining Coupled Similarity

Coupled simulation is often defined in terms of two *weak simulations*, but it is more convenient to use just a single one [10], which extends weak simulation with a weak form of symmetry, we shall call *coupling* (Fig. 3).

Definition 3 (Weak simulation). *A* weak simulation *is a relation $\mathcal{R} \subseteq S \times S$ such that, for all $(p,q) \in \mathcal{R}$, $p \overset{\alpha}{\rightarrow} p'$ implies that there is a q' such that $q \overset{\hat{\alpha}}{\Rightarrow} q'$ and $(p', q') \in \mathcal{R}$.*

Definition 4 (Coupled simulation). *A* coupled simulation *is a weak simulation $\mathcal{R} \subseteq S \times S$ such that, for all $(p,q) \in \mathcal{R}$, there exists a q' such that $q \Rightarrow q'$ and $(q', p) \in \mathcal{R}$ (coupling).*

The coupled simulation preorder *relates two processes,* $p \sqsubseteq_{CS} q$, *iff there is a coupled simulation* $\mathcal{R}$ *such that* $(p, q) \in \mathcal{R}$. Coupled similarity *relates two processes,* $p \equiv_{CS} q$, *iff* $p \sqsubseteq_{CS} q$ *and* $q \sqsubseteq_{CS} p$.

Adapting words from [10], $p \sqsubseteq_{CS} q$ intuitively does not only mean that "p is *ahead* of q" (weak simulation), but also that "q can *catch up* to p" (coupling). The weak simulation on the philosopher transition system from Example 1 is coupled.

Coupled similarity can also be characterized employing an effectively stronger concept than weak simulation, namely *delay simulation*. Delay simulations [11, 28] are defined in terms of a "shortened" weak step relation $\overset{\alpha}{\Rightarrow}$ where $\overset{\tau}{\Rightarrow} := \mathrm{id}$ and $\overset{a}{\Rightarrow} := \Rightarrow \overset{a}{\rightarrow}$. So the difference between $\overset{a}{\Rightarrow}$ and $\overset{\hat{a}}{\Rightarrow}$ lies in the fact that the latter can move on with τ-steps after the strong $\overset{a}{\rightarrow}$-step in its construction.

Definition 5 (Coupled delay simulation). *A* coupled delay simulation *is a relation* $\mathcal{R} \subseteq S \times S$ *such that, for all* $(p, q) \in \mathcal{R}$,

– $p \overset{\alpha}{\rightarrow} p'$ *implies there is a* q' *such that* $q \overset{\alpha}{\Rightarrow} q'$ *and* $(p', q') \in \mathcal{R}$ *(delay simulation),*
– *and there exists a* q' *such that* $q \Rightarrow q'$ *and* $(q', p) \in \mathcal{R}$ *(coupling).*

The only difference to Definition 4 is the use of $\overset{\alpha}{\Rightarrow}$ instead of $\overset{\hat{\alpha}}{\Rightarrow}$. Some coupled simulations are no (coupled) delay simulations, for example, consider $\mathcal{R} = \{(c.\tau, c.\tau), (\tau, \mathbf{0}), (\mathbf{0}, \tau), (\mathbf{0}, \mathbf{0})\}$ on CCS processes. Still, the *greatest* coupled simulation $\sqsubseteq_{CS}$ is a coupled delay simulation, which enables the following characterization:

Lemma 1. $p \sqsubseteq_{CS} q$ *precisely if there is a coupled delay simulation* $\mathcal{R}$ *such that* $(p, q) \in \mathcal{R}$.

2.3   Order Properties and Coinduction

Lemma 2. $\sqsubseteq_{CS}$ *forms a preorder, that is, it is reflexive and transitive. Coupled similarity* $\equiv_{CS}$ *is an equivalence relation.*

Lemma 3. *The coupled simulation preorder can be characterized coinductively by the rule:*

$$\frac{\forall p', \alpha.\ p \overset{\alpha}{\rightarrow} p' \longrightarrow \exists q'.\ q \overset{\alpha}{\Rightarrow} q' \wedge p' \sqsubseteq_{CS} q' \qquad \exists q'.\ q \Rightarrow q' \wedge q' \sqsubseteq_{CS} p}{p \sqsubseteq_{CS} q}.$$

This coinductive characterization motivates the fixed-point algorithm (Sect. 3) and the game characterization (Sect. 4) central to this paper.

Lemma 4. *If* $q \Rightarrow p$, *then* $p \sqsubseteq_{CS} q$.

Corollary 1. *If* p *and* q *are on a* τ-cycle, *that means* $p \Rightarrow q$ *and* $q \Rightarrow p$, *then* $p \equiv_{CS} q$.

Ordinary coupled simulation is blind to divergence. In particular, it cannot distinguish two states whose outgoing transitions only differ in an additional τ-loop at the second state:

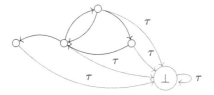

Fig. 4. Example for $\mathcal{S}^\perp$ from Theorem 1 ($\mathcal{S}$ in black, $\mathcal{S}^\perp\backslash\mathcal{S}$ in red). (Color figure online)

Lemma 5. *If* $p \xrightarrow{\alpha} p' \longleftrightarrow q \xrightarrow{\alpha} p' \vee p' = p \wedge \alpha = \tau$ *for all* α, p', *then* $p \equiv_{CS} q$.

Due to the previous two results, finite systems with divergence can be transformed into $\equiv_{CS}$-equivalent systems without divergence. This connects the original notion of stability-coupled similarity [23,24] to our modern formulation and motivates the usefulness of the next lemma.

Coupling can be thought of as "weak symmetry." For a relation to be symmetric, $\mathcal{R}^{-1} \subseteq \mathcal{R}$ must hold whereas coupling means that $\mathcal{R}^{-1} \subseteq \Rightarrow\mathcal{R}$. This weakened symmetry of coupled similarity can guarantee weak bisimulation on steps to stable states:

Lemma 6. *Assume* $\mathcal{S}$ *is finite and has no* τ-*cycles. Then* $p \sqsubseteq_{CS} q$ *and* $p \xrightarrow{\hat{\alpha}} p'$ *with stable* p' *imply there is a stable* q' *such that* $q \xrightarrow{\hat{\alpha}} q'$ *and* $p' \equiv_{CS} q'$.

2.4   Reduction of Weak Simulation to Coupled Simulation

Theorem 1. *Every decision algorithm for the coupled simulation preorder in a system* $\mathcal{S}$, $\sqsubseteq_{CS}^{\mathcal{S}}$, *can be used to decide the weak simulation preorder,* $\sqsubseteq_{WS}^{\mathcal{S}}$, *(without relevant overhead with respect to space or time complexity).*

Proof. Let $\mathcal{S} = (S, \Sigma_\tau, \rightarrow)$ be an arbitrary transition system and $\perp \notin S$. Then

$$\mathcal{S}^\perp := \left(S \cup \{\perp\}, \quad \Sigma_\tau, \quad \rightarrow \cup \{(p, \tau, \perp) \mid p \in S \cup \{\perp\}\}\right)$$

extends $\mathcal{S}$ with a sink $\perp$ that can be reached by a τ-step from everywhere. For an illustration see Fig. 4. Note that for $p, q \neq \perp, p \sqsubseteq_{WS}^{\mathcal{S}} q$ exactly if $p \sqsubseteq_{WS}^{\mathcal{S}^\perp} q$. On $\mathcal{S}^\perp$, coupled simulation preorder and weak simulation preorder coincide, $\sqsubseteq_{WS}^{\mathcal{S}^\perp} = \sqsubseteq_{CS}^{\mathcal{S}^\perp}$, because $\perp$ is τ-reachable everywhere, and, for each p, $\perp \sqsubseteq_{CS}^{\mathcal{S}^\perp} p$ discharges the coupling constraint of coupled simulation.

Because $\sqsubseteq_{WS}^{\mathcal{S}}$ can be decided by deciding $\sqsubseteq_{CS}^{\mathcal{S}^\perp}$, a decision procedure for $\sqsubseteq_{CS}$ also induces a decision procedure for $\sqsubseteq_{WS}$. The transformation has linear time in terms of state space size $|S|$ and adds only one state to the problem size.

```
1  def fp_step_(S,Σ_τ,→)(R):
2      return  {(p, q) ∈ R |
3          (∀p', α. p →ᵅ p' ⟶ ∃q'. (p', q') ∈ R ∧ q ⇒ᵅ q')
4          ∧ (∃q'. q ⇒ q' ∧ (q', p) ∈ R)}
5  def fp_compute_cs(S = (S, Σ_τ, →)):
6      R := S × S
7      while fp_step_S(R) ≠ R:
8          |  R := fp_step_S(R)
9      return R
```

Algorithm 1: Fixed-point algorithm for the coupled simulation preorder.

3 Fixed-Point Algorithm for Coupled Similarity

The coinductive characterization of $\sqsubseteq_{CS}$ in Lemma 3 induces an extremely simple polynomial-time algorithm to compute the coupled simulation preorder as a *greatest fixed point*. This section introduces the algorithm and proves its correctness.

3.1 The Algorithm

Roughly speaking, the algorithm first considers the universal relation between states, $S \times S$, and then proceeds by removing every pair of states from the relation that would contradict the coupling or the simulation property. Its pseudo code is depicted in Algorithm 1.

fp_step plays the role of removing the tuples that would immediately violate the simulation or coupling property from the relation. Of course, such a pruning might invalidate tuples that were not rejected before. Therefore, fp_compute_cs repeats the process until $\text{fp\_step}_S(R) = R$, that is, until R is a fixed point of fp_step_S.

3.2 Correctness and Complexity

It is quite straight-forward to show that Algorithm 1 indeed computes $\sqsubseteq_{CS}$ because of the resemblance between fp_step and the coupled simulation property itself, and because of the monotonicity of fp_step.

Lemma 7. *If R is the greatest fixed point of* fp_step, *then $R = \sqsubseteq_{CS}$.*

On finite labeled transition systems, that is, with finite S and $→$, the while loop of fp_compute_cs is guaranteed to terminate at the greatest fixed point of fp_step (by a dual variant of the Kleene fixed-point theorem).

Lemma 8. *For finite S,* fp_compute_cs(S) *computes the greatest fixed point of* fp_step_S.

Theorem 2. *For finite* $\mathcal{S}$, fp_compute_cs$(\mathcal{S})$ *returns* $\sqsubseteq^{\mathcal{S}}_{CS}$.

We verified the proof using Isabelle/HOL. Due to its simplicity, we can trust implementations of Algorithm 1 to faithfully return sound and complete $\sqsubseteq_{CS}$-relations. Therefore, we use this algorithm to generate reliable results within test suites for the behavior of other $\sqsubseteq_{CS}$-implementations.

The space complexity, given by the maximal size of $\mathcal{R}$, clearly is in $\mathcal{O}(|S|^2)$. Time complexity takes some inspection of the algorithm. For our considerations, we assume that $\dot{\Rightarrow}$ has been pre-computed, which can slightly increase the space complexity to $\mathcal{O}(|\Sigma||S|^2)$.

Lemma 9. *The running time of* fp_compute_cs *is in* $\mathcal{O}(|\Sigma||S|^6)$.

Proof. Checking the simulation property for a tuple $(p, q) \in \mathcal{R}$ means that for all $\mathcal{O}(|\Sigma||S|)$ outgoing $p\overset{\cdot}{\rightarrow}$-transitions, each has to be matched by a $q\dot{\Rightarrow}$-transition with identical action, of which there are at most $|S|$. So, simulation checking costs $\mathcal{O}(|\Sigma||S|^2)$ time per tuple. Checking the coupling can be approximated by $\mathcal{O}(|S|)$ per tuple. Simulation dominates coupling. The amount of tuples that have to be checked is in $\mathcal{O}(|S|^2)$. Thus, the overall complexity of one invocation of fp_step is in $\mathcal{O}(|\Sigma||S|^4)$.

Because every invocation of fp_step decreases the size of $\mathcal{R}$ or leads to termination, there can be at most $\mathcal{O}(|S|^2)$ invocations of fp_step in fp_compute_cs. Checking whether fp_step changes $\mathcal{R}$ can be done without notable overhead. In conclusion, we arrive at an overall time complexity of $\mathcal{O}(|\Sigma||S|^6)$.

Now, it does not take much energy to spot that applying the filtering in fp_step to each and every tuple in $\mathcal{R}$ in every step, would not be necessary. Only after a tuple (p, q) has been removed from $\mathcal{R}$, the algorithm does really need to find out whether this was the last witness for the $\exists$-quantification in the clause of another tuple. While this observation could inspire various improvements, let us fast-forward to the game-theoretic approach in the next section, which elegantly explicates the witness structure of a coupled similarity problem.

4   Game Algorithm for Coupled Similarity

Checking whether two states are related by a (bi-)simulation preorder $\sqsubseteq_X$ can be seen as a *game* along the lines of coinductive characterizations [30]. One player, the *attacker*, challenges that $p \sqsubseteq_X q$, while the other player, the *defender*, has to name witnesses for the existential quantifications of the definition.

Based on the coinductive characterization from Lemma 3, we here define such a game for the coupled simulation preorder and transform it into an algorithm, which basically only amounts to a more clever way of computing the fixed point of the previous section. We show how this additional layer of abstraction enables optimizations.

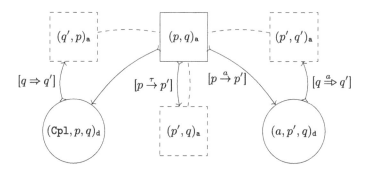

Fig. 5. Schematic coupled simulation game. Boxes stand for attacker nodes, circles for defender nodes, arrows for moves. From the dashed boxes, the moves are analogous to the ones of the solid box.

4.1   The Coupled Simulation Game

The *coupled simulation game* proceeds as follows: For $p \sqsubseteq_{CS} q$, the attacker may question that simulation holds by selecting p' and $a \in \Sigma$ with $p \xrightarrow{a} p'$. The defender then has to name a q' with $q \xRightarrow{a} q'$, whereupon the attacker may go on to challenge $p' \sqsubseteq_{CS} q'$. If $p \xrightarrow{\tau} p'$, the attacker can directly skip to question $p' \sqsubseteq_{CS} q$. For coupled simulation, the attacker may moreover demand the defender to name a coupling witness q' with $q \Rightarrow q'$ whereafter $q' \sqsubseteq_{CS} p$ stands to question. If the defender runs out of answers, they lose; if the game continues forever, they win. This can be modeled by a simple game, whose schema is given in Fig. 5, as follows.

Definition 6 (Games). *A simple game* $\mathcal{G}[p_0] = (G, G_d, \rightarrowtail, p_0)$ *consists of*

- *a (countable) set of* game positions G,
  - *partitioned into a set of* defender positions $G_d \subseteq G$
  - *and* attacker positions $G_a := G \setminus G_d$,
- *a graph of* game moves $\rightarrowtail \subseteq G \times G$, *and*
- *an* initial position $p_0 \in G$.

Definition 7 ($\sqsubseteq_{CS}$ game). *For a transition system* $\mathcal{S} = (S, \Sigma_\tau, \rightarrow)$, *the coupled simulation game* $\mathcal{G}^{\mathcal{S}}_{CS}[p_0] = (G, G_d, \rightarrowtail, p_0)$ *consists of*

- attacker nodes $(p, q)_a \in G_a$ *with* $p, q \in S$,
- simulation defender nodes $(a, p, q)_d \in G_d$ *for situations where a simulation challenge for* $a \in \Sigma$ *has been formulated, and*
- coupling defender nodes $(\mathtt{Cpl}, p, q)_d \in G_d$ *when coupling is challenged,*

and five kinds of moves

- simulation challenges $(p, q)_a \rightarrowtail (a, p', q)_d$ *if* $p \xrightarrow{a} p'$ *with* $a \neq \tau$,
- simulation internal moves $(p, q)_a \rightarrowtail (p', q)_a$ *if* $p \xrightarrow{\tau} p'$,

- simulation answers $(a, p', q)_{\mathsf{d}} \rightarrowtail (p', q')_{\mathsf{a}}$ if $q \overset{a}{\Rightarrow} q'$,
- coupling challenges $(p, q)_{\mathsf{a}} \rightarrowtail (\mathtt{Cpl}, p, q)_{\mathsf{d}}$,   and
- coupling answers $(\mathtt{Cpl}, p, q)_{\mathsf{d}} \rightarrowtail (q', p)_{\mathsf{a}}$ if $q \Rightarrow q'$.

Definition 8 (Plays and wins). *We call the paths $p_0 p_1 ... \in G^{\infty}$ with $p_i \rightarrowtail p_{i+1}$ plays of $\mathcal{G}[p_0]$. The defender wins all infinite plays. If a finite play $p_0 \ldots p_n$ is stuck, that is, if $p_n \nrightarrow$, then the stuck player loses: The defender wins if $p_n \in G_a$, and the attacker wins if $p_n \in G_d$.*

Definition 9 (Strategies and winning strategies). *A defender strategy is a (usually partial) mapping from initial play fragments to next moves $f \subseteq \{(p_0 ... p_n, p') \mid p_n \in G_d \wedge p_n \rightarrowtail p'\}$. A play p follows a strategy f iff, for each move $p_i \rightarrowtail p_{i+1}$ with $p_i \in G_d$, $p_{i+1} = f(p_0 ... p_i)$. If every such play is won by the defender, f is a winning strategy for the defender. The player with a winning strategy for $\mathcal{G}[p_0]$ is said to win $\mathcal{G}[p_0]$.*

Definition 10 (Winning regions and determinacy). *The winning region W_σ of player $\sigma \in \{a, d\}$ for a game $\mathcal{G}$ is the set of states p_0 from which player σ wins $\mathcal{G}[p_0]$.*

Let us now see that the defender's winning region of $\mathcal{G}^{\mathcal{S}}_{CS}$ indeed corresponds to $\sqsubseteq^{\mathcal{S}}_{CS}$. To this end, we first show how to construct winning strategies for the defender from a coupled simulation, and then establish the opposite direction.

Lemma 10. *Let $\mathcal{R}$ be a coupled delay simulation and $(p_0, q_0) \in \mathcal{R}$. Then the defender wins $\mathcal{G}^{\mathcal{S}}_{CS}[(p_0, q_0)_{\mathsf{a}}]$ with the following positional strategy:*

- *If the current play fragment ends in a simulation defender node $(a, p', q)_{\mathsf{d}}$, move to some attacker node $(p', q')_{\mathsf{a}}$ with $(p', q') \in \mathcal{R}$ and $q \overset{a}{\Rightarrow} q'$;*
- *if the current play fragment ends in a coupling defender node $(\mathtt{Cpl}, p, q)_{\mathsf{d}}$, move to some attacker node $(q', p)_{\mathsf{a}}$ with $(q', p) \in \mathcal{R}$ and $q \Rightarrow q'$.*

Lemma 11. *Let f be a winning strategy for the defender in $\mathcal{G}^{\mathcal{S}}_{CS}[(p_0, q_0)_{\mathsf{a}}]$. Then $\{(p, q) \mid \text{ some } \mathcal{G}^{\mathcal{S}}_{CS}[(p_0, q_0)_{\mathsf{a}}]\text{-play fragment consistent with } f \text{ ends in } (p, q)_{\mathsf{a}}\}$ is a coupled delay simulation.*

Theorem 3. *The defender wins $\mathcal{G}^{\mathcal{S}}_{CS}[(p, q)_{\mathsf{a}}]$ precisely if $p \sqsubseteq_{CS} q$.*

4.2 Deciding the Coupled Simulation Game

It is well-known that the winning regions of finite simple games can be computed in linear time. Variants of the standard algorithm for this task can be found in [12] and in our implementation [1]. Intuitively, the algorithm first assumes that the defender wins everywhere and then sets off a chain reaction beginning in defender deadlock nodes, which "turns" all the nodes won by the attacker. The algorithm runs in linear time of the game moves because every node can only turn once.

```
1 def game_compute_cs(S):
2     G^S_CS = (G, G_a, ↦) := obtain_cs_game(S)
3     win := compute_winning_region(G^S_CS)
4     R := {(p, q) | (p, q)_a ∈ G_a ∧ win[(p, q)_a] = d}
5     return R
```

Algorithm 2: Game algorithm for the coupled simulation preorder $\sqsubseteq_{CS}$.

With such a winning region algorithm for simple games, referred to as compute_winning_region in the following, it is only a matter of a few lines to determine the coupled simulation preorder for a system S as shown in game_compute_cs in Algorithm 2. One starts by constructing the corresponding game G^S_{CS} using a function obtain_cs_game, we consider given by Definition 7. Then, one calls compute_winning_region and collects the attacker nodes won by the defender for the result.

Theorem 4. *For a finite labeled transition systems* S, game_compute_cs(S) *from Algorithm 2 returns* $\sqsubseteq^S_{CS}$.

Proof. Theorem 3 states that the defender wins $G^S_{CS}[(p, q)_a]$ exactly if $p \sqsubseteq^S_{CS} q$. As compute_winning_region(G^S_{CS}), according to [12], returns where the defender wins, line 4 of Algorithm 2 precisely assigns $R = \sqsubseteq^S_{CS}$. □

The complexity arguments from [12] yield linear complexity for deciding the game by compute_winning_region.

Proposition 1. *For a game* $G = (G, G_a, ↦)$, compute_winning_region *runs in* $O(|G| + |↦|)$ *time and space.*

In order to tell the overall complexity of the resulting algorithm, we have to look at the size of G^S_{CS} depending on the size of S.

Lemma 12. *Consider the coupled simulation game* $G^S_{CS} = (G, G_a, ↦)$ *for varying* $S = (S, \Sigma_\tau, →)$. *The growth of the game size* $|G| + |↦|$ *is in* $O(|\overset{.}{\Rightarrow}| |S|)$.

Proof. Let us reexamine Definition 7. There are $|S|^2$ attacker nodes. Collectively, they can formulate $O(|\overset{.}{→}| |S|)$ simulation challenges including internal moves and $|S|^2$ coupling challenges. There are $O(|\overset{.}{\Rightarrow}| |S|)$ simulation answers and $O(|\Rightarrow| |S|)$ coupling answers. Of these, $O(|\overset{.}{\Rightarrow}| |S|)$ dominates the others. □

Lemma 13. game_compute_cs *runs in* $O(|\overset{.}{\Rightarrow}| |S|)$ *time and space.*

Proof. Proposition 1 and Lemma 12 already yield that line 3 is in $O(|\overset{.}{\Rightarrow}| |S|)$ time and space. Definition 7 is completely straight-forward, so the complexity of building G^S_{CS} in line 2 equals its output size $O(|\overset{.}{\Rightarrow}| |S|)$, which coincides with the complexity of computing $\overset{.}{\Rightarrow}$. The filtering in line 4 is in $O(|S|^2)$ (upper bound for attacker nodes) and thus does not influence the overall complexity. □

4.3   Tackling the τ-closure

We have mentioned that there can be some complexity to computing the τ-closure $\Rightarrow = \xrightarrow{\tau}{}^{*}$ and the derived $\xRightarrow{}$. In theory, both the weak delay transition relation $\xRightarrow{}$ and the conventional transition relation $\rightarrow$ are bounded in size by $|\Sigma_\tau|\,|S|^2$. But for most transition systems, the weak step relations tend to be much bigger in size. Sparse $\rightarrow$-graphs can generate dense $\xRightarrow{}$-graphs. The computation of the transitive closure also has significant time complexity. Algorithms for transitive closures usually are cubic, even though the theoretical bound is a little lower.

There has been a trend to skip the construction of the transitive closure in the computation of weak forms of bisimulation [3,13,19,26]. With the game approach, we can follow this trend. The transitivity of the game can emulate the transitivity of $\xRightarrow{}$ (for details see [1, Sec. 4.5.4]). With this trick, the game size, and thus time and space complexity, reduces to $\mathcal{O}(|\Sigma_\tau|\,|\xrightarrow{\tau}|\,|S|+|\rightarrow|\,|S|)$. Though this is practically better than the bound from Lemma 13, both results amount to cubic complexity $\mathcal{O}(|\Sigma|\,|S|^3)$, which is in line with the reduction result from Theorem 1 and the time complexity of existing similarity algorithms.

4.4   Optimizing the Game Algorithm

The game can be downsized tremendously once we take additional over- and under-approximation information into account.

Definition 11. *An* over-approximation *of $\sqsubseteq_{CS}$ is a relation $\mathcal{R}_O$ of that we know that $\sqsubseteq_{CS} \subseteq \mathcal{R}_O$. Conversely, an* under-approximation *of $\sqsubseteq_{CS}$ is a relation $\mathcal{R}_U$ where $\mathcal{R}_U \subseteq \sqsubseteq_{CS}$.*

Regarding the game, over-approximations tell us where the defender *can* win, and under-approximations tell us where the attacker is doomed to lose. They can be used to eliminate "boring" parts of the game. Given an over-approximation $\mathcal{R}_O$, when unfolding the game, it only makes sense to add moves from defender nodes to attacker nodes $(p, q)_a$ if $(p, q) \in \mathcal{R}_O$. There just is no need to allow the defender moves we already know cannot be winning for them. Given an under-approximation $\mathcal{R}_U$, we can ignore all the outgoing moves of $(p, q)_a$ if $(p, q) \in \mathcal{R}_U$. Without moves, $(p, q)_a$ is sure to be won by the defender, which is in line with the claim of the approximation.

Corollary 2. $\Rightarrow^{-1}$ *is an under-approximation of $\sqsubseteq_{CS}$. (Cf. Lemma 4)*

Lemma 14. $\{(p, q)\,|$ *all actions weakly enabled in p are weakly enabled in $q\}$ is an over-approximation of $\sqsubseteq_{CS}$.*

The fact that coupled simulation is "almost bisimulation" on steps to stable states in finite systems (Lemma 6) can be used for a comparably cheap and precise over-approximation. The idea is to compute strong bisimilarity for the system $\mathcal{S}_{\xRightarrow{}|} = (S, \Sigma_\tau, \xRightarrow{}|)$, where *maximal weak steps*, $p \xRightarrow{\alpha}| p'$, exist iff $p \xRightarrow{\hat{\alpha}} p'$ and p' is stable, that is, $p' \xrightarrow{\tau}\!\!\!\!/\,$. Let $\equiv_{\xRightarrow{}|}$ be the biggest symmetric relation where $p \equiv_{\xRightarrow{}|} q$ and $p \xRightarrow{\alpha}| p'$ implies there is q' such that $p' \equiv_{\xRightarrow{}|} q'$ and $q \xRightarrow{\alpha}| q'$.

Lemma 15. $\mathcal{R}_{\Rightarrow|} = \{(p,q) \mid \forall p'. p \overset{\alpha}{\Rightarrow}| p' \longrightarrow q \overset{\alpha}{\Rightarrow}| \equiv_{\Rightarrow|} p'\}$ *is an over-approximation of* $\sqsubseteq_{CS}$ *on finite systems.*

Computing $\equiv_{\Rightarrow|}$ can be expected to be cheaper than computing weak bisimilarity $\equiv_{WB}$. After all, $\Rightarrow|$ is just a subset of $\overset{\cdot}{\Rightarrow}$. However, filtering $S \times S$ using subset checks to create $\mathcal{R}_{\Rightarrow|}$ might well be *quartic*, $\mathcal{O}(|S|^4)$, or worse. Nevertheless, one can argue that with a reasonable algorithm design and for many real-world examples, $\overset{\alpha}{\Rightarrow}|\equiv_{\Rightarrow|}$ will be sufficiently bounded in branching degree, in order for the over-approximation to do more good than harm.

For everyday system designs, $\mathcal{R}_{\Rightarrow|}$ is a tight approximation of $\sqsubseteq_{CS}$. On the philosopher system from Example 1, they even coincide. In some situations, $\mathcal{R}_{\Rightarrow|}$ degenerates to the shared enabledness relation (Lemma 14), which is to say it becomes comparably useless. One example for this are the systems created by the reduction from weak simulation to coupled simulation in Theorem 1 after τ-cycle removal. There, all $\Rightarrow|$-steps are bound to end in the same one τ-sink state $\bot$.

5   A Scalable Implementation

The experimental results by Ranzato and Tapparo [27] suggest that their simulation algorithm and the algorithm by Henzinger, Henzinger, and Kopke [15] only work on comparably small systems. The necessary data structures quickly consume gigabytes of RAM. So, the bothering question is not so much whether some highly optimized C++-implementation can do the job in milliseconds for small problems, but how to implement the algorithm such that large-scale systems are feasible at all.

To give first answers, we implemented a scalable and distributable prototype of the coupled simulation game algorithm using the stream processing framework *Apache Flink* [4] and its *Gelly* graph API, which enable computations on large data sets built around a universal data-flow engine. Our implementation can be found on https://coupledsim.bbisping.de/code/flink/.

5.1   Prototype Implementation

We base our implementation on the game algorithm and optimizations from Sect. 4. The implementation is a vertical prototype in the sense that every feature to get from a transition system to its coupled simulation preorder is present, but there is no big variety of options in the process. The phases are:

Import Reads a CSV representation of the transition system $\mathcal{S}$.

Minimize Computes an equivalence relation under-approximating $\equiv_{CS}$ on the transition system and builds a quotient system $\mathcal{S}_M$. This stage should at least compress τ-cycles if there are any. The default minimization uses a parallelized signature refinement algorithm [20,33] to compute delay bisimilarity ($\equiv_{DB}^{\mathcal{S}}$).

Table 1. Sample systems, sizes, and benchmark results.

system	S	$\stackrel{\cdot}{\rightarrow}$	$\Rightarrow S_{/\equiv_{DB}}$		$\rightarrowtail$	$\rightarrowtail_\sigma \cdot\ S_{/\equiv_{CS}}$		$\sqsubseteq_{CS}^{S_{/\equiv_{CS}}}$	time/s
phil	10	14	86	6	234	201	5	11	5.1
ltbts	88	98	2,599	27	4,100	399	25	38	5.5
vasy_0_1	289	1,224	52,641	9	543	67	9	9	5.7
vasy_1_4	1,183	4,464	637,585	4	73	30	4	4	5.3
vasy_5_9	5,486	9,676	1,335,325	112	63,534	808	112	112	6.0
cwi_1_2	1,952	2,387	593,734	67	29,049	1,559	67	137	6.9
cwi_3_14	3,996	14,552	15,964,021	2	15	10	2	2	7.8
vasy_8_24	8,879	24,411	2,615,500	170	225,555	3,199	169	232	6.7
vasy_8_38	8,921	38,424	46,232,423	193	297,643	2,163	193	193	6.7
vasy_10_56	10,849	56,156	842,087	2,112	o.o.m.	72,617	2,112	3,932	13.8
vasy_25_25	25,217	25,216	50,433	25,217	o.o.m.	126,083	25,217	25,217	117.4

Compute over-approximation Determines an equivalence relation over-approximating $\equiv_{CS}^{S_M}$. The result is a mapping σ from states to *signatures* (sets of colors) such that $p \sqsubseteq_{CS}^{S_M} q$ implies $\sigma(p) \subseteq \sigma(q)$. The prototype uses the maximal weak step equivalence $\equiv_{\Rightarrow\!\mid}$ from Subsect. 4.4.

Build game graph Constructs the τ-closure-free coupled simulation game $\mathcal{G}_{CS}^{S_M}$ for S_M with attacker states restricted according to the over-approximation signatures σ.

Compute winning regions Decides for $\mathcal{G}_{CS}^{S_M}$ where the attacker has a winning strategy following the scatter-gather scheme [16]. If a game node is discovered to be won by the attacker, it *scatters* the information to its predecessors. Every game node *gathers* information on its winning successors. Defender nodes count down their degrees of freedom starting at their game move outdegrees.

Output Finally, the results can be output or checked for soundness. The winning regions directly imply $\sqsubseteq_{CS}^{S_M}$. The output can be de-minimized to refer to the original system S.

5.2 Evaluation

Experimental evaluation shows that the approach can cope with the smaller examples of the "Very Large Transition Systems (VLTS) Benchmark Suite" [6] (vasy_* and cwi_* up to 50,000 transitions). On small examples, we also tested that the output matches the return values of the verified fixed-point $\sqsubseteq_{CS}$-algorithm from Sect. 3. These samples include, among others, the philosopher system phil containing P_g and P_o from Example 1 and ltbts, which consists of the finitary separating examples from the linear-time branching-time spectrum [9, p. 73].

Table 1 summarizes the results for some of our test systems with pre-minimization by delay bisimilarity and over-approximation by maximal weak step equivalence. The first two value columns give the system sizes in number of states

S and transitions $\xrightarrow{\cdot}$. The next two columns present derived properties, namely an upper estimate of the size of the (weak) delay step relation $\Rightarrow$, and the number of partitions with respect to delay bisimulation $S_{/\equiv_{DB}}$. The next columns list the sizes of the game graphs without and with maximal weak step over-approximation ($\rightarrowtail$ and $\rightarrowtail_\sigma$, some tests without the over-approximation trick ran out of memory, "o.o.m."). The following columns enumerate the sizes of the resulting coupled simulation preorders represented by the partition relation pair $(S_{/\equiv_{CS}}, \sqsubseteq_{CS}^{S_{/\equiv_{CS}}})$, where $S_{/\equiv_{CS}}$ is the partitioning of S with respect to coupled similarity $\equiv_{CS}$, and $\sqsubseteq_{CS}^{S_{/\equiv_{CS}}}$ the coupled simulation preorder projected to this quotient. The last column reports the running time of the programs on an Intel i7-8550U CPU with four threads and 2 GB Java Virtual Machine heap space.

The systems in Table 1 are a superset of the VLTS systems for which Ranzato and Tapparo [27] report their algorithm SA to terminate. Regarding complexity, SA is the best simulation algorithm known. In the [27]-experiments, the C++ implementation ran out of 2 GB RAM for vasy_10_56 and vasy_25_25 but finished much faster than our setup for most smaller examples. Their time advantage on small systems comes as no surprise as the start-up of the whole Apache Flink pipeline induces heavy overhead costs of about 5 s even for tiny examples like phil. However, on bigger examples such as vasy_18_73 their and our implementation both fail. This is in stark contrast to bi-simulation implementations, which usually cope with much larger systems single-handedly [3,19].

Interestingly, for all tested VLTS systems, the weak bisimilarity quotient system $S_{/\equiv_{WB}}$ equals $S_{/\equiv_{CS}}$ (and, with the exception of vasy_8_24, $S_{/\equiv_{DB}}$). The preorder $\sqsubseteq_{CS}^{S_{/\equiv_{CS}}}$ also matches the identity in 6 of 9 examples. This observation about the effective closeness of coupled similarity and weak bisimilarity is two-fold. On the one hand, it brings into question how meaningful coupled similarity is for minimization. After all, it takes a lot of space and time to come up with the output that the cheaper delay bisimilarity already minimized everything that could be minimized. On the other hand, the observation suggests that the considered VLTS samples are based around models that do not need—or maybe even do avoid—the expressive power of weak bisimilarity. This is further evidence for the case from the introduction that coupled similarity has a more sensible level of precision than weak bisimilarity.

6   Conclusion

The core of this paper has been to present a game-based algorithm to compute coupled similarity in cubic time and space. To this end, we have formalized coupled similarity in Isabelle/HOL and merged two previous approaches to defining coupled similarity, namely using single relations with weak symmetry [10] and the relation-pair-based coupled delay simulation from [28], which followed the older tradition of two weak simulations [24,29]. Our characterization seems to be the most convenient. We used the entailed coinductive characterization to devise a game characterization and an algorithm. Although we could show that deciding coupled similarity is as hard as deciding weak similarity, our Apache Flink implementation is able to exploit the closeness between coupled similarity and weak bisimilarity to at least handle slightly bigger systems than comparable similarity algorithms. Through the application to the VLTS suite, we have established that coupled similarity and weak bisimilarity match for the considered systems. This points back to a line of thought [11] that, for many applications, branching, delay and weak bisimilarity will coincide with coupled similarity. Where they do not, usually coupled similarity or a coarser notion of equivalence is called for. To gain deeper insights in that direction, real-world case studies—and maybe an embedding into existing tool landscapes like FDR [8], CADP [7], or LTSmin [17]—would be necessary.

References

1. Bisping, B.: Computing coupled similarity. Master's thesis, Technische Universität Berlin (2018). https://coupledsim.bbisping.de/bisping_computingCoupledSimilarity_thesis.pdf
2. Bisping, B.: Isabelle/HOL proof and Apache Flink program for TACAS 2019 paper: Computing Coupled Similarity (artifact). Figshare (2019). https://doi.org/10.6084/m9.figshare.7831382.v1
3. Boulgakov, A., Gibson-Robinson, T., Roscoe, A.W.: Computing maximal weak and other bisimulations. Formal Aspects Comput. **28**(3), 381–407 (2016). https://doi.org/10.1007/s00165-016-0366-2
4. Carbone, P., Katsifodimos, A., Ewen, S., Markl, V., Haridi, S., Tzoumas, K.: Apache Flink: stream and batch processing in a single engine. In: Bulletin of the IEEE Computer Society Technical Committee on Data Engineering, vol. 36, no. 4 (2015)
5. Derrick, J., Wehrheim, H.: Using coupled simulations in non-atomic refinement. In: Bert, D., Bowen, J.P., King, S., Waldén, M. (eds.) ZB 2003. LNCS, vol. 2651, pp. 127–147. Springer, Heidelberg (2003). https://doi.org/10.1007/3-540-44880-2_10
6. Garavel, H.: The VLTS benchmark suite (2017). https://doi.org/10.18709/perscido.2017.11.ds100. Jointly created by CWI/SEN2 and INRIA/VASY as a CADP resource
7. Garavel, H., Lang, F., Mateescu, R., Serwe, W.: CADP 2011: a toolbox for the construction and analysis of distributed processes. Int. J. Softw. Tools Technol. Transfer **15**(2), 89–107 (2013). https://doi.org/10.1007/s10009-012-0244-z
8. Gibson-Robinson, T., Armstrong, P., Boulgakov, A., Roscoe, A.W.: FDR3 — a modern refinement checker for CSP. In: Ábrahám, E., Havelund, K. (eds.) TACAS 2014. LNCS, vol. 8413, pp. 187–201. Springer, Heidelberg (2014). https://doi.org/10.1007/978-3-642-54862-8_13
9. van Glabbeek, R.J.: The linear time — branching time spectrum II. In: Best, E. (ed.) CONCUR 1993. LNCS, vol. 715, pp. 66–81. Springer, Heidelberg (1993). https://doi.org/10.1007/3-540-57208-2_6
10. van Glabbeek, R.J.: A branching time model of CSP. In: Gibson-Robinson, T., Hopcroft, P., Lazić, R. (eds.) Concurrency, Security, and Puzzles. LNCS, vol. 10160, pp. 272–293. Springer, Cham (2017). https://doi.org/10.1007/978-3-319-51046-0_14

11. van Glabbeek, R.J., Weijland, W.P.: Branching time and abstraction in bisimulation semantics. J. ACM (JACM) **43**(3), 555–600 (1996). https://doi.org/10.1145/233551.233556
12. Grädel, E.: Finite model theory and descriptive complexity. In: Grädel, E., et al. (eds.) Finite Model Theory and Its Applications. Texts in Theoretical Computer Science an EATCS Series, pp. 125–130. Springer, Heidelberg (2007). https://doi.org/10.1007/3-540-68804-8_3
13. Groote, J.F., Jansen, D.N., Keiren, J.J.A., Wijs, A.J.: An $\mathcal{O}(m \log n)$ algorithm for computing stuttering equivalence and branching bisimulation. ACM Trans. Comput. Logic (TOCL) **18**(2), 13:1–13:34 (2017). https://doi.org/10.1145/3060140
14. Hatzel, M., Wagner, C., Peters, K., Nestmann, U.: Encoding CSP into CCS. In: Proceedings of the Combined 22th International Workshop on Expressiveness in Concurrency and 12th Workshop on Structural Operational Semantics, and 12th Workshop on Structural Operational Semantics, EXPRESS/SOS, pp. 61–75 (2015). https://doi.org/10.4204/EPTCS.190.5
15. Henzinger, M.R., Henzinger, T.A., Kopke, P.W.: Computing simulations on finite and infinite graphs. In: 36th Annual Symposium on Foundations of Computer Science, Milwaukee, Wisconsin, pp. 453–462 (1995). https://doi.org/10.1109/SFCS.1995.492576
16. Kalavri, V., Vlassov, V., Haridi, S.: High-level programming abstractions for distributed graph processing. IEEE Trans. Knowl. Data Eng. **30**(2), 305–324 (2018). https://doi.org/10.1109/TKDE.2017.2762294
17. Kant, G., Laarman, A., Meijer, J., van de Pol, J., Blom, S., van Dijk, T.: LTSmin: high-performance language-independent model checking. In: Baier, C., Tinelli, C. (eds.) TACAS 2015. LNCS, vol. 9035, pp. 692–707. Springer, Heidelberg (2015). https://doi.org/10.1007/978-3-662-46681-0_61
18. Kučera, A., Mayr, R.: Why is simulation harder than bisimulation? In: Brim, L., Křetínský, M., Kučera, A., Jančar, P. (eds.) CONCUR 2002. LNCS, vol. 2421, pp. 594–609. Springer, Heidelberg (2002). https://doi.org/10.1007/3-540-45694-5_39
19. Li, W.: Algorithms for computing weak bisimulation equivalence. In: Third IEEE International Symposium on Theoretical Aspects of Software Engineering, 2009. TASE 2009, pp. 241–248. IEEE (2009). https://doi.org/10.1109/TASE.2009.47
20. Luo, Y., de Lange, Y., Fletcher, G.H.L., De Bra, P., Hidders, J., Wu, Y.: Bisimulation reduction of big graphs on MapReduce. In: Gottlob, G., Grasso, G., Olteanu, D., Schallhart, C. (eds.) BNCOD 2013. LNCS, vol. 7968, pp. 189–203. Springer, Heidelberg (2013). https://doi.org/10.1007/978-3-642-39467-6_18
21. Milner, R.: Communication and Concurrency. Prentice-Hall Inc., Upper Saddle River (1989)
22. Nestmann, U., Pierce, B.C.: Decoding choice encodings. Inf. Comput. **163**(1), 1–59 (2000). https://doi.org/10.1006/inco.2000.2868
23. Parrow, J., Sjödin, P.: Multiway synchronization verified with coupled simulation. In: Cleaveland, W.R. (ed.) CONCUR 1992. LNCS, vol. 630, pp. 518–533. Springer, Heidelberg (1992). https://doi.org/10.1007/BFb0084813
24. Parrow, J., Sjödin, P.: The complete axiomatization of Cs-congruence. In: Enjalbert, P., Mayr, E.W., Wagner, K.W. (eds.) STACS 1994. LNCS, vol. 775, pp. 555–568. Springer, Heidelberg (1994). https://doi.org/10.1007/3-540-57785-8_171
25. Peters, K., van Glabbeek, R.J.: Analysing and comparing encodability criteria. In: Proceedings of the Combined 22th International Workshop on Expressiveness in Concurrency and 12th Workshop on Structural Operational Semantics, EXPRESS/SOS, pp. 46–60 (2015). https://doi.org/10.4204/EPTCS.190.4

26. Ranzato, F., Tapparo, F.: Generalizing the Paige-Tarjan algorithm by abstract interpretation. Inf. Comput. **206**(5), 620–651 (2008). https://doi.org/10.1016/j.ic.2008.01.001. Special Issue: The 17th International Conference on Concurrency Theory (CONCUR 2006)
27. Ranzato, F., Tapparo, F.: An efficient simulation algorithm based on abstract interpretation. Inf. Comput. **208**(1), 1–22 (2010). https://doi.org/10.1016/j.ic.2009.06.002
28. Rensink, A.: Action contraction. In: Palamidessi, C. (ed.) CONCUR 2000. LNCS, vol. 1877, pp. 290–305. Springer, Heidelberg (2000). https://doi.org/10.1007/3-540-44618-4_22
29. Sangiorgi, D.: Introduction to Bisimulation and Coinduction. Cambridge University Press, New York (2012). https://doi.org/10.1017/CBO9780511777110
30. Stirling, C.: Modal and Temporal Properties of Processes. Springer, New York (2001). https://doi.org/10.1007/978-1-4757-3550-5
31. Voorhoeve, M., Mauw, S.: Impossible futures and determinism. Inf. Process. Lett. **80**(1), 51–58 (2001). https://doi.org/10.1016/S0020-0190(01)00217-4
32. Wenzel, M.: The Isabelle/Isar Reference Manual (2018). https://isabelle.in.tum.de/dist/Isabelle2018/doc/isar-ref.pdf
33. Wimmer, R., Herbstritt, M., Hermanns, H., Strampp, K., Becker, B.: SIGREF – a symbolic bisimulation tool box. In: Graf, S., Zhang, W. (eds.) ATVA 2006. LNCS, vol. 4218, pp. 477–492. Springer, Heidelberg (2006). https://doi.org/10.1007/11901914_35

Reachability Analysis for Termination and Confluence of Rewriting

Christian Sternagel[1]([⊠]) [iD] and Akihisa Yamada[2]([⊠]) [iD]

[1] University of Innsbruck, Innsbruck, Austria
`christian.sternagel@uibk.ac.at`
[2] National Institute of Informatics, Tokyo, Japan
`akihisayamada@nii.ac.jp`

Abstract. In term rewriting, reachability analysis is concerned with the problem of deciding whether or not one term is reachable from another by rewriting. Reachability analysis has several applications in termination and confluence analysis of rewrite systems. We give a unified view on reachability analysis for rewriting with and without conditions by means of what we call reachability constraints. Moreover, we provide several techniques that fit into this general framework and can be efficiently implemented. Our experiments show that these techniques increase the power of existing termination and confluence tools.

Keywords: Reachability analysis · Termination · Confluence · Conditional term rewriting · Infeasibility

1 Introduction

Reachability analysis for term rewriting [6] is concerned with the problem of, given a rewrite system $\mathcal{R}$, a source term s and a target term t, deciding whether the source reduces to the target by rewriting, which is usually written $s \to_{\mathcal{R}}^* t$. A useful generalization of this problem is the (un)satisfiability of the following reachability problem: given terms s and t containing variables, decide whether there is a substitution σ such that $s\sigma \to_{\mathcal{R}}^* t\sigma$ or not. This problem, also called (in)feasibility by Lucas and Guitiérrez [11], has various applications in termination and confluence analysis for plain and conditional rewriting.

This can be understood as a form of safety analysis, as illustrated below.

Example 1. Let $\mathcal{R}$ be a term rewrite system consisting of the following rules for division (where s stands for "successor"):

$$x - 0 \to x \qquad \mathsf{s}(x) - \mathsf{s}(y) \to x - y \qquad 0 \div \mathsf{s}(y) \to 0$$
$$\mathsf{s}(x) \div \mathsf{s}(y) \to \mathsf{s}((x-y) \div \mathsf{s}(y)) \qquad x \div 0 \to \mathsf{err}(\texttt{"division by zero"})$$

The question "Can division yield an error?" is naturally formulated as the satisfiability of reachability from $x \div y$ to $\mathsf{err}(z)$. Unsurprisingly, the solution

T. Vojnar and L. Zhang (Eds.): TACAS 2019, Part I, LNCS 11427, pp. 262–278, 2019.
https://doi.org/10.1007/978-3-030-17462-0_15

$$\sigma = [y \mapsto 0, z \mapsto \texttt{"division by zero"}]$$

shows that it is actually possible to obtain an error.

In termination analysis we are typically interested in unsatisfiability of reachability and can thereby rule out certain recursive calls as potential source of non-termination. For confluence analysis of conditional term rewriting, infeasibility is crucial: some other techniques do not apply before critical pairs are shown infeasible, and removal of infeasible rules simplifies proofs.

In this work we provide a formal framework that allows us to uniformly speak about (un)satisfiability of reachability for plain and conditional rewriting, and give several techniques that are useful in practice.

More specifically, our contributions are as follows:

- We introduce the syntax and semantics of *reachability constraints* (Sect. 3) and formulate their satisfiability problem. We recast several concrete techniques for reachability analysis in the resulting framework.
- We present a new, simple, and efficient technique for reachability analysis based on what we call the *symbol transition graph* of a rewrite system (Sect. 4.1) and extend it to conditional rewriting (Sect. 5.2).
- Additionally, we generalize the prevalent existing technique for term rewriting to what we call *look-ahead reachability* (Sect. 4.2) and extend it to the conditional case (Sect. 5.3).
- Then, we present a new result for conditional rewriting that is useful for proving conditional rules infeasible (Sect. 5.1).
- Finally, we evaluate the impact of our work on existing automated tools NaTT [16] and ConCon [13] (Sect. 6).

2 Preliminaries

In the remainder, we assume some familiarity with term rewriting. Nevertheless, we recall required concepts and notations below. For further details on term rewriting, we refer to standard textbooks [3,14].

Throughout the paper $\mathcal{F}$ denotes a set of function symbols with associated arities, and $\mathcal{V}$ a countably infinite set of variables (so that fresh variables can always be picked) such that $\mathcal{F} \cap \mathcal{V} = \varnothing$. A *term* is either a variable $x \in \mathcal{V}$ or of the form $f(t_1, \ldots, t_n)$, where n is the arity of $f \in \mathcal{F}$ and the arguments $t_1, \ldots, t_n$ are terms. The set of all terms over $\mathcal{F}$ and $\mathcal{V}$ is denoted by $\mathcal{T}(\mathcal{F}, \mathcal{V})$. The set of variables occurring in a term t is denoted by $\mathsf{Var}(t)$. The *root symbol* of a term $t = f(t_1, \ldots, t_n)$ is f and denoted by $\mathsf{root}(t)$. When we want to indicate that a term is not a variable, we sometimes write $f(\ldots)$, where "..." denotes an arbitrary list of terms.

A *substitution* is a mapping $\sigma : \mathcal{V} \to \mathcal{T}(\mathcal{F}, \mathcal{V})$. Given a term t, $t\sigma$ denotes the term obtained by replacing every occurrence of variable x in t by $\sigma(x)$. The *domain* of a substitution σ is $\mathsf{Dom}(\sigma) := \{x \in \mathcal{V} \mid x\sigma \neq x\}$, and σ is *idempotent* if $\mathsf{Var}(x\sigma) \cap \mathsf{Dom}(\sigma) = \varnothing$ for every $x \in \mathcal{V}$. A *renaming* is a bijection $\alpha : \mathcal{V} \to \mathcal{V}$.

Two terms s and t are *unifiable* if $s\sigma = t\sigma$ for some substitution σ, which is called a *unifier* of s and t.

A *context* is a term with exactly one occurrence of the special symbol $\square$. We write $C[t]$ for the term resulting from replacing $\square$ in context C by term t.

A *rewrite rule* is a pair of terms, written $l \to r$, such that the *variable conditions* $l \notin \mathcal{V}$ and $\mathsf{Var}(l) \supseteq \mathsf{Var}(r)$ hold. By a *variant* of a rewrite rule we mean a rule that is obtained by consistently renaming variables in the original rule to fresh ones. A *term rewrite system (TRS)* is a set $\mathcal{R}$ of rewrite rules. A function symbol $f \in \mathcal{F}$ is *defined* in $\mathcal{R}$ if $f(...) \to r \in \mathcal{R}$, and the set of defined symbols in $\mathcal{R}$ is $\mathcal{D}_{\mathcal{R}} := \{f \mid f(...) \to r \in \mathcal{R}\}$. We call $f \in \mathcal{F} \setminus \mathcal{D}_{\mathcal{R}}$ a *constructor*.

There is an *$\mathcal{R}$-rewrite step* from s to t, written $s \to_{\mathcal{R}} t$, iff there exist a context C, a substitution σ, and a rule $l \to r \in \mathcal{R}$ such that $s = C[l\sigma]$ and $t = C[r\sigma]$. We write $s \xrightarrow{\epsilon}_{\mathcal{R}} t$ if $C = \square$ (called a *root step*), and $s \xrightarrow{>\epsilon}_{\mathcal{R}} t$ (called a *non-root step*), otherwise. We say a term s_0 is *$\mathcal{R}$-terminating* if it starts no infinite rewrite sequence $s_0 \to_{\mathcal{R}} s_1 \to_{\mathcal{R}} s_2 \to_{\mathcal{R}} \cdots$, and say $\mathcal{R}$ is *terminating* if every term is $\mathcal{R}$-terminating.

For a relation $\rightarrowtail \subseteq A \times A$, we denote its transitive closure by $\rightarrowtail^+$ and reflexive transitive closure by $\rightarrowtail^*$. We say that $a_1, \ldots, a_n \in A$ are *joinable* (*meetable*) at $b \in A$ with respect to $\rightarrowtail$ if $a_i \rightarrowtail^* b$ ($b \rightarrowtail^* a_i$) for every $i \in \{1, \ldots, n\}$.

3   Reachability Constraint Satisfaction

In this section we introduce the syntax and semantics of reachability constraints, a framework that allows us to unify several concrete techniques for reachability analysis on an abstract level. Reachability constraints are first-order formulas[1] with a single binary predicate symbol whose intended interpretation is reachability by rewriting with respect to a given rewrite system.

Definition 1 (Reachability Constraints). *Reachability constraints are given by the following grammar (where $s, t \in \mathcal{T}(\mathcal{F}, \mathcal{V})$ and $x \in \mathcal{V}$)*

$$\phi, \psi, \cdots ::= \top \mid \bot \mid s \rightarrowtail t \mid \phi \vee \psi \mid \phi \wedge \psi \mid \neg\phi \mid \forall x.\, \phi \mid \exists x.\, \phi$$

To save some space, we use conventional notation like $\bigwedge_{i \in I} \phi_i$ and $\exists x_1, \ldots, x_n.\, \phi$.

As mentioned above, the semantics of reachability constraints is defined with respect to a given rewrite system. In the following we define satisfiability of constraints with respect to a TRS. (This definition will be extended to conditional rewrite systems in Sect. 5).

Definition 2 (Satisfiability). *We define[2] inductively when a substitution σ satisfies a reachability constraint ϕ modulo a TRS $\mathcal{R}$, written $\sigma \models_{\mathcal{R}} \phi$, as follows:*

---

[1] While in general we allow an arbitrary first-order logical structure for formulas, for the purpose of this paper, negation and universal quantification are not required.

[2] It is also possible to give a model-theoretic account for these notions. However, the required preliminaries are outside the scope of this paper.

- $\sigma \models_{\mathcal{R}} \top$;
- $\sigma \models_{\mathcal{R}} s \twoheadrightarrow t$ if $s\sigma \to^*_{\mathcal{R}} t\sigma$;
- $\sigma \models_{\mathcal{R}} \phi \vee \psi$ if $\sigma \models_{\mathcal{R}} \phi$ or $\sigma \models_{\mathcal{R}} \psi$;
- $\sigma \models_{\mathcal{R}} \phi \wedge \psi$ if $\sigma \models_{\mathcal{R}} \phi$ and $\sigma \models_{\mathcal{R}} \psi$;
- $\sigma \models_{\mathcal{R}} \neg\phi$ if $\sigma \models_{\mathcal{R}} \phi$ does not hold;
- $\sigma \models_{\mathcal{R}} \forall x. \phi$ if $\sigma' \models_{\mathcal{R}} \phi$ for every σ' that coincides with σ on $\mathcal{V} \setminus \{x\}$.
- $\sigma \models_{\mathcal{R}} \exists x. \phi$ if $\sigma' \models_{\mathcal{R}} \phi$ for some σ' that coincides with σ on $\mathcal{V} \setminus \{x\}$.

We say ϕ and ψ are equivalent modulo $\mathcal{R}$, written $\phi \equiv_{\mathcal{R}} \psi$, when $\sigma \models_{\mathcal{R}} \phi$ iff $\sigma \models_{\mathcal{R}} \psi$ for all σ. We say ϕ and ψ are (logically) equivalent, written $\phi \equiv \psi$, if they are equivalent modulo any $\mathcal{R}$. We say ϕ is satisfiable modulo $\mathcal{R}$, written $\mathsf{SAT}_{\mathcal{R}}(\phi)$, if there is a substitution σ that satisfies ϕ modulo $\mathcal{R}$, and call σ a solution of ϕ with respect to $\mathcal{R}$.

Checking for satisfiability of reachability constraints is for example useful for proving termination of term rewrite systems via the *dependency pair method* [2], or more specifically in *dependency graph* analysis. For the dependency pair method, we assume a fresh *marked* symbol $f^\sharp$ for every $f \in \mathcal{D}_{\mathcal{R}}$, and write $s^\sharp$ to denote the term $f^\sharp(s_1, \ldots, s_n)$ for $s = f(s_1, \ldots, s_n)$. The set of *dependency pairs* of a TRS $\mathcal{R}$ is $\mathsf{DP}(\mathcal{R}) := \{ l^\sharp \to r^\sharp \mid l \to C[r] \in \mathcal{R},\ r \notin \mathcal{V},\ \mathsf{root}(r) \in \mathcal{D}_{\mathcal{R}} \}$. The standard definition of the dependency graph of a TRS [2] can be recast using reachability constraints as follows:

Definition 3 (Dependency Graph). *Given a TRS $\mathcal{R}$, its dependency graph $\mathsf{DG}(\mathcal{R})$ is the directed graph over $\mathsf{DP}(\mathcal{R})$ where there is an edge from $l^\sharp \to s^\sharp$ to $t^\sharp \to r^\sharp$ iff $\mathsf{SAT}_{\mathcal{R}}(s^\sharp \twoheadrightarrow t^\sharp \alpha)$, where α is a renaming of variables such that $\mathsf{Var}(t^\sharp \alpha) \cap \mathsf{Var}(s^\sharp) = \varnothing$.*

The nodes of the dependency graph correspond to the possible recursive calls in a program (represented by a TRS), while its edges encode the information which recursive calls can directly follow each other in arbitrary program executions. This is the reason why dependency graphs are useful for investigating the termination behavior of TRSs, as captured by the following result.

Theorem 1 ([10]). *A TRS $\mathcal{R}$ is terminating iff for every strongly connected component $\mathcal{C}$ of an over approximation of $\mathsf{DG}(\mathcal{R})$, there is no infinite chain $s_0 \xrightarrow{\epsilon}_{\mathcal{C}} t_0 \to^*_{\mathcal{R}} s_1 \xrightarrow{\epsilon}_{\mathcal{C}} t_1 \to^*_{\mathcal{R}} \cdots$ where every t_i is $\mathcal{R}$-terminating.*

Example 2. Consider the TRS $\mathcal{R}$ of Toyama [15] consisting of the single rule $\mathsf{f}(0, 1, x) \to \mathsf{f}(x, x, x)$. Its dependency graph $\mathsf{DG}(\mathcal{R})$ consists of the single node:

$$\mathsf{f}^\sharp(0, 1, x) \to \mathsf{f}^\sharp(x, x, x) \tag{1}$$

To show $\mathcal{R}$ terminates it suffices to show that $\mathsf{DG}(\mathcal{R})$ has no edge from (1) back to (1), that is, the unsatisfiability of the constraint (with a fresh variable x')

$$\mathsf{f}^\sharp(x, x, x) \twoheadrightarrow \mathsf{f}^\sharp(0, 1, x') \tag{2}$$

The most popular method today for checking reachability during dependency graph analysis is unifiability between the target and an approximation of the topmost part of the source (its "cap") that does not change under rewriting, which is computed by the $\mathsf{tcap}_{\mathcal{R}}$ function [9].

Definition 4 (tcap). *Let $\mathcal{R}$ be a TRS. We recursively define $\mathsf{tcap}_{\mathcal{R}}(t)$ for a given term t as follows: $\mathsf{tcap}_{\mathcal{R}}(x)$ is a fresh variable if $x \in \mathcal{V}$; $\mathsf{tcap}_{\mathcal{R}}(f(t_1, \ldots, t_n))$ is a fresh variable if $u = f(\mathsf{tcap}_{\mathcal{R}}(t_1), \ldots, \mathsf{tcap}_{\mathcal{R}}(t_n))$ unifies with some left-hand side of the rules in $\mathcal{R}$; otherwise, it is u.*

The standard way of checking for nonreachability that is implemented in most tools is captured by of the following proposition.

Proposition 1. *If $\mathsf{tcap}_{\mathcal{R}}(s)$ and t are not unifiable, then $s \twoheadrightarrow t \equiv_{\mathcal{R}} \bot$.*

Example 3. Proposition 1 cannot prove the unsatisfiability of (2) of Example 2, since the term cap of the source $\mathsf{tcap}_{\mathcal{R}}(\mathsf{f}^\sharp(x, x, x)) = \mathsf{f}^\sharp(z, z', z'')$, where z, z', z'' are fresh variables, is unifiable with the target $\mathsf{f}^\sharp(0, 1, x')$.

4   Reachability in Term Rewriting

In this section we introduce some techniques for analyzing (un)satisfiability of reachability constraints. The first one described below formulates an obvious observation: no root rewrite step is applicable when starting from a term whose root is a constructor.

Definition 5 (Non-Root Reachability). *For terms $s = f(\ldots)$ and $t = g(\ldots)$, we define the non-root reachability constraint $s \xrightarrow{>\epsilon} t$ as follows:*

- *$s \xrightarrow{>\epsilon} t = \bot$ if $f \neq g$, and*
- *$f(s_1, \ldots, s_n) \xrightarrow{>\epsilon} f(t_1, \ldots, t_n) = s_1 \twoheadrightarrow t_1 \wedge \ldots \wedge s_n \twoheadrightarrow t_n$.*

The intention of non-root reachability constraints is to encode zero or more steps of non-root rewriting, in the following sense.

Lemma 1. *For $s, t \notin \mathcal{V}$, $s\sigma \xrightarrow{>\epsilon}{}^*_{\mathcal{R}} t\sigma$ iff $\sigma \models_{\mathcal{R}} s \xrightarrow{>\epsilon} t$.*

Proof. The claim vacuously follows if $\mathsf{root}(s) \neq \mathsf{root}(t)$. So let $s = f(s_1, \ldots, s_n)$ and $t = f(t_1, \ldots, t_n)$. We have $f(s_1, \ldots, s_n)\sigma \xrightarrow{>\epsilon}{}^*_{\mathcal{R}} f(t_1, \ldots, t_n)\sigma$ iff $s_1\sigma \to^*_{\mathcal{R}} t_1\sigma, \ldots, s_n\sigma \to^*_{\mathcal{R}} t_n\sigma$ iff $\sigma \models_{\mathcal{R}} s_1 \twoheadrightarrow t_1 \wedge \ldots \wedge s_n \twoheadrightarrow t_n$. $\qquad\square$

Combined with the observation that no root step is applicable to a term whose root symbol is a constructor, we obtain the following reformulation of a folklore result that reduces reachability to direct subterms.

Proposition 2. *If $s = f(\ldots)$ with $f \notin \mathcal{D}_{\mathcal{R}}$ and $t \notin \mathcal{V}$, then $s \twoheadrightarrow t \equiv_{\mathcal{R}} s \xrightarrow{>\epsilon} t$.*

Proposition 2 is directly applicable in the analysis of dependency graphs.

Example 4. Consider again the constraint $\mathsf{f}^\sharp(x, x, x) \twoheadrightarrow \mathsf{f}^\sharp(0, 1, x')$ from Example 2. Since $\mathsf{f}^\sharp$ is not defined in $\mathcal{R}$, Proposition 2 reduces this constraint to $\mathsf{f}^\sharp(x, x, x) \xrightarrow{>\epsilon} \mathsf{f}^\sharp(0, 1, x')$, that is,

$$x \twoheadrightarrow 0 \wedge x \twoheadrightarrow 1 \wedge x \twoheadrightarrow x' \tag{3}$$

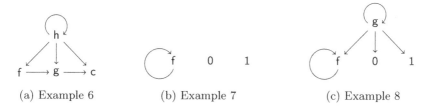

(a) Example 6   (b) Example 7   (c) Example 8

Fig. 1. Example symbol transition graphs.

4.1 Symbol Transition Graphs

Here we introduce a new, simple and efficient way of overapproximating reachability by tracking the relation of root symbols of terms according to a given set of rewrite rules. We first illustrate the intuition by an example.

Example 5. Consider a TRS $\mathcal{R}$ consisting of rules of the following form:

$$\mathsf{f}(...) \to \mathsf{g}(...) \qquad\qquad \mathsf{g}(...) \to \mathsf{c}(...) \qquad\qquad \mathsf{h}(...) \to x$$

Moreover, suppose $s \to_{\mathcal{R}}^* t$. Then we can make the following observations:

- If $\mathsf{root}(s) = \mathsf{c}$, then $\mathsf{root}(t) = \mathsf{c}$ since non-root steps preserve the root symbol and no root steps are applicable to terms of the form $\mathsf{c}(...)$.
- If $\mathsf{root}(s) = \mathsf{g}$, then $\mathsf{root}(t) \in \{\mathsf{g}, \mathsf{c}\}$ since non-root steps preserve the root symbol and the only possible root step is $\mathsf{g}(...) \to \mathsf{c}(...)$.
- If $\mathsf{root}(s) = \mathsf{f}$, then $\mathsf{root}(t) \in \{\mathsf{f}, \mathsf{g}, \mathsf{c}\}$ by the same reasoning.
- If $\mathsf{root}(s) = \mathsf{h}$, then t can be any term and $\mathsf{root}(t)$ can be arbitrary.

This informal argument is captured by the following definition.

Definition 6 (Symbol Transition Graphs). *The* symbol transition graph $\mathsf{SG}(\mathcal{R})$ *of a TRS $\mathcal{R}$ over signature $\mathcal{F}$ is the graph $\langle \mathcal{F}, \rightarrowtail_{\mathcal{R}} \rangle$, where $f \rightarrowtail_{\mathcal{R}} g$ iff $\mathcal{R}$ contains a rule of form $f(...) \to g(...)$ or $f(...) \to x$ with $x \in \mathcal{V}$.*

The following result tells us that for non-variable terms the symbol transition graph captures the relation between the root symbols of root rewrite steps.

Lemma 2. *If $s \xrightarrow{\epsilon}_{\mathcal{R}} t$ then $t \in \mathcal{V}$ or $\mathsf{root}(s) \rightarrowtail_{\mathcal{R}} \mathsf{root}(t)$.*

Proof. By assumption there exist $l \to r \in \mathcal{R}$ and σ such that $s = l\sigma$ and $r\sigma = t$. If $r \in \mathcal{V}$ then either $t \in \mathcal{V}$ or $\mathsf{root}(s) = \mathsf{root}(l) \rightarrowtail_{\mathcal{R}} \mathsf{root}(t)$. Otherwise, $\mathsf{root}(s) = \mathsf{root}(l) \rightarrowtail_{\mathcal{R}} \mathsf{root}(r) = \mathsf{root}(t)$. □

Since every rewrite sequence is composed of subsequences that take place entirely below the root (and hence do not change the root symbol) separated by root steps, we can extend the previous result to rewrite sequences.

Lemma 3. *If $s = f(...) \to_{\mathcal{R}}^* g(...) = t$ then $f \rightarrowtail_{\mathcal{R}}^* g$.*

Proof. We prove the claim for arbitrary s and f by induction on the derivation length of $s \to_{\mathcal{R}}^* t$. The base case is trivial, so consider $s \to_{\mathcal{R}} s' \to_{\mathcal{R}}^n t\sigma$. Since $t \notin \mathcal{V}$, we have $f' \in \mathcal{F}$ with $s' = f'(\ldots)$. Thus the induction hypothesis yields $f' \rightarrowtail_{\mathcal{R}}^* g$. If $s \xrightarrow{\epsilon}_{\mathcal{R}} s'$ then by Lemma 2 we conclude $f \rightarrowtail_{\mathcal{R}} f' \rightarrowtail_{\mathcal{R}}^* g$, and otherwise $f = f' \rightarrowtail_{\mathcal{R}}^* g$. □

It is now straightforward to derive the following from Lemma 3.

Corollary 1. *If $f \rightarrowtail_{\mathcal{R}}^* g$ does not hold, then $f(\ldots) \twoheadrightarrow g(\ldots) \equiv_{\mathcal{R}} \bot$.*

Example 6. The symbol transition graph for Example 5 is depicted in Fig. 1(a). By Corollary 1 we can conclude, for instance, $\mathsf{g}(\ldots) \twoheadrightarrow \mathsf{f}(\ldots)$ is unsatisfiable.

Corollary 1 is useful for checking (un)satisfiability of $s \twoheadrightarrow t$, only if neither s nor t is a variable. However, the symbol transition graph is also useful for unsatisfiability in the case when s and t may be variables.

Proposition 3. *If $\mathsf{SAT}_{\mathcal{R}}(x \twoheadrightarrow t_1 \wedge \ldots \wedge x \twoheadrightarrow t_n)$ for $t_1 = g_1(\ldots), \ldots, t_n = g_n(\ldots)$, then $g_1, \ldots, g_n$ are meetable with respect to $\rightarrowtail_{\mathcal{R}}$.*

Proof. By assumption there is a substitution σ such that $x\sigma \to_{\mathcal{R}}^* t_1\sigma, \ldots, x\sigma \to_{\mathcal{R}}^* t_n\sigma$. Clearly $x\sigma \in \mathcal{V}$ is not possible. Thus, suppose $x\sigma = f(\ldots)$ for some f. Finally, from Lemma 3, we have $f \rightarrowtail_{\mathcal{R}}^* g_1, \ldots, f \rightarrowtail_{\mathcal{R}}^* g_n$ and thereby conclude that $g_1, \ldots, g_n$ are meetable at f. □

The dual of Proposition 3 is proved in a similar way, but with some special care to ensure $x\sigma \in \mathcal{V}$.

Proposition 4. *If $\mathsf{SAT}_{\mathcal{R}}(s_1 \twoheadrightarrow x \wedge \ldots \wedge s_n \twoheadrightarrow x)$ for $s_1 = f_1(\ldots), \ldots, s_n = f_n(\ldots)$, then $f_1, \ldots, f_n$ are joinable with respect to $\rightarrowtail_{\mathcal{R}}$.*

Example 7 (Continuation of Example 4). Due to Proposition 3, proving (3) unsatisfiable reduces to proving that 0 and 1 are not meetable with respect to $\rightarrowtail_{\mathcal{R}}$. This is obvious from the symbol transition graph depicted in Fig. 1(b). Hence, we conclude the termination of $\mathcal{R}$.

Example 8. Consider the following extension of $\mathcal{R}$ from Example 2.

$$\mathsf{f}(0, 1, x) \to \mathsf{f}(x, x, x) \qquad \mathsf{g}(x, y) \to x \qquad \mathsf{g}(x, y) \to y$$

The resulting system is not terminating [15]. The corresponding symbol transition graph is depicted in Fig. 1(c), where 0 and 1 are meetable, as expected.

4.2 Look-Ahead Reachability

Here we propose another method for overapproximating reachability, which eventually subsumes the `tcap`-unifiability method when target terms are linear. Note that this condition is satisfied in the dependency graph approximation of left-linear TRSs. Our method is based on the observation that any rewrite sequence either contains at least one root step, or takes place entirely below the root. This observation can be captured using our reachability constraints.

Definition 7 (Root Narrowing Constraints). *Let $l \to r$ be a rewrite rule with $\mathsf{Var}(l) = \{x_1, \ldots, x_n\}$. Then for terms s and t not containing $x_1, \ldots, x_n$, the* root narrowing constraint *from s to t via $l \to r$ is defined by*

$$s \leadsto_{l \to r} t := \exists x_1, \ldots, x_n. \ s \xrightarrow{> \epsilon} l \wedge r \twoheadrightarrow t$$

We write $s \leadsto_{\mathcal{R}} t$ for $\bigvee_{l \to r \in \mathcal{R}'} s \leadsto_{l \to r} t$, where $\mathcal{R}'$ is a variant of $\mathcal{R}$ in which variables occurring in s or t are renamed to fresh ones.

In the definition above, the intuition is that if there are any root steps inside a rewrite sequence then we can pick the first one, which is only preceded by non-root steps. The following theorem justifies this intuition.

Theorem 2. *If $s, t \notin \mathcal{V}$, then $s \twoheadrightarrow t \equiv_{\mathcal{R}} s \xrightarrow{> \epsilon} t \vee s \leadsto_{\mathcal{R}} t$.*

Proof. Let $s = f(s_1, \ldots, s_n)$ and σ be a substitution. We show $\sigma \models_{\mathcal{R}} s \twoheadrightarrow t$ iff $\sigma \models_{\mathcal{R}} s \xrightarrow{> \epsilon} t \vee s \leadsto_{\mathcal{R}} t$. For the "if" direction suppose the latter. If $\sigma \models_{\mathcal{R}} s \xrightarrow{> \epsilon} t$, then t is of form $f(t_1, \ldots, t_n)$ and $s_i \sigma \to_{\mathcal{R}}^* t_i \sigma$ for every $i \in \{1, \ldots, n\}$, and thus $s\sigma \to_{\mathcal{R}}^* t\sigma$. If $\sigma \models_{\mathcal{R}} s \leadsto_{\mathcal{R}} t$, then we have a renamed variant $l \to r$ of a rule in $\mathcal{R}$ such that $\sigma \models_{\mathcal{R}} s \leadsto_{l \to r} t$. This indicates that there exists a substitution σ' that coincides with σ on $\mathcal{V} \setminus \mathsf{Var}(l)$, and satisfies

- $\sigma' \models_{\mathcal{R}} s \xrightarrow{> \epsilon} l$, that is, $l = f(l_1, \ldots, l_n)$ and $s_i \sigma' \to_{\mathcal{R}}^* l_i \sigma'$;
- $\sigma' \models_{\mathcal{R}} r \twoheadrightarrow t$, that is, $r\sigma' \to_{\mathcal{R}}^* t\sigma'$.

In combination, we have $s\sigma = s\sigma' \xrightarrow{> \epsilon}_{\mathcal{R}}^* l\sigma' \xrightarrow{\epsilon}_{\mathcal{R}} r\sigma' \to_{\mathcal{R}}^* t\sigma' = t\sigma$.

Now consider the "only if" direction. Suppose that σ is an idempotent substitution such that $s\sigma \to_{\mathcal{R}}^* t\sigma$. We may assume idempotence, since from any solution σ' of $s \twoheadrightarrow t$, we obtain idempotent solution σ by renaming variables in $\mathsf{Var}(s) \cup \mathsf{Var}(t)$ to fresh ones. We proceed by the following case analysis:

- *No root step is involved:* $s\sigma \xrightarrow{> \epsilon}_{\mathcal{R}}^* t\sigma$. Then Lemma 1 implies $\sigma \models_{\mathcal{R}} s \xrightarrow{> \epsilon} t$.
- *At least one root step is involved:* there is a rule $l \to r \in \mathcal{R}$ and a substitution θ such that $s\sigma \xrightarrow{> \epsilon}_{\mathcal{R}}^* l\theta$ and $r\theta \to_{\mathcal{R}}^* t\sigma$. Since variables in $l\theta$ must occur in $s\sigma$ (due to our assumptions on rewrite rules), we have $l\theta = l\theta\sigma$ since σ is idempotent. Thus from Lemma 1 we have $\sigma \models_{\mathcal{R}} s \xrightarrow{> \epsilon} l\theta$. Further, variables in $r\theta$ must occur in $l\theta$ and thus in $s\theta$, we also have $r\theta\sigma = r\theta \to_{\mathcal{R}}^* t\sigma$, and hence $\sigma \models_{\mathcal{R}} r\theta \twoheadrightarrow t$. This concludes $\sigma \models_{\mathcal{R}} s \leadsto_{l \to r} t$. $\square$

Proposition 2 is a corollary of Theorem 2 together with the following easy lemma, stating that if the root symbol of the source term is not a defined symbol, then no root step can occur.

Lemma 4. *If $c \notin \mathcal{D}_{\mathcal{R}}$ then $c(\ldots) \leadsto_{\mathcal{R}} t \equiv \bot$.*

Example 9. Consider the TRS $\mathcal{R}$ consisting of the following rules:

$$0 > x \to \mathsf{false} \qquad \mathsf{s}(x) > 0 \to \mathsf{true} \qquad \mathsf{s}(x) > \mathsf{s}(y) \to x > y$$

Applying Theorem 2 once reduces the reachability constraint $0 > z \twoheadrightarrow \mathsf{true}$ to the disjunction of

1. $0 > z \xrightarrow{>\epsilon} \text{true}$,
2. $\exists x.\ 0 > z \xrightarrow{>\epsilon} 0 > x \ \wedge \ \text{false} \twoheadrightarrow \text{true}$
3. $\exists x.\ 0 > z \xrightarrow{>\epsilon} \mathsf{s}(x) > 0 \ \wedge \ \text{true} \twoheadrightarrow \text{true}$
4. $\exists x, y.\ 0 > z \xrightarrow{>\epsilon} \mathsf{s}(x) > \mathsf{s}(y) \ \wedge \ x > y \twoheadrightarrow \text{true}$

Disjuncts 1, 3, and 4 expand to $\bot$ by definition of $\xrightarrow{>\epsilon}$. For disjunct 2, applying Theorem 2 or Proposition 2 to $\text{false} \twoheadrightarrow \text{true}$ yields $\bot$.

Note that Theorem 2 can be applied arbitrarily often. Thus, to avoid nontermination in an implementation, we need to control how often it is applied. For this purpose we introduce the following definition.

Definition 8 (k-**Fold Look-Ahead**). *We define the k-fold look-ahead transformation with respect to a TRS $\mathcal{R}$ as follows:*

$$\mathsf{L}_{\mathcal{R}}^k(s \twoheadrightarrow t) := \begin{cases} \mathsf{L}_{\mathcal{R}}^k(s \xrightarrow{>\epsilon} t) \vee s \rightsquigarrow_{\mathcal{R}}^k t & \text{if } k \geq 1 \text{ and } s, t \notin \mathcal{V} \\ s \twoheadrightarrow t & \text{otherwise} \end{cases}$$

which is homomorphically extended to reachability constraints. Here, $\rightsquigarrow_{\mathcal{R}}^k$ is defined as in Definition 7, but k controls the number of root steps to be expanded:

$$s \rightsquigarrow_{l \rightarrow r}^k t := \exists x_1, \ldots, x_n.\ \mathsf{L}_{\mathcal{R}}^k(s \xrightarrow{>\epsilon} l) \wedge \mathsf{L}_{\mathcal{R}}^{k-1}(r \twoheadrightarrow t)$$

It easily follows from Theorem 2 and induction on k that the k-fold look-ahead preserves the semantics of reachability constraints.

Corollary 2. $\mathsf{L}_{\mathcal{R}}^k(\phi) \equiv_{\mathcal{R}} \phi$.

The following results indicate that, whenever $\mathsf{tcap}_{\mathcal{R}}$-unifiability (Proposition 1) proves $s \twoheadrightarrow t$ unsatisfiable for linear t, $\mathsf{L}_{\mathcal{R}}^1$ can also conclude it.

Lemma 5. *Let $s = f(s_1, \ldots, s_n)$ and $t \notin \mathcal{V}$ be a linear term, and suppose that $f(\mathsf{tcap}_{\mathcal{R}}(s_1), \ldots, \mathsf{tcap}_{\mathcal{R}}(s_n))$ does not unify with t or any left-hand side in $\mathcal{R}$. Then $\mathsf{L}_{\mathcal{R}}^1(s \twoheadrightarrow t) \equiv \bot$.*

Proof. By structural induction on s. First, we show $\mathsf{L}_{\mathcal{R}}^1(s \xrightarrow{>\epsilon} t) \equiv \bot$. This is trivial if $\mathsf{root}(t) \neq f$. So let $t = f(t_1, \ldots, t_n)$. By assumption there is an $i \in \{1, \ldots, n\}$ such that $\mathsf{tcap}_{\mathcal{R}}(s_i)$ does not unify with t_i. Hence $\mathsf{tcap}_{\mathcal{R}}(s_i)$ cannot be a fresh variable, and thus s_i is of the form $g(u_1, \ldots, u_m)$ and $\mathsf{tcap}_{\mathcal{R}}(s_i) = g(\mathsf{tcap}_{\mathcal{R}}(u_1), \ldots, \mathsf{tcap}_{\mathcal{R}}(u_m))$ is not unifiable with any left-hand side in $\mathcal{R}$. Therefore, the induction hypothesis applies to s_i, yielding $\mathsf{L}_{\mathcal{R}}^1(s_i \twoheadrightarrow t_i) \equiv \bot$. This concludes $\mathsf{L}_{\mathcal{R}}^1(s \xrightarrow{>\epsilon} t) = \mathsf{L}_{\mathcal{R}}^1(s_1 \twoheadrightarrow t_1) \wedge \ldots \wedge \mathsf{L}_{\mathcal{R}}^1(s_n \twoheadrightarrow t_n) \equiv \bot$.

Second, we show $\mathsf{L}_{\mathcal{R}}^1(s \rightsquigarrow_{\mathcal{R}}^1 t) \equiv \bot$. To this end, we show for an arbitrary variant $l \rightarrow r$ of a rule in $\mathcal{R}$ that $\mathsf{L}_{\mathcal{R}}^1(s \xrightarrow{>\epsilon} l) \equiv \bot$. This is clear if $\mathsf{root}(l) \neq f$. So let $l = f(l_1, \ldots, l_n)$. By assumption there is an $i \in \{1, \ldots, n\}$ such that $\mathsf{tcap}_{\mathcal{R}}(s_i)$ and l_i are not unifiable. By a similar reasoning as above the induction hypothesis applies to s_i and yields $\mathsf{L}_{\mathcal{R}}^1(s_i \twoheadrightarrow l_i) \equiv \bot$. This concludes $\mathsf{L}_{\mathcal{R}}^1(s \xrightarrow{>\epsilon} l) \equiv \bot$. $\square$

Corollary 3. *If $\mathsf{tcap}_{\mathcal{R}}(s)$ and t are not unifiable, then $\mathsf{L}_{\mathcal{R}}^1(s \twoheadrightarrow t) \equiv \bot$.*

5 Conditional Rewriting

Conditional rewriting is a flavor of rewriting where rules are guarded by conditions. On the one hand, this gives us a boost in expressiveness in the sense that it is often possible to directly express equations with preconditions and that it is easier to directly express programming constructs like the where-clauses of Haskell. On the other hand, the analysis of conditional rewrite systems is typically more involved than for plain rewriting.

In this section we first recall the basics of conditional term rewriting. Then, we motivate the importance of reachability analysis for the conditional case. Finally, we extend the techniques of Sect. 4 to conditional rewrite systems.

Preliminaries. A *conditional rewrite rule* $l \to r \Leftarrow \phi$ consists of two terms $l \notin \mathcal{V}$ and r (the left-hand side and right-hand side, respectively) and a list ϕ of pairs of terms (its *conditions*). A *conditional term rewrite system* (CTRS for short) is a set of conditional rewrite rules. Depending on the interpretation of conditions, conditional rewriting can be separated into several classes. For the purposes of this paper we are interested in *oriented* CTRSs, where conditions are interpreted as reachability constraints with respect to conditional rewriting. Hence, from now on we identify conditions $\langle s_1, t_1 \rangle, \ldots, \langle s_n, t_n \rangle$ with the reachability constraint $s_1 \twoheadrightarrow t_1 \wedge \ldots \wedge s_n \twoheadrightarrow t_n$, and the empty list with $\top$ (omitting "$\Leftarrow \top$" from rules).

The rewrite relation of a CTRS is layered into *levels*: given a CTRS $\mathcal{R}$ and level $i \in \mathbb{N}$, the corresponding (unconditional) TRS $\mathcal{R}_i$ is defined recursively:

$$\mathcal{R}_0 := \varnothing$$
$$\mathcal{R}_{i+1} := \{l\sigma \to r\sigma \mid l \to r \Leftarrow \phi \in \mathcal{R},\ \sigma \models_{\mathcal{R}_i} \phi\}$$

Then the *(conditional) rewrite relation at level* i, written $\to_{\mathcal{R},i}$ (or $\to_i$ whenever $\mathcal{R}$ is clear from the context), is the plain rewrite relation $\to_{\mathcal{R}_i}$ induced by the TRS $\mathcal{R}_i$. Finally, the *induced (conditional) rewrite relation* of a CTRS $\mathcal{R}$ is defined by $\to_{\mathcal{R}} := \bigcup\{\to_i \mid i \geq 0\}$. At this point Definition 2 is extended to the conditional case in a straightforward manner.

Definition 9 (Level Satisfiability). *Let $\mathcal{R}$ be a CTRS and ϕ a reachability constraint. We say that a substitution σ satisfies ϕ modulo $\mathcal{R}$ at level i, whenever $\sigma \models_{\mathcal{R},i} \phi$. If we are not interested in a specific satisfying substitution we say that ϕ is satisfiable modulo $\mathcal{R}$ at level i and write $\mathsf{SAT}_{\mathcal{R},i}(\phi)$ (or just $\mathsf{SAT}_i(\phi)$ whenever $\mathcal{R}$ is clear from the context).*

5.1 Infeasibility

The main area of interest for reachability analysis in the conditional case is checking for *infeasibility*. While a formal definition of this concept follows below, for the moment, think of it as unsatisfiability of conditions. The two predominant applications of infeasibility are: (1) if the conditions of a rule are unsatisfiable, the rule can never be applied and thus safely be removed without changing the induced rewrite relation; (2) if the conditions of a conditional critical pair (which arises from confluence analysis of CTRSs) are unsatisfiable, then it poses no problem to confluence and can safely be ignored.

Definition 10 (Infeasibility). *We say that a conditional rewrite rule $l \to r \Leftarrow \phi$ is* applicable at level i *with respect to a CTRS $\mathcal{R}$ iff* $\mathsf{SAT}_{\mathcal{R},i-1}(\phi)$. *A set $\mathcal{S}$ of rules is* infeasible *with respect to $\mathcal{R}$ when no rule in $\mathcal{S}$ is applicable at any level.*

The next theorem allows us to remove some rules from a CTRS while checking for infeasibility of rules.

Theorem 3. *A set $\mathcal{S}$ of rules is infeasible with respect to a CTRS $\mathcal{R}$ iff it is infeasible with respect to $\mathcal{R} \setminus \mathcal{S}$.*

Proof. The 'only if' direction is trivial. Thus we concentrate on the 'if' direction. To this end, assume that $\mathcal{S}$ is infeasible with respect to $\mathcal{R} \setminus \mathcal{S}$, but not infeasible with respect to $\mathcal{R}$. That is, at least one rule in $\mathcal{S}$ is applicable at some level with respect to $\mathcal{R}$. Let m be the minimum level such that there is a rule $l \to r \Leftarrow \phi \in \mathcal{S}$ that is applicable at level m with respect to $\mathcal{R}$. Now if $m = 0$ then $l \to r \Leftarrow \phi$ is applicable at level 0 and thus $\mathsf{SAT}_{\mathcal{R},0}(\phi)$, which trivially implies $\mathsf{SAT}_{\mathcal{R}\setminus\mathcal{S},0}(\phi)$, contradicting the assumption that all rules in $\mathcal{S}$ are infeasible with respect to $\mathcal{R} \setminus \mathcal{S}$. Otherwise, $m = k+1$ for some $k \geq 0$ and since $l \to r \Leftarrow \phi$ is applicable at level m we have $\mathsf{SAT}_{\mathcal{R},k}(\phi)$. Moreover, the rewrite relations $\to_{\mathcal{R},k}$ and $\to_{\mathcal{R}\setminus\mathcal{S},k}$ coincide (since all rules in $\mathcal{S}$ are infeasible at levels smaller than m by our choice of m). Thus we also have $\mathsf{SAT}_{\mathcal{R}\setminus\mathcal{S},k}(\phi)$, again contradicting the assumption that all rules in $\mathcal{S}$ are infeasible with respect to $\mathcal{R} \setminus \mathcal{S}$.   □

The following example from *the confluence problems data base* (Cops)[3] shows that Theorem 3 is beneficial for showing infeasibility of conditional rewrite rules.

Example 10 (Cops 794). Consider the CTRS $\mathcal{R}$ consisting of the two rules:

$$a \to c \Leftarrow f(a) \twoheadrightarrow f(b) \qquad\qquad f(b) \to b$$

The tcap-method does not manage to conclude infeasibility of the first rule, since $\mathsf{tcap}_{\mathcal{R}}(f(a)) = x$ for some fresh variable x and thus unifies with $f(b)$. The reason for this result was that for computing $\mathsf{tcap}_{\mathcal{R}}$ we had to recursively (in a bottom-up fashion) try to unify arguments of functions with left-hand sides of rules, which succeeded for the left-hand side of the first rule and the argument a of $f(a)$, thereby obtaining $f(x)$ which, in turn, unifies with the left-hand side of the second rule. But by Theorem 3 we do not need to consider the first rule for computing the term cap and thus obtain $\mathsf{tcap}_{\{f(b)\to b\}}(f(a)) = f(a)$ which does not unify with $f(b)$ and thereby shows that the first rule is infeasible.

---

[3] http://cops.uibk.ac.at/?q=ctrs+oriented.

Fig. 2. Inductive and plain symbol transition graph of Example 11.

5.2 Symbol Transition Graphs in the Presence of Conditions

In the presence of conditions in rules we replace Definition 6 by the following inductive definition:

Definition 11 (Inductive Symbol Transition Graphs). *The symbol transition graph* $SG(\mathcal{R})$ *of a CTRS* $\mathcal{R}$ *over a signature* $\mathcal{F}$ *is the graph* $\langle \mathcal{F}, \rightarrowtail_{\mathcal{R}} \rangle$ *where* $\rightarrowtail_{\mathcal{R}}$ *is defined inductively by the following two inference rules:*

$$\frac{f(\ldots) \to x \Leftarrow \phi \in \mathcal{R} \quad \forall \langle s, t \rangle \in \phi.\, s \in \mathcal{V} \vee t \in \mathcal{V} \vee \mathsf{root}(s) \rightarrowtail_{\mathcal{R}}^{*} \mathsf{root}(t)}{f \rightarrowtail_{\mathcal{R}} g}\, g \in \mathcal{F}$$

$$\frac{f(\ldots) \to g(\ldots) \Leftarrow \phi \in \mathcal{R} \quad \forall \langle s, t \rangle \in \phi.\, s \in \mathcal{V} \vee t \in \mathcal{V} \vee \mathsf{root}(s) \rightarrowtail_{\mathcal{R}}^{*} \mathsf{root}(t)}{f \rightarrowtail_{\mathcal{R}} g}$$

The example below shows the difference between the symbol transition graph for TRSs (which can be applied as a crude overapproximation also to CTRSs by dropping all conditions) and the inductive symbol transition graph for CTRSs.

Example 11 (Cops 293). Consider the CTRS consisting of the three rules:

$$a \to b \qquad\qquad a \to c \qquad\qquad b \to c \Leftarrow b \twoheadrightarrow c$$

The corresponding inductive symbol transition graph is depicted in Fig. 2(a) and implies unsatisfiability of $b \twoheadrightarrow c$. Note that this conclusion cannot be drawn from the plain symbol transition graph of the TRS obtained by dropping the condition of the third rule, shown in Fig. 2(b).

The inductive symbol transition graph gives us a sufficient criterion for concluding nonreachability with respect to a given CTRS, as shown in the following.

Lemma 6. *If* $f(\ldots) \to_{\mathcal{R}}^{*} g(\ldots)$ *then* $f \rightarrowtail_{\mathcal{R}}^{*} g$.

Proof. Let $s = f(\ldots)$ and $u = g(\ldots)$ and assume that s rewrites to u at level i, that is, $s \to_{i}^{*} u$. We prove the statement by induction on the level i. If $i = 0$ then we are done, since $\to_{0}$ is empty and therefore $f(\ldots) = s = u = g(\ldots)$, which trivially implies $f \rightarrowtail_{\mathcal{R}}^{*} g$. Otherwise, $i = j + 1$ and we obtain the induction hypothesis (IH) that $s \to_{j}^{*} t$ implies $\mathsf{root}(s) \rightarrowtail_{\mathcal{R}}^{*} \mathsf{root}(t)$ for arbitrary non-variable terms s and t. We proceed to show that $s \to_{i}^{*} u$ implies $f \rightarrowtail_{\mathcal{R}}^{*} g$ by an inner induction on the length of this derivation. If the derivation is empty, then $f(\ldots) = s =$

$u = g(...)$ and therefore trivially $f \rightarrowtail_{\mathcal{R}}^* g$. Otherwise, the derivation is of the shape $s \rightarrow_i^* t \rightarrow_i u$ for some non-variable term $t = h(...)$ and we obtain the inner induction hypothesis that $f \rightarrowtail_{\mathcal{R}}^* h$. It remains to show $h \rightarrowtail_{\mathcal{R}}^* g$ in order to conclude the proof. To this end, consider the step $t = C[l\sigma] \rightarrow_i C[r\sigma] = u$ for some context C, substitution σ, and rule $l \rightarrow r \Leftarrow \phi \in \mathcal{R}$ such that $\sigma \models_j \phi$. Now, by IH, we obtain that $s' \in \mathcal{V}$ or $t' \in \mathcal{V}$ or $\mathsf{root}(s') \rightarrowtail_{\mathcal{R}}^* \mathsf{root}(t')$ for all $\langle s', t' \rangle \in \phi$. Thus, by Definition 11, we obtain that $\mathsf{root}(l\sigma) \rightarrowtail_{\mathcal{R}} \mathsf{root}(r\sigma)$. We conclude by a case analysis on the structure of the context C. If C is empty, that is $C = \square$, then $h = \mathsf{root}(l\sigma) \rightarrowtail_{\mathcal{R}}^* \mathsf{root}(r\sigma) = g$ and we are done. Otherwise, $h = \mathsf{root}(t) = \mathsf{root}(u) = g$ and therefore trivially $h \rightarrowtail_{\mathcal{R}}^* g$.   □

Corollary 4. *If $f \rightarrowtail_{\mathcal{R}}^* g$ does not hold, then $f(...) \twoheadrightarrow g(...) \equiv_{\mathcal{R}} \bot$.*

5.3   Look-Ahead Reachability in the Presence of Conditions

In the following definition we extend our look-ahead technique from plain rewriting to conditional rewriting.

Definition 12 (Conditional Root Narrowing Constraints). *Let $l \rightarrow r \Leftarrow \phi$ be a conditional rewrite rule with $\mathsf{Var}(l) = \{x_1, ..., x_n\}$. Then for terms s and t not containing $x_1, ..., x_n$, the conditional root narrowing constraint from s to t via $l \rightarrow r \Leftarrow \phi$ is defined by*

$$s \rightsquigarrow_{l \rightarrow r \Leftarrow \phi} t := \exists x_1, ..., x_n. \, s \xrightarrow{\geq \epsilon} l \wedge r \twoheadrightarrow t \wedge \phi$$

We write $s \rightsquigarrow_{\mathcal{R}} t$ for $\bigvee_{l \rightarrow r \Leftarrow \phi \in \mathcal{R}'} s \rightsquigarrow_{l \rightarrow r \Leftarrow \phi} t$, where $\mathcal{R}'$ is a variant of $\mathcal{R}$ in which variables occurring in s or t are renamed to fresh ones.

And we obtain a result similar to Theorem 2.

Lemma 7. *If $s, t \notin \mathcal{V}$, then $s \twoheadrightarrow t \equiv_{\mathcal{R}} s \xrightarrow{\geq \epsilon} t \vee s \rightsquigarrow_{\mathcal{R}} t$.*

Example 12 (Cops 793). Consider the CTRS $\mathcal{R}$ consisting of the two rules:

$$\mathsf{a} \rightarrow \mathsf{a} \Leftarrow \mathsf{f(a)} \twoheadrightarrow \mathsf{a} \qquad \qquad \mathsf{f}(x) \rightarrow \mathsf{a} \Leftarrow x \twoheadrightarrow \mathsf{b}$$

To show infeasibility of the first rule we can safely remove it from $\mathcal{R}$ by Theorem 3, resulting in the modified CTRS $\mathcal{R}'$. Then we have to check $\mathsf{SAT}_{\mathcal{R}'}(\mathsf{f(a)} \twoheadrightarrow \mathsf{a})$ which is made easier by the following chain of equivalences:

$$
\begin{aligned}
\mathsf{f(a)} \twoheadrightarrow \mathsf{a} \equiv_{\mathcal{R}'} \; & \mathsf{f(a)} \xrightarrow{\geq \epsilon} \mathsf{a} \vee \mathsf{f(a)} \rightsquigarrow_{\mathsf{f}(x) \rightarrow \mathsf{a} \Leftarrow x \twoheadrightarrow \mathsf{b}} \mathsf{a} && \text{(by Lemma 7)} \\
\equiv_{\mathcal{R}'} \; & \mathsf{f(a)} \rightsquigarrow_{\mathsf{f}(x) \rightarrow \mathsf{a} \Leftarrow x \twoheadrightarrow \mathsf{b}} \mathsf{a} && \text{(by Definition 5)} \\
\equiv_{\mathcal{R}'} \; & \exists x. \, \mathsf{f(a)} \xrightarrow{\geq \epsilon} \mathsf{f}(x) \wedge \mathsf{a} \twoheadrightarrow \mathsf{a} \wedge x \twoheadrightarrow \mathsf{b} && \text{(by Definition 12)} \\
\equiv_{\mathcal{R}'} \; & \exists x. \, \mathsf{a} \twoheadrightarrow x \wedge \mathsf{a} \twoheadrightarrow \mathsf{a} \wedge x \twoheadrightarrow \mathsf{b} && \text{(by Definition 5)}
\end{aligned}
$$

Since satisfiability of the final constraint above implies $\mathsf{SAT}_{\mathcal{R}'}(\mathsf{a} \twoheadrightarrow \mathsf{b})$ and we also have $\mathsf{a} \not\rightarrowtail_{\mathcal{R}}^* \mathsf{b}$, we can conclude unsatisfiability of the original constraint by Corollary 4 and hence that the first rule of $\mathcal{R}$ is infeasible.

Table 1. Experimental results for dependency graph analysis (TRSs).

		Look-ahead				
		$\mathsf{L}^0_{\mathcal{R}}$	$\mathsf{L}^1_{\mathcal{R}}$	$\mathsf{L}^2_{\mathcal{R}}$	$\mathsf{L}^3_{\mathcal{R}}$	$\mathsf{L}^8_{\mathcal{R}}$
None	UNSAT	0	104 050	105 574	105 875	105 993
	time (s)	33.96	38.98	38.13	39.15	116.52
Corollary 1	UNSAT	307 207	328 216	328 430	328 499	328 636
	time (s)	38.50	42.71	42.72	43.00	66.82

6 Assessment

We implemented our techniques in the TRS termination prover NaTT [16][4] version 1.8 for dependency graph analysis, and the CTRS confluence prover Con-Con [13][5] version 1.7 for infeasibility analysis. In both cases we only need a complete satisfiability checker, or equivalently, a sound unsatisfiability checker. Hence, to conclude unsatisfiability of given reachability constraints, we apply Corollary 2 with appropriate k together with a complete approximation of constraints. One such approximation is the symbol transition graph (Corollary 1). In the following we describe the experimental results on TRS termination and CTRS confluence. Further details of our experiments can be found at http://cl-informatik.uibk.ac.at/experiments/reachability/.

TRS Termination. For plain rewriting, we take all the 1498 TRSs from the TRS standard category of the *termination problem data base* version 10.6,[6] the benchmark used in the annual *Termination Competition* [8], and over-approximate their dependency graphs. This results in 1 133 963 reachability constraints, which we call "edges" here. Many of these edges are actually satisfiable, but we do not know the exact number (the problem is undecidable in general).

For checking unsatisfiability of edges, we combine Corollary 2 for various values of k (0, 1, 2, 3, and 8), and either Corollary 1 or 'None'. Here 'None' concludes unsatisfiability only for constraints that are logically equivalent to $\bot$. In Table 1 we give the number of edges that could be shown unsatisfiable. Here, the 'UNSAT' row indicates the number of detected unsatisfiable edges and the 'time' row indicates the total runtime in seconds. (We ran our experiments on an Amazon EC2 instance model `c5.xlarge`: 4 virtual 3.0 GHz Intel Xeon Platinum CPUs on 8 GB of memory).

The starting point is $\mathsf{L}^1_{\mathcal{R}}$ + None, which corresponds to the `tcap` technique, the method that was already implemented in NaTT before. The benefit of symbol transition graphs turns out to be quite significant, while the overhead in runtime seems acceptable. Moreover, increasing k of the look-ahead reasonably improves the power of unsatisfiability checks, both with and without the symbol transition

---

[4] https://www.trs.css.i.nagoya-u.ac.jp/NaTT/.
[5] http://cl-informatik.uibk.ac.at/software/concon/.
[6] http://www.termination-portal.org/wiki/TPDB.

graph technique. In terms of the overall termination proving power, NaTT using only tcap solves 1039 out of the 1498 termination problems, while using L_R^8 and Corollary 1, it proves termination of 18 additional problems.

CTRS Confluence. For conditional rewriting, we take the 148 oriented CTRSs of Cops,[7] a benchmark of confluence problems used in the annual *Confluence Competition* [1]. Compared to version 1.5 of ConCon (the winner of the CTRS category in the last competition in 2018) our new version (1.7) can solve five more systems (that is a gain of roughly 3%) by incorporating a combination of Theorem 3, inductive symbol transition graphs (Corollary 4), and k-fold look-ahead (Lemma 7), where for the latter we fixed $k = 1$ since we additionally have to control the level of conditional rewriting.

7   Related Work

Reachability is a classical topic in term rewriting; cf. Genet [7] for a survey. Some modern techniques include the tree-automata-completion approach [5,6] and a Knuth-Bendix completion-like approach [4]. Compared to these lines of work, first of all our interest is not directly in reachability problems but their (un)satisfiability. Middeldorp [12] proposed tree-automata techniques to approximate dependency graphs and made a theoretical comparison to an early term-cap-unifiability method [2], a predecessor of the tcap-based method. It is indeed possible (after some approximations of input TRSs) to encode our satisfiability problems into reachability problems between regular tree languages. However, our main motivation is to efficiently test reachability when analyzing other properties like termination and confluence. In that setting, constructing tree automata often leads to excessive overhead.

Our work is inspired by the work of Lucas and Gutiérrez [11]. Their *feasibility sequences* serve the same purpose as our reachability constraints, but are limited to atoms and conjunctions. Our formulation, allowing other constructions of logic formulas, is essential for introducing look-ahead reachability.

8   Conclusion

We introduced reachability constraints and their satisfiability problem. Such problems appear in termination and confluence analysis of plain and conditional rewriting. Moreover, we proposed two efficient techniques to prove (un)satisfiability of reachability constraints, first for plain and then for conditional rewriting. Finally, we implemented these techniques in the termination prover NaTT and the confluence prover ConCon, and experimentally verified their significance.

---

[7] http://cops.uibk.ac.at/?q=oriented+ctrs.

Acknowledgments. We thank Aart Middeldorp and the anonymous reviewers for their insightful comments. This work is supported by the Austrian Science Fund (FWF) project P27502 and ERATO HASUO Metamathematics for Systems Design Project (No. JPMJER1603), JST.

References

1. Aoto, T., Hirokawa, N., Nagele, J., Nishida, N., Zankl, H.: Confluence competition 2015. In: Felty, A.P., Middeldorp, A. (eds.) CADE 2015. LNCS (LNAI), vol. 9195, pp. 101–104. Springer, Cham (2015). https://doi.org/10.1007/978-3-319-21401-6_5
2. Arts, T., Giesl, J.: Termination of term rewriting using dependency pairs. Theor. Compt. Sci. **236**(1–2), 133–178 (2000). https://doi.org/10.1016/S0304-3975(99)00207-8
3. Baader, F., Nipkow, T.: Term Rewriting and All That. Cambridge University Press, Cambridge (1998)
4. Burel, G., Dowek, G., Jiang, Y.: A completion method to decide reachability in rewrite systems. In: Lutz, C., Ranise, S. (eds.) FroCoS 2015. LNCS (LNAI), vol. 9322, pp. 205–219. Springer, Cham (2015). https://doi.org/10.1007/978-3-319-24246-0_13
5. Felgenhauer, B., Thiemann, R.: Reachability, confluence, and termination analysis with state-compatible automata. Inf. Comput. **253**, 467–483 (2017). https://doi.org/10.1016/j.ic.2016.06.011
6. Feuillade, G., Genet, T., Viet Triem Tong, V.: Reachability analysis over term rewriting systems. J. Autom. Reason. **33**(341), 341–383 (2004). https://doi.org/10.1007/s10817-004-6246-0
7. Genet, T.: Reachability analysis of rewriting for software verification. Habilitation à diriger des recherches, Université de Rennes 1 (2009)
8. Giesl, J., Mesnard, F., Rubio, A., Thiemann, R., Waldmann, J.: Termination competition (termCOMP 2015). In: Felty, A.P., Middeldorp, A. (eds.) CADE 2015. LNCS (LNAI), vol. 9195, pp. 105–108. Springer, Cham (2015). https://doi.org/10.1007/978-3-319-21401-6_6
9. Giesl, J., Thiemann, R., Schneider-Kamp, P.: Proving and disproving termination of higher-order functions. In: Gramlich, B. (ed.) FroCoS 2005. LNCS (LNAI), vol. 3717, pp. 216–231. Springer, Heidelberg (2005). https://doi.org/10.1007/11559306_12
10. Hirokawa, N., Middeldorp, A.: Dependency pairs revisited. In: van Oostrom, V. (ed.) RTA 2004. LNCS, vol. 3091, pp. 249–268. Springer, Heidelberg (2004). https://doi.org/10.1007/978-3-540-25979-4_18
11. Lucas, S., Gutiérrez, R.: Use of logical models for proving infeasibility in term rewriting. Inf. Process. Lett. **136**, 90–95 (2018). https://doi.org/10.1016/j.ipl.2018.04.002
12. Middeldorp, A.: Approximating dependency graphs using tree automata techniques. In: Goré, R., Leitsch, A., Nipkow, T. (eds.) IJCAR 2001. LNCS, vol. 2083, pp. 593–610. Springer, Heidelberg (2001). https://doi.org/10.1007/3-540-45744-5_49
13. Sternagel, T., Middeldorp, A.: Conditional confluence (system description). In: Dowek, G. (ed.) RTA 2014. LNCS, vol. 8560, pp. 456–465. Springer, Cham (2014). https://doi.org/10.1007/978-3-319-08918-8_31

14. TeReSe: Term Rewriting Systems. Cambridge Tracts in Theoretical Computer Science, vol. 55. Cambridge University Press, Cambridge (2003)
15. Toyama, Y.: Counterexamples to termination for the direct sum of term rewriting systems. Inf. Process. Lett. **25**(3), 141–143 (1987). https://doi.org/10.1016/0020-0190(87)90122-0
16. Yamada, A., Kusakari, K., Sakabe, T.: Nagoya termination tool. In: Dowek, G. (ed.) RTA 2014. LNCS, vol. 8560, pp. 466–475. Springer, Cham (2014). https://doi.org/10.1007/978-3-319-08918-8_32

Model Checking

VoxLogicA: A Spatial Model Checker for Declarative Image Analysis

Gina Belmonte[1], Vincenzo Ciancia[2(✉)],
Diego Latella[2], and Mieke Massink[2]

[1] Azienda Ospedaliera Universitaria Senese, Siena, Italy
[2] Consiglio Nazionale delle Ricerche - Istituto di Scienza e Tecnologie
dell'Informazione 'A. Faedo', CNR, Pisa, Italy
vincenzo.ciancia@isti.cnr.it

Abstract. Spatial and spatio-temporal model checking techniques have a wide range of application domains, among which large scale distributed systems and signal and image analysis. We explore a new domain, namely (semi-)automatic contouring in Medical Imaging, introducing the tool VoxLogicA which merges the state-of-the-art library of computational imaging algorithms ITK with the unique combination of declarative specification and optimised execution provided by spatial logic model checking. The result is a *rapid*, logic based analysis development methodology. The analysis of an existing benchmark of medical images for segmentation of brain tumours shows that simple VoxLogicA analysis can reach state-of-the-art accuracy, competing with best-in-class algorithms, with the advantage of *explainability* and easy *replicability*. Furthermore, due to a two-orders-of-magnitude speedup compared to the existing *general-purpose* spatio-temporal model checker topochecker, VoxLogicA enables *interactive* development of analysis of 3D medical images, which can greatly facilitate the work of professionals in this domain.

Keywords: Spatial logics · Closure spaces · Model checking · Medical Imaging

1 Introduction and Related Work

Spatial and Spatio-temporal model checking have gained an increasing interest in recent years in various domains of application ranging from Collective Adaptive Systems [11,15,18] and networked systems [27], to *signals* [32] and *digital images* [14,26]. Research in this field has its origin in the *topological* approach to spatial logics, dating back to the work of Alfred Tarski (see [9] for a thorough introduction). More recently these early theoretical foundations have been extended to encompass reasoning about *discrete* spatial structures, such as graphs and images, extending the theoretical framework of topology to *(quasi discrete) closure spaces* (see for instance [1,23,24]). That framework has subsequently been taken further in recent work by Ciancia et al. [13,14,17] resulting in the definition of the *Spatial Logic for Closure Spaces* (SLCS), temporal extensions (see [12,32,36]), and related model checking algorithms and tools.

© The Author(s) 2019
T. Vojnar and L. Zhang (Eds.): TACAS 2019, Part I, LNCS 11427, pp. 281–298, 2019.
https://doi.org/10.1007/978-3-030-17462-0_16

The main idea of spatial (and spatio-temporal) model checking is to use specifications written in a suitable logical language to describe spatial properties and to automatically identify patterns and structures of interest in a variety of domains (see e.g., [5,16,18]). In this paper we focus on one such domain, namely medical imaging for radiotherapy, and brain tumour segmentation in particular, which is an important and currently very active research domain of its own. One of the technical challenges of the development of automated (brain) tumour segmentation is that lesion areas are only defined through differences in the intensity (luminosity) in the (black & white) images that are *relative* to the intensity of the surrounding normal tissue. A further complication is that even (laborious and time consuming) manual segmentation by experts shows significant variations when intensity gradients between adjacent tissue structures are smooth or partially obscured [31]. Moreover, there is a considerable variation across images from different patients and images obtained with different Magnetic Resonance Images (MRI) scanners. Several automatic and semi-automatic methods have been proposed in this very active research area (see e.g., [20–22,29,34,37]).

This paper continues the research line of [3,7,8], introducing the free and open source tool VoxLogicA (*Voxel-based Logical Analyser*)[1], catering for a novel approach to image segmentation, namely a *rapid-development*, declarative, logic-based method, supported by *spatial model checking*. This approach is particularly suitable to reason at the "macro-level", by exploiting the *relative* spatial relations between tissues or organs at risk. VoxLogicA is similar, in the accepted logical language, and functionality, to the spatio-temporal model checker topochecker[2], but specifically designed for the analysis of (possibly multi-dimensional, e.g. 3D) *digital images* as a specialised image analysis tool. It is tailored to usability and efficiency by employing state-of-the-art algorithms and open source libraries, borrowed from computational image processing, in combination with efficient spatial model checking algorithms.

We show the application of VoxLogicA on BraTS 2017[3] [2,31,35], a publicly available set of benchmark MRI images for brain tumour segmentation, linked to a yearly challenge. For each image, a manual segmentation of the tumour by domain experts is available, enabling rigorous and objective qualitative comparisons via established similarity indexes. We propose a simple, yet effective, high-level specification for glioblastoma segmentation. The procedure, partly derived from the one presented in [3], directly competes in accuracy with the state-of-the-art techniques submitted to the BraTS 2017 challenge, most of which based on machine learning. Our approach to segmentation has the unique advantage of *explainability*, and is easy to replicate; in fact, the structure of a logically specified procedure can be explained to domain experts, and improved to encompass new observations. A mathematically formalised, unambiguous semantics permits results to be replicated not only by executing them in the multi-platform, open source tool that has been provided, but also by computing them via different implementations.

---

[1] VoxLogicA: https://github.com/vincenzoml/VoxLogicA.

[2] Topochecker: *a topological model checker*, see http://topochecker.isti.cnr.it, https://github.com/vincenzoml/topochecker.

[3] See https://www.med.upenn.edu/sbia/brats2017/data.html.

2   The Spatial Logic Framework

In this section, we briefly recall the logical language ImgQL (*Image Query Language*) proposed in [3], which is based on the *Spatial Logic for Closure Spaces* SLCS [13,14] and which forms the *kernel* of the framework we propose in the present paper. In Sect. 4 we will see how the resulting logic can be used for actual analysis via spatial model checking.

2.1   Foundations: Spatial Logics for Closure Spaces

The logic for closure spaces we use in the present paper is closely related to SLCS [13,14] and, in particular, to the SLCS extension with distance-based operators presented in [3]. As in [3], the resulting logic constitutes the *kernel* of a solid logical framework for reasoning about texture features of digital images, when interpreted as closure spaces. In the context of our work, a *digital image* is not only a 2-dimensional grid of *pixels*, but, more generally, a multi-dimensional (very often, 3-dimensional) grid of hyper-rectangular elements that are called *voxels* ("volumetric picture elements"). When voxels are not *hypercubes*, images are said to be *anisotropic*; this is usually the case in medical imaging. Furthermore, a digital image may contain information about its "real world" spatial dimensions, position (origin) and rotation, permitting one to compute the real-world coordinates of the centre and edges of each voxel. In medical imaging, such information is typically encapsulated into data by machines such as MRI scanners. In the remainder of the paper, we make no dimensionality assumptions. From now on, we refer to picture elements either as voxels or simply as points.

Definition 1. *A* closure space *is a pair* $(X, \mathcal{C})$ *where* X *is a non-empty set (of points) and* $\mathcal{C} : 2^X \to 2^X$ *is a function satisfying the following axioms:* $\mathcal{C}(\emptyset) = \emptyset$; $Y \subseteq \mathcal{C}(Y)$ *for all* $Y \subseteq X$; $\mathcal{C}(Y_1 \cup Y_2) = \mathcal{C}(Y_1) \cup \mathcal{C}(Y_2)$ *for all* $Y_1, Y_2 \subseteq X$.   •

Given any relation $R \subseteq X \times X$, function $\mathcal{C}_R : 2^X \to 2^X$ with $\mathcal{C}_R(Y) \triangleq Y \cup \{x \mid \exists y \in Y . y\, R\, x\}$ satisfies the axioms of Definition 1 thus making $(X, \mathcal{C}_R)$ a closure space. Whenever a closure space is generated by a relation as above, it is called a *quasi-discrete* closure space. A quasi-discrete closure space $(X, \mathcal{C}_R)$, can be used as the basis for a mathematical model of a digital image. X represents the finite set of *voxels* and R is the reflexive and symmetric *adjacency* relation between voxels [25]. A closure space $(X, \mathcal{C})$ can be enriched with a notion of *distance*, i.e. a function $d : X \times X \to \mathbb{R}_{\geq 0} \cup \{\infty\}$ such that $d(x, y) = 0$ iff $x = y$, leading to the *distance closure space* $((X, \mathcal{C}), d)$.[4]

---

[4] We recall that for $\emptyset \neq Y \subseteq X$, $d(x, Y) \triangleq \inf\{d(x, y) \mid y \in Y\}$, with $d(x, \emptyset) = \infty$. In addition, as the definition of d might require the elements of R to be weighted, quasi-discrete distance closure spaces may be enriched with a R-weighting function $\mathcal{W} : R \to \mathbb{R}$ assigning the weight $\mathcal{W}(x, y)$ to each $(x, y) \in R$. In the sequel we will keep $\mathcal{W}$ implicit, whenever possible and for the sake of simplicity.

It is sometimes convenient to equip the points of a closure space with *attributes*; for instance, in the case of images, such attributes could be the color or intensity of voxels. We assume sets A and V of attribute *names* and *values*, and an *attribute valuation* function $\mathcal{A}$ such that $\mathcal{A}(x, a) \in V$ is the value of attribute a of point x. Attributes can be used in *assertions* α, i.e. boolean expressions, with standard syntax and semantics. Consequently, we abstract from related details here and assume function $\mathcal{A}$ extended in the obvious way; for instance, $\mathcal{A}(x, a \leq c) = \mathcal{A}(x, a) \leq c$, for appropriate constant c.

A (quasi-discrete) *path* π in $(X, \mathcal{C}_R)$ is a function $\pi : \mathbb{N} \to X$, such that for all $Y \subseteq \mathbb{N}$, $\pi(\mathcal{C}_{Succ}(Y)) \subseteq \mathcal{C}_R(\pi(Y))$, where $(\mathbb{N}, \mathcal{C}_{Succ})$ is the closure space of natural numbers with the *successor* relation: $(n, m) \in Succ \Leftrightarrow m = n + 1$. Intuitively: the ordering in the path imposed by $\mathbb{N}$ is compatible with relation R, i.e. $\pi(i) \, R \, \pi(i+1)$. For given set P of *atomic predicates* p, and interval of $\mathbb{R}$ I, the syntax of the logic we use in this paper is given below:

$$\Phi ::= p \mid \neg \Phi \mid \Phi_1 \wedge \Phi_2 \mid \mathcal{N}\Phi \mid \rho \, \Phi_1[\Phi_2] \mid \mathcal{D}^I \Phi \tag{1}$$

We assume that space is modelled by the set of points of a distance closure space; each atomic predicate $p \in P$ models a specific *feature* of *points* and is thus associated with the points that have this feature[5]. A point x satisfies $\mathcal{N} \Phi$ if a point satisfying Φ can be reached from x in at most one (closure) step, i.e. if x is *near* (or *close*) to a point satisfying Φ; x satisfies $\rho \, \Phi_1[\Phi_2]$ if x *may reach* a point satisfying Φ_1 via a path passing only by points satisfying Φ_2; it satisfies $\mathcal{D}^I \Phi$ if its distance from the set of points satisfying Φ falls in interval I. The logic includes logical negation ($\neg$) and conjunction ($\wedge$). In the following we formalise the semantics of the logic. A *distance closure model* $\mathcal{M}$ is a tuple $\mathcal{M} = (((X, \mathcal{C}), d), \mathcal{A}, \mathcal{V})$, where $((X, \mathcal{C}), d)$ is a distance closure space, $\mathcal{A} : X \times A \to V$ an attribute valuation, and $\mathcal{V} : P \to 2^X$ is a valuation of atomic propositions.

Definition 2. Satisfaction $\mathcal{M}, x \models \Phi$ *of a formula* Φ *at point* $x \in X$ *in model* $\mathcal{M} = (((X, \mathcal{C}), d), \mathcal{A}, \mathcal{V})$ *is defined by induction on the structure of formulas:*

$$\mathcal{M}, x \models p \in P \quad \Leftrightarrow x \in \mathcal{V}(p)$$
$$\mathcal{M}, x \models \neg \Phi \quad\quad \Leftrightarrow \mathcal{M}, x \models \Phi \text{ does not hold}$$
$$\mathcal{M}, x \models \Phi_1 \wedge \Phi_2 \Leftrightarrow \mathcal{M}, x \models \Phi_1 \text{ and } \mathcal{M}, x \models \Phi_2$$
$$\mathcal{M}, x \models \mathcal{N} \Phi \quad\quad \Leftrightarrow x \in \mathcal{C}(\{y \mid \mathcal{M}, y \models \Phi\})$$
$$\mathcal{M}, x \models \rho \, \Phi_1[\Phi_2] \Leftrightarrow \text{ there is path } \pi \text{ and index } \ell \text{ s.t. } \pi(0) = x \text{ and } \mathcal{M}, \pi(\ell) \models \Phi_1$$
$$\text{and for all indexes } j : 0 < j < \ell \text{ implies } \mathcal{M}, \pi(j) \models \Phi_2$$
$$\mathcal{M}, x \models \mathcal{D}^I \Phi \quad \Leftrightarrow d(x, \{y \mid \mathcal{M}, y \models \Phi\}) \in I$$

where, when $p := \alpha$ *is a definition for* p, *we let* $x \in \mathcal{V}(p)$ *iff* $\mathcal{A}(x, \alpha)$ *is true.* ●

---

[5] In particular, a predicate p can be a *defined* one, by means of a definition as $p := \alpha$, meaning that the feature of interest is characterized by the (boolean) value of α.

In the logic proposed in [13,14], the "may reach" operator is not present, and the *surrounded* operator $\mathcal{S}$ has been defined as basic operator as follows: x satisfies $\Phi_1 \, \mathcal{S} \, \Phi_2$ if and only if x belongs to an area of points satisfying Φ_1 and one cannot "escape" from such an area without hitting a point satisfying Φ_2. Several types of *reachability* predicates can be derived from $\mathcal{S}$. However, reachability is in turn a widespread, more basic primitive, implemented in various forms (e.g., *flooding, connected components*) in programming libraries. Thus, in this work, we prefer to use reachability as a basic predicate of the logic, as in [4], which is dedicated to extending the *Spatial Signal Temporal Logic* of [32]. In the sequel we show that $\mathcal{S}$ can be derived from the operators defined above, employing a definition patterned after the model-checking algorithm of [13]. This change simplifies the definition of several derived connectives, including that of *touch* (see below), and resulted in notably faster execution times for analyses using such derived connectives. We recall the definition of $\mathcal{S}$ from [14]: $\mathcal{M}, x \models \Phi_1 \, \mathcal{S} \, \Phi_2$ if and only if $\mathcal{M}, x \models \Phi_1$ and for all paths π and indexes ℓ we have: if $\pi(0) = x$ and $\mathcal{M}, \pi(\ell) \models \neg\Phi_1$, then there is j such that $0 < j \leq \ell$ and $\mathcal{M}, \pi(j) \models \Phi_2$.

Proposition 1. *For all closure models* $\mathcal{M} = ((X, \mathcal{C}), \mathcal{A}, \mathcal{V})$ *and all formulas* Φ_1, Φ_2 *the following holds:* $\Phi_1 \, \mathcal{S} \, \Phi_2 \equiv \Phi_1 \wedge \neg(\rho \, \neg(\Phi_1 \vee \Phi_2)[\neg\Phi_2])$ ◇

Definition 3. *We define some derived operators that are of particular use in medical image analysis:* $touch(\Phi_1, \Phi_2) \triangleq \Phi_1 \wedge \rho \, \Phi_2[\Phi_1]; grow(\Phi_1, \Phi_2) \triangleq \Phi_1 \vee touch(\Phi_2, \Phi_1); flt(r, \Phi_1) \triangleq \mathcal{D}^{<r}(\mathcal{D}^{\geq r}\neg\Phi_1)$ •

The formula $touch(\Phi_1, \Phi_2)$ is satisfied by points that satisfy Φ_1 and that are on a path of points satisfying Φ_1 that reaches a point satisfying Φ_2. The formula $grow(\Phi_1, \Phi_2)$ is satisfied by points that satisfy Φ_1 and by points that satisfy Φ_2 which are on a path of points satisfying Φ_2 that reaches a point satisfying Φ_1. The formula $flt(r, \Phi_1)$ is satisfied by points that are at a distance of less than r from a point that is at least at distance r from points that do not satisfy Φ_1. This operator works as a filter; only contiguous areas satisfying Φ_1 that have a minimal diameter of at least $2r$ are preserved; these are also smoothened if they have an irregular shape (e.g. protrusions of less than the indicated distance).

Example 1. In Fig. 1, the top row shows four pictures using colours *blue* and *red*, interpreted as atomic propositions. Each picture in the bottom row shows in white the points that satisfy a given formula. In particular: Fig. 1e is $blue \, \mathcal{S} \, red$ of (a); Fig. 1f is touch($red, blue$) of (b); Fig. 1g is grow($red, blue$) of (c); Fig. 1h is $red \, \mathcal{S} \, (\mathcal{D}^{\leq 11} blue)$ of (d). For more details the reader is referred to [6].

2.2   Region Similarity via Statistical Cross-correlation

In the sequel, we provide some details on a logical operator, first defined in [3], that we use in the context of Texture Analysis (see for example [10,19,28,30]) for defining a notion of *statistical similarity* between image regions. The statistical distribution of an area Y of a black and white image is approximated

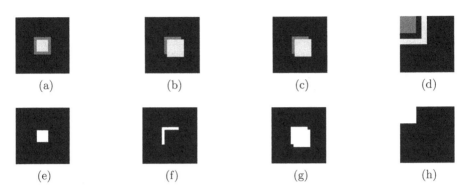

Fig. 1. Some examples of `ImgQL` operators (see Example 1). (Color figure online)

by the *histogram* of the grey levels of points (voxels) belonging to Y, limiting the representation to those levels laying in a certain interval $[m, M]$, the latter being split into k *bins*. In the case of images modelled as closure models, where each point may have several attributes, the histogram can be defined for different attributes. Given a closure model $\mathcal{M} = ((X, \mathcal{C}), \mathcal{A}, \mathcal{V})$, define function $\mathcal{H} : A \times 2^X \times \mathbb{R} \times \mathbb{R} \times \mathbb{N} \to (\mathbb{N} \to \mathbb{N})$ such that for all $m < M$, $k > 0$ and $i \in \{1, \ldots, k\}$, $\mathcal{H}(a, Y, m, M, k)(i) = \left| \{y \in Y \mid (i-1) \cdot \Delta \le \mathcal{A}(y, a) - m < i \cdot \Delta\} \right|$ where $\Delta = \frac{M-m}{k}$. We call $\mathcal{H}(a, Y, m, M, k)$ the *histogram* of Y (for attribute a), with k bins and m, M min and max values respectively. The *mean* $\overline{h}$ of a histogram h with k *bins* is the quantity $\frac{1}{k} \sum_{i=1}^{k} h(i)$. The *cross correlation* between two histograms h_1, h_2 with the same number k of *bins* is defined as follows: $\mathbf{r}(h_1, h_2) = \frac{\sum_{i=1}^{k}\left(h_1(i) - \overline{h_1}\right)\left(h_2(i) - \overline{h_2}\right)}{\sqrt{\sum_{i=1}^{k}\left(h_1(i) - \overline{h_1}\right)^2}\sqrt{\sum_{i=1}^{k}\left(h_2(i) - \overline{h_2}\right)^2}}$. The value of $\mathbf{r}$ is *normalised* so that $-1 \le \mathbf{r} \le 1$; $\mathbf{r}(h_1, h_2) = 1$ indicates that h_1 and h_2 are *perfectly correlated* (that is, $h_1 = ah_2 + b$, with $a > 0$); $\mathbf{r}(h_1, h_2) = -1$ indicates *perfect anti-correlation* (that is, $h_1 = ah_2 + b$, with $a < 0$). On the other hand, $\mathbf{r}(h_1, h_2) = 0$ indicates no correlation.

We embed *statistical similarity* $\triangle_{\bowtie c}\left[\begin{smallmatrix} m & M & k \\ r & a & b \end{smallmatrix}\right]$ in the logic by adding it to the grammar defined by (1) and extending the definition of the satisfaction relation (Definition 2) with the following equation, for m, M, k as above:

$$\mathcal{M}, x \models \triangle_{\bowtie c}\left[\begin{smallmatrix} m & M & k \\ r & a & b \end{smallmatrix}\right]\Phi \Leftrightarrow \mathbf{r}(h_a, h_b) \bowtie c$$

where $h_a = \mathcal{H}(a, S(x, r), m, M, k)$, $h_b = \mathcal{H}(b, \{y \mid \mathcal{M}, y \models \Phi\}, m, M, k)$, c is a constant in $[-1, 1]$, $\bowtie \in \{<, \le, =, \ge, >\}$ and $S(x, r) = \{y \in X \mid d(x, y) \le r\}$ is the *sphere* of radius r centred in x. Note that, differently from `topochecker` that was used in [3], in `VoxLogicA`, for efficiency reasons, $S(x, r)$ is actually the *hypercube* with edge size $2r$, which, for anisotropic images, becomes a hyperrectangle. So $\triangle_{\bowtie c}\left[\begin{smallmatrix} m & M & k \\ r & a & b \end{smallmatrix}\right]\Phi$ compares the region of the image constituted by the sphere (hypercube) of radius r centred in x against the region characterised by Φ. The comparison is based on the cross correlation of the histograms of the chosen attributes of (the points of) the two regions, namely a and b and both histograms share the same range ($[m, M]$) and the same bins ($[1, k]$). In summary, the operator allows to check *to which extent* the *sphere (hypercube) around the point of interest* is *statistically similar* to a given region (specified by) Φ.

3 The Tool VoxLogicA

VoxLogicA is a framework for image analysis, that embeds the logic ImgQL into a user-oriented expression language to manipulate images. More precisely, the VoxLogicA type system distinguishes between *boolean-valued* images, that can be arguments or results of the application of ImgQL operators, and *number-valued* images, resulting from imaging primitives. Underlying such expression language is a *global model checker*, that is, the set of points satisfying a logic formula is computed at once; this is done implicitly when an expression corresponding to a logic formula is saved to an image. Functionality-wise, VoxLogicA specialises topochecker to the case of spatial analysis of *multi-dimensional images*. It interprets a specification written in the ImgQL language, using a set of multi-dimensional images[6] as models of the spatial logic, and produces as output a set of multi-dimensional images representing the valuation of user-specified expressions. For logical operators, such images are Boolean-valued, that is, *regions of interest* in medical imaging terminology, which may be loaded as *overlays* in medical image viewers. Non-logical operators may generate number-valued images. VoxLogicA augments ImgQL with file loading and saving primitives, and a set of additional commodity operators, specifically aimed at image analysis, that is destined to grow along with future developments of the tool. The main execution modality of VoxLogicA is *batch execution*. A (currently experimental) *graphical user interface* is under development.

Implementation-wise, the tool achieves a two-orders-of-magnitude speedup with respect to topochecker. Such speedup has permitted the rapid development of a novel procedure for automatic segmentation of *glioblastoma* that, besides being competitive with respect to the state-of-the-art in the field (see Sect. 4), is also easily *replicable* and *explainable* to humans, and therefore amenable of improvement by the community of medical imaging practitioners.

3.1 Functionality

We provide an overview of the tool functionality, starting from its syntax. For space reasons, we omit details on parsing rules (delegated to the tool documentation). In the following, f, x1,..., xN, x are identifiers, "s" is a string, and e1, ..., eN, e are expressions (to be detailed later). A VoxLogicA specification consists of a text file containing a sequence of **commands** (see Specification 1 in Sect. 4 as an example). Five commands are currently implemented:

---

[6] Besides common bitmap formats, the model loader of VoxLogicA currently supports the NIfTI (Neuro-imaging Informatics Technology Initiative) format (https://nifti.nimh.nih.gov/, version 1 and 2). 3D MR-FLAIR images in this format very often have a slice size of 256 by 256 pixels, multiplied by 20 to 30 slices.

– `let f(x1,...,xN) = e` is used for *function declaration*, also in the form `let f = e` *(constant declaration)*, and with special syntactic provisions to define *infix* operators. After execution of the command, name `f` is bound to a function or constant that evaluates to `e` with the appropriate substitutions of parameters;
– `load x = "s"` loads an image from file `"s"` and binds it to `x` for subsequent usage;
– `save "s" e` stores the image resulting from evaluation of expression `e` to file `"s"`;
– `print "s" e` prints to the log the string `s` followed by the numeric, or boolean, result of computing `e`;
– `import "s"` imports a library of declarations from file `"s"`; subsequent import declarations for the *same* file are not processed; furthermore, such imported files can only contain `let` or `import` commands.

`VoxLogicA` comes equipped with a set of built-in functions, such as arithmetic operators, logic primitives as described in Sect. 2, and imaging operators, for instance for computing the gray-scale intensity of a colour image, or its colour components, or the percentiles of its values (see Sect. 4.1). An exhaustive list of the available built-ins is provided in the user manual[7]. Furthermore, a "standard library" is provided containing short-hands for commonly used functions, and for derived operators. An **expression** may be a numeric literal (no distinction is made between floating point and integer constants), an identifier (e.g. `x`), a function application (e.g. `f(x1,x2)`), an infix operator application (e.g. `x1 + x2`), or a parenthesized (sub-)expression (e.g. `(x1 + x2)`).

The language features **strong dynamic typing**, that is, types of expressions are unambiguously checked and errors are precisely reported, but such checks are only performed at "run time", that is, when evaluating closed-form expressions with no free variables. The type system has currently been kept lightweight (the only typing rules regard constants and function application), in order to leave the design space open to future improvements. For instance, a planned development is function and operator *overloading*, as well as some form of static typing not interfering with the usability of the tool.

However, it is *not* the case that a type error may waste a long-running analysis. Type checking occurs after loading and parsing, but before analysis is run. Actual program execution after parsing is divided into two phases. First (usually, in a negligible amount of time), all the "save" and "print" instructions are examined to determine what expressions actually *need* to be computed; in this phase, name binding is resolved, all constant and function applications are substituted with closed expressions, types are checked and the environment binding expressions to names is discarded. Finally, the set of closed expressions to be evaluated is transformed into a set of tasks to be executed, possibly in parallel, and dependencies among them. After this phase, no further syntax processing or name resolution are needed, and it is guaranteed that the program is free from type errors. The second phase simply runs each task – in an order compliant with dependencies – parallelising execution on multiple CPU cores.

Each built-in logical operator has an associated type of its input parameters and output result. The available types are inductively defined as `Number`, `Bool`,

---

[7] See https://github.com/vincenzoml/VoxLogicA.

String, Model, and Valuation(t), where t is in turn a type. The type Model is the type assigned to x in load x = "f"; operations such as the extraction of RGB components take this type as input, and return as output the only parametric type: Valuation(t), which is the type of a multi-dimensional image in which each voxel contains a value of type t. For instance, the red component of a loaded model has type Valuation(Number), whereas the result of evaluating a logic formula has type Valuation(Bool)[8].

An important aspect of the execution semantics of VoxLogicA specifications is *memoization*, constituting the core of its execution engine, and used to achieve maximal sharing of subformulas. In VoxLogicA, no expression is ever computed twice, freeing the user from worrying about how many times a given function is called, and making execution of complex macros and logical operators feasible.

3.2   Implementation Details

VoxLogicA is implemented in the functional, object-oriented programming language FSharp, using the .NET Core implementation of the .NET specification[9]. This permits a single code base with minimal environment-dependent setup to be cross-compiled and deployed as a standalone executable, for the major desktop operating systems, namely *Linux*, *macOS*, and *Windows*. Despite .NET code is compiled for an intermediate machine, this does not mean that efficiency of VoxLogicA is somehow "non-native". There are quite a number of measures in place to maximise efficiency. First and foremost, the execution time is heavily dominated by the time spent in native libraries (more details below), and VoxLogicA acts as a higher-level, declarative front-end for such libraries, adding a logical language, memoization, parallel execution, and abstraction from a plethora of technical details that a state-of-the-art imaging library necessarily exposes. In our experiments, parsing, memoization, and preparation of the tasks to be run may take a fraction of a second; the rest of the execution time (usually, several seconds, unless the analysis is extremely simple) is spent in *foreign function calls*. The major performance boosters in VoxLogicA are: a state-of-the-art computational imaging library (ITK); the optimised implementation of the *may reach* operator; a new algorithm for statistical cross-correlation; an efficient memoizing execution engine; parallel evaluation of independent tasks, exploiting modern multi-core CPUs. Moreover, special care has been put in making all performance-critical loops *allocationless*. All used memory along the loops is pre-allocated, avoiding the risk to trigger garbage collection during computation. We will address each of them briefly in the following.

ITK Library. VoxLogicA uses the state-of-the-art imaging library ITK, via the SimpleITK glue library[10]. Most of the operators of VoxLogicA are implemented

---

[8] Although such type system would permit "odd" types such as Valuation(Model), there is no way to construct them; in the future this may change when appropriate.
[9] See https://fsharp.org and https://dotnet.github.io.
[10] See https://itk.org and http://www.simpleitk.org.

directly by a library call. Notably, this includes the *Maurer distance transform*, used to efficently implement the distance operators of ImgQL.

Novel Algorithms. The two most relevant operators that do not have a direct implementation in ITK are `mayReach` and `crossCorrelation`, implementing, respectively, the logical operator ρ, and statistical comparison described in Sect. 2.2. The computation of the voxels satisfying $\rho\ \phi_1[\phi_2]$ can be implemented either using the (classical, in computer graphics) *flood-fill* primitive, or by exploiting the *connected components* of ϕ_2 as a reachability primitive; both solutions are available in `SimpleITK`. In our experiments, connected components perform better using this library from `FSharp`, for large input seeds. Several critical logical connectives (e.g. *surrounded* and *touch*), are defined in terms of `mayReach`. Therefore, an optimised algorithm for `mayReach` is a key performance improvement. The `crossCorrelation` operation is resource-intensive, as it uses the histogram of a multi-dimensional hyperrectangle at each voxel. Pre-computation methods such as the *integral histogram* [33], would not yield the expected benefits, because cross-correlation is called only few times on the same image. In this work, we designed a parallel algorithm exploiting *additivity* of histograms. Given two sets of values P_1, P_2, let h_1, h_2 be their respective histograms, and let h_1', h_2' be the histograms of $P_1 \backslash P_2$ and $P_2 \backslash P_1$. For i a bin, we have $h_2(i) = h_1(i) - h_1'(i) + h_2'(i)$. This property leads to a particularly efficient algorithm when P_1 and P_2 are two hyperrectangles centred over adjacent voxels, as $P_1 \backslash P_2$ and $P_2 \backslash P_1$ are *hyperfaces*, having one dimension less than hyperrectangles. Our algorithm divides the image into as many partitions as the number of available processors, and then computes a *Hamiltonian path* for each partition, passing by each of its voxels exactly once. All partitions are visited in parallel, in the order imposed by such Hamiltonian paths; the histogram is computed incrementally as described above; finally cross-correlation is also computed and stored in the resulting image. The *asymptotic algorithmic complexity* of the implementation of ImgQL primitives in `VoxLogicA` is linear in the number of voxels, with the exception of `crossCorrelation`, which, by the above explanation, has complexity $O(k \cdot n)$, where n is the number of voxels, and k is the size of the largest hyperface of the considered hypercube.

Memoizing Execution Semantics. Sub-expressions in `VoxLogicA` are *by construction* identified up-to syntactic equality and assigned a number, representing a unique identifier (UID). UIDs start from 0 and are contiguous, therefore admitting an array of all existing sub-formulas to be used to pre-computed valuations of expressions without further hashing.

3.3   Design and Data Structures

The design of `VoxLogicA` defines three implementation layers. The *core* execution engine implements the concurrent, memoizing semantics of the tool. The *interpreter* is responsible for translating source code into core library invocations. These two layers only include some basic arithmetic and boolean primitives.

Operators can be added by inheriting from the abstract base class `Model`. The third implementation layer is the instantiation of the core layer to define operators from ImgQL, and loading and saving of graphical models, using the `ITK` library. We provide some more detail on the design of the core layer, which is the most critical part of `VoxLogicA`. At the time of writing, the core consists of just 350 lines of `FSharp` code, that has been carefully engineered not only for performance, but also for ease of maintenance and future extensions.

The essential **classes** are `ModelChecker`, `FormulaFactory`, `Formula`, and `Operator`, of which `Constant` is a subclass. Class `Operator` describes the available operators and their evaluation method. Class `Formula` is a symbolic representation of a syntactic sub-expression. Each instance of `Formula` has a unique numeric id (UID), an instance of `Operator`, and (inductively) a list of `Formula` instances, denoting its arguments. The UID of a formula is determined by the operator name (which is unique across the application), and the list of parameter UIDs. Therefore, by construction, it is not possible to build two different instances of `Formula` that are syntactically equal. UIDs are contiguous and start from 0. By this, all created formulas can be inserted into an array. Furthermore, UIDs are allocated in such a way that the natural number order is a topological sort of the dependency graph between subformulas (that is, if f_1 is a parameter of f_2, the UID of f_1 is greater than the UID of f_2). This is exploited in class `ModelChecker`; internally, the class uses an array to store the results of evaluating each `Formula` instance, implementing memoization. The class `ModelChecker` turns each formula into a task to be executed. Whenever a formula with UID i is a parameter of the formula with UID j, a dependency is noted between the associated tasks. The high-level, lightweight concurrent programming library `Hopac`[11] and its abstractions are used to evaluate the resulting task graph, in order to maximise CPU usage on multi-core machines.

4 Experimental Evaluation

The performance of `VoxLogicA` has been evaluated on the Brain Tumor Image Segmentation Benchmark (BraTS) of 2017 [2,31] containing 210 multi contrast MRI scans of high grade glioma patients that have been obtained from multiple institutions and were acquired with different clinical protocols and various scanners. All the imaging data sets provided by BraTS 2017 have been segmented manually and approved by experienced neuro-radiologists. In our evaluation we used the T2 Fluid Attenuated Inversion Recovery (FLAIR) type of scans, which is one of the four provided modalities in the benchmark. Use of other modalities is planned for future work. For training, the numeric parameters of the `VoxLogicA` specification presented in Sect. 4.1 were manually calibrated against a subset of 20 cases. Validation of the method was conducted as follows. A priori, 17 of the 210 cases can be excluded because the current procedure is not suitable for these images. This is because of the presence of multi-focal tumours (different tumours in different areas of the brain), or due to clearly distinguishable artifacts in the

---

[11] See https://github.com/Hopac/Hopac.

FLAIR acquisition, or because the hyperintense area is too large and clearly not significant (possibly by incorrect acquisition). Such cases require further investigation. For instance, the current procedure may be improved to identify specific types of artefacts, whereas multi-modal analysis can be used to complement the information provided by the FLAIR image in cases where FLAIR hyperintensity is not informative enough. In Sect. 4.2, we present the results both for the full dataset (210 cases), and for the subset without these problematic cases (193 cases). We considered both the *gross tumour volume* (GTV), corresponding to what can actually be seen on an image, and the *clinical target volume* (CTV) which is an extension of the GTV. For glioblastomas this margin is a 2–2.5 cm isotropic expansion of the GTV volume within the brain.

4.1   ImgQL Segmentation Procedure

Specification 1 shows the tumour segmentation procedure that we used for the evaluation[12]. The syntax is that of `VoxLogicA`, namely: `|`,`&`,`!` are boolean *or*, *and*, *not*; `distlt(c,phi)` is the set $\{y \mid \mathcal{M}, y \models \mathcal{D}^{<c}phi\}$ (similarly, `distgeq`; distances are in millimiters); `crossCorrelation(r,a,b,phi,m,M,k)` yields a cross-correlation coefficient for each voxel, to which a predicate c may be applied to obtain the *statistical similarity* function of Sect. 2.2; the > operator performs thresholding of an image; `border` is true on voxels that lay at the border of the image. Operator `percentiles(img,mask)`, where `img` is a number-valued image, and `mask` is boolean-valued, considers the points identified by `mask`, and assigns to each such point x the fraction of points that have an intensity below that of x in `img`. Other operators are explained in Definition 3 (see also Fig. 1). Figure 2 shows the intermediate phases of the procedure, for axial view of one specific 2D slice of an example 3D MRI scan of the BraTS 2017 data set.

We briefly discuss the specification (see [6] for more details). Lines 1–8 merely define utility functions and load the image, calling it `flair`. Lines 9–10 define the `background` as all voxels in the area of intensity less than 0.1 that touches the border of the image, and the `brain` as the complement of the background. The application of `percentiles` in line 11 assigns to each point of the brain the percentile rank of its intensity among those that are part of `brain`. Based on these percentiles, hyper-intense and very-intense points are identified that satisfy hI and vI, respectively (lines 12–13). Hyper-intense points have a very high likelihood to belong to tumour tissue; very-high intensity points are likely to belong to the tumour as well, or to the oedema that is usually surrounding the tumour. However, not all hyper-intense and very-intense points are part of a tumour. The idea is to identify the actual tumour using further spatial information. In lines 14–15 the hyper-intense and very-intense points are filtered, thus removing noise, and considering only areas of a certain relevant size.

---

[12] Note that, although the procedure is loosely inspired by the one in [3], there are major differences, partly due to a different method for identification of hyperintensities (using percentiles), and partly since the task in this work is simpler, as we only identify the CTV and GTV (avoiding, for instance, to label the oedema).

The points that satisfy hyperIntense and veryIntense are shown in red in Fig. 2a and in Fig. 2b, respectively. In line 16 the areas of hyper-intense points are extended via the grow operator, with those areas that are very intense (possibly belonging to the oedema), and in turn touch the hyper-intense areas. The points that satisfy growTum are shown in red in Fig. 2c. In line 17 the previously-defined (line 8) similarity operator is used to assign to all voxels a texture-similarity score with respect to growTum. In line 18 this operator is used to find those voxels that have a high cross correlation coefficient and thus are likely part of the tumour. The result is shown in Fig. 2d. Finally (line 19), the voxels that are identified as part of the whole tumour are those that satisfy growTum extended with those that are statistically similar to it via the grow operator. Points that satisfy tumFinal are shown in red in Fig. 2e and points identified by manual segmentation are shown for comparison in blue in the same figure (overlapping areas are purple).

ImgQL Specification 1: Full specification of tumour segmentation

```
1  import "stdlib.imgql"

2  let grow(a,b) = (a | touch(b,a))
3  let flt(r,a) = distlt(r,distgeq(r,!a))
4  load imgFLAIR = "Brats17_2013_2_1_flair.nii.gz"
5  load imgManualSeg = "Brats17_2013_2_1_seg.nii.gz"
6  let manualContouring = intensity(imgManualSeg) > 0
7  let flair = intensity(imgFLAIR)
8  let similarFLAIRTo(a) =
   crossCorrelation(5,flair,flair,a,min(flair),max(flair),100)

9  let background = touch(flair < 0.1,border)
10 let brain = !background
11 let pflair = percentiles(flair,brain)

12 let hI = pflair > 0.95
13 let vI = pflair > 0.86
14 let hyperIntense = flt(5.0,hI)
15 let veryIntense = flt(2.0,vI)

16 let growTum = grow(hyperIntense,veryIntense)
17 let tumSim = similarFLAIRTo(growTum)
18 let tumStatCC = flt(2.0,(tumSim > 0.6))
19 let tumFinal= grow(growTum,tumStatCC)

20 save "output_Brats17_2013_2_1/complete-FLAIR_FL-seg.nii" tumFinal
```

Interesting aspects of the ImgQL specification are its relative simplicity and abstraction level, fitting that of neuro-radiologists, its explainability, its time-efficient verification, admitting a rapid development cycle, and its independence of normalisation procedures through the use of percentiles rather than absolute values for the intensity of voxels.

4.2   Validation Results

Results of tumour segmentation are evaluated based on a number of indexes commonly used to compare the quality of different techniques (see [31]). These indexes are based on the true positive (TP) voxels (voxels that are identified as part of a tumour in both manual and VoxLogicA segmentation), true negatives (TN) voxels (those that are *not* identified as part of a tumour in both manual and VoxLogicA segmentation), false positives (FP) voxels (those identified as part of a tumour by VoxLogicA but not by manual segmentation) and false negatives (FN) voxels (those identified as part of a tumour by manual segmentation but not by VoxLogicA). Based on these four types the following indexes are defined: *sensitivity*: $TP/(TP + FN)$; *specificity*: $TN/(TN + FP)$; *Dice*: $2 * TP/(2 * TP + FN + FP)$. Sensitivity measures the fraction of voxels that are correctly identified as part of a tumour. Specificity measures the fraction of voxels that are correctly identified as *not* being part of a tumour. The Dice similarity coefficient is used to provide a measure of the similarity of two segmentations. Table 1 shows the mean values of the above indexes both for GTV and CTV volumes for Specification 1 applied to the BraTS 2017 training phase collection. The top-scoring methods of the BraTS 2017 Challenge [35] can be considered a good sample of the state-of-the-art in this domain. Among those, in order to collect significant statistics, we selected the 18 techniques that have been applied to at least 100 cases of the dataset. The *median* and *range of values* of the sensitivity, specificity and Dice indexes for the GTV segmentation of the whole tumour are, respectively, 0.88 (ranging from 0.55 to 0.97), 0.99 (0.98 to 0.999) and 0.88 (0.64 to 0.96). The 3D images used in this experiment have size $240 \times 240 \times 155$ (about 9 million voxels). The evaluation of each case study takes about 10 s on a desktop computer equipped with an Intel Core I7 7700 processor (with 8 cores) and 16 GB of RAM.

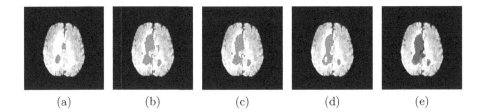

(a)   (b)   (c)   (d)   (e)

Fig. 2. Tumour segmentation of image Brats17_2013_2_1, FLAIR, axial 2D slice at X = 155, Y = 117 and Z = 97. (a) hyperIntense (b) veryIntense (c) growTum (d) tumStatCC (e) tumFinal (red) and manual (blue, overlapping area is purple). (Color figure online)

Table 1. VoxLogicA evaluation on the BraTS 2017 benchmark.

	Sensitivity (193 cases)	Specificity (193 cases)	Dice (193 cases)	Sensitivity (210 cases)	Specificity (210 cases)	Dice (210 cases)
GTV	0.89(0.10)	1.0(0.00)	0.85(0.10)	0.86(0.16)	1.0(0.0)	0.81(0.18)
CTV	0.95(0.07)	0.99(0.01)	0.90(0.09)	0.93(0.14)	0.99(0.2)	0.87(0.15)

4.3   Comparison with topochecker

The evaluation of VoxLogicA that we presented in this section uses features that are present in VoxLogicA, but not in topochecker. On the other hand, the example specification in [3], and its variant aimed at 3D images, are quite similar to the one we presented, and can be readily used to compare the performance of VoxLogicA and topochecker. The specifications consist of two human-authored text files of about 30 lines each. The specifications were run on a desktop computer equipped with an Intel Core I7 7700 processor (with 8 cores) and 16 GB of RAM. In the 2D case (image size: 512×512), topochecker took 52 s to complete the analysis, whereas VoxLogicA took 750 ms. In the 3D case (image size: $512 \times 512 \times 24$), topochecker took about 30 min, whereas VoxLogicA took 15 s. As we mentioned before, this huge improvement is due to the combination of a specialised imaging library, new algorithms (e.g., for statistical similarity of regions), parallel execution and other optimisations. More details could be obtained by designing a specialised set of benchmarks, where some of which can also be run using topochecker; however, for the purposes of the current paper, the performance difference is so large that we do not deem such detailed comparison necessary.

5   Conclusions and Future Work

We presented VoxLogicA, a spatial model checker designed and optimised for the analysis of multi-dimensional digital images. The tool has been successfully evaluated on 193 cases of an international brain tumour 3D MRI segmentation benchmark. The obtained results are well-positioned w.r.t. the performance of state-of-the-art segmentation techniques, both efficiency-wise and accuracy-wise. Future research work based on the tool will focus on further benchmarking (e.g. various other types of tumours and tumour tissue such as necrotic and non-enhancing parts), and clinical application. On the development side, planned future work includes a graphical (web) interface for interactive parameter calibration (for that, execution times will need to be further improved, possibly employing *GPU computing*); improvements in the type-system (e.g. *operator overloading*); turning the core design layer into a reusable library available for other projects. Finally, the (currently small, albeit useful) library of logical and imaging-related primitives available will be enhanced, based on input from case studies. Calibration of the numerical parameters of our Glioblastoma segmentation was done manually. Future work aims at exploring different possibilities for human-computer interaction in designing such procedures (e.g. via ad-hoc graphical interfaces), to improve user friendliness for domain experts. Experimentation in combining *machine-learning* methods with the logic-based approach of `VoxLogicA` are also worth being explored in this respect.

References

1. Aiello, M., Pratt-Hartmann, I., van Benthem, J.: Handbook of Spatial Logics. Springer, Dordrecht (2007). https://doi.org/10.1007/978-1-4020-5587-4
2. Bakas, S., et al.: Advancing the cancer genome atlas glioma MRI collections with expert segmentation labels and radiomic features. Sci. Data **4** (2017). https://doi.org/10.1038/sdata.2017.117. Accessed 05 Sept 2017
3. Banci Buonamici, F., Belmonte, G., Ciancia, V., et al.: Int. J. Softw. Tools Technol. Transfer (2019). https://doi.org/10.1007/s10009-019-00511-9
4. Bartocci, E., Bortolussi, L., Loreti, M., Nenzi, L.: Monitoring mobile and spatially distributed cyber-physical systems. In: Proceedings of the 15th ACM-IEEE International Conference on Formal Methods and Models for System Design, MEMOCODE 2017, pp. 146–155. ACM, New York (2017). http://doi.acm.org/10.1145/3127041.3127050
5. Bartocci, E., Gol, E.A., Haghighi, I., Belta, C.: A formal methods approach to pattern recognition and synthesis in reaction diffusion networks. IEEE Trans. Control Netw. Syst. 1 (2016). https://doi.org/10.1109/tcns.2016.2609138
6. Belmonte, G., Ciancia, V., Latella, D., Massink, M.: VoxLogicA: a spatial model checker for declarative image analysis (Extended Version). ArXiv e-prints, November 2018. https://arxiv.org/abs/1811.05677
7. Belmonte, G., et al.: A topological method for automatic segmentation of glioblastoma in MRI flair for radiotherapy. Magn. Reson. Mater. Phys. Biol. Med. **30**(S1), 437 (2017). https://doi.org/10.1007/s10334-017-0634-z. In ESMRMB 2017, 34th annual scientific meeting
8. Belmonte, G., Ciancia, V., Latella, D., Massink, M.: From collective adaptive systems to human centric computation and back: spatial model checking for medical imaging. In: ter Beek, M.H., Loreti, M. (eds.) Proceedings of the Workshop on FORmal Methods for the Quantitative Evaluation of Collective Adaptive Systems, FORECAST@STAF 2016, Vienna, Austria, 8 July 2016. EPTCS, vol. 217, pp. 81–92 (2016). https://doi.org/10.4204/EPTCS.217.10
9. van Benthem, J., Bezhanishvili, G.: Modal logics of space. In: Aiello, M., Pratt-Hartmann, I., Van Benthem, J. (eds.) Handbook of Spatial Logics, pp. 217–298. Springer, Dordrecht (2007). https://doi.org/10.1007/978-1-4020-5587-4_5
10. Castellano, G., Bonilha, L., Li, L., Cendes, F.: Texture analysis of medical images. Clin. Radiol. **59**(12), 1061–1069 (2004)
11. Ciancia, V., Gilmore, S., Latella, D., Loreti, M., Massink, M.: Data verification for collective adaptive systems: spatial model-checking of vehicle location data. In: Eighth IEEE International Conference on Self-Adaptive and Self-Organizing Systems Workshops, SASOW, pp. 32–37. IEEE Computer Society (2014)
12. Ciancia, V., Grilletti, G., Latella, D., Loreti, M., Massink, M.: An experimental spatio-temporal model checker. In: Bianculli, D., Calinescu, R., Rumpe, B. (eds.) SEFM 2015. LNCS, vol. 9509, pp. 297–311. Springer, Heidelberg (2015). https://doi.org/10.1007/978-3-662-49224-6_24

13. Ciancia, V., Latella, D., Loreti, M., Massink, M.: Specifying and verifying properties of space. In: Diaz, J., Lanese, I., Sangiorgi, D. (eds.) TCS 2014. LNCS, vol. 8705, pp. 222–235. Springer, Heidelberg (2014). https://doi.org/10.1007/978-3-662-44602-7_18

14. Ciancia, V., Latella, D., Loreti, M., Massink, M.: Model checking spatial logics for closure spaces. Log. Methods Comput. Sci. **12**(4), October 2016. http://lmcs.episciences.org/2067

15. Ciancia, V., Latella, D., Massink, M., Pakauskas, R.: Exploring spatio-temporal properties of bike-sharing systems. In: 2015 IEEE International Conference on Self-Adaptive and Self-Organizing Systems Workshops, SASO Workshops, pp. 74–79. IEEE Computer Society (2015)

16. Ciancia, V., Gilmore, S., Grilletti, G., Latella, D., Loreti, M., Massink, M.: Spatio-temporal model checking of vehicular movement in public transport systems. Int. J. Softw. Tools Technol. Transfer (2018). https://doi.org/10.1007/s10009-018-0483-8

17. Ciancia, V., Latella, D., Loreti, M., Massink, M.: Spatial logic and spatial model checking for closure spaces. In: Bernardo, M., De Nicola, R., Hillston, J. (eds.) SFM 2016. LNCS, vol. 9700, pp. 156–201. Springer, Cham (2016). https://doi.org/10.1007/978-3-319-34096-8_6

18. Ciancia, V., Latella, D., Massink, M., Paškauskas, R., Vandin, A.: A tool-chain for statistical spatio-temporal model checking of bike sharing systems. In: Margaria, T., Steffen, B. (eds.) ISoLA 2016, Part I. LNCS, vol. 9952, pp. 657–673. Springer, Cham (2016). https://doi.org/10.1007/978-3-319-47166-2_46

19. Davnall, F., et al.: Assessment of tumor heterogeneity: an emerging imaging tool for clinical practice? Insights Imaging **3**(6), 573–589 (2012)

20. Despotović, I., Goossens, B., Philips, W.: MRI segmentation of the human brain: challenges, methods, and applications. Comput. Math. Methods Med. **2015**, 1–23 (2015). https://doi.org/10.1155/2015/450341

21. Dupont, C., Betrouni, N., Reyns, N., Vermandel, M.: On image segmentation methods applied to glioblastoma: state of art and new trends. IRBM **37**(3), 131–143 (2016). https://doi.org/10.1016/j.irbm.2015.12.004

22. Fyllingen, E.H., Stensjøen, A.L., Berntsen, E.M., Solheim, O., Reinertsen, I.: Glioblastoma segmentation: comparison of three different software packages. PLOS ONE **11**(10), e0164891 (2016). https://doi.org/10.1371/journal.pone.0164891

23. Galton, A.: The mereotopology of discrete space. In: Freksa, C., Mark, D.M. (eds.) COSIT 1999. LNCS, vol. 1661, pp. 251–266. Springer, Heidelberg (1999). https://doi.org/10.1007/3-540-48384-5_17

24. Galton, A.: A generalized topological view of motion in discrete space. Theor. Comput. Sci. **305**(1–3), 111–134 (2003). https://doi.org/10.1016/S0304-3975(02)00701-6

25. Galton, A.: Discrete mereotopology. In: Calosi, C., Graziani, P. (eds.) Mereology and the Sciences: Parts and Wholes in the Contemporary Scientific Context, pp. 293–321. Springer, Cham (2014). https://doi.org/10.1007/978-3-319-05356-1_11

26. Grosu, R., Smolka, S., Corradini, F., Wasilewska, A., Entcheva, E., Bartocci, E.: Learning and detecting emergent behavior in networks of cardiac myocytes. Commun. ACM **52**(3), 97–105 (2009)

27. Haghighi, I., Jones, A., Kong, Z., Bartocci, E., Grosu, R., Belta, C.: Spatel: a novel spatial-temporal logic and its applications to networked systems. In: Proceedings of the 18th International Conference on Hybrid Systems: Computation and Control, HSCC 2015, pp. 189–198. ACM, New York (2015)

28. Kassner, A., Thornhill, R.E.: Texture analysis: a review of neurologic MR imaging applications. Am. J. Neuroradiol. **31**(5), 809–816 (2010)

29. Lemieux, L., Hagemann, G., Krakow, K., Woermann, F.: Fast, accurate, and reproducible automatic segmentation of the brain in t1-weighted volume mri data. Magn. Reson. Med. **42**(1), 127–135 (1999)

30. Lopes, R., et al.: Prostate cancer characterization on MR images using fractal features. Med. Phys. **38**(1), 83 (2011)

31. Menze, B.H., et al.: The multimodal brain tumor image segmentation benchmark (brats). IEEE Trans. Med. Imaging **34**(10), 1993–2024 (2015)

32. Nenzi, L., Bortolussi, L., Ciancia, V., Loreti, M., Massink, M.: Qualitative and quantitative monitoring of spatio-temporal properties. In: Bartocci, E., Majumdar, R. (eds.) RV 2015. LNCS, vol. 9333, pp. 21–37. Springer, Cham (2015). https://doi.org/10.1007/978-3-319-23820-3_2

33. Porikli, F.M.: Integral histogram: a fast way to extract histograms in Cartesian spaces. 2005 IEEE Computer Society Conference on Computer Vision and Pattern Recognition (CVPR 2005), vol. 1, pp. 829–836 (2005)

34. Simi, V., Joseph, J.: Segmentation of glioblastoma multiforme from MR images-a comprehensive review. Egypt. J. Radiol. Nucl. Med. **46**(4), 1105–1110 (2015). https://doi.org/10.1016/j.ejrnm.2015.08.001

35. Spyridon (Spyros) Bakas, et al. (Ed.): 2017 international MICCAI BraTS Challenge: Pre-conference Proceedings, September 2017. https://www.cbica.upenn.edu/sbia/Spyridon.Bakas/MICCAI_BraTS/MICCAI_BraTS_2017_proceedings_shortPapers.pdf

36. Tsigkanos, C., Kehrer, T., Ghezzi, C.: Modeling and verification of evolving cyber-physical spaces. In: Proceedings of the 2017 11th Joint Meeting on Foundations of Software Engineering, ESEC/FSE 2017, pp. 38–48. ACM, New York (2017). http://doi.acm.org/10.1145/3106237.3106299

37. Zhu, Y., et al.: Semi-automatic segmentation software for quantitative clinical brain glioblastoma evaluation. Acad. Radiol. **19**(8), 977–985 (2012). https://doi.org/10.1016/j.acra.2012.03.026

On Reachability in Parameterized Phaser Programs

Zeinab Ganjei[1], Ahmed Rezine[1($\boxtimes$)], Ludovic Henrio[2], Petru Eles[1], and Zebo Peng[1]

[1] Linköping University, Linköping, Sweden
{zeinab.ganjei,ahmed.rezine,petru.eles,zebo.peng}@liu.se
[2] Univ Lyon, EnsL, UCBL, CNRS, Inria, LIP, 69342 Lyon Cedex 07, France
ludovic.henrio@ens-lyon.fr

Abstract. We address the problem of statically checking safety properties (such as assertions or deadlocks) for parameterized *phaser programs*. Phasers embody a non-trivial and modern synchronization construct used to orchestrate executions of parallel tasks. This generic construct supports dynamic parallelism with runtime registrations and deregistrations of spawned tasks. It generalizes many synchronization patterns such as collective and point-to-point schemes. For instance, phasers can enforce barriers or producer-consumer synchronization patterns among all or subsets of the running tasks. We consider in this work programs that may generate arbitrarily many tasks and phasers. We propose an exact procedure that is guaranteed to terminate even in the presence of unbounded phases and arbitrarily many spawned tasks. In addition, we prove undecidability results for several problems on which our procedure cannot be guaranteed to terminate.

1 Introduction

We focus on the parameterized verification problem of parallel programs that adopt the phasers construct for synchronization [15]. This coordination construct unifies collective and point-to-point synchronization. Parameterized verification is particularly relevant for mainstream parallel programs as the number of inter-dependent tasks in many applications, from scientific computing to web services or e-banking, may not be known apriori. Parameterized verification of phaser programs is a challenging problem due to the arbitrary numbers of involved tasks and phasers. In this work, we address this problem and provide an exact symbolic verification procedure. We identify parameterized problems for which our procedure is guaranteed to terminate and prove the undecidability of several variants on which our procedure cannot be guaranteed to terminate in general.

Phasers build on the clock construct from the X10 programming language [5] and are implemented in Habanero Java [4]. They can be added to any parallel programming language with a shared address space. Conceptually, phasers are synchronization entities to which tasks can be registered or unregistered.

© The Author(s) 2019
T. Vojnar and L. Zhang (Eds.): TACAS 2019, Part I, LNCS 11427, pp. 299–315, 2019.
https://doi.org/10.1007/978-3-030-17462-0_17

Registered tasks may act as producers, consumers, or both. Tasks can individually issue `signal`, `wait`, and `next` commands to a phaser they are registered to. Intuitively, a `signal` command is used to inform other tasks registered to the same phaser that the issuing task is done with its current phase. It increments the *signal* value associated to the issuing task on the given phaser. The `wait` command on the other hand checks whether all *signal* values in the phaser are strictly larger than the number of `waits` issued by this task, i.e. all registered tasks have passed the issuing task's *wait* phase. It then increments the *wait* value associated to the task on the phaser. As a result, the `wait` command might block the issuing task until other tasks issue enough `signal`s. The `next` command consists in a `signal` followed by a `wait`. The `next` command may be associated to a sequence of statements that are to be executed in isolation by one of the registered tasks participating in the command. A program that does not use this feature of the next statement is said to be *non-atomic*. A task deregisters from a phaser by issuing a `drop` command on it.

The dynamic synchronization allowed by the construct suits applications that need dynamic load balancing (e.g., for solving non-uniform problems with unpredictable load estimates [17]). Dynamic behavior is enabled by the possible runtime creation of tasks and phasers and their registration/de-registration. Moreover, the spawned tasks can work in different phases, adding flexibility to the synchronization pattern. The generality of the construct makes it also interesting from a theoretical perspective, as many language constructs can be expressed using phasers. For example, synchronization barriers of Single Program Multiple Data programs, the Bulk Synchronous Parallel computation model [16], or promises and futures constructs [3] can be expressed using phasers.

We believe this paper provides general (un)decidability results that will guide verification of other synchronization constructs. We identify combinations of features (e.g., unbounded differences between signal and wait phases, atomic statements) and properties to be checked (e.g., assertions, deadlocks) for which the parameterized verification problem becomes undecidable. These help identify synchronization constructs with enough expressivity to result in undecidable parameterized verification problems. We also provide a symbolic verification procedure that terminates even on fragments with arbitrary phases and numbers of spawned tasks. We get back to possible implications in the conclusion:

- We show an operational model for phaser programs based on [4,6,9,15].
- We propose an exact symbolic verification procedure for checking reachability of sets of configurations for non-atomic phaser programs even when arbitrarily many tasks and phasers may be generated.
- We prove undecidability results for several reachability problems.
- We show termination of our procedure when checking assertions for non-atomic programs even when arbitrary many tasks may be spawned.
- We show termination of our procedure when checking deadlock-freedom and assertions for non-atomic programs with bounded gaps between *signal* and *wait* values, even when arbitrary many tasks may be spawned.

Related work. The closest work to ours is [9]. It is the only work on automatic and static formal verification of phaser programs. It does not consider the parameterized case. The current work studies decidability of different parameterized reachability problems and proposes a symbolic procedure that, for example, decides program assertions even in the presence of arbitrary many tasks. This is well beyond [9]. The work of [6] considers dynamic deadlock verification of phaser programs and can therefore only detect deadlocks at runtime. The work in [2] uses Java Path Finder [11] to explore all concrete execution paths. A more general description of the phasers mechanism has also been formalized in Coq [7].

Outline. We describe phasers in Sect. 2. The construct is formally introduced in Sect. 3 where we show a general reachability problem to be undecidable. We describe in Sect. 4 our symbolic representation and state some of its non-trivial properties. We use the representation in Sect. 5 to instantiate a verification procedure and establish decidability results. We refine our undecidability results in Sect. 6 and summarize our findings in Sect. 7. Proofs can be found in [10].

```
1  bool a, done;              14  Prod(p:SIG,c:WAIT)    27  Cons(p:WAIT,c:SIG)
2  main(){                    15  {                     28  {
3    done = false;            16    while(¬done)        29    while(¬done){
4    p= newPhaser(SIG_WAIT);  17    {                   30      p.wait();
5    c= newPhaser(SIG_WAIT);  18      p.signal();       31      if(ndet())
6    while(ndet()){           19      c.wait();         32        done = true;
7      asynch(Prod,p:SIG,c:WAIT); 20    assert(a);      33      a = true;
8      asynch(Cons,p:WAIT,c:SIG); 21    a = false;      34      c.signal();
9    }                        22    };                  35    };
10   p.drop();                23    p.drop();           36    p.drop();
11   c.drop();                24    c.drop();           37    c.drop();
12 }                          25  }                     38  }
```

Fig. 1. An unbounded number of producers and consumers are synchronized using two phasers. In this construction, each consumer requires all producers to be ahead of it (wrt. the p phaser) in order for it to consume their respective products. At the same time, each consumer needs to be ahead of all producers (wrt. the c phaser) in order for the producers to be able to move to the next phase and produce new items.

2   Motivating Example

The program listed in Fig. 1 uses Boolean shared variables $B = \{a, done\}$. The main task creates two phasers (line 4–5). When creating a phaser, the task gets automatically registered to it. The main task also creates an unbounded number of other task instances (lines 7–8). When a task t is registered to a phaser p, a pair (w_t^p, s_t^p) in $\mathbb{N}^2$ can be associated to the couple (t, p). The pair represents the individual *wait* and *signal* phases of task t on phaser p.

Registration of a task to a phaser can occur in one of three modes: SIG_WAIT, WAIT and SIG. In SIG_WAIT mode, a task may issue both **signal** and **wait** commands. In WAIT (resp. SIG) mode, a task may only issue **wait** (resp. **signal**) commands on the phaser. Issuing a **signal** command by a task on a phaser results in the task incrementing its signal phase associated to the phaser. This is non-blocking. On the other-hand, issuing a `wait` command by a task on a phaser p will block until **all** tasks registered to p get signal values on p that are strictly larger than the wait value of the issuing task. The wait phase of the issuing task is then incremented. Intuitively, signals allow issuing tasks to state other tasks need not wait for them. In retrospect, waits allow tasks to make sure all registered tasks have moved past their wait phases.

Upon creation of a phaser, wait and signal phases are initialized to 0 (except in WAIT mode where no signal phase is associated to the task in order to not block other waiters). The only other way a task may get registered to a phaser is if an already registered task spawns and registers it in the same mode (or in WAIT or SIG if the registrar is registered in SIG_WAIT). In this case, wait and signal phases of the newly registered task are initialized to those of the registrar. Tasks are therefore dynamically registered (e.g., lines 7–8). They can also dynamically deregister themselves (e.g., line 10–11).

Here, an unbounded number of producers and consumers synchronize using two phasers. Consumers require producers to be ahead wrt. the phaser they point to with `p`. At the same time, consumers need to be ahead of all producers wrt. the phaser pointed to with `c`. It should be clear that phasers can be used as barriers for synchronizing dynamic subsets of concurrent tasks. Observe that tasks need not, in general, proceed in a lock step fashion. The difference between the largest signal value and the smallest wait value can be arbitrarily large (several signals before waits catch up). This allows for more flexibility.

We are interested in checking: (a) control reachability as in assertions (e.g., line 20), race conditions (e.g., mutual exclusion of lines 20 and 33) or registration errors (e.g., signaling a dropped phaser), and (b) plain reachability as in deadlocks (e.g., a producer at line 19 and a consumer at line 30 with equal phases waiting for each other). Both problems deal with reachability of sets of configurations. The difference is that control state reachability defines the targets with the states of the tasks (their control locations and whether they are registered to some phasers). Plain reachability can, in addition, constrain values of the phases in the target configurations (e.g., requiring equality between wait and signal values for deadlocks).

3   Phaser Programs and Reachability

We describe syntax and semantics of a core language. We make sure the language is representative of general purpose languages with phasers so that our results have a practical impact. A phaser program `prg` $= (B, V, T)$ involves a set T of tasks including a unique "main" task `main(){stmt}`. Arbitrary many instances of each task might be spawned during a program execution. All task instances share a set B of Boolean variables and make use of a set V of phaser variables that are local to individual task instances. Arbitrary many phasers might also be generated during program execution. Syntax of programs is as follows.

```
prg  ::= bool b₁,...,bₚ;
         task₁(v₁₁,...,vₖ₁) {stmt₁};
         ...
         taskₙ(v₁ₙ,...,vₖₙ) {stmtₙ};
```

$$\mathtt{stmt} ::= \mathtt{v = newPhaser()}; \mid \mathtt{asynch(task, v_1,...,v_k)}; \mid \mathtt{v.drop()}; \mid \mathtt{v.signal()};$$
$$\mid \mathtt{v.wait()}; \mid \mathtt{v.next()}; \mid \mathtt{v.next()\{stmt\}}; \mid \mathtt{b := cond}; \mid \mathtt{assert(cond)};$$
$$\mid \mathtt{while(cond)\{stmt\}}; \mid \mathtt{stmt\ stmt} \mid \mathtt{exit};$$

$$\mathtt{cond} ::= \mathtt{ndet()} \mid \mathtt{true} \mid \mathtt{false} \mid \mathtt{b} \mid \mathtt{cond} \vee \mathtt{cond} \mid \mathtt{cond} \wedge \mathtt{cond} \mid \neg\mathtt{cond}$$

Initially, a unique task instance starts executing the $\mathtt{main()\{stmt\}}$ task. A phaser can recall a pair of values (i.e., wait and signal) for each task instance registered to it. A task instance can create a new phaser with $\mathtt{v = newPhaser()}$, get registered to it (i.e., gets zero as wait and signal values associated to the new phaser) and refer to the phaser with its local variable $\mathtt{v}$. We simplify the presentation by assuming all registrations to be in SIG_WAIT mode. Including the other modes is a matter of depriving WAIT-registered tasks of a signal value (to ensure they do not block other registered tasks) and of ensuring issued commands respect registration modes. We use $\mathtt{V}$ for the union of all local phaser variables. A task $\mathtt{task(v_1,...,v_k)\{stmt\}}$ in T takes the phaser variables $\mathtt{v_1,...v_k}$ as parameters (write $\mathtt{paramOf(task)}$ to mean these parameters). A task instance can spawn another task instance with $\mathtt{asynch(task, v_1,...,v_n)}$. The issuing task instance registers the spawned task to the phasers pointed to by $\mathtt{v_1,...,v_n}$, with its own wait and signal values. Spawner and Spawnee execute concurrently. A task instance can deregister itself from a phaser with $\mathtt{v.drop()}$.

A task instance can issue signal or wait commands on a phaser referenced by $\mathtt{v}$ and on which it is registered. A wait command on a phaser blocks until the wait value of the task instance executing the wait on the phaser is strictly smaller than the signal value of all task instances registered to the phaser. In other words, $\mathtt{v.wait()}$ blocks if $\mathtt{v}$ points to a phaser such that at least one of the signal values stored by the phaser is equal to the wait value of the task that tries to perform the wait. A signal command does not block. It only increments the signal value of the task instance executing the signal command on the phaser. $\mathtt{v.next()}$ is syntactic sugar for a signal followed by a wait. Moreover, $\mathtt{v.next()\{stmt\}}$ is similar to $\mathtt{v.next()}$ but the block of code $\mathtt{stmt}$ is executed atomically by exactly one of the tasks participating in the synchronization before all tasks continue the execution that follows the barrier. $\mathtt{v.next()\{stmt\}}$ thus requires all tasks to be synchronized on exactly the same statement and is less flexible. Absence of a $\mathtt{v.next()\{stmt\}}$ makes a program *non-atomic*.

Note that assignment of phaser variables is excluded from the syntax; additionally, we restrict task creation $\mathtt{asynch(task, v_1,...,v_n)}$ and require that parameter variables $\mathtt{v_i}$ are all different. This prevents two variables from pointing to the same phaser and avoids the need to deal with aliasing: we can reason on the single variable in a process that points to a phaser. Extending our work to deal with aliasing is easy but would require heavier notations.

We will need the notions of configurations, partial configurations and inclusion in order to define the reachability problems we consider in this work. We introduce them in the following and assume a phaser program $\mathtt{prg} = (\mathtt{B}, \mathtt{V}, \mathtt{T})$.

Configurations. Configurations of a phaser program describe valuations of its variables, control sequences of its tasks and registration details to the phasers.

Control sequences. We define the set $\mathtt{Suff}$ of control sequences of $\mathtt{prg}$ to be the set of suffixes of all sequences $\mathtt{stmt}$ appearing in some statement $\mathtt{task}(\ldots)\{\mathtt{stmt}\}$. In addition, we define $\mathtt{UnrSuff}$ to be the smallest set containing $\mathtt{Suff}$ in addition to the suffixes of all (i) $\mathtt{s_1;while(cond)}\{\mathtt{s_1}\};\mathtt{s_2}$ if $\mathtt{while(cond)}\{\mathtt{s_1}\};\mathtt{s_2}$ is in $\mathtt{UnrSuff}$, and of all (ii) $\mathtt{s_1;s_2}$ if $\mathtt{if(cond)}\{\mathtt{s_1}\};\mathtt{s_2}$ is in $\mathtt{UnrSuff}$, and of all (iii) $\mathtt{s_1;v.next()}\{\};\mathtt{s_2}$ if $\mathtt{v.next()}\{\mathtt{s_1}\};\mathtt{s_2}$ in $\mathtt{UnrSuff}$, and finally of all (iv) $\mathtt{v.signal();v.wait();s_2}$ if $\mathtt{v.next()}\{\};\mathtt{s_2}$ is in $\mathtt{UnrSuff}$. We write $\mathtt{hd(s)}$ and $\mathtt{tl(s)}$ to respectively mean the head and the tail of a sequence $\mathtt{s}$.

Partial configurations. Partial configurations allow the characterization of sets of configurations by partially stating some of their common characteristics. A *partial configuration* c of $\mathtt{prg} = (\mathtt{B}, \mathtt{V}, \mathtt{T})$ is a tuple $\big(\mathcal{T}, \mathcal{P}, bv, seq, phase\big)$ where:

- $\mathcal{T}$ is a finite set of task identifiers. We let t, u range over the values in $\mathcal{T}$.
- $\mathcal{P}$ is a finite set of phaser identifiers. We let p, q range over the values in $\mathcal{P}$.
- $bv : \mathtt{B} \to \mathbb{B}^{\{*\}}$ fixes the values of some of the shared variables.[1]
- $seq : \mathcal{T} \to \mathtt{UnrSuff}^{\{*\}}$ fixes the control sequences of some of the tasks.
- $phase : \mathcal{T} \to \mathtt{partialFunctions}\big(\mathcal{P}, \mathtt{V}^{\{-,*\}} \times \big(\mathbb{N}^2 \cup \{(*,*), \mathtt{nreg}\}\big)\big)$ is a mapping that associates to each task t in $\mathcal{T}$ a partial mapping stating which phasers are known by the task and with which registration values.

Intuitively, partial configurations are used to state some facts about the valuations of variables and the control sequences of tasks and their registrations. Partial configurations leave some details unconstrained using partial mappings or the symbol $*$. For instance, if $bv(\mathtt{b}) = *$ in a partial configuration $\big(\mathcal{T}, \mathcal{P}, bv, seq, phase\big)$, then the partial configuration does not constrain the value of the shared variable $\mathtt{b}$. Moreover, a partial configuration does not constrain the relation between a task t and a phaser p when $phase(t)(p)$ is undefined. Instead, when the partial mapping $phase(t)$ is defined on phaser p, it associates a pair $phase(t)(p) = (\mathtt{var}, \mathtt{val})$ to p. If $\mathtt{var} \in \mathtt{V}^{\{-,*\}}$ is a variable $\mathtt{v} \in \mathtt{V}$ then the task t in $\mathcal{T}$ uses its variable $\mathtt{v}$ to refer to the phaser p in $\mathcal{P}$.[2] If $\mathtt{var}$ is the symbol $-$ then the task t does not refer to $\mathtt{v}$ with any of its variables in $\mathtt{V}$. If $\mathtt{var}$ is the symbol $*$, then the task might or might not refer to p. The value $\mathtt{val}$ in $phase(t)(p) = (\mathtt{var}, \mathtt{val})$ is either the value $\mathtt{nreg}$ or a pair (w, s). The value $\mathtt{nreg}$ means the task t is not registered to phaser p. The pair (w, s) belongs to $(\mathbb{N} \times \mathbb{N}) \cup \{(*,*)\}$. In this case, task t is registered to phaser p with a wait phase

---

[1] For any set S, $S^{\{a,b,\ldots\}}$ denotes $S \cup \{a, b, \ldots\}$.
[2] The uniqueness of this variable is due to the absence of aliasing discussed above.

$$\frac{\mathtt{hd}(seq(t)) = \mathtt{assert(cond)} \quad [\![\mathtt{cond}]\!]_{bv} = \mathtt{false}}{(T, P, bv, seq, phase) \in \mathtt{AssertErrors}} \text{ (assertion)}$$

$$\frac{\mathtt{hd}(seq(t)) = \mathtt{b}' := \mathtt{cond}' \quad (b' \text{ coincides with } b \text{ or appears in cond})}{\mathtt{hd}(seq(u)) \in \{\mathtt{b} := \mathtt{cond}, \mathtt{if(cond)}\,\{\mathtt{stmt}\}, \mathtt{while(cond)}\,\{\mathtt{stmt}\}, \mathtt{assert(cond)}\}}{(T, P, bv, seq, phase) \in \mathtt{RaceErrors}} \text{ (race)}$$

$$\frac{t \in T \quad v \in V \quad p \in P \quad phase(t)(p) = (v, \mathtt{nreg})}{\mathtt{hd}(seq(t)) \in \{\mathtt{asynch(task}, \ldots v \ldots)\{\mathtt{stmt}\}, \mathtt{v.signal()}, \mathtt{v.wait()}, \mathtt{v.drop()}\}}{(T, P, bv, seq, phase) \in \mathtt{RegisterErrors}} \text{ (registration)}$$

$$\frac{\begin{array}{c} t_0, \ldots t_n \in T \quad v_0, \ldots v_n \in V \quad var_0, \ldots var_n \in V^{\{-\}} \quad p_0, \ldots p_n \in P \\ s_0 \cdots s_n, s_0' \cdots s_n' \in \mathbb{N} \quad w_0 \cdots w_n, w_0' \cdots w_n' \in \mathbb{N} \quad \forall i : 0 \le i \le n. \ \mathtt{hd}(seq(t_i)) = v_i.\mathtt{wait()} \\ phase(t_i)(p_i) = (v_i, (w_i, s_i)) \quad phase(t_i)(p_{(i+1)\%(n+1)}) = (var_i, (w_i', s_i')) \quad s_i' = w_{(i+1)\%(n+1)} \end{array}}{(T, P, bv, seq, phase) \in \mathtt{DeadlockErrors}} \text{ (deadlock)}$$

Fig. 2. Definition of error configurations. For instance, a deadlock is obtained in $(T, P, bv, seq, phase)$ if tasks $\{t_0, \ldots, t_n\} \subseteq T$ form a cycle where each t_i blocks the wait being executed by $t_{(i+1)\%(n+1)}$ on phaser $p_{(i+1)\%(n+1)}$.

w and a signal phase s. The value $*$ means that the wait phase w (resp. signal phase s) can be any value in $\mathbb{N}$. For instance, $phase(t)(p) = (v, \mathtt{nreg})$ means variable v of the task t refers to phaser p but the task is not registered to p. On the other hand, $phase(t)(p) = (-, (*, *))$ means the task t does not refer to p but is registered to it with arbitrary wait and signal phases.

Concrete configurations. A concrete configuration (or configuration for short) is a partial configuration $(T, P, bv, seq, phase)$ where $phase(t)$ is total for each $t \in T$ and where the symbol $*$ does not appear in any range. It is a tuple $(T, P, bv, seq, phase)$ where $bv : B \to \mathbb{B}$, $seq : T \to \mathtt{UnrSuff}$, and $phase : T \to \mathtt{totalFunctions}\,(P, V^{\{-\}} \times ((\mathbb{N} \times \mathbb{N}) \cup \{\mathtt{nreg}\}))$. For a concrete configuration $(T, P, bv, seq, phase)$, we write $\mathtt{isReg}(phase, t, p)$ to mean the predicate $phase(t)(p) \notin (V^{\{-\}} \times \{\mathtt{nreg}\})$. The predicate $\mathtt{isReg}(phase, t, p)$ captures whether the task t is registered to phaser p according to the mapping $phase$.

Inclusion of configurations. A configuration $c' = (T', P', bv', seq', phase')$ *includes* a partial configuration $c = (T, P, bv, seq, phase)$ if renaming and deleting tasks and phasers from c' can give a configuration that "matches" c. More formally, c' includes c if $((bv(b) \ne bv'(b)) \implies (bv(b) = *))$ for each $b \in B$ and there are injections $\tau : T \to T'$ and $\pi : P \to P'$ s.t. for each $t \in T$ and $p \in P$: (1) $((seq(t) \ne seq'(\tau(t))) \implies (seq(t) = *))$, and either (2.a) $phase(t)(p)$ is undefined, or (2.b) $phase(t)(p) = (var, val)$ and $phase'(\tau(t))(\pi(p)) = (var', val')$ with $((var \ne var') \implies (var = *))$ and either $(val = val' = \mathtt{nreg})$ or $val = (w, s)$ and $val' = (w', s')$ with $((w \ne w') \implies (w = *))$ and $((s \ne s') \implies (s = *))$.

Semantics and reachability. Given a program $\mathtt{prg} = (B, V, T)$, the main task $\mathtt{main()}\{\mathtt{stmt}\}$ starts executing $\mathtt{stmt}$ from an initial configuration $c_{init} = (T_{init}, P_{init}, bv_{init}, seq_{init}, phase_{init})$ where T_{init} is a singleton, P_{init} is empty, bv_{init} sends all shared variables to $\mathtt{false}$ and seq_{init} associates $\mathtt{stmt}$ to the unique task in T_{init}. We write $c \xrightarrow[\mathtt{stmt}]{t} c'$ to mean a task t in c can fire statement $\mathtt{stmt}$

$$\frac{\begin{array}{c} hd(seq(t)) = \texttt{v := newPhaser()} \quad p \notin \mathcal{P} \quad \mathcal{P}' = \mathcal{P} \cup \{p\} \quad phase' = phase[t \leftarrow \{p \leftarrow (\texttt{v},(0,0))\}] \\ phase'' = phase'\left[\{u \leftarrow phase'(u)[p \leftarrow (-,\texttt{nreg})] \mid u \in \mathcal{T} \setminus \{t\}\}\right] \end{array}}{(\mathcal{T},\mathcal{P},bv,seq,phase) \xrightarrow[\texttt{v:=newPhaser()}]{t} (\mathcal{T},\mathcal{P}',bv,seq[t \leftarrow \texttt{tl}(seq(t))],phase'')} \text{ (newPhaser)}$$

$$\frac{\begin{array}{c} hd(seq(t)) = \texttt{asynch(task,v}_1,\ldots\texttt{v}_k)\{\texttt{stmt}\} \quad \texttt{paramOf(task)} = (\texttt{w}_1,\ldots\texttt{w}_k) \quad u \notin \mathcal{T} \quad \mathcal{T}' = \mathcal{T} \cup \{u\} \\ \text{for each } i : 1 \leq i \leq k.\ phase(t)(p_i) = (\texttt{v}_i,(w_i,s_i)) \quad \text{for each } i,j : 1 \leq i,j \leq k.\ i \neq j \Rightarrow \texttt{v}_i \neq \texttt{v}_j \\ phase' = phase[u \leftarrow \{p_i \leftarrow (\texttt{w}_i,(w_i,s_i)) \mid 1 \leq i \leq k\} \cup \{p \leftarrow (-,\texttt{nreg}) \mid p \notin \{p_i \mid 1 \leq i \leq k\}\}] \end{array}}{(\mathcal{T},\mathcal{P},bv,seq,phase) \xrightarrow[\texttt{asynch(task,v}_1,\ldots\texttt{v}_k)\{\texttt{stmt}\}]{t} (\mathcal{T}',\mathcal{P},bv,seq'[\{u \leftarrow \texttt{stmt}\} \cup \{t \leftarrow \texttt{tl}(seq(t))\}],phase')} \text{ (asynch)}$$

$$\frac{hd(seq(t)) = \texttt{v.signal()} \quad phase(t)(p) = (\texttt{v},(w,s)) \quad phase' = phase[t \leftarrow \{p \leftarrow (\texttt{v},(w,1+s))\}]}{(\mathcal{T},\mathcal{P},bv,seq,phase) \xrightarrow[\texttt{v.signal()}]{t} (\mathcal{T},\mathcal{P},bv,seq[t \leftarrow \texttt{tl}(seq(t))],phase')} \text{ (signal)}$$

$$\frac{\begin{array}{c} hd(seq(t)) = \texttt{v.wait()} \quad phase(t)(p) = (\texttt{v},(w_t,s_t)) \quad phase' = phase[t \leftarrow \{p \leftarrow (\texttt{v},(1+w_t,s_t))\}] \\ \forall u \in \mathcal{T}, var \in \texttt{V}^{\{-\}}.\ (phase(u)(p) = (var,(w_u,s_u)) \Rightarrow w_t < s_u) \end{array}}{(\mathcal{T},\mathcal{P},bv,seq,phase) \xrightarrow[\texttt{v.wait()}]{t} (\mathcal{T},\mathcal{P},bv,seq[t \leftarrow \texttt{tl}(seq(t))],phase')} \text{ (wait)}$$

$$\frac{hd(seq(t)) = \texttt{v.next()} \quad seq' = seq[t \leftarrow \texttt{v.signal();v.wait();tl}(seq(t))]}{(\mathcal{T},\mathcal{P},bv,seq,phase) \xrightarrow[\texttt{v.next()}]{t} (\mathcal{T},\mathcal{P},bv,seq',phase)} \text{ (next)}$$

$$\frac{\mathcal{U} = \{u \mid isReg(phase,u,p)\} \quad \forall u \in \mathcal{U}.hd(seq(u)) = \texttt{v.next()}\{\texttt{stmt}\} \quad t \in \mathcal{U}}{seq' = seq[t \leftarrow \texttt{stmt;v.next();tl}(seq(t))][\{u \leftarrow \texttt{v.next();tl}(seq(u)) \mid u \in \mathcal{U} \setminus \{t\}\}]}{(\mathcal{T},\mathcal{P},bv,seq,phase) \xrightarrow[\texttt{v.next()}\{\texttt{stmt}\}]{t} (\mathcal{T},\mathcal{P},bv,seq',phase)} \text{ (next\{stmt\})}$$

$$\frac{hd(seq(t)) = \texttt{v.drop()} \quad phase(t)(p) = (\texttt{v},(w,s)) \quad phase' = phase[t \leftarrow phase(t)[p \leftarrow (\texttt{v},\texttt{nreg})]]}{(\mathcal{T},\mathcal{P},bv,seq,phase) \xrightarrow[\texttt{v.drop()}]{t} (\mathcal{T},\mathcal{P},bv,seq[t \leftarrow \texttt{tl}(seq(t))],phase')} \text{ (drop)}$$

Fig. 3. Operational semantics of phaser statements. Each transition corresponds to a task $t \in \mathcal{T}$ executing a statement from a configuration $(\mathcal{T},\mathcal{P},bv,seq,phase)$. For instance, the **drop** transition corresponds to a task t executing $\texttt{v.drop()}$ when registered to phaser $p \in \mathcal{P}$ (with phases (w,s)) and refering to it with variable $\texttt{v}$. The result is the same configuration where task t moves to its next statement without being registered to p.

resulting in configuration c'. See Fig. 3 for a description of phaser semantics. We write $c \xrightarrow[\text{stmt}]{} c'$ if $c \xrightarrow[\text{stmt}]{t} c'$ for some task t and $c \to c'$ if $c \xrightarrow[\text{stmt}]{} c'$ for some stmt. We write $\xrightarrow[\text{stmt}]{}^+$ for the transitive closure of $\xrightarrow[\text{stmt}]{}$ and let $\to^*$ be the reflexive transitive closure of $\to$. Figure 2 identifies erroneous configurations.

We are interested in the reachability of sets of configurations (i.e., checking safety properties). We differentiate between two reachability problems depending on whether the target sets of configurations constrain the registration phases or not. The *plain reachability* problem may constrains the registration phases of the target configurations. The *control reachability* problem may not. We will see that decidability of the two problems can be different. The two problems are defined in the following.

Plain reachability. First, we define equivalent configurations. A configuration $c = (\mathcal{T},\mathcal{P},bv,seq,phase)$ is equivalent to configuration $c' = (\mathcal{T}',\mathcal{P}',bv',seq',phase')$ if $bv = bv'$ and there are bijections $\tau : \mathcal{T} \to \mathcal{T}'$ and $\pi : \mathcal{P} \to \mathcal{P}'$ such that, for all $t \in T$, $p \in P$ and $var \in V^{\{-\}}$, $seq(t) = seq'(\tau(t))$ and there are some integers $(k_p)_{p \in P}$ such that $phase(t)(p) = (var, (w, s))$ iff $phase'(\tau(t))(\pi(p)) = (var, (w + k_p, s + k_p))$. We write $c \sim c'$ to mean that c and c' are equivalent. Intuitively, equivalent configurations simulate each other. We can establish the following:

Lemma 1 (Equivalence). *Assume two configurations c_1 and c_2. If $c_1 \to c_2$ and $c'_1 \sim c_1$ then there is a configuration c'_2 s.t. $c'_2 \sim c_2$ and $c'_1 \to c'_2$.*

Observe that if the wait value of a task t on a phaser p is equal to the signal of a task t' on the same phaser p in some configuration c, then this is also the case, up to a renaming of the phasers and tasks, in all equivalent configurations. This is particularly relevant for defining deadlock configurations where a number of tasks are waiting for each other. The plain reachability problem is given a program and a target partial configuration and asks whether a configuration (equivalent to a configuration) that includes the target partial configuration is reachable.

More formally, given a program **prg** and a partial configuration c, let c_{init} be the initial configuration of **prg**, then reach(**prg**, c) if and only if $c_{init} \to^* c_1$ for $c_1 \sim c_2$ and c_2 includes c.

Definition 1 (Plain reachability). *For a program* **prg** *and a partial configuration c, decide whether* reach(**prg**, c) *holds.*

Control reachability. A partial configuration $c = (T, P, bv, seq, phase)$ is said to be a *control partial configuration* if for all $t \in T$ and $p \in P$, either $phase(t)(p)$ is undefined or $phase(t)(p) \in (V^{\{-,*\}} \times \{(*, *)\}, \text{nreg}\})$. Intuitively, control partial configurations do not constrain phase values. They are enough to characterize, for example, configurations where an assertion is violated (see Fig. 2).

Definition 2 (Control reachability). *For a program* **prg** *and a <u>control</u> partial configuration c, decide whether* reach(**prg**, c) *holds.*

Observe that plain reachability is at least as hard to answer as control reachability since any control partial configuration is also a partial configuration. It turns out the control reachability problem is undecidable for programs resulting in arbitrarily many tasks and phasers as stated by the theorem below. This is proven by reduction of the state reachability problem for 2-counter Minsky machines. A 2-counter Minsky machine $(S, \{x_1, x_2\}, \Delta, s_0, s_F)$ has a finite set S of states, two counters $\{x_1, x_2\}$ with values in $\mathbb{N}$, an initial state s_0 and a final state s_F. Transitions may increment, decrement or test a counter. For example $(s_0, \text{test}(x_1), s_F)$ takes the machine from s_0 to s_F if the counter x_1 is zero.

Theorem 1 (Minsky machines [14]). *Checking whether s_F is reachable from configuration $(s_0, 0, 0)$ for 2-counter machines is undecidable in general.*

Theorem 2. *Control reachability is undecidable in general.*

Proof sketch. State reachability of an arbitrary 2-counters Minsky machine is encoded as the control reachability problem of a phaser program. The phaser program (see [10]) has three tasks main, xUnit and yUnit. It uses Boolean shared variables to encode the state $s \in S$ and to pass information between different task instances. The phaser program builds two chains, one with xUnit instances for the x-counter, and one with yUnit instances for the y-counter. Each chain alternates a phaser and a task and encodes the values of its counter with its length. The idea is to have the phaser program simulate all transitions of the counter machine, i.e., increments, decrements and tests for zero. Answering state reachability of the counter machine amounts to checking whether there are reachable configurations where the boolean variables encoding the counter machine can evaluate to the target machine state s_F.

4 A Gap-Based Symbolic Representation

The symbolic representation we propose builds on the following intuitions. First, observe the language semantics impose, for each phaser, the invariant that signal values are always larger or equal to wait values. We can therefore assume this fact in our symbolic representation. In addition, our reachability problems from Sect. 3 are defined in terms of reachability of equivalence classes, not of individual configurations. This is because configurations violating considered properties (see Fig. 2) are not defined in terms of concrete phase values but rather in terms of relations among them (in addition to the registration status, control sequences and variable values). Finally, we observe that if a wait is enabled with smaller gaps on a given phaser, then it will be enabled with larger ones. We therefore propose to track the gaps of the differences between signal and wait values wrt. to an existentially quantified level (per phaser) that lies between wait and signal values of all tasks registered to the considered phaser.

We formally define our symbolic representation and describe a corresponding entailment relation. We also establish a desirable property (namely being a $\mathcal{WQO}$, i.e., well-quasi-ordering [1,8]) on some classes of representations. This is crucial for the decidability of certain reachability problems (see Sect. 5).

Named gaps. A *named gap* is associated to a task-phaser pair. It consists in a tuple (var, val) in $\mathbb{G} = \left(\mathtt{V}^{\{-,*\}} \times \left(\left(\mathbb{N}^4 \cup \left(\mathbb{N}^2 \times \{\infty\}^2 \right) \right) \cup \{\mathtt{nreg}\} \right) \right)$. Like for partial configurations in Sect. 3, $var \in \mathtt{V}^{\{-,*\}}$ constrains variable values. The *val* value describes task registration to the phaser. If registered, then *val* is a 4-tuple $(\mathtt{lw}, \mathtt{ls}, \mathtt{uw}, \mathtt{us})$. This intuitively captures, together with some level l common to all tasks registered to the considered phaser, all concrete wait and signal values (w, s) satisfying $\mathtt{lw} \leq (l - w) \leq \mathtt{uw}$ and $\mathtt{ls} \leq (s - l) \leq \mathtt{us}$. A named gap $(var, (\mathtt{lw}, \mathtt{ls}, \mathtt{uw}, \mathtt{us}))$ is said to be *free* if $\mathtt{uw} = \mathtt{us} = \infty$. It is said to be B-*gap-bounded*, for $B \in \mathbb{N}$, if both $\mathtt{uw} \leq B$ and $\mathtt{us} \leq B$ hold. A set $\mathcal{G} \subseteq \mathbb{G}$ is said to be free (resp. B-gap-bounded) if all its named gaps are free (resp. B-gap-bounded). The set $\mathcal{G}$ is said to be B-*good* if each one of its named gaps is either free or B-gap-bounded. Finally, $\mathcal{G}$ is said to be *good* if it is B-good for some $B \in \mathbb{N}$. Given a set $\mathcal{G}$ of named gaps, we define the partial order $\trianglelefteq$ on $\mathcal{G}$, and write $(var, val) \trianglelefteq (var', val')$, to mean (i) $(var \neq var' \Rightarrow var = *)$, and (ii)

$(val = \mathtt{nreg}) \iff (val' = \mathtt{nreg})$, and (iii) if $val = (\mathtt{lw}, \mathtt{ls}, \mathtt{uw}, \mathtt{us})$ and $val' = (\mathtt{lw}', \mathtt{ls}', \mathtt{uw}', \mathtt{us}')$ then $\mathtt{lw} \leq \mathtt{lw}'$, $\mathtt{ls} \leq \mathtt{ls}'$, $\mathtt{uw}' \leq \mathtt{uw}$ and $\mathtt{us}' \leq \mathtt{us}$. Intuitively, named gaps are used in the definition of constraints to capture relations (i.e., reference, registration and possible phases) of tasks and phasers. The partial order $(var, val) \trianglelefteq (var', val')$ ensures relations allowed by (var', val') are also allowed by (var, val).

Constraints. A constraint ϕ of $\mathtt{prg} = (\mathsf{B}, \mathsf{V}, \mathsf{T})$ is a tuple $(\mathcal{T}, \mathcal{P}, bv, seq, gap, egap)$ that denotes a possibly infinite set of configurations. Intuitively, $\mathcal{T}$ and $\mathcal{P}$ respectively represent a minimal set of tasks and phasers that are required in any configuration denoted by the constraint. In addition:

- $bv : \mathsf{B} \to \mathbb{B}^{\{*\}}$ and $seq : \mathcal{T} \to \mathtt{UnrSuff}^{\{*\}}$ respectively represent, like for partial configurations, a valuation of the shared Boolean variables and a mapping of tasks to their control sequences.
- $gap : \mathcal{T} \to \mathtt{totalFunctions}\,(\mathcal{P}, \mathbb{G})$ constrains relations between $\mathcal{T}$-tasks and $\mathcal{P}$-phasers by associating to each task t a mapping $gap(t)$ that defines for each phaser p a named gap $(var, val) \in \mathbb{G}$ capturing the relation of t and p.
- $egap : \mathcal{P} \to \mathbb{N}^2$ associates *lower bounds* $(\mathtt{ew}, \mathtt{es})$ on gaps of tasks that are registered to $\mathcal{P}$-phasers but which are not explicitly captured by $\mathcal{T}$. This is described further in the constraints denotations below.

We write $\mathtt{isReg}(gap, t, p)$ to mean the task t is registered to the phaser p, i.e., $gap(t)(p) \notin (\mathsf{V}^{\{-,*\}} \times \{\mathtt{nreg}\})$. A constraint ϕ is said to be free (resp. B-gap-bounded or B-good) if the set $G = \{gap(t)(p) \mid t \in \mathcal{T}, p \in \mathcal{P}\}$ is free (resp. B-gap-bounded or B-good). The dimension of a constraint is the number of phasers it requires (i.e., $|\mathcal{P}|$). A set of constraints Φ is said to be free, B-gap-bounded, B-good or K-dimension-bounded if each of its constraints are.

Denotations. We write $c \models \phi$ to mean constraint $\phi = \left(\mathcal{T}_\phi, \mathcal{P}_\phi, bv_\phi, seq_\phi, gap_\phi, egap_\phi \right)$ denotes configuration $c = (\mathcal{T}_c, \mathcal{P}_c, bv_c, seq_c, phase_c)$. Intuitively, the configuration c should have at least as many tasks (captured by a surjection τ from a subset $\mathcal{T}_c^1$ of $\mathcal{T}_c$ to $\mathcal{T}_\phi$) and phasers (captured by a bijection π from a subset $\mathcal{P}_c^1$ of $\mathcal{P}_c$ to $\mathcal{P}_\phi$). Constraints on the tasks and phasers in $\mathcal{T}_c^1$ and $\mathcal{P}_c^1$ ensure target configurations are reachable. Additional constraints on the tasks in $\mathcal{T}_c^2 = \mathcal{T}_c \setminus \mathcal{T}_c^1$ ensure this reachability is not blocked by tasks not captured by $\mathcal{T}_\phi$. More formally:

1. for each $\mathsf{b} \in \mathsf{B}$, $(bv_\phi(\mathsf{b}) \neq bv_c(\mathsf{b})) \implies (bv_\phi(\mathsf{b}) = *)$, and
2. $\mathcal{T}_c$ and $\mathcal{P}_c$ can be written as $\mathcal{T}_c = \mathcal{T}_c^1 \uplus \mathcal{T}_c^2$ and $\mathcal{P}_c = \mathcal{P}_c^1 \uplus \mathcal{P}_c^2$, with
3. $\tau : \mathcal{T}_c^1 \to \mathcal{T}_\phi$ is a surjection and $\pi : \mathcal{P}_c^1 \to \mathcal{P}_\phi$ is a bijection, and
4. for $t_c \in \mathcal{T}_c^1$ with $t_\phi = \tau(t_c)$, $(seq_\phi(t_\phi) \neq seq_c(t_c)) \implies (seq_\phi(t_\phi) = *)$, and
5. for each $p_\phi = \pi(p_c)$, there is a natural level $\ell : 0 \leq \ell$ such that:
   - (a) if $t_c \in \mathcal{T}_c^1$ with $t_\phi = \tau(t_c)$, $phase_c(t_c)(p_c) = (var_c, val_c)$ and $gap_\phi(t_\phi)(p_\phi) = (var_\phi, val_\phi)$, then it is the case that:
     - i. $(var_c \neq var_\phi) \implies (var_\phi = *)$, and

ii. $(val_c = \mathtt{nreg}) \Longleftrightarrow (val_\phi = \mathtt{nreg})$, and

iii. if $(val_c = (w, s))$ and $(val_\phi = (\mathtt{lw}, \mathtt{ls}, \mathtt{uw}, \mathtt{us}))$ then $\mathtt{lw} \leq l - w \leq \mathtt{uw}$ and $\mathtt{ls} \leq s - l \leq \mathtt{us}$.

(b) if $t_c \in T_c^2$, then for each $p_\phi = \pi(p_c)$ with $phase_c(t_c)(p_c) = (var_c, (w, s))$ and $egap(p_\phi) = (\mathtt{ew}, \mathtt{es})$, we have: $(\mathtt{es} \leq s - l)$ and $(\mathtt{ew} \leq l - w)$

Intuitively, for each phaser, the bounds given by gap constrain the values of the phases belonging to tasks captured by T_ϕ (i.e., those in T_c^1) and registered to the given phaser. This is done with respect to some non-negative level, one per phaser. The same level is used to constrain phases of tasks registered to the phaser but not captured by T_ϕ (i.e., those in T_c^2). For these tasks, lower bounds are enough as we only want to ensure they do not block executions to target sets of configurations. We write $[\![\phi]\!]$ for $\{c \mid c \models \phi\}$.

Entailment. We write $\phi_a \sqsubseteq \phi_b$ to mean $\phi_a = (T_a, P_a, bv_a, seq_a, gap_a, egap_a)$ is entailed by $\phi_b = (T_b, P_b, bv_b, seq_b, gap_b, egap_b)$. This will ensure that configurations denoted by ϕ_b are also denoted by ϕ_a. Intuitively, ϕ_b should have at least as many tasks (captured by a surjection τ from a subset T_b^1 of T_b to T_a) and phasers (captured by a bijection π from a subset P_b^1 of P_b to P_a). Conditions on tasks and phasers in T_b^1 and P_b^1 ensure the conditions in ϕ_a are met. Additional conditions on the tasks in $T_b^2 = T_b \setminus T_b^1$ ensure at least the $egap_a$ conditions in ϕ_a are met. More formally:

1. $(bv_a(\mathbf{b}) \neq bv_b(\mathbf{b})) \Longrightarrow (bv_a(\mathbf{b}) = *)$, for each $\mathbf{b} \in \mathrm{B}$ and
2. T_b and P_b can be written as $T_b = T_b^1 \uplus T_b^2$ and $P_b = P_b^1 \uplus P_b^2$ with
3. $\tau : T_b^1 \to T_a$ is a surjection and $\pi : P_b^1 \to P_a$ is a bijection, and
4. $(seq_b(t_b) \neq seq_a(t_a)) \Longrightarrow (seq_b(t_b) = *)$ for each $t_b \in T_b^1$ with $t_a = \tau(t_b)$, and
5. for each phaser $p_a = \pi(p_b)$ in P_a:
   (a) if $egap_a(p_a) = (\mathtt{ew}_a, \mathtt{es}_a)$ and $egap_b(p_b) = (\mathtt{ew}_b, \mathtt{es}_b)$ then $\mathtt{ew}_a \leq \mathtt{ew}_b$ and $\mathtt{es}_a \leq \mathtt{es}_b$
   (b) for each $t_b \in T_b^1$ with $t_a = \tau(t_b)$ and $gap_a(t_a)(p_a) = (var_a, val_a)$, and $gap_b(t_b)(p_b) = (var_b, val_b)$, it is the case that:
      i. $(var_b \neq var_a) \Longrightarrow (var_a = *)$, and
      ii. $(val_b = \mathtt{nreg}) \Longleftrightarrow (val_a = \mathtt{nreg})$, and
      iii. if $val_a = (\mathtt{lw}_a, \mathtt{ls}_a, \mathtt{uw}_a, \mathtt{us}_a)$ and $val_b = (\mathtt{lw}_b, \mathtt{ls}_b, \mathtt{uw}_b, \mathtt{us}_b)$, then $(\mathtt{lw}_a \leq \mathtt{lw}_b)$, $(\mathtt{ls}_a \leq \mathtt{ls}_b)$, $(\mathtt{uw}_b \leq \mathtt{uw}_a)$ and $(\mathtt{us}_b \leq \mathtt{us}_a)$.
   (c) for each $t_b \in T_b^2$ with $gap_b(t_b)(p_b) = (var, (\mathtt{lw}_a, \mathtt{ls}_a, \mathtt{uw}_a, \mathtt{us}_a))$, with $egap_a(p_a) = (\mathtt{ew}_a, \mathtt{es}_a)$, both $(\mathtt{ew}_a \leq \mathtt{lw}_b)$ and $(\mathtt{es}_a \leq \mathtt{ls}_b)$ hold.

The following lemma shows that it is safe to eliminate entailing constraints in the working list procedure of Sect. 5.

Lemma 2 (Constraint entailment). $\phi_a \sqsubseteq \phi_b$ *implies* $[\![\phi_b]\!] \subseteq [\![\phi_a]\!]$

A central contribution that allows establishing the positive results of Sect. 5 is to show $\sqsubseteq$ is actually $\mathcal{WQO}$ on any K-dimension-bounded and B-good set of constraints. For this, we prove $(\mathcal{M}(\mathtt{UnrSuff} \times \mathcal{G}^K), \exists \preceq_\forall)$ is $\mathcal{WQO}$ if $\mathcal{G}$ is B-good, where $\mathcal{M}(\mathtt{UnrSuff} \times \mathcal{G}^K)$ is the set of multisets over $\mathtt{UnrSuff} \times \mathcal{G}^K$

and $M \; \exists \preceq_\forall \; M'$ requires each $(\mathbf{s}', g_1', \dots, g_K') \in M'$ may be mapped to some $(\mathbf{s}, g_1, \dots, g_K) \in M$ for which $\mathbf{s} = \mathbf{s}'$ and $g_i \unlhd g_i'$ for each $i : 1 \leq i \leq K$ (written $(\mathbf{s}, g_1, \dots, g_K) \preceq (\mathbf{s}', g_1', \dots, g_K')$). Intuitively, we need to use $\exists \preceq_\forall$, and not simply $\forall \preceq_\exists$, in order to "cover all registered tasks" in the larger constraint as otherwise some tasks may block the path to the target configurations. Rado's structure [12,13] shows that, in general, $(\mathcal{M}(S), \; \exists \preceq_\forall)$ need not be $\mathcal{WQO}$ just because $\preceq$ is $\mathcal{WQO}$ over S. The proof details can be found in [10].

Theorem 3. $(\Phi, \sqsubseteq)$ is $\mathcal{WQO}$ if Φ is K-dimension-bounded and B-good for some pre-defined $K, B \in \mathbb{N}$.

5   A Symbolic Verification Procedure

We use the constraints defined in Sect. 4 as a symbolic representation in an instantiation of the classical framework of Well-Structured-Transition-Systems [1,8]. The instantiation (described in [10]) is a working-list procedure that takes as arguments a program **prg** and a $\sqsubseteq$-minimal set Φ of constraints denoting the targeted set of configurations. Such constraints can be easily built from the partial configurations described in Fig. 2.

The procedure computes a fixpoint using the entailment relation of Sect. 4 and a predecessor computation that results, for a constraint ϕ and a statement **stmt**, in a finite set $\mathrm{pre}_{\mathtt{stmt}} = \left\{ \phi' \mid \phi \xrightarrow{\mathtt{stmt}} \phi' \right\}$. Figure 4 describes part of the computation for the **v.signal()** instruction (see [10] for other instructions). For all but atomic statements, the set $\mathrm{pre}_{\mathtt{stmt}} = \left\{ \phi' \mid \phi \xrightarrow{\mathtt{stmt}} \phi' \right\}$ is exact in the sense that $\left\{ c' \mid c \in \llbracket \phi \rrbracket \text{ and } c' \xrightarrow{\mathtt{stmt}} c \right\} \subseteq \bigcup_{\phi' \in \mathrm{pre}_{\mathtt{stmt}}} \llbracket \phi' \rrbracket \subseteq \left\{ c' \mid c \in \llbracket \phi \rrbracket \text{ and } c' \xrightarrow{\mathtt{stmt}}^+ c \right\}$. Intuitively, the predecessors calculation for the atomic **v.next(){stmt}** is only an over-approximation because such an instruction can encode a test-and-set operation. Our representation allows for more tasks, but the additional tasks may not be able to carry the atomic operation. We would therefore obtain a non-exact over-approximation and avoid this issue by only applying the procedure to non-atomic programs. We can show the following theorems.

$$\begin{array}{c} \mathbf{s}', \mathbf{s} \in \mathsf{UnrSuff} \quad \mathbf{s}' = \mathtt{v.signal}(); \mathbf{s} \quad seq' = seq[t \leftarrow \mathbf{s}'] \quad gap(t)(p) = (\mathtt{v}, (\mathtt{lw}_t, \mathtt{ls}_t, \mathtt{uw}_t, \mathtt{us}_t)) \\ \mathcal{U} = \{u \mid u \in \mathcal{T} \text{ and } gap(u)(p) = (var_u, (\mathtt{lw}_u, \mathtt{ls}_u, \mathtt{uw}_u, \mathtt{us}_u))\} \quad \text{for each } u \in \mathcal{U}. \; \mathtt{uw}_u \geq 1 \\ gap_1 = gap[\{u \leftarrow gap(u)[p \leftarrow (var_u, ((\mathtt{lw}_u - 1)^+, \mathtt{ls}_u + 1, \mathtt{uw}_u - 1, \mathtt{us}_u + 1))] \mid u \in \mathcal{U} \setminus \{t\}\}] \\ gap' = gap_1[t \leftarrow gap_1[p \leftarrow (var_t, ((\mathtt{lw}_t - 1)^+, \mathtt{ls}_t, \mathtt{uw}_t - 1, \mathtt{us}_t))]] \quad egap' = egap[p \leftarrow (\mathtt{ew} - 1)^+, \mathtt{es} + 1] \\ \hline (\mathcal{T}, \mathcal{P}, bv, seq, gap, egap) \xrightarrow{\mathtt{v.signal}()} (\mathcal{T}', \mathcal{P}', bv, seq', gap', egap') \end{array}$$

Fig. 4. Part of the predecessors computation for the **v.signal()** phaser statement where x^+ stands for $max(0, x)$. Task $t \in \mathcal{T}$ is registered to $p \in \mathcal{P}$ and refers to it with v with all registered tasks having a non-zero upper bound on their waiting phases.

Theorem 4. *Control reachability is decidable for non-atomic phaser programs generating a finite number of phasers.*

The idea is to systematically drop, in the instantiated backward procedure, constraints violating K-dimension-boundedness (as none of the denoted configurations is reachable). Also, the set of target constraints is free (since we are checking control reachability) and this is preserved by the predecessors computation (see [10]). Finally, we use the exactness of the $\mathtt{pre}_{\mathtt{stmt}}$ computation, the soundness of the entailment relation and Theorem 3. We can use a similar reasoning for plain reachability of programs generating a finite number of phasers and bounded gap-values for each phaser.

Theorem 5. *Plain reachability is decidable for non-atomic phaser programs generating a finite number of phasers with, for each phaser, bounded phase gaps.*

6   Limitations of Deciding Reachability

Assume a program $\mathtt{prg} = (\mathtt{B}, \mathtt{V}, \mathtt{T})$ and its initial configuration c_{init}. We show a number of parameterized reachability problems to be undecidable. First, we address checking control reachability when restricting to configurations with at most K task-referenced phasers. We call this K-control-reachability.

Definition 3 (K-control-reachability). *Given a partial control configuration c, we write $\mathtt{reach}_K(\mathtt{prg}, c)$, and say c is K-control-reachable, to mean there are $n + 1$ configurations $(c_i)_{i:0\leq i\leq n}$, each with at most K reachable phasers (i.e., phasers referenced by at least a task variable) s.t. $c_{init} = c_0$ and $c_i \longrightarrow c_{i+1}$ for $i : 0 \leq i < n - 1$ with c_n equivalent to a configuration that includes c.*

Theorem 6. *K-control-reachability is undecidable in general.*

Proof sketch. Encode state reachability of an arbitrary Minsky machine with counters x and y using K-control-reachability of a suitable phaser program. The program (see [10]) has five tasks: $\mathtt{main}$, $\mathtt{xTask}$, $\mathtt{yTask}$, $\mathtt{child1}$ and $\mathtt{child2}$. Machine states are captured with shared variables and counter values with phasers $\mathtt{xPh}$ for counter x (resp. $\mathtt{yPh}$ for counter y). Then, (1) spawn an instance of $\mathtt{xTask}$ (resp. $\mathtt{yTask}$) and register it to $\mathtt{xPh}$ (resp. $\mathtt{yPh}$) for increments, and (2) perform a wait on $\mathtt{xPh}$ (resp. $\mathtt{yPh}$) to test for zero. Decrementing a counter, say x, involves asking an $\mathtt{xTask}$, via shared variables, to exit (hence, to deregister from $\mathtt{xPh}$). However, more than one task might participate in the decrement operation. For this reason, each participating task builds a path from $\mathtt{xPh}$ to $\mathtt{child2}$ with two phasers. If more than one $\mathtt{xTask}$ participates in the decrement, then the number of reachable phasers of an intermediary configuration will be at least five.

Theorem 7. *Control reachability is undecidable if atomic statements are allowed even if only a finite number of phasers is generated.*

Proof sketch. Encode state reachability of an arbitrary Minsky machine with counters x and y using a phaser program with atomic statements. The phaser program (see [10]) has three tasks: `main`, `xTask` and `yTask` and encodes machine states with shared variables. The idea is to associate a phaser `xPh` to counter x (resp. `yPh` to y) and to perform a signal followed by a wait on `xPh` (resp. `yPh`) to test for zero. Incrementing and decrementing is performed by asking spawned tasks to spawn a new instance or to deregister. Atomic-next statements are used to ensure exactly one task is spawned or deregistered.

Finally, even with finite numbers of tasks and phasers, but with arbitrary gap-bounds, we can show [9] the following.

Theorem 8. *Plain reachability is undecidable if generated gaps are not bounded even when restricting to non-atomic programs with finite numbers of phasers.*

Table 1. Findings summary: *ctrl* stands for control reachability and *plain* for plain reachability; *atomic* stands for allowing the `v.next(){stmt}` atomic instruction and *non-atomic* for forbidding it (resulting in non-atomic programs). Decidable problems are marked with ✓ and undecidable ones with ✗.

	Arbitrary numbers of tasks			
	Finite dimension		K-reachability	Arbitrary dimension
Bounded gaps	ctrl atomic ✗ (Theorem 7)	plain non-atomic ✓ (Theorem 5)	ctrl non-atomic ✗ (Theorem 6)	ctrl non-atomic ✗ (Theorem 2)
Arbitrary gaps	ctrl non-atomic ✓ (Theorem 4)	plain non-atomic ✗ (From [9])		

7 Conclusion

We have studied parameterized plain (e.g., deadlocks) and control (e.g., assertions) reachability problems. We have proposed an exact verification procedure for non-atomic programs. We summarize our findings in Table 1. The procedure is guaranteed to terminate, even for programs that may generate arbitrary many tasks but finitely many phasers, when checking control reachability or when checking plain reachability with bounded gaps. These results were obtained using a non-trivial symbolic representation for which termination had required showing an $\exists \preceq_\forall$ preorder on multisets on gaps on natural numbers to be a $\mathcal{WQO}$. We are working on a tool that implements the procedure to verify phaser programs that dynamically spawn tasks. We believe our general decidability results are useful to reason about synchronization constructs other than phasers. For instance, a traditional static barrier can be captured with one phaser and with bounded gaps (in fact one). Similarly, one phaser with one producer and arbitrary many consumers can capture futures where "gets" are modeled with waits. Also, test-and-set operations can model atomic instructions and may result in undecidability of reachability. This suggests more general applications of the work are to be investigated.

References

1. Abdulla, P.A., Cerans, K., Jonsson, B., Tsay, Y.K.: General decidability theorems for infinite-state systems. In: Proceedings of the Eleventh Annual IEEE Symposium on Logic in Computer Science, LICS 1996, pp. 313–321. IEEE (1996)
2. Anderson, P., Chase, B., Mercer, E.: JPF verification of Habanero Java programs. SIGSOFT Softw. Eng. Notes **39**(1), 1–7 (2014). https://doi.org/10.1145/2557833. 2560582. http://doi.acm.org/10.1145/2557833.2560582
3. de Boer, F.S., Clarke, D., Johnsen, E.B.: A complete guide to the future. In: De Nicola, R. (ed.) ESOP 2007. LNCS, vol. 4421, pp. 316–330. Springer, Heidelberg (2007). https://doi.org/10.1007/978-3-540-71316-6_22
4. Cavé, V., Zhao, J., Shirako, J., Sarkar, V.: Habanero-Java: the new adventures of old x10. In: Proceedings of the 9th International Conference on Principles and Practice of Programming in Java, pp. 51–61. ACM (2011)
5. Charles, P., et al.: X10: an object-oriented approach to non-uniform cluster computing. SIGPLAN Not. **40**(10), 519–538 (2005). https://doi.org/10.1145/1103845. 1094852. http://doi.acm.org/10.1145/1103845.1094852
6. Cogumbreiro, T., Hu, R., Martins, F., Yoshida, N.: Dynamic deadlock verification for general barrier synchronisation. In: 20th ACM SIGPLAN Symposium on Principles and Practice of Parallel Programming, PPoPP 2015, pp. 150–160. ACM, New York (2015). https://doi.org/10.1145/2688500.2688519. http://doi.acm.org/ 10.1145/2688500.2688519
7. Cogumbreiro, T., Shirako, J., Sarkar, V.: Formalization of Habanero phasers using Coq. J. Log. Algebraic Methods Program. **90**, 50–60 (2017). https://doi.org/10. 1016/j.jlamp.2017.02.006. http://www.sciencedirect.com/science/article/pii/S23 52220816300839
8. Finkel, A., Schnoebelen, P.: Well-structured transition systems everywhere!. Theoret. Comput. Sci. **256**(1), 63–92 (2001). https://doi.org/10.1016/S0304-3975(00)00102-X. http://www.sciencedirect.com/science/article/pii/S0304397 50000102X
9. Ganjei, Z., Rezine, A., Eles, P., Peng, Z.: Safety verification of phaser programs. In: Proceedings of the 17th Conference on Formal Methods in Computer-Aided Design, FMCAD 2017, pp. 68–75. FMCAD Inc., Austin (2017). http://dl.acm. org/citation.cfm?id=3168451.3168471
10. Ganjei, Z., Rezine, A., Henrio, L., Eles, P., Peng, Z.: On reachability in parameterized phaser programs. arXiv:1811.07142 (2019)
11. Havelund, K., Pressburger, T.: Model checking Java programs using Java pathfinder. Int. J. Softw. Tools Technol. Transfer (STTT) **2**(4), 366–381 (2000)
12. Jancar, P.: A note on well quasi-orderings for powersets. Inf. Process. Lett. **72**(5–6), 155–160 (1999). https://doi.org/10.1016/S0020-0190(99)00149-0
13. Marcone, A.: Fine analysis of the quasi-orderings on the power set. Order **18**(4), 339–347 (2001). https://doi.org/10.1023/A:1013952225669
14. Minsky, M.L.: Computation: Finite and Infinite Machines. Prentice-Hall Inc., Englewood Cliffs (1967)
15. Shirako, J., Peixotto, D.M., Sarkar, V., Scherer, W.N.: Phasers: a unified deadlock-free construct for collective and point-to-point synchronization. In: 22nd Annual International Conference on Supercomputing, pp. 277–288. ACM (2008)
16. Valiant, L.G.: A bridging model for parallel computation. CACM **33**(8), 103 (1990)
17. Willebeek-LeMair, M.H., Reeves, A.P.: Strategies for dynamic load balancing on highly parallel computers. IEEE Trans. Parallel Distrib. Syst. **4**(9), 979–993 (1993)

Abstract Dependency Graphs and Their Application to Model Checking

Søren Enevoldsen, Kim Guldstrand Larsen, and Jiří Srba[⊠]

Department of Computer Science,
Aalborg University, Selma Lagerlofs Vej 300,
9220 Aalborg East, Denmark
srba@cs.aau.dk

Abstract. Dependency graphs, invented by Liu and Smolka in 1998, are oriented graphs with hyperedges that represent dependencies among the values of the vertices. Numerous model checking problems are reducible to a computation of the minimum fixed-point vertex assignment. Recent works successfully extended the assignments in dependency graphs from the Boolean domain into more general domains in order to speed up the fixed-point computation or to apply the formalism to a more general setting of e.g. weighted logics. All these extensions require separate correctness proofs of the fixed-point algorithm as well as a one-purpose implementation. We suggest the notion of *abstract dependency graphs* where the vertex assignment is defined over an abstract algebraic structure of Noetherian partial orders with the least element. We show that existing approaches are concrete instances of our general framework and provide an open-source C++ library that implements the abstract algorithm. We demonstrate that the performance of our generic implementation is comparable to, and sometimes even outperforms, dedicated special-purpose algorithms presented in the literature.

1 Introduction

Dependency Graphs (DG) [1] have demonstrated a wide applicability with respect to verification and synthesis of reactive systems, e.g. checking behavioural equivalences between systems [2], model checking systems with respect to temporal logical properties [3–5], as well as synthesizing missing components of systems [6]. The DG approach offers a general and often performance-optimal way to solve these problem. Most recently, the DG approach to CTL model checking of Petri nets [7], implemented in the model checker TAPAAL [8], won the gold medal at the annual Model Checking Contest 2018 [9].

A DG consists of a finite set of vertices and a finite set of hyperedges that connect a vertex to a number of children vertices. The computation problem is to find a point-wise minimal assignment of vertices to the Boolean values 0 and 1 such that the assignment is stable: whenever there is a hyperedge where all children have the value 1 then also the father of the hyperedge has the value 1. The main contribution of Liu and Smolka [1] is a linear-time, on-the-fly algorithm to find such a minimum stable assignment.

© The Author(s) 2019
T. Vojnar and L. Zhang (Eds.): TACAS 2019, Part I, LNCS 11427, pp. 316–333, 2019.
https://doi.org/10.1007/978-3-030-17462-0_18

Recent works successfully extend the DG approach from the Boolean domain to more general domains, including synthesis for timed systems [10], model checking for weighted systems [3] as well as probabilistic systems [11]. However, each of these extensions have required separate correctness arguments as well as ad-hoc specialized implementations that are to a large extent similar with other implementations of dependency graphs (as they are all based on the general principle of computing fixed points by local exploration). The contribution of our paper is a notion of Abstract Dependency Graph (ADG) where the values of vertices come from an abstract domain given as an Noetherian partial order (with least element). As we demonstrate, this notion of ADG covers many existing extensions of DG as concrete instances. Finally, we implement our abstract algorithms in C++ and make it available as an open-source library. We run a number of experiments to justify that our generic approach does not sacrifice any significant performance and sometimes even outperforms existing implementations.

Related Work. The aim of Liu and Smolka [1] was to find a unifying formalism allowing for a local (on-the-fly) fixed-point algorithm running in linear time. In our work, we generalize their formalism from the simple Boolean domain to general Noetherian partial orders over potentially infinite domains. This requires a non-trivial extension to their algorithm and the insight of how to (in the general setting) optimize the performance, as well as new proofs of the more general loop invariants and correctness arguments.

Recent extensions of the DG framework with certain-zero [7], integer [3] and even probabilistic [11] domains generalized Liu and Smolka's approach, however they become concrete instances of our abstract dependency graphs. The formalism of Boolean Equation Systems (BES) provides a similar and independently developed framework [12–15] pre-dating that of DG. However, BES may be encoded as DG [1] and hence they also become an instance of our abstract dependency graphs.

2   Preliminaries

A set D together with a binary relation $\sqsubseteq \subseteq D \times D$ that is reflexive ($x \sqsubseteq x$ for any $x \in D$), transitive (for any $x, y, z \in D$, if $x \sqsubseteq y$ and $y \sqsubseteq x$ then also $x \sqsubseteq z$) and anti-symmetric (for any $x, y \in D$, if $x \sqsubseteq y$ and $y \sqsubseteq x$ then $x = y$) is called a *partial order* and denoted as a pair $(D, \sqsubseteq)$. We write $x \sqsubset y$ if $x \sqsubseteq y$ and $x \neq y$. A function $f : D \to D'$ from a partial order $(D, \sqsubseteq)$ to a partial order $(D', \sqsubseteq')$ is *monotonic* if whenever $x \sqsubseteq y$ for $x, y \in D$ then also $f(x) \sqsubseteq' f(y)$. We shall now define a particular partial order that will be used throughout this paper.

Definition 1 (NOR). Noetherian Ordering Relation with least element *(NOR) is a triple $\mathcal{D} = (D, \sqsubseteq, \bot)$ where $(D, \sqsubseteq)$ is a partial order, $\bot \in D$ is its least element such that for all $d \in D$ we have $\bot \sqsubseteq d$, and $\sqsubseteq$ satisfies the ascending chain condition: for any infinite chain $d_1 \sqsubseteq d_2 \sqsubseteq d_3 \sqsubseteq \ldots$ there is an integer k such that $d_k = d_{k+j}$ for all $j > 0$.*

We can notice that any finite partial order with a least element is a NOR; however, there are also such relations with infinitely many elements in the domain as shown by the following example.

Example 1. Consider the partial order $\mathcal{D} = (\mathbb{N}^0 \cup \{\infty\}, \geq, \infty)$ over the set of natural numbers extended with ∞ and the natural larger-than-or-equal comparison on integers. As the relation is reversed, this implies that ∞ is the least element of the domain. We observe that $\mathcal{D}$ is NOR. Consider any infinite sequence $d_1 \geq d_2 \geq d_3 \ldots$. Then either $d_i = \infty$ for all i, or there exists i such that $d_i \in \mathbb{N}^0$. Clearly, the sequence must in both cases eventually stabilize, i.e. there is a number k such that $d_k = d_{k+j}$ for all $j > 0$.

New NORs can be constructed by using the Cartesian product. Let $\mathcal{D}_i = (D_i, \sqsubseteq_i, \perp_i)$ for all i, $1 \leq i \leq n$, be NORs. We define $\mathcal{D}^n = (D^n, \sqsubseteq^n, \perp^n)$ such that $D^n = D_1 \times D_2 \times \cdots \times D_n$ and where $(d_1, \ldots, d_n) \sqsubseteq^n (d'_1, \ldots, d'_n)$ if $d_i \sqsubseteq_i d'_i$ for all i, $1 \leq i \leq k$, and where $\perp^n = (\perp_1, \ldots, \perp_n)$.

Proposition 1. *Let $\mathcal{D}_i$ be a NOR for all i, $1 \leq i \leq n$. Then $\mathcal{D}^n = (D^n, \sqsubseteq^n, \perp^n)$ is also a NOR.*

In the rest of this paper, we consider only NOR $(D, \sqsubseteq, \perp)$ that are *effectively computable*, meaning that the elements of D can be represented by finite strings, and that given the finite representations of two elements x and y from D, there is an algorithm that decides whether $x \sqsubseteq y$. Similarly, we consider only functions $f : D \to D'$ from an effectively computable NOR $(D, \sqsubseteq, \perp)$ to an effectively computable NOR $(D', \sqsubseteq', \perp')$ that are *effectively computable*, meaning that there is an algorithm that for a given finite representation of an element $x \in D$ terminates and returns the finite representation of the element $f(x) \in D'$. Let $\mathcal{F}(\mathcal{D}, n)$, where $\mathcal{D} = (D, \sqsubseteq, \perp)$ is an effectively computable NOR and n is a natural number, stand for the collection of all effectively computable functions $f : D^n \to D$ of arity n and let $\mathcal{F}(\mathcal{D}) = \bigcup_{n \geq 0} \mathcal{F}(\mathcal{D}, n)$ be a collection of all such functions.

For a set X, let X^* be the set of all finite strings over X. For a string $w \in X^*$ let $|w|$ denote the length of w and for every i, $1 \leq i \leq |w|$, let w^i stand for the i'th symbol in w.

3   Abstract Dependency Graphs

We are now ready to define the notion of an abstract dependency graph.

Definition 2 (Abstract Dependency Graph). *An* abstract dependency graph *(ADG) is a tuple $G = (V, E, \mathcal{D}, \mathcal{E})$ where*

- *V is a finite set of vertices,*
- *$E : V \to V^*$ is an edge function from vertices to sequences of vertices such that $E(v)^i \neq E(v)^j$ for every $v \in V$ and every $1 \leq i < j \leq |E(v)|$, i.e. the co-domain of E contains only strings over V where no symbol appears more than once,*

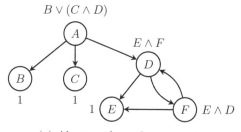

$B \vee (C \wedge D)$

(a) Abstract dependency graph

	A	B	C	D	E	F
$A_\perp$	0	0	0	0	0	0
$F(A_\perp)$	0	1	1	0	1	0
$F^2(A_\perp)$	1	1	1	0	1	0
$F^3(A_\perp)$	1	1	1	0	1	0

(b) Fixed-point computation

Fig. 1. Abstract dependency graph over NOR $(\{0,1\}, \leq, 0)$

- $\mathcal{D}$ is an effectively computable NOR, and
- $\mathcal{E}$ is a labelling function $\mathcal{E} : V \to \mathcal{F}(\mathcal{D})$ such that $\mathcal{E}(v) \in \mathcal{F}(\mathcal{D}, |E(v)|)$ for each $v \in V$, i.e. each edge $E(v)$ is labelled by an effectively computable function f of arity that corresponds to the length of the string $E(v)$.

Example 2. An example of ADG over the NOR $\mathcal{D} = (\{0,1\}, \{(0,1)\}, 0)$ is shown in Fig. 1a. Here 0 (interpreted as false) is below the value 1 (interpreted as true) and the monotonic functions for vertices are displayed as vertex annotations. For example $E(A) = B \cdot C \cdot D$ and $\mathcal{E}(A)$ is a ternary function such that $\mathcal{E}(A)(x, y, z) = x \vee (y \wedge z)$, and $E(B) = \epsilon$ (empty sequence of vertices) such that $\mathcal{E}(B) = 1$ is a constant labelling function. Clearly, all functions used in our example are monotonic and effectively computable.

Let us now assume a fixed ADG $G = (V, E, \mathcal{D}, \mathcal{E})$ over an effectively computable NOR $\mathcal{D} = (D, \sqsubseteq, \perp)$. We first define an assignment of an ADG.

Definition 3 (Assignment). *An* assignment *on G is a function $A : V \to D$.*

The set of all assignments is denoted by $\mathcal{A}$. For $A, A' \in \mathcal{A}$ we define $A \leq A'$ iff $A(v) \sqsubseteq A'(v)$ for all $v \in V$. We also define the bottom assignment $A_\perp(v) = \perp$ for all $v \in V$ that is the least element in the partial order $(\mathcal{A}, \leq)$. The following proposition is easy to verify.

Proposition 2. *The partial order $(\mathcal{A}, \leq, A_\perp)$ is a NOR.*

Finally, we define the *minimum fixed-point assignment* A_{min} for a given ADG $G = (V, E, \mathcal{D}, \mathcal{E})$ as the minimum fixed point of the function $F : \mathcal{A} \to \mathcal{A}$ defined as follows: $F(A)(v) = \mathcal{E}(v)(A(v_1), A(v_2), \dots, A(v_k))$ where $E(v) = v_1 v_2 \dots v_k$.

In the rest of this section, we shall argue that A_{min} of the function F exists by following the standard reasoning about fixed points of monotonic functions [16].

Lemma 1. *The function F is monotonic.*

Let us define the notation of multiple applications of the function F by $F^0(A) = A$ and $F^i(A) = F(F^{i-1}(A))$ for $i > 0$.

Lemma 2. *For all $i \geq 0$ the assignment $F^i(A_\perp)$ is effectively computable, $F^i(A_\perp) \leq F^j(A_\perp)$ for all $i \leq j$, and there exists a number k such that $F^k(A_\perp) = F^{k+j}(A_\perp)$ for all $j > 0$.*

We can now finish with the main observation of this section.

Theorem 1. *There exists a number k such that $F^j(A_\perp) = A_{min}$ for all $j \geq k$.*

Example 3. The computation of the minimum fixed point for our running example from Fig. 1a is given in Fig. 1b. We can see that starting from the assignment where all nodes take the least element value 0, in the first iteration all constant functions increase the value of the corresponding vertices to 1 and in the second iteration the value 1 propagates from the vertex B to A, because the function $B \vee (C \wedge D)$ that is assigned to the vertex A evaluates to true due to the fact that $F(A_\perp)(B) = 1$. On the other hand, the values of the vertices D and F keep the assignment 0 due to the cyclic dependencies between the two vertices. As $F^2(A_\perp) = F^3(A_\perp)$, we know that we found the minimum fixed point.

As many natural verification problems can be encoded as a computation of the minimum fixed point on an ADG, the result in Theorem 1 provides an algorithmic way to compute such a fixed point and hence solve the encoded problem. The disadvantage of this *global* algorithm is that it requires that the whole dependency graph is a priory generated before the computation can be carried out and this approach is often inefficient in practice [3]. In the following section, we provide a *local*, on-the-fly algorithm for computing the minimum fixed-point assignment of a specific vertex, without the need to always explore the whole abstract dependency graph.

4   On-the-Fly Algorithm for ADGs

The idea behind the algorithm is to progressively explore the vertices of the graph, starting from a given root vertex for which we want to find its value in the minimum fixed-point assignment. To search the graph, we use a waiting list that contains configurations (vertices) whose assignment has the potential of being improved by applying the function $\mathcal{E}$. By repeated applications of $\mathcal{E}$ on the vertices of the graph in some order maintained by the algorithm, the minimum fixed-point assignment for the root vertex can be identified without necessarily exploring the whole dependency graph.

To improve the performance of the algorithm, we make use of an optional user-provided function $\text{IGNORE}(A, v)$ that computes, given a current assignment A and a vertex v of the graph, the set of vertices on an edge $E(v)$ whose current and any potential future value no longer effect the value of $A_{min}(v)$. Hence, whenever a vertex v' is in the set $\text{IGNORE}(A, v)$, there is no reason to explore the subgraph rooted by v' for the purpose of computing $A_{min}(v)$ since an improved assignment value of v' cannot influence the assignment of v. The soundness property of the ignore function is formalized in the following definition. As before, we assume a fixed ADG $G = (V, E, \mathcal{D}, \mathcal{E})$ over an effectively computable NOR $\mathcal{D} = (D, \sqsubseteq, \perp)$.

Definition 4 (Ignore Function). *A function:* IGNORE $: \mathcal{A} \times V \to 2^V$ *is sound if for any two assignments* $A, A' \in \mathcal{A}$ *where* $A \leq A'$ *and every* i *such that* $E(v)^i \in$ IGNORE(A, v) *holds that*

$$\mathcal{E}(v)(A'(v_1), A'(v_2), \ldots, A(v_i), \ldots, A'(v_{|E(v)-1|}), A'(v_{|E(v)|}))$$
$$= \mathcal{E}(v)(A'(v_1), A'(v_2), \ldots, A'(v_i), \ldots, A'(v_{|E(v)-1|}), A'(v_{|E(v)|})).$$

From now on, we shall consider only sound and effectively computable ignore functions. Note that there is always a trivially sound IGNORE function that returns for every assignment and every vertex the empty set. A more interesting and universally sound ignore function may be defined by

$$\text{IGNORE}(A, v) = \begin{cases} \{E(v)^i \mid 1 \leq i \leq |E(v)|\} & \text{if } d \leq A(v) \text{ for all } d \in D \\ \emptyset & \text{otherwise} \end{cases}$$

that returns the set of all vertices on an edge $E(v)$ once $A(v)$ reached its maximal possible value. This will avoid the exploration of the children of the vertex v once the value of v in the current assignment cannot be improved any more. Already this can have a significant impact on the improved performance of the algorithm; however, for concrete instances of our general framework, the user can provide more precise and case-specific ignore functions in order to tune the performance of the fixed-point algorithm, as shown by the next example.

Example 4. Consider the ADG from Fig. 1a in an assignment where the value of B is already known to be 1. As the vertex A has the labelling function $B \lor (C \land D)$, we can see that the assignment of A will get the value 1, irrelevant of what are the assignments for the vertices C and D. Hence, in this assignment, we can move the vertices C and D to the ignore set of A and avoid the exploration of the subgraphs rooted by C and D.

The following lemma formalizes the fact that once the ignore function of a vertex contains all its children and the vertex value has been relaxed by applying the associated monotonic function, then its current assignment value is equal to the vertex value in the minimum fixed-point assignment.

Lemma 3. *Let* A *be an assignment such that* $A \leq A_{min}$. *If* $v_i \in$ IGNORE(A, v) *for all* $1 \leq i \leq k$ *where* $E(v) = v_1 \cdots v_k$ *and* $A(v) = \mathcal{E}(v)(A(v_1), \ldots, A(v_k))$ *then* $A(v) = A_{min}(v)$.

In Algorithm 1 we now present our local (on-the-fly) minimum fixed-point computation. The algorithm uses the following internal data structures:

- A is the currently computed assignment that is initialized to $A_\perp$,
- W is the waiting list containing the set of pending vertices to be explored,
- PASSED is the set of explored vertices, and
- $Dep : V \to 2^V$ is a function that for each vertex v returns a subset of vertices that should be reevaluated whenever the assignment value of v improves.

Input: An effectively computable ADG $G = (V, E, \mathcal{D}, \mathcal{E})$ and $v_0 \in V$.
Output: $A_{min}(v_0)$
1 $A := A_\perp$; $Dep(v) := \emptyset$ for all v
2 $W := \{v_0\}$; PASSED $:= \emptyset$
3 **while** $W \neq \emptyset$ **do**
4 | let $v \in W$; $W := W \setminus \{v\}$
5 | UPDATEDEPENDENTS (v)
6 | **if** $v = v_0$ or $Dep(v) \neq \emptyset$ **then**
7 | | let $v_1 v_2 \cdots v_k = E(v)$
8 | | $d := \mathcal{E}(v)(A(v_1), \ldots, A(v_k))$
9 | | **if** $A(v) \sqsubset d$ **then**
10 | | | $A(v) := d$
11 | | | $W := W \cup \{u \in Dep(v) \mid v \notin \text{IGNORE}(A, u)\}$
12 | | | **if** $v = v_0$ and $\{v_1, \ldots, v_k\} \subseteq \text{IGNORE}(A, v_0)$ **then**
13 | | | | "break out of the while loop"
14 | | **if** $v \notin$ PASSED **then**
15 | | | PASSED $:=$ PASSED $\cup \{v\}$
16 | | | **for** all $v_i \in \{v_1, \ldots, v_k\} \setminus \text{IGNORE}(A, v)$ **do**
17 | | | | $Dep(v_i) := Dep(v_i) \cup \{v\}$
18 | | | | $W := W \cup \{v_i\}$
19 return $A(v_0)$
20 **Procedure** UPDATEDEPENDENTS(v):
21 | $C := \{u \in Dep(v) \mid v \in \text{IGNORE}(A, u)\}$
22 | $Dep(v) := Dep(v) \setminus C$
23 | **if** $Dep(v) = \emptyset$ and $C \neq \emptyset$ **then**
24 | | PASSED $:=$ PASSED $\setminus \{v\}$
25 | | UPDATEDEPENDENTSREC (v)
26 **Procedure** UPDATEDEPENDENTSREC(v):
27 | **for** $v' \in E(v)$ **do**
28 | | $Dep(v') := Dep(v') \setminus \{v\}$
29 | | **if** $Dep(v') = \emptyset$ **then**
30 | | | UPDATEDEPENDENTSREC (v')
31 | | | PASSED $:=$ PASSED $\setminus \{v'\}$

Algorithm 1. Minimum Fixed-Point Computation on an ADG

The algorithm starts by inserting the root vertex v_0 into the waiting list. In each iteration of the while-loop it removes a vertex v from the waiting list and performs a check whether there is some other vertex that depends on the value of v. If this is not the case, we are not going to explore the vertex v and recursively propagate this information to the children of v. After this, we try to improve the current assignment of $A(v)$ and if this succeeds, we update the waiting list by adding all vertices that depend on the value of v to W, and we test if the algorithm can early terminate (should the root vertex v_0 get its final value). Otherwise, if the vertex v has not been explored yet, we add all its children to the waiting list and update the dependencies. We shall now state the termination and correctness of our algorithm.

Lemma 4 (Termination). *Algorithm 1 terminates.*

Lemma 5 (Soundness). *Algorithm 1 at all times satisfies $A \leq A_{min}$.*

Lemma 6 (While-Loop Invariant). *At the beginning of each iteration of the loop in line 1 of Algorithm 1, for any vertex $v \in V$ it holds that either:*

1. *$A(v) = A_{min}(v)$, or*
2. *$v \in W$, or*
3. *$v \neq v_0$ and $Dep(v) = \emptyset$, or*
4. *$A(v) = \mathcal{E}(v)(A(v_1), \ldots, A(v_k))$ where $v_1 \cdots v_k = E(v)$ and for all i, $1 \leq i \leq k$, whenever $v_i \notin \text{IGNORE}(A, v)$ then also $v \in Dep(v_i)$.*

Theorem 2. *Algorithm 1 terminates and returns the value $A_{min}(v_0)$.*

5   Applications of Abstract Dependency Graphs

We shall now describe applications of our general framework to previously studied settings in order to demonstrate the direct applicability of our framework. Together with an efficient implementation of the algorithm, this provides a solution to many verification problems studied in the literature. We start with the classical notion of dependency graphs suggested by Liu and Smolka.

5.1   Liu and Smolka Dependency Graphs

In the dependency graph framework introduced by Liu and Smolka [17], a dependency graph is represented as $G = (V, H)$ where V is a finite set of vertices and $H \subseteq V \times 2^V$ is the set of *hyperedges*. An *assignment* is a function $A : V \rightarrow \{0, 1\}$. A given assignment is a *fixed-point assignment* if $(A)(v) = \max_{(v,T) \in H} \min_{v' \in T} A(v')$ for all $v \in V$. In other words, A is a fixed-point assignment if for every hyperedge (v, T) where $T \subseteq V$ holds that if $A(v') = 1$ for every $v' \in T$ then also $A(v) = 1$. Liu and Smolka suggest both a global and a local algorithm [17] to compute the minimum fixed-point assignment for a given dependency graph.

We shall now argue how to instantiate their framework into abstract dependency graphs. Let (V, H) be a fixed dependency graph. We consider a NOR $\mathcal{D} = (\{0, 1\}, \leq, 0)$ where $0 < 1$ and construct an abstract dependency graph $G' = (V, E, \mathcal{D}, \mathcal{E})$. Here $E : V \rightarrow V^*$ is defined

$$E(v) = v_1 \cdots v_k \text{ s.t. } \{v_1, \ldots, v_k\} = \bigcup_{(v,T) \in H} T$$

such that $E(v)$ contains (in some fixed order) all vertices that appear on at least one hyperedge rooted with v. The labelling function $\mathcal{E}$ is now defined as expected

$$\mathcal{E}(v)(d_1, \ldots, d_k) = \max_{(v,T) \in H} \min_{v_i \in T} d_i$$

mimicking the computation in dependency graphs. For the efficiency of fixed-point computation in abstract dependency graphs it is important to provide an IGNORE function that includes as many vertices as possible. We shall use the following one

$$\text{IGNORE}(A, v) = \begin{cases} \{E(v)^i \mid 1 \leq i \leq |E(v)|\} & \text{if } \exists(v, T) \in H.\forall u \in T.A(u) = 1 \\ \emptyset & \text{otherwise} \end{cases}$$

meaning that once there is a hyperedge with all the target vertices with value 1 (that propagates the value 1 to the root of the hyperedge), then the vertices of all other hyperedges can be ignored. This ignore function is, as we observed when running experiments, more efficient than this simpler one

$$\text{IGNORE}(A, v) = \begin{cases} \{E(v)^i \mid 1 \leq i \leq |E(v)|\} & \text{if } A(v) = 1 \\ \emptyset & \text{otherwise} \end{cases}$$

because it avoids the exploration of vertices that can be ignored before the root v is picked from the waiting list. Our encoding hence provides a generic and efficient way to model and solve problems described by Boolean equations [18] and dependency graphs [17].

5.2   Certain-Zero Dependency Graphs

Liu and Smolka's on-the-fly algorithm for dependency graphs significantly benefits from the fact that if there is a hyperedge with all target vertices having the value 1 then this hyperedge can propagate this value to the source of the hyperedge without the need to explore the remaining hyperedges. Moreover, the algorithm can early terminate should the root vertex v_0 get the value 1. On the other hand, if the final value of the root is 0 then the whole graph has to be explored and no early termination is possible. Recently, it has been noticed [19] that the speed of fixed-point computation by Liu and Smolka's algorithm can been considerably improved by considering also certain-zero value in the assignment that can, in certain situations, propagate from children vertices to their parents and once it reaches the root vertex, the algorithm can early terminate.

We shall demonstrate that this extension can be directly implemented in our generic framework, requiring only a minor modification of the abstract dependency graph. Let $G = (V, H)$ be a given dependency graph. We consider now a NOR $\mathcal{D} = (\{\bot, 0, 1\}, \sqsubseteq, \bot)$ where $\bot \sqsubseteq 0$ and $\bot \sqsubseteq 1$ but 0 and 1, the 'certain' values, are incomparable. We use the labelling function

$$\mathcal{E}(v)(d_1, \ldots, d_k) = \begin{cases} 1 & \text{if } \exists(v, T) \in H.\forall v_i \in T.d_i = 1 \\ 0 & \text{if } \forall(v, T) \in H.\exists v_i \in T.d_i = 0 \\ \bot & \text{otherwise} \end{cases}$$

so that it rephrases the method described in [19]. In order to achieve a competitive performance, we use the following ignore function.

$$\text{IGNORE}(A, v) = \begin{cases} \{E(v)^i \mid 1 \leq i \leq |E(v)|\} & \text{if } \exists(v, T) \in H. \forall u \in T.A(u) = 1 \\ \{E(v)^i \mid 1 \leq i \leq |E(v)|\} & \text{if } \forall(v, T) \in H. \exists u \in T.A(u) = 0 \\ \emptyset & \text{otherwise} \end{cases}$$

Our experiments presented in Sect. 6 show a clear advantage of the certain-zero algorithm over the classical one, as also demonstrated in [19].

5.3 Weighted Symbolic Dependency Graphs

In this section we show an application that instead of a finite NOR considers an ordering with infinitely many elements. This allows us to encode e.g. the model checking problem for weighted CTL logic as demonstrated in [3,20]. The main difference, compared to the dependency graphs in Sect. 5.1, is the addition of cover-edges and hyperedges with weight.

A *weighted symbolic dependency graph*, as introduced in [20], is a triple $G = (V, H, C)$, where V is a finite set of vertices, $H \subseteq V \times 2^{(\mathbb{N}^0 \times V)}$ is a finite set of hyperedges and $C \subseteq V \times \mathbb{N}^0 \times V$ a finite set of cover-edges. We assume the natural ordering relation $>$ on natural numbers such that $\infty > n$ for any $n \in \mathbb{N}^0$. An *assignment* $A : V \to \mathbb{N}^0 \cup \{\infty\}$ is a mapping from configurations to values. A *fixed-point assignment* is an assignment A such that

$$A(v) = \begin{cases} 0 & \text{if there is } (v, w, u) \in C \text{ such that } A(u) \leq w \\ \min_{(v,T)\in H} \left(\max\{A(u) + w \mid (w, u) \in T\} \right) & \text{otherwise} \end{cases}$$

where we assume that $\max \emptyset = 0$ and $\min \emptyset = \infty$. As before, we are interested in computing the value $A_{min}(v_0)$ for a given vertex v_0 where A_{min} is the minimum fixed-point assignment.

In order to instantiate weighted symbolic dependency graphs in our framework, we use the NOR $\mathcal{D} = (\mathbb{N}^0 \cup \{\infty\}, \geq, \infty)$ as introduced in Example 1 and define an abstract dependency graph $G' = (V, E, \mathcal{D}, \mathcal{E})$. We let $E : V \to V^*$ be defined as $E(v) = v_1 \cdots v_m c_1 \cdots c_n$ where $\{v_1, \ldots, v_m\} = \bigcup_{(v,T)\in H} \bigcup_{(w,v_i)\in T}\{v_i\}$ is the set (in some fixed order) of all vertices that are used in hyperedges and $\{c_1, \ldots, c_n\} = \bigcup_{(v,w,u)\in C}\{u\}$ is the set (in some fixed order) of all vertices connected to cover-edges. Finally, we define the labelling function $\mathcal{E}$ as

$$\mathcal{E}(v)(d_1, \ldots, d_m, e_1, \ldots, e_n) =$$

$$\begin{cases} 0 & \text{if } \exists(v, w, c_i) \in C. \ w \geq e_i \\ \min_{(v,T)\in H} \max_{(w,v_i)\in T} w + d_i & \text{otherwise.} \end{cases}$$

In our experiments, we consider the following ignore function.

$$\text{IGNORE}(A, v) = \begin{cases} \{E(v)^i \mid 1 \leq i \leq |E(v)|\} & \text{if } \exists(v, w, u) \in C.A(u) \leq w \\ \{E(v)^i \mid 1 \leq i \leq |E(v)|, A(E(v)^i) = 0\} & \text{otherwise} \end{cases}$$

```
struct Value {                          struct VertexRef {
  bool operator==(const Value&);          bool operator==(const VertexRef&);
  bool operator!=(const Value&);          bool operator<(const VertexRef&);
  bool operator<(const Value&);         };
};


struct ADG {
  using Value = Value;
  using VertexRef = VertexRef;
  using EdgeTuple = vector<VertexRef>;
  static Value BOTTOM;
  VertexRef initialVertex();
  EdgeTuple getEdge(VertexRef& v);
  using VRA = typename algorithm:VertexRefAssignment<ADG>;
  Value compute(const VRA*, const VRA**, size_t n);
  void updateIgnored(const VRA*, const VRA**, size_t n, vector<bool>& ignore);
  bool ignoreSingle(const VRA* v, const VRA* u);
};
```

Fig. 2. The C++ interface

This shows that also the formalism of weighted symbolic dependency graphs can be modelled in our framework and the experimental evaluation documents that it outperforms the existing implementation.

6   Implementation and Experimental Evaluation

The algorithm is implemented in C++ and the signature of the user-provided interface in order to use the framework is shown in Fig. 2. The structure ADG is the main interface the algorithm uses. It assumes the definition of the type Value that represents the NOR, and the type VertexRef that represents a light-weight reference to a vertex and the bottom element. The type aliased as VRA contains both a Value and a VertexRef and represents the assignment of a vertex. The user must also provide the implementation of the functions: initialVertex that returns the root vertex v_0, getEdge that returns ordered successors for a given vertex, compute that computes $\mathcal{E}(v)$ for a given assignment of v and its successors, and updateIgnored that receives the assignment of a vertex and its successors and sets the ignore flags.

We instantiated this interface to three different applications as discussed in Sect. 5. The source code of the algorithm and its instantiations is available at https://launchpad.net/adg-tool/.

We shall now present a number of experiments showing that our generic implementation of abstract dependency graph algorithm is competitive with single-purpose implementations mentioned in the literature. The first two experiments (bisimulation checking for CCS processes and CTL model checking of Petri nets) were run on a Linux cluster with AMD Opteron 6376 processors running Ubuntu 14.04. We marked an experiment as OOT if it run for more than one hour and OOM if it used more than 16 GB of RAM. The final experiment for WCTL model checking required to be executed on a personal computer as the tool we compare to is written in JavaScript, so each problem instance was run on

Size	Time [s]				Memory [MB]		
	DG	ADG	Speedup		DG	ADG	Reduction
Lossy Alternating Bit Protocol – Bisimilar							
3	83.03	78.08	+6%		71	58	22%
4	2489.08	2375.10	+5%		995	810	23%
Lossy Alternating Bit Protocol — Nonbisimilar							
4	6.04	5.07	+19%		25	18	39%
5	4.10	5.08	−19%		69	61	13%
6	9.04	6.06	+49%		251	244	3%
Ring Based Leader-Election — Bisimilar							
8	21.09	18.06	+17%		31	23	35%
9	190.01	186.05	+2%		79	71	11%
10	2002.05	1978.04	+1%		298	233	28%
Ring Based Leader-Election — Nonbisimilar							
8	4.09	2.01	+103%		59	52	13%
9	16.02	15.07	+6%		185	174	6%
10	125.06	126.01	−1%		647	638	1%

Fig. 3. Weak bisimulation checking comparison

a Lenovo ThinkPad T450s laptop with an Intel Core i7-5600U CPU @ 2.60 GHz and 12 GB of memory.

6.1 Bisimulation Checking for CCS Processes

In our first experiment, we encode using ADG a number of weak bisimulation checking problems for the process algebra CCS. The encoding was described in [2] where the authors use classical Liu and Smolka's dependency graphs to solve the problems and they also provide a C++ implementation (referred to as DG in the tables). We compare the verification time needed to answer both positive and negative instances of the test cases described in [2].

Figure 3 shows the results where DG refers to the implementation from [2] and ADG is our implementation using abstract dependency graphs. It displays the verification time in seconds and peak memory consumptions in MB for both implementations as well as the relative improvement in percents. We can see that the performance of both algorithms is comparable, slightly in favour of our algorithm, sometimes showing up to 103% speedup like in the case of nonbisimilar processes in leader election of size 8. For nonbisimilar processes modelling alternating bit protocol of size 5 we observe a 19% slowdown caused by the different search strategies so that the counter-example to bisimilarity is found faster by the implementation from [2]. Memory-wise, the experiments are slightly in favour of our implementation.

We further evaluated the performance for weak simulation checking on task graph scheduling problems. We verified 180 task graphs from the Standard Task Graph Set as used in [2] where we check for the possibility to complete all tasks

Name	VerifyPN	ADG	Speedup
VerifyPN/ADG *Best 2*			
Diffusion2D-PT-D05N350:12	OOM	42.07	∞
Diffusion2D-PT-D05N350:01	332.70	0.01	+3326900%
VerifyPN/ADG *Middle 7*			
IOTPpurchase-PT-C05M04P03D02:08	4.15	2.13	+95%
Solitaire-PT-SqrNC5x5:09	340.31	180.47	+89%
Railroad-PT-010:08	155.34	83.92	+85%
IOTPpurchase-PT-C05M04P03D02:13	0.16	0.09	+78%
PolyORBLF-PT-S02J04T06:11	2.66	1.67	+59%
Diffusion2D-PT-D10N050:01	168.17	110.59	+52%
MAPK-PT-008:05	454.50	325.24	+40%
VerifyPN/ADG *Worst 2*			
ResAllocation-PT-R020C002:06	0.02	OOM	−∞
MAPK-PT-008:06	0.01	OOM	−∞

Fig. 4. Time comparison for CTL model checking (in seconds)

within a fixed number of steps. Both DG and ADG solved 35 task graphs using the classical Liu Smolka approach. However, once we allow for the certain-zero optimization in our approach (requiring to change only a few lines of code in the user-defined functions), we can solve 107 of the task graph scheduling problems.

6.2   CTL Model Checking of Petri Nets

In this experiment, we compare the performance of the tool TAPAAL [8] and its engine VerifyPN [21], version 2.1.0, on the Petri net models and CTL queries from the 2016 Model Checking Contest [22]. From the database of models and queries, we selected all those that do not contain logical negation in the CTL query (as they are not supported by the current implementation of abstract dependency graphs). This resulted in 267 model checking instances[1].

The results comparing the speed of model checking are shown in Fig. 4. The 267 model checking executions are ordered by the ratio of the verification time of VerifyPN vs. our implementation referred to as ADG. In the table we show the best two instances for our tool, the middle seven instances and the worst two instances. The results significantly vary on some instances as both algorithms are on-the-fly with early termination and depending on the search strategy the verification times can be largely different. Nevertheless, we can observe that on the average (middle) experiment IOTPpurchase-PT-C05M04P03D02:13, we are 78% faster than VerifyPN. However, we can also notice that in the two worst cases, our implementation runs out of memory.

---

[1] During the experiments we turned off the query preprocessing using linear programming as it solves a large number of queries by applying logical equivalences instead of performing the state-space search that we are interested in.

Name	VerifyPN	ADG	Reduction
VerifyPN/ADG *Best 2*			
Diffusion2D-PT-D05N350:12	OOM	4573	$+\infty$
Diffusion2D-PT-D05N350:01	9882	7	141171%
VerifyPN/ADG *Middle 7*			
PolyORBLF-PT-S02J04T06:13	17	23	−35%
ParamProductionCell-PT-0:02	1846	2556	−38%
ParamProductionCell-PT-0:07	1823	2528	−39%
ParamProductionCell-PT-4:13	1451	2064	−42%
SharedMemory-PT-000010:12	21	30	−43%
Angiogenesis-PT-15:04	51	74	−45%
Peterson-PT-3:03	1910	2792	−46%
VerifyPN/ADG *Worst 2*			
ParamProductionCell-PT-5:13	6	OOT	$-\infty$
ParamProductionCell-PT-0:10	6	OOT	$-\infty$

Fig. 5. Memory comparison for CTL model checking (in MB)

In Fig. 5 we present an analogous table for the peak memory consumption of the two algorithms. In the middle experiment ParamProductionCell-PT-4:13 we use 42% extra memory compared to VerifyPN. Hence we have a trade-off between the verification speed and memory consumption where our implementation is faster but consumes more memory. We believe that this is due to the use of the waiting list where we store directly vertices (allowing for a fast access to their assignment), compared to storing references to hyperedges in the VerifyPN implementation (saving the memory). Given the 16 GB memory limit we used in our experiments, this results in the fact that we were able to solve only 144 instances, compared to 218 answers provided by VerifyPN and we run 102 times out of memory while VerifyPN did only 45 times.

6.3   Weighted CTL Model Checking

Our last experiment compares the performance on the model checking of weighted CTL against weighted Kripke structures as used in the WKTool [3]. We implemented the weighted symbolic dependency graphs in our generic interface and run the experiments on the benchmark from [3]. The measurements for a few instances are presented in Fig. 6 and clearly show significant speedup in favour of our implementation. We remark that because WKTool is written in JavaScript, it was impossible to gather its peek memory consumption.

Instance	Time [s]			Satisfied?
	WKTool	ADG	Speedup	
Alternating Bit Protocol: $EF[\leq Y]$ delivered $= X$				
B=5 X=7 Y=35	7.10	0.83	+755%	yes
B=5 X=8 Y=40	4.17	1.05	+297%	yes
B=6 X=5 Y=30	7.58	1.44	+426%	yes
Alternating Bit Protocol: EF (send0 && deliver1) $\parallel$ (send1 && deliver0)				
B=5, M=7	7.09	1.39	+410%	no
B=5, M=8	4.64	1.60	+190%	no
B=6, M=5	7.75	2.37	+227%	no
Leader Election: EF leader > 1				
N=10	5.88	1.98	+197%	no
N=11	25.19	9.35	+169%	no
N=12	117.00	41.57	+181%	no
Leader Election: $EF[\leq X]$ leader				
N=11 X=11	24.36	2.47	+886%	yes
N=12 X=12	101.22	11.02	+819%	yes
N=11 X=10	25.42	9.00	+182%	no
Task Graphs: $EF[\leq 10]$ done $= 9$				
T=0	26.20	22.17	+18%	no
T=1	6.13	5.04	+22%	no
T=2	200.69	50.78	+295%	no

Fig. 6. Speed comparison for WCTL (B–buffer size, M–number of messages, N–number of processes, T–task graph number)

7   Conclusion

We defined a formal framework for minimum fixed-point computation on dependency graphs over an abstract domain of Noetherian orderings with the least element. This framework generalizes a number of variants of dependency graphs recently published in the literature. We suggested an efficient, on-the-fly algorithm for computing the minimum fixed-point assignment, including performance optimization features, and we proved the correctness of the algorithm.

On a number of examples, we demonstrated the applicability of our framework, showing that its performance is matching those of specialized algorithms already published in the literature. Last but not least, we provided an open source C++ library that allows the user to specify only a few domain-specific functions in order to employ the generic algorithm described in this paper. Experiential results show that we are competitive with e.g. the tool TAPAAL, winner of the 2018 Model Checking Contest in the CTL category [9], showing 78% faster performance on the median instance of the model checking problem, at the expense of 42% higher memory consumption.

In the future work, we shall apply our approach to other application domains (in particular probabilistic model checking), develop and test generic heuristic search strategies as well as provide a parallel/distributed implementation of our general algorithm (that is already available for some of its concrete instances [7, 23]) in order to further enhance the applicability of the framework.

Acknowledgments. The work was funded by the center IDEA4CPS, Innovation Fund Denmark center DiCyPS and ERC Advanced Grant LASSO. The last author is partially affiliated with FI MU in Brno.

References

1. Liu, X., Smolka, S.A.: Simple linear-time algorithms for minimal fixed points (extended abstract). In: Larsen, K.G., Skyum, S., Winskel, G. (eds.) ICALP 1998. LNCS, vol. 1443, pp. 53–66. Springer, Heidelberg (1998). https://doi.org/10.1007/BFb0055040
2. Dalsgaard, A.E., Enevoldsen, S., Larsen, K.G., Srba, J.: Distributed computation of fixed points on dependency graphs. In: Fränzle, M., Kapur, D., Zhan, N. (eds.) SETTA 2016. LNCS, vol. 9984, pp. 197–212. Springer, Cham (2016). https://doi.org/10.1007/978-3-319-47677-3_13
3. Jensen, J.F., Larsen, K.G., Srba, J., Oestergaard, L.K.: Efficient model checking of weighted CTL with upper-bound constraints. Int. J. Softw. Tools Technol. Transfer (STTT) **18**(4), 409–426 (2016)
4. Keiren, J.J.A.: Advanced reduction techniques for model checking. Ph.D thesis, Eindhoven University of Technology (2013)
5. Christoffersen, P., Hansen, M., Mariegaard, A., Ringsmose, J.T., Larsen, K.G., Mardare, R.: Parametric verification of weighted systems. In: André, É., Frehse, G. (eds.) SynCoP 2015, OASIcs, vol. 44, pp. 77–90. Schloss Dagstuhl–Leibniz-Zentrum fuer Informatik, Dagstuhl, Germany (2015)
6. Larsen, K.G., Liu, X.: Equation solving using modal transition systems. In: Proceedings of the Fifth Annual Symposium on Logic in Computer Science (LICS 1990), Philadelphia, Pennsylvania, USA, 4–7 June 1990, pp. 108–117. IEEE Computer Society (1990)
7. Dalsgaard, A.E., et al.: Extended dependency graphs and efficient distributed fixed-point computation. In: van der Aalst, W., Best, E. (eds.) PETRI NETS 2017. LNCS, vol. 10258, pp. 139–158. Springer, Cham (2017). https://doi.org/10.1007/978-3-319-57861-3_10
8. David, A., Jacobsen, L., Jacobsen, M., Jørgensen, K.Y., Møller, M.H., Srba, J.: TAPAAL 2.0: integrated development environment for timed-arc Petri nets. In: Flanagan, C., König, B. (eds.) TACAS 2012. LNCS, vol. 7214, pp. 492–497. Springer, Heidelberg (2012). https://doi.org/10.1007/978-3-642-28756-5_36
9. Kordon, F., et al.: Complete Results for the 2018 Edition of the Model Checking Contest, June 2018. http://mcc.lip6.fr/2018/results.php
10. Cassez, F., David, A., Fleury, E., Larsen, K.G., Lime, D.: Efficient on-the-fly algorithms for the analysis of timed games. In: Abadi, M., de Alfaro, L. (eds.) CONCUR 2005. LNCS, vol. 3653, pp. 66–80. Springer, Heidelberg (2005). https://doi.org/10.1007/11539452_9

11. Mariegaard, A., Larsen, K.G.: Symbolic dependency graphs for PCTL$^\geq_\leq$ model-checking. In: Abate, A., Geeraerts, G. (eds.) FORMATS 2017. LNCS, vol. 10419, pp. 153–169. Springer, Cham (2017). https://doi.org/10.1007/978-3-319-65765-3_9

12. Larsen, K.G.: Efficient local correctness checking. In: von Bochmann, G., Probst, D.K. (eds.) CAV 1992. LNCS, vol. 663, pp. 30–43. Springer, Heidelberg (1993). https://doi.org/10.1007/3-540-56496-9_4

13. Andersen, H.R.: Model checking and boolean graphs. In: Krieg-Brückner, B. (ed.) ESOP 1992. LNCS, vol. 582, pp. 1–19. Springer, Heidelberg (1992). https://doi.org/10.1007/3-540-55253-7_1

14. Mader, A.: Modal μ-calculus, model checking and Gauß elimination. In: Brinksma, E., Cleaveland, W.R., Larsen, K.G., Margaria, T., Steffen, B. (eds.) TACAS 1995. LNCS, vol. 1019, pp. 72–88. Springer, Heidelberg (1995). https://doi.org/10.1007/3-540-60630-0_4

15. Mateescu, R.: Efficient diagnostic generation for Boolean equation systems. In: Graf, S., Schwartzbach, M. (eds.) TACAS 2000. LNCS, vol. 1785, pp. 251–265. Springer, Heidelberg (2000). https://doi.org/10.1007/3-540-46419-0_18

16. Tarski, A.: A lattice-theoretical fixpoint theorem and its applications. Pacific J. Math. **5**(2), 285–309 (1955)

17. Liu, X., Ramakrishnan, C.R., Smolka, S.A.: Fully local and efficient evaluation of alternating fixed points. In: Steffen, B. (ed.) TACAS 1998. LNCS, vol. 1384, pp. 5–19. Springer, Heidelberg (1998). https://doi.org/10.1007/BFb0054161

18. Andersen, H.R.: Model checking and boolean graphs. Theoret. Comput. Sci. **126**(1), 3–30 (1994)

19. Dalsgaard, A.E., et al.: A distributed fixed-point algorithm for extended dependency graphs. Fundamenta Informaticae **161**(4), 351–381 (2018)

20. Jensen, J.F., Larsen, K.G., Srba, J., Oestergaard, L.K.: Local model checking of weighted CTL with upper-bound constraints. In: Bartocci, E., Ramakrishnan, C.R. (eds.) SPIN 2013. LNCS, vol. 7976, pp. 178–195. Springer, Heidelberg (2013). https://doi.org/10.1007/978-3-642-39176-7_12

21. Jensen, J.F., Nielsen, T., Oestergaard, L.K., Srba, J.: TAPAAL and reachability analysis of P/T nets. In: Koutny, M., Desel, J., Kleijn, J. (eds.) Transactions on Petri Nets and Other Models of Concurrency XI. LNCS, vol. 9930, pp. 307–318. Springer, Heidelberg (2016). https://doi.org/10.1007/978-3-662-53401-4_16

22. Kordon, F., et al.: Complete Results for the 2016 Edition of the Model Checking Contest, June 2016. http://mcc.lip6.fr/2016/results.php

23. Joubert, C., Mateescu, R.: Distributed local resolution of Boolean equation systems. In: 13th Euromicro Workshop on Parallel, Distributed and Network-Based Processing (PDP 2005), 6–11 February 2005, Lugano, Switzerland, pp. 264–271. IEEE Computer Society (2005)

Tool Demos

nonreach – A Tool for Nonreachability Analysis

Florian Meßner and Christian Sternagel$^{(\boxtimes)}$

University of Innsbruck, Innsbruck, Austria
{florian.g.messner,
christian.sternagel}@uibk.ac.at

Abstract. We introduce nonreach, an automated tool for nonreachability analysis that is intended as a drop-in addition to existing termination and confluence tools for term rewriting. Our preliminary experimental data suggests that nonreach can improve the performance of existing termination tools.

Keywords: Term rewriting · Nonreachability analysis · Narrowing · Termination · Confluence · Infeasibility

1 Introduction

Nonreachability analysis is an important part of automated tools like $\mathsf{T_TT_2}$ [1] (for proving termination of rewrite systems) and ConCon [2] (for proving confluence of conditional rewrite systems). Many similar systems compete against each other in the annual termination (TermComp)[1] and confluence (CoCo)[2] competitions, both of which will run as part of TACAS's TOOLympics[3] in 2019.

Our intention for nonreach is to become a valuable component of all of the above mentioned tools by providing a fast and powerful back end for reachability analysis. This kind of analysis is illustrated by the following example.

Example 1. Suppose we have a simple program for multiplication represented by a term rewrite system (TRS, for short) consisting of the following rules:

$$\mathsf{add}(0, y) \to y \qquad\qquad \mathsf{add}(\mathsf{s}(x), y) \to \mathsf{s}(\mathsf{add}(x, y))$$
$$\mathsf{mul}(0, y) \to 0 \qquad\qquad \mathsf{mul}(\mathsf{s}(x), y) \to \mathsf{add}(\mathsf{mul}(x, y), y)$$

For checking termination we have to make sure that there is no infinite sequence of recursive calls. One specific subproblem for doing so is to check whether it is

This work is supported by the Austrian Science Fund (FWF): project P27502.

[1] http://termination-portal.org/wiki/Termination_Competition.

[2] http://project-coco.uibk.ac.at/.

[3] https://tacas.info/toolympics.php.

T. Vojnar and L. Zhang (Eds.): TACAS 2019, Part I, LNCS 11427, pp. 337–343, 2019.
https://doi.org/10.1007/978-3-030-17462-0_19

possible to reach $t = \mathsf{MUL}(\mathsf{s}(y), z)^4$ from $s = \mathsf{ADD}(\mathsf{mul}(w, x), x)$ for arbitrary instantiations of the variables w, x, y, and z. In other words, we have to check *nonreachability* of the target t from the source s.

In the remainder we will: comment on the role we intend for nonreach (Sect. 2), describe how nonreach is built and used (Sect. 3), give an overview of the techniques that went into nonreach (Sect. 4), and finally provide some experimental data (Sect. 5).

2   Role

When looking into implementations of current termination and confluence tools it soon becomes apparent that many tools use the same techniques for proving nonreachability. In light of this observation, one of our main goals for nonreach was to provide a dedicated stand-alone tool for nonreachability that can be reused for example in termination and confluence tools and can in principle replace many existing implementations.

In order to make such a reuse desirable for authors of other tools two things are important: (1) we have to provide a simple but efficient interface, and (2) we should support all existing techniques that can be implemented efficiently.[5]

At the time of writing, we already successfully use nonreach as back end in the termination tool T┬T₂ [1]. To this end, we incorporated support for external nonreachability tools into T┬T₂, with interaction purely via standard input and output. More specifically, while at the moment only YES/NO/MAYBE answers are required, the interface is general enough to support more detailed certificates corroborating such answers. The external tool is launched once per termination proof and supplied with those nonreachability problems that could not be handled by the existing techniques of T┬T₂. Our next goal is to achieve the same for the confluence tool ConCon [2].

Furthermore, a new *infeasibility* category will be part of CoCo 2019.[6] Infeasibility is a concept from conditional term rewriting but can be seen as a variant of nonreachability [3]. Thus, we plan to enter the competition with nonreach.

Another potential application of nonreach is dead code detection or showing that some error can never occur.

3   Installation and Usage

Our tool nonreach is available from a public *bitbucket*[7] repository which can be obtained using the following command:

---

[4] We differentiate between recursive calls and normal argument evaluation by capitalization of function symbols.

[5] Efficiency is especially important under the consideration that, for example, termination tools may sometimes have to check thousands of nonreachability problems within a single termination proof.

[6] http://project-coco.uibk.ac.at/2019/categories/infeasibility.php.

[7] https://bitbucket.org/fmessner/nonreach.

```
git clone git@bitbucket.org:fmessner/nonreach.git
```

To compile and run nonreach, you need an up to date installation of *Haskell's stack*.[8] The source code is compiled by invoking `stack build` in the project directory containing the `stack.yaml` file. In order to install the executable in the local `bin` path (`~/.local/bin/` on Linux), run `stack install` instead.

Usage. The execution of nonreach is controlled by several command line flags. The only mandatory part is a rewrite system (with respect to which nonreachability should be checked). This may be passed either as literal string (flag `-d "..."`) or as file (flag `-f filename`). Either way, the input follows the formats for (conditional) rewrite systems that are used for TermComp and CoCo.

In addition to a rewrite system we may provide the nonreachability problems to be worked on (if we do not provide any problems, nonreach will wait indefinitely). For a single nonreachability problem the simple format `s -> t` is used, where s and t are terms and we are interested in nonreachability of the target t from the source s. Again, there are several ways to pass problems to nonreach:

- We can provide white-space-separated lists of problems either literally on the command line (flag `-P "..."`) or through a file (flag `-p filename`).
- Alternatively, a single infeasibility problem can be provided as part of the input rewrite system as specified by the new infeasibility category of CoCo 2019.
- Otherwise, nonreach waits for individual problems on standard input.

For each given problem nonreach produces one line of output: In its default mode the output is `NO` whenever nonreachability can be established and either `MAYBE` or `TIMEOUT`, otherwise. When given an infeasibility problem, the output is `YES` if the problem is infeasible and either `MAYBE` or `TIMEOUT`, otherwise.

Further flags may be used to specify a timeout (in microseconds; flag `-t`) or to give finer control over the individual techniques that are implemented in nonreach (we will mention those in Sect. 4).

It is high time for an example. Let us check Example 1 using nonreach.

Example 2. Assuming that the TRS of Example 1 is in a file `mul.trs` we can have the following interaction (where we indicate user input by a preceding >):

```
nonreach -f mul.trs
> ADD(mul(w,x),x) -> MUL(s(y),z)
NO
```

4   Design and Techniques

In this section we give a short overview of the general design decisions and specific nonreachability techniques that went into nonreach.

---

[8] https://docs.haskellstack.org/en/stable/README.

Design. Efficiency was at the heart of our concern. On the one hand, from a user-interface perspective, this was the reason to provide the possibility that a single invocation of nonreach for a fixed TRS can work on arbitrarily many reachability problems. On the other hand, this lead us to mostly concentrate on techniques that are known to be fast in practice. The selection of techniques we present below (with the exception of narrowing) satisfies this criterion.

Techniques. Roughly speaking, nonreach uses two different kinds of techniques: (1) *transformations* that result in disjunctions or conjunctions of easier nonreachability problems, and (2) actual *nonreachability checks*. We use the notation $s \twoheadrightarrow t$ for a nonreachability problem with source s and target t.

Reachability checks. The first check we recapitulate is implemented by most termination tools and based on the idea of computing the topmost part of a term that does not change under rewriting (its *cap*) [4]. If the cap of the source s does not unify with the target t, then there are no substitutions σ and τ such that $s\sigma \to^* t\tau$. There are different algorithms to underapproximate such caps. We use etcap, developed by Thiemann together with the second author [5], due to its linear time complexity (by reducing unification to *ground context matching*) but nevertheless simple implementation. With etcap subterms are matched bottom-up with left-hand sides of rules. In case of a match, the corresponding subterm is potentially rewritable and thus replaced by a *hole*, written $\square$, representing a fresh variable. We illustrate etcap on the first two (addition) rules of Example 1.

Example 3. We have $\mathsf{etcap}(\mathsf{s}(0)) = \mathsf{s}(0)$ and $\mathsf{etcap}(\mathsf{s}(\mathsf{add}(\mathsf{s}(z),\mathsf{s}(0)))) = \mathsf{s}(\square)$, since the subterm headed by add matches the second addition rule. Using etcap, we obtain the following nonreachability check

$$\mathsf{reach}_{\mathsf{etcap}}(s \twoheadrightarrow t) = \begin{cases} \mathtt{MAYBE} & \text{if } \mathsf{etcap}(s) \sim t \\ \mathtt{NO} & \text{otherwise} \end{cases}$$

where $\sim$ denotes unifiability of terms.

The second reachability check implemented in nonreach [3,6] is based on the so called *symbol transition graph* (SG for short) of a TRS. Here, the basic idea is to build a graph that encodes the dependencies between root symbols induced by the rules of a TRS. This is illustrated by the following example:

Example 4. Given the TRS $\mathcal{R}$ consisting of the four rules

$$f(x, x) \to g(x) \qquad g(x) \to a \qquad h(a) \to b \qquad h(x) \to x$$

we generate the corresponding SG shown in Fig. 1(a) on page 5.

For each rule we generate an edge from the node representing the root symbol of the left-hand side to the node representing the root symbol of the right-hand side. Since in the last rule, the right-hand side is a variable (which can in principle

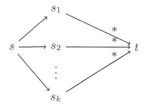

(a) SG of TRS R from Example 4.   (b) Decomposition by narrowing.

Fig. 1. A symbol transition graph and the idea of narrowing.

be turned into an arbitrary term by applying a substitution), we have to add edges from h to all nodes (including h itself).

From the graph it is apparent that $f(x, y)$ is not reachable from $g(z)$, no matter the substitutions for x, y and z, since there is no path from g to f.

We obtain the following SG based nonreachability check:

$$\mathrm{reach}_{\mathrm{stg}}(s \twoheadrightarrow t) = \begin{cases} \mathtt{MAYBE} & \text{if there is a path from } \mathrm{root}(s) \text{ to } \mathrm{root}(t) \text{ in the graph} \\ \mathtt{NO} & \text{otherwise} \end{cases}$$

Which reachability checks are applied by nonreach can be controlled by its -s flag, which expects a list of checks (in Haskell syntax). Currently the two checks TCAP and STG are supported.

Transformations. We call the first of our transformations *(problem) decomposition*. This technique relies on root-reachability checks to decompose a problem into a *conjunction* of strictly smaller subproblems. Thus, we are done if any of these subproblems is nonreachable.

Decomposition of a problem $s \twoheadrightarrow t$ only works if source and target are of the form $s = f(s_1, \ldots, s_n)$ and $t = f(t_1, \ldots, t_n)$, respectively. Now the question is whether t can be reached from s involving at least one root-rewrite step. If this is not possible, we know that for reachability from s to t, we need all t_i to be reachable from the corresponding s_i.

For the purpose of checking root-nonreachability, we adapt the two reachability checks from above:

$$\mathrm{rootreach}_{\mathrm{etcap}}(s, t) = \begin{cases} \mathtt{True} & \text{if there is a rule } \ell \to r \text{ such that } \mathrm{etcap}(s) \sim \ell \\ \mathtt{False} & \text{otherwise} \end{cases}$$

$$\mathrm{rootreach}_{\mathrm{stg}}(s, t) = \begin{cases} \mathtt{True} & \text{if there is a non-empty path from } \mathrm{root}(s) \\ & \text{to } \mathrm{root}(t) \text{ in the SG} \\ \mathtt{False} & \text{otherwise} \end{cases}$$

If at least one of these checks returns `False`, we can decompose the initial problem $s \twoheadrightarrow t$ into a conjunction of problems $s_1 \twoheadrightarrow t_1, \ldots, s_n \twoheadrightarrow t_n$.

The second transformation is based on *narrowing*. Without going into too much technical detail let us start from the following consideration. Given a reachability problem $s \rightarrow t$, assume that t is reachable from s. Then either the corresponding rewrite sequence is empty (in which case s and t are unifiable) or there is at least one initial rewrite step. Narrowing is the tool that allows us to capture all possible first steps (one for each rule $l \rightarrow r$ and each subterm of s that unifies with l), of the form $s \rightarrow s_i \rightarrow^* t$. This idea is captured in Fig. 1(b).

Now, decomposition (which is always applicable and thus has to be handled with care), transforms a given reachability problem $s \rightarrow t$ into a disjunction of new problems (that is, this time we have to show NO for all of these problems in order to conclude NO for the initial one) $s \overset{?}{\sim} t$ or $s_1 \rightarrow t$ or ... or $s_k \rightarrow t$, where the first one is a unifiability problem and the remaining ones are again reachability problems.

The maximal number of narrowing applications is specified by the -1 flag.

5   Experiments

In order to obtain test data for nonreach we started from the *Termination Problem Data Base* (TPDB, for short),[9] the data base of problems that are used also in TermComp. Then we used a patched version of the termination tool $\mathsf{T_TT_2}$ to obtain roughly 20,000 non-trivial reachability problems with respect to 730 TRSs. These are available from a public *bitbucket* repository[10] alongside a small script, that runs nonreach on all the problems and displays the overall results. All these problems could, at the time of creating the dataset, not be solved with the reachability checks used in the competition strategy of $\mathsf{T_TT_2}$. The current version[11] of nonreach in its default configuration can prove nonreachability of 369 problems of this set. While this does not seem much, we strongly suspect that the majority of problems in our set are actually reachable.

References

1. Korp, M., Sternagel, C., Zankl, H., Middeldorp, A.: Tyrolean termination tool 2. In: Treinen, R. (ed.) RTA 2009. LNCS, vol. 5595, pp. 295–304. Springer, Heidelberg (2009). https://doi.org/10.1007/978-3-642-02348-4_21
2. Sternagel, T., Middeldorp, A.: Conditional confluence (system description). In: Dowek, G. (ed.) RTA 2014. LNCS, vol. 8560, pp. 456–465. Springer, Cham (2014). https://doi.org/10.1007/978-3-319-08918-8_31
3. Sternagel, C., Yamada, A.: Reachability analysis for termination and confluence of rewriting. In: Vojnar, T., Zhang, L. (eds.) TACAS 2019. LNCS, vol. 11427, pp. 262–278 (2019)
4. Giesl, J., Thiemann, R., Schneider-Kamp, P.: Proving and disproving termination of higher-order functions. In: Gramlich, B. (ed.) FroCoS 2005. LNCS (LNAI), vol. 3717, pp. 216–231. Springer, Heidelberg (2005). https://doi.org/10.1007/11559306_12

---

[9] http://cl2-informatik.uibk.ac.at/mercurial.cgi/TPDB.
[10] https://bitbucket.org/fmessner/nonreach-testdata.
[11] https://bitbucket.org/fmessner/nonreach/src/77945a5/?at=master.

5. Thiemann, R., Sternagel, C.: Certification of termination proofs using CeTA. In: Berghofer, S., Nipkow, T., Urban, C., Wenzel, M. (eds.) TPHOLs 2009. LNCS, vol. 5674, pp. 452–468. Springer, Heidelberg (2009). https://doi.org/10.1007/978-3-642-03359-9_31
6. Yamada, A.: Reachability for termination. In: 4th AJSW (2016). http://cl-informatik.uibk.ac.at/users/ayamada/AJSW2016-slides.pdf

The Quantitative Verification Benchmark Set

Arnd Hartmanns[1]([✉])[ID], Michaela Klauck[2],
David Parker[3][ID], Tim Quatmann[4][ID],
and Enno Ruijters[1][ID]

[1] University of Twente, Enschede, The Netherlands
a.hartmanns@utwente.nl
[2] Saarland University, Saarbrücken, Germany
[3] University of Birmingham, Birmingham, UK
[4] RWTH Aachen, Aachen, Germany

Abstract. We present an extensive collection of quantitative models to
facilitate the development, comparison, and benchmarking of new verification algorithms and tools. All models have a formal semantics in terms
of extensions of Markov chains, are provided in the JANI format, and
are documented by a comprehensive set of metadata. The collection is
highly diverse: it includes established probabilistic verification and planning benchmarks, industrial case studies, models of biological systems,
dynamic fault trees, and Petri net examples, all originally specified in
a variety of modelling languages. It archives detailed tool performance
data for each model, enabling immediate comparisons between tools and
among tool versions over time. The collection is easy to access via a
client-side web application at qcomp.org with powerful search and visualisation features. It can be extended via a Git-based submission process,
and is openly accessible according to the terms of the CC-BY license.

1 Introduction

Quantitative verification is the analysis of formal models and requirements that
capture probabilistic behaviour, hard and soft real-time aspects, or complex continuous dynamics. Its applications include probabilistic programs, safety-critical
and fault-tolerant systems, biological processes, queueing systems, and planning in uncertain environments. Quantitative verification tools can, for example,
compute the worst-case probability of failure within a time bound, the minimal
expected cost to achieve a goal, or a Pareto-optimal control strategy balancing
energy consumption versus the probability of unsafe behaviour. Two prominent
such tools are PRISM [15] for probabilistic and UPPAAL [17] for real-time systems.

Over the past decade, various improvements and extensions have been made
to quantitative model checking algorithms, with different approaches implemented in an increasing number of tools, e.g. [7,8,11,13,18]. Researchers, tool

Authors are listed alphabetically. This work was supported by DFG grant 389792660
(part of CRC 248), ERC Advanced Grants 695614 (POWVER) and 781914 (FRAPPANT),
NWO and BetterBe grant 628.010.006, and NWO VENI grant 639.021.754.

T. Vojnar and L. Zhang (Eds.): TACAS 2019, Part I, LNCS 11427, pp. 344–350, 2019.
https://doi.org/10.1007/978-3-030-17462-0_20

developers, non-academic users, and reviewers can all greatly benefit from a common set of realistic and challenging examples that new algorithms and tools are consistently benchmarked and compared on and that may indicate the practicality of a new method or tool. Such sets, and the associated push to standardised semantics, formats, and interfaces, have proven their usefulness in other areas such as software verification [4] and SMT solving [3].

In quantitative verification, the PRISM Benchmark Suite (PBS) [16] has served this role for the past seven years. It provides 24 distinct examples in the PRISM language covering discrete- and continuous time Markov chains (DTMC and CTMC), discrete-time Markov decision processes (MDP), and probabilistic timed automata (PTA). To date, it has been used in over 60 scientific papers. Yet several developments over the past seven years are not adequately reflected or supported by the PBS. New tools (1) support other modelling languages and semantics (in particular, several tools have converged on the JANI model exchange format [6]), and (2) exploit higher-level formalisms like Petri nets or fault trees. In addition, (3) today's quantitative verification tools employ a wide range of techniques, whereas the majority of models in the PBS work best with PRISM's original BDD-based approach. Furthermore, (4) probabilistic verification and planning have been connected (e.g. [14]), and (5) MDP have gained in prominence through recent breakthroughs in AI and learning.

We present the Quantitative Verification Benchmark Set (QVBS): a new and growing collection of currently 72 models (Sect. 2) in the JANI format, documented by comprehensive metadata. It includes all models from the PBS plus a variety of new examples originally specified in significantly different modelling languages. It also covers decision processes in continuous stochastic time via Markov automata (MA [9]). The QVBS aggregates performance results obtained by different tools on its models (Sect. 3). All data is accessible via a client-side web application with powerful search and visualisation capabilities (Sect. 4).

2   A Collection of Quantitative Models

The Quantitative Verification Benchmark Set is characterised by commonality and diversity. All models are available in the JANI model exchange format [6], and they all have a well-defined formal semantics in terms of five related automata-based probabilistic models based on Markov chains. At the same time, the models of the QVBS originate from a number of different application domains, were specified in six modelling languages (with the original models plus information on the JANI conversion process being preserved in the QVBS), and pose different challenges including state space explosion, numeric difficulties, and rare events.

Syntax and semantics. The QVBS accepts any interesting model with a JANI translation to the DTMC, CTMC, MDP, MA, and PTA model types. Its current models were originally specified in Galileo for fault trees [20], GREATSPN [2] for Petri nets, the MODEST language [5], PGCL for probabilistic programs [10], PPDDL for planning domains [21], and the PRISM language [15]. By also storing

Table 1. Sources and domains of models

	all	source			application domain					
		PBS	IPPC	TA	com	rda	dpe	pso	bio	sec
all	72	24	10	7	12	9	17	16	6	5
DTMC	9	7			2	3	1			2
CTMC	13	7					4	1	6	
MDP	25	5	10		5	5		13		
MA	18			7		1	12	2		1
PTA	7	5			5					2

Table 2. Properties and valuations

	all	properties					all	parameter valuations			
		P	Pb	E	Eb	S		10^4	10^6	10^7	$>10^7$
all	229	90	57	52	12	18	589	135	127	94	28
DTMC	20	10	1	9			91	40	23	14	14
CTMC	49	6	22	4	11	6	161	43	52	28	5
MDP	61	40	3	17	1		82	31	24	21	6
MA	61	14	18	17		12	218	7	28	26	3
PTA	38	20	13	5			37	14		5	

the original model, structural information (such as in Petri nets or fault trees) that is lost by a conversion to an automata-based model is preserved for tools that can exploit it. We plan to broaden the scope to e.g. stochastic timed automata [5] or stochastic hybrid systems [1] in coordination with interested tool authors.

Sources and application domains. 41 of the QVBS's current 72 models stem from existing smaller and more specialised collections: 24 from the PRISM Benchmark Suite (PBS) [16], 10 from the probabilistic/uncertainty tracks of the 2006 and 2008 International Planning Competitions (IPPC) [21], and 7 repairable dynamic fault trees from the Twente Arberretum (TA) [19]. 65 of the models can be categorised as representing systems from six broad application domains: models of communication protocols (com), of more abstract randomised and distributed algorithms (rda), for dependability and performance evaluation (dpe), of planning, scheduling and operations management scenarios (pso), of biological processes (bio), and of mechanisms for security and privacy (sec). We summarise the sources and application domains of the QVBS models in Table 1.

Metadata. Alongside each model, in original and JANI format, we store a comprehensive set of structured JSON metadata to facilitate browsing and data mining the benchmark set. This includes basic information such as a description of the model, its version history, and references to the original source and relevant literature. Almost all models are parameterised such that the difficulty of analysing the model can be varied: some parameters influence the size of the state spaces, others may be time bounds used in properties, etc. The metadata documents all parameters and the ranges of admissible values. It includes sets of "proposed" parameter valuations with corresponding state space sizes and reference results. Each model contains a set of properties to be analysed; they are categorised into probabilistic unbounded and bounded reachability (P and Pb), unbounded and bounded expected rewards (E and Eb), and steady-state queries (S). Table 2 summarises the number of properties of each type (left), and the number of suggested parameter valuations (right) per resulting state space size (if available), where e.g. column "10^6" lists the numbers of valuations yielding 10^4 to 10^6 states.

3   An Archive of Results

The Quantitative Verification Benchmark Set collects not only models, but also *results*: the values of the properties that have been checked and performance data on runtime and memory usage. For every model, we archive results obtained with different tools/tool versions and settings on different hardware in a structured JSON format. The aim is to collect a "big dataset" of performance information that can be mined for patterns over tools, models, and time. It also gives developers of new tools and algorithms a quick indication of the relative performance of their implementation, saving the often cumbersome process of installing and running many third-party tools locally. Developers of existing tools may profit from an archive of the performance of their own tool, helping to highlight performance improvements—or pinpoint regressions—over time. The QVBS includes a graphical interface to aggregate and visualise this data (see Sect. 4 below).

4   Accessing the Benchmark Set

The models and results data of the Quantitative Verification Benchmark Set are managed in a Git repository at github.com/ahartmanns/qcomp. A user-friendly interface is provided at qcomp.org/benchmarks via a web application that dynamically loads the JSON data and presents it in two views:

The model browser presents a list of all models with key metadata. The list can be refined by a full-text search over the models' names, descriptions and notes, and by filters for model type, original modelling language, property types, and state space size. For example, a user could request the list of all MODEST MDP models with an expected-reward property and at least ten million states. Every model can be opened in a detail view that links to the JANI and original files, shows all metadata including parameters, proposed valuations,

Fig. 1. The model browser and detail view

and properties with reference results, and provides access to all archived results. Figure 1 shows the model browser filtered to GREATSPN models that include a bounded probabilistic reachability property. The flexible-manufacturing model is open in detail view.

The results browser is accessed by selecting one or more models in the model browser and opening the "compare results" link. It provides a flexible, summarising view of the performance data collected from all archived results for the selected models. The data can be filtered to include select properties or parameter valuations only. It is visualised as a table or different types of charts, including bar charts and scatter plots. Figure 2 shows the result browser for the beb and breakdown-queues models, comparing the performance of MCSTA [13] with default

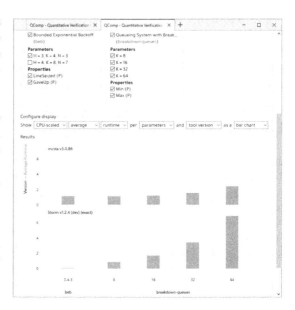

Fig. 2. The results browser showing a bar chart

settings to STORM [8] in its slower "exact" mode. The performance data can optionally be normalised by the benchmark scores of the CPU used to somewhat improve comparability, although this still disregards many other important factors (like memory bandwidth and storage latency), of course.

The web application is entirely client-side: all data is loaded into the user's browser as needed. All aggregation, filtering, and visualisation is implemented in Javascript. The application thus has no requirements on the server side. It is part of the Git repository and can be downloaded and opened offline by anyone.

5   Conclusion

Building upon the successful foundation of the PRISM Benchmark Suite, the new Quantitative Verification Benchmark Set not only expands the number and diversity of easily accessible benchmarks, but also professionalises the collection and provision of benchmark data through its JSON-based formats for metadata and results. We expect its associated web application to become a valuable tool for researchers, tool authors, and users alike. The QVBS is also an *open* dataset: all content is available under the CC-BY license, and new content—new models, updates, and results—can be contributed via a well-defined Git-based process. The Quantitative Verification Benchmark Set is the sole source of models for QCOMP 2019 [12], the first friendly competition of quantitative verification tools.

Acknowledgments. The authors thank Paul Gainer (University of Liverpool), Sebastian Junges (RWTH Aachen), Joachim Klein (Technische Universität Dresden), Matthias Volk (RWTH Aachen), and Zhen Zhang (Utah State University) for submitting models to the QVBS, Gethin Norman (University of Glasgow) for his contributions to the PRISM Benchmark Suite, and Marcel Steinmetz (Saarland University) for translating the IPPC benchmarks.

References

1. Abate, A., Blom, H., Cauchi, N., Haesaert, S., Hartmanns, A., Lesser, K., Oishi, M., Sivaramakrishnan, V., Soudjani, S., Vasile, C.I., Vinod, A.P.: ARCH-COMP18 category report: stochastic modelling. In: ARCH Workshop at ADHS. EPiC Series in Computing, vol. 54, pp. 71–103. EasyChair (2018)

2. Amparore, E.G., Balbo, G., Beccuti, M., Donatelli, S., Franceschinis, G.: 30 years of GreatSPN. In: Fiondella, L., Puliafito, A. (eds.) Principles of Performance and Reliability Modeling and Evaluation. SSRE, pp. 227–254. Springer, Cham (2016). https://doi.org/10.1007/978-3-319-30599-8_9

3. Barrett, C., Fontaine, P., Tinelli, C.: SMT-LIB benchmarks. http://smtlib.cs.uiowa.edu/benchmarks.shtml

4. Beyer, D.: Software verification with validation of results. In: Legay, A., Margaria, T. (eds.) TACAS 2017. LNCS, vol. 10206, pp. 331–349. Springer, Heidelberg (2017). https://doi.org/10.1007/978-3-662-54580-5_20

5. Bohnenkamp, H.C., D'Argenio, P.R., Hermanns, H., Katoen, J.P.: MoDeST: a compositional modeling formalism for hard and softly timed systems. IEEE Trans. Software Eng. **32**(10), 812–830 (2006)

6. Budde, C.E., Dehnert, C., Hahn, E.M., Hartmanns, A., Junges, S., Turrini, A.: JANI: quantitative model and tool interaction. In: Legay, A., Margaria, T. (eds.) TACAS 2017. LNCS, vol. 10206, pp. 151–168. Springer, Heidelberg (2017). https://doi.org/10.1007/978-3-662-54580-5_9

7. David, A., Jensen, P.G., Larsen, K.G., Mikučionis, M., Taankvist, J.H.: UPPAAL STRATEGO. In: Baier, C., Tinelli, C. (eds.) TACAS 2015. LNCS, vol. 9035, pp. 206–211. Springer, Heidelberg (2015). https://doi.org/10.1007/978-3-662-46681-0_16

8. Dehnert, C., Junges, S., Katoen, J.-P., Volk, M.: A STORM is coming: a modern probabilistic model checker. In: Majumdar, R., Kunčak, V. (eds.) CAV 2017. LNCS, vol. 10427, pp. 592–600. Springer, Cham (2017). https://doi.org/10.1007/978-3-319-63390-9_31

9. Eisentraut, C., Hermanns, H., Zhang, L.: On probabilistic automata in continuous time. In: LICS, pp. 342–351. IEEE Computer Society (2010)

10. Gordon, A.D., Henzinger, T.A., Nori, A.V., Rajamani, S.K.: Probabilistic programming. In: FOSE, pp. 167–181. ACM (2014)

11. Hahn, E.M., Li, Y., Schewe, S., Turrini, A., Zhang, L.: iscasMc: a web-based probabilistic model checker. In: Jones, C., Pihlajasaari, P., Sun, J. (eds.) FM 2014. LNCS, vol. 8442, pp. 312–317. Springer, Cham (2014). https://doi.org/10.1007/978-3-319-06410-9_22

12. Hartmanns, A., Hensel, C., Klauck, M., Klein, J., Kretínský, J., Parker, D., Quatmann, T., Ruijters, E., Steinmetz, M.: The 2019 comparison of tools for the analysis of quantitative formal models. In: Beyer, D., Huisman, M., Kordon, F., Steffen, B. (eds.) TACAS 2019. LNCS, vol. 11429, pp. 69–92. Springer, Cham (2019)

13. Hartmanns, A., Hermanns, H.: The Modest Toolset: an integrated environment for quantitative modelling and verification. In: Ábrahám, E., Havelund, K. (eds.) TACAS 2014. LNCS, vol. 8413, pp. 593–598. Springer, Heidelberg (2014). https://doi.org/10.1007/978-3-642-54862-8_51

14. Klauck, M., Steinmetz, M., Hoffmann, J., Hermanns, H.: Compiling probabilistic model checking into probabilistic planning. In: ICAPS. AAAI Press (2018)

15. Kwiatkowska, M., Norman, G., Parker, D.: PRISM 4.0: verification of probabilistic real-time systems. In: Gopalakrishnan, G., Qadeer, S. (eds.) CAV 2011. LNCS, vol. 6806, pp. 585–591. Springer, Heidelberg (2011). https://doi.org/10.1007/978-3-642-22110-1_47

16. Kwiatkowska, M.Z., Norman, G., Parker, D.: The PRISM benchmark suite. In: QEST, pp. 203–204. IEEE Computer Society (2012)

17. Larsen, K.G., Lorber, F., Nielsen, B.: 20 years of UPPAAL enabled industrial model-based validation and beyond. In: Margaria, T., Steffen, B. (eds.) ISoLA 2018. LNCS, vol. 11247, pp. 212–229. Springer, Cham (2018). https://doi.org/10.1007/978-3-030-03427-6_18

18. Legay, A., Sedwards, S., Traonouez, L.-M.: Plasma Lab: a modular statistical model checking platform. In: Margaria, T., Steffen, B. (eds.) ISoLA 2016. LNCS, vol. 9952, pp. 77–93. Springer, Cham (2016). https://doi.org/10.1007/978-3-319-47166-2_6

19. Ruijters, E., et al.: The Twente Arberretum. https://dftbenchmarks.utwente.nl/

20. Sullivan, K.J., Dugan, J.B., Coppit, D.: The Galileo fault tree analysis tool. In: FTCS-29, pp. 232–235. IEEE Computer Society (1999)

21. Younes, H.L.S., Littman, M.L., Weissman, D., Asmuth, J.: The first probabilistic track of the International Planning Competition. J. Artif. Intell. Res. **24**, 851–887 (2005)

ILAng: A Modeling and Verification Platform for SoCs Using Instruction-Level Abstractions

Bo-Yuan Huang[(✉)], Hongce Zhang,
Aarti Gupta, and Sharad Malik

Princeton University, Princeton, USA
{byhuang,hongcez,aartig,sharad}@princeton.edu

Abstract. We present ILAng, a platform for modeling and verification of systems-on-chip (SoCs) using Instruction-Level Abstractions (ILA). The ILA formal model targeting the hardware-software interface enables a clean separation of concerns between software and hardware through a unified model for heterogeneous processors and accelerators. Top-down it provides a specification for functional verification of hardware, and bottom-up it provides an abstraction for software/hardware co-verification. ILAng provides a programming interface for (i) constructing ILA models (ii) synthesizing ILA models from templates using program synthesis techniques (iii) verifying properties on ILA models (iv) behavioral equivalence checking between different ILA models, and between an ILA specification and an implementation. It also provides for translating models and properties into various languages (e.g., Verilog and SMT LIB2) for different verification settings and use of third-party verification tools. This paper demonstrates selected capabilities of the platform through case studies. Data or code related to this paper is available at: [9].

1 Introduction

Modern computing platforms are increasingly heterogeneous, having both programmable processors and application-specific accelerators. These accelerator-rich platforms pose two distinct verification challenges. The first challenge is constructing meaningful specifications for accelerators that can be used to verify the implementation. Higher-level executable models used in early design stages are not suitable for this task. The second challenge is to reason about hardware-software interactions from the viewpoint of software. The traditional approach in system-level/hardware modeling using detailed models, e.g., Register-Transfer Level (RTL) descriptions, is not amenable to scalable formal analysis.

This work was supported by the Applications Driving Architectures (ADA) Research Center, a JUMP Center co-sponsored by SRC and DARPA. This research is also funded in part by NSF award number 1628926, XPS: FULL: Hardware Software Abstractions: Addressing Specification and Verification Gaps in Accelerator-Oriented Parallelism, and the DARPA POSH Program Project: Upscale: Scaling up formal tools for POSH Open Source Hardware.

© The Author(s) 2019
T. Vojnar and L. Zhang (Eds.): TACAS 2019, Part I, LNCS 11427, pp. 351–357, 2019.
https://doi.org/10.1007/978-3-030-17462-0_21

The Instruction-Level Abstraction (ILA) has been proposed to address these challenges [4]. The ILA model is a uniform formal abstraction for processors and accelerators that captures their software-visible functionality as a set of instructions. It facilitates behavioral equivalence checking of an implementation against its ILA specification. This, in turn, supports accelerator upgrades using the notion of ILA compatibility similar to that of ISA compatibility for processors [4]. It also enables firmware/hardware co-verification [3]. Further, it enables reasoning about memory consistency models for system-wide properties [8].

In this paper, we present ILAng, a platform for Systems-on-chip (SoC) verification where ILAs are used as the formal model for processors and accelerators. ILAng provides for (i) ILA modeling and synthesis, (ii) ILA model verification, and (iii) behavioral equivalence checking between ILA models, and between an ILA specification and an implementation. The tool is open source and available online on https://github.com/Bo-Yuan-Huang/ILAng.

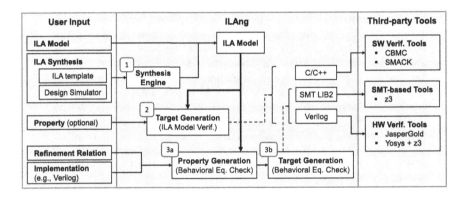

Fig. 1. ILAng work flow

2   The ILAng Platform

Figure 1 illustrates the modeling and verification capabilities of ILAng.

1. It allows constructing ILA formal models using a programming interface. It also allows semi-automated ILA synthesis using program synthesis techniques [5] and a template language [6].
2. It provides a set of utilities for ILA model verification, such as SMT-based transition unrolling and bounded model checking. Further, ILAng is capable of translating ILA formal models into various languages for verification, including Verilog, C, C++, and SMT LIB2, targeting other off-the-shelf verification tools and platforms.
3. It supports behavioral equivalence checking between ILA models and between an ILA specification and an implementation based on the standard commutative diagram approach [1].

2.1 Background

ILA. The ILA is a formal, uniform, modular, and hierarchical model for modeling both programmable processors and accelerators [4].

An ILA model is **modular** (state updates defined per instruction) and can be viewed as a generalization of the processor ISA in the heterogeneous context, where the commands on an accelerator's interface are defined as instructions. Generally, these appear as memory-mapped IO (MMIO) instructions in programs. The MMIO instruction lacks the actual semantics of what the instruction is doing in the accelerator; the ILA instruction captures exactly that.

It is an operational model that captures updates to *program-visible states* (i.e., states that are accessible or observable by programs). For processors, these include the architectural registers, flag bits, data, and program memory. An `ADD` instruction ($R1 = R2 + R3$), for example, of a processor defines the update to the $R1$ program-visible register. For accelerators, the program visible state includes memory-mapped registers, internal buffers, output ports to on-chip interconnect, etc. An ILA instruction for a crypto-accelerator could define the setting of an encryption key or even the encryption of an entire block using this key.

An ILA model is **hierarchical**, where an instruction at a high level can be expressed as a program of *child-instructions* (like micro-instructions). For example, the `START_ENCRYPT` instruction of a crypto-accelerator can be described as a program of reading data, encrypting it, and writing the result.

2.2 Constructing ILAs

ILAng provides a programming interface to define ILA models. For each component, the program-visible (aka architectural) states are specified. For each instruction, the state updates are specified independently as transition relations. Currently, ILAng supports state variables of type Boolean, bit-vector, and array. Uninterpreted functions are also supported for modeling complex operations.

Synthesis Capability. To alleviate the manual effort in constructing ILAs, ILAng provides a synthesis engine for synthesizing ILAs from a partial description called a template [6] using program synthesis techniques [5]. This is shown as Block 1 in Fig. 1. The synthesis algorithm requires two user inputs: an ILA template, and a design simulator/emulator. A template is a partially defined ILA model that specifies the program-visible states, the set of instructions, and also the *possible* operations for each instruction. The simulator can be a software/hardware prototype and is used as an oracle during ILA synthesis. The synthesis algorithm fills in the missing parts in the set of instructions.

2.3 Verification Using ILAs

The ILA formal model is a modular (per instruction) transition system, enabling the use of verification techniques such as model checking. We now discuss a selected list of verification capabilities provided by ILAng.

ILA Model Verification. As shown in Block 2 in Fig. 1, ILAng supports verification of user-provided safety properties on ILAs. It generates verification targets (including the design and property assertions) into different languages, as discussed in Sect. 2.4.

Behavioral Equivalence Checking. The modularity and hierarchy in the ILA models simplify behavioral equivalence checking through decomposition. Based on the standard commutative diagram approach [1], behavioral equivalence checking in ILAng supports two main settings: (i) ILA vs. ILA, and (ii) ILA vs. finite state machine (FSM) model (e.g., RTL implementation). As shown in Blocks 3a and 3b in Fig. 1, ILAng takes as input the two models (two ILA models, or an ILA model and an implementation model) and the user-provided refinement relation. The refinement relation specifies:

1. how to apply an instruction (e.g., instruction decode),
2. how to flush the state machine if required (e.g., stalling), and
3. how to identify if an instruction has completed (e.g., commit point).

The refinement map is then used with the two models to generate the property assertions using the standard commutative diagram approach [1]. The verification targets (the design and property assertions) are then generated in Verilog or SMT LIB2 for further reasoning, as described in Sect. 2.4.

SMT-Based Verification Utilities

Unrolling. Given an ILA, ILAng provides utilities to unroll the transition relation up to a finite bound, with options for different encodings and simplifications. Users can unroll a sequence of given instructions with a fixed instruction ordering. They can also unroll all possible instructions as a monolithic state machine.

Bounded Model Checking (BMC). With the unrolling utility, ILAng supports BMC of safety properties using an SMT solver. Users can specify initial conditions, invariants, and the properties. They can use a fixed bound for BMC or use on-the-fly BMC that iteratively increases the bound.

2.4   Generating Verification Targets

To utilize off-the-shelf verification tools, ILAng can export ILA models into different languages, including Verilog, C, C++, and SMT-LIB2.

Verilog. Many hardware implementations use RTL descriptions in Verilog. To support ILA vs. FSM equivalence checking, ILAng supports exporting ILA to Verilog. This also allows the use of third-party verification tools, since most such tools support Verilog. The memory module in the exported ILA can be configured as internal registers or external memory modules for different requirements.

C/C++. Given an ILA model, ILAng can generate a hardware simulator (in C or C++) for use in system/software development. This simulator can be verified against an implementation to check that it is a reliable executable model.

SMT LIB2. The ILAng platform is integrated with the SMT solver z3 [2]. It can generate SMT formulas for the transition relation and other verification conditions using the utilities described in Sect. 2.3.

3   Tutorial Case Studies

We demonstrate the applicability of ILAng through two case studies discussed in this section.[1] Table 1 provides information for each case study, including implementation size, ILA (template) size, synthesis time, and verification time (Ubuntu 18.04 VM on Intel i5-8300H with 2 GB memory). Note that these case studies are for demonstration, ILAng is capable of handling designs with significant complexity, as discussed and referenced in Sect. 4.

Table 1. Experimental Results

Design Statistics			ILA		Verif.
Reference	Ref. Size	# of Insts. (parent/child)	ILA Size	Synth. Time (s)	Time (s)
AES_V RTL Impl. (Verilog)	1756	8/5	324[†]	110	63
AES_C Software Model (C)	328	8/7	292[†]	63	
$Pipe_I$ RTL Impl. (Verilog)	218	4/0	78	-	25

† ILA synthesis template. Note: sizes are LoC w.r.t the corresponding language.

3.1   Advanced Encryption Standard (AES)

In this case study, we showcase the synthesis engine (Sect. 2.2) and the verification utilities (Sect. 2.3) for ILA vs. ILA behavioral equivalence checking.

We synthesized two ILAs for the AES crypto-engine, AES_C and AES_V, based on C and Verilog implementations respectively. They have the same instruction set, but with differences in block-level and round-level algorithms. As shown in Table 1, the sizes of ILAs (synthesis templates) are *significantly smaller* than the final RTL implementation, making this an attractive entry point for verification.

The equivalence between AES_C and AES_V is checked modularly, i.e., per instruction. Table 1 shows the verification time for checking behavioral equivalence using the SMT solver z3.

3.2   A Simple Instruction Execution Pipeline

In this case study, we demonstrate the steps in manually defining an ILA (Sect. 2.2) and exporting it in Verilog (Sect. 2.4) for ILA vs. FSM behavioral equivalence checking using existing hardware verification tools.

---

[1] All tutorial case studies are available in the submitted artifact and on GitHub.

This pipeline case study is a simple version of the back-end of a pipelined processor. We manually define an ILA model Pipe$_I$ as the specification of the design. This specification can be verified against a detailed RTL implementation, using a given refinement relation. We exported the Verilog model (including Pipe$_I$ and property assertions) and utilized Yosys and z3 for hardware verification. The equivalence is checked modularly per instruction, and took 22 s in total for all four instructions, as shown in Table 1.

4   Other ILAng Applications

Firmware/Hardware Co-verification. The ILA models program-visible hardware behavior while abstracting out lower-level implementation details. This enables scalable firmware/hardware co-verification, as demonstrated in our previous work on security verification of firmware in industrial SoCs using ILAs [3].

Reasoning about Concurrency and Memory Consistency. The ILA model is an operational model that captures program-visible state updates. When integrated with axiomatic memory consistency models that specify orderings between memory operations, the transition relation defined in ILAs (Sect. 2.3) can be used to reason about concurrent interactions between heterogeneous components [8].

Data Race Checking of GPU Programs. Besides general-purpose processors and accelerators, an ILA model has been synthesized for the nVidia GPU PTX instruction set using the synthesis engine (Sect. 2.2) [7]. This model has then been used for data race checking for GPU programs using the BMC utility (Sect. 2.3).

References

1. Burch, J.R., Dill, D.L.: Automatic verification of pipelined microprocessor control. In: Dill, D.L. (ed.) CAV 1994. LNCS, vol. 818, pp. 68–80. Springer, Heidelberg (1994). https://doi.org/10.1007/3-540-58179-0_44
2. de Moura, L., Bjørner, N.: Z3: an efficient SMT solver. In: Ramakrishnan, C.R., Rehof, J. (eds.) TACAS 2008. LNCS, vol. 4963, pp. 337–340. Springer, Heidelberg (2008). https://doi.org/10.1007/978-3-540-78800-3_24
3. Huang, B.Y., Ray, S., Gupta, A., Fung, J.M., Malik, S.: Formal security verification of concurrent firmware in SoCs using instruction-level abstraction for hardware. In: DAC, pp. 1–6 (2018)
4. Huang, B.Y., Zhang, H., Subramanyan, P., Vizel, Y., Gupta, A., Malik, S.: Instruction-Level Abstraction (ILA): a uniform specification for System-on-Chip (SoC) verification. ACM TODAES **24**(1), 10 (2018)
5. Jha, S., Gulwani, S., Seshia, S.A., Tiwari, A.: Oracle-guided component-based program synthesis. In: ICSE, pp. 215–224 (2010)
6. Subramanyan, P., Huang, B.Y., Vizel, Y., Gupta, A., Malik, S.: Template-based parameterized synthesis of uniform instruction-level abstractions for SoC verification. IEEE TCAD **37**(8), 1692–1705 (2018)

7. Xing, Y., Huang, B.Y., Gupta, A., Malik, S.: A formal instruction-level GPU model for scalable verification. In: ICCAD, pp. 130–135 (2018)
8. Zhang, H., Trippel, C., Manerkar, Y.A., Gupta, A., Martonosi, M., Malik, S.: ILA-MCM: integrating memory consistency models with instruction-level abstractions for heterogeneous system-on-chip verification. In: FMCAD (2018)
9. Huang, B.-Y., Zhang, H., Gupta, A., Malik, S.: ILAng: A Modeling and Verification Platform for SoCs using Instruction-Level Abstractions (artifact). Figshare (2019). https://doi.org/10.6084/m9.figshare.7808960.v1

METAcsl: Specification and Verification of High-Level Properties

Virgile Robles[1]([⊠]) [ID], Nikolai Kosmatov[1] [ID], Virgile Prevosto[1] [ID],
Louis Rilling[2] [ID], and Pascale Le Gall[3] [ID]

[1] Institut LIST, CEA, Université Paris-Saclay,
Palaiseau, France
{virgile.robles,nikolai.kosmatov,
virgile.prevosto}@cea.fr
[2] DGA, Bruz, France
louis.rilling@irisa.fr
[3] Laboratoire de Mathématiques et Informatique pour la Complexité et les Systèmes
CentraleSupélec, Université Paris-Saclay, Gif-Sur-Yvette, France
pascale.legall@centralesupelec.fr

Abstract. Modular deductive verification is a powerful technique capable to show that each function in a program satisfies its contract. However, function contracts do not provide a global view of which high-level (e.g. security-related) properties of a whole software module are actually established, making it very difficult to assess them. To address this issue, this paper proposes a new specification mechanism, called meta-properties. A meta-property can be seen as an enhanced global invariant specified for a set of functions, and capable to express predicates on values of variables, as well as memory related conditions (such as separation) and read or write access constraints. We also propose an automatic transformation technique translating meta-properties into usual contracts and assertions, that can be proved by traditional deductive verification tools. This technique has been implemented as a Frama-C plugin called MetAcsl and successfully applied to specify and prove safety- and security-related meta-properties in two illustrative case studies.

1 Introduction

Modular deductive verification is a well-known technique for formally proving that a program respects some user-defined properties. It consists in providing for each function of the program a *contract*, which basically contains a *precondition* describing what the function expects from its callers, and a *postcondition* indicating what it guarantees when it successfully returns. Logical formulas, known as *verification conditions* or *proof obligations* (POs), can then be generated and given to automated theorem provers. If all POs are validated, the body of the function fulfills its contract. Many deductive verification frameworks exist for various programming and formal specification languages. We focus here on

© The Author(s) 2019
T. Vojnar and L. Zhang (Eds.): TACAS 2019, Part I, LNCS 11427, pp. 358–364, 2019.
https://doi.org/10.1007/978-3-030-17462-0_22

Frama-C [1] and its deductive verification plugin Wp, which allows proving a C program correct with respect to a formal specification expressed in ACSL [1].

However, encoding *high-level* properties spanning across the entire program in a set of Pre/Post-based contracts is not always immediate. In the end, such high-level properties get split among many different clauses in several contracts, without an explicit link between them. Therefore, even if each individual clause is formally proved, it might be very difficult for a verification engineer, a code reviewer or a certification authority to convince themselves that the provided contracts indeed ensure the expected high-level properties. Moreover, a software product frequently evolves during its lifetime, leading to numerous modifications in the code and specifications. Maintaining a high-level (e.g. security-related) property is extremely complex without a suitable mechanism to formally specify and automatically verify it after each update.

The purpose of the present work is to propose such a specification mechanism for high-level properties, which we call *meta-properties*, and to allow their automatic verification on C code in Frama-C thanks to a new plugin called MetAcsl.

Motivation. This work was motivated by several previous projects. During the verification of a hypervisor, we observed the need for a mechanism of specification and automatic verification of high-level properties, in particular, for global properties related to isolation and memory separation. Isolation properties are known as key properties in many verification projects, in particular, for hypervisors and micro-kernels.

A similar need for specific high-level properties recently arose from a case study on a confidentiality-oriented page management system submitted by an industrial partner. In this example, each page and each user (process) are given a confidentiality level, and we wish to specify and verify that in particular:

- (P_{read}) a user cannot read data from a page with a confidentiality level higher than its own;
- (P_{write}) a user cannot write data to a page with a confidentiality level lower than its own.

This case study will be used as a running example in this paper. As a second case study (also verified, but not detailed in this paper), we consider a simple smart house manager with several interesting properties such as: "a door can only be unlocked after a proper authentication or in case of alarm" or "whenever the alarm is ringing, all doors must be unlocked". Again, these examples involve properties that are hard to express with function contracts since they apply to the entire program rather than a specific function.[1]

Contributions. The contributions of this paper[2] include:

- a new form of high-level properties, which we call *meta-properties*, and an extension of the ACSL language able to express them (Sect. 2),

---

[1] These examples are publicly available at https://huit.re/metacas.
[2] A longer version is available at https://arxiv.org/abs/1811.10509.

- a set of code transformations to translate meta-properties into native ACSL annotations that can be proved via the usual methods (Sect. 3),
- a FRAMA-C plugin METACSL able to parse C code annotated with meta-properties and to perform the aforementioned code transformations (Sect. 4),
- a case study: a confidentiality-oriented page system, where important security guarantees were expressed using meta-properties and automatically verified thanks to the code transformation with METACSL (Sect. 4).

```
1  struct Page { //Page handler structure
2    char* data; //First address of the page
3    enum allocation status; //ALLOCATED or FREE (ensured by M_1, lines 10-12)
4    enum confidentiality level; /*Page level, CONFIDENTIAL or PUBLIC*/ }
5  enum confidentiality user_level; //Current user process level
6  struct Page metadata[PAGE_NB]; //All pages
7  struct Page* page_alloc(void); //Allocates a page
8  void page_read(struct Page*, char* buffer); //Reads a page
9  void page_encrypt(struct Page*); //Encrypts a page in place, makes it PUBLIC
10 /*@ meta M_1: ∀function f; \strong_invariant(f),
11     ∀ int page; 0 ≤ page < PAGE_NB ⇒
12     metadata[page].status == FREE ∨ metadata[page].status == ALLOCATED;
13   meta M_2: ∀function f; //Only page_encrypt can change levels of allocated
                          pages
14     ! \subset(f, {page_encrypt}) ⇒ \writing(f),
15     ∀ int page; 0 ≤ page < PAGE_NB ∧ metadata[page].status == ALLOCATED
16     ⇒ \separated(\written, &metadata[page].level);
17   meta M_3: ∀function f; \reading(f), //Ensures P_read
18     ∀ int page; 0 ≤ page < PAGE_NB ∧ metadata[page].status == ALLOCATED
19     ∧ user_level == PUBLIC ∧ metadata[page].level == CONFIDENTIAL
20     ⇒ \separated(\read, metadata[page].data + (0 .. PAGE_LENGTH - 1));
21 */ //Meta-property ensuring P_write is defined similarly to M_3
```

Fig. 1. Partial meta-specification of a confidentiality case study

2   Specification of Meta-properties

A meta-property is a property meant to express high-level requirements. As such, it is not attached to any particular function but instead to a set of functions. It is thus defined in the global scope and can only refer to global objects.

To define a meta-property, the user must provide (i) the set of functions it will be applied to, (ii) a property (expressed in ACSL) and (iii) the *context, i.e.* a characterization of the situations in which they want the property to hold in each of these functions (everywhere in the function, only at the beginning and the end, upon writing in a variable, etc.). Furthermore, depending on the context, the property can refer to some special variables which we call *meta-variables*. Figure 1 features a few examples of meta-properties further explained below.

Let $\mathcal{F}$ denote the set of functions defined in the current program, and $\mathcal{P}$ the set of native ACSL properties. Formally, we can define a meta-property as a triple (c, F, P), where c is a context (see Sect. 2.2), $F \subseteq \mathcal{F}$ and $P \in \mathcal{P}$. Intuitively, we can interpret this triple as "$\forall f \in F$, P holds for f in the context c". For the meta-property to be well-formed, P must be a property over a subset of $\mathcal{G} \cup \mathcal{M}(c)$, where $\mathcal{G}$ is the set of variables available in the global scope of the program and $\mathcal{M}(c)$ is the set of meta-variables provided by the context c.

The actual METACSL syntax for defining a meta-property (c, F, P) is `meta [specification of F] c, P;` An example is given by property M_1 (cf. lines 10–12 in Fig. 1), where $F = \mathcal{F}$, $c = $ `strong_invariant` and P is the predicate stating that the status of any page should be either `FREE` or `ALLOCATED`.

2.1   Target Functions and Quantification

Meta-properties are applied to a given *target set* of functions F defined as $F = F_+ \backslash F_-$ by providing explicit lists of considered and excluded functions $F_+, F_- \subseteq \mathcal{F}$. If not provided, F_+ and F_- are respectively equal to $\mathcal{F}$ and $\emptyset$ by default, *i.e.* the meta-property should hold for all functions of the program. F_- is useful when the user wants to target every function except a few, since they do not have to explicitly provide every resulting target function.

The METACSL syntax for the specification of F uses the built-in ACSL construction `\forall`, possibly followed by `\subset` with or without logic negation ! (to express $f \in F_+$ and $f \notin F_-$). It can be observed in property M_2 (lines 13–16), where $F_+ = \mathcal{F}$ and $F_- = \{$`page_encrypt`$\}$ excludes only one function.

2.2   Notion of Context

The *context* c of a meta-property defines the states in which property P must hold, and may introduce *meta-variables* that can be used in the definition of P.

Beginning/Ending Context (Weak Invariant). A *weak invariant* indicates that P must hold at the beginning and at the end of each target function $f \in F$.

Everywhere Context (Strong invariant). A *strong invariant* is similar to a weak invariant, except that it ensures that P holds at *every point*[3] of each target function. For example, property M_1 specifies that at every point of the program, the status of any page must be either `FREE` or `ALLOCATED`.

Writing Context. This ensures that P holds upon any modification of the memory (both stack and heap). It provides a meta-variable `\written` that refers to the variable (and, more generally, the memory location) being written to.

A simple usage of this context can be to forbid any direct modification of some global variable, as in property M_2. This property states that for any function that is not `page_encrypt`, the left-hand side of any assignment must be *separated* from (that is, disjoint with) the global variable `metadata[page].level` for any `page` with the `ALLOCATED` status. In other words, only the `page_encrypt` function is allowed to modify the confidentiality level of an allocated page.

An important benefit of this setting is a *non-transitive restriction of modifications* that cannot be specified using the ACSL clause `assigns`, since the latter is transitive over function calls and necessarily permits to modify a variable when

---

[3] More precisely, every *sequence point* as defined by the C standard.

at least one callee has the right to modify it. Here, since we only focus on *direct* modifications, a call to `page_encrypt` (setting to public the level of the page it has encrypted) from another function does not violate meta-property M_2.

Furthermore, modification can be forbidden *under some condition* (i.e. that the page is allocated), while `assigns` has no such mechanism readily available.

Reading Context. Similar to the writing context, this ensures that the property holds whenever some memory location is read, and provides a meta-variable `\read` referring to the read location. It is used in property M_3 (lines 17–20), which expresses the guarantee P_{read} of the case study (see Motivation in Sect. 1) by imposing a separation of a read location and the contents of allocated confidential pages when the user does not have sufficient access rights. As another example, an isolation of a page can be specified as separation of all reads and writes from it.

These few simple contexts, combined with the native features of ACSL, turn out to be powerful enough to express quite interesting properties, including memory isolation and all properties used in our two motivating case studies.

3   Verification of Meta-properties

Figure 2 shows an (incorrect) toy implementation of two functions of Fig. 1 that we will use to illustrate the verification of meta-properties M_1–M_3.

The key idea of the verification is the translation of meta-properties into native ACSL annotations, which are then verified using existing FRAMA-C analyzers. To that end, the property P of a meta-property (c, F, P) must be inserted as an assertion in relevant locations (as specified by context c) in each target function $f \in F$, and the meta-variables (if any) must be instantiated.

We define a specific translation for each context. For weak invariants, property P is simply added as both a precondition and a postcondition in the contract of f. This is also done for the strong invariant, for which P is additionally inserted after each instruction potentially modifying the values of the free variables in P[4] For example, Fig. 3a shows the translation of M_1 on `page_alloc`. Our property (defined on lines 11–12 in Fig. 1, denoted P_{M_1} here) is inserted after the modification of a `status` field

```
1  struct Page* page_alloc() {
2    //try to find a free page
3    struct Page* fp = find_free_page();
4    //if a free page is found,
5    //allocate it with current user
       level
6    if(fp ≠ NULL) {
7      fp->status = ALLOCATED;
8      fp->level = user_level;
9    }
10   return fp;
11 }
12 void page_read(struct Page* from,
       char* buffer) {
13   for(i ∈ ℕ = 0 ; i < PAGE_LENGTH ;
       ++i)
14     buffer[i] = from->data[i];
15 }
```

Fig. 2. Incorrect code w.r.t. M_2 and M_3

---

[4] The AST is normalized so that every memory modification happens through an assignment. Then we conservatively determine if the object being assigned is one of the free variables of P: in presence of pointers, we assume the worst case.

(line 6) since the property involves these objects, but not after the modification of a `level` field (line 8).

For *Writing* (resp. *Reading*) contexts, P is inserted before any instruction potentially making a write (resp. read) access to the memory, with the exception of function calls. In addition, each meta-variable is replaced by its actual value. For example, in the translation of M_2 on `page_alloc` (Fig. 3b), the property is inserted before the two modifications of `fp`, and `\written` is replaced respectively by `fp->status` and `fp->level`. In this case M_2 does not hold. While its first instantiation (lines 4–6) is easily proved, it is not the case for the second one (lines 8–10). Indeed, there exists a `page` (the one being modified) that has a status set to ALLOCATED because of the previous instruction (line 7) and for which the `\separated` clause is obviously false. Hence, the assertion fails, meaning that the whole meta-property M_2 cannot be proved. The fix consists in swapping lines 6 and 7 in Fig. 2. After that, all assertions generated from M_2 are proved.

A similar transformation for M_3 on `page_read` shows that the proof fails since the implementation allows an agent to read from any page without any check. Adding proper guards allows the meta-property to be proved. Conversely, if a meta-property is broken by an erroneous code update, a proof failure after *automatically* re-running METACSL helps to easily detect it.

```
1  /*@ requires P_M₁;
2      ensures P_M₁; */
3  struct Page* page_alloc() {
4      struct Page* fp =
            find_free_page();
5      if(fp ≠ NULL) {
6          fp->status = ALLOCATED;
7          /*@ assert P_M₁;*/
8          fp->level = user_level;
9          //Line 8 cannot break P_M₁
10     }
11 }
```

(a) Transformation for M_1

```
1  struct Page* page_alloc() {
2      struct Page* fp = find_free_page();
3      if(fp ≠ NULL) {
4          /*@ assert ∀ int page; 0 ≤ page < PAGE_NB
5          ⇒ metadata[page].status == ALLOCATED
6          ⇒ \separated(fp->status,
                          &metadata[page].level);*/
7          fp->status = PAGE_ALLOCATED;
8          /*@ assert ∀ int page; 0 ≤ page < PAGE_NB
9          ⇒ metadata[page].status == ALLOCATED
10         ⇒ \separated(fp->level,
                          &metadata[page].level);*/
11         fp->level = user_level;
12     }
13 }
```

(b) Transformation for M_2

Fig. 3. Examples of code transformations for functions of Fig. 2

4 Results on Case Studies and Conclusion

Experiments. The support of meta-properties and the proposed methodology for their verification were fully implemented in OCaml as a FRAMA-C plugin called METACSL. We realized a simple implementation of the two case studies mentioned in Sect. 1 and were able to fully specify and automatically verify all aforementioned properties (in particular P_{read} and P_{write}) using METACSL. The transformation step is performed in less than a second while the automatic proof takes generally less than a minute.

Conclusion. We proposed a new specification mechanism for high-level properties in FRAMA-C, as well as an automatic transformation-based technique to verify these properties by a usual deductive verification approach. The main idea of this technique is similar to some previous efforts e.g. [2]. Meta-properties provide a useful extension to function contracts offering the possibility to express a variety of high-level safety- and security-related properties. They also provide a verification engineer with an explicit global view of high-level properties being really proved, avoiding the risk to miss some part of an implicit property which is not formally linked to relevant parts of several function contracts, thus facilitating code review and certification. Another benefit of the new mechanism is the possibility to easily re-execute a proof after a code update. Initial experiments confirm the interest of the proposed solution.

Future Work. We plan to establish a formal soundness proof for our transformation technique, thereby allowing METACSL to be reliably used for critical code verification. Other future work directions include further experiments to evaluate the proposed approach on real-life software and for more complex properties.

Acknowledgment. This work was partially supported by the project VESSEDIA, which has received funding from the EU Horizon 2020 research and innovation programme under grant agreement No 731453. The work of the first author was partially funded by a Ph.D. grant of the French Ministry of Defense. Many thanks to the anonymous referees for their helpful comments.

References

1. Kirchner, F., Kosmatov, N., Prevosto, V., Signoles, J., Yakobowski, B.: Frama-C: a software analysis perspective. FAOC **27**, 573–609 (2015)
2. Pavlova, M., Barthe, G., Burdy, L., Huisman, M., Lanet, J.L.: Enforcing high-level security properties for applets. In: Quisquater, J.J., Paradinas, P., Deswarte, Y., El Kalam, A.A. (eds.) Smart Card Research and Advanced Applications VI. IFIP International Federation for Information Processing, vol. 153. Springer, Boston (2004). https://doi.org/10.1007/1-4020-8147-2_1

ROLL 1.0: ω-Regular Language Learning Library

Yong Li[1,2] , Xuechao Sun[1,2],
Andrea Turrini[1,3(✉)],
Yu-Fang Chen[4], and Junnan Xu[1,2]

[1] State Key Laboratory of Computer Science,
Institute of Software, Chinese Academy of Sciences, Beijing, China
turrini@ios.ac.cn
[2] University of Chinese Academy of Sciences, Beijing, China
[3] Institute of Intelligent Software, Guangzhou, China
[4] Institute of Information Science, Academia Sinica, Taipei, Taiwan

Abstract. We present ROLL 1.0, an ω-regular language learning library with command line tools to learn and complement Büchi automata. This open source Java library implements all existing learning algorithms for the complete class of ω-regular languages. It also provides a learning-based Büchi automata complementation procedure that can be used as a baseline for automata complementation research. The tool supports both the Hanoi Omega Automata format and the BA format used by the tool RABIT. Moreover, it features an interactive Jupyter notebook environment that can be used for educational purpose.

1 Introduction

In her seminal work [3], Angluin introduced the well-known algorithm L^* to learn regular languages by means of deterministic finite automata (DFAs). In the learning setting presented in [3], there is a *teacher*, who knows the target language L, and a *learner*, whose task is to learn the target language, represented by an automaton. The learner interacts with the teacher by means of two kinds of queries: *membership queries* and *equivalence queries*. A membership query $\mathrm{MQ}(w)$ asks whether a string w belongs to L while an equivalence query $\mathrm{EQ}(A)$ asks whether the conjectured DFA A recognizes L. The teacher replies with a witness if the conjecture is incorrect otherwise the learner completes its job. This learning setting now is widely known as *active automata learning*. In recent years, active automata learning algorithms have attracted increasing attention in the computer aided verification community: it has been applied in *black-box model checking* [24], *compositional verification* [12], *program verification* [10], *error localization* [8], and *model learning* [26].

Due to the increasing importance of automata learning algorithms, many efforts have been put into the development of automata learning libraries such as libalf [6] and LearnLib [18]. However, their focus is only on automata accepting

T. Vojnar and L. Zhang (Eds.): TACAS 2019, Part I, LNCS 11427, pp. 365–371, 2019.
https://doi.org/10.1007/978-3-030-17462-0_23

finite words, which correspond to safety properties. The ω-regular languages are the standard formalism to describe liveness properties. The problem of learning the complete class of ω-regular languages was considered open until recently, when it has been solved by Farzan *et al.* [15] and improved by Angluin *et al.* [4].

However, the research on applying ω-regular language learning algorithms for verification problems is still in its infancy. Learning algorithms for ω-regular languages are admittedly much more complicated than their finite regular language counterparts. This becomes a barrier for the researchers doing further investigations and experiments on such topics. We present ROLL 1.0, an open-source library implementing all existing learning algorithms for the complete class of ω-regular languages known in literature, which we believe can be an enabling tool for this direction of research. To the best of our knowledge, ROLL 1.0 is the only publicly available tool focusing on ω-regular language learning.

ROLL, a preliminary version of ROLL 1.0, was developed in [22] to compare the performance of different learning algorithms for Büchi automata (BAs). The main improvements made in ROLL 1.0 compared to its previous version are as follows. ROLL 1.0 rewrites the algorithms in the core part of ROLL and obtains high modularity to allow for supporting the learning algorithms for more types of ω-automata than just BAs, algorithms to be developed in future. In addition to the BA format [1,2,11], ROLL 1.0 now also supports the Hanoi Omega Automata (HOA) format [5]. Besides the learning algorithms, ROLL 1.0 also contains complementation [23] and a new language inclusion algorithm. Both of them are built on top of the BAs learning algorithms. Experiments [23] have shown that the resulting automata produced by the learning-based complementation can be much smaller than those built by structure-based algorithms [7,9,19,21,25]. Therefore, the learning-based complementation is suitable to serve as a baseline for Büchi automata complementation researches. The language inclusion checking algorithm implemented in ROLL 1.0 is based on learning and a Monte Carlo word sampling algorithm [17]. ROLL 1.0 features an interactive mode which is used in the ROLL Jupyter notebook environment. This is particularly helpful for teaching and learning how ω-regular language learning algorithms work.

2   **ROLL 1.0** Architecture and Usage

ROLL 1.0 is written entirely in Java and its architecture, shown in Fig. 1, comprises two main components: the **Learning Library**, which provides all known existing learning algorithms for Büchi automata, and the **Control Center**, which uses the learning library to complete the input tasks required by the user.

Learning Library. The learning library implements all known BA learning algorithms for the full class of ω-regular languages: the $L^\$$ learner [15], based on DFA learning [3], and the L^ω learner [22], based on three canonical *family of DFAs* (FDFAs) learning algorithms [4,22]. ROLL 1.0 supports both *observation tables* [3] and *classification trees* [20] to store membership query answers. All learning algorithms provided in ROLL 1.0 implement the `Learner` interface; their

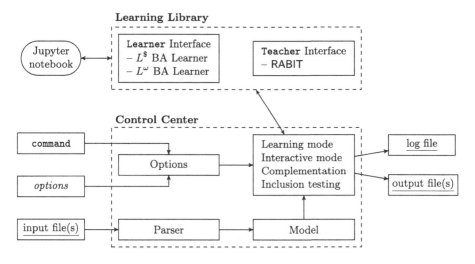

Fig. 1. Architecture of ROLL 1.0

corresponding teachers implement the `Teacher` interface. Any Java object that implements `Teacher` and can decide the equivalence of two Büchi automata is a valid teacher for the BA learning algorithms. Similarly, any Java object implementing `Learner` can be used as a learner, making ROLL 1.0 easy to extend with new learning algorithms and functionalities. The BA teacher implemented in ROLL 1.0 uses RABIT [1,2,11] to answer the equivalence queries posed by the learners since the counterexamples RABIT provides tend to be short and hence are easier to analyze; membership queries are instead answered by implementing the ASCC algorithm from [16].

Control Center. The control center is responsible for calling the appropriate learning algorithm according to the user's command and options given at command line, which is used to set the `Options`. The file formats supported by ROLL 1.0 for the input automata are the RABIT BA format [1,2,11] and the standard Hanoi Omega Automata (HOA) format [5], identified by the file extensions .ba and .hoa, respectively. Besides managing the different execution modes, which are presented below, the control center allows for saving the learned automaton into a given file (option *-out*), for further processing, and to save execution details in a log file (option *-log*). The output automaton is generated in the same format of the input. The standard way to call ROLL 1.0 from command line is

`java -jar ROLL.jar command` input file(s) [*options*]

Learning mode (command `learn`) makes ROLL 1.0 learn a Büchi automaton equivalent to the given Büchi automaton; this can be used, for instance, to get a possibly smaller BA. The default option for storing answers to membership queries is *-table*, which selects the observation tables; classification trees can be chosen instead by means of the *-tree* option.

```
java -jar ROLL.jar learn aut.hoa
```

for instance runs ROLL 1.0 in learning mode against the input BA aut.hoa; it learns aut.hoa by means of the L^ω learner using observation tables. The three canonical FDFA learning algorithms given in [4] can be chosen by means of the options *-syntactic* (default), *-recurrent*, and *-periodic*. Options *-under* (default) and *-over* control which approximation is used in the L^ω learner [22] to transform an FDFA to a BA. By giving the option *-ldollar*, ROLL 1.0 switches to use the $L^\$$ learner instead of the default L^ω learner.

Interactive mode (command `play`) allows users to play as the teacher guiding ROLL 1.0 in learning the language they have in mind. To show how the learning procedure works, ROLL 1.0 outputs each intermediate result in the Graphviz dot layout format[1]; users can use Graphviz's tools to get a graphical view of the output BA so to decide whether it is the right conjecture.

Complementation (command `complement`) of the BA $\mathcal{B}$ in ROLL 1.0 is based on the algorithm from [23] which learns the complement automaton $\mathcal{B}^c$ from a teacher who knows the language $\Sigma^\omega \setminus \mathcal{L}(\mathcal{B})$. This allows ROLL 1.0 to disentangle $\mathcal{B}^c$ from the structure of $\mathcal{B}$, avoiding the $\Omega((0.76n)^n)$ blowup [27] of the structure-based complementation algorithms (see., e.g., [7,19,21,25]).

Inclusion testing (command `include`) between two BAs $\mathcal{A}$ and $\mathcal{B}$ is implemented in ROLL 1.0 as follows: (1) first, sample several ω-words $w \in \mathcal{L}(\mathcal{A})$ and check whether $w \notin \mathcal{L}(\mathcal{B})$ to prove $\mathcal{L}(\mathcal{A}) \not\subseteq \mathcal{L}(\mathcal{B})$; (2) then, try simulation techniques [11,13,14] to prove inclusion; (3) finally, use the learning based complementation algorithm to check inclusion. The ROLL 1.0's ω-word sampling algorithm is an extension of the one proposed in [17]. The latter only samples paths visiting any state at most twice while ROLL 1.0's variant allows for sampling paths visiting any state at most K times, where K is usually set to the number of states in $\mathcal{A}$. In this way, ROLL 1.0 can get a larger set of ω-words accepted by $\mathcal{A}$ than the set from the original algorithm.

Online availability of ROLL 1.0. ROLL 1.0 is an open-source library freely available online at https://iscasmc.ios.ac.cn/roll/, where more details are provided about its commands and options, its use as a Java library, and its GitHub repository[2]. Moreover, from the roll page, it is possible to access an online Jupyter notebook[3] allowing to interact with ROLL 1.0 without having to download and compile it. Each client gets a new instance of the notebook, provided by Jupyter-Hub[4], so to avoid unexpected interactions between different users. Figure 2 shows few screenshots of the notebook for learning in interactive mode the language $\Sigma^* \cdot b^\omega$ over the alphabet $\Sigma = \{a, b\}$. As we can see, the membership query

---

[1] https://www.graphviz.org/.
[2] https://github.com/ISCAS-PMC/roll-library.
[3] https://iscasmc.ios.ac.cn/roll/jupyter.
[4] https://jupyterhub.readthedocs.io/.

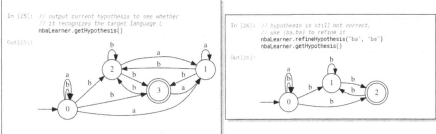

```
In [24]: import roll.jupyter.*;
         import java.util.function.BiFunction;
         import roll.words.*;

         // now we define a function mqOracle : (string, string) -> boolean  and this
         // function is used to determine whether a string is in the target language L
         mqOracle = {
             stem, loop ->
             if (loop.length() < 1) return false;      // this is a finite word
             for (int i = 0; i < loop.length(); i++) {
                 // check whether the periodic word is b'+
                 if (loop.charAt(i) != 'b') {
                     return false;
                 }
             }
             return true;
         };

         // now we create a table-based recurrent NBA learner to learn the language L
         nbaLearner = JupyterROLL.createNBALearner("recurrent", "table", mqOracle);
         // we can also see the table data structure of the learner
         nbaLearner
```

```
Out[24]:  Leading Learner:
             || (ε, ε) |
          =============
          ε || -      |
          =============
          a || -      |
          b || -      |

          Progress Learner for ε:
             || ε      |
          =============
          ε  || (+, -) |
          b  || (+, +) |
          =============
          a  || (+, -) |
          ba || (+, -) |
          bb || (+, +) |
```

Fig. 2. ROLL 1.0 running in the Jupyter notebook for interactively learning $\Sigma^* \cdot b^\omega$

$MQ(w)$ is answered by means of the `mqOracle` function: it gets as input two finite words, the `stem` and the `loop` of the ultimately periodic word w, and it checks whether `loop` contains only b. Then one can create a BA learner with the oracle `mqOracle`, say the BA learner `nbaLearner`, based on observation tables and the recurrent FDFAs, as shown in the top-left screenshot. One can check the internal table structures of `nbaLearner` by printing out the learner, as in the top-right screenshot. The answer to an equivalence query is split in two parts: first, the call to `getHypothesis()` shows the currently conjectured BA; then, the call to `refineHypothesis("ba", "ba")` simulates a negative answer with counterexample $ba \cdot (ba)^\omega$. After the refinement by `nbaLearner`, the new conjectured BA is already the right conjecture.

Acknowledgement. This work has been supported by the National Natural Science Foundation of China (Grants Nos. 61532019, 61761136011) and by the CAP project GZ1023.

References

1. Abdulla, P.A., et al.: Simulation subsumption in Ramsey-based Büchi automata universality and inclusion testing. In: Touili, T., Cook, B., Jackson, P. (eds.) CAV 2010. LNCS, vol. 6174, pp. 132–147. Springer, Heidelberg (2010). https://doi.org/10.1007/978-3-642-14295-6_14

2. Abdulla, P.A., et al.: Advanced Ramsey-based Büchi automata inclusion testing. In: Katoen, J.-P., König, B. (eds.) CONCUR 2011. LNCS, vol. 6901, pp. 187–202. Springer, Heidelberg (2011). https://doi.org/10.1007/978-3-642-23217-6_13

3. Angluin, D.: Learning regular sets from queries and counterexamples. Inf. Comput. **75**(2), 87–106 (1987)

4. Angluin, D., Fisman, D.: Learning regular omega languages. Theoret. Comput. Sci. **650**, 57–72 (2016)

5. Babiak, T., et al.: The Hanoi Omega-Automata format. In: Kroening, D., Păsăreanu, C.S. (eds.) CAV 2015. LNCS, vol. 9206, pp. 479–486. Springer, Cham (2015). https://doi.org/10.1007/978-3-319-21690-4_31

6. Bollig, B., Katoen, J.-P., Kern, C., Leucker, M., Neider, D., Piegdon, D.R.: libalf: the automata learning framework. In: Touili, T., Cook, B., Jackson, P. (eds.) CAV 2010. LNCS, vol. 6174, pp. 360–364. Springer, Heidelberg (2010). https://doi.org/10.1007/978-3-642-14295-6_32

7. Büchi, J.R.: On a decision method in restricted second order arithmetic. In: International Congress on Logic, Methodology and Philosophy of Science, pp. 1–11 (1962)

8. Chapman, M., Chockler, H., Kesseli, P., Kroening, D., Strichman, O., Tautschnig, M.: Learning the language of error. In: Finkbeiner, B., Pu, G., Zhang, L. (eds.) ATVA 2015. LNCS, vol. 9364, pp. 114–130. Springer, Cham (2015). https://doi.org/10.1007/978-3-319-24953-7_9

9. Chen, Y.-F., et al.: Advanced automata-based algorithms for program termination checking. In: PLDI, pp. 135–150 (2018)

10. Chen, Y.-F., et al.: PAC learning-based verification and model synthesis. In: ICSE, pp. 714–724 (2016)

11. Clemente, L., Mayr, R.: Advanced automata minimization. In: POPL, pp. 63–74 (2013)

12. Cobleigh, J.M., Giannakopoulou, D., Păsăreanu, C.S.: Learning assumptions for compositional verification. In: Garavel, H., Hatcliff, J. (eds.) TACAS 2003. LNCS, vol. 2619, pp. 331–346. Springer, Heidelberg (2003). https://doi.org/10.1007/3-540-36577-X_24

13. Dill, D.L., Hu, A.J., Wong-Toi, H.: Checking for language inclusion using simulation preorders. In: Larsen, K.G., Skou, A. (eds.) CAV 1991. LNCS, vol. 575, pp. 255–265. Springer, Heidelberg (1992). https://doi.org/10.1007/3-540-55179-4_25

14. Etessami, K., Wilke, T., Schuller, R.A.: Fair simulation relations, parity games, and state space reduction for Büchi automata. In: Orejas, F., Spirakis, P.G., van Leeuwen, J. (eds.) ICALP 2001. LNCS, vol. 2076, pp. 694–707. Springer, Heidelberg (2001). https://doi.org/10.1007/3-540-48224-5_57

15. Farzan, A., Chen, Y.-F., Clarke, E.M., Tsay, Y.-K., Wang, B.-Y.: Extending automated compositional verification to the full class of omega-regular languages. In: Ramakrishnan, C.R., Rehof, J. (eds.) TACAS 2008. LNCS, vol. 4963, pp. 2–17. Springer, Heidelberg (2008). https://doi.org/10.1007/978-3-540-78800-3_2

16. Gaiser, A., Schwoon, A.: Comparison of algorithms for checking emptiness of Büchi automata. In: MEMICS (2009)

17. Grosu, R., Smolka, S.A.: Monte carlo model checking. In: Halbwachs, N., Zuck, L.D. (eds.) TACAS 2005. LNCS, vol. 3440, pp. 271–286. Springer, Heidelberg (2005). https://doi.org/10.1007/978-3-540-31980-1_18
18. Isberner, M., Howar, F., Steffen, B.: The open-source LearnLib. In: Kroening, D., Păsăreanu, C.S. (eds.) CAV 2015. LNCS, vol. 9206, pp. 487–495. Springer, Cham (2015). https://doi.org/10.1007/978-3-319-21690-4_32
19. Kähler, D., Wilke, T.: Complementation, disambiguation, and determinization of Büchi automata unified. In: Aceto, L., Damgård, I., Goldberg, L.A., Halldórsson, M.M., Ingólfsdóttir, A., Walukiewicz, I. (eds.) ICALP 2008. LNCS, vol. 5125, pp. 724–735. Springer, Heidelberg (2008). https://doi.org/10.1007/978-3-540-70575-8_59
20. Kearns, M.J., Vazirani, U.V.: An Introduction to Computational Learning Theory. MIT Press, Cambridge (1994)
21. Kupferman, O., Vardi, M.Y.: Weak alternating automata are not that weak. ACM Trans. Comput. Logic **2**(3), 408–429 (2001)
22. Li, Y., Chen, Y.-F., Zhang, L., Liu, D.: A novel learning algorithm for Büchi automata based on family of DFAs and classification trees. In: Legay, A., Margaria, T. (eds.) TACAS 2017. LNCS, vol. 10205, pp. 208–226. Springer, Heidelberg (2017). https://doi.org/10.1007/978-3-662-54577-5_12
23. Li, Y., Turrini, A., Zhang, L., Schewe, S.: Learning to complement Büchi automata. In: Dillig, I., Palsberg, J. (eds.) VMCAI 2018. LNCS, vol. 10747, pp. 313–335. Springer, Cham (2018). https://doi.org/10.1007/978-3-319-73721-8_15
24. Peled, D., Vardi, M.Y., Yannakakis, M.: Black box checking. J. Autom. Lang. Comb. **7**(2), 225–246 (2001)
25. Piterman, N.: From nondeterministic Büchi and Streett automata to deterministic parity automata. In: LICS, pp. 255–264 (2006)
26. Vaandrager, F.: Model learning. Commun. ACM **60**(2), 86–95 (2017)
27. Yan, Q.: Lower bounds for complementation of omega-automata via the full automata technique. Logical Methods Comput. Sci. **4**(1) (2008)

Symbolic Regex Matcher

Olli Saarikivi[1], Margus Veanes[1(✉)], Tiki Wan[2],
and Eric Xu[2]

[1] Microsoft Research, Redmond, USA
margus@microsoft.com
[2] Microsoft Azure, Redmond, USA

Abstract. Symbolic regex matcher is a new open source .NET regular expression matching tool and match generator in the Microsoft Automata framework. It is based on the .NET regex parser in combination with a set based representation of character classes. The main feature of the tool is that the core matching algorithms are based on symbolic derivatives that support extended regular expression operations such as intersection and complement and also support a large set of commonly used features such as bounded loop quantifiers. The particularly useful features of the tool are that it supports full UTF16 encoded strings, the match generation is backtracking free, thread safe, and parallelizes with low overhead in multithreaded applications. We discuss the main design decisions behind the tool, explain the core algorithmic ideas and how the tool works, discuss some practical usage scenarios, and compare it to existing state of the art.

1 Motivation

We present a new tool called *Symbolic Regex Matcher* or *SRM* for fast match generation from extended regular expressions. The development of SRM has been motivated by some concrete industrial use cases and should meet the following *expectations*. Regarding *performance*, the overall algorithm complexity of match generation should be *linear* in the length of the input string. Regarding *expressivity*, it should handle common types of .NET regexes, including support for *bounded quantifiers* and *Unicode categories*; while nonregular features of regexes, such as back-references, are not required. Regarding *semantics*, the tool should be .NET compliant regarding strings and regexes, and the main type of match generation is: *earliest eager nonoverlapping* matches in the input string. Moreover, the tool should be safe to use in distributed and *multi threaded* development environments. Compilation time should be reasonable but it is not a critical factor because the intent is that the regexes are used frequently but updated infrequently. A concrete application of SRM is in an internal tool at Microsoft that scans for credentials and other sensitive content in cloud service software, where the search patterns are stated in form of individual regexes or in certain scenarios as intersections of regexes.

© The Author(s) 2019
T. Vojnar and L. Zhang (Eds.): TACAS 2019, Part I, LNCS 11427, pp. 372–378, 2019.
https://doi.org/10.1007/978-3-030-17462-0_24

The built-in .NET regex engine uses a backtracking based match search algorithm and does not meet the above expectations; in particular, some patterns may cause *exponential* search time. While SRM uses the *same parser* as the .NET regex engine, its back-end is a new engine that is built on the notion of *derivatives* [1], is developed as a tool in the open source Microsoft Automata framework [5], the framework was originally introduced in [8]. SRM meets *all* of the above expectations. Derivatives of regular expressions have been studied before in the context of matching of regular expressions, but only in the functional programming world [2,6] and in related domains [7]. Compared to earlier derivative based matching engines, the new contribution of SRM is that it supports *match generation* not only match detection, it supports extended features, such as *bounded quantifiers*, *Unicode categories*, and *case insensitivity*, it is .NET compliant, and is implemented in an imperative language. As far as we are aware of, SRM is the first tool that supports derivative based match generation for extended regular expressions. In our evaluation SRM shows significant performance improvements over .NET, with more predictable performance than RE2 [3], a state of the art automata based regex matcher.

In order to use SRM in a .NET application instead of the built-in match generator, `Microsoft.Automata.dll` can be built from [5] on a .NET platform version 4.0 or higher. The library extends the built-in `Regex` class with methods that expose SRM, in particular through the `Compile` method.

2 Matching with Derivatives

Here we work with derivatives of *symbolic extended regular expressions* or *regexes* for short. *Symbolic* means that the basic building blocks of single character regexes are *predicates* as opposed to singleton characters. In the case of standard .NET regexes, these are called *character classes*, such as the class of digits or \d. In general, such predicates are drawn from a given effective Boolean algebra and are here denoted generally by α and β; $\bot$ denotes the *false* predicate and . the *true* predicate. For example, in .NET $\bot$ can be represented by the empty character class `[0-[0]]`.[1] *Extended* here means that we allow *intersection*, *complement*, and *bounded quantifiers*.

The abstract syntax of regexes assumed here is the following, assuming the usual semantics where () denotes the empty sequence ϵ and $\langle \alpha \rangle$ denotes any singleton sequence of character that belongs to the set $[\![\alpha]\!] \subseteq \Sigma$, where Σ is the alphabet, and n and m are nonnegative integers such that $n \leq m$:

$$() \quad \langle \alpha \rangle \quad R_1 R_2 \quad R\{n,m\} \quad R\{n,*\} \quad R_1 | R_2 \quad R_1 \& R_2 \quad \neg R$$

where $[\![R\{n,m\}]\!] \overset{\text{def}}{=} \{v \in [\![R]\!]^i \mid n \leq i \leq m\}$, $[\![R\{n,*\}]\!] \overset{\text{def}}{=} \{v \in [\![R]\!]^i \mid n \leq i\}$. The expression $R*$ is a shorthand for $R\{0,*\}$. We write $\bot$ also for $\langle \bot \rangle$. We assume that $[\![R_1 | R_2]\!] = [\![R_1]\!] \cup [\![R_2]\!]$, $[\![R_1 \& R_2]\!] = [\![R_1]\!] \cap [\![R_2]\!]$, and $[\![\neg R]\!] = \Sigma^* \setminus [\![R]\!]$.

---

[1] The more intuitive syntax [] is unfortunately not allowed.

A less known feature of the .NET regex grammar is that it also supports *if-then-else* expressions over regexes, so, when combined appropriately with $\perp$ and $.$, it also supports intersection and complement. R is *nullable* if $\epsilon \in [\![R]\!]$. Nullability is defined recursively, e.g., $R\{n, m\}$ is nullable iff R is nullable or $n = 0$.

Given a concrete character x in the underlying alphabet Σ, and a regex R, the x-*derivative of R*, denoted by $\partial_x R$, is defined on the right. Given a language $L \subseteq \Sigma^*$, the x-derivative of L, $\boldsymbol{\partial}_x L \overset{\text{def}}{=} \{v \mid xv \in L\}$. It is well-known that $[\![\partial_x R]\!] = \boldsymbol{\partial}_x[\![R]\!]$. The abstract derivation rules provide a way to decide if an input u matches a regex R as follows. If $u = \epsilon$ then u matches R iff R is nullable; else, if $u =$ xv for some $x \in \Sigma, v \in \Sigma^*$ then u matches R iff v matches $\partial_x R$. In other words, the derivation rules can be unfolded lazily to create the transitions of the underlying DFA. In this setting we are considering Brzozowski derivatives [1].

$$\partial_x() \overset{\text{def}}{=} \perp$$

$$\partial_x\langle\alpha\rangle \overset{\text{def}}{=} \begin{cases} (), & \text{if } x \in [\![\alpha]\!]; \\ \perp, & \text{otherwise.} \end{cases}$$

$$\partial_x(R_1 R_2) \overset{\text{def}}{=} \begin{cases} ((\partial_x R_1)R_2)|\partial_x R_2, & \text{if } R_1 \text{ is nullable}; \\ (\partial_x R_1)R_2, & \text{otherwise.} \end{cases}$$

$$\partial_x R\{n, m\} \overset{\text{def}}{=} \begin{cases} (\partial_x R)R\{n-1, m-1\}, & \text{if } n>0; \\ (\partial_x R)R\{0, m-1\}, & \text{if } n=0 \text{ and } m>0; \\ \perp, & \text{otherwise (since } R\{0, 0\} \overset{\text{def}}{=} ()). \end{cases}$$

$$\partial_x R\{n, *\} \overset{\text{def}}{=} \begin{cases} (\partial_x R)R\{n-1, *\}, & \text{if } n > 0; \\ (\partial_x R)R\{0, *\}, & \text{otherwise.} \end{cases}$$

$$\partial_x(R_1|R_2) \overset{\text{def}}{=} (\partial_x R_1)|(\partial_x R_2)$$

$$\partial_x(R_1 \& R_2) \overset{\text{def}}{=} (\partial_x R_1)\&(\partial_x R_2)$$

$$\partial_x \neg R \overset{\text{def}}{=} \neg \partial_x R$$

Match Generation. The main purpose of the tool is to *generate* matches. While match generation is a topic that has been studied extensively for classical regular expressions, we are not aware of efforts that have considered the use of derivatives and extended regular expressions in this context, while staying *backtracking free* in order to guarantee *linear complexity* in terms of the length of the input. Our matcher implements by default *nonoverlapping earliest eager* match semantics. An important property in the matcher is that the above set of regular expressions is closed under *reversal*. The reversal of regex R is denoted $R^{\mathbf{r}}$. Observe that:

$$(R_1 R_2)^{\mathbf{r}} \overset{\text{def}}{=} (R_2^{\mathbf{r}} R_1^{\mathbf{r}}) \quad R\{n, m\}^{\mathbf{r}} \overset{\text{def}}{=} R^{\mathbf{r}}\{n, m\} \quad R\{n, *\}^{\mathbf{r}} \overset{\text{def}}{=} R^{\mathbf{r}}\{n, *\}$$

It follows that $[\![R^{\mathbf{r}}]\!] = [\![R]\!]^{\mathbf{r}}$ where $L^{\mathbf{r}}$ denotes the reversal of $L \subseteq \Sigma^*$. The match generation algorithm can now be described at a high level as follows. Given a regex R, find all the (nonoverlapping earliest eager) matches in a given input string u. This procedure uses the three regexes: R, $R^{\mathbf{r}}$ and $.*R$:

1. Initially $i = 0$ is the start position of the first symbol u_0 of u.
2. Let $i_{\text{orig}} = i$. Find the *earliest* match starting from i and $q = .*R$: Compute $q := \partial_{u_i} q$ and $i := i + 1$ until q is nullable. **Terminate** if no such q exists.
3. Find the *start position* for the above match closest to i_{orig}: Let $p = R^{\mathbf{r}}$. While $i > i_{\text{orig}}$ let $p := \partial_{u_i} p$ and $i := i - 1$, if p is nullable let $i_{\text{start}} := i$.

4. Find the *end position* for the match: Let $q = R$ and $i = i_{\text{start}}$. Compute $q := \partial_{u_i} q$ and $i := i + 1$ and let $i_{\text{end}} := i$ if q is nullable; repeat until $q = \bot$.
5. **Return** the match from i_{start} to i_{end}.
6. Repeat step 2 from $i := i_{\text{end}} + 1$ for the next *nonoverlapping* start position.

Observe that step 4 guarantees *longest* match in R from the position i_{start} found in step 3 for the earliest match found in step 2. In order for the above procedure to be practical there are several optimizations that are required. We discuss some of the implementation aspects next.

3   Implementation

SRM is implemented in `C#`. The input to the tool is a .NET regex (or an array of regexes) that is compiled into a serializable object R that implements the main matching interface `IMatcher`. Initially, this process uses a Binary Decision Diagram (*BDD*) based representation of predicates in order to efficiently canonicalize various conditions such as *case insensitivity* and *Unicode categories*. The use of BDDs as character predicates is explained in [4]. Then all the BDDs that occur in R are collected and their *minterms* (satisfiable Boolean combinations) are calculated, called the *atoms* $(\alpha_1, \ldots, \alpha_k)$ *of* R, where $\{[\![\alpha_i]\!]_{\text{BDD}}\}_{i=1}^{k}$ forms a partition of Σ. Each BDD-predicate α in R is now translated into a k-bit bit-vector (or BV) value β whose i'th bit is 1 iff $\alpha \wedge_{\text{BDD}} \alpha_i$ is nonempty. Typically k is small (often $k \le 64$) and allows BV to be implemented very efficiently (often by `ulong`), where $\wedge_{\text{BV}}$ is bit-wise-and. All subsequent Boolean operations are performed on this more efficient and *thread safe* data type. The additional step required during input processing is that each concrete input character c (`char` value) is now first mapped into an atom id i that determines the bit position in the BV predicate. In other words, $c \in [\![\beta]\!]_{\text{BV}}$ is implemented by finding the index i such that $c \in [\![\alpha_i]\!]_{\text{BDD}}$ and testing if the i'th bit of β is 1, where the former search is hardcoded into a precomputed lookup table or decision tree.

For example let R be constructed for the regex `\w\d*`. Then R has three atoms: $[\![\alpha_1]\!] = \Sigma \setminus [\![\backslash\text{w}]\!]$, $[\![\alpha_2]\!] = [\![\backslash\text{d}]\!]$, and $[\![\alpha_3]\!] = [\![\backslash\text{w}]\!] \setminus [\![\backslash\text{d}]\!]$, since $[\![\backslash\text{d}]\!] \subset [\![\backslash\text{w}]\!]$. For example BV 110_2 represents `\w` and 010_2 represents `\d`.

The symbolic regex AST type is treated as a value type and is handled similarly to the case of derivative based matching in the context of functional languages [2,6]. A key difference though, is that *weak equivalence* [6] checking is not enough to avoid state-space explosion when *bounded quantifiers* are allowed. A common situation during derivation is appearance of subexpressions of the form $(A\{0, k\}B)|(A\{0, k - 1\}B)$ that, when kept unchecked, keep reintroducing disjuncts of the same subexpression but with smaller value of the upper bound, potentially causing a substantial blowup. However, we know that $A\{0, n\}B$ is *subsumed* by $A\{0, m\}B$ when $n \le m$, thus $(A\{0, m\}B)|(A\{0, n\}B)$ can be simplified to $A\{0, m\}B$. To this end, a disjunct $A\{0, k\}B$, where $k > 0$, is represented internally as a *multiset element* $\langle A, B \rangle \mapsto k$ and the expression $(\langle A, B \rangle \mapsto m)|(\langle A, B \rangle \mapsto n)$ reduces to $(\langle A, B \rangle \mapsto \max(m, n))$. This is a form of *weak subsumption checking* that provides a crucial optimization step during derivation. Similarly, when A and B are both singletons, say $\langle \alpha \rangle$ and $\langle \beta \rangle$, then $\langle \alpha \rangle | \langle \beta \rangle$ reduces to $\langle \alpha \vee_{BV} \beta \rangle$ and $\langle \alpha \rangle \& \langle \beta \rangle$ reduces to $\langle \alpha \wedge_{BV} \beta \rangle$. Here thread safety of the Boolean operations is important in a multi threaded application.

Finally, two more key optimizations are worth mentioning. First, during the main match generation loop, symbolic regex nodes are internalized into integer state ids and a DFA is maintained in form of an integer array δ indexed by $[i, q]$ where $1 \leq i \leq k$ is an atom index, and q is a state integer id, such that old state ids are immediately looked up as $\delta[i, q]$ and not rederived. Second, during step 2, initial search for the *relevant initial prefix*, when applicable, is performed using `string.IndexOf` to completely avoid the trivial initial state transition corresponding to the loop $\partial_c .*R = .*R$ in the case when $\partial_c R = \bot$.

4 Evaluation

We have evaluated the performance of SRM on two benchmarks:

Twain: 15 regexes matched against a 16 MB file containing the collected works of Mark Twain.

Assorted: 735 regexes matched against a synthetic input that includes some matches for each regex concatenated with random strings to produce an input file of 32 MB. The regexes are from the Automata library's samples and were originally collected from an online database of regular expressions.

We compare the performance of our matcher against the built-in .NET regex engine and Google's RE2 [3], a state of the art backtracking free regex match generation engine. RE2 is written in `C++` and internally based on automata. It eliminates bounded quantifiers in a preprocessing step by unwinding them, which may cause the regex to be rejected if the unwinding exceeds a certain limit. RE2 does not support extended operations over regexes such as intersection or complement. We use RE2 through a `C#` wrapper library.

The input to the built-in .NET regex engine and SRM is in UTF16, which is the encoding for NET's built-in strings, while RE2 is called with UTF8 encoded input. This implies for example that a regex such as `[\uD800-\uDFFF]` that tries to locate a single UTF16 surrogate is not meaningful in the context UTF8. All experiments were run on a machine with dual Intel Xeon E5-2620v3 CPUs running Windows 10 with .NET Framework 4.7.1. The reported running times for **Twain** are averages of 10 samples, while the statistics for **Assorted** are based on a single sample for each regex.

Figure 1 presents running times for each regex in **Twain**, while Fig. 2 presents a selection of metrics for the **Assorted** benchmark.

Both SRM and RE2 are faster than .NET on most regexes. This highlights the advantages of automata based regular expression matching when the richer features of a backtracking matcher are not required.

Compilation of regular expressions into matcher objects takes more time in SRM than RE2 or .NET. The largest contributor to this is finding the minterms of all predicates in the regex. For use cases where initialization time is critical

Regex	.NET	RE2	SRM
Twain	0.20s	**0.02s**	0.05s
(?i)Twain	0.66s	**0.26s**	0.39s
[a-z]shing	4.11s	**0.21s**	0.78s
Huck[a-zA-Z]+|Saw[a-zA-Z]+	1.47s	0.21s	**0.11s**
[a-q][^u-z]{13}x	10.20s	16.64s	**3.07s**
Tom|Sawyer|Huckleberry|Finn	1.53s	0.24s	**0.12s**
(?i)Tom|Sawyer|Huckleberry|Finn	6.73s	**0.22s**	0.51s
.{0,2}(Tom|Sawyer|Huckleberry|Finn)	15.84s	**0.22s**	0.64s
.{2,4}(Tom|Sawyer|Huckleberry|Finn)	16.15s	**0.22s**	0.62s
Tom.{10,25}river|river.{10,25}Tom	1.83s	0.21s	**0.21s**
[a-zA-Z]+ing	9.62s	**0.73s**	0.92s
\s[a-zA-Z]{0,12}ing\s	5.56s	**0.30s**	0.82s
([A-Za-z]awyer|[A-Za-z]inn)\s	6.26s	**0.21s**	0.87s
["'][^"']{0,30}[?!\.][\"']	2.00s	0.25s	**0.19s**
\p{Sm}	1.71s	0.21s	**0.10s**

Fig. 1. Time to generate all matches for each regex in **Twain**.

Metric	.NET	RE2	SRM
# of regexes with best time	0	305	**430**
Total compilation time for all regexes	0.8s	**0.1s**	13.9s
Average matching time	7.93s	0.36s	**0.25s**
80th percentile matching time	2.24s	**0.08s**	0.13s

Fig. 2. Metrics for the **Assorted** benchmark.

and inputs are known in advance, SRM provides support for pre-compilation and fast deserialization of matchers.

Comparing SRM to RE2 we can see that both matchers have regexes they do better on. While SRM achieves a lower average matching time on **Assorted**, this is due to the more severe outliers in RE2's performance profile, as shown by the lower 80th percentile matching time. Overall SRM offers performance that is comparable to RE2 while being implemented in C# without any unsafe code.

Application to Security Leak Scanning. SRM has been adopted in an internal tool at Microsoft that scans for credentials and other sensitive content in cloud service software. With the built-in .NET regex engine the tool was susceptible to catastrophic backtracking on files with long lines, such as minified JavaScript and SQL server seeding files. SRM's linear matching complexity has helped address these issues, while maintaining compatibility for the large set of .NET regexes used in the application.

References

1. Brzozowski, J.A.: Derivatives of regular expressions. JACM **11**, 481–494 (1964)
2. Fischer, S., Huch, F., Wilke, T.: A play on regular expressions: functional pearl. SIGPLAN Not. **45**(9), 357–368 (2010)
3. Google: RE2. https://github.com/google/re2

4. Hooimeijer, P., Veanes, M.: An evaluation of automata algorithms for string analysis. In: Jhala, R., Schmidt, D. (eds.) VMCAI 2011. LNCS, vol. 6538, pp. 248–262. Springer, Heidelberg (2011). https://doi.org/10.1007/978-3-642-18275-4_18
5. Microsoft: Automata. https://github.com/AutomataDotNet/
6. Owens, S., Reppy, J., Turon, A.: Regular-expression derivatives re-examined. J. Funct. Program. **19**(2), 173–190 (2009)
7. Traytel, D., Nipkow, T.: Verified decision procedures for MSO on words based on derivatives of regular expressions. SIGPLAN Not. **48**(9), 3–12 (2013)
8. Veanes, M., Bjørner, N.: Symbolic automata: the toolkit. In: Flanagan, C., König, B. (eds.) TACAS 2012. LNCS, vol. 7214, pp. 472–477. Springer, Heidelberg (2012). https://doi.org/10.1007/978-3-642-28756-5_33

COMPASS 3.0

Marco Bozzano[1]([✉]), Harold Bruintjes[2], Alessandro Cimatti[1],
Joost-Pieter Katoen[2], Thomas Noll[2], and Stefano Tonetta[1]

[1] Embedded Systems Unit, Fondazione Bruno Kessler, Trento, Italy
bozzano@fbk.eu
[2] Software Modeling and Verification Group, RWTH Aachen University,
Aachen, Germany

Abstract. COMPASS (COrrectness, Modeling and Performance of
AeroSpace Systems) is an international research effort aiming to ensure
system-level correctness, safety, dependability and performability of on-
board computer-based aerospace systems. In this paper we present
COMPASS 3.0, which brings together the results of various development
projects since the original inception of COMPASS. Improvements have
been made both to the frontend, supporting an updated modeling language and user interface, as well as to the backend, by adding new functionalities and improving the existing ones. New features include Timed
Failure Propagation Graphs, contract-based analysis, hierarchical fault
tree generation, probabilistic analysis of non-deterministic models and
statistical model checking.

1 Introduction

The COMPASS toolset provides an integrated model-based approach for System-
Software Co-Engineering in the aerospace domain. It uses formal verification
techniques, notably model checking, and originates from an ESA initiative dating
back to 2008 [6]. Over the past eight years, various projects followed which
extended the toolset. In a recent effort funded by ESA, the results of this work
have been thoroughly consolidated into a single release, which is now available.

COMPASS 3.0 includes features originally included in distinct tool releases
that diverged from the original development trunk[1]. The AUTOGEF and
FAME projects focused on Fault Detection, Identification, and Recovery (FDIR)
requirements modeling and development, and on fault propagation analysis;
HASDEL extended formal analysis techniques to deal with the specific needs
of launcher systems, with a strong focus on timed aspects of the model; and
finally CATSY had the goal of improving the requirements specification process.

This paper presents an overview of the toolset, as well as a description of the
enhancements made since its last official release in 2013 (v2.3). For a more detailed
description of the (pre-)existing features and capabilities, we refer to [5,6].

---

[1] See www.compass-toolset.org.

This work has been funded by the European Space Agency (ESA-ESTEC) under contract 4000115870/15/NL/FE/as.

T. Vojnar and L. Zhang (Eds.): TACAS 2019, Part I, LNCS 11427, pp. 379–385, 2019.
https://doi.org/10.1007/978-3-030-17462-0_25

2   Toolset Overview

The COMPASS toolset can be divided into the user facing side (the frontend), and the verification engines used (the backend). The frontend provides a GUI that offers access to all the analysis functions of the toolset, as well as command-line scripts. The backend tools are chosen and invoked by the toolset automatically.

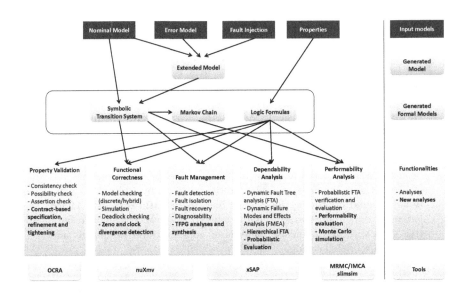

Fig. 1. Overview of the COMPASS toolset

The functionalities of COMPASS are summarized in Fig. 1, where arrows represent I/O relationships for model transformations, and link models with the corresponding analyses. User inputs are models written in a dialect of AADL [18] and properties. COMPASS is based on the concept of *model extension*, i.e., the possibility to automatically inject faults into a nominal model, by specifying error models and a set of fault injections. The extended model is internally converted into a symbolic model amenable to formal verification and to a Markov chain (for probabilistic analyses). Properties are automatically translated into temporal logic formulas. Given the models and the properties, COMPASS provides a full set of functionalities, including property validation, functional correctness, fault management, dependability and performability analyses.

The analyses are supported by the following verification engines: nuXmv [9] for correctness checking; OCRA [10] for contract-based analysis; IMCA [19] and MRMC [20] for performance analysis by probabilistic model checking; slimsim [8] for statistical model checking and xSAP [1] for safety analysis.

COMPASS is licensed under a variant of the GPL license, restricted to ESA member states. It is distributed on a pre-configured and ready-to-use virtual machine, or as two different code bundles.

In a typical workflow, one would start with both a nominal and an error specification of the system and then use simulation to interactively explore its dynamic behavior. In a next step, verification of functional correctness based on user-defined properties can be performed, followed by more specialized analyses as indicated in Fig. 1. For a complete overview of the COMPASS toolset, we refer to the COMPASS tutorial [15] and user manual [16].

3   Input Language

Input models for COMPASS use a variant of the AADL language [18], named SLIM. AADL is standardized and used in e.g., the aerospace and automotive industries. SLIM provides extensions for behavior and error specification. A model is described in terms of components, which may specify subcomponents, forming a component hierarchy. Components interact with each other by means of ports, which send either discrete events or data values. Components may furthermore specify modes, which may render subcomponents active or inactive, thus enabling system reconfiguration. Error behavior is specified in terms of error components, which define error states, (probabilistic) events and propagations which may trigger a synchronization between error components. The impact of faults occurring in the error model onto the nominal model is described by means of *fault injections*, which specify the fault effect by update operations on data components. This has been extended by supporting specifications that can inhibit certain events from occurring, or specifying a set of modes that is available in a certain failure state. The language's semantics and syntax are described in [14].

Language Updates. COMPASS 3.0 supports the property system used by AADL. This makes it possible to annotate various elements in the model by using SLIM specific attributes, and makes the language more compatible with the core AADL specification, improving interoperability. New features also include timed error models (that is, error components may contain clocks), non-blocking ports and separation of configuration and behavior. The latter entails that composite components can only specify modes and cannot change data values or generate events by means of transitions, whereas atomic components may specify states.

Property Specification. Properties can be specified in three different ways. The first two options are simpler to use, since they hide the details of the underlying temporal logic, but less expressive. *Design attributes* [3] represent a specific property of a model's element, such as the delay of an event or the invariant of a mode. They are directly associated to model elements. Formal properties are automatically derived based on the Catalogue of System and Software Properties (CSSP) [3]. The *pattern-based* system uses pre-defined patterns with placeholders to define formal properties. Time bounds and probabilities can optionally be specified. As a last option, the user can encode properties directly using *logical expressions*. This enables the modeler to exploit the full power of the underlying temporal logics, and offers the highest expressivity.

4   New Functionalities in COMPASS 3.0

In this section, we discuss the main functionalities of the COMPASS 3.0 toolset.

Correctness Checking. COMPASS supports checking for correctness of the model by providing properties. The toolset indicates for each property whether it holds or not, and gives a counter example in the latter case. Verification relies on edge technologies based on BDD- and SAT-based model checking, including *K-liveness verification* [12]. In order to assist the user in the specification of timed models, COMPASS 3.0 offers functionality to check the timed correctness of the model w.r.t. *Zenoness* and *clock divergence*. The former is caused by cycles in the system's state space that do not require progressing of time. The latter is caused by clocks that can attain an arbitrarily large value. The toolset can automatically check Zenoness for all modes in the system, and divergence for all clocks.

Contract-Based Analysis. COMPASS 3.0 offers the possibility to perform *contract-based analysis* [11]. Contracts must be specified in the model and attached to components. Each contract consists of an *assumption* (a property of the environment of the component) and a *guarantee* (a property of the implementation of the component, which must hold as long as the assumption holds). In order to perform compositional analysis, a contract refinement must be further specified, which links a contract to a set of contracts of the subcomponents. COMPASS 3.0 supports the following analyses. *Validation* is performed on assumptions and guarantees. The user can choose a subset of these properties and check consistency or entailment. *Refinement checking* verifies whether the contract refinements are correct. Namely, that whenever the implementations of the subcomponents satisfy their contracts and the environment satisfies its assumption, then the guarantee of the supercomponent and the assumptions of its subcomponents are satisfied. Finally, *tightening* looks for a weakening and/or strengthening of the assumptions/guarantees, respectively, such that the refinement still holds.

Fault Trees. COMPASS 3.0 can generate fault trees associated with particular error states in the model. Standard fault trees are flat in nature (being two- or three-leveled), hiding some of the nested dependencies. Contract-based analysis can be used to generate a *hierarchical fault tree*, which captures the hierarchy of the model. This approach makes use of the specified contracts, and checks which events may cause them to be invalidated. COMPASS 3.0 offers further alternatives to analyze fault trees. Static probabilities can be calculated for the entire tree by specifying the probabilities of basic events. Fault Tree Evaluation calculates the probability of failure for a given time span. Finally, Fault Tree Verification checks a probabilistic property specified for the fault tree.

Performability. COMPASS 3.0 offers two model checking approaches to probabilistic analysis (which, using a probabilistic property, determine the probability of failure within a time period): using numerical analysis or using Monte-Carlo simulation. The former originally only supported Continuous Time Markov Chains (CTMCs) using the MRMC [20] tool. This has now been extended to Interactive Markov Chains (IMCs) using IMCA [19], which makes it possible to analyze continuous-time stochastic models which exhibit *non-determinism*. However, neither approach supports hybrid models containing clocks. For the analysis of these models, statistical model checking techniques [7,8] are employed, which use Monte-Carlo simulation to determine, within a certain margin of likelihood and error, the probability of quantitative properties.

Timed Failure Propagation Graphs. Timed Failure Propagation Graphs (TFPGs) [2] support various aspects of diagnosis and prognosis, such as modeling the temporal dependency between the occurrence of events and their dependence on system modes. A TFPG is a labeled directed graph where nodes represent either fault modes or discrepancies, which are off-nominal conditions that are effects of fault modes. COMPASS 3.0 supports three kinds of analyses based on TFPGs: *synthesis*, where a TFPG is automatically derived from the model, *behavioral validation*, which checks whether a given TFPG is complete (i.e., a faithful abstraction) w.r.t. the model; and *effectiveness validation*, which checks whether the TFPG is sufficiently accurate for allowing diagnosability of failures.

5   Related Work and Conclusion

Closely related to COMPASS is the TASTE toolset, dedicated to the development of embedded, real-time systems. It focuses on the integration of heterogeneous technologies for modeling and verification (including AADL), code generation and integration (e.g., written in C and ADA) and deployment. Another ESA initiative is COrDeT-2, part of which defines OSRA (On-board Software Reference Architecture), which aims to improve software reuse by defining a standardized architecture. Security extensions in COMPASS 3.0 have been added as part of the D-MILS project [21], enabling reasoning on data security.

Various case studies have been performed using COMPASS 3.0. The first one was targeting at the Preliminary Design Review stage of a satellite's design [17]. The study lasted for six months and encompassed a model of about 90 components. A second case study followed during the Critical Design Review stage, focusing on modeling practices and diagnosability [4], with a scale twice the size of [17]. A smaller scale case study was later performed as part of the HASDEL project [8]. Recently, the CubETH nano-satellite was represented as a model with 82 components and analyzed using COMPASS 3.0 [7].

The case studies demonstrate that the key benefit of the COMPASS approach is the culmination of a single comprehensive system model that covers all aspects (discrete, real-time, hybrid, probabilistic). This ensures consistency of the analyses, which is a major benefit upon current practices where various (tailored) models are constructed each covering different aspects. For further directions, we refer to the COMPASS roadmap [13], which thoroughly discusses goals for the toolset as well as the development process, research directions, community outreach and further integration with other ESA initiatives.

References

1. Bittner, B., et al.: The XSAP safety analysis platform. In: Chechik, M., Raskin, J.-F. (eds.) TACAS 2016. LNCS, vol. 9636, pp. 533–539. Springer, Heidelberg (2016). https://doi.org/10.1007/978-3-662-49674-9_31

2. Bittner, B., Bozzano, M., Cimatti, A.: Automated synthesis of timed failure propagation graphs. In: Proceedings of IJCAI, pp. 972–978 (2016)

3. Bos, V., Bruintjes, H., Tonetta, S.: Catalogue of system and software properties. In: Skavhaug, A., Guiochet, J., Bitsch, F. (eds.) SAFECOMP 2016. LNCS, vol. 9922, pp. 88–101. Springer, Cham (2016). https://doi.org/10.1007/978-3-319-45477-1_8

4. Bozzano, M., et al.: Spacecraft early design validation using formal methods. Reliab. Eng. Syst. Saf. **132**, 20–35 (2014)

5. Bozzano, M., Cimatti, A., Katoen, J.P., Nguyen, V.Y., Noll, T., Roveri, M.: Safety, dependability and performance analysis of extended AADL models. Comput. J. **54**(5), 754–775 (2011)

6. Bozzano, M., et al.: A model checker for AADL. In: Touili, T., Cook, B., Jackson, P. (eds.) CAV 2010. LNCS, vol. 6174, pp. 562–565. Springer, Heidelberg (2010). https://doi.org/10.1007/978-3-642-14295-6_48

7. Bruintjes, H.: Model-based reliability analysis of aerospace systems. Ph.D. thesis, RWTH Aachen University (2018)

8. Bruintjes, H., Katoen, J.P., Lesens, D.: A statistical approach for timed reachability in AADL models. In: Proceedings of DSN, pp. 81–88. IEEE (2015)

9. Cavada, R., et al.: The NUXMV symbolic model checker. In: Biere, A., Bloem, R. (eds.) CAV 2014. LNCS, vol. 8559, pp. 334–342. Springer, Cham (2014). https://doi.org/10.1007/978-3-319-08867-9_22

10. Cimatti, A., Dorigatti, M., Tonetta, S.: OCRA: a tool for checking the refinement of temporal contracts. In: Proceedings of ASE, pp. 702–705 (2013)

11. Cimatti, A., Tonetta, S.: Contracts-refinement proof system for component-based embedded systems. Sci. Comput. Program. **97**, 333–348 (2015)

12. Claessen, K., Sörensson, N.: A liveness checking algorithm that counts. In: Proceedings of FMCAD, pp. 52–59 (2012)

13. COMPASS Consortium: COMPASS roadmap. Technical report (2016). http://www.compass-toolset.org/docs/compass-roadmap.pdf

14. COMPASS Consortium: SLIM 3.0 - syntax and semantics. Technical report (2016). http://www.compass-toolset.org/docs/slim-specification.pdf

15. COMPASS Consortium: COMPASS tutorial - version 3.0.1. Technical report (2018). http://www.compass-toolset.org/docs/compass-tutorial.pdf

16. COMPASS Consortium: COMPASS user manual - version 3.0.1. Technical report (2018). http://www.compass-toolset.org/docs/compass-manual.pdf

17. Esteve, M.A., Katoen, J.P., Nguyen, V.Y., Postma, B., Yushtein, Y.: Formal correctness, safety, dependability and performance analysis of a satellite. In: Proceeding of ICSE, pp. 1022–1031. ACM and IEEE (2012)

18. Feiler, P.H., Gluch, D.P.: Model-Based Engineering with AADL: An Introduction to the SAE Architecture Analysis & Design Language. Addison-Wesley, Upper Saddle River (2012)

19. Guck, D., Han, T., Katoen, J.-P., Neuhäußer, M.R.: Quantitative timed analysis of interactive Markov Chains. In: Goodloe, A.E., Person, S. (eds.) NFM 2012. LNCS, vol. 7226, pp. 8–23. Springer, Heidelberg (2012). https://doi.org/10.1007/978-3-642-28891-3_4

20. Katoen, J.P., Zapreev, I.S., Hahn, E.M., Hermanns, H., Jansen, D.N.: The ins and outs of the probabilistic model checker MRMC. Perform. Eval. **68**(2), 90–104 (2011)

21. van der Pol, K., Noll, T.: Security type checking for MILS-AADL specifications. In: International MILS Workshop. Zenodo (2015). http://mils-workshop-2015.euromils.eu/

Debugging of Behavioural Models
with CLEAR

Gianluca Barbon[1], Vincent Leroy[2], and Gwen Salaün[1(✉)]

[1] Univ. Grenoble Alpes, CNRS, Grenoble INP, Inria,
LIG, 38000 Grenoble, France
`gwen.salaun@inria.fr`
[2] Univ. Grenoble Alpes, CNRS, Grenoble INP, LIG, 38000 Grenoble, France

Abstract. This paper presents a tool for debugging behavioural models being analysed using model checking techniques. It consists of three parts: (i) one for annotating a behavioural model given a temporal formula, (ii) one for visualizing the erroneous part of the model with a specific focus on decision points that make the model to be correct or incorrect, and (iii) one for abstracting counterexamples thus providing an explanation of the source of the bug.

1 Introduction

Model checking [2] is an established technique for automatically verifying that a behavioural model satisfies a given temporal property, which specifies some expected requirement of the system. In this work, we use Labelled Transition Systems (LTS) as behavioural models of concurrent programs. An LTS consists of states and labelled transitions connecting these states. An LTS can be produced from a higher-level specification of the system described with a process algebra for instance. Temporal properties are usually divided into two main families: safety and liveness properties [2]. Both are supported in this work. If the LTS does not satisfy the property, the model checker returns a counterexample, which is a sequence of actions leading to a state where the property is not satisfied.

Understanding this counterexample for debugging the specification is a complicated task for several reasons: (i) the counterexample may consist of many actions; (ii) the debugging task is mostly achieved manually (satisfactory automatic debugging techniques do not yet exist); (iii) the counterexample does not explicitly point out the source of the bug that is hidden in the model; (iv) the most relevant actions are not highlighted in the counterexample; (v) the counterexample does not give a global view of the problem.

The CLEAR tools (Fig. 1) aims at simplifying the debugging of concurrent systems whose specification compiles into a behavioural model. To do so, we propose a novel approach for improving the comprehension of counterexamples by highlighting some of the states in the counterexample that are of prime importance because from those states the specification can reach a correct part of the model or an incorrect one. These states correspond to decisions or choices that are particularly interesting because they usually provide an explanation of the

© The Author(s) 2019
T. Vojnar and L. Zhang (Eds.): TACAS 2019, Part I, LNCS 11427, pp. 386–392, 2019.
https://doi.org/10.1007/978-3-030-17462-0_26

source of the bug. The first component of the CLEAR toolset computes these specific states from a given LTS (AUT format) and a temporal property (MCL logic [5]). Second, visualization techniques are provided in order to graphically observe the whole model and see how those states are distributed over that model. Third, explanations of the bug are built by abstracting away irrelevant parts of the counterexample, which results in a simplified counterexample.

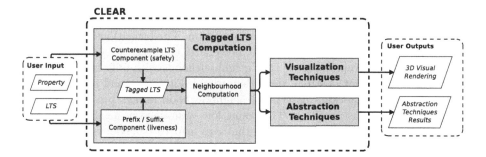

Fig. 1. Overview of the CLEAR toolset.

The CLEAR toolset has been developed mainly in Java and consists of more than 10K lines of code. All source files and several case studies are available online [1]. CLEAR has been applied to many examples and the results turn out to be quite positive as presented in an empirical evaluation which is also available online.

The rest of this paper is organised as follows. Section 2 overviews the LTS and property manipulations in order to compute annotated or tagged LTSs. Sections 3 and 4 present successively our techniques for visualizing tagged models and for abstracting counterexamples with the final objective in both cases to simplify the debugging steps. Section 5 describes experiments we carried out for validating our approach on case studies. Section 6 concludes the paper.

2   Tagged LTSs

The first step of our approach is to identify in the LTS parts of it corresponding to correct or incorrect behaviours. This is achieved using several algorithms that we define and that are presented in [3,4]. We use different techniques depending on the property family. As far as safety properties are concerned, we compute an LTS consisting of all counterexamples and compare it with the full LTS. As for liveness properties, for each state, we compute the set of prefixes and suffixes. Then, we use this information for tagging transitions as correct, incorrect or neutral in the full LTS. A correct transition leads to a behaviour that always satisfies the property, while an incorrect one leads to a behaviour that always violates the property. A neutral transition is common to correct and incorrect behaviours.

Once we have this information about transitions, we can identify specific states in the LTS where there is a choice in the LTS that directly affects the compliance with the property. We call these states and the transitions incoming to/outgoing from those states *neighbourhoods*.

There are four kinds of neighbourhoods, which differ by looking at their outgoing transitions (Fig. 2 from left to right): (1) with at least one correct transition (and no incorrect transition), (2) with at least one incorrect transition (and no correct transition), (3) with at least one correct transition and one incorrect transition, but no neutral transition, (4) with at least one correct transition, one incorrect transition and one neutral transition. The transitions contained in neighbourhood of type (1) highlight a choice that can lead to behaviours that always satisfy the property. Note that neighbourhoods with only correct outgoing transitions are not possible, since they would not correspond to a problematic choice. Consequently, this type of neighbourhood always presents at least one outgoing neutral transition. The transitions contained in neighbourhood of type (2), (3) or (4) highlight a choice that can lead to behaviours that always violate the property.

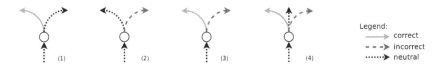

Fig. 2. The four types of neighbourhoods. (Color figure online)

It is worth noting that both visualization and counterexample abstraction techniques share the computation of the tagged LTS (correct/incorrect/neutral transitions) and of the neighbourhoods.

3   Visualization Techniques

The CLEAR visualizer provides support for visualizing the erroneous part of the LTS and emphasizes all the states (a.k.a. neighbourhoods) where a choice makes the specification either head to correct or incorrect behaviour. This visualization is very useful from a debugging perspective to have a global point of view and not only to focus on a specific erroneous trace (that is, a counterexample).

More precisely, the CLEAR visualizer supports the visualization of tagged LTSs enriched with neighbourhoods. These techniques have been developed using Javascript, the AngularJS framework, the bootstrap CSS framework, and the 3D force graph library. These 3D visualization techniques make use of different colors to distinguish correct (green), incorrect (red) and neutral (black) transitions on the one hand, and all kinds of neighbourhoods (represented with different shades of yellow) on the other hand. The tool also provides several functionalities in order to explore tagged LTSs for debugging purposes, the main one being the step-by-step animation starting from the initial state or from any chosen state in the LTS. This animation keeps track of the already traversed states/transitions and it is possible to move backward in that trace. Beyond visualizing the whole erroneous LTS, another functionality allows one to focus on one specific counterexample and rely on the animation features introduced beforehand for exploring the details of that counterexample (correct/incorrect transitions and neighbourhoods).

Figure 3 gives a screenshot of the CLEAR visualizer. The legend on the left hand side of this figure depicts the different elements and colors used in the LTS visualization. All functionalities appear in the bottom part. When the LTS is loaded, one can also load a counterexample. On the right hand side, there is the name of the file and the list of states/transitions of the current animation. Note that transitions labels are not shown, they are only displayed through mouseover. This choice allows the tool to provide a clearer view of the LTS.

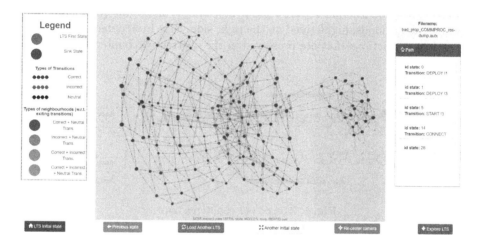

Fig. 3. Screenshot of the CLEAR visualizer. (Color figure online)

From a methodological point of view, it is adviced to use first the CLEAR visualizer during the debugging process for taking a global look at the erroneous part of the LTS and possibly notice interesting structures in that LTS that may guide the developer to specific kinds of bug. Step-by-step animation is also helpful for focusing on specific traces and for looking more carefully at some transitions and neighbourhoods on those traces. If the developer does not identify the bug using these visualization techniques, (s)he can make use of the CLEAR abstraction techniques presented in the next section.

4   Abstraction Techniques

In this section, once the LTS has been tagged using algorithms overviewed in Sect. 2, the developer can use abstraction techniques that aim at simplifying a counterexample produced from the LTS and a given property. To do so we make a joint analysis of the counterexample and of the LTS enriched with neighbourhoods computed previously. This analysis can be used for obtaining different kinds of simplifications, such as: (i) an abstracted counterexample, that allows one to remove from a counterexample actions that do not belong to neighbourhoods (and thus represent noise); (ii) a shortest path to a neighbourhood, which retrieves the shortest sequence of actions that leads to a neighbourhood; (iii) improved versions of (i) and (ii), where the developer provides a pattern representing a sequence of non-contiguous actions, in order to allow the developer to focus on a specific part of the model; (iv) techniques focusing on a notion of distance to the bug in terms of neighbourhoods. For the sake of space, we focus on the abstracted counterexample in this paper.

Abstracted Counterexample. This technique takes as input an LTS where neighbourhoods have been identified and a counterexample. Then, it removes all the actions in the counterexample that do not represent incoming or outgoing transitions of neighbourhoods. Figure 4 shows an example of a counterexample where two neighbourhoods, highlighted on the right side, have been detected and allow us to identify actions that are preserved in the abstracted counterexample.

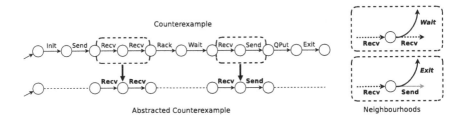

Fig. 4. Abstracted counterexample.

5   Experiments

We carried out experiments on about 100 examples. For each one, we use as input a process algebraic specification that was compiled into an LTS model, and a temporal property. As far as computation time is concerned, the time is quite low for small examples (a few seconds), while it tends to increase w.r.t. the size of the LTS when we deal with examples with hundreds of thousands of transitions and states (a few minutes). In this case, it is mainly due to the computation of tagged LTSs, which is quite costly because it is based on several graph traversals. Visualization techniques allowed us to identify several examples of typical bugs with their corresponding visual models. This showed that the visualizations exhibit specific structures that characterize the bug and are helpful for supporting the developer during his/her debugging tasks. As for abstraction techniques, we observed some clear gain in length (up to 90%) between the original counterexample and the abstracted one, which keeps only relevant actions using our approach and thus facilitates the debugging task for the developer.

We also carried out an empirical study to validate our approach. We asked 17 developers, with different degrees of expertise, to find bugs on two test cases by taking advantage of the abstracted counterexample techniques. The developers were divided in two groups, in order to evaluate both test cases with and without the abstracted counterexample. The developers were asked to discover the bug and measure the total time spent in debugging each test case. We measured the results in terms of time, comparing for both test cases the time spent with and without the abstracted counterexample. We observed a gain of about 25% of the total average time spent in finding the bug for the group using our approach. We finally asked developers' opinion about the benefit given by our method in detecting the bug. Most of them agreed considering our approach helpful.

The CLEAR toolset is available online [1] jointly with several case studies and the detailed results of the empirical study.

6   Concluding Remarks

In this paper, we have presented the CLEAR toolset for simplifying the comprehension of erroneous behavioural specifications under validation using model checking techniques. To do so, we are able to detect the choices in the model (neighbourhood) that may lead to a correct or incorrect behaviour, and generate a tagged LTS as result. The CLEAR visualizer takes as input a tagged LTS and provides visualization techniques of the whole erroneous part of the model as well as animation techniques that help the developer to navigate in the model for better understanding what is going on and hopefully detect the source of the bug. The counterexample abstraction techniques are finally helpful for building abstractions from counterexamples by keeping only relevant actions from a debugging perspective. The experiments we carried out show that our approach is useful in practice to help the designer in finding the source of the bug(s).

References

1. CLEAR Debugging Tool. https://github.com/gbarbon/clear/
2. Baier, C., Katoen, J.: Principles of Model Checking. MIT Press, Cambridge (2008)
3. Barbon, G., Leroy, V., Salaün, G.: Debugging of concurrent systems using counterexample analysis. In: Dastani, M., Sirjani, M. (eds.) FSEN 2017. LNCS, vol. 10522, pp. 20–34. Springer, Cham (2017). https://doi.org/10.1007/978-3-319-68972-2_2
4. Barbon, G., Leroy, V., Salaün, G.: Counterexample simplification for liveness property violation. In: Johnsen, E.B., Schaefer, I. (eds.) SEFM 2018. LNCS, vol. 10886, pp. 173–188. Springer, Cham (2018). https://doi.org/10.1007/978-3-319-92970-5_11
5. Mateescu, R., Thivolle, D.: A model checking language for concurrent value-passing systems. In: Cuellar, J., Maibaum, T., Sere, K. (eds.) FM 2008. LNCS, vol. 5014, pp. 148–164. Springer, Heidelberg (2008). https://doi.org/10.1007/978-3-540-68237-0_12

Machine Learning

Omega-Regular Objectives in Model-Free Reinforcement Learning

Ernst Moritz Hahn[1,2], Mateo Perez[3],
Sven Schewe[4], Fabio Somenzi[3],
Ashutosh Trivedi[5(✉)], and Dominik Wojtczak[4]

[1] School of EEECS, Queen's University Belfast, Belfast, UK
[2] State Key Laboratory of Computer Science,
Institute of Software, CAS, Beijing, People's Republic of China
[3] Department of ECEE, University of Colorado Boulder, Boulder, USA
[4] Department of Computer Science, University of Liverpool, Liverpool, UK
[5] Department of Computer Science, University of Colorado Boulder, Boulder, USA
ashutosh.trivedi@colorado.edu

Abstract. We provide the first solution for model-free reinforcement learning of ω-regular objectives for Markov decision processes (MDPs). We present a constructive reduction from the almost-sure satisfaction of ω-regular objectives to an almost-sure reachability problem, and extend this technique to learning how to control an unknown model so that the chance of satisfying the objective is maximized. We compile ω-regular properties into limit-deterministic Büchi automata instead of the traditional Rabin automata; this choice sidesteps difficulties that have marred previous proposals. Our approach allows us to apply model-free, off-the-shelf reinforcement learning algorithms to compute optimal strategies from the observations of the MDP. We present an experimental evaluation of our technique on benchmark learning problems.

1 Introduction

Reinforcement learning (RL) [3,37,40] is an approach to sequential decision making in which agents rely on reward signals to choose actions aimed at achieving prescribed objectives. Model-free RL refers to a class of techniques that are asymptotically space-efficient [36] because they do not construct a full model of the environment. These techniques include classic algorithms like Q-learning [37] as well as their extensions to deep neural networks [14,31]. Some objectives, like running a maze, are naturally expressed in terms of scalar rewards; in other cases the translation is less obvious. We solve the problem of ω-regular rewards, that

This work is supported in part by the Marie Skłodowska Curie Fellowship *Parametrised Verification and Control*, NSFC grants 61761136011 and 61532019, an ASIRT grant by the College of Engineering and Applied Sciences of CU Boulder, and EPSRC grants EP/M027287/1 and EP/P020909/1.

T. Vojnar and L. Zhang (Eds.): TACAS 2019, Part I, LNCS 11427, pp. 395–412, 2019.
https://doi.org/10.1007/978-3-030-17462-0_27

is, the problem of defining scalar rewards for the transitions of a Markov decision process (MDP) so that strategies that maximize the probability to satisfy an ω-regular objective may be computed by off-the-shelf, *model-free* RL algorithms.

Omega-regular languages [28,38] provide a rich formalism to unambiguously express qualitative safety and progress requirements of MDPs [2]. A common way to describe an ω-regular language is via a formula in Linear Time Logic (LTL); other specification mechanisms include extensions of LTL, various types of automata, and monadic second-order logic. A typical requirement that is naturally expressed as an ω-regular objective prescribes that the agent should eventually control the MDP to stay within a given set of states, while at all times avoiding another set of states. In LTL this would be written (F G goal) ∧ (G ¬trap), where goal and trap are labels attached to the appropriate states, F stands for "finally," and G stands for "globally."

For verification or synthesis, an ω-regular objective is usually translated into an automaton that monitors the traces of the MDP [10]. Successful executions cause the automaton to take certain (accepting) transitions infinitely often, and ultimately avoid certain (rejecting) transitions. That is, ω-regular objectives are about the long-term behavior of an MDP; the frequency of reward collected is not what matters. A policy that guarantees no rejecting transitions and an accepting transition every ten steps, is better than a policy that promises an accepting transition at each step, but with probability 0.5 does not accept at all.

The problem of ω-regular rewards in the context of model-free RL was first tackled in 2014 by translating the objective into a deterministic Rabin automaton and deriving positive and negative rewards directly from the acceptance condition of the automaton [32]. In Sect. 3 we show that their algorithm, and the extensi of [18] may fail to find optimal strategies, and may underestimate the probability of satisfaction of the objective. In [16,17] the use of limit-deterministic Büchi automata avoids the problems connected with the use of a Rabin acceptance condition. However, as shown in Sect. 3, that approach may still produce incorrect results.

We avoid the problems inherent in the use of deterministic Rabin automata for model-free RL by resorting to *limit-deterministic* Büchi automata, which, under mild restrictions, were shown by [8,15,33] to be suitable for both qualitative and quantitative analysis of MDPs under all ω-regular objectives. The Büchi acceptance condition, which, unlike the Rabin condition, does not use rejecting transitions, allows us to constructively reduce the almost-sure satisfaction of ω-regular objectives to an almost-sure reachability problem. It is also suitable for quantitative analysis: the value of a state converges to the maximum probability of satisfaction of the objective from that state as a parameter approaches 1.

We concentrate on model-free approaches and infinitary behaviors for finite MDPs. Related problems include model-based RL [13], RL for finite-horizon objectives [22,23], and learning for efficient verification [4].

This paper is organized as follows. Section 2 recalls definitions and notations. Section 3 shows the problems that arise when the reward of the RL algorithm is derived from the acceptance condition of a deterministic Rabin automaton. In Sect. 4 we prove the main results. Finally, Sect. 5 discusses our experiments.

2 Preliminaries

2.1 Markov Decision Processes

Let $\mathcal{D}(S)$ be the set of distributions over S. A *Markov decision process* $\mathcal{M}$ is a tuple (S, A, T, AP, L) where S is a finite set of states, A is a finite set of *actions*, $T: S \times A \rightarrow \mathcal{D}(S)$ is the probabilistic transition (partial) function, AP is the set of *atomic propositions*, and $L: S \rightarrow 2^{AP}$ is the *proposition labeling function*.

For any state $s \in S$, we let $A(s)$ denote the set of actions that can be selected in state s. For states $s, s' \in S$ and $a \in A(s)$, $T(s, a)(s')$ equals $p(s'|s, a)$. A *run* of $\mathcal{M}$ is an ω-word $\langle s_0, a_1, s_1, \ldots \rangle \in S \times (A \times S)^\omega$ such that $p(s_{i+1}|s_i, a_{i+1}) > 0$ for all $i \geq 0$. A finite run is a finite such sequence. For a *run* $r = \langle s_0, a_1, s_1, \ldots \rangle$ we define the corresponding labeled run as $L(r) = \langle L(s_0), L(s_1), \ldots \rangle \in (2^{AP})^\omega$. We write $Runs^{\mathcal{M}}(FRuns^{\mathcal{M}})$ for the set of runs (finite runs) of the MDP $\mathcal{M}$ and $Runs^{\mathcal{M}}(s)(FRuns^{\mathcal{M}}(s))$ for the set of runs (finite runs) of the MDP $\mathcal{M}$ starting from state s. We write $last(r)$ for the last state of a finite run r.

A strategy in $\mathcal{M}$ is a function $\sigma: FRuns \rightarrow \mathcal{D}(A)$ such that $supp(\sigma(r)) \subseteq A(last(r))$, where $supp(d)$ denotes the support of the distribution d. Let $Runs_\sigma^{\mathcal{M}}(s)$ denote the subset of runs $Runs^{\mathcal{M}}(s)$ that correspond to strategy σ with initial state s. Let $\Sigma_\mathcal{M}$ be the set of all strategies. A strategy σ is *pure* if $\sigma(r)$ is a point distribution for all runs $r \in FRuns^{\mathcal{M}}$ and we say that σ is *stationary* if $last(r) = last(r')$ implies $\sigma(r) = \sigma(r')$ for all runs $r, r' \in FRuns^{\mathcal{M}}$. A strategy that is not pure is *mixed*. A strategy is *positional* if it is both pure and stationary.

The behavior of an MDP $\mathcal{M}$ under a strategy σ is defined on a probability space $(Runs_\sigma^{\mathcal{M}}(s), \mathcal{F}_{Runs_\sigma^{\mathcal{M}}(s)}, \Pr_\sigma^{\mathcal{M}}(s))$ over the set of infinite runs of σ with starting state s. Given a real-valued random variable over the set of infinite runs $f: Runs^{\mathcal{M}} \rightarrow \mathbb{R}$, we denote by $\mathbb{E}_\sigma^{\mathcal{M}}(s)\{f\}$ the expectation of f over the runs of $\mathcal{M}$ originating at s that follow strategy σ.

Given an MDP $\mathcal{M} = (S, A, T, AP, L)$, we define its directed underlying graph $\mathcal{G}_\mathcal{M} = (V, E)$ where $V = S$ and $E \subseteq S \times S$ is such that $(s, s') \in E$ if $T(s, a)(s') > 0$ for some $a \in A(s)$. A sub-MDP of $\mathcal{M}$ is an MDP $\mathcal{M}' = (S', A', T', AP, L')$, where $S' \subset S$, $A' \subseteq A$ is such that $A'(s) \subseteq A(s)$ for every $s \in S'$, and T' and L' are analogous to T and L when restricted to S' and A'. In particular, $\mathcal{M}'$ is closed under probabilistic transitions, i.e. for all $s \in S'$ and $a \in A'$ we have that $T(s, a)(s') > 0$ implies that $s' \in S'$. An *end-component* [10] of an MDP $\mathcal{M}$ is a sub-MDP $\mathcal{M}'$ of $\mathcal{M}$ such that $\mathcal{G}_{\mathcal{M}'}$ is strongly connected.

Theorem 1 (End-Component Properties [10]**).** *Once an end-component C of an MDP is entered, there is a strategy that visits every state-action combination in C with probability 1 and stays in C forever. Moreover, for every strategy the union of the end-components is visited with probability 1.*

A Markov chain is an MDP whose set of actions is singleton. A *bottom strongly connected component* (BSCC) of a Markov chain is any of its end-components. A BSCC is accepting if it contains an accepting transition (see below) and otherwise it is rejecting. For any MDP $\mathcal{M}$ and positional strategy σ, let $\mathcal{M}_\sigma$ be the Markov chain resulting from resolving the nondeterminism in $\mathcal{M}$ using σ.

A *rewardful* MDP is a pair $(\mathcal{M}, \rho)$, where $\mathcal{M}$ is an MDP and $\rho \colon S \times A \to \mathbb{R}$ is a reward function assigning utility to state-action pairs. A rewardful MDP $(\mathcal{M}, \rho)$ under a strategy σ determines a sequence of random rewards $\rho(X_{i-1}, Y_i)_{i \geq 1}$, where X_i and Y_i are the random variables denoting the i-th state and action, respectively. Depending upon the problem of interest, different performance objectives may be of interest. The *reachability probability* objective $Reach(T)_{\sigma}^{\mathcal{M}}(s)$ (with $T \subseteq S$) is defined as $\mathrm{Pr}_{\sigma}^{\mathcal{M}}(s)\{\langle s, a_1, s_1, \ldots \rangle \in Runs_{\sigma}^{\mathcal{M}}(s) \colon \exists i . s_i \in T\}$. For a given discount factor $\lambda \in [0, 1[$, the *discounted reward* objective $Disct(\lambda)_{\sigma}^{\mathcal{M}}(s)$ is defined as $\lim_{N \to \infty} \mathbb{E}_{\sigma}^{\mathcal{M}}(s)\left\{\sum_{1 \leq i \leq N} \lambda^{i-1} \rho(X_{i-1}, Y_i)\right\}$, while the *average reward* $Avg_{\sigma}^{\mathcal{M}}(s)$ is defined as $\limsup_{N \to \infty}(1/N)\mathbb{E}_{\sigma}^{\mathcal{M}}(s)\left\{\sum_{1 \leq i \leq N} \rho(X_{i-1}, Y_i)\right\}$. For an objective $Reward^{\mathcal{M}} \in \{Reach(T)^{\mathcal{M}}, Disct(\lambda)^{\mathcal{M}}, Avg^{\mathcal{M}}\}$ and an initial state s, we define the optimal reward $Reward_{*}^{\mathcal{M}}(s)$ as $\sup_{\sigma \in \Sigma_{\mathcal{M}}} Reward_{\sigma}^{\mathcal{M}}(s)$. A strategy $\sigma \in \Sigma_{\mathcal{M}}$ is optimal for $Reward^{\mathcal{M}}$ if $Reward_{\sigma}^{\mathcal{M}}(s) = Reward_{*}^{\mathcal{M}}(s)$ for all $s \in S$.

2.2 ω-Regular Performance Objectives

A *nondeterministic ω-automaton* is a tuple $\mathcal{A} = (\Sigma, Q, q_0, \delta, \mathsf{Acc})$, where Σ is a finite *alphabet*, Q is a finite set of *states*, $q_0 \in Q$ is the *initial state*, $\delta \colon Q \times \Sigma \to 2^Q$ is the *transition function*, and Acc is the *acceptance condition*. A *run* r of $\mathcal{A}$ on $w \in \Sigma^{\omega}$ is an ω-word $r_0, w_0, r_1, w_1, \ldots$ in $(Q \cup \Sigma)^{\omega}$ such that $r_0 = q_0$ and, for $i > 0$, $r_i \in \delta(r_{i-1}, w_{i-1})$. Each triple (r_{i-1}, w_{i-1}, r_i) is a *transition* of $\mathcal{A}$.

We consider Büchi and Rabin acceptance conditions, which depend on the transitions that occur infinitely often in a run of an automaton. We write $\inf(r)$ for the set of transitions that appear infinitely often in the run r. The *Büchi* acceptance condition defined by $F \subseteq Q \times \Sigma \times Q$ is the set of runs $\{r \in (Q \cup \Sigma)^{\omega} \colon \inf(r) \cap F \neq \emptyset\}$. A *Rabin* acceptance condition is defined in terms of k pairs of subsets of $Q \times \Sigma \times Q$, $(B_0, G_0), \ldots, (B_{k-1}, G_{k-1})$, as the set $\{r \in (Q \cup \Sigma)^{\omega} \colon \exists i < k . \inf(r) \cap B_i = \emptyset \wedge \inf(r) \cap G_i \neq \emptyset\}$. The *index* of a Rabin condition is its number of pairs.

A run r of $\mathcal{A}$ is *accepting* if $r \in \mathsf{Acc}$. The *language*, $L_{\mathcal{A}}$, of $\mathcal{A}$ (or, *accepted* by $\mathcal{A}$) is the subset of words in Σ^{ω} that have accepting runs in $\mathcal{A}$. A language is *ω-regular* if it is accepted by an ω-automaton.

Given an MDP $\mathcal{M}$ and an ω-regular objective φ given as an ω-automaton $\mathcal{A}_{\varphi} = (\Sigma, Q, q_0, \delta, \mathsf{Acc})$, we are interested in computing an optimal strategy satisfying the objective. We define the satisfaction probability of a strategy σ from initial state s as: $\mathrm{Pr}_{\sigma}^{\mathcal{M}}(s \models \varphi) = \mathrm{Pr}_{\sigma}^{\mathcal{M}}(s)\{r \in Runs_{\sigma}^{\mathcal{M}}(s) \colon L(r) \in L_{\mathcal{A}}\}$. The optimal satisfaction probability $\mathrm{Pr}_{*}^{\mathcal{M}}(s \models \varphi)$ is defined as $\sup_{\sigma \in \Sigma_{\mathcal{M}}} \mathrm{Pr}_{\sigma}^{\mathcal{M}}(s \models \varphi)$ and we say that $\sigma \in \Sigma_{\mathcal{M}}$ is an optimal strategy for φ if $\mathrm{Pr}_{*}^{\mathcal{M}}(s \models \varphi) = \mathrm{Pr}_{\sigma}^{\mathcal{M}}(s \models \varphi)$.

An automaton $\mathcal{A} = (\Sigma, Q, q_0, \delta, \mathsf{Acc})$ is *deterministic* if $|\delta(q, \sigma)| \leq 1$ for all $q \in Q$ and all $\sigma \in \Sigma$. $\mathcal{A}$ is *complete* if $|\delta(q, \sigma)| \geq 1$. A word in Σ^{ω} has exactly one run in a deterministic, complete automaton. We use common three-letter abbreviations to distinguish types of automata. The first (D or N) tells whether the automaton is deterministic; the second denotes the acceptance condition (B for Büchi and R for Rabin). The third letter (W) says that the automaton reads ω-words. For example, an NBW is a nondeterministic Büchi automaton, and a DRW is a deterministic Rabin automaton.

Every ω-regular language is accepted by some DRW and by some NBW. In contrast, there are ω-regular languages that are not accepted by any DBW. The *Rabin index* of a Rabin automaton [6, 20] is the index of its acceptance condition. The Rabin index of an ω-regular language $\mathcal{L}$ is the minimum index among those of the DRWs that accept $\mathcal{L}$. For each $n \in \mathbb{N}$ there exist ω-regular languages of Rabin index n. The languages accepted by DBWs, however, form a proper subset of the languages of index 1.

2.3   The Product MDP

Given an MDP $\mathcal{M} = (S, A, T, AP, L)$ with a designated initial state $s_0 \in S$, and a deterministic ω-automaton $\mathcal{A} = (2^{AP}, Q, q_0, \delta, \mathsf{Acc})$, the *product* $\mathcal{M} \times \mathcal{A}$ is the tuple $(S \times Q, (s_0, q_0), A, T^{\times}, \mathsf{Acc}^{\times})$. The probabilistic transition function $T^{\times} : (S \times Q) \times A \to \mathcal{D}(S \times Q)$ is such that $T^{\times}((s, q), a)((\hat{s}, \hat{q})) = T(s, a)(\hat{s})$ if $\{\hat{q}\} = \delta(q, L(s))$ and is 0 otherwise. If $\mathcal{A}$ is a DBW, Acc is defined by $F \subseteq Q \times 2^{AP} \times Q$; then $F^{\times} \subseteq (S \times Q) \times A \times (S \times Q)$ defines $\mathsf{Acc}^{\times}$ as follows: $((s, q), a, (s', q')) \in F^{\times}$ if and only if $(q, L(s), q') \in F$ and $T(s, a)(s') \neq 0$. If $\mathcal{A}$ is a DRW of index k, $\mathsf{Acc}^{\times} = \{(B_0^{\times}, G_0^{\times}), \ldots, (B_{k-1}^{\times}, G_{k-1}^{\times})\}$. To set B_i of Acc, there corresponds $B_i^{\times}$ of $\mathsf{Acc}^{\times}$ such that $((s, q), a, (s', q')) \in B_i^{\times}$ if and only if $(q, L(s), q') \in B_i$ and $T(s, a)(s') \neq 0$. Likewise for $G_i^{\times}$.

If $\mathcal{A}$ is a nondeterministic automaton, the actions in the product are enriched to identify both the actions of the original MDP and the choice of the successor state of the nondeterministic automaton.

End-components and runs are defined for products just like for MDPs. A run of $\mathcal{M} \times \mathcal{A}$ is accepting if it satisfies the product's acceptance condition. An *accepting end-component* of $\mathcal{M} \times \mathcal{A}$ is an end-component such that every run of the product MDP that eventually dwells in it is accepting.

In view of Theorem 1, satisfaction of an ω-regular objective φ by an MDP $\mathcal{M}$ can be formulated in terms of the accepting end-components of the product $\mathcal{M} \times \mathcal{A}_{\varphi}$, where $\mathcal{A}_{\varphi}$ is an automaton accepting φ. The maximum probability of satisfaction of φ by $\mathcal{M}$ is the maximum probability, over all strategies, that a run of the product $\mathcal{M} \times \mathcal{A}_{\varphi}$ eventually dwells in one of its accepting end-components.

It is customary to use DRWs instead of DBWs in the construction of the product, because the latter cannot express all ω-regular objectives. On the other hand, general NBWs are not used since causal strategies cannot optimally resolve nondeterministic choices because that requires access to future events [39].

2.4   Limit-Deterministic Büchi Automata

In spite of the large gap between DRWs and DBWs in terms of indices, even a very restricted form of nondeterminism is sufficient to make DBWs as expressive as DRWs. Broadly speaking, an LDBW behaves deterministically once it has seen an accepting transition. Formally, a *limit-deterministic* Büchi automaton

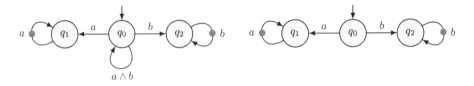

Fig. 1. Suitable (left) and unsuitable (right) LDBWs for the LTL formula $(G\,a) \vee (G\,b)$.

(LDBW) is an NBW $\mathcal{A} = (\Sigma, Q_i \cup Q_f, q_0, \delta, F)$ such that

- $Q_i \cap Q_f = \emptyset$, $F \subseteq Q_f \times \Sigma \times Q_f$;
- $|\delta(q, \sigma) \cap Q_i| \leq 1$ for all $q \in Q_i$ and $\sigma \in \Sigma$;
- $|\delta(q, \sigma)| \leq 1$ for all $q \in Q_f$ and $\sigma \in \Sigma$;
- $\delta(q, \sigma) \subseteq Q_f$ for all $q \in Q_f$ and $\sigma \in \Sigma$.

LDBWs are as expressive as general NBWs. Moreover, NBWs can be translated into LDBWs that can be used for the qualitative and quantitative analysis of MDPs [8,15,33,39]. We use the translation from [15], which uses LDBWs that consist of two parts: an initial deterministic automaton (without accepting transitions) obtained by a subset construction; and a final part produced by a breakpoint construction. They are connected by a single "guess", where the automaton guesses a singleton subset of the reachable states to start the breakpoint construction. Like in other constructions (e.g. [33]), one can compose the resulting automata with an MDP, such that the optimal control of the product defines a control on the MDP that maximizes the probability of obtaining a word from the language of the automaton. We refer to LDBWs with this property as *suitable* limit-deterministic automata (SLDBWs).

Definition 1 (Suitable LDBW). *An SLDBW $\mathcal{A}$ for property φ is an LDBW that recognizes φ and such that, for every finite MDP $\mathcal{M}$, there exists a positional strategy $\sigma \in \Sigma_{\mathcal{M} \times \mathcal{A}}$ such that the probability of satisfying the Büchi condition in the Markov chain $(\mathcal{M} \times \mathcal{A})_\sigma$ is $\mathrm{Pr}_*^{\mathcal{M}}(s \models \varphi)$.*

Although the construction of a suitable LDBW reaches back to the 80s [39], not all LDBWs are suitable. Broadly speaking, the nondeterministic decisions taken in the initial part may not depend on the future—though it may depend on the state of an MDP. The example LDBW from Fig. 1 (left) satisfies the property: it can try to delay to progress to one of the accepting states to when an end-component in an MDP is reached that always produces a's or b's, respectively. In contrast, the LDBW from Fig. 1 (right)—which recognizes the same language—will have to make the decision of seeing only a's or only b's immediately, without the option to wait for reaching an end-component. This makes it unsuitable for the use in MDPs.

Theorem 2 [8,15,33,39]. *Suitable limit-deterministic Büchi automata exist for all ω-regular languages.*

SLDBWs—and their properties described in Definition 1—are used in the qualitative and quantitative model checking algorithms in [8,15,33,39]. The accepting end-components of the product MDPs are all using only states from the final part of the SLDBW. Büchi acceptance then allows for using memoryless almost sure winning strategies in the accepting end-components, while outside of accepting end-components a memoryless strategy that maximizes the chance of reaching such an end-component can be used. The distinguishing property is the guarantee that they provide the correct probability, while using a product with a general NBW would only provide a value that cannot exceed it.

2.5   Linear Time Logic Objectives

LTL (Linear Time Logic) is a temporal logic whose formulae describe a subset of the ω-regular languages, which is often used to specify objectives in human-readable form. Translations exist from LTL to various forms of automata, including NBW, DRW, and SLDBW. Given a set of atomic propositions AP, a is an LTL formula for each $a \in AP$. Moreover, if φ and ψ are LTL formulae, so are $\neg\varphi, \varphi \vee \psi, \mathsf{X}\,\varphi, \psi\,\mathsf{U}\,\varphi$. Additional operators are defined as abbreviations: $\top \stackrel{\text{def}}{=} a \vee \neg a$; $\bot \stackrel{\text{def}}{=} \neg\top$; $\varphi \wedge \psi \stackrel{\text{def}}{=} \neg(\neg\varphi \vee \neg\psi)$; $\varphi \to \psi \stackrel{\text{def}}{=} \neg\varphi \vee \psi$; $\mathsf{F}\,\varphi \stackrel{\text{def}}{=} \top\,\mathsf{U}\,\varphi$; and $\mathsf{G}\,\varphi \stackrel{\text{def}}{=} \neg\,\mathsf{F}\,\neg\varphi$. We write $w \models \varphi$ if ω-word w over 2^{AP} satisfies LTL formula φ. The satisfaction relation is defined inductively [2,24].

2.6   Reinforcement Learning

For an MDP $\mathcal{M}$ and an objectives $Reward^{\mathcal{M}} \in \{Reach(T)^{\mathcal{M}}, Disct(\lambda)^{\mathcal{M}}, Avg^{\mathcal{M}}\}$, the optimal reward and an optimal strategy can be computed using value iteration, policy iteration, or, in polynomial time, using linear programming [12,30]. On the other hand, for ω-regular objectives (given as DRW, SLDBW, or LTL formulae) optimal satisfaction probabilities and strategies can be computed using graph-theoretic techniques (computing accepting end-component and then maximizing the probability to reach states in such components) over the product structure. However, when the MDP transition/reward structure is unknown, such techniques are not applicable.

For MDPs with unknown transition/reward structure, *reinforcement learning* [37] provides a framework to compute optimal strategies from repeated interactions with the environment. Of the two main approaches to reinforcement learning in MDPs, *model-free* approaches and *model-based* approaches the former, which is asymptotically space-efficient [36], has been demonstrated to scale well [14,25,35]. In a model-free approach such as Q-learning [31,37], the learner computes optimal strategies without explicitly estimating the transition probabilities and rewards. We focus on making it possible for model-free RL to learn a strategy that maximizes the probability of satisfying a given ω-regular objective.

3   Problem Statement and Motivation

Given MDP $\mathcal{M}$ with unknown transition structure and ω-regular objective φ, we seek a strategy that maximizes the probability that $\mathcal{M}$ satisfies φ.

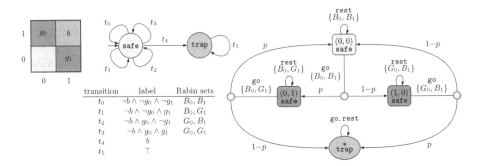

Fig. 2. A grid-world example (left), a Rabin automaton for $[(\mathsf{F\,G}\,g_0) \vee (\mathsf{F\,G}\,g_1)] \wedge \mathsf{G}\,\neg b$ (center), and product MDP (right).

To apply model-free RL algorithms to this task, one needs to define rewards that depend on the observations of the MDP and reflect the satisfaction of the objective. It is natural to use the product of the MDP and an automaton monitoring the satisfaction of the objective to assign suitable rewards to various actions chosen by the learning algorithm.

Sadigh *et al.* [32] were the first to apply model-free RL to a qualitative-version of this problem, i.e., to learn a strategy that satisfies the property with probability 1. For an MDP $\mathcal{M}$ and a DRW $\mathcal{A}_\varphi$ of index k, they formed the product MDP $\mathcal{M} \times \mathcal{A}_\varphi$ with k different "Rabin" reward functions $\rho_1, \ldots, \rho_k$. The function ρ_i corresponds to the Rabin pair $(B_i^\times, G_i^\times)$: it assigns a fixed negative reward $-R_- < 0$ to all edges in $B_i^\times$ and a fixed positive reward $R_+ > 0$ to all edges in $G_i^\times$. [32] claimed that if there exists a strategy satisfying an ω-regular objective φ with probability 1, then there exists a Rabin pair i, discount factor $\lambda_* \in [0, 1[$, and suitably high ratio R_*, such that for all $\lambda \in [\lambda_*, 1[$ and $R_-/R_+ \geq R_*$, any strategy maximizing λ-discounted reward for the MDP $(\mathcal{M} \times \mathcal{A}_\varphi, \rho_i)$ also satisfies the ω-regular objective φ with probability 1. Using Blackwell-optimality theorem [19], a paraphrase of this claim is that if there exists a strategy satisfying an ω-regular objective φ with probability 1, then there exists a Rabin pair i and suitably high ratio R_*, such that for all $R_-/R_+ \geq R_*$, any strategy maximizing expected average reward for the MDP $(\mathcal{M} \times \mathcal{A}_\varphi, \rho_i)$ also satisfies the ω-regular objective φ with probability 1. This approach has two faults, the second of which also affects approaches that replace DRWs with LDBWs [16,17].

1. We provide in Example 1 an MDP and an ω-regular objective φ with Rabin index 2, such that, although there is a strategy that satisfies the property with probability 1, optimal average strategies from any Rabin reward do not satisfy the objective with probability 1.
2. Even for an ω-regular objective with one Rabin pair (B, G) and $B=\emptyset$—i.e., one that can be specified by a DBW—we demonstrate in Example 2 that the problem of finding a strategy that satisfies the property with probability 1 may not be reduced to finding optimal average strategies.

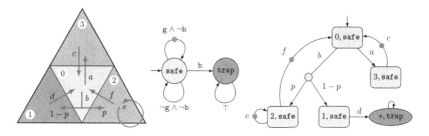

Fig. 3. A grid-world example. The arrows represent actions (left). When action b is performed, Cell 2 is reached with probability p and Cell 1 is reached with probability $1-p$, for $0 < p < 1$. Deterministic Büchi automaton for $\varphi = (\mathsf{G}\,\neg b) \wedge (\mathsf{G}\,\mathsf{F}\,g)$ (center). The dotted transition is the only accepting transition. Product MDP (right).

Example 1 (Two Rabin Pairs). Consider the MDP given as a simple grid-world example shown in Fig. 2. Each cell (state) of the MDP is labeled with the atomic propositions that are true there. In each cell, there is a choice between two actions `rest` and `go`. With action `rest` the state of the MDP does not change. However, with action `go` the MDP moves to the other cell in the same row with probability p, or to the other cell in the same column with probability $1-p$. The initial cell is $(0,0)$.

The specification is given by LTL formula $\varphi = [(\mathsf{F}\,\mathsf{G}\,g_0) \vee (\mathsf{F}\,\mathsf{G}\,g_1)] \wedge \mathsf{G}\,\neg b$. A DRW that accepts φ is shown in Fig. 2. The DRW has two accepting pairs: (B_0, G_0) and (B_1, G_1). The table besides the automaton gives, for each transition, its label and the B and G sets to which it belongs.

The optimal strategy that satisfies the objective φ with probability 1 chooses `go` in Cell $(0,0)$ and chooses `rest` subsequently. However, for both Rabin pairs, the optimal strategy for expected average reward is to maximize the probability of reaching one of the $(0,1)$, `safe` or $(1,0)$, `safe` states of the product and stay there forever. For the first accepting pair the maximum probability of satisfaction is $\frac{1}{2-p}$, while for the second pair it is $\frac{1}{1+p}$.

Example 2 (DBW to Expected Average Reward Reduction). This counterexample demonstrates that even for deterministic Büchi objectives, the problem of finding an optimal strategy satisfying an objective may not be reduced to the problem of finding an optimal average strategy. Consider the simple grid-world example of Fig. 3 with the specification $\varphi = (\mathsf{G}\,\neg b) \wedge (\mathsf{G}\,\mathsf{F}\,g)$, where atomic proposition b (blue) labels Cell 1 and atomic proposition g (green) labels Cells 2 and 3. Actions enabled in various cells and their probabilities are depicted in the figure.

The strategy from Cell 0 that chooses Action a guarantees satisfaction of φ with probability 1. An automaton with accepting transitions for φ is shown in Fig. 3; it is a DBW (or equivalently a DRW with one pair (B, G) and $B = \emptyset$).

The product MDP is shown at the bottom of Fig. 3. All states whose second component is `trap` have been merged. Notice that there is no negative reward since the set B is empty. If reward is positive and equal for all accepting transitions, and 0 for all other transitions, then when $p > 1/2$, the strategy that

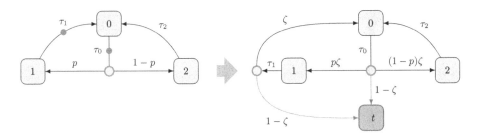

Fig. 4. Adding transitions to the target in the augmented product MDP.

maximizes expected average reward chooses Action b in the initial state and Action e from State $(2, \mathtt{safe})$. Note that, for large values of λ, the optimal expected average reward strategies are also optimal strategies for the λ-discounted reward objective. However, these strategies are not optimal for ω-regular objectives.

Example 1 shows that one cannot select a pair from a Rabin acceptance condition ahead of time. This problem can be avoided by the use of Büchi acceptance conditions. While DBWs are not sufficiently expressive, SLDBWs express all ω-regular properties and are suitable for probabilistic model checking. In the next section, we show that they are also "the ticket" for model-free reinforcement learning, because they allow us to maximize the probability of satisfying an ω-regular specification by solving a reachability probability problem that can be solved efficiently by off-the-shelf RL algorithms.

4   Model-Free RL from Omega-Regular Rewards

We now reduce the model checking problem for a given MDP and SLDBW to a reachability problem by slightly changing the structure of the product: We add a target state t that can be reached with a given probability $1 - \zeta$ whenever visiting an accepting transition of the original product MDP.

Our reduction avoids the identification of winning end-components and thus allows a natural integration to a wide range of model-free RL approaches. Thus, while the proofs do lean on standard model checking properties that are based on identifying winning end-components, they serve as a justification not to consider them when running the learning algorithm. In the rest of this section, we fix an MDP $\mathcal{M}$ and an SLDBW $\mathcal{A}$ for the ω-regular property φ.

Definition 2 (Augmented Product). *For any $\zeta \in]0,1[$, the augmented MDP $\mathcal{M}^\zeta$ is an MDP obtained from $\mathcal{M} \times \mathcal{A}$ by adding a new state t with a self-loop to the set of states of $\mathcal{M} \times \mathcal{A}$, and by making t a destination of each accepting transition τ of $\mathcal{M} \times \mathcal{A}$ with probability $1 - \zeta$. The original probabilities of all other destinations of an accepting transition τ are multiplied by ζ.*

An example of an augmented MDP is shown in Fig. 4. With a slight abuse of notation, if σ is a strategy on the augmented MDP $\mathcal{M}^\zeta$, we denote by σ also the strategy on $\mathcal{M} \times \mathcal{A}$ obtained by removing t from the domain of σ.

We let $p_s^\sigma(\zeta)$ denote the probability of reaching t in $\mathcal{M}_\sigma^\zeta$ when starting at state s. Notice that we can encode this value as the expected average reward in the following rewardful MDP $(\mathcal{M}^\zeta, \rho)$, where we set the reward function $\rho(t, a) = 1$ for all $a \in A$ and $\rho(s, a) = 0$ otherwise. For any strategy σ, the probability $p_s^\sigma(\zeta)$ and the reward of σ from s in $(\mathcal{M}^\zeta, \rho)$ are the same. We also let a_s^σ be the probability that a run that starts from s in $(\mathcal{M} \times \mathcal{A})_\sigma$ is accepting.

Lemma 1. *If σ is a positional strategy on $\mathcal{M}^\zeta$, then, for every state s of the Markov chain $(\mathcal{M} \times \mathcal{A})_\sigma$, the following holds:*

1. *if the state s is in a rejecting BSCC of $(\mathcal{M} \times \mathcal{A})_\sigma$, then $p_s^\sigma(\zeta) = 0$;*
2. *if the state s is in an accepting BSCC of $(\mathcal{M} \times \mathcal{A})_\sigma$, then $p_s^\sigma(\zeta) = 1$;*
3. *the probability $p_s^\sigma(\zeta)$ of reaching t is greater than a_s^σ; and*
4. *if $p_s^\sigma(\zeta){=}1$ then no rejecting BSCC is reachable from s in $(\mathcal{M} \times \mathcal{A})_\sigma$ and $a_s^\sigma = 1$.*

Proof. (1) holds as there are no accepting transition in a rejecting BSCC of $(\mathcal{M} \times \mathcal{A})_\sigma$, and so t cannot be reached when starting at s in $\mathcal{M}_\sigma^\zeta$. (2) holds because t (with its self-loop) is the only BSCC reachable from s in $\mathcal{M}^\zeta$. In other words, t (with its self-loop) and the rejecting BSCCs of $(\mathcal{M} \times \mathcal{A})_\sigma$ are the only BSCCs in $\mathcal{M}_\sigma^\zeta$. (3) then follows, because the same paths lead to a rejecting BSCCs in $(\mathcal{M} \times \mathcal{A})_\sigma$ and $\mathcal{M}_\sigma^\zeta$, while the probability of each such a path is no larger—and strictly smaller iff it contains an accepting transition—than in $\mathcal{M}_\sigma^\zeta$. (4) holds because, if $p_s^\sigma(\zeta) = 1$, then t (with its self-loop) is the only BSCC reachable from s in $\mathcal{M}_\sigma^\zeta$. Thus, there is no path to a rejecting BSCC in $\mathcal{M}_\sigma^\zeta$, and therefore no path to a rejecting BSCC in $(\mathcal{M} \times \mathcal{A})_\sigma$. $\square$

Lemma 2. *Let σ be a positional strategy on $\mathcal{M}^\zeta$. For every state s of $\mathcal{M}^\zeta$, we have that $\lim_{\zeta \uparrow 1} p_s^\sigma(\zeta) = a_s^\sigma$.*

Proof. As shown in Lemma 1(3) for all ζ, we have $p_s^\sigma(\zeta) \geq a_s^\sigma$. For a coarse approximation of their difference, we recall that $(\mathcal{M} \times \mathcal{A})_\sigma$ is a finite Markov chain. The expected number of transitions taken before reaching a BSCC from s in $(\mathcal{M} \times \mathcal{A})_\sigma$ is therefore a finite number. Let us refer to the—no larger—expected number of accepting transitions taken before reaching a BSCC when starting at s in $(\mathcal{M} \times \mathcal{A})_\sigma$ as f_s^σ. We claim that $a_s^\sigma \geq p_s^\sigma(\zeta) - (1 - \zeta) \cdot f_s^\sigma$. This is because the probability of reaching a rejecting BSCC in $(\mathcal{M} \times \mathcal{A})_\sigma$ is at most the probability of reaching a rejecting BSCC in $\mathcal{M}_\sigma^\zeta$, which is at most $1 - p_s^\sigma(\zeta)$, plus the probability of moving on to t from a state that is not in any BSCC in $(\mathcal{M} \times \mathcal{A})_\sigma$, which we are going to show next is at most $f_s^\sigma \cdot (1 - \zeta)$.

First, a proof by induction shows that $(1 - \zeta^k) \leq k(1 - \zeta)$ for all $k \geq 0$. Let $P_s^\sigma(\zeta, k)$ be the probability of generating a path from s with k accepting transitions before t or a node in some BSCC of $(\mathcal{M} \times \mathcal{A})_\sigma$ is reached in $\mathcal{M}_\sigma^\zeta$. The probability of seeing k accepting transitions and not reaching t is at least ζ^k. Therefore, probability of moving to t from a state not in any BSCC is at most

$$\sum_k P_s^\sigma(\zeta, k)(1 - \zeta^k) \leq \sum_k P_s^\sigma(\zeta, k) k \cdot (1 - \zeta) \leq f_s^\sigma \cdot (1 - \zeta).$$

The proof is now complete.   □

This provides us with our main theorem.

Theorem 3. *There exists a threshold $\zeta' \in]0,1[$ such that, for all $\zeta > \zeta'$ and every state s, any strategy σ that maximizes the probability $p_s^\sigma(\zeta)$ of reaching the sink in $\mathcal{M}^\zeta$ is (1) an optimal strategy in $\mathcal{M} \times \mathcal{A}$ from s and (2) induces an optimal strategy for the original MDP $\mathcal{M}$ from s with objective φ.*

Proof. We use the fact that it suffices to study positional strategies, and there are only finitely many of them. Let σ_1 be an optimal strategy of $\mathcal{M} \times \mathcal{A}$, and let σ_2 be a strategy that has the highest likelihood of creating an accepting run among all non-optimal memoryless ones. (If σ_2 does not exist, then all strategies are equally good, and it does not matter which one is chosen.) Let $\delta = a_s^{\sigma_1} - a_s^{\sigma_2}$.

Let $f_{\max} = \max_\sigma \max_s f_s^\sigma$, where σ ranges over positional strategies only, and f_s^σ is defined as in Lemma 2. We claim that it suffices to pick $\zeta' \in]0,1[$ such that $(1 - \zeta') \cdot f_{\max} < \delta$. Suppose that σ is a positional strategy that is optimal in $\mathcal{M}^\zeta$ for $\zeta > \zeta'$, but is not optimal in $\mathcal{M} \times \mathcal{A}$. We then have

$$a_s^\sigma \le p_s^\sigma(\zeta) \le a_s^\sigma + (1 - \zeta)f_s^\sigma < a_s^\sigma + \delta \le a_s^{\sigma_1} \le p_s^{\sigma_1}(\zeta),$$

where these inequalities follow, respectively, from: Lemma 1(3), the proof of Lemma 2, the definition of ζ', the assumption that σ is not optimal and the definition of δ, and the last one from Lemma 1(3). This shows that $p_s^\sigma(\zeta) < p_s^{\sigma_1}(\zeta)$, i.e., σ is not optimal in $\mathcal{M}^\zeta$; a contradiction. Therefore, any positional strategy that is optimal in $\mathcal{M}^\zeta$ for $\zeta > \zeta'$ is also optimal in $\mathcal{M} \times \mathcal{A}$.

Now, suppose that σ is a positional strategy that is optimal in $\mathcal{M} \times \mathcal{A}$. Then the probability of satisfying φ in $\mathcal{M}$ when starting at s is at least[1] a_s^σ. At the same time, if there was a strategy for which the probability of satisfying φ in $\mathcal{M}$ is $> a_s^\sigma$, then the property of $\mathcal{A}$ to be an SLDBW (Definition 1) would guarantee the existence of strategy σ' for which $a_s^{\sigma'} > a_s^\sigma$; a contradiction with the assumption that σ is optimal. Therefore any positional strategy that is optimal in $\mathcal{M} \times \mathcal{A}$ induces an optimal strategy in $\mathcal{M}$ with objective φ.   □

Corollary 1. *Due to Lemma 1(4), $\mathcal{M}$ satisfies φ almost surely if and only if the sink is almost surely reachable in $\mathcal{M}^\zeta$ for all $0 < \zeta < 1$.*

Theorem 3 leads to a very simple model-free RL algorithm. The augmented product is not built by the RL algorithm, which does not know the transition structure of the environment MDP. Instead, the observations of the MDP are used by an *interpreter* process to compute a run of the objective automaton. The interpreter also extracts the set of actions for the learner to choose from. If the automaton is not deterministic and it has not taken the one nondeterministic transition it needs to take yet, the set of actions the interpreter provides to the learner includes the choice of special "jump" actions that instruct the automaton to move to a chosen accepting component.

---

[1] This holds for all nondeterministic automata that recognize the models of φ: an accepting run establishes that the path was a model of φ.

When the automaton reports an accepting transition, the interpreter gives the learner a positive reward with probability $1 - \zeta$. When the learner actually receives a reward, the training episode terminates. Any RL algorithm that maximizes this probabilistic reward is guaranteed to converge to a policy that maximizes the probability of satisfaction of the ω-regular objective.

5   Experimental Results

We implemented the construction described in the previous sections in a tool named MUNGOJERRIE [11], which reads MDPs described in the PRISM language [21], and ω-regular automata written in the HOA format [1,9]. MUNGOJERRIE builds the augmented product $\mathcal{M}^\zeta$, provides an interface for RL algorithms akin to that of [5] and supports probabilistic model checking. Our algorithm computes, for each pair (s, a) of state and action, the maximum probability of satisfying the given objective after choosing action a from state s by using off-the-shelf, temporal difference algorithms. Not all actions with maximum probability are part of positional optimal strategies—consider a product MDP with one state and two actions, a and b, such that a enables an accepting self-loop, and b enables a non-accepting one: both state/action pairs are assigned probability 1. In b's case, because choosing b once—or a finite number of times—does not preclude acceptance. Since the probability values alone do not identify a pure optimal strategy, MUNGOJERRIE computes an optimal mixed strategy, uniformly choosing all maximum probability actions from a state.

The MDPs on which we tested our algorithms [26] are listed in Table 1. For each model, the numbers of decision states in the MDP, the automaton, and the product MDP are given. Next comes the probability of satisfaction of the objective for the strategy chosen by the RL algorithm as computed by the model checker (which has full access to the MDP). This is followed by the estimate of the probability of satisfaction of the objective computed by the RL algorithm and the time taken by learning. The last six columns report values of the hyperparameters when they deviate from the default values: ζ controls the probability of reward, ϵ is the exploration rate, α is the learning rate, and tol is the tolerance for probabilities to be considered different. Finally, ep-l controls the episode length (it is the maximum allowed length of a path in the MDP that does contain an accepting edge) and ep-n is the number of episodes. All performance data are the averages of three trials with Q-learning. Rewards are undiscounted, so that the value of a state-action pair computed by Q-learning is a direct estimate of the probability of satisfaction of the objective from that state when taking that action.

Models twoPairs and riskReward are from Examples 1 and 2, respectively. Model deferred is discussed later. Models grid5x5 and trafficNtk are from [32]. The three "windy" MDPs are taken from [37]. The "frozen" examples are from [27]. Some ω-regular objectives are simple reachability requirements (e.g., frozenSmall and frozenLarge). The objective for the othergrid models is to collect three types of coupons, while incurring at most one of two types of penalties. In doublegrid two agents simultaneously move across the grid.

Table 1. Q-learning results. The default values of the learner hyperparameters are: $\zeta = 0.99$, $\epsilon = 0.1$, $\alpha = 0.1$, tol= 0.01, ep-l= 30, and ep-n= 20000. Times are in seconds.

Name	states	aut.	prod.	prob.	est.	time	ζ	ϵ	α	tol	ep-l	ep-n
twoPairs	4	4	16	1	1	0.26						
riskReward	4	2	8	1	1	1.47						
deferred	41	1	41	1	1	1.01						
grid5x5	25	3	75	1	1	10.82		0.01	0.2		400	30k
trafficNtk	122	13	462	1	1	2.89						
windy	123	2	240	1	1	12.35	0.95	0.001	0.05	0	900	200k
windyKing	130	2	256	1	1	14.34	0.95	0.02	0.2	0	300	120k
windyStoch	130	2	260	1	1	47.70	0.95	0.02	0.2	0	300	200k
frozenSmall	16	3	48	0.823	0.83	0.51			0.05	0	200	
frozenLarge	64	3	192	1	1	1.81			0.05	0	700	
othergrid6	36	25	352	1	1	10.80				0	300	75k
othergrid20	400	25	3601	1	1	78.00	0.9999	0.07	0.2	0	5k	
othergrid40	1600	25	14401	1	0.99	87.90	0.9999	0.05	0.2	0	14k	25k
doublegrid8	4096	3	12287	1	1	45.50				0	3k	100k
doublegrid12	20736	3	62207	1	1	717.6				0	20k	300k
slalom	36	5	84	1	1	0.98						
rps1	121	2	130	0.768	0.76	5.21		0.12	0.006	0		500k
dpenny	52	2	65	0.5	0.5	1.99		0.001	0.2	0	50	120k
devious	11	1	11	1	1	0.81						
arbiter2	32	3	72	1	1	5.16			0.5	0.02	200	
knuthYao	13	3	39	1	1	0.31					100	
threeWayDuel	10	3	13	0.397	0.42	0.08						
mutual4-14	27600	128	384386	1	1	2.74						
mutual4-15	27600	527	780504	1	1	3.61						

The objective for `slalom` is given by the LTL formula $G(p \to X\,G\,\neg q) \wedge G(q \to X\,G\,\neg p)$. For model `rps1` the strategy found by RL is (slightly) suboptimal. The difference in probability of 0.01 is explained by the existence of many strategies of nearly identical values. Model `mutual` [7,15,34] describes the mutual exclusion protocol of Pnueli and Zuck [29]. Though large, this model is easy for learning.

Figure 5 illustrates how increasing the parameter ζ makes the RL algorithm less sensitive to the presence of transient (not in an end-component) accepting transitions. Model `deferred` consists of two chains of states: one, which the agent choses with action a, has accepting transitions throughout, but leads to an end-component that is not accepting. The other chain, selected with action b, leads to an accepting end-component, but has no other accepting transitions. There are no other decisions in the model; hence only two strategies are possible, which we denote by a and b, depending on the action chosen.

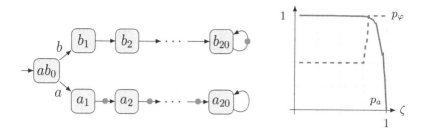

Fig. 5. Model `deferred` and effect of ζ on it.

The curve labeled p_a in Fig. 5 gives the probability of satisfaction under strategy a of the MDP's objective as a function of ζ as computed by Q-learning. The number of episodes is kept fixed at $20,000$ and each episode has length 80. Each data point is the average of five experiments for the same value of ζ.

For values of ζ close to 0, the chance is high that the sink is reached directly from a transient state. Consequently, Q-learning considers strategies a and b equally good. For this reason, the probability of satisfaction of the objective, p_φ, according to the strategy that mixes a and b, is computed by MUNGOJERRIE's model checker as 0.5. As ζ approaches 1, the importance of transient accepting transitions decreases, until the probability computed for strategy a is no longer considered to be approximately the same as the probability of strategy b. When that happens, p_φ abruptly goes from 0.5 to its true value of 1, because the pure strategy b is selected. The value of p_a continues to decline for larger values of ζ until it reaches its true value of 0 for $\zeta = 0.9999$. Probability p_b, not shown in the graph, is 1 throughout.

The change in value of p_φ does not contradict Theorem 3, which says that $p_b = 1 > p_a$ for all values of ζ. In practice a high value of ζ may be needed to reliably distinguish between transient and recurrent accepting transitions in numerical computation. Besides, Theorem 3 suggests that even in the almost-sure case there is a meaningful path to the target strategy where the likelihood of satisfying φ can be expected to grow. This is important, as it comes with the promise of a generally increasing quality of intermediate strategies.

6 Conclusion

We have reduced the problem of maximizing the satisfaction of an ω-regular objective in a MDP to reachability on a product graph augmented with a sink state. This change is so simple and elegant that it may surprise that it has not been used before. But the reason for this is equally simple: it does not help in a model checking context, as it does not remove any analysis step there. In a reinforcement learning context, however, it simplifies our task significantly. In previous attempts to use suitable LDBW [4], the complex part of the model checking problem—identifying the accepting end-components—is still present. Only after this step, which is expensive and requires knowledge of the structure of the underlying MDP, can these methods reduce the search for optimal satisfaction to the problem of maximizing the chance to reach those components. Our reduction avoids the identification of accepting end-components entirely and thus allows a natural integration with a wide range of model-free RL approaches.

References

1. Babiak, T., et al.: The Hanoi omega-automata format. In: Kroening, D., Păsăreanu, C.S. (eds.) CAV 2015. LNCS, vol. 9206, pp. 479–486. Springer, Cham (2015). https://doi.org/10.1007/978-3-319-21690-4_31
2. Baier, C., Katoen, J.-P.: Principles of Model Checking. MIT Press, Cambridge (2008)
3. Bertsekas, D.P., Tsitsiklis, J.N.: Neuro-Dynamic Programming. Athena Scientific, Belmont (1996)
4. Brázdil, T., et al.: Verification of Markov decision processes using learning algorithms. In: Cassez, F., Raskin, J.-F. (eds.) ATVA 2014. LNCS, vol. 8837, pp. 98–114. Springer, Cham (2014). https://doi.org/10.1007/978-3-319-11936-6_8
5. Brockman, G., et al.: OpenAI Gym. CoRR, abs/1606.01540 (2016)
6. Carton, O., Maceiras, R.: Computing the Rabin index of a parity automaton. Theoret. Inf. Appl. **33**, 495–505 (1999)
7. Chatterjee, K., Gaiser, A., Křetínský, J.: Automata with generalized Rabin pairs for probabilistic model checking and LTL synthesis. In: Sharygina, N., Veith, H. (eds.) CAV 2013. LNCS, vol. 8044, pp. 559–575. Springer, Heidelberg (2013). https://doi.org/10.1007/978-3-642-39799-8_37
8. Courcoubetis, C., Yannakakis, M.: The complexity of probabilistic verification. J. ACM **42**(4), 857–907 (1995)
9. cpphoafparser (2016). https://automata.tools/hoa/cpphoafparser. Accessesd 05 Sept 2018
10. de Alfaro, L.: Formal Verification of Probabilistic Systems. Ph.D. thesis, Stanford University (1998)
11. Eliot, T.S.: Old Possum's Book of Practical Cats. Harcourt Brace Jovanovich, San Diego (1939)
12. Feinberg, E.A., Shwartz, A. (eds.): Handbook of Markov Decision Processes. Springer, New York (2002). https://doi.org/10.1007/978-1-4615-0805-2
13. Fu, J., Topcu, U.: Probably approximately correct MDP learning and control with temporal logic constraints. In: Robotics: Science and Systems, July 2014
14. Guez, A., et al.: An investigation of model-free planning. CoRR, abs/1901.03559 (2019)
15. Hahn, E.M., Li, G., Schewe, S., Turrini, A., Zhang, L.: Lazy probabilistic model checking without determinisation. In: Concurrency Theory (CONCUR), pp. 354–367 (2015)
16. Hasanbeig, M., Abate, A., Kroening, D.: Logically-correct reinforcement learning. CoRR, abs/1801.08099v1, January 2018
17. Hasanbeig, M., Abate, A., Kroening, D.: Certified reinforcement learning with logic guidance. arXiv e-prints, arXiv:1902.00778, February 2019
18. Hiromoto, M., Ushio, T.: Learning an optimal control policy for a Markov decision process under linear temporal logic specifications. In: Symposium Series on Computational Intelligence, pp. 548–555, December 2015

19. Hordijk, A., Yushkevich, A.A.: Blackwell optimality. In: Feinberg, E.A., Shwartz, A. (eds.) Handbook of Markov Decision Processes: Methods and Applications, pp. 231–267. Springer, Boston (2002). https://doi.org/10.1007/978-1-4615-0805-2_8

20. Krishnan, S.C., Puri, A., Brayton, R.K., Varaiya, P.P.: The Rabin index and chain automata, with applications to automata and games. In: Wolper, P. (ed.) CAV 1995. LNCS, vol. 939, pp. 253–266. Springer, Heidelberg (1995). https://doi.org/10.1007/3-540-60045-0_55

21. Kwiatkowska, M., Norman, G., Parker, D.: PRISM 4.0: verification of probabilistic real-time systems. In: Gopalakrishnan, G., Qadeer, S. (eds.) CAV 2011. LNCS, vol. 6806, pp. 585–591. Springer, Heidelberg (2011). https://doi.org/10.1007/978-3-642-22110-1_47

22. Lahijanian, M., Andersson, S.B., Belta, C.: Temporal logic motion planning and control with probabilistic satisfaction guarantees. IEEE Trans. Robot. **28**(2), 396–409 (2012)

23. Li, X., Vasile, C.I., Belta, C.: Reinforcement learning with temporal logic rewards. In: International Conference on Intelligent Robots and Systesm (IROS), pp. 3834–3839 (2017)

24. Manna, Z., Pnueli, A.: The Temporal Logic of Reactive and Concurrent Systems *Specification*. Springer, New York (1991). https://doi.org/10.1007/978-1-4612-0931-7

25. Mnih, V., et al.: Human-level control through reinforcement learning. Nature **518**, 529–533 (2015)

26. Mungojerrie ω-regular reinforcement learning benchmarks (2019). https://plv.colorado.edu/omega-regular-rl-benchmarks-2019

27. OpenAI Gym (2018). https://gym.openai.com. Accessed 05 Sept 2018

28. Perrin, D., Pin, J.É.: Infinite Words: Automata, Semigroups, Logic and Games. Elsevier, Amsterdam (2004)

29. Pnueli, A., Zuck, L.: Verification of multiprocess probabilistic protocols. Distrib. Comput. **1**, 53–72 (1986)

30. Puterman, M.L.: Markov Decision Processes: Discrete Stochastic Dynamic Programming. Wiley, New York (1994)

31. Riedmiller, M.: Neural fitted Q iteration – first experiences with a data efficient neural reinforcement learning method. In: Gama, J., Camacho, R., Brazdil, P.B., Jorge, A.M., Torgo, L. (eds.) ECML 2005. LNCS (LNAI), vol. 3720, pp. 317–328. Springer, Heidelberg (2005). https://doi.org/10.1007/11564096_32

32. Sadigh, D., Kim, E., Coogan, S., Sastry, S.S., Seshia, S.A.: A learning based approach to control synthesis of Markov decision processes for linear temporal logic specifications. In: IEEE Conference on Decision and Control (CDC), pp. 1091–1096, December 2014

33. Sickert, S., Esparza, J., Jaax, S., Křetínský, J.: Limit-deterministic Büchi automata for linear temporal logic. In: Chaudhuri, S., Farzan, A. (eds.) CAV 2016. LNCS, vol. 9780, pp. 312–332. Springer, Cham (2016). https://doi.org/10.1007/978-3-319-41540-6_17

34. Sickert, S., Křetínský, J.: MoChiBA: probabilistic LTL model checking using limit-deterministic Büchi automata. In: Artho, C., Legay, A., Peled, D. (eds.) ATVA 2016. LNCS, vol. 9938, pp. 130–137. Springer, Cham (2016). https://doi.org/10.1007/978-3-319-46520-3_9

35. Silver, D., et al.: Mastering the game of go with deep neural networks and tree search. Nature **529**, 484–489 (2016)

36. Strehl, A.L., Li, L., Wiewiora, E., Langford, J., Littman, M.L.: PAC model-free reinforcement learning. In: International Conference on Machine Learning ICML, pp. 881–888 (2006)
37. Sutton, R.S., Barto, A.G.: Reinforcement Learning: An Introduction, 2nd edn. MIT Press, Cambridge (2018)
38. Thomas, W.: Automata on infinite objects. In: Handbook of Theoretical Computer Science, pp. 133–191. The MIT Press/Elsevier, Cambridge (1990)
39. Vardi, M.Y.: Automatic verification of probabilistic concurrent finite state programs. In: Foundations of Computer Science, pp. 327–338 (1985)
40. Wiering, M., van Otterlo, M. (eds.): Reinforcement Learning: State of the Art. Springer, Heidelberg (2012). https://doi.org/10.1007/978-3-642-27645-3

Verifiably Safe Off-Model Reinforcement Learning

Nathan Fulton[✉] and André Platzer

Computer Science Department, Carnegie Mellon University,
Pittsburgh, USA
{nathanfu,aplatzer}@cs.cmu.edu

Abstract. The desire to use reinforcement learning in safety-critical settings has inspired a recent interest in formal methods for learning algorithms. Existing formal methods for learning and optimization primarily consider the problem of constrained learning or constrained optimization. Given a single correct model and associated safety constraint, these approaches guarantee efficient learning while provably avoiding behaviors outside the safety constraint. Acting well given an accurate environmental model is an important pre-requisite for safe learning, but is ultimately insufficient for systems that operate in complex heterogeneous environments. This paper introduces verification-preserving model updates, the first approach toward obtaining formal safety guarantees for reinforcement learning in settings where multiple possible environmental models must be taken into account. Through a combination of inductive data and deductive proving with design-time model updates and runtime model falsification, we provide a first approach toward obtaining formal safety proofs for autonomous systems acting in heterogeneous environments.

1 Introduction

The desire to use reinforcement learning in safety-critical settings has inspired several recent approaches toward obtaining formal safety guarantees for learning algorithms. Formal methods are particularly desirable in settings such as self-driving cars, where testing alone cannot guarantee safety [22]. Recent examples of work on formal methods for reinforcement learning algorithms include justified speculative control [14], shielding [3], logically constrained learning [17], and constrained Bayesian optimization [16]. Each of these approaches provide formal safety guarantees for reinforcement learning and/or optimization algorithms by stating assumptions and specifications in a formal logic, generating monitoring conditions based upon specifications and environmental assumptions, and then

This research was sponsored by the Defense Advanced Research Projects Agency (DARPA) under grant number FA8750-18-C-0092. The views and conclusions contained in this document are those of the author and should not be interpreted as representing the official policies, either expressed or implied, of any sponsoring institution, the U.S. government or any other entity.

T. Vojnar and L. Zhang (Eds.): TACAS 2019, Part I, LNCS 11427, pp. 413–430, 2019.
https://doi.org/10.1007/978-3-030-17462-0_28

leveraging these monitoring conditions to constrain the learning/optimization process to a known-safe subset of the state space.

Existing formal methods for learning and optimization consider the problem of constrained learning or constrained optimization [3,14,16,17]. They address the question: assuming we have a single accurate environmental model with a given specification, how can we learn an efficient control policy respecting this specification?

Correctness proofs for control software in a single well-modeled environment are necessary but not sufficient for ensuring that reinforcement learning algorithms behave safely. Modern cyber-physical systems must perform a large number of subtasks in many different environments and must safely cope with situations that are not anticipated by system designers. These design goals motivate the use of reinforcement learning in safety-critical systems. Although some formal methods suggest ways in which formal constraints might be used to inform control even when modeling assumptions are violated [14], none of these approaches provide formal safety guarantees when environmental modeling assumptions are violated.

Holistic approaches toward safe reinforcement learning should provide formal guarantees even when a single, a priori model is not known at design time. We call this problem *verifiably safe off-model learning*. In this paper we introduce a first approach toward obtaining formal safety proofs for off-model learning. Our approach consists of two components: (1) a model synthesis phase that constructs a set of candidate models together with provably correct control software, and (2) a runtime model identification process that selects between available models at runtime in a way that preserves the safety guarantees of all candidate models.

Model update learning is initialized with a set of models. These models consist of a set of differential equations that model the environment, a control program for selecting actuator inputs, a safety property, and a formal proof that the control program constrains the overall system dynamics in a way that correctly ensures the safety property is never violated.

Instead of requiring the existence of a single accurate initial model, we introduce *model updates* as syntactic modifications of the differential equations and control logic of the model. We call a model update *verification-preserving* if there is a corresponding modification to the formal proof establishing that the modified control program continues to constrain the system of differential equations in a way that preserves the original model's safety properties.

Verification-preserving model updates are inspired by the fact that different parts of a model serve different roles. The continuous portion of a model is often an assumption about how the world behaves, and the discrete portion of a model is derived from these equations and the safety property. For this reason, many of our updates inductively synthesize ODEs (i.e., in response to data from previous executions of the system) and then deductively synthesize control logic from the resulting ODEs and the safety objective.

Our contributions enabling verifiably safe off-model learning include: (**1**) A set of verification preserving model updates (VPMUs) that systematically update differential equations, control software, and safety proofs in a way that preserves verification guarantees while taking into account possible deviations between an initial model and future system behavior. (*2*) A reinforcement learning algorithm, called model update learning (μlearning), that explains how to transfer safety proofs for a set of feasible models to a learned policy. The learned policy will actively attempt to falsify models at runtime in order to reduce the safety constraints on actions. These contributions are evaluated on a set of hybrid systems control tasks. Our approach uses a combination of program repair, system identification, offline theorem proving, and model monitors to obtain formal safety guarantees for systems in which a single accurate model is not known at design time. This paper fully develops an approach based on an idea that was first presented in an invited vision paper on Safe AI for CPS by the authors [13].

The approach described in this paper is model-based but does not assume that a single correct model is known at design time. Model update learning allows for the possibility that all we can know at design time is that there are many feasible models, one of which might be accurate. Verification-preserving model updates then explain how a combination of data and theorem proving can be used at design time to enrich the set of feasible models.

We believe there is a rich space of approaches toward safe learning in-between model-free reinforcement learning (where formal safety guarantees are unavailable) and traditional model-based learning that assumes the existence of a single ideal model. This paper provides a first example of such an approach by leveraging inductive data and deductive proving at both design time and runtime.

The remainder of this paper is organized as follows. We first review the logical foundations underpinning our approach. We then introduce verification-preserving model updates and discuss how experimental data may be used to construct a set of explanatory models for the data. After discussing several model updates, we introduce the μlearning algorithm that selects between models at runtime. Finally, we discuss case studies that validate both aspects of our approach. We close with a discussion of related work.

2   Background

This section reviews existing approaches toward safe on-model learning and discusses the fitness of each approach for obtaining guarantees about off-model learning. We then introduce the specification language and logic used throughout the rest of this paper.

Alshiekh et al. and Hasanbeig et al. propose approaches toward safe reinforcement learning based on Linear Temporal Logic [3,17]. Alshiekh et al. synthesize monitoring conditions based upon a safety specification and an environmental abstraction. In this formalism, the goal of off-model learning is to systematically expand the environmental abstraction based upon both design-time insights about how the system's behavior might change over time and based upon observed data at runtime. Jansen et al. extend the approach of Alshiekh et al. by observing that constraints should adapt whenever runtime data suggests that a safety constraint is too restrictive to allow progress toward an over-arching objective [20]. Herbert et al. address the problem of safe motion planning by using offline reachability analysis of pursuit-evasion games to pre-compute an overapproximate monitoring condition that then constrains online planners [9,19].

The above-mentioned approaches have an implicit or explicit environmental model. Even when these environmental models are accurate, reinforcement learning is still necessary because these models focus exclusively on safety and are often nondeterministic. Resolving this nondeterminism in a way that is not only safe but is also effective at achieving other high-level objectives is a task that is well-suited to reinforcement learning.

We are interested in how to provide formal safety guarantees even when there is not a single accurate model available at design time. Achieving this goal requires two novel contributions. We must first find a way to generate a robust set of feasible models given some combination of an initial model and data on previous runs of the system (because formal safety guarantees are stated with respect to a model). Given such a set of feasible models, we must then learn how to safely identify which model is most accurate so that the system is not over-constrained at runtime.

To achieve these goals, we build on the safe learning work for a single model by Fulton et al. [14]. We choose this approach as a basis for verifiably safe learning because we are interested in safety-critical systems that combine discrete and continuous dynamics, because we would like to produce explainable models of system dynamics (e.g., systems of differential equations as opposed to large state machines), and, most importantly, because our approach requires the ability to systematically modify a model together with that model's safety proof.

Following [14], we recall Differential Dynamic Logic [26,27], a logic for verifying properties about safety-critical hybrid systems control software, the ModelPlex synthesis algorithm in this logic [25], and the KeYmaera X theorem prover [12] that will allow us to systematically modify models and proofs together.

Hybrid (dynamical) systems [4,27] are mathematical models that incorporate both discrete and continuous dynamics. Hybrid systems are excellent models for safety-critical control tasks that combine the discrete dynamics of control software with the continuous motion of a physical system such as an aircraft, train, or automobile. Hybrid programs [26–28] are a programming language for hybrid systems. The syntax and informal semantics of hybrid programs is summarized in Table 1. The continuous evolution program is a continuous evolution along the differential equation system $x_i' = \theta_i$ for an arbitrary duration within the region described by formula F.

Hybrid Program Semantics. The semantics of the hybrid programs described by Table 1 are given in terms of transitions between states [27,28], where a state s assigns a real number $s(x)$ to each variable x. We use $s[\![t]\!]$ to refer to the value of a term t in a state s. The semantics of a program α, written $[\![\alpha]\!]$, is the set of pairs (s_1, s_2) for which state s_2 is reachable by running α from state s_1. For example, $[\![x := t_1 \cup x := t_2]\!]$ is:

$$\{(s_1, s_2) \mid s_1 = s_2 \text{ except } s_2(x) = s_1[\![t_1]\!]\} \ \cup \ \{(s_1, s_2) \mid s_1 = s_2 \text{ except } s_2(x) = s_1[\![t_2]\!]\}$$

Table 1. Hybrid programs

Program statement	Meaning
$\alpha; \beta$	Sequentially composes β after α.
$\alpha \cup \beta$	Executes either α or β nondeterministically.
α^*	Repeats α zero or more times nondeterministically.
$x := \theta$	Evaluates term θ and assigns result to variable x.
$x := *$	Nondeterministically assign arbitrary real value to x.
$\{x'_1 = \theta_1, ..., x'_n = \theta_n \& F\}$	Continuous evolution for any duration within domain F.
$?F$	Aborts if formula F is not true.

for a hybrid program α and state s where $[\![\alpha]\!](s)$ is set of all states t such that $(s, t) \in [\![\alpha]\!]$.

Differential Dynamic Logic. Differential dynamic logic ($d\mathcal{L}$) [26–28] is the dynamic logic of hybrid programs. The logic associates with each hybrid program α modal operators $[\alpha]$ and $\langle\alpha\rangle$, which express state reachability properties of α. The formula $[\alpha]\phi$ states that the formula ϕ is true in *all* states reachable by the hybrid program α, and the formula $\langle\alpha\rangle\phi$ expresses that the formula ϕ is true after *some* execution of α. The $d\mathcal{L}$ formulas are generated by the grammar

$$\phi ::= \ \theta_1 \smile \theta_2 \mid \neg\phi \mid \phi \wedge \psi \mid \phi \vee \psi \mid \phi \rightarrow \psi \mid \forall x\, \phi \mid \exists x\, \phi \mid [\alpha]\phi \mid \langle\alpha\rangle\phi$$

where θ_i are arithmetic expressions over the reals, ϕ and ψ are formulas, α ranges over hybrid programs, and $\smile$ is a comparison operator $=, \neq, \geq, >, \leq, <$. The quantifiers quantify over the reals. We denote by $s \models \phi$ the fact that formula ϕ is true in state s; e.g., we denote by $s \models [\alpha]\phi$ the fact that $(s, t) \in [\![\alpha]\!]$ implies $t \models \phi$ for all states t. Similarly, $\vdash \phi$ denotes the fact that ϕ has a proof in $d\mathcal{L}$. When ϕ is true in every state (i.e., valid) we simply write $\models \phi$.

Example 1 (Safety specification for straight-line car model).

$$\underbrace{v \geq 0 \wedge A > 0}_{\text{initial condition}} \rightarrow [(\underbrace{(a := A \cup a := 0)}_{\text{ctrl}} ; \underbrace{\{p' = v, v' = a\}}_{\text{plant}})^*] \underbrace{v \geq 0}_{\text{post cond.}}$$

This formula states that if a car begins with a non-negative velocity, then it will also always have a non-negative velocity after repeatedly choosing new acceleration (A or 0), or coasting and moving for a nondeterministic period of time.

Throughout this paper, we will refer to sets of actions. An **action** is simply the effect of a loop-free deterministic discrete program without tests. For example, the programs $a := A$ and $a := 0$ are the actions available in the above program. Notice that **actions** can be equivalently thought of as mappings from variables to terms. We use the term action to refer to both the mappings themselves and the hybrid programs whose semantics correspond to these mappings. For an action u, we write $u(s)$ to mean the effect of taking action u in state s; i.e., the unique state t such that $(s, t) \in [\![u]\!]$.

ModelPlex. Safe off-model learning requires noticing when a system deviates from model assumptions. Therefore, our approach depends upon the ability to check, at runtime, whether the current state of the system can be explained by a hybrid program.

The KeYmaera X theorem prover implements the ModelPlex algorithm [25]. For a given d$\mathcal{L}$ specification ModelPlex constructs a correctness proof for monitoring conditions expressed as a formula of quantifier-free real arithmetic. The monitoring condition is then used to extract provably correct monitors that check whether observed transitions comport with modeling assumptions. ModelPlex can produce monitors that enforce models of control programs as well as monitors that check whether the model's ODEs comport with observed state transitions.

ModelPlex *controller monitors* are boolean functions that return false if the controller portion of a hybrid systems model has been violated. A *controller monitor* for a model $\{\texttt{ctrl};\texttt{plant}\}^*$ is a function $\texttt{cm} : \mathcal{S} \times \mathcal{A} \to \mathbb{B}$ from states $\mathcal{S}$ and actions $\mathcal{A}$ to booleans $\mathbb{B}$ such that if $\texttt{cm}(s,a)$ then $(s, a(s)) \in [\![\texttt{ctrl}]\!]$. We sometimes also abuse notation by using controller monitors as an implicit filter on $\mathcal{A}$; i.e., $\texttt{cm} : \mathcal{S} \to \mathcal{A}$ such that $a \in \texttt{cm}(s)$ iff $\texttt{cm}(s,a)$ is true.

ModelPlex also produces *model monitors*, which check whether the model is accurate. A *model monitor* for a safety specification $\phi \to [\alpha^*]\psi$ is a function $\texttt{mm} : \mathcal{S} \times \mathcal{S} \to \mathbb{B}$ such that $(s_0, s) \in [\![\alpha]\!]$ if $\texttt{mm}(s_0, s)$. For the sake of brevity, we also define $\texttt{mm} : \mathcal{S} \times \mathcal{A} \times \mathcal{S} \to \mathbb{B}$ as the model monitor applied after taking an action $(a \in A)$ in a state and then following the plant in a model of form $\alpha \equiv \texttt{ctrl};\texttt{plant}$. Notice that if the model has this canonical form and if if $\texttt{mm}(s, a, a(s))$ for an action a, then $\texttt{cm}(s, a(s))$.

The KeYmaera X system is a theorem prover [12] that provides a language called Bellerophon for scripting proofs of d$\mathcal{L}$ formulas [11]. Bellerophon programs, called tactics, construct proofs of d$\mathcal{L}$ formulas. This paper proposes an approach toward updating models in a way that preserves safety proofs. Our approach simultaneously changes a system of differential equations, control software expressed as a discrete loop-free program, and the formal proof that the controller properly selects actuator values such that desired safety constraints are preserved throughout the flow of a system of differential equations.

3   Verification-Preserving Model Updates

A *verification-preserving model update* (VPMU) is a transformation of a hybrid program accompanied by a proof that the transformation preserves key safety properties [13]. VPMUs capture situations in which a model and/or a set of data can be updated in a way that captures possible runtime behaviors which are not captured by an existing model.

Definition 1 (VPMU). *A* verification-preserving model update *is a mapping which takes as input an initial* d$\mathcal{L}$ *formula* φ *with an associated Bellerophon tactic* e *of* φ, *and produces as output a new* d$\mathcal{L}$ *formula* ψ *and a new Bellerophon tactic* f *such that* f *is a proof of* ψ.

Before discussing our VPMU library, we consider how a set of feasible models computed using VPMUs can be used to provide verified safety guarantees for a family of reinforcement learning algorithms. The primary challenge is to maintain safety with respect to all feasible models while also avoiding overly conservative monitoring constraints. We address this challenge by falsifying some of these models at runtime.

4   Verifiably Safe RL with Multiple Models

VPMUs may be applied whenever system designers can characterize likely ways in which an existing model will deviate from reality. Although applying model updates at runtime is possible and sometimes makes sense, model updates are easiest to apply at design time because of the computational overhead of computing both model updates and corresponding proof updates. This section introduces model update learning, which explains how to take a set of models generated using VPMUs at design time to provide safety guarantees at runtime.

Model update learning is based on a simple idea: begin with a set of *feasible models* and act safely with respect to all feasible models. Whenever a model does not comport with observed dynamics, the model becomes infeasible and is therefore removed from the set of feasible models. We introduce two variations of μlearning: a basic algorithm that chooses actions without considering the underlying action space, and an algorithm that prioritizes actions that rule out feasible models (adding an *eliminate* choice to the classical explore/exploit tradeoff [32]).

All μlearning algorithms use monitored models; i.e., models equipped with ModelPlex controller monitors and model monitors.

Definition 2 (Monitored   Model). *A   **monitored   model**   is   a   tuple (m, cm, mm) such that m is a d$\mathcal{L}$ formula of the form*

$$init \rightarrow [\{ctrl; plant\}^*]safe$$

where ctrl *is a loop-free program, the entire formula m contains exactly one modality, and the formulas cm and mm are the control monitor and model monitor corresponding to m, as defined in Sect. 2.*

Monitored models may have a continuous action space because of both tests and the nondeterministic assignment operator. We sometimes introduce additional assumptions on the structure of the monitored models. A monitored model over a finite action space is a monitored model where $\{t : (s, t) \in [\![ctrl]\!]\}$ is finite for all $s \in S$. A time-aware monitored model is a monitored model whose differential equations contain a local clock which is reset at each control step.

Model update learning, or μlearning, leverages verification-preserving model updates to maintain safety while selecting an appropriate environmental model. We now state and prove key safety properties about the μlearning algorithm.

Definition 3 (μlearning Process). *A learning process P_M for a finite set of monitored models M is defined as a tuple of countable sequences $(\boldsymbol{U}, \boldsymbol{S}, \boldsymbol{Mon})$ where $\boldsymbol{U}$ are actions in a finite set of actions $\mathcal{A}$ (i.e., mappings from variables to values), elements of the sequence $\boldsymbol{S}$ are states, and $\boldsymbol{Mon}$ are monitored models with $\boldsymbol{Mon}_0 = M$. Let $specOK_m(\boldsymbol{U}, \boldsymbol{S}, i) \equiv mm(\boldsymbol{S}_{i-1}, \boldsymbol{U}_{i-1}, \boldsymbol{S}_i) \rightarrow cm(\boldsymbol{S}_i, \boldsymbol{U}_i)$ where cm and mm are the monitors corresponding to the model m. Let $specOK$ always return true for $i = 0$.*

A μlearning process is a learning process satisfying the following additional conditions: (a) action availability: in each state $\boldsymbol{S}_i$ there is at least one action u such that for all $m \in \boldsymbol{Mon}_i$, $u \in specOK_m(\boldsymbol{U}, \boldsymbol{S}, i)$, (b) actions are safe for all feasible models: $\boldsymbol{U}_{i+1} \in \{u \in A \mid \forall(m, cm, mm) \in \boldsymbol{Mon}_i, cm(\boldsymbol{S}_i, u)\}$, (c) feasible models remain in the feasible set: if $(\varphi, cm, mm) \in \boldsymbol{Mon}_i$ and $mm(\boldsymbol{S}_i, \boldsymbol{U}_i, \boldsymbol{S}_{i+1})$ then $(\varphi, cm, mm) \in \boldsymbol{Mon}_{i+1}$.

Note that μlearning processes are defined over an environment $E : \mathcal{A} \times \mathcal{S} \rightarrow \mathcal{S}$ that determines the sequences $\mathbf{U}$ and $\mathbf{S}^1$, so that $\mathbf{S}_{i+1} = E(\mathbf{U}_i, \mathbf{S}_i)$. In our algorithms, the set $\boldsymbol{Mon}_i$ never retains elements that are inconsistent with the observed dynamics at the previous state. We refer to the set of models in $\boldsymbol{Mon}_i$ as the set of feasible models for the ith state in a μlearning process.

Notice that the safe actions constraint is not effectively checkable without extra assumptions on the range of parameters. Two canonical choices are discretizing options for parameters or including an effective identification process for parameterized models.

Our safety theorem focuses on time-aware μlearning processes, i.e., those whose models are all time-aware; similarly, a *finite action space μlearning process* is a μlearning process in which all models $m \in M$ have a finite action space. The basic correctness property for a μlearning process is the safe reinforcement learning condition: the system never takes unsafe actions.

Definition 4 (μlearning process with an accurate model). *Let $P_M = (\boldsymbol{S}, \boldsymbol{U}, \boldsymbol{Mon})$ be a μlearning process. Assume there is some element $m^* \in \boldsymbol{Mon}_0$ with the following properties. First,*

$$m^* \equiv (\mathtt{init}_m \rightarrow [\{\mathtt{ctrl}_m; \mathtt{plant}_m\}^*]\mathtt{safe}).$$

Second, $\vdash m^*$. Third, $(s, u(s)) \in [\![\mathtt{ctrl}_m]\!]$ implies $(u(s), E(u, s)) \in [\![plant]\!]$ for a mapping $E : \mathcal{S} \times \mathcal{A} \rightarrow \mathcal{S}$ from states and actions to new states called environment. When only one element of $\boldsymbol{Mon}_0$ satisfies these properties we call that element m^* the distinguished *and/or* accurate *model and say that the process P_M is* accurately modeled *with respect to E.*

We will often elide the environment E for which the process P_M is accurate when it is obvious from context.

Theorem 1 (Safety). *If P_M is a μlearning process with an accurate model, then $\boldsymbol{S}_i \models \mathtt{safe}$ for all $0 < i < |\boldsymbol{S}|$.*

---

[1] Throughout the paper, we denote by $\mathbf{S}$ a specific sequence of states and by $\mathcal{S}$ the set of all states.

Listing 1.1 presents the μlearning algorithm. The inputs are: (a) A set M of models each with an associated function m.models : $\mathcal{S} \times \mathcal{A} \times \mathcal{S} \to \mathbb{B}$ that implements the evaluation of its model monitor in the given previous and next state and actions and a method m.safe : $\mathcal{S} \times \mathcal{A} \to \mathbb{B}$ which implements evaluation of its controller monitor, (b) an action space A and an initial state init $\in S$, (c) an environment function env : $\mathcal{S} \times \mathcal{A} \to \mathcal{S} \times \mathbb{R}$ that computes state updates and rewards in response to actions, and (d) a function choose : $\wp(\mathcal{A}) \to \mathcal{A}$ that selects an action from a set of available actions and update updates a table or approximation. Our approach is generic and works for any reinforcement learning algorithm; therefore, we leave these functions abstract. It augments an existing reinforcement learning algorithm, defined by update and choose, by restricting the action space at each step so that actions are only taken if they are safe with respect to *all* feasible models. The feasible model set is updated at each control set by removing models that are in conflict with observed data.

The μlearning algorithm rules out incorrect models from the set of possible models by taking actions and observing the results of those actions. Through these experiments, the set of relevant models is winnowed down to either the distinguished correct model m^*, or a set of models M^* containing m^* and other models that cannot be distinguished from m^*.

Listing 1.1. The basic μlearning algorithm

```
def μlearn(M,A,init,env,choose,update):
  s_pre = s_curr = init
  act    = None
  while(not done(s_curr)):
    if act is not None:
      M = {m ∈ M : m.models(s_pre,act,s_curr)}
      avail = {a ∈ A : ∀ m ∈ M, m.safe(s_curr, a)}
    act = choose(avail)
    s_pre = s_curr
    (s_curr, reward) = env(s_curr, act)
    update(s_pre, act, s_curr, reward)
```

4.1   Active Verified Model Update Learning

Removing models from the set of possible models relaxes the monitoring condition, allowing less conservative and more accurate control decisions. Therefore, this section introduces an active learning refinement of the μlearning algorithm that prioritizes taking actions that help rule out models $m \in M$ that are not m^*. Instead of choosing a random safe action, μlearning prioritizes actions that differentiate between available models. We begin by explaining what it means for an algorithm to perform good experiments.

Definition 5 (Active Experimentation). *A μlearning process with an accurate model m^* has* locally active experimentation *provided that: if $\bm{Mon}_i > 1$*

and there exists an action a that is safe for all feasible models (see Definition 3) in state s_i such that taking action a results in the removal of m from the model set[2], then $|\boldsymbol{Mon}_{i+1}| < |\boldsymbol{Mon}_i|$. Experimentation is er-*active if the following conditions hold: there exists an action a that is safe for all feasible models (see Definition 3) in state s_i, and taking action a resulted in the removal of m from the model set, then $|\boldsymbol{Mon}_{i+1}| < |\boldsymbol{Mon}_i|$ with probability $0 < $ er $ < 1$.*

Definition 6 (Distinguishing Actions). *Consider a µlearning process $(\boldsymbol{U}, \boldsymbol{S}, \boldsymbol{Mon})$ with an accurate model m^* (see Definition 4). An action a distinguishes m from m^* if $a = \boldsymbol{U}_i$, $m \in \boldsymbol{Mon}_i$ and $m \notin \boldsymbol{Mon}_{i+1}$ for some $i > 0$.*

The *active µlearning algorithm* uses model monitors to select distinguishing actions, thereby performing active experiments which winnow down the set of feasible models. The inputs to `active-µlearn` are the same as those to Listing 1.1 with two additions: (**1**) models are augmented with an additional prediction method p that returns the model's prediction of the next state given the current state, a candidate action, and a time duration. (**2**) An elimination rate er is introduced, which plays a similar role as the classical explore-exploit rate except that we are now deciding whether to insist on choosing a good experiment. The `active-µlearn` algorithm is guaranteed to make some progress toward winnowing down the feasible model set whenever $0 < $ er $ < 1$.

Theorem 2. *Let $P_M = (\boldsymbol{S}, \boldsymbol{U}, \boldsymbol{Mon})$ be a finite action space µlearning process with an accurate model m^*. Then $m^* \in \boldsymbol{Mon}_i$ for all $0 \leq i \leq |\boldsymbol{Mon}|$.*

Theorem 3. *Let P_M be a finite action space er-active µlearning process under environment E and with an accurate model m^*. Consider any model $m \in \boldsymbol{Mon}_0$ such that $m \neq m^*$. If every state s has an action a_s that is safe for all models and distinguishes m from m^*, then $\lim_{i \to \infty} Pr(m \notin \boldsymbol{Mon}_i) = 1$.*

Corollary 1. *Let $P_M = (\boldsymbol{S}, \boldsymbol{U}, \boldsymbol{Mon})$ be a finite action space er-active µlearning process under environment E and with an accurate model m^*. If each model $m \in \boldsymbol{Mon}_0 \setminus \{m^*\}$ has in each state s an action a_s that is safe for all models and distinguishes m from m^*, then $\boldsymbol{Mon}$ converges to $\{m^*\}$ a.s.*

Although locally active experimentation is not strong enough to ensure that P_M eventually converges to a minimal set of models[3], our experimental validation demonstrates that this heuristic is none-the-less effective on some representative examples of model update learning problems.

5   A Model Update Library

So far, we have established how to obtain safety guarantees for reinforcement learning algorithms given a set of formally verified dℒ models. We now turn

---

[2] We say that taking action a_i in state s_i results in the removal of a model m from the model set if $m \in \mathbf{Mon}_i$ but $m \notin \mathbf{Mon}_{i+1}$.

[3] $x \geq 0 \wedge t = 0 \rightarrow [\{\{?t = 0; x := 1 \cup x := 0\}; \{x' = F, t' = 1\}\}^*] x \geq 0$ with the parameters $F = 0, F = 5$, and $F = x$ are a counter example [10, Section 8.4.4].

our attention to the problem of generating such a set of models by systematically modifying d$\mathcal{L}$ formulas and their corresponding Bellerophon tactical proof scripts. This section introduces five generic model updates that provide a representative sample of the kinds of computations that can be performed on models and proofs to predict and account for runtime model deviations[4].

The simplest example of a VPMU instantiates a parameter whose value is not known at design time but can be determined at runtime via system identification. Consider a program p modeling a car whose acceleration depends upon both a known control input *accel* and parametric values for maximum braking force $-B$ and maximum acceleration A. Its proof is

$$\text{implyR}(1); \text{loop}(\text{pos} - \text{obsPos} > \frac{\text{vel}^2}{2B}, 1); \text{onAll}(\text{master})$$

This model and proof can be updated with concrete experimentally determined values for each parameter by uniformly substituting the variables B and A with concrete values in both the model and the tactic.

The **Automatic Parameter Instantiation** update improves the basic parameter instantiation update by automatically detecting which variables are parameters and then constraining instantiation of parameters by identifying relevant initial conditions.

The **Replace Worst-Case Bounds with Approximations** update improves models designed for the purpose of safety verification. Often a variable occurring in the system is bounded above (or below) by its worst-case value. Worst-case analyses are sufficient for establishing safety but are often overly conservative. The approximation model update replaces worst-case bounds with approximate bounds obtained via series expansions. The proof update then introduces a tactic on each branch of the proof that establishes our approximations are upper/lower bounds by performing.

Models often assume perfect sensing and actuation. A common way of robustifying a model is to add a piecewise constant noise term to the system's dynamics. Doing so while maintaining safety invariants requires also updating the controller so that safety envelope computations incorporate this noise term. The **Add Disturbance Term** update introduces noise terms to differential equations, systematically updates controller guards, and modifies the proof accordingly.

Uncertainty in object classification is naturally modeled in terms of sets of feasible models. In the simplest case, a robot might need to avoid an obstacle that is either static, moves in a straight line, or moves sinusoidally. Our generic model update library contains an update that changes the model by making a static point (x, y) dynamic. For example, one such update introduces the equations $\{x' = -y, y' = -x\}$ to a system of differential equations in which the variables x, y do not have differential equations. The controller is updated so that any statements about separation between (a, b) and (x, y) require global separation of (a, b) from the circle on which (x, y) moves. The proof is also updated by

---

[4] Extended discussion of these model updates is available in [10, Chapters 8 and 9].

prepending to the first occurrence of a differential tactic on each branch with a sequence of differential cuts that characterize circular motion.

Model updates also provide a framework for characterizing algorithms that combine model identification and controller synthesis. One example is our synthesis algorithm for systems whose ODEs have solutions in a decidable fragment of real arithmetic (a subset of linear ODEs). Unlike other model updates, we do not assume that any initial model is provided; instead, we learn a model (and associated control policy) entirely from data. The **Learn Linear Dynamics** update takes as input: (1) data from previous executions of the system, and (2) a desired safety constraint. From these two inputs, the update computes a set of differential equations `odes` that comport with prior observations, a corresponding controller `ctrl` that enforces the desired safety constraint with corresponding initial conditions `init`, and a Bellerophon tactic `prf` which proves $\text{init} \to [\{\text{ctrl}; \text{odes}\}^*]\text{safe}$. Computing the model requires an exhaustive search of the space of possible ODEs followed by a computation of a safe control policy using solutions to the resulting ODEs. Once a correct controller is computed, the proof proceeds by symbolically decomposing the control program and solving the ODEs on each resulting control branch. The full mechanism is beyond the scope of this paper but explained in detail elsewhere [10, Chapter 9].

Significance of Selected Updates. The updates described in this section demonstrate several possible modes of use for VPMUs and μlearning. VPMUS can update existing models to account for systematic modeling errors (e.g., missing actuator noise or changes in the dynamical behavior of obstacles). VPMUs can automatically optimize control logic in a proof-preserving fashion. VPMUS can also be used to generate accurate models and corresponding controllers from experimental data made available at design time, without access to any prior model of the environment.

6   Experimental Validation

The μlearning algorithms introduced in this paper are designed to answer the following question: given a set of possible models that contains the one true model, how can we *safely* perform a set of experiments that allow us to efficiently discover a minimal safety constraint? In this section we present two experiments which demonstrate the use of μlearning in safety-critical settings. Overall, these experiments empirically validate our theorems by demonstrating that μlearning processes with accurate models do not violate safety constraints.

Our simulations use a conservative discretization of the hybrid systems models, and we translated monitoring conditions by hand into Python from ModelPlex's C output. Although we evaluate our approach in a research prototype implemented in Python for the sake of convenience, there is a verified compilation pipeline for models implemented in d$\mathcal{L}$ that eliminates uncertainty introduced by discretization and hand-translations [7].

Adaptive Cruise Control. Adaptive Cruise Control (ACC) is a common feature in new cars. ACC systems change the speed of the car in response to the changes in the speed of traffic in front of the car; e.g., if the car in front of an ACC-enabled car begins slowing down, then the ACC system will decelerate to match the velocity of the leading car. Our first set of experiments consider a simple linear model of ACC in which the acceleration set-point is perturbed by an unknown parameter p; i.e., the relative position of the two vehicles is determined by the equations $\text{pos}'_{\text{rel}} = \text{vel}_{\text{rel}}, \text{vel}'_{\text{rel}} = \text{acc}_{\text{rel}}$.

In [14], the authors consider the collision avoidance problem when a noise term is added so that $\text{vel}'_{\text{rel}} = p\text{acc}_{\text{rel}}$. We are able to outperform the approach in [14] by combining the **Add Noise Term** and **Parameter Instantiation** updates; we outperform in terms of both avoiding unsafe states and in terms of cumulative reward. These two updates allow us to insert a multiplicative noise term p into these equations, synthesize a provably correct controller, and then choose the correct value for this noise term at runtime. Unlike [14], μlearning avoids all safety violations. The graph in Fig. 1 compares the Justified Speculative Control approach of [14] to our approach in terms of cumulative reward; in addition to substantially outperforming the JSC algorithm of [14], μlearning also avoids 204 more crashes throughout a 1,000 episode training process.

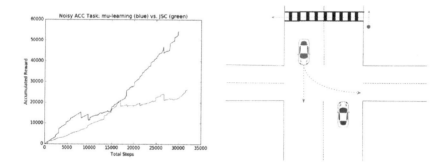

Fig. 1. Left: The cumulative reward obtained by Justified Speculative Control [14] (green) and μlearning (blue) during training over 1,000 episodes with each episode truncated at 100 steps. Each episode used a randomly selected error term that remains constant throughout each episode but may change between episodes. Right: a visualization of the hierarchical safety environment. (Color figure online)

A Hierarchical Problem. Model update learning can be extended to provide formal guarantees for hierarchical reinforcement learning algorithms [6]. If each feasible model m corresponds to a subtask, and if all states satisfying termination conditions for subtask m_i are also safe initial states for any subtask m_j reachable from m_i, then μlearning directly supports safe hierarchical reinforcement learning by re-initializing M to the initial (maximal) model set whenever reaching a termination condition for the current subtask.

We implemented a variant of μlearning that performs this re-initialization and validated this algorithm in an environment where a car must first navigate an intersection containing another car and then must avoid a pedestrian in a crosswalk (as illustrated in Fig. 1). In the crosswalk case, the pedestrian at (ped_x, ped_y) may either continue to walk along a sidewalk indefinitely or may enters the crosswalk at some point between $c_{min} \leq ped_y \leq c_{max}$ (the boundaries of the crosswalk). This case study demonstrates that safe hierarchical reinforcement learning is simply safe μlearning with safe model re-initialization.

7   Related Work

Related work falls into three broad categories: safe reinforcement learning, runtime falsification, and program synthesis.

Our approach toward safe reinforcement learning differs from existing approaches that do not include a formal verification component (e.g., as surveyed by García and Fernández [15] and the SMT-based constrained learning approach of Junges et al. [21]) because we focused on *verifiably* safe learning; i.e., instead of relying on oracles or conjectures, constraints are derived in a provably correct way from formally verified safety proofs. The difference between verifiably safe learning and safe learning is significant, and is equivalent to the difference between verified and unverified software. Unlike most existing approaches our safety guarantees apply to both the learning process and the final learned policy.

Section 2 discusses how our work relates to the few existing approaches toward *verifiably* safe reinforcement learning. Unlike those [3,14,17,20], as well as work on model checking and verification for MDPs [18], we introduce an approach toward verifiably safe off-model learning. Our approach is the first to combine model synthesis at design time with model falsification at runtime so that safety guarantees capture a wide range of possible futures instead of relying on a single accurate environmental model. Safe off-model learning is an important problem because autonomous systems must be able to cope with unanticipated scenarios. Ours is the first approach toward verifiably safe off-model learning.

Several recent papers focus on providing safety guarantees for model-free reinforcement learning. Trust Region Policy Optimization [31] defines safety as monotonic policy improvement, a much weaker notion of safety than the constraints guaranteed by our approach. Constrained Policy Optimization [1] extends TRPO with guarantees that an agent nearly satisfies safety constraints during learning. Brázdil et al. [8] give probabilistic guarantees by performing a heuristic-driven exploration of the model. Our approach is model-based instead of model-free, and instead of focusing on learning safely without a model we focus on identifying accurate models from data obtained both at design time and at runtime. Learning concise dynamical systems representations has one substantial advantage over model-free methods: safety guarantees are stated with respect to an explainable model that captures the safety-critical assumptions about the system's dynamics. Synthesizing explainable models is important because safety guarantees are always stated with respect to a model; therefore, engineers must be able to understand inductively synthesized models in order to understand what safety properties their systems do (and do not) ensure.

Akazaki et al. propose an approach, based on deep reinforcement learning, for efficiently discovering defects in models of cyber-physical systems with specifications stated in signal temporal logic [2]. Model falsification is an important component of our approach; however, unlike Akazaki et al., we also propose an approach toward obtaining more robust models and explain how runtime falsification can be used to obtain safety guarantees for off-model learning.

Our approach includes a model synthesis phase that is closely related to program synthesis and program repair algorithms [23,24,29]. Relative to work on program synthesis and repair, VPMUs are unique in several ways. We are the first to explore *hybrid* program repair. Our approach combines program verification with mutation. We treat programs as *models* in which one part of the model is varied according to interactions with the environment and another part of the model is systematically derived (together with a correctness proof) from these changes. This separation of the dynamics into inductively synthesized models and deductively synthesized controllers enables our approach toward using programs as representations of dynamic safety constraints during reinforcement learning.

Although we are the first to explore hybrid program repair, several researchers have explored the problem of synthesizing hybrid systems from data [5,30]. This work is closely related to our **Learn Linear Dynamics** update. Sadraddini and Belta provide formal guarantees for data-driven model identification and controller synthesis [30]. Relative to this work, our **Learn Linear Dynamics** update is continuous-time, synthesizes a computer-checked correctness proof but does not consider the full class of linear ODEs. Unlike Asarin et al. [5], our full set of model updates is sometimes capable of synthesizing nonlinear dynamical systems from data (e.g., the static → circular update) and produces computer-checked correctness proofs for permissive controllers.

8   Conclusions

This paper introduces an approach toward verifiably safe off-model learning that uses a combination of design-time verification-preserving model updates and runtime model update learning to provide safety guarantees even when there is no single accurate model available at design time. We introduced a set of model updates that capture common ways in which models can deviate from reality, and introduced an update that is capable of synthesizing ODEs and provably correct controllers without access to an initial model. Finally, we proved safety and efficiency theorems for active μlearning and evaluated our approach on some representative examples of hybrid systems control tasks. Together, these contributions constitute a first approach toward verifiably safe off-model learning.

References

1. Achiam, J., Held, D., Tamar, A., Abbeel, P.: Constrained policy optimization. In: Precup, D., Teh, Y.W. (eds.) Proceedings of the 34th International Conference on Machine Learning (ICML 2017), Proceedings of Machine Learning Research, vol. 70, pp. 22–31. PMLR (2017)
2. Akazaki, T., Liu, S., Yamagata, Y., Duan, Y., Hao, J.: Falsification of cyber-physical systems using deep reinforcement learning. In: Havelund, K., Peleska, J., Roscoe, B., de Vink, E. (eds.) FM 2018. LNCS, vol. 10951, pp. 456–465. Springer, Cham (2018). https://doi.org/10.1007/978-3-319-95582-7_27
3. Alshiekh, M., Bloem, R., Ehlers, R., Könighofer, B., Niekum, S., Topcu, U.: Safe reinforcement learning via shielding. In: McIlraith, S.A., Weinberger, K.Q (eds.) Proceedings of the Thirty-Second AAAI Conference on Artificial Intelligence (AAAI 2018). AAAI Press (2018)
4. Alur, R., Courcoubetis, C., Henzinger, T.A., Ho, P.-H.: Hybrid automata: an algorithmic approach to the specification and verification of hybrid systems. In: Grossman, R.L., Nerode, A., Ravn, A.P., Rischel, H. (eds.) HS 1991–1992. LNCS, vol. 736, pp. 209–229. Springer, Heidelberg (1993). https://doi.org/10.1007/3-540-57318-6_30
5. Asarin, E., Bournez, O., Dang, T., Maler, O., Pnueli, A.: Effective synthesis of switching controllers for linear systems. Proc. IEEE **88**(7), 1011–1025 (2000)
6. Barto, A.G., Mahadevan, S.: Recent advances in hierarchical reinforcement learning. Discret. Event Dyn. Syst. **13**(1–2), 41–77 (2003)
7. Bohrer, B., Tan, Y.K., Mitsch, S., Myreen, M.O., Platzer, A.: VeriPhy: verified controller executables from verified cyber-physical system models. In: Grossman, D. (ed.) Proceedings of the 39th ACM SIGPLAN Conference on Programming Language Design and Implementation (PLDI 2018), pp. 617–630. ACM (2018)
8. Brázdil, T., et al.: Verification of Markov decision processes using learning algorithms. In: Cassez, F., Raskin, J.-F. (eds.) ATVA 2014. LNCS, vol. 8837, pp. 98–114. Springer, Cham (2014). https://doi.org/10.1007/978-3-319-11936-6_8
9. Fridovich-Keil, D., Herbert, S.L., Fisac, J.F., Deglurkar, S., Tomlin, C.J.: Planning, fast and slow: a framework for adaptive real-time safe trajectory planning. In: IEEE International Conference on Robotics and Automation (ICRA), pp. 387–394 (2018)
10. Fulton, N.: Verifiably safe autonomy for cyber-physical systems. Ph.D. thesis, Computer Science Department, School of Computer Science, Carnegie Mellon University (2018)
11. Fulton, N., Mitsch, S., Bohrer, B., Platzer, A.: Bellerophon: tactical theorem proving for hybrid systems. In: Ayala-Rincón, M., Muñoz, C.A. (eds.) ITP 2017. LNCS, vol. 10499, pp. 207–224. Springer, Cham (2017). https://doi.org/10.1007/978-3-319-66107-0_14
12. Fulton, N., Mitsch, S., Quesel, J.-D., Völp, M., Platzer, A.: KeYmaera X: an axiomatic tactical theorem prover for hybrid systems. In: Felty, A.P., Middeldorp, A. (eds.) CADE 2015. LNCS (LNAI), vol. 9195, pp. 527–538. Springer, Cham (2015). https://doi.org/10.1007/978-3-319-21401-6_36
13. Fulton, N., Platzer, A.: Safe AI for CPS (invited paper). In: IEEE International Test Conference (ITC 2018) (2018)
14. Fulton, N., Platzer, A.: Safe reinforcement learning via formal methods: toward safe control through proof and learning. In: McIlraith, S., Weinberger, K. (eds.) Proceedings of the Thirty-Second AAAI Conference on Artificial Intelligence (AAAI 2018), pp. 6485–6492. AAAI Press (2018)

15. García, J., Fernández, F.: A comprehensive survey on safe reinforcement learning. J. Mach. Learn. Res. **16**, 1437–1480 (2015)
16. Ghosh, S., Berkenkamp, F., Ranade, G., Qadeer, S., Kapoor, A.: Verifying controllers against adversarial examples with Bayesian optimization. CoRR abs/1802.08678 (2018)
17. Hasanbeig, M., Abate, A., Kroening, D.: Logically-correct reinforcement learning. CoRR abs/1801.08099 (2018)
18. Henriques, D., Martins, J.G., Zuliani, P., Platzer, A., Clarke, E.M.: Statistical model checking for Markov decision processes. In: QEST, pp. 84–93. IEEE Computer Society (2012). https://doi.org/10.1109/QEST.2012.19
19. Herbert, S.L., Chen, M., Han, S., Bansal, S., Fisac, J.F., Tomlin, C.J.: FaSTrack: a modular framework for fast and guaranteed safe motion planning. In: IEEE Annual Conference on Decision and Control (CDC)
20. Jansen, N., Könighofer, B., Junges, S., Bloem, R.: Shielded decision-making in MDPs. CoRR abs/1807.06096 (2018)
21. Junges, S., Jansen, N., Dehnert, C., Topcu, U., Katoen, J.-P.: Safety-constrained reinforcement learning for MDPs. In: Chechik, M., Raskin, J.-F. (eds.) TACAS 2016. LNCS, vol. 9636, pp. 130–146. Springer, Heidelberg (2016). https://doi.org/10.1007/978-3-662-49674-9_8
22. Kalra, N., Paddock, S.M.: Driving to Safety: How Many Miles of Driving Would It Take to Demonstrate Autonomous Vehicle Reliability?. RAND Corporation, Santa Monica (2016)
23. Kitzelmann, E.: Inductive programming: a survey of program synthesis techniques. In: Schmid, U., Kitzelmann, E., Plasmeijer, R. (eds.) AAIP 2009. LNCS, vol. 5812, pp. 50–73. Springer, Heidelberg (2010). https://doi.org/10.1007/978-3-642-11931-6_3
24. Le Goues, C., Nguyen, T., Forrest, S., Weimer, W.: Genprog: a generic method for automatic software repair. IEEE Trans. Softw. Eng. **38**(1), 54–72 (2012)
25. Mitsch, S., Platzer, A.: ModelPlex: verified runtime validation of verified cyber-physical system models. Form. Methods Syst. Des. **49**(1), 33–74 (2016). Special issue of selected papers from RV'14
26. Platzer, A.: Differential dynamic logic for hybrid systems. J. Autom. Reas. **41**(2), 143–189 (2008)
27. Platzer, A.: Logics of dynamical systems. In: LICS, pp. 13–24. IEEE (2012)
28. Platzer, A.: A complete uniform substitution calculus for differential dynamic logic. J. Autom. Reas. **59**(2), 219–266 (2017)
29. Rothenberg, B.-C., Grumberg, O.: Sound and complete mutation-based program repair. In: Fitzgerald, J., Heitmeyer, C., Gnesi, S., Philippou, A. (eds.) FM 2016. LNCS, vol. 9995, pp. 593–611. Springer, Cham (2016). https://doi.org/10.1007/978-3-319-48989-6_36
30. Sadraddini, S., Belta, C.: Formal guarantees in data-driven model identification and control synthesis. In: Proceedings of the 21st International Conference on Hybrid Systems: Computation and Control (HSCC 2018), pp. 147–156 (2018)
31. Schulman, J., Levine, S., Abbeel, P., Jordan, M.I., Moritz, P.: Trust region policy optimization. In: Bach, F.R., Blei, D.M. (eds.) Proceedings of the 32nd International Conference on Machine Learning (ICML 2015), JMLR Workshop and Conference Proceedings, vol. 37, pp. 1889–1897 (2015)
32. Sutton, R.S., Barto, A.G.: Reinforcement Learning: An Introduction. MIT Press, Cambridge (1998)

Correction to: WAPS: Weighted and Projected Sampling

Rahul Gupta, Shubham Sharma, Subhajit Roy, and Kuldeep S. Meel

Correction to:
Chapter "WAPS: Weighted and Projected Sampling"
in: T. Vojnar and L. Zhang (Eds.): *Tools and Algorithms*
for the Construction and Analysis of Systems, **LNCS 11427,**
https://doi.org/10.1007/978-3-030-17462-0_4

In the version of this paper that was originally published, there was an error in the acknowledgement at the bottom of the first page. "AI Singapore Grant [R-252-000-A16-490]" was mentioned instead of "National Research Foundation Singapore under its AI Singapore Programme [Award Number: AISG-RP-2018-005]". This has now been corrected.

The updated version of this chapter can be found at
https://doi.org/10.1007/978-3-030-17462-0_4

T. Vojnar and L. Zhang (Eds.): TACAS 2019, Part I, LNCS 11427, p. C1, 2019.
https://doi.org/10.1007/978-3-030-17462-0_29

Author Index

Printed in the United States
By Bookmasters